Psychology of Women
Selected Readings

Second Edition

Juanita H. Williams is the author of

Psychology of Women: Behavior in a Biosocial Context, Second Edition

Psychology of Women

Selected Readings

Second Edition

Edited by

Juanita H. Williams

University of South Florida

W · W · NORTON & COMPANY

New York · London

Published simultaneously in Canada by Penguin Books Canada Ltd, 2801 John Street, Markham, Ontario L3R 1B4.

PRINTED IN THE UNITED STATES OF AMERICA.

The text of this book is composed in Baskerville, with display type set in Friz Quadrata. Composition by Vail-Ballou Press, Inc. Manufacturing by Maple-Vail Book Manufacturing Group.

Library of Congress Cataloging in Publication Data
Main entry under title:
Psychology of women. Selected Readings, 2nd edition.
    Includes bibliographical references.
    1. Women—Psychology—Addresses, essays, lectures.
I. Williams, Juanita Hingst, 1922–   .
HQ1206.P77   1985   305.4   84-18899

ISBN 0-393-95379-3

W. W. Norton & Company, Inc.,
500 Fifth Avenue, New York, N.Y. 10110

W. W. Norton & Company Ltd.,
37 Great Russell Street, London WC1B 3NU

1 2 3 4 5 6 7 8 9 0

Contents

Preface

The appearance of this second edition of *Psychology of Women: Selected Readings* is testimony to the surge of research interest and continued growth in the field of psychology of women and of women's studies in general. Since the publication in 1979 of the first edition, I have continued my teaching and research activities in the field and have used that experience to select for this volume important papers that I expect to make lasting contributions to this area of study. I have used many of these papers in both undergraduate and graduate courses and see them as valuable for courses on the psychology of women, the sociology of women, sex roles, and other women's studies courses. As supplementary reading, they can bring much-needed balance to traditional courses in psychology and sociology. Only five of the articles in this book appeared in the first edition. Most of the others have been published since 1979. The purpose of this book, then, is to bring together a selection of the most recent scholarship, set in historical perspective.

This book may be used either alone or as a supplement to *Psychology of Women: Behavior in a Biosocial Context.* Its organization is parallel to that of *Psychology of Women,* and the readings are keyed to the major topics in the textbook. The student and the instructor will have convenient access to important theoretical, empirical, and review articles in critical areas of the subject.

Each of the eleven parts of the book is preceded by an introduction that identifies the relevant issues of the topic and briefly describes each of the papers included in it. Part 1 presents some early philosophical and psychological ideas about woman and her behavior and a contemporary commentary on both scientific and social mythology as they pertain to the psychology of women. The second part presents some major psychoanalytic views and counterviews that show how thinking about women was influenced by the status and roles of women and men and by the social values attached to them.

Beginning with Part 3, the book consists of recent research organized by a life-cycle approach to the study of women. Papers on biological influences on behavior in Part 3 are followed in Part 4 by others on the meaning of sex and gender and on some areas of gender differences. Implications of the experience of growing up female are explored in Part 5, including a review article on the black female adolescent and a vivid description of her girlhood by a woman of the desert-dwelling !Kung.

The papers on female sexuality in Part 6 attest to the diversity of women's experiences, from our Victorian past to the varied styles of sexual expression observed today. Issues of birth control and abortion, with particular reference to the future and what it may bring, are explored in Part 7. Pregnancy, birth, and bonding are the subjects of the papers in Part 8. Included here is a controversial article on the possible biological substratum of parenthood for both sexes.

The papers in Part 9 are concerned with both tradition and change as they affect women's lives today. Differences between men and women in career decisions and in friendships are examined, as well as the meaning of the contemporary value of female equality for the old institution of the family. Some aspects of the work lives of black women and of Lesbians are also explored.

Atypical and problem behavior of women, its effects on the individual and its social significance, are subjects of the papers in Part 10. Each of these papers, while not infused with ideology, reflects to some extent a feminist perspective as an organizing principle.

The last group of papers, in Part 11, deals with women and aging in our society. They include a study of older single women, a reflective essay on the intimacy needs of widows, and a look at what the future may bring for older women.

The field of psychology of women, its subject matter the scientific study of female behavior, must draw from disciplines other than its own to bring understanding to the complex issues involved. The papers in this book include data from history, biology, anthropology, economics, and philosophy, among other disciplines. This field is also unique in psychology because it cuts across many of the subdisciplines: developmental, social, personality, comparative, physiological. Thus the psychology of women integrates many sources of knowledge. As an interdisciplinary and integrative field, it has the potential for facilitating community, for lowering the walls that separate scholars and disciplines from each other. Thus, by its existence, it introduces values that are woman-identified into the world of science.

The energy of the women's movement has generated a flood of academic research. Equally important, it has caused the reanalysis and reinterpretation of older concepts in psychology and other disciplines. The papers in this book demonstrate the changed awareness of scholars as they reexamine theories of personality, psychotherapy, and sex roles. Also, they exemplify the introduction of new theories and research, all of which help us more adequately to understand the phenomena of behavior.

Once again, I want to thank my editor at Norton, Don Fusting, and his assistant, Caroline McKinley, for their attention, care, and knowledgeable assistance. I have benefited, too, from the reactions of many students to the selections. I hope the book will make a contribution to their future.

J.H.W.
Tampa

PART I

Myths, Stereotypes, and the Psychology of Women

Though serious attention to the scientific study of women by psychologists is less than two decades old, beliefs about the nature of woman and her behavior have always been part of the human record. Across the centuries, she has variously been described as earth mother, seductive witch, necessary evil, ministering angel, and unfathomable mystery.

Philosophers since Aristotle have held man to be the prototype of a human being and woman to be a special case, the "Other." Thinkers have described woman by contrasting her differences from man, the standard. From this vantage point, they have seen her as intellectually inferior. And further, they believed that her destiny as sexual creature and propagator limited her talent and kept her from doing anything else.

Psychology, as it began to develop around the turn of the century, attempted to turn the pure light of science on such matters as sex differences in brain and behavior. But the early researchers were still mired in old assumptions about human nature. Examination of the writings of philosophers, scientists, and laymen alike reveals the hidden agendas: their preconceptions about woman, which guided their thinking, their interpretations of their findings, and their proposals for dealing with her.

This section includes both archival and contemporary comments on the nature of woman, her social roles, and the ways these have been explained. "On Women," an essay written in 1893 by German philosopher Arthur Schopenhauer, is a good example of the misogynistic view of woman as sex object and childbearer, her mind unclouded by ideas, her life unmarked by achievement. Vain, prodigal of man's resources, she is devious, scheming, and utterly dependent on him whom she deludes with her youthful beauty into taking her on as his life's burden.

In a less vitriolic article, "The Psychology of Woman" (1895), Professor

G. T. W. Patrick shared certain assumptions with Schopenhauer. He examined woman's physical and psychological characteristics in order to determine their bearing, if any, on the movement for woman's political, educational, and economic equality. Sex differences in variability, brain size, intellectual functioning, and character were interpreted by Patrick as unsupportive of the doctrine of woman's inferiority. Woman was biologically less vulnerable to stress and disease. Though her brain was smaller than man's, her brain/body ratio was equal to his. She excelled in quickness of perception, memory, and language development, but was deficient in logical powers, in the ability to think analytically and critically. Morally she was man's superior, being more altruistic and self-sacrificing than he, but a fallen woman easily surpassed man in her capacity for cruelty and depravity.

Such data led Patrick to his central thesis, which was that woman was a case of arrested development. Physically and mentally she was closer to the primitive archetype of the race. For example, the division of labor that marked progress in the civilized world was not found in the work of women; their work was undiversified and their tools primitive. Though richly endowed with the essentials of humanity, woman did not share man's variability, by which he adapted so readily to his environment. These observations, thought Patrick, formed the scientific basis for granting a woman a "reverent exemption" from those worldly duties requiring the "restless and active" nature of her consort, man.

In 1914, the Nebraska Men's Association of Omaha published a manifesto setting forth the reasons for their opposition to the pending Nineteenth amendment to the U.S. Constitution, which would give women the right to vote. This brief document, signed by business and professional men of the community, is of interest to us because it expresses perfectly a sentimental ideal of woman-as-angel, deserving always the protection of man, too fragile for the duties of public life. But the darker side appears: fear of the consequences of giving women the political power of the vote. Cloaked in the notion that women are too emotional to be trusted with political responsibility, there emerges the prediction, if she is given this power, of insurrection, revolution, and the end of our form of government. Embedded in this statement by middle-class, midwestern, ordinary males is man's ancient fear of woman, her seeming unpredictability—and thus, the need for guarding and limiting her actions.

In a contemporary paper entitled "Functionalism, Darwinism, and the Psychology of Women," Stephanie Shields examines the influence of Darwin's theory of evolution on the young science of psychology. She shows how beliefs about women's special qualities, such as those expressed in Patrick's paper, were incorporated into the scientific enterprise as psychologists tried to explain women's roles by looking for their origins in woman's special nature and in her differences from man. Differences in male and female brains were held to account for differences in mental capacities and in cultural achievement. In addition, the belief that women were more alike than men were explained the greater representation of men among the eminent as well as among the mentally handicapped. Finally, the concept of the maternal instinct, already popular, received strong support from the extension of evolutionary biology to behavior; woman was related to the other primates, not only in her reproductive functions, but in her nurturing behavior as well. The tenacity of such ideas, Shields says, is witness to the service that science performed for social values: it provided justification for the status quo.

Beliefs about the relation of woman to her body, to nature, and to man, and about her place in the scheme of life have profoundly influenced the ways in which she has been treated and the accommodations that have been made for her. The articles in this section demonstrate the continuity and coherence of ideas about women through history, linking today's myths to their roots in the past.

1

On Women

Arthur Schopenhauer

Schiller's poem in honour of women, *Würde der Frauen*, is the result of much careful thought, and it appeals to the reader by its antithetic style and its use of contrast; but as an expression of the true praise which should be accorded to them, it is, I think, inferior to these few words of Jouy's: *Without women the beginning of our life would be helpless; the middle, devoid of pleasure; and the end, of consolation.* . . .

You need only look at the way in which she is formed to see that woman is not meant to undergo great labour, whether of the mind or of the body. She pays the debt of life not by what she does but by what she suffers; by the pains of childbearing and care for the child, and by submission to her husband, to whom she should be a patient and cheering companion. The keenest sorrows and joys are not for her, nor is she called upon to display a great deal of strength. The current of her life should be more gentle, peaceful and trivial than man's, without being essentially happier or unhappier.

Women are directly fitted for acting as the nurses and teachers of our early childhood by the fact that they are themselves childish, frivolous and shortsighted; in a word, they are big children all their life long—a kind of intermediate stage between the child and the full-grown man, who is man in the strict sense of the word. See how a girl will fondle a child for days together, dance with it and sing to it; and then think what a man, with the best will in the world, could do if he were put in her place.

With young girls Nature seems to have had in view what, in the language of the drama, is called *a coup de théâtre*. For a few years she dowers

"On Women" by Arthur Schopenhauer in *Studies in Pessimism: A Series of Essays*. London: S. Sonnenschein, 1893.

them with a wealth of beauty and is lavish in her gift of charm, at the
expense of the rest of their life, in order that during those years they may
capture the fantasy of some man to such a degree that he is hurried into
undertaking the honourable care of them, in some form or other, as long
as they live—a step for which there would not appear to be any sufficient
warranty if reason only directed his thoughts. Accordingly Nature has
equipped woman, as she does all her creatures, with the weapons and
implements requisite for the safeguarding of her existence, and for just as
long as it is necessary for her to have them. Here, as elsewhere, Nature
proceeds with her usual economy; for just as the female ant, after fecun-
dation, loses her wings, which are then superfluous, nay, actually a danger
to the business of breeding; so, after giving birth to one or two children, a
woman generally loses her beauty; probably, indeed, for similar reasons.

And so we find that young girls, in their hearts, look upon domestic
affairs or work of any kind as of secondary importance, if not actually as a
mere jest. The only business that really claims their earnest attention is
love, making conquests, and everything connected with this—dress, dancing, and so on.

The nobler and more perfect a thing is, the later and slower it is in
arriving at maturity. A man reaches the maturity of his reasoning powers
and mental faculties hardly before the age of twenty-eight; at woman, at
eighteen. And then, too, in the case of woman, it is only reason of a sort—
very niggard in its dimensions. That is why women remain children their
whole life long; never seeing anything but what is quite close to them, cleav-
ing to the present moment, taking appearance for reality, and preferring
trifles to matters of the first importance. For it is by virtue of his reasoning
faculty that man does not live in the present only, like the brute, but looks
about him and considers the past and the future; and this is the origin of
prudence, as well as of that care and anxiety which so many people exhibit.
Both the advantages and the disadvantages which this involves, are shared
in by the woman to a smaller extent because of her weaker power of reasoning. She may, in fact, be described as intellectually shortsighted, because,
while she has an intuitive understanding of what lies quite close to her, her
field of vision is narrow and does not reach to what is remote: so that things
which are absent or past or to come have much less effect upon women
than upon men. This is the reason why women are more often inclined to
be extravagant, and sometimes carry their inclination to a length that bor-
ders upon madness. In their hearts women think that it is men's business
to earn money and theirs to spend it—if possible during their husband's
life, but, at any rate, after his death. The very fact that their husband hands
them over his earnings for purposes of housekeeping strengthens them in
this belief.

However many disadvantages all this may involve, there is at least this
to be said in its favour: that the woman lives more in the present than the
man, and that, if the present is at all tolerable, she enjoys it more eagerly.
This is the source of that cheerfulness which is peculiar to woman, fitting
her to amuse man in his hours of recreation, and, in case of need, to con-
sole him when he is borne down by the weight of his cares. . . .

The weakness of their reasoning faculty also explains why it is that
women show more sympathy for the unfortunate than men do, and so treat

them with more kindness and interest; and why it is that, on the contrary, they are inferior to men in point of justice, and less honourable and conscientious. For it is just because their reasoning power is weak that present circumstances have such a hold over them, and those concrete things which lie directly before their eyes exercise a power which is seldom counteracted to any extent by abstract principles of thought, by fixed rules of conduct, firm resolutions, or, in general, by consideration for the past and the future, or regard for what is absent and remote. . . .

Hence it will be found that the fundamental fault of the female character is that it has *no sense of justice*. This is mainly due to the fact, already mentioned, that women are defective in the powers of reasoning and deliberation; but it is also traceable to the position which Nature has assigned to them as the weaker sex. They are dependent, not upon strength, but upon craft; and hence their instinctive capacity for cunning, and their ineradicable tendency to say what is not true. . . . Perjury in a court of justice is more often committed by women than by men. It may, indeed, be generally questioned whether women ought to be sworn at all. From time to time one finds repeated cases everywhere of ladies, who want for nothing, taking things from shop-counters when no one is looking and making off with them.

Nature has appointed that the propagation of the species shall be the business of men who are young, strong and handsome; so that the race may not degenerate. This is the firm will and purpose of Nature in regard to the species, and it finds its expression in the passions of women. There is no law that is older or more powerful than this. Woe, then, to the man who sets up claims and interests that will conflict with it; whatever he may say and do, they will be unmercifully crushed at the first serious encounter. For the innate rule that governs women's conduct, though it is secret and unformulated, nay, unconscious in its working, is this: *We are justified in deceiving those who think they have acquired rights over the species by paying little attention to the individual, that is, to us. The constitution and, therefore, the welfare of the species have been placed in our hands and committed to our care, through the control we obtain over the next generation, which proceeds from us; let us discharge our duties conscientiously.* But women have no abstract knowledge of this leading principle; they are conscious of it only as a concrete fact; and they have no other method of giving expression to it than the way in which they act when the opportunity arrives. . . .

And since women exist in the main solely for the propagation of the species, and are not destined for anything else, they live, as a rule, more for the species than for the individual, and in their hearts take the affairs of the species more seriously than those of the individual. This gives their whole life and being a certain levity; the general bent of their character is in a direction fundamentally different from that of man; and it is this which produces that discord in married life which is so frequent, and almost the normal state. . . .

It is only the man whose intellect is clouded by his sexual impulses that could give the name of *the fair sex* to that undersized, narrow-shouldered, broad-hipped, and short-legged race: for the whole beauty of the sex is bound up with this impulse. Instead of calling them beautiful, there would be more warrant for describing women as the unaesthetic sex. Neither for music, nor for poetry, nor for fine art, have they really and truly any sense or susceptibility; it is a mere mockery if they make a pretence of it in order to assist their endeavour to please. Hence, as a result of this, they are incapable of taking a *purely objective interest* in anything; and the reason of it seems to me to be as follows. A man tries to acquire *direct* mastery over things, either by understanding them or by forcing them to do his will. But a woman is always and everywhere reduced to obtaining this mastery *indirectly*, namely through a man; and whatever direct mastery she may have is entirely confined to him. And so it lies in woman's nature to look upon everything only as a means for conquering man; and if she takes an interest in anything else it is simulated—a mere roundabout way of gaining her ends by coquetry and feigning what she does not feel. . . .

And you cannot expect anything else of women if you consider that the most distinguished intellects among the whole sex have never managed to produce a single achievement in the fine arts that is really great, genuine, and original; or given to the world any work of permanent value in any sphere. . . . They form the *sexus sequior*—the second sex, inferior in every respect to the first; their infirmities should be treated with consideration; but to show them great reverence is extremely ridiculous, and lowers us in their eyes. When Nature made two divisions of the human race, she did not draw the line exactly through the middle. These divisions are polar and opposed to each other, it is true; but the difference between them is not qualitative merely, it is also quantitative.

This is just the view which the ancients took of woman, and the view which people in the East take now; and their judgment as to her proper position is much more correct than ours, with our old French notions of gallantry and our preposterous system of reverence—that highest product of Teutonico-Christian stupidity. These notions have served only to make women more arrogant and overbearing; so that one is occasionally reminded of the holy apes in Benares, who in the consciousness of their sanctity and inviolable position think they can do exactly as they please.

But in the West the woman, and expecially the *lady*, finds herself in a false position; for woman, rightly called by the ancients *sexus sequior*, is by no means fit to be the object of our honour and veneration, or to hold her head higher than man and be on equal terms with him. The consequences of this false position are sufficiently obvious. Accordingly it would be a very desirable thing if this Number Two of the human race were in Europe also relegated to her natural place, and an end put to that lady-nuisance, which not only moves all Asia to laughter but would have been ridiculed by Greece and Rome as well. It is impossible to calculate the good effects which such a change would bring about in our social, civil and political arrangements. . . . In Europe the *lady*, strictly so-called, is a being who should not exist at all; she should be either a housewife or a girl who hopes to become one; and she should be brought up, not to be arrogant, but to be thrifty and submissive. It is just because there are such people as *ladies* in Europe that the women of the lower classes, that is to say, the great majority of the sex, are much more unhappy than they are in the East. . . .

The laws of marriage prevailing in Europe consider the woman as the equivalent of the man—start, that is to say, from a wrong position. In our part of the world where monogamy is the rule, to marry means to halve one's rights and double one's duties. Now when the laws gave women equal rights with man, they ought to have also endowed her with a masculine intellect. . . . For the institution of monogamy, and the laws of marriage which it entails, bestow upon the woman an unnatural position of privilege, by considering her throughout as the full equivalent of the man, which is by no means the case; and seeing this men who are shrewd and prudent very often scruple to make so great a sacrifice and to acquiesce in so unfair an arrangement. . . .

Moreover, the bestowal of unnatural rights upon women has imposed upon them unnatural duties, and nevertheless a breach of these duties makes them unhappy. Let me explain. A man may often think that his social or financial position will suffer if he marries, unless he makes some brilliant alliance. His desire will then be to win a woman of his own choice under conditions other than those of marriage, such as will secure her position and that of the children. However fair, reasonable, fit and proper these conditions may be, if the woman consents by foregoing that undue amount of privilege which marriage alone can bestow, she to some extent loses her honour, because marriage is the basis of civic society; and she will lead an unhappy life, since human nature is so constituted that we pay an attention to the opinion of other people which is out of all proportionate to its value. On the other hand, if she does not consent, she runs the risk either of having to be given in marriage to a man whom she does not like, or of being landed high and dry as an old maid; for the period during which she has a chance of being settled for life is very short. . . .

The first love of a mother for her child is, with the lower animals as with men, of a purely *instinctive* character, and so it ceases when the child is no longer in a physically helpless condition. After that, the first love should give way to one that is based on habit and reason; but this often fails to make its appearance, especially where the mother did not love the father. The love of a father for his child is of a different order, and more likely to last; because it has its foundation in the fact that in the child he recognises his own inner self; that is to say, his love for it is metaphysical in its origin.

In almost all nations, whether of the ancient or the modern world, . . . property is inherited by the male descendants alone; it is only in Europe that a departure has taken place; but not amongst the nobility, however. That the property which has cost men long years of toil and effort, and been won with so much difficulty, should afterwards come into the hands of women, who then, in their lack of reason, squander it in a short time, or otherwise fool it away, is a grievance and a wrong, as serious as it is common, which should be prevented by limiting the right of women to inherit. In my opinion the best arrangement would be that by which women, whether widows or daughters, should never receive anything beyond the interest for life on property secured by mortgage, and in no case the property itself, or the capital, except where all male descendants fail. The people who make money are men, not women; and it follows from this that women are neither justified in having unconditional possession of it, nor fit persons to be entrusted with its administration. When wealth, in any true sense of the word, that is to say, funds, houses or land, is to go to them as an inheritance, they should never be allowed the free disposition of it. In their case a guardian should always be appointed; and hence they should never be given the free control of their own children, wherever it can be avoided. The vanity of women, even though it should not prove to be greater than that of men, has this much danger in it that it takes an entirely material direction. They are vain, I mean, of their personal beauty, and then of finery, show and magnificence. That is just why they are so much in their element in society. It is this, too, which makes them so inclined to be extravagant, all the more as their reasoning power is low. . . . But with men vanity often takes the direction of non-material advantages, such as intellect, learning, courage. . . .

That woman is by nature meant to obey may be seen by the fact that every woman who is placed in the unnatural position of complete independence, immediately attaches herself to some man, by whom she allows herself to be guided and ruled. It is because she needs a lord and master. If she is young, it will be a lover; if she is old, a priest.

2

The Psychology of Woman

G. T. W. Patrick

Every thoughtful observer of both the popular and the scientific movements of the day must have noticed the frequent lack of harmony or cooperation between them. Such lack of co-operation, if not of harmony, is
well illustrated in the woman question. Two vigorous movements are now
in progress. The first is a popular movement, whose end, apparently being
very rapidly realized, is the advancement of woman to a position of complete political, legal, educational, and social parity with man—a position
which means much more than mere equality of rights for woman; it means
for her a changed sphere of activity, with new duties and new burdens, and
may in the end involve radical changes in the state and in the family. The
second is a scientific movement in anthropology, conducted by laborious
and painstaking research, whose end is to ascertain the constitutional differences, both physical and psychical, between man and woman. It may be
that these two movements will be found to support each other; but, if so, it
is to be feared that it will be by happy chance rather than by intelligent cooperation.

It is the purpose of this article to bring together some of the results of
these anthropological studies relating especially to the psychology of woman,
in order that we may see what bearing, if any, they may have upon the
above-mentioned popular movement. The most devoted patron of woman's political and educational advancement would hardly deny that the success and permanence of the reform will depend in the end upon the fact
that there shall be no inherent contradiction between her new duties and
her natural physical and mental constitution. It should be borne in mind,

"The Psychology of Woman" by G. T. W. Patrick. *Popular Science Monthly*, 47 (1895), 209–
225.

however, that the mere fact of woman's present intellectual or physical weakness, should such be shown, would not be a justifiable ground for denying to her full political and educational privileges. It might be quite the reverse, if it should appear that such weakness were itself the result of the subordinate position which she has been compelled to hold. It would, however, be a justifiable ground for advising woman to assume her new duties gradually, in order that disaster to her cause might not follow the overtaxing of her strength.

In outlining some of the psychological peculiarities of woman as revealed by modern anthropological researches, I shall endeavor to confine myself to those points upon which investigators generally agree, simply omitting those still in dispute, or mentioning them only as questioned.

All facts are best studied in the light of an idea. It may be conducive to clearness, therefore, to mention first the leading theories now in the field concerning woman's peculiarities. It has often been asserted since Aristotle that woman is a stunted or inferior man and represents arrested development. Again, it has been said that woman is a grown-up child, that she belongs to the child type, and must ever to some extent retain the child relation. Again, more recently, it has been maintained that although woman belongs to the child type, yet the child type is in truth the race type and represents greater perfection than is represented by man, whose natural characteristic is senility. Finally, it has been said that throughout the whole animal world, where artificial circumstances have not modified natural relations, the female stands for physical superiority in size and vitality, and more truly represents the essential qualities of the species. Without prejudice for or against any of these theories, let us see what evidence there may be for each. . . .

Some interesting differences are now clearly made out between man and woman in respect to birth, death, and disease. Statistics show that about one hundred and five boys are born to every one hundred girls in Europe and America. The proportion in other countries and among uncivilized races is said to be nearly the same. The greater mortality of males, however, begins with birth and continues throughout childhood and adolescence and the greater proportion of adult years. If, therefore, a count be made of boys and girls or men and women at any age after the first year, the females are found to be in a considerable excess, and this notwithstanding the decimation of women by diseases incidental to the child-bearing stage of their lives. These results, formerly attributed to accidental causes, are now known to be due to the greater natural mortality of males, and this is found to be in harmony with another series of sexual differences, namely, the greater power of woman to resist nearly all diseases. . . . Sudden deaths from internal causes are much less frequent among women. They endure surgical operations better than men, and recover more easily from the effects of wounds. They also grow old less rapidly and live longer. Among centenarians there are twice as many women as men. Women retain longer the use of their legs and of their hands. Their hair becomes gray later, and they suffer less from senile irritability and from loss of sight, hearing, and memory. In brief, contrary to popular opinion, woman is more hardy than man, and possesses a larger reserve of vitality. . . .

The long-disputed questions about woman's brain are now approaching solution in a few leading points. In the first place, woman's brain is of less absolute weight than man's, the proportion among modern civilized races being about nine to ten. This fact in itself has little significance, as man is heavier and taller than woman. If we consider the weight of the brain relatively to the height of the body, it still appears that woman's brain is smaller; but if, as is more just, we consider the weight of the brain relatively to the weight of the body, it appears that there is nearly perfect equality, the difference, if any, being in favor of woman. . . . Of more significance in its bearing upon woman's mental capacity is the relative size of the different parts of the brain. Here it is shown that the lower centers as compared with the hemispheres are larger in the female brain. In the cerebrum itself the frontal region is not, as has been supposed, smaller in woman, but rather larger relatively. The same is true of the occipital lobe. But the parietal lobe is somewhat smaller. It is now believed, however, that a preponderance of the frontal region does not imply intellectual superiority, as was formerly supposed, but that the parietal region is really the more important. As a balance, perhaps, to these female deficiencies, we may note that the circulation of the blood seems to be somewhat greater in woman's brain. In respect to her whole physical structure woman is less modified than man and shows less tendency to variation. Women are more alike than men. . . .

We come now to the well-worn theme of the purely mental differences between the sexes, and here I shall make a brief summary of the more important and well-recognized differences, citing experiments and statistics where they are possible. In perception, woman is in general decidedly quicker than man. She reads a paragraph or book more quickly, and, knowledge of the subject being equal, she grasps more of it. In perception of objects she grasps more quickly a number of wholes or groups, and has a rapid unreasoned perception of relations which has the appearance of intuition. Her perception of details, however, is less accurate than man's, and her rapid reference of things to their proper classes extends only to matters of common human experience. In apperception the subjective factor is larger in woman, and she sees things more from the standpoint of her own experience, wishes, and prejudices. Even more than a man, where feeling is strong, objective perception is blind. Hence women make poorer critics than men, and more rarely are they impartial judges. For the formation of concepts, especially the more abstract ones, woman's mind is less adapted than man's. She thinks more in terms of the concrete and individual. . . .

In respect to memory, as far as any general statements can be made, woman is superior. In memory tests college girls surpass boys. In Gilbert's tests on New Haven school children, however, the boys were superior in the exact reproduction of an interval of time. In reasoning of the quick associative kind women are more apt than men, but in slow logical reasoning, whether deductive or inductive, they are markedly deficient. They lack logical feeling, and are less disturbed by inconsistency. Analysis is relatively distasteful to them, and they less readily comprehend the relation of the part to the whole. They are thus less adapted to the plodding, analytical work of science, discovery, or invention. Their interest lies rather with the finished product. Of the 483,517 patents issued by the U.S. Patent Office prior to October, 1892, 3,458 were granted to women. In general, woman's thought is less methodical and less deep. The arts, sciences, and philosophy owe their progress more to man than to woman. Whether one studies the history of logic, mathematics, or philosophic thought, of the special sciences or scientific discovery and invention, of poetry or general literature, of musical composition or technique, of painting, sculpture, or architecture, one is engaged more with the names of men than of women. Even in those spheres for which woman by her peculiar physical or mental qualities is particularly adapted, such as vocal music, the stage, and the writing of novels, it is doubtful whether a list of the greatest artists would include more women than men. Even in the arts of cooking and dressmaking, when men undertake them they often excel. Woman, owing to her greater patience, her intuition, and her retentive memory, as well as her constant association with the young, is especially qualified for teaching and has equal or greater success in this work than man. Yet all educational reforms, from the kindergarten to the university, have originated with the latter.

What woman loses in profundity she gains in quickness. She excels in tact, and extricates herself from a difficulty with astonishing adroitness. In language she is more apt than man. Girls learn to speak earlier than boys, and old women are more talkative than old men. Among the uneducated the wife can express herself more intelligently than the husband. Experience in coeducational institutions shows that women are more faithful and punctilious than men, and at least equally apt. In colleges where a record of standing is kept the women gain probably a somewhat higher average. In the years immediately following graduation the men make much greater intellectual progress. Women reach their mental maturity at an earlier age, and develop relatively less after maturity. In many kinds of routine work, especially that requiring patience, women are superior, but they are less able to endure protracted overwork. . . .

One of the most marked differences between man and woman is the greater excitability of the nerve centers in the latter. Woman possesses in a higher degree than man the fundamental property of all nervous tissue, irritability, or response to any stimulus. The vasomotor system is particularly excitable, and this fact is in immediate connection with her emotional life. That woman is more emotional than man is only another way of stating the same fact. Various expressions and bodily changes which are really the ground of emotions, such, for instance, as laughing, crying, blushing, quickening of the heart-beat, are more common in woman, and in general her face is more mobile and witnesses more to her mental states. Various forms of abnormal mental conditions, closely connected with the emotions, such as hysteria, are more frequent among women. Women are more easily influenced by suggestion than men, and a larger percentage of them may be hypnotized. Trance mediums are usually women. The word witch has been narrowed almost wholly to the female, and this may be explained by the fact that various forms of mental disturbance connected with superstitious notions are more frequently manifested in women. Sympathy, pity, and charity are stronger in woman, and she is more prominent in works that spring from these sentiments, such as philanthropy and humane and charitable movements. Woman is more generous than man. Her maternal instincts lead her to lend her sympathy to the weak and helpless. She cares for the sick and protects the friendless, and, seeing present rather than remote consequences, she feeds the pauper and pardons the criminal.

In morals a few distinctions between the sexes are well determined. Male criminals outnumber female criminals about six to one. Woman's sympathy and love, her physical weakness and timid nature, her domestic and quiet habits, ill adapt her to the criminal life. Morally bad women too usually find other more attractive fields open to them. Some forms of crime, indeed, such as murder by poisoning, domestic theft, and infanticide, are much more common among women. When women do become criminals their crimes are often marked by greater heinousness, cruelty, and depravity. It is said by Lombroso and his school that in respect to cruelty in general woman surpasses man, particularly in her conduct to her own sex. Woman's appetites are not so strong and her passions are less intense. She is freer from intemperance and related forms of vice. The most marked moral superiority of woman appears in her altruism; her greatest moral defect is her untruthfulness. In her altruistic life of love and self-sacrifice woman shows herself the leader in the supreme virtue of Christian civilization. As far as she leads in this, so far does she fall behind in veracity. She has not the same conception of abstract truth as man, but thinks more of the good to be attained. . . .

Woman's religious nature is stronger than man's. She possesses in a marked degree the qualities of reverence, dependence, devotion, trust, and fidelity. Fear and timidity are feminine qualities, while faith is so natural to woman that she is disposed to credulity rather than to skepticisim.

Let us pause a second time to see what theory, if any, our results establish. Here, again, from her mental differences the doctrine of woman's inferiority receives no support—inferior, no doubt, in philosophy, science, and invention, and in her conception of abstract truth and justice, but superior in intuition, in charity, in temperance, in fidelity, in balance. But here again, as in her physical peculiarities, woman approaches the child type. This is seen in the preponderance of the emotional life over the discriminative, and of the impulsive over the voluntary. So also the quick perception and the retentive memory remind us of the child more than do the stern logical processes of the man. Woman's mental associations, selecting the concrete, the individual, the whole rather than the part, relations in space rather than in time, are also those of the child. Woman's receptivity, her faith and trust, her naïve freedom from skepticism, her fear and timidity, her feeling of dependence, her religious instincts, are all child traits. Children, like women, have slower reaction-time and lesser motor ability, are more easily hypnotized, have more number forms and color associations, have less power of inhibition, express their emotions more in their faces, and more readily give way to tears and smiles. Modern child study has shown that children are more cruel than adults and have little power to discriminate between truth and falsehood. They also are sympathetic and changeable, and act with reference to present rather than remote ends. Woman in respect to her altruism, pity, and charity has less resemblance to the child, but these traits are so intimately connected with her duties of motherhood as to have little bearing upon the theory of her naturally infantile constitution.

The hypothesis that woman approximates to the primitive rather than to the child type, that she represents arrested development, may be said to receive a certain amount of confirmation from her mental traits. Indifference to physical and psychical pain, freedom from color blindness, the preponderance of memory and intuition over reason, lack of mechanical inventiveness, conservatism and adherence to custom, precocity, changeableness, cruelty, tact, deceitfulness, emotional expression, religious feeling, are all traits conspicuous among primitive races, and, as we have seen, are more noticeable in women than in men. That women are less modified mentally and are more alike than men also argues for arrested development. It is well known that in insane asylums the female patients are more destructive, noisy, abusive, and vicious than the male patients, although their insanity is less serious and more curable. This fact, together with the other, that when women become bad they become more hopelessly bad, has led some too hastily to conclude that women, like children, are natural savages. The fact that woman has less logical and philosophical ability and has taken so little part in the development of the sciences, arts, and inventions, which are considered to represent human progress, is adduced as further confirmation of this theory. But in many of her mental traits woman departs further than man from the savage type. In her moral qualities she represents higher evolution. This is notably true in respect to her altruism, charity, sympathy, and pity. Woman's greater humanity, philanthropy, conscientiousness, fidelity, self-sacrifice, modesty, and patience, as well as her lesser disposition to crime, are qualities which separate her further than man from the savage. The same may be said of certain other subtle and scarcely definable feminine qualities, such, for instance, as grace and refinement. Woman's development along these lines certainly has not been arrested, and although it may be argued that these qualities are the logical outcome partly of her physical weakness and partly of her maternal duties, still it would be difficult to show that evolution in this direction represents less progress than in the more intellectual direction in which man has developed. It must be admitted, however, that woman's purely intellectual development has been retarded, and this may have a practical significance considering that on these qualities the struggle for existence now so largely turns. . . .

Certain other facts . . . point, it is said, to woman's arrested development. The division of labor which marks the progress of civilization has reached no such extent in the work of woman as in that of man. In fact, it may be said that there is in woman's work hardly any division of labor, except in so far as, in recent years, she has entered upon pursuits formerly followed only by men. As we have seen that women are more alike physically and mentally than men, so their work is more alike. In domestic life, which still includes the mass of representative women, each one either does her own housework, or has it done by female servants whose labor is equally unspecialized. No man now in civilized communities makes his own clothes, yet this is not uncommon among women, and in primitive communities they may even spin and weave the material. Not only is their work and manner of work more primitive, but also their tools. In the German cities on market day, for instance, may be seen numbers of men and women bringing their produce from the country, the men using carts or wagons propelled by themselves or their horses, but the women bearing their burdens in baskets upon their backs in quite the primitive fashion. . . . It has been suggested that the greater size and strength of the male among the higher vertebrates may be explained as the indirect result, in part, of his combats with rivals, and, in part, of his greater activity in protecting and supporting himself and his mate when the maternal duties of the latter incapacitate her for these actions, and furthermore that the retarded development of woman is due to artificial and unnatural restrictions arising from a sort of bondage which the above conditions have made possible. Again, if it should be shown that woman conspicuously resembles the infant in body and mind, very unwarranted inferences might be drawn from this. It is true that the infant of the human species has certain curious points of resemblance to the lower animals, notably the ape, but it is equally true that the infant ape has certain marked resemblances to the human species which the adult ape does not have. By analogy we may infer that the human infant has closer resemblance to the more highly developed being of the future than the human adult has, and if woman is more like the child than man is, then she is more representative of the future being. The matter, in fact, reduces itself probably to this: that woman, like the child, represents the race type, while man represents those variable qualities by which mankind adapts itself to its surroundings. Every woman is, as it were, a composite picture of the race, never much worse nor much better than all. Man is, as it were, Nature's experiment, modified to reflect, if possible, the varying conditions of his environment. If superiority consists in adaptation to present environment, then man is superior; if it consists in the possession of those underlying qualities which are essential to the race—past, present, and future—then woman is superior.

. . . Woman's more intimate connection with the life history of the race, her childlike, representative, and typical nature, her embodiment of the everlasting essentials of humanity, her at present arrested or retarded development—all these are indicated by modern anthropological studies. These results are indicated, not proved. They must be verified, supplemented, and no doubt, in some instances, corrected by future studies along these lines.

From these studies there would be no want of lessons for political and social reformers, if they would learn them. From woman's rich endowment with all that is essentially human, the most devoted enthusiast for woman's rights and equality might gain new inspiration. From her retarded development the educational and political reformer might learn that woman's cause may suffer irretrievable damage if she is plunged too suddenly into duties demanding the same strain and nervous expenditure that is safely borne by man, and if it is attempted to correct in a century the evil of ages. From woman's childlike nature the thoughtful "spectator of all time and all existence" might learn yet a deeper and more significant lesson. May it not be that woman, representative of the past and future of humanity, whose qualities are concentration, passivity, calmness, and reserve of force, and upon whom, more than upon man, rest the burdens and responsibilities of the generations, is too sacred to be jostled roughly in the struggle for existence, and that she deserves from man a reverent exemption from some of the duties for which his restless and active nature adapts him?

3
Nebraska Men's Association Opposed to Woman Suffrage

To the Electors of the State of Nebraska:

At a meeting of men lately held in the city of Omaha the following resolution was unanimously adopted: "Resolved, That it is the sense of this meeting that a Manifesto be prepared, issued and circulated, setting forth the reasons for our opposition to the pending constitutional amendment providing for equal (woman) suffrage and requesting the cooperation of the voters of the State, and that such Manifesto be signed by all the men present."

We yield to none in our admiration, veneration and respect for woman. We recognize in her admirable and adorable qualities and sweet and noble influences which make for the betterment of mankind and the advancement of civilization. We have ever been willing and ready to grant to woman every right and protection, even to favoritism in the law, and to give her every opportunity that makes for development and true womanhood. We have a full appreciation of all the great things which have been accomplished by women in education, in charity and in benevolent work and in other channels of duty too numerous to mention, by which both men and women have been benefited, society improved and the welfare of the human race advanced. We would take from women none of their privileges as citizens but we do not believe that women are adapted to the political work of the world.

The discussion of all questions growing out of the social and family relations and local economic conditions has no direct relationship to the right of women to participate in the political affairs of government. The right of suffrage does not attach of right to the owners of property, for, if so, all other persons should be disfranchised. It is not a fundamental right of taxpayers, for a great body of men are not taxpayers, and nine-tenths of the women who would become voters, if woman suffrage were adopted, would be non-taxpayers. It is not an inherent right of citizenship, for the time never was in the whole history of the world when the franchise was granted to all citizens. . . . Franchise is a privilege of government granted only to those to whom the Government sees fit to grant it. As a law-abiding people men and women alike should recognize once and for all that the right of suffrage is not a natural or inherent right of citizenship but can only come by grant from the Government. [Legal authorities quoted.]

We must also recognize that woman suffrage is inconsistent with the fundamental principles upon which our representative government was founded and to accept it now involves revolutionary changes. The framers of the Federal Constitution, a body of the wisest men the country has ever produced, did not recognize or provide for woman suffrage. No one of the original thirteen States which adopted it provided in their constitutions for woman suffrage. True it was permitted in New Jersey from 1776 to 1807, a period of thirty-one years, when it was taken away by statute, by reason of unsatisfactory conditions and results. After the close of the Civil War, the southern States which had gone into rebellion were admitted back into the Union under constitutions limiting suffrage to men. These precedents in our governmental history were never departed from until in recent years. The greatest danger to the Republic of the United States today, as it always has been in governments where the people rule, is in an excitable and emotional suffrage. If the women of this country would always think coolly and deliberate calmly, if they could always be controlled and act by judgment and not under passion, they might help us to keep our institutions "eternal as the foundations of the continent itself"; but the philosophers of history and the experience of the ages past and present tell us in unanswerable arguments and teach us by illustrations drawn from actual experience, that governments have been overturned or endangered in periods of great excitement by emotional suffrage and the speech and writings of intolerant people. . . .

Open that terrible page of the French Revolution and the days of terror, when the click of the guillotine and the rush of blood through the streets of Paris demonstrated to what extremities the ferocity of human nature can be driven by political passion. Who led those bloodthirsty mobs? Who shrieked loudest in that hurricane of passion? Woman. Her picture upon the page of history is indelible. In the city of Paris, in those ferocious mobs, the controlling agency, nay, not agency but the controlling and principal power, came from those whom God had intended to be the soft and gentle angels of mercy throughout the world. . . .

It has been said that if woman suffrage should become universal in the United States, in times of great excitement arising out of sectional questions or local conditions this country would be in danger of State insurrections and seditions and that in less than a hundred years revolutions would occur and our republican form of government would come to an end. The United States should guard against emotional suffrage. What we need is to put more logic and less feeling into public affairs. This country has already extended suffrage beyond reasonable bounds. Instead of enlarging it there are strong reasons why it should be curtailed. It would have been better for wise and safe government and the welfare of all the people if there had been some reasonable standard of fitness for the ballot.

During the intense feeling and turbulent conditions growing out of the Civil War, suffrage was so extended that many of the southern States were turned over to the political control of those not sufficiently informed to conduct good government. It has taken half-a-century of strenuous effort to correct that mistake. The granting of universal woman suffrage would greatly increase the existing evil and put it beyond the possibility of correction except by an ultimate revolution.

We hear it frequently stated that there is no argument against woman suffrage except sentiment. We can reply with equal force that there is no argument for woman suffrage except sentiment, and that often misguided and uninformed. Some suffragists insist that if woman suffrage became universal "it would set in motion the machinery of an earthly paradise." It was a woman of high standing in the literary and journalistic field who answered, "It is my opinion it would let loose the wheels of purgatory." . . . Suffragists frequently ask the question, "If we want to vote why should other people object?" If it is wrong they should not ask it any more than they should ask the privilege of committing a crime. If it is a wrong against the State every other man and woman has a right to object and it is their duty to object. . . .

There are spheres in which feeling should be paramount. There are kingdoms in which the heart should reign supreme. That kingdom belongs to woman—the realm of sentiment, the realm of love, the realm of gentler and holier and kindlier attributes that make the name of wife, mother and sister next to the name of God himself, but it is not in harmony with suffrage and has no place in government.

We submit these considerations in all candor to the men of this State. Ultimately the decision of this question at the polls is a man's question. We ask your cooperation. . . .

Omaha, July 6, 1914.

Joseph H. Millard, ex-U. S. Senator and president Omaha National Bank. (Largest creditor of Willow Springs Distillery.)

John A. McShane, ex-Congressman and retired capitalist.

John Lee Webster, lawyer, representing Omaha Street Railway.

Luther Drake, president Merchants' National Bank.

John C. Cowin, prominent lawyer.

William F. Gurley, prominent lawyer.

William D. McHugh, lawyer representing Standard Oil Company.

Frank T. Hamilton, president Omaha Gas Co. and officer Street Railway Co.

William Wallace, former cashier Omaha National Bank.

John A. Munroe, vice-president Union Pacific Railway Company.

Frank Boyd, employee Omaha National Bank.

Gerrit Fort, Union Pacific Railway official.

Joseph Barker, insurance official.

EDWARD A. PECK, general manager Omaha Grain Elevator Company.
HENRY W. YATES, president Nebraska National Bank.
MILTON C. PETERS, president Alfalfa Milling Co.
WILLIAM H. KOENIC, of firm of Kilpatrick & Co., dry goods merchants.
W. H. BOCHOLZ, vice-president Omaha National Bank.
FRED H. DAVIS, president First National Bank.
BENJAMIN S. BAKER, lawyer.
L. F. CROFOOT, lawyer for Omaha Smelting Co. and Chicago & Milwaukee R. R.
E.E. BRUCE, wholesale druggist
GEORGE W. HOLDREDGE, manager Burlington & Missouri River R. R. Co.
FRED A. NASH, President Omaha Electric Light Co.
NELSON H. LOOMIS, General Attorney Union Pacific R. R.
EDSON RICH, assistant attorney Union Pacific R. R.
FRANK B. JOHNSON, president Omaha Printing Co.
THOMAS C. BYRNE, president Wholesale Dry Goods Co.
REV. THOMAS J. MACKAY, Minister All Saints' Church (Episcopal).
REV. JOHN W. WILLIAMS, Minister St. Barnabas' Church (Episcopal).

————

This Manifesto with the signatures is given almost in full because in language and in the business interests of the signers it is thoroughly typical of the open opposition to woman suffrage. The other classes who were opposed—the "machine" politicians, the liquor interests and those directly or indirectly connected with them—for the most part worked more secretly.

4

Functionalism, Darwinism, and the Psychology of Women
A Study in Social Myth

Stephanie A. Shields

The psychology of women is acquiring the character of an academic entity as witnessed by the proliferation of research on sex differences, the appearance of textbooks devoted to the psychology of women, and the formation of a separate APA division, Psychology of Women. Nevertheless, there is almost universal ignorance of the psychology of women as it existed prior to its incorporation into psychoanalytic theory. If the maxim "A nation without a history is like a man without a memory" can be applied, then it would behoove the amnesiacs interested in female psychology to investigate its pre-Freudian past.

This article focuses on one period of that past (from the latter half of the 19th century to the first third of the 20th) in order to clarify the important issues of the time and trace their development to the position they occupy in current psychological theory. Even a limited overview leads the reader to appreciate Helen Thompson Woolley's (1910) early appraisal of the quality of the research on sex differences:

> There is perhaps no field aspiring to be scientific where flagrant personal bias, logic martyred in the cause of supporting a prejudice, unfounded assertions, and even sentimental rot and drivel, have run riot to such an extent as here. (p. 340)

The Functionalist Milieu

Although the nature of woman had been an academic and social concern of philosopher psychologists throughout the ages, formed psychology (its inception usually dated 1879) was relatively slow to take up the topic of female psychology. The "woman question" was a social one, and social problems did not fall within the sharply defined limits of Wundt's "new" psychology. The business of psychology was the description of the "generalized adult mind," and it is not at all clear whether "adult" was meant to include both sexes. When the students of German psychology did venture outside of the laboratory, however, there is no evidence that they were sympathetic to those defending the equality of male and female ability (cf. Wundt, 1901).

It was the functionalist movement in the United States that fostered academic psychology's study of sex differences and, by extension, a prototypic psychology of women. The incorporation of evolutionary theory into the practice of psychology made the study of the female legitimate, if not imperative. It would be incorrect to assume that the psychology of women existed as a separate specialty within the discipline. The female was discussed only in relation to the male, and the function of the female was thought to be distinctly different from and complementary to the function of the male. The leitmotiv of evolutionary theory as it came to be applied to the social sciences was the evolutionary supremacy of the Caucasian male. The notion of the supplementary, subordinate role of the female was ancillary to the development of that theme.

The influence of evolutionary theory on the psychology of women can be traced along two major conceptual lines: (a) by emphasizing the biological foundations of temperament, evolutionary theory led to serious academic discussion of maternal instinct (as one facet of the general topic of instinct); and (b) by providing a theoretical justification of the study of individual differences, evolutionary theory opened the door to the study of sex differences in sensory, motor, and intellectual abilities. As a whole, the concept of evolution with its concomitant emphasis on biological determinism provided ample "scientific" reason for cataloging the "innate" differences in male and female nature.

This article examines three topics that were of special significance to the psychology of women during the functionalist era: (a) structural differences in the brains of males and females and the implications of these differences for intelligence and temperament, (b) the hypothesis of greater male variability and its relation to social and educational issues, and (c) maternal instinct and its meaning for a psychology of female "nature." As the functionalist paradigm gave way to behaviorism and psychoanalytic theory, the definition and "meaning" of each of these issues changed to fit the times. When issues faded in importance, it was not because they were resolved but because they ceased to serve as viable scientific "myths" in the changing social and scientific milieu. As the times change, so must the myths change.

The Female Brain

The topic of female intelligence came to 19th-century psychology via phrenology and the neuroanatomists. Philosophers of the time (e.g., Hegel, Kant, Schopenhauer) had demonstrated, to their satisfaction, the justice of woman's subordinate social position, and it was left to the men of science to discover the particular physiological determinants of female inadequacy. In earlier periods, woman's inferiority had been defined as a general "state" intimately related to the absence of qualities that would have rendered her a male and to the presence of reproductive equipment that destined her to be female. For centuries the mode of Eve's creation and her greater guilt for the fall from grace had been credited as the cause of woman's imperfect nature, but this was not an adequate explanation in a scientific age. Thus, science sought explanations for female inferiority that were more in keeping with contemporary scientific philosophy.

Although it had long been believed that the brain was the chief organ of the mind, the comparison of male and female mental powers traditionally included only allusions to vague "imperfections" of the female brain. More precise definition of the sites of these imperfections awaited the advancement of the concept of cortical localization of function. Then, as finer distinctions of functional areas were noted, there was a parallel recognition of the differences between those sites as they appeared in each sex.

At the beginning of the 19th century, the slowly increasing interest in the cerebral gyri rapidly gathered momentum with the popularization of phrenology. Introduced by Franz Joseph Gall, "cranioscopy," as he preferred to call it, postulated that the seat of various mental and moral faculties was located in specific areas of the brain's surface such that a surfeit or deficiency could be detected by an external examination of the cranium. Phrenology provided the first objective method for determining the neurological foundation of sex differences in intelligence and temperament that had long been promulgated. Once investigation of brain structure had begun, it was fully anticipated that visible sex differences would be found: Did not the difference between the sexes pervade every other aspect of physique and physiological function? Because physical differences were so obvious in every other organ of the body, it was unthinkable that the brain could have escaped the stamp of sex.

Gall was convinced that he could, from gross anatomical observation, discriminate between male and female brains, claiming that "if there had been presented to him in water, the fresh brains of two adult animals of any species, one male and the other female, he could have distinguished the two sexes" (Walker, 1850, p. 317). Gall's student and colleague, Johann Spurzheim, elaborated on this basic distinction by noting that the frontal lobes were less developed in females, "the organs of the perceptive faculties being commonly larger than those of the reflective powers." Gall also observed sex differences in the nervous tissue itself, "confirming" Malebranche's belief that the female "cerebral fibre" is softer than that of the male, and that it is also "slender and long rather than thick" (Walker, 1850, p. 318). Spurzheim also listed the cerebral "organs" whose appearance differed commonly in males and females: females tended to have the areas devoted to philoprogenetiveness and other "tender" traits most prominent, while in males, areas of aggressiveness and constructiveness dominated. Even though cranioscopy did not survive as a valid system of describing cortical function, the practice of comparing the appearance of all or part of the brain for anatomical evidence of quality of function remained one of the most popular means of providing proof of female mental inferiority. Most comparisons used adult human brains, but with the rise of evolutionary theory, increasing emphasis was placed on the value of developmental and cross-species comparisons. The argument for female mental inferiority took two forms: some argued that quality of intellect was proportional to absolute or relative brain size; others, more in the tradition of cortical localization, contended that the presence of certain mental qualities was dependent upon the development of corresponding brain centers.

The measurement of cranial capacity had long been in vogue as one method of determining intellectual ability. That women had smaller heads than men was taken by some as clear proof of a real disparity between male and female intelligence. The consistently smaller brain size of the female was cited as another anatomical indicator of its functional inferiority. More brain necessarily meant better brain; the exception only proved this rule. Alexander Bain (1875) was among those who believed that the smaller absolute brain size of females accounted for a lesser mental ability. George Romanes (1887) enumerated the "secondary sex characteristics" of mental abilities attributable to brain size. The smaller brain of women was directly responsible for their mental inferiority, which "displays itself most conspicuously in a comparative absence of originality, and this more especially in the higher levels of intellectual work" (p. 655). He, like many, allowed that women were to some degree compensated for intellectual inferiority by a superiority of instinct and perceptual ability. These advantages carried with them the germ of female failure, however, by making women more subject to emotionality.

Proof of the male's absolute brain-size superiority was not enough to secure his position of intellectual superiority, since greater height and weight tended to offset the brain-size advantage. Reams of paper were, therefore, dedicated to the search for the most "appropriate" relative measures, but results were equivocal: if the ratio of brain weight to body weight is considered, it is found that women possess a proportionately larger brain than men; if the ratio of brain surface to body surface is computed, it is found to favor men. That some of the ratios "favored" males while others "favored" females led some canny souls to conclude that there was no legitimate solution to the problem. That they had ever hoped for a solution seems remarkable; estimates of brain size from cranial capacity involve a large margin of error because brains differing as much as 15% have been found in heads of the same size (Elliott, 1969, p. 316).

Hughlings Jackson has been credited as the first to regard the frontal cortex as the repository of the highest mental capacities, but the notion must have held popular credence as early as the 1850s because that period saw sporadic references to the comparative development of the frontal lobes in men and women. Once the function of the frontal lobes had been established, many researchers reported finding that the male possessed noticeably larger and more well-developed frontal lobes than females. The neuroanatomist Hischke came to the conclusion in 1854 that woman is *homo parietalis* while man is *homo frontalis* (Ellis, 1934). Likewise, Rudinger in 1877 found the frontal lobes of man in every way more extensive than those of women, and reported that these sex differences were evident even in the unborn fetus (Mobius, 1901).

At the turn of the century, the parietal lobes (rather than the frontal lobes) came to be regarded by some as the seat of intellect, and the necessary sex difference in parietal development was duly corroborated by the neuroanatomists. The change in cerebral hierarchy involved a bit of revisionism:

> the frontal region is not, as has been supposed smaller in woman, but rather larger relatively. . . . But the parietal lobe is somewhat smaller, [furthermore,] a preponderance of the frontal region does not imply intellectual superiority . . . the parietal region is really the more important. (Patrick, 1895, p. 212)

Once beliefs regarding the relative importance of the frontal and parietal lobes had shifted, it became critical to reestablish congruence between neuroanatomical findings and accepted sex differences. Among those finding parietal predominance in men were Paul Broca,[1] Theodore Meynert, and the German Rudinger (see Ellis, 1934, p. 217).

Other neuroanatomical "deficiencies" of the female were found in (a) the area of the corpus callosum, (b) the complexity of the gyri and sulci, (c) the conformation of gyri and sulci, and (d) the rate of development of the cortex of the fetus (Woolley, 1910, p. 335). Franklin Mall (1909) objected to the use of faulty research methods that gave spurious differences the appearance of being real. Among the most serious errors he noted was the practice of making observations with a knowledge of the sex of the brain under consideration.

The debate concerning the importance of brain size and anatomy as indicators of intelligence diminished somewhat with the development of mental tests; nevertheless, the brain-size difference was a phenomenon that many felt obligated to interpret. Max Meyer (1921) attempted to settle the matter by examining the various measures of relative difference that had been employed. After finding these methods far too equivocal, he concluded, in the best behavioristic terms, that sex differences in intelligence were simply "accidents of habits acquired."

Characteristics of the female brain were thought not simply to render women less intelligent but also to allow more "primitive" parts of human nature to be expressed in her personality. Instinct was thought to dominate woman, as did her emotions, and the resulting "affectability" was considered woman's greatest weakness, the reason for her inevitable failure. Affectability was typically defined as a general state, the manifestation of instinctive and emotional predispositions that in men were kept in check by a superior intellect.[2]

One of the most virulent critics of woman was the German physiologist Paul Mobius (1901), who argued that her mental incapacity was a necessary condition for the survival of the race. Instinct rendered her easily led and easily pleased, so much the better for her to give her all to bearing and rearing children. The dependence of woman also extracted a high price from man:

> All progress is due to man. Therefore the woman is like a dead weight on him, she prevents much restlessness and meddlesome inquisitiveness, but she also restrains him from noble actions, for she is unable to distinguish good from evil. (p. 629)

Mobius observed that woman was essentially unable to think independently, had strong inclinations to be mean and untrustworthy, and spent a
good deal of her time in an emotionally unbalanced state. From this he was
forced to conclude that: "If woman was not physically and mentally weak, if
she was not as a rule rendered harmless by circumstances, she would be extremely dangerous" (Mobius, 1901, p. 630). Diatribes of this nature were
relatively common German importations; woman's severest critics in this
country seldom achieved a similar level of acerbity. Mobius and his ilk (e.g.,
Weininger, 1906) were highly publicized and widely read in the United
States, and not a little of their vituperation crept into serious scientific discussions of woman's nature. For example, Porteus and Babcock (1926)
resurrected the brain-size issue, discounting the importance of size to intelligence and instead associating it with the "maturing of other powers."
Males, because of their larger brains would be more highly endowed with
these "other powers," and so more competent and achieving. Proposals
such as these, which were less obviously biased than those of Mobius, Weininger, and others, fit more easily into the current social value system and so
were more easily assimilated as "good science" (cf. Allen, 1927, p. 294).

The Variability Hypothesis

The first systematic treatment of individual differences in intelligence appeared in 1575. Juan Huarte attributed sex differences in intelligence to
the different humoral qualities that characterized each sex, a notion that
had been popular in Western thought since ancient Greece. Heat and
dryness were characteristic of the male principle, while moisture and
coolness were female attributes. Because dryness of spirit was necessary for
intelligence, males naturally possessed greater "wit." The maintenance of
dryness and heat was the function of the testicles, and Huarte (1959) noted
that if a man were castrated the effects were the same "as if he had received
some notable dammage in his very braine" (p. 279). Because the principles
necessary for cleverness were only possessed by males, it behooved parents
to conduct their life-style, diet, and sexual intercourse in such a manner as
to insure the conception of a male. The humoral theory of sex differences
was widely accepted through the 17th century, but with the advent of more
sophisticated notions of anatomy and physiology, it was replaced by other,
more specific, theories of female mental defect: the lesser size and hypothesized simpleness of the female brain, affectability as the source of inferiority, and complementarity of abilities in male and female. It was the developing evolutionary theory that provided an overall explanation for why
these sex differences existed and why they were necessary for the survival
of the race.

The theory of evolution as proposed by Darwin had little to say
regarding the intellectual capacity of either sex. It was in Francis Galton's
(Charles Darwin's cousin) anthropometric laboratory that the investigation
of intellectual differences took an empirical form (Galton, 1907). The
major conclusion to come from Galton's research was that women tend in
all their capacities to be inferior to men. He looked to common experience
for confirmation, reasoning that:

If the sensitivity of women were superior to that of men, the self interest of
merchants would lead to their being always employed; but as the reverse is the
case, the opposite supposition is likely to be the true one. (pp. 20–21)

This form of logic—women have not excelled, therefore they cannot
excel—was often used to support arguments denigrating female intellectual ability. The fact of the comparative rarity of female social achievement
was also used as "evidence" in what was later to become a widely debated
issue concerning the range of female ability.

Prior to the formulation of evolutionary theory, there had been little
concern with whether deviation from the average or "normal" occurred
more frequently in either sex. One of the first serious discussions of the
topic appeared in the early 19th century when the anatomist Meckel concluded on pathological grounds that the human female showed greater
variability than the human male. He reasoned that because man is the superior animal and variability a sign of inferiority, this conclusion was justified (in Ellis, 1903, p. 237). The matter was left at that until 1871. At that
time Darwin took up the question of variability in *The Descent of Man* while
attempting to explain how it could be that in many species males had developed greatly modified secondary sexual characteristics while females of the
same species had not. He determined that this was originally caused by the
males' greater activity and "stronger passions" that were in turn more likely
(he believed) to be transmitted to male offspring. Because the females
would prefer to mate with the strong and passionate, sexual selection
would insure the survival of those traits. A tendency toward greater variation per se was not thought to be responsible for the appearance of unusual
characteristics, but "development of such characters would be much aided,
if the males were more liable to vary than the females" (Darwin, 1922, p.
344). To support this hypothesis of greater male variability, he cited recent
data obtained by anatomists and biologists that seemed to confirm the relatively more frequent occurrence of physical anomaly among males.

Because variation from the norm was already accepted as the mechanism of evolutionary progress (survival and transmission of adaptive variations) and because it seemed that the male was the more variable sex, it
soon was universally concluded that the male is the progressive element in
the species. Variation for its own sake took on a positive value because
greatness, whether of an individual or a society, could not be achieved
without variation. Once deviation from the norm became legitimized by
evolutionary theory, the hypothesis of greater male variability became a
convenient explanation for a number of observed sex differences, among
them the greater frequency with which men achieved "eminence." By the
1890s it was popularly believed that greater male variability was a principle
that held true, not only for physical traits but for mental abilities as well:

That men should have greater cerebral variability and therefore more originality, while women have greater stability and therefore more "common
sense," are facts both consistent with the general theory of sex and verifiable in
common experience. (Geddes & Thomson, 1890, p. 271)

Havelock Ellis (1894), an influential sexologist and social philosopher,
brought the variability hypothesis to the attention of psychologists in the

first edition of *Man and Woman*. After examining anatomical and pathological data that indicated a greater male *variational tendency* (Ellis felt this term was less ambiguous than *variability*), he examined the evidence germane to a discussion of range of intellectual ability. After noting that there were more men than women in homes for the mentally deficient, which indicated a higher incidence of retardation among males, and that there were more men than women on the roles of the eminent, which indicated a higher incidence of genius among males, he concluded that greater male variability probably held for all qualities of character and ability. Ellis (1903) particularly emphasized the wide social and educational significance of the phenomenon, claiming that greater male variability was "a fact which has affected the whole of our human civilization" (p. 238), particularly through the production of men of genius. Ellis (1934) was also adamant that the female's tendency toward the average did not necessarily imply inferiority of talent; rather, it simply limited her expertise to "the sphere of concrete practical life" (p. 436).

The variability hypothesis was almost immediately challenged as a "pseudo-scientific superstition" by the statistician Karl Pearson (1897). Though not a feminist, Pearson firmly believed that the "woman question" deserved impartial, scientific study. He challenged the idea of greater male variability primarily because he thought it contrary to the fact and theory of evolution and natural selection. According to evolutionary theory (Pearson, 1897), "the more intense the struggle the less is the variability, the more nearly are individuals forced to approach the type fittest to their surroundings, if they are to survive" (p. 258). In a "civilized" community one would expect that because men have a "harder battle for life," any difference in variation should favor women. He took Ellis to task by arguing it was (a) meaningless to consider secondary sex characteristics (as Ellis had done) and, likewise, (b) foolish to contrast the sexes on the basis of abnormalities (as Ellis had done). By redefining the problem and the means for its solution, he was able to dismiss the entire corpus of data that had been amassed: "the whole trend of investigations concerning the relative variability of men and women up to the present seems to be erroneous" (Pearson, 1897, p. 261). Confining his measurements to "normal variations in organs or characteristics not of a secondary sexual character," he assembled anthropometric data on various races, from Neolithic skeletons to modern French peasants. He also challenged the adequacy of statistical comparison of only the extremes of the distribution, preferring to base his contrasts on the dispersion of measures around the mean. Finding a slight tendency toward greater female variability, he concluded that the variability hypothesis as stated remained a "quite unproven principle."

Ellis countered Pearson in a lengthy article, one more vicious than that ordinarily due an intellectual affront.[3] Pearson's greatest sins (according to Ellis) were his failure to define "variability" and his measurement of characteristics that were highly subject to environmental influence. Ellis, of course, overlooked his own failure to define variability and his inclusion of environmentally altered evidence.

In the United States the variability hypothesis naturally found expression in the new testing movement, its proponents borrowing liberally from the theory of Ellis and the statistical technique of Pearson. The favor that was typically afforded the hypothesis did not stem from intellectual commitment to the scientific validity of the proposal as much as it did from personal commitment to the social desirability of its acceptance. The variability hypothesis was most often thought of in terms of its several corollaries: (a) genius (seldom, and then poorly, defined) is a peculiarly male trait; (b) men of genius naturally gravitate to positions of power and prestige (i.e., achieve eminence) by virtue of their talent; (c) an equally high ability level should not be expected of females; and (d) the education of women should, therefore, be consonant with their special talents and special place in society as wives and mothers.

Woman's Education

The "appropriate" education for women had been at issue since the Renaissance, and the implications of the variability hypothesis favored those who had been arguing for a separate female education. Late in the 18th century, Mary Wollstonecraft Godwin (1759–1797) questioned the "natural" roles of each sex, contending that for both the ultimate goal was the same: "the first object of laudable ambition is to obtain a character as a human being, regardless of the distinction of sex" (Wollstonecraft, 1955, p. 5). Without education, she felt, women could not contribute to social progress as mature individuals, and this would be a tragic loss to the community. Though not the first to recognize the social restrictions arbitrarily placed on women, she was the first to hold those restrictions as directly responsible for the purported "defective nature" of women. She emphasized that women had never truly been given an equal chance to prove or disprove their merits. Seventy years later, John Stuart Mill (1955) also took up the cause of women's education, seeing it as one positive action to be taken in the direction of correcting the unjust social subordination of women. He felt that what appeared as woman's intellectual inferiority was actually no more than the effort to maintain the passive-dependent role relationship with man, her means of support:

> When we put together three things—first, the natural attraction between the sexes; secondly, the wife's entire dependence on the husband . . . and lastly, that the principal object of human pursuit, consideration, and all objects of social ambition, can in general be sought or obtained by her only through him, it would be a miracle if the object of being attractive to men had not become the polar star of feminine education and formation of character. (pp. 232–233)[4]

Although Mill objected to fostering passivity and dependency in girls, other educators felt that this was precisely their duty. One of the more influential of the 19th century, Hannah More, rejected outright the proposal that women should share the same type of education as men, because "the chief end to be proposed in cultivating the understanding of women" was "to qualify them for the practical purposes of life" (see Smith, 1970, p. 101). To set one's sights on other than harmonious domesticity was to defy the natural order. Her readers were advised to be excellent women rather than indifferent men; to follow the "plain path which Providence has obviously marked out to the sex . . . rather than . . . stray awkwardly, unbecomingly, and unsuccessfully, in a forbidden road" (Smith, 1970, pp.

100–101). Her values were consonant with those held by most of the middle class, and so her *Strictures on the Modern System of Female Education* (More, 1800) enjoyed widespread popularity for some time.

By the latter part of the century, the question had turned from whether girls should be educated like boys to how much they should be educated like boys. With the shift in emphasis came the question of coeducation. One of the strongest objections to coeducation in adolescence was the threat it posed to the "normalization" of the menstrual period. G. Stanley Hall (1906) waxed poetic on the issue:

> At a time when her whole future life depends upon normalizing the lunar month, is there not something not only unnatural and unhygienic, but a little monstrous, in daily school associations with boys, where she must suppress and conceal her instincts and feelings, at those times when her own promptings suggest withdrawal or stepping a little aside to let Lord Nature do his magnificent work of efflorescence. (p. 590)

Edward Clarke (see Sinclair, 1965, p. 123) had earlier elucidated the physiological reason for the restraint of girls from exertion in their studies: by forcing their brains to do work at puberty, they would use up blood later needed for menstruation.

Hall proposed an educational system for girls that would not only take into consideration their delicate physical nature but would also be tailored to prepare them for their special role in society. He feared that women's competition with men "in the world" would cause them to neglect their instinctive maternal urges and so bring about "race suicide." Because the glory of the female lay in motherhood, Hall believed that all educational and social institutions should be structured with that end in mind. Domestic arts would therefore be emphasized in special schools for adolescent girls, and disciplines such as philosophy, chemistry, and mathematics would be treated only superficially. If a girl had a notion to stay in the "male" system, she should be able to, but, Hall warned, such a woman selfishly interested in self-fulfillment would also be less likely to bear children and so be confined to an "agamic" life, thus failing to reproduce those very qualities that made her strong (Hall, 1918).

Throughout Hall's panegyric upon the beauties of female domestic education, there runs an undercurrent of the *real* threat that he perceived in coeducation, and that was the "feminization" of the American male. David Starr Jordan (1902) shared this objection but felt that coeducation would nevertheless make young men more "civilized" and young women less frivolous, tempering their natural pubescent inclinations. He was no champion of female ability though, stressing that women "on the whole, lack originality" (p. 100). The educated woman, he said, "is likely to master technic rather than art; method, rather than substance. She may know a good deal, but she can do nothing" (p. 101). In spite of this, he did assert that their training is just as serious and important as that of men. His position strongly favored the notion that the smaller range of female ability was the cause of lackluster female academic performance.

The issue of coeducation was not easily settled, and even as late as 1935, one finds debates over its relative merits (*Encyclopedia of the Social Sciences*, 1935, pp. 614–617).

The Biological Bases of Sex Differences

The variability hypothesis was compatible not only with prevailing attitudes concerning the appropriate form of female education but also with a highly popular theory of the biological complementarity of the sexes. The main tenet of Geddes and Thomson's (1890) theory was that males are primarily "catabolic," females "anabolic." From this difference in metabolism, all other sex differences in physical, intellectual, and emotional makeup were derived. The male was more agile, creative, and variable; the female was truer to the species type and therefore, in all respects, less variable. The conservatism of the female insured the continuity of the species. The authors stressed the metabolic antecedents of female conservatism and male differentiation rather than variational tendency per se, and also put emphasis on the complementarity of the two natures:

> The feminine passivity is expressed in greater patience, more open-mindedness, greater appreciation of subtle details, and consequently what we call more rapid intuition. The masculine activity lends a greater power of maximum effort, of scientific insight, or cerebral experiment with impressions, and is associated with an unobservant or impatient disregard of minute details, but with a more stronger grasp of generalities. (p. 271)

The presentation of evolutionary theory anchored in yin–yang concepts of function represents the most positive evaluation of the female sex offered by 19th-century science. Whatever woman's shortcomings, they were necessary to complete her nature, which itself was necessary to complete man's: "Man thinks more, woman feels more. He discovers more, but remembers less; she is more receptive, and less forgetful" (Geddes & Thomson, 1890, p. 271).

Variability and the Testing Movement

Helen Thompson (later Woolley) put Geddes and Thomson's and other theories of sex differences in ability to what she felt was a crucial experimental test (see Thompson, 1903). Twenty-five men and 25 women participated in nearly 20 hours of individual testing of their intellectual, motor, and sensory abilities. Of more importance than her experimental results (whether men or women can tap a telegraph key more times per minute has lost its significance to psychology) was her discussion of the implications of the resulting negligible differences for current theories of sex differences. She was especially critical of the mass of inconsistencies inherent in contemporary biological theories:

> Women are said to represent concentration, patience, and stability in emotional life. One might logically conclude that prolonged concentration of attention and unbiased generalization would be their intellectual characteristics, but these are the very characteristics assigned to men. (p. 173)

In the face of such contradictions, she was forced to conclude that "if the author's views as to the mental differences of sex had been different, they might as easily have derived a very different set of characteristics" (pp. 173–174). Thompson singled out the variability hypothesis for special criticism, objecting not only to the use of physical variation as evidence for intellectual variation but also to the tendency to minimize environmental influences. She held that training was responsible for sex differences in variation, and to those who countered that it is really a fundamental difference of instincts and characteristics that determines the differences in training, she replied that if this were true, "it would not be necessary to spend so much time and effort in making boys and girls follow the lines of conduct proper to their sex" (p. 181).

Thompson's recommendation to look at environmental factors went unheeded, as more and more evidence of woman's incapability of attaining eminence was amassed. In the surveys of eminent persons that were popular at the turn of the century, more credence was given to nature (à la Hall) than nurture (à la Thompson) for the near absence of eminent women (Cattell, 1903; Ellis, 1904). Cattell (1903) found a ready-made explanation in the variability hypothesis: "Women depart less from the normal than man," ergo "the distribution of women is represented by a narrower bell-shaped curve" (p. 375). Cora Castle's (1913) survey of eminent women was no less critical of woman's failure to achieve at the top levels of power and prestige.

One of the most influential individuals to take up the cause of the variability hypothesis was Edward Thorndike. Much of the early work in the testing movement was done at Columbia University, which provided the perfect milieu for Thorndike's forays into the variability problem as applied to mental testing and educational philosophy. Thorndike based his case for the acceptance of the variability hypothesis on the reevaluation of the results of two studies (Thompson, 1903; Wissler, 1901) that had not themselves been directed toward the issue. Thorndike insisted that greater male variability only became meaningful when one examined the distribution of ability at the highest levels of giftedness. Measurement of more general sex differences could only "prove that the sexes are closely alike and that sex can account for only a very small fraction of human mental differences in the abilities listed" (Thorndike, 1910, p. 185). Since the range of female ability was narrower, he reasoned, the talents of women should be channeled into fields in which they would be most needed and most successful because "this one fundamental difference in variability is more important than all the differences between the average male and female capacities" (Thorndike, 1906):

> Not only the probability and the desirability of marriage and the training of children as an essential feature of woman's career, but also the restriction of women to the mediocre grades of ability and achievement should be reckoned with by our educational systems. The education of women for . . . professions . . . where a very few gifted individuals are what society requires, is far less needed than for such professions as nursing, teaching, medicine, or architecture, where the average level is the essential. (p. 213)

He felt perfectly justified in this recommendation because of "the patent fact that in the great achievements of the world in science, as, invention, and management, women have been far excelled by men" (Thorndike, 1910, p. 35). In Thorndike's view, environmental factors scarcely mattered. Others, like Joseph Jastrow (1915), seemed to recognize the tremendous influence that societal pressures had upon achievement. He noted that even when women had been admitted to employment from which they had previously been excluded, new prejudices arose; "allowances and considerations for sex intrude, favorably or unfavorably; the avenues of preferment, though ostensibly open are really barred by invisible barriers of social prejudice" (pp. 567–568). This was little more than lip service because he was even more committed to the importance of variational tendency and its predominance over any possible extenuating factors: the effects of the variability of the male and the biological conservatism of the female "radiates to every distinctive aspect of their contrasted natures and expressions" (p. 568).

A small but persistent minority challenged the validity of the variability hypothesis, and it is not surprising that this minority was composed mainly of women. Although the "woman question" was, to some degree, at issue, the larger dispute was between those who stressed "nature" as the major determinant of ability (and therefore success) and those who rejected nature and its corollary, instead emphasizing the importance of environmental factors. Helen Thompson Woolley, while remaining firmly committed to the investigation of the differential effects of social factors on each sex, did not directly involve herself in the variability controversy. Leta Stetter Hollingworth, first a student and then a colleague of Thorndike's at Teachers College of Columbia University, actively investigated the validity of the hypothesis and presented sound objections to it. She argued that there was no real basis for assuming that the distribution of "mental traits" in the population conforms without exception to the Gaussian distribution. The assumption of normality was extremely important to the validity of the variability hypothesis, because only in a normal distribution would a difference in variability indicate a difference in range. It was the greater range of male ability that was used to "prove" the ultimate superiority of male ability. Greater range of male ability was usually verified by citing lists of eminent persons (dominated by men) and the numbers and sex of those in institutions for the feebleminded (also dominated by men). Hollingworth (1914) saw no reason to resort to biological theory for an explanation of the phenomenon when a more parsimonious one was available in social fact. Statistics reporting a larger number of males among the feebleminded could be explained by the fact that the supporting data had been gathered in institutions, where men were more likely to be admitted than women of an equal degree of retardation. The better ability of feebleminded women to survive outside the institutional setting was simply a function of female social role:

> Women have been and are a dependent and non-competitive class, and when defective can more easily survive outside of institutions, since they do not have to compete *mentally* with normal individuals, as men do, to maintain themselves in the social *milieu*. (Hollingworth, 1914, p. 515)

Women would therefore be more likely to be institutionalized at an older age than men, after they had become too old to be "useful" or self-supporting. A survey of age and sex ratios in New York institutions supported her hypothesis: the ratio of females to males increased with the age of the inmates (Hollingworth, 1913). As for the rarity of eminence among women,

Hollingworth (1914) argued that because the social role of women was defined in terms of housekeeping and child-rearing functions, "a field where eminence is not possible," and because of concomitant constraints placed on the education and employment of women by law, custom, and the demands of the role, one could not possibly validly compare the achievements of women with those of men who "have followed the greatest possible range of occupations, and have at the same time procreated unhindered" (p. 528). She repeatedly emphasized (Hollingworth, 1914, 1916) that the true potential of woman could only be known when she began to receive social acceptance of her right to choose career, maternity, or both.

Hollingworth's argument that unrecognized differences in social training had misdirected the search for *inherent* sex differences had earlier been voiced by Mary Calkins (1896). Just as Hollingworth directed her response particularly at Thorndike's formulation of the variability hypothesis, Calkins objected to Jastrow's (1896) intimations that one finds "greater uniformity amongst women than amongst men" (p. 431).

Hollingworth's work was instrumental in bringing the variability issue to a crisis point, not only because she presented persuasive empirical data to support her contentions but also because this was simply the first major opposition that the variability hypothesis had encountered. Real resolution of this crisis had to await the development of more sophisticated testing and statistical techniques. With the United States' involvement in World War I, most testing efforts were redirected to wartime uses. This redirection effectively terminated the variability debate, and although it resumed during the postwar years, the renewed controversy never attained the force of conviction that had characterized the earlier period. "Variational tendency" became a statistical issue, and the pedagogic implications that had earlier colored the debate were either minimized or disguised in more egalitarian terms.

After its revival in the mid-1920s, investigation of the variability hypothesis was often undertaken as part of larger intelligence testing projects. Evidence in its favor began to look more convincing than it ever had. The use of larger samples, standardized tests, and newer methods of computing variation gave an appearance of increased accuracy, but conclusions were still based on insubstantial evidence of questionable character. Most discussions of the topic concluded that there were not enough valid data to resolve the issue and that even if that data were available, variation within each sex is so much greater than the difference in variation between sexes that the "meaning" of the variability hypothesis was trivial (Shields, Note 1).

Maternal Instinct

The concept of maternal instinct was firmly entrenched in American psychology before American psychology itself existed as an entity. The first book to appear in the United States with "psychology" in its title outlined the psychological sex differences arising from the physical differences between men and women. Differences in structure were assumed to imply differences in function, and therefore differences in abilities, temperament, and intelligence. In each sex a different set of physical systems was thought to predominate: "In man the arterial and cerebral systems prevail, and with them irritability; in woman the venous and ganglion systems and with them plasticity and sensibility" (Rausch, 1841, p. 81). The systems dominant in woman caused her greatest attributes to lie in the moral sphere in the form of love, patience, and chastity. In the intellectual sphere, she was not equally blessed, "and this is not accidental, not because no opportunity has offered itself to their productive genius . . . but because it is their highest happiness to be mothers" (Rausch, 1841, p. 83).[5]

Although there was popular acceptance of a maternal instinct in this country, the primary impetus for its incorporation into psychology came by way of British discussion of social evolution. While the variability hypothesis gained attention because of an argument, the concept of maternal instinct evolved without conflict. There was consistent agreement as to its existence, if not its precise nature or form. Typical of the evolutionary point of view was the notion that woman's emotional nature (including her tendency to nurturance) was a direct consequence of her reproductive physiology. As Herbert Spencer (1891) explained it, the female's energies were directed toward preparation for pregnancy and lactation, reducing the energy available for the development of other qualities. This resulted in a "rather earlier cessation of individual evolution" in the female. Woman was, in essence, a stunted man. Her lower stage of development was evident not only in her interior mental and emotional powers but also in the resulting expression of the parental instinct. Whereas the objectivity of the male caused his concern to be extended "to all the relatively weak who are dependent upon him" (p. 375), the female's propensity to "dwell on the concrete and proximate rather than on the abstract and remote" made her incapable of the generalized protective attitude assumed by the male. Instead, she was primarily responsive to "infantile helplessness."

Alexander Sutherland (1898) also described a parental instinct whose major characteristic (concern for the weak) was "the basis of all other sympathy," which is itself "the ultimate basis of all moral feeling" (p. 156). Like his contemporaries (e.g., McDougall, 1913, 1923; Shand, 1920; Spencer, 1891), Sutherland revered maternal sentiment but thought the expression of parental instinct in the male, that is, a protective attitude, was a much more significant factor in social evolution, an attitude of benevolent paternalism more in keeping with Victorian social ethic than biological reality. The expression of the parental instinct in men, Sutherland thought, must necessarily lead to deference toward women out of "sympathetic regard for women's weakness." He noted that male protectiveness had indeed wrought a change in the relations between the sexes, evident in a trend away from sexual motivations and toward a general improvement in moral tone, witness the "large number of men who lead perfectly chaste lives for ten or twenty years after puberty before they marry," which demonstrated that the "sensuous side of man's nature is slowly passing under the control of sympathetic sentiments" (p. 288).[6]

Whatever facet of the activity that was emphasized, there was common agreement that the maternal (or parental) instinct was truly an instinct. A. F. Shand (1920) argued that the maternal instinct is actually composed of an ordered "system" of instincts and characterized by a number of emotions. Despite its complexity, "maternal love" was considered to be a hereditary trait "in respect not only of its instincts, but also of the bond connecting its primary emotions, and of the end which the whole system pursues, namely, the preservation of the offspring" (p. 42). The sociologist L. T. Hobhouse (1916) agreed that maternal instinct was a "true" instinct, "not only in the drive but in some of the detail." He doubted the existence of a corresponding paternal instinct, however, since he had observed that few men have a natural aptitude with babies.

The unquestioning acceptance of the maternal instinct concept was just as prevalent in this country as it was in Britain. William James (1950) listed parental love among the instincts of humans and emphasized the strength with which it was expressed in women. He was particularly impressed with the mother-infant relationship and quoted at length from a German psychologist concerning the changes wrought in a woman at the birth of her child: "She has, in one word, transferred her entire egoism to the child, and lives only in it" (p. 439). Even among those who employed a much narrower definition of instinct than James, maternal behavior was thought to be mediated by inherent neural connections. R. P. Halleck (1895) argued that comparatively few instincts are fully developed in humans, because reason intervenes and modifies their expression to fit the circumstances. Maternal instinct qualified as a clear exception, and its expression seemed as primitive and unrefined as that of infants' reflexive behavior.

Others (e.g., Jastrow, 1915; Thorndike, 1914a, 1914b) treated instinct more as a quality of character than of biology. Edward Thorndike (1911) considered the instincts peculiar to each sex to be the primary source of sex differences: "it appears that if the primary sex characters—the instincts directly related to courtship, love, child-bearing, and nursing—are left out of account, the average man differs from the average woman far less than many men differ from one another" (p. 30). Thorndike taught that the tendency to display maternal concern was universal among women, although social pressures could "complicate or deform" it. He conceded that males share in an instinctive "good will toward children," but other instincts, such as the "hunting instinct," predominated (Thorndike, 1914b). He was so sure of the innate instinctual differences between men and women that it was his contention (Thorndike, 1914b) that even "if we should keep the environment of boys and girls absolutely similar these instincts would produce sure and important differences between the mental and moral activities of boys and girls" (p. 203). The expression of instincts therefore was thought to have far-reaching effects on seemingly unrelated areas of ability and conduct. For example, woman's "nursing instinct," which was most often exhibited in "unreasoning tendencies to pet, coddle, and 'do for' others," was also "the chief source of woman's superiorities in the moral life" (Thorndike, 1914a, p. 203). Another of the female's instinctive tendencies was described as "submission to mastery":

> Women in general are thus by original nature submissive to men in general. Submissive behavior is apparently not annoying when assumed as the instinctive response to its natural stimulus. Indeed, it is perhaps a common satisfier. (Thorndike, 1914b, p. 34)

The existence of such an "instinct" would, of course, validate the social norm of female subservience and dependence. An assertive woman would be acting contrary to instinct and therefore contrary to *nature*. There is a striking similarity between Thorndike's description of female nature and that of the Freudians with their mutual emphasis on woman's passivity, dependency, and masochism. For Thorndike, however, the *cause* of such a female attitude was thought to be something quite different from mutilation fears and penis envy.

The most vocal proponent of instinct, first in England and later in this country, was William McDougall (1923). Unlike Shand, he regarded "parental sentiment" as a primary instinct and did not hesitate to be highly critical of those who disagreed with him. When his position was maligned by the behaviorists, his counterattack was especially strong:

> And, when we notice how in so many ways the behavior of the human mother most closely resembles that of the animal-mother, can we doubt that . . . if the animal-mother is moved by the impulse of a maternal instinct, so also is the woman? To repudiate this view as baseless would seem to me the height of blindness and folly, yet it is the folly of a number of psychologists who pride themselves on being strictly "scientific." (p. 136)

In McDougall's system of instincts, each of the primary instincts in humans was accompanied by a particular emotional quality. The parental instinct had as its primary emotional quality the "tender emotion" vaguely defined as love, tenderness, and tender feeling. Another of the primary instincts was that of "pairing," its primary emotional quality that of sexual emotion or excitement, "sometimes called love—an unfortunate and confusing usage" (p. 234). Highly critical of what he called the "Freudian dogma that all love is sexual," McDougall proposed that it was the interaction of the parental and pairing instincts that was the basis of heterosexual "love." "Female coyness," which initiated the courtship ritual, was simply the reproductively oriented manifestation of the instincts of self-display and self-abasement. The appearance of a suitable male would elicit coyness from the female, and at that point the male's parental instinct would come into play:

> A certain physical weakness and delicacy (probably moral also) about the normal young woman or girl constitute in her a resemblance to a child. This resemblance . . . throws the man habitually into the protective attitude, evokes the impulse and emotion of the parental instinct. He feels that he wants to protect and shield and help her in every way. (p. 425)

Once the "sexual impulse" had added its energy to the relationship, the young man was surely trapped, and the survival of the species was insured. McDougall, while firmly committed to the importance of instinct all the way up the evolutionary ladder, never lost his sense of Victorian delicacy: while pairing simply meant reproduction in lower animals, in humans it was accorded a tone of gallantry and concern.

The fate of instinct at the hands of the radical behaviorists is a well-known tale. Perhaps the most adamant, as well as notorious, critic of the instinct concept was J. B. Watson (1926). Like those before him who had relied upon observation to prove the existence of maternal instinct, he used observation to confirm its nonexistence:

We have observed the nursing, handling, bathing, etc. of the first baby of a good many mothers. Certainly there are no new ready-made activities appearing except nursing. The mother is usually as awkward about that as she can well be. The instinctive factors are practically nil. (p. 54)

Watson attributed the appearance of instinctive behavior to the mother's effort to conform to societal expectations of her successful role performance. He, like the 19th-century British associationist Alexander Bain, speculated that not a little of the mother's pleasure in nursing and caring for the infant was due to the sexually stimulating effect of those activities.[7]

Even the most dedicated behaviorists hedged a bit when it came to discarding the idea of instinct altogether. Although the teleology and redundancy of the concept of instinct were sharply criticized, some belief in "instinctive activity" was typically retained (cf. Dunlap, 1919–1920). W. B. Pillsbury (1926), for example, believed that the parental instinct was a "secondary" instinct. Physical attraction to the infant guided the mother's first positive movements toward the infant, but trial and error guided her subsequent care. Instinct was thought of as that quality which set the entire pattern of maternal behavior in motion.

In time instinct was translated into *drive* and *motivation,* refined concepts more in keeping with behavioristic theory. Concomitantly, interest in the maternal instinct of human females gave way to the study of mothering behavior in rodents. The concept of maternal instinct did find a place in psychoanalytic theory, but its definition bore little resemblance to that previously popular. Not only did maternal instinct lose the connotation of protectiveness and gentility that an earlier generation of psychologists had ascribed to it, but it was regarded as basically sexual, masochistic, and even destructive in nature (cf. Rheingold, 1964).

The Ascendancy of Psychoanalytic Theory

The functionalists, because of their emphasis on "nature," were predictably indifferent to the study of social sex roles and cultural concepts of masculine and feminine. The behaviorists, despite their emphasis on "nurture," were slow to recognize those same social forces. During the early 1930s, there was little meaningful ongoing research in female psychology: the point of view taken by the functionalists was no longer a viable one, and the behaviorists with their emphasis on nonsocial topics (i.e., learning and motivation) had no time for serious consideration of sex differences. While the functionalists had defined laws of behavior that mirrored the society of the times, behaviorists concentrated their efforts on defining universal laws that operated in any time, place, or organism. Individual differences in nature were expected during the functionalist era because they were the sine qua non of a Darwinian view of the world and of science. The same individual differences were anathema to early learning-centered psychology because, no longer necessary or expedient, they were a threat to the formulation of universal laws of behavior.

In the hiatus created by the capitulation of functionalism to behaviorism, the study of sex differences and female nature fell within the domain of psychoanalytic theory—the theory purported to have all the answers. Freudian theory (or some form of it) had for some years already served as the basis for a psychology of female physiological function (cf. Benedek & Rubenstein, 1939). The application of principles popular in psychiatry and medicine (and their inescapable identification with pathology) to academic psychology was easily accomplished. Psychoanalytic theory provided psychology with the first comprehensive theoretical explanation of sex differences. Its novelty in that respect aided its assimilation.

Psychology proper, as well as the general public, had been well-prepared for a biological, and frankly sexual, theory of male and female nature. Havelock Ellis, although himself ambivalent and even hostile toward Freudian teachings, had done much through his writing to encourage openness in the discussion of sexuality. He brought a number of hitherto unmentionable issues to open discussion, couching them in the commonly accepted notion of the complementarity of the sexes, thus insuring their popular acceptance. Emphasis on masculinity and femininity as real dimensions of personality appeared in the mid-1930s in the form of the Terman Masculinity-Femininity Scale (Terman & Miles, 1968). Although Lewis Terman himself avoided discussion of whether masculinity and femininity were products of nature or nurture, social determinants of masculinity and femininity were commonly deemphasized in favor of the notion that they were a type of psychological secondary sexual characteristic. Acceptance of social sex role soon came to be perceived as an indicator of one's mental health.

The traps inherent in a purely psychoanalytic concept of female nature were seldom recognized. John Dewey's (1957) observation, made in 1922, merits attention, not only for its accuracy but because its substance can be found in present-day refutations of the adequacy of psychaoanlytic theory as an explanation of woman's behavior and "nature":

> The treatment of sex by psycho-analysts is most instructive, for it flagrantly exhibits both the consequences of artificial simplification and the transformation of social results into psychic causes. Writers, usually male, hold forth on the psychology of women, as if they were dealing with a Platonic universal entity, although they habitually treat men as individuals, varying with structure and environment. They treat phenomena which are peculiarly symptoms of civilization of the West at the present time as if they were the necessary effects of fixed nature impulses of human nature. (pp. 143–144)

The identification of the psychology of women with psychoanalytic theory was nearly complete by the mid-1930s and was so successful that many psychologists today, even those most deeply involved in the current movement for a psychology of women, are not aware that there was a psychology of women long before there was a Sigmund Freud. This article has dealt only with a brief period in that history, and then only with the most significant topics of that period. Lesser issues were often just as hotly debated, for example, whether there is an innate difference in the style of handwriting of men and women (cf. Allen, 1927; Downey, 1910).

And what has happened to the issues of brain size, variability, and maternal instinct since the 1930s? Where they are politically and socially useful, they have an uncanny knack of reappearing, albeit in an altered form.

For example, the search for central nervous system differences between males and females has continued. Perhaps the most popular form this search has taken is the theory of prenatal hormonal "organization" of the hypothalamus into exclusively male or female patterns of function (Harris & Levine, 1965). The proponents of this theory maintain an Aristotelian view of woman as an incomplete man:

> In the development of the embryo, nature's first choice or primal impulse is to differentiate a female. . . . The principle of differentiation is always that to obtain a male, something must be added. Subtract that something, and the result will be a female. (Money, 1970, p. 428)

The concept of maternal instinct, on the other hand, has recently been taken up and refashioned by a segment of the woman's movement. Pregnancy and childbirth are acclaimed as important expressions of womanliness whose satisfactions cannot be truly appreciated by males. The idea that women are burdened with "unreasoning tendencies to pet, coddle, and 'do for' others" has been disposed of by others and replaced by the semiserious proposal that if any "instinctive" component of parental concern exists, it is a peculiarly male attribute (Stannard, 1970). The variability hypothesis is all but absent from contemporary psychological work, but if it ever again promises a viable justification for existing social values, it will be back as strongly as ever. Conditions which would favor its revival include the renaissance of rugged individualism or the "need" to suppress some segment of society, for example, women's aspirations to positions of power. In the first case the hypothesis would serve to reaffirm that there are those "born to lead," and in the latter that there are those "destined to follow."

Of more importance than the issues themselves or their fate in contemporary psychology is the recognition of the role that they have played historically in the psychology of women: the role of social myth. Graves (1968, p. v) included among the functions of mythologizing that of justification of existing social systems. This function was clearly operative throughout the evolutionist-functionalist treatment of the psychology of women: the "discovery" of sex differences in brain structure to correspond to "appropriate" sex differences in brain function; the biological justification (via the variability hypothesis) for the enforcement of woman's subordinate social status; the Victorian weakness and gentility associated with maternity; and pervading each of these themes, the assumption of an innate emotional, sexless, unimaginative female character that played the perfect foil to the Darwinian male. That science played handmaiden to social values cannot be denied. Whether a parallel situation exists in today's study of sex differences is open to question.

NOTES

1. Ellis (1934) claimed that Broca's opinion changed over time. Broca

   > became inclined to think that it [the hypothesized male superiority of intellect] was merely a matter of education—of muscular . . . not merely mental, education—and he thought that if left to their spontaneous impulses men and women would tend to resemble each other, as happens in the savage condition. (p. 222)

2. Burt and Moore (1912, p. 385), inspired by contemporary theories of cortical localization of function, proposed a neurological theory of female affectability. On the basis of the popular belief that the thalamus was "the centre for the natural expression of the emotions" while "control of movements and the association of ideas" was localized in the cortex and the common assumption that the male was more inclined to be intellectual and rational and the female more passionate and emotional, they concluded that in the adult male the cortex would tend to be "more completely organized," while in the adult female "the thalamus tends to appear more completely organized." They came to the general conclusion that "the mental life of man is predominantly cortical; that of woman predominantly thalamic."

3. One of Ellis's biographers (Calder-Marshall, 1959, pp. 97–98) has suggested that Ellis was "wildly jealous" of Karl Pearson's influence on Olive Schreiner, the controversial South African writer. Schreiner first met Pearson in 1885, over a year after she had met Ellis, and according to Calder-Marshall "was vastly attracted to him [Pearson] in what she considered to be a selfless Hintonian sense. . . . She regarded him as a brilliant young man, dying of tuberculosis, whose few remaining years it was her selfless duty to solace" (Pearson died in 1936). Calder-Marshall summed up the triangle in few, but insinuating, phrases:

> Exactly what was happening between Karl Pearson and Olive Schreiner during these months [August 1885–December 1886] is a matter more for any future biographer of Olive Schreiner . . . it is enough to know that Olive did her best to remain loyal to both her friends without telling too many lies, and that while Olive remained the most important person in Havelock's life, the most important person in Olive's was Karl Pearson from the time she first met him to a considerable time after she left England. (p. 98)

Ellis's rivalry with Pearson could explain his bitter and supercilious treatment of Pearson's venture into "variational tendency," since Ellis was not one to easily accept an assault on his ego. For his part Pearson "despised the Hinton group, including Ellis. He thought they were flabby-minded, unhealthy and immoral" (p. 97). But these opinions, while possibly influencing him to write on variation originally, did not intrude upon a fair-minded scientific discussion of the matter.

4. One of the severest critics of Mill's defense of women was Sigmund Freud. He felt Mill's propositions were in direct contradiction to woman's "true" nature:

> It is really a stillborn thought to send women into the struggle for existence exactly as men. . . . I believe that all reforming action in law and education would break down in front of the fact that, long before the age at which a man can earn a position in society, Nature has determined woman's destiny through beauty, charm, and sweetness. Law and custom have much to give women that has been withheld from them, but the position of women will surely be what it is: in youth an adored darling and in mature years a loved wife. (quoted in Reeves, 1971, pp. 163–164)

5. This sentiment was echoed by Bruno Bettelheim (1965) over 100 years later: "as much as women want to be good scientists or engineers, they want first and foremost to be womanly companions of men and to be mothers" (p. 15).

6. Similar observations were made concerning women. Sutherland (1898) noted that because social morality had developed to such a high level, women "now largely enter upon marriage out of purely sympathetic attractions, in which sex counts for something, but with all its grosser aspects gone." He happily reported another's finding that "sexual desire enters not at all into the minds of a very large proportion of women when contemplating matrimony" (p. 288).

7. Bain's (1875) position was similar except that he believed that there *was* an innate tendency to nurture that initiated the entire cycle of positive affect-positive action. The instinct was thought to be a natural "sentiment," which was fostered by the long period of gestation and the "special energies" required of the mother to sustain the infant. The positive affect arising from activity connected with the infant then brought about increased nurturance and increased pleasure. At least part of this pleasure was thought to be physical in nature.

REFERENCES

ALLEN, C. N. Studies in sex differences. *Psychological Bulletin*, 1927, *24*, 294–304.

BAIN, A. *Mental science*. New York: Appleton, 1875.

BENEDEK, T., & RUBENSTEIN, B. B. The correlations between ovarian activity and psychodynamic processes. II. The menstrual phase. *Psychosomatic Medicine*, 1939, *1*, 461–485.

BETTELHEIM, B. The commitment required of a woman entering a scientific profession in present-day American society. In J. A. Mattfield & C. G. Van Aken (Eds.), *Women and the scientific professions*. Cambridge, Mass.: M.I.T. Press, 1965.

BURT, C., & MOORE, R. C. The mental differences between the sexes. *Journal of Experimental Pedagogy*, 1912, *1*, 355–388.

CALDER-MARSHALL, A. *The sage of sex.* New York: Putnam, 1959.

CALKINS, M. W. Community of ideas of men and women. *Psychological Review*, 1896, *3*, 426–430.

CASTLE, C. A. A statistical study of eminent women. *Columbia Contributions to Philosophy and Psychology*, 1913, *22*(27).

CATTELL, J. MCK. A statistical study of eminent men. *Popular Science Monthly*, 1903, *62*, 359–377.

DARWIN, C. *The descent of man* (2nd ed.). London: John Murray, 1922. (Originally published, 1871; 2nd edition originally published, 1874.)

DEWEY, J. *Human nature and conduct.* New York: Random House, 1957.

DOWNEY, J. E. Judgment on the sex of handwriting. *Psychological Review*, 1910, *17*, 205–216.

DUNLAP, J. Are there any instincts? *Journal of Abnormal and Social Psychology*, 1919–1920, *14*, 307–311.

ELLIOTT, H. C. *Textbook of neuroanatomy* (2nd ed.). Philadelphia: Lippincott, 1969.

ELLIS, H. *Man and woman: A study of human secondary sexual characters.* London: Walter Scott; New York: Scribner's, 1894.

ELLIS, H. Variation in man and woman. *Popular Science Monthly*, 1903, *62*, 237–253.

ELLIS, H. *A study of British genius.* London: Hurst & Blackett, 1904.

ELLIS, H. *Man and woman, a study of secondary and tertiary sexual characteristics* (8th rev. ed.). London: Heinemann, 1934.

Encyclopedia of the Social Sciences. New York: Macmillan, 1935.

GALTON, F. *Inquiries into the human faculty and its development.* London: Dent, 1907.

GEDDES, P., & THOMSON, J. A. *The evolution of sex.* New York: Scribner & Welford, 1890.

GRAVES, R. Introduction. In *New Larousse encyclopedia of mythology* (Rev. ed.). London: Paul Hamlyn, 1968.

HALL, G. S. The question of coeducation. *Munsey's Magazine*, 1906, *34*, 588–592.

HALL, G. S. *Youth, its education, regimen and hygiene.* New York: Appleton, 1918.

HALLECK, R. *Psychology and psychic culture.* New York: American Book, 1895.

HARRIS, G. W., & LEVINE, S. Sexual differentiation of the brain and its experimental control. *Journal of Physiology*, 1965, *181*, 379–400.

HOBHOUSE, L. *Morals in evolution.* New York: Holt, 1916.

HOLLINGWORTH, L. S. The frequency of amentia as related to sex. *Medical Record*, 1913, *84*, 753–756.

HOLLINGWORTH, L. S. Variability as related to sex differences in achievement. *American Journal of Sociology*, 1914, *19*, 510–530.

HOLLINGWORTH, L. S. Social devices for impelling women to bear and rear children. *American Journal of Sociology*, 1916, *22*, 19–29.

HUARTE, J. *The examination of mens wits* (trans. from Spanish to Italian by M. Camilli; trans. from Italian to English by R. Carew). Gainesville, Fla.: Scholars' Facsimiles and Reprints, 1959.

JAMES, W. *The principles of psychology.* New York: Dover, 1950.

JASTROW, J. Note on Calkins' "Community of ideas of men and women." *Psychological Review*, 1896, *3*, 430–431.

JASTROW, J. *Character and temperament.* New York: Appleton, 1915.

JORDAN, D. S. The higher education of women. *Popular Science Monthly*, 1902, *62*, 97–107.

MALL, F. P. On several anatomical characters of the human brain, said to vary according to race and sex, with especial reference to the weight of the frontal lobe. *American Journal of Anatomy*, 1909, *9*, 1–32.

MC DOUGALL, W. *An introduction to social psychology* (7th ed.). London: Methuen, 1913.

MC DOUGALL, MEYER, M. *Psychology of the other-one.* Columbia: Missouri Book, 1921.

MILL, J. S. *The subjection of women.* London: Dent, 1955.

MOBIUS, P. J. The physiological mental weakness of woman (A. McCorn, Trans.). *Alienist and Neurologist*, 1901, *22*, 624–642.

MONEY, J. Sexual dimorphism and homosexual gender identity. *Psychological Bulletin*, 1970, *74*, 425–440.

MORE, H. *Strictures on the modern system of female education. With a view of the principles and conduct prevalent among women of rank and fortune.* Philadelphia, Pa.: Printed by Budd and Bertram for Thomas Dobson, 1800.

PATRICK, G. T. W. The psychology of woman. *Popular Science Monthly*, 1895, *47*, 209–225.

PEARSON, K. Variation in man and woman. In *The chances of death* (Vol. 1). London: Edward Arnold, 1897.

PILLSBURY, W. B. *Education as the psychologist sees it.* New York: Macmillan, 1926.

PORTEUS, S., & BABCOCK, M. E. *Temperament and race.* Boston: Gorham Press, 1926.

RAUSCH, F. A. *Psychology; Or, a view of the human soul including anthropology* (2nd rev. ed.). New York: Dodd, 1841.

REEVES, N. *Womankind.* Chicago: Aldine-Atherton, 1971.

RHEINGOLD, J. *The fear of being a woman.* New York: Grune & Stratton, 1964.

ROMANES, G. J. Mental differences between men and women. *Nineteenth Century,* 1887, *21,* 654–672.

SHAND, A. F. *The foundations of character.* London: Macmillan, 1920.

SINCLAIR, A. *The better half: The emancipation of the American woman.* New York: Harper & Row, 1965.

SMITH, P. *Daughters of the promised land.* Boston: Little, Brown, 1970.

SPENCER, H. *The study of sociology.* New York: Appleton, 1891.

STANNARD, U. Adam's rib, or the woman within. *Trans-Action,* 1970, *8,* 24–35.

SUTHERLAND, A. *The origin and growth of the moral instinct* (Vol. 1). London: Longmans, Green, 1898.

TERMAN, L., & MILES, C. C. *Sex and personality.* New York: Russell and Russell, 1968.

THOMPSON, H. B. *The mental traits of sex.* Chicago: University of Chicago Press, 1903.

THORNDIKE, E. L. Sex in education. *The Bookman,* 1906, *23,* 211–214.

THORNDIKE, E. L. *Educational psychology* (2nd ed.). New York: Teachers College, Columbia University, 1910.

THORNDIKE, E. L. *Individuality.* Boston: Houghton Mifflin, 1911.

THORNDIKE, E. L. *Educational psychology* (Vol. 3). New York: Teachers College, Columbia University, 1914. (a)

THORNDIKE, E. L. *Educational psychology briefer course.* New York: Teachers College, Columbia University, 1914. (b)

WALKER, A. *Woman physiologically considered.* New York: J. & H. G. Langley, 1850.

WATSON, J. B. Studies on the growth of the emotions. In *Psychologies of 1925.* Worcester, Mass.: Clark University Press, 1926.

WEININGER, O. *Sex and character* (trans.). London: Heinemann, 1906.

WISSLER, C. The correlation of mental and physical tests. *Psychological Review Monograph Supplements,* 1899–1901, *3*(6, Whole No. 16).

WOLLSTONECRAFT, M. *A vindication of the rights of woman.* New York: Dutton, 1955.

WOOLLEY, H. T. Psychological literature: A review of the recent literature on the psychology of sex. *Psychological Bulletin,* 1910, *7,* 335–342.

WUNDT, W. *Ethics.* Vol. 3: *The principles of morality, and the departments of the moral life* (M. F. Washburn, Trans.). London: Sonnenschein, 1901.

PART II
Psychoanalysis and the Woman Question

At the turn of the century, a Viennese physician named Sigmund Freud developed a complex theory of human behavior that has come to be known as psychoanalytic theory. It has since evolved into the Western world's most influential theory of human development. Freud's theory rests upon the idea of unconscious motivation, the belief that much of our behavior is motivated by psychic forces of which we are unaware. These forces, or drives, originate in the developmental events of early childhood, which, according to the theory, are fraught with conflicts. If not successfully resolved and integrated into the personality, these conflicts can disrupt normal development, resulting in neuroses and other maladaptive outcomes. An example is the well-known *Oedipal conflict*, whose resolution requires the child to abandon the unrealistic desire for exclusive possession of the opposite-sex parent, to identify with the same-sex parent, and, later, to transfer the old desire to an appropriate mate.

The therapeutic application of psychoanalytic theory is psychoanalysis. This is a treatment by which patients are supposed to come to an understanding of their inner conflicts. By doing so, they are relieved of their neurotic symptoms. Techniques such as dream interpretation and the free expression of thoughts in a relaxed state (free association) were developed by Freud and his followers in order to elicit material buried in the unconscious. The theory provides a framework for the understanding of such material, thus giving the patient and the therapist insight into the nature of the long-repressed conflicts.

The psychology of women was not a central concern of Freud's theory. In fact, he commented more than once that the topic was an enigma and that the mental life of women was less accessible than that of men. Nevertheless, he wrote three papers on the psychology of women, and his ideas were enormously influential in directing the thinking of his colleagues and followers, many of whom elaborated upon and expanded what he had to say.

Freud first dealt with the psychology of women in his article "Some Psychological Consequences of the Anatomical Distinction between the Sexes." In it he set forth his famous concept of penis envy, the various ways it could be resolved, and their fateful determination of the woman's future adjustment. In the normal course, he thought, she would accept her lack of a penis, substitute for it the wish for a child, and thereby attain a resolution of her conflict over being not-male when she became a wife and mother. As a corollary to this, she would give up her infantile gratification from the "masculine" clitoris, her recognition of its inferiority being a "necessary precondition for the development of femininity."

Freud thought that traces of penis envy persisted in the adult woman in the character trait of jealousy, which he said women manifest more than men do. Too, the development of the superego in women is less rigorous than it is in men, so that women have less sense of justice and are more emotional in their judgments than men are. Here Freud acknowledged the opposition of the feminists of his day, "who are anxious to force us to regard the two sexes as completely equal in position and worth." But Freud did not present these ideas as final truths about women. They stand, he said, "in urgent need of confirmation" before their value can be decided. He commented that his findings were based on only a handful of cases, needing validation from those who would come after him.

Psychoanalytic views about women have been widely disseminated and criticized. It is ironic that dissenting and refuting statements that began to appear within Freud's own time have never attracted as much attention as Freud's work. Current feminist criticism of Freud, for example, often completely ignores the fact that Freud had critics who took sharp exception to his theories of female personality and sexuality. These individuals are known as the neo-Freudians and are represented here by Karen Horney and Clara Thompson.

In "The Problem of Feminine Masochism" Karen Horney directly attacked the Freudian position that masochism was biologically inherent in the female condition and that it was thus normal for women to exhibit masochistic trends in their approach to life and in their relations with others. Horney wrote that such ideas were based on studies of small samples of neurotic women and that there were no substantive data to support generalizations of such personality characteristics to normal women. In addition to calling attention to this important methodological error, Horney argued for the power of cultural conditioning as a causal factor for the appearance of masochism in women. Inhibiting self-assertion, presenting oneself as weak and helpless and in need of special consideration, and permitting oneself to be exploited are all observable in masochistic women. But such phenomena could be expected, she said, in societies that restricted opportunities for women, held them to be inferior, made sure that they were economically dependent, and confined them to a life consisting of emotional bonds and the duties of caring and expressing compassion for others. Furthermore, in such societies, ideologies about woman's "true nature"—that she was weak, emotional, dependent, and so on—would arise, and her value as an erotic partner would then become dependent upon her conformity to the beliefs about her. The marvel is, Horney said, that any woman could escape becoming masochistic under such conditions: Yet many did escape. Thus it is clear, Horney argued, that biological factors have been greatly overestimated as determinants of female personality.

The American psychoanalyst Clara Thompson refuted the doctrine of penis envy in "Cultural Pressures in the Psychology of Women," published in 1942. Sometimes, she said, such envy was recalled by women in analysis. Even so, penis envy could be interpreted symbolically, "in this culture where the advantages go to the possessor of the penis"; Thompson analysed the changes in the girl's life, imposed by the culture, when she reaches puberty. She is restricted in her activities and must inhibit her natural aggression and hide her interest in males and in sex—all contributing to a diminished sense of self. As for her narcissism, her greater need for love, and the other character traits seen by classic theorists to be part of her biological makeup, she is required to incorporate these into her personality because of her insecure status and her economic dependency on man. Being sexually attractive to him becomes her profession, one which requires her to practice narcissistic concern and to appear to overvalue that which is in reality a dire necessity. In a further examinatition of the so-called "masculinity complex," Thompson shows how this, too, can develop in a culture that now holds out the promise to women of equality if they step forward to compete. But since women have no models of their own, it is not surprising if they sometimes appear to copy men and their behavior. "Imitating of a person superior to one is by no means unusual." Thompson's contribution was not confined to showing how female personality could be affected by culture. She insisted that her profession knew practically nothing about the sexuality and the "basic nature" of women. Her paper, then, was both a new perspective on the psychology of women and a challenge to ignorance.

As theory, the early psychoanalytic view of female personality represented here by Freud's paper is easy to criticize. Its importance lies in its explanation of behavior within a social order and in its widespread acceptance and application by professionals whose task it was to provide understanding and advice to women and men on the subject of the psychology and sexuality of women. Alternative views and critical reappraisals are now in the ascendancy and set the stage for new theoretical developments, based on empirical research conducted in a different sociocultural climate. In no other literature can we see the relation between scientific inquiry and social values so clearly revealed.

5

Some Psychological Consequences of the Anatomical Distinction between the Sexes

Sigmund Freud

In my own writings and in those of my followers more and more stress is laid upon the necessity for carrying the analyses of neurotics back into the remotest period of their childhood, the time of the early efflorescence of sexual life. It is only by examining the first manifestations of the patient's innate instinctual constitution and the effects of his earliest experiences that we can accurately gauge the motive forces that have led to his neurosis and can be secure against the errors into which we might be tempted by the degree to which they have become remodelled and overlaid in adult life. This requirement is not only of theoretical but also of practical importance, for it distinguishes our efforts from the work of those physicians whose interests are focussed exclusively upon therapeutic results and who employ analytic methods, but only up to a certain point. An analysis of early childhood such as we are considering is tedious and laborious and makes demands both upon the physician and upon the patient which cannot always be met. Moreover it leads us into dark regions where there are as yet no sign-posts. Indeed, analysts may feel reassured, I think, that there is no risk of their work becoming mechanical, and so of losing its interest, during the next few decades.

In the following pages I bring forward some findings of analytical research which would be of great importance if they could be proved to apply universally. Why do I not postpone publication of them until further experience has given me the necessary proof, if such proof is obtainable? Because the conditions under which I work have undergone a change, with implications which I cannot disguise. Formerly, I was never one of those who are unable to hold back what seems to be a new discovery until it has been either confirmed or corrected. My *Interpretation of Dreams* [1900], and my 'Fragment of an Analysis of a Case of Hysteria [1905*c*] (the case of Dora) were suppressed by me—if not for the nine years enjoined by Horace—at all events for four or five years before I allowed them to be published. But in those days I had unlimited time before me and material poured in upon me in such quantities that fresh experiences were hardly to be escaped. Moreover, I was the only worker in a new field, so that my reticence involved no danger to myself and no risk of loss to others.

But now everything has changed. The time before me is limited. The whole of it is no longer spent in working, so that my opportunities for making fresh observations are not so numerous. If I think I see something new, I am uncertain whether I can wait for it to be confirmed. And further, everything that is to be seen upon the surface has already been exhausted; what remains has to be slowly and laboriously dragged up from the depths. Finally, I am no longer alone. An eager crowd of fellow-workers is ready to make use of what is unfinished or doubtful, and I can leave to them that part of the work which I should otherwise have done myself. On this occasion, therefore, I feel justified in publishing something which stands in urgent need of confirmation before its value or lack of value can be decided.

In examining the earliest mental shapes assumed by the sexual life of children we have been in the habit of taking as the subject of our investigations the male child, the little boy. With little girls, so we have supposed, things must be similar, through in some way or other they must nevertheless be different. The point in development at which this difference lay could not clearly be determined.

In boys the situation of the Oedipus complex is the first stage that can be recognized with certainty. It is easy to understand, because at that stage a child retains the same object which he previously cathected with his pre-genital libido during the preceding period while he was being suckled and nursed. The further fact that in this situation he regards his father as a disturbing rival and would like to get rid of him and take his place is a straightforward consequence of the actual state of affairs. I have shown elsewhere (1924*b*) how the Oedipus attitude in little boys belongs to the phallic phase, and how it succumbs to the fear of castration, that is, to narcissistic interest in their own genitals. The matter is made more difficult to grasp by the complicating circumstance that even in boys the Oedipus complex has a double orientation, active and passive, in accordance with their bisexual constitution; a boy also wants to take his *mother's* place as the love-object of his *father*—a fact which we describe as the feminine attitude.

As regards the prehistory of the Oedipus complex in boys we are far from complete clarity. We know that that period includes an identification of an affectionate sort with the boy's father, an identification which is still free from any sense of rivalry in regard to his mother. Another element of that stage is invariably, I believe, a masturbatory stimulation of the genitals, the masturbation of early childhood, the more or less violent suppression of which by the persons in charge of the child sets the castration complex in action. It is to be assumed that this masturbation is attached to the Oedipus complex and serves as a discharge for the sexual excitation belonging to it. It is, however, uncertain whether the masturbation has this character from the first, or whether on the contrary it makes its first appearance spontaneously as an activity of a bodily organ and is only brought into relation with the Oedipus complex at some later date; this second possibility is by far the more probable. Another doubtful question is the part played by bed-wetting and by the breaking of that habit through the intervention of training measures. We are inclined to adopt the simple generalization that continued bed-wetting is a result of masturbation and that its suppression is regarded by boys as an inhibition of their genital activity, that is, as having the meaning of a threat of castration; but whether we are always right in supposing this remains to be seen. Finally, analysis shows us in a shadowy way how the fact of a child at a very early age listening to his parents copulating may set up his first sexual excitation, and how that event may, owing to its after-effects, act as a starting-point for the child's whole sexual development. Masturbation, as well as the two attitudes in the Oedipus complex, later on become attached to this early experience, the child having subsequently interpreted its meaning. It is impossible, however, to suppose that these observations of coitus are of universal occurrence, so that at this point we are faced with the problem of 'primal phantasies'. Thus the prehistory of the Oedipus complex, even in boys, raises all of these questions for sifting and explanation; and there is the further problem of whether we are to suppose that the process invariably follows the same course, or whether a great variety of different preliminary stages may not converge upon the same terminal situation.

In little girls the Oedipus complex raises one problem more than in boys. In both cases the mother is the original object; and there is no cause for surprise that boys retain that object in the Oedipus complex. But how does it happen that girls abandon it and instead take their father as an object? In pursuing this question I have been able to reach some conclusions which may throw light upon the prehistory of the Oedipus relation in girls.

Every analyst has come across certain women who cling with especial intensity and tenacity to the bond with their father and to the wish in which it culminates of having a child by him. We have good reason to suppose that the same wishful phantasy was also the motive force of their infantile masturbation, and it is easy to form an impression that at this point we have been brought up against an elementary and unanalysable fact of infantile sexual life. But a thorough analysis of these very cases brings something different to light, namely, that here the Oedipus complex has a long prehistory and is in some respects a secondary formation.

The old paediatrician Lindner [1879] once remarked that a child discovers the genital zones (the penis or the clitoris) as a source of pleasure while indulging in sensual sucking (thumb-sucking). I shall leave it an open question whether it is really true that the child takes the newly found source of pleasure in exchange for the recent loss of the mother's nipple—a possibility to which later phantasies (fellatio) seem to point. Be that as it may, the genital zone is discovered at some time or other, and there seems no justification for attributing any psychical content to its first stimulations. But the first step in the phallic phase which begins in this way is not the linking-up of the masturbation with the object-cathexes of the Oedipus situation, but a momentous discovery which little girls are destined to make. They notice the penis of a brother or playmate, strikingly visible and of large proportions, at once recognize it as the superior counterpart of their own small and inconspicuous organ, and from that time forward fall a victim to envy for the penis.

There is an interesting contrast between the behaviour of the two sexes. In the analogous situation, when a little boy first catches sight of a girl's genital region, he begins by showing irresolution and lack of interest; he sees nothing or disowns what he has seen, he softens it down or looks about for expedients for bringing it into line with his expectations. It is not until later, when some threat of castration has obtained a hold upon him, that the observation becomes important to him: if he then recollects or repeats it, it arouses a terrible storm of emotion in him and forces him to believe in the reality of the threat which he has hitherto laughed at. This combination of circumstances leads to two reactions, which may become fixed and will in that case, whether separately or together or in conjunction with other factors, permanently determine the boy's relations to women: horror of the mutilated creature or triumphant contempt for her. These developments, however, belong to the future, though not to a very remote one.

A little girl behaves differently. She makes her judgement and her decision in a flash. She has seen it and knows that she is without it and wants to have it.[1]

From this point there branches off what has been named the masculinity complex of women, which may put great difficulties in the way of their regular development towards femininity, if it cannot be got over soon enough. The hope of some day obtaining a penis in spite of everything and so of becoming like a man may persist to an incredibly late age and may become a motive for the strangest and otherwise unaccountable actions. Or again, a process may set in which might be described as a 'denial', a process which in the mental life of children seems neither uncommon nor very dangerous but which in an adult would mean the beginning of a psychosis. Thus a girl may refuse to accept the fact of being castrated, may harden herself in the conviction that she *does* possess a penis and may subsequently be compelled to behave as though she were a man.

The psychical consequences of penis-envy, in so far as it does not become absorbed in the reaction-formation of the masculinity complex, are various and far-reaching. After a woman has become aware of the wound to her narcissism, she develops, like a scar, a sense of inferiority. When she has passed beyond her first attempt at explaining her lack of a penis as being a punishment personal to herself and has realized that that sexual character is a universal one, she begins to share the contempt felt by men for a sex which is the lesser in so important a respect, and, at least in the holding of that opinion, insists upon being like a man.[2]

Even after penis-envy has abandoned its true object, it continues to exist: by an easy displacement it persists in the character-trait of *jealousy*. Of course, jealousy is not limited to one sex and has a wider foundation than this, but I am of opinion that it plays a far larger part in the mental life of women than of men and that that is because it is enormously reinforced from the direction of displaced penis-envy. While I was still unaware of this source of jealousy and was considering the phantasy 'A Child is Being Beaten' (1919), which occurs so commonly in girls, I constructed a first phase for it in which its meaning was that another child, a rival of whom the subject was jealous, was to be beaten. This phantasy seems to be a relic of the phallic period in girls. The peculiar rigidity which struck me so much in the monotonous formula 'a child is being beaten' can probably be interpreted in a special way. The child which is being beaten (or caressed) may at bottom be nothing more nor less than the clitoris itself, so that at its very lowest level the statement will contain a confession of masturbation, which has remained attached to the content of t..e formula from its beginning in the phallic phase up to the present time.

A third consequence of penis-envy seems to be a loosening of the girl's relation with her mother as a love-object. The situation as a whole is not very clear, but it can be seen that in the end the girl's mother, who sent her into the world so insufficiently equipped, is almost always held responsible for her lack of a penis. The way in which this comes about historically is often that soon after the girl has discovered that her genitals are unsatisfactory she begins to show jealousy of another child on the ground that her mother is fonder of it than her, which serves as a reason for her giving up her affectionate relation to her mother. It will fit in with this if the child which has been preferred by her mother is made into the first object of the beating-phantasy which ends in masturbation.

There is yet another surprising effect of penis-envy, or of the discovery of the inferiority of the clitoris, which is undoubtedly the most important of all. In the past I had often formed an impression that in general women tolerate masturbation worse than men, that they more frequently fight against it and that they are unable to make use of it in circumstances in which a man would seize upon it as a way of escape without any hesitation. Experience would no doubt elicit innumerable exceptions to this statement, if we attempted to turn it into a rule. The reactions of human individuals of both sexes are of course made up of masculine and feminine traits. But it appeared to me nevertheless as though masturbation were further removed from the nature of women than of men, and the solution of the problem could be assisted by the reflection that masturbation, at all events of the clitoris, is a masculine activity and that the elimination of clitoridal sexuality is a necessary pre-condition for the development of femininity. Analyses of the remote phallic period have now taught me that in girls, soon after the first signs of penis-envy, an intense current of feeling against masturbation makes its appearance, which cannot be attributed exclusively to the educational influence of those in charge of the child. This impulse is clearly a forerunner of the wave of repression which at puberty will do away with a large amount of the girl's masculine sexuality in order to make room for the development of her femininity. It may happen that this first opposition to auto-erotic stimulation fails to attain its end. And this was in fact the case in the instances which I analysed. The conflict continued, and both then and later the girl did everything she could to free herself from the compulsion to masturbate. Many of the later manifestations of sexual life in women remain unintelligible unless this powerful motive is recognized.

I cannot explain the opposition which is raised in this way by little girls to phallic masturbation except by supposing that there is some concurrent factor which turns her violently against that pleasurable activity. Such a factor lies close at hand in the narcissistic sense of humiliation which is bound up with penis-envy, the girl's reflection that after all this is a point on which she cannot compete with boys and that it would therefore be best for her to give up the idea of doing so. Thus the little girl's recognition of the anatomical distinction between the sexes forces her away from masculinity and masculine masturbation on to new lines which lead to the development of femininity.

So far there has been no question of the Oedipus complex, nor has it up to this point played any part. But now the girl's libido slips into a new position by means—there is no other way of putting it—of the equation 'penis = child'. She gives up her wish for a penis and puts in place of it a wish for a child: and *with this purpose in view* she takes her father as a love-object. Her mother becomes the object of her jealousy. The girl has turned into a little woman. If I am to credit a single exaggerated analytic instance, this new situation can give rise to physical sensations which would have to be regarded as a premature awakening of the female genital apparatus. If the girl's attachment to her father comes to grief later on and has to be abandoned, it may give place to an identification with him and the girl may thus return to her masculinity complex and perhaps remain fixated in it.

I have now said the essence of what I had to say: I will stop, therefore, and cast an eye over our findings. We have gained some insight into the prehistory of the Oedipus complex in girls. The corresponding period in boys is more or less unknown. In girls the Oedipus complex is a secondary formation. The operations of the castration complex precede it and prepare for it. As regards the relation between the Oedipus and castration complexes there is a fundamental contrast between the two sexes, *Whereas in boys the Oedipus complex succumbs to the castration complex, in girls it is made possible and led up to by the castration complex.* This contradiction is cleared up if we reflect that the castration complex always operates in the sense dictated by its subject-matter: it inhibits and limits masculinity and encourages femininity. The difference between the sexual development of males and females at the stage we have been considering is an intelligible consequence of the anatomical distinction between their genitals and of the psychical situation involved in it; it corresponds to the difference between a castration that has been carried out and one that has merely been threatened. In their essentials, therefore, our findings are self-evident and it should have been possible to foresee them.

The Oedipus complex, however, is such an important thing that the manner in which one enters and leaves it cannot be without its effects. In boys (as I have shown at length in the paper to which I have just referred and to which all of my present remarks are closely related) the complex is not simply repressed, it is literally smashed to pieces by the shock of threatened castration. Its libidinal cathexes are abandoned, desexualized and in part sublimated; its objects are incorporated into the ego, where they form the nucleus of the super-ego and give that new structure its characteristic qualities. In normal, or rather in ideal cases, the Oedipus complex exists no longer, even in the unconscious; the super-ego has become its heir. Since the penis (to follow Ferenczi) owes its extraordinarily high narcissistic cath-exis to its organic significance for the propagation of the species, the catas-trophe of the Oedipus complex (the abandonment of incest and the institution of conscience and morality) may be regarded as a victory of the race over the individual. This is an interesting point of view when one considers that neurosis is based upon a struggle of the ego against the demands of the sexual function. But to leave the standpoint of individual psychology is not likely to be of any immediate help in clarifying this com-plicated situation.

In girls the motive for the destruction of the Oedipus complex is lack-ing. Castration has already had its effect, which was to force the child into the situation of the Oedipus complex. Thus the Oedipus complex escapes the fate which it meets with in boys: it may either be slowly abandoned or got rid of by repression, or its effects may persist far into women's normal mental life. I cannot escape the notion (though I hesitate to give it expres-sion) that for women the level of what is ethically normal is different from what it is in men. Their super-ego is never so inexorable, so impersonal, so independent of its emotional origins as we require it to be in men. Char-acter-traits which critics of every epoch have brought up against women—that they show less sense of justice than men, that they are less ready to submit to the great necessities of life, that they are more often influenced in their judgments by feelings of affection or hostility—all these would be amply accounted for by the modification in the formation of their super-ego which we have already inferred. We must not allow ourselves to be deflected from such conclusions by the denials of the feminists, who are anxious to force us to regard the two sexes as completely equal in position and worth; but we shall, of course, willingly agree that the majority of men are also far behind the masculine ideal and that all human individuals, as a result of their bisexual disposition and of cross-inheritance, combine in themselves both masculine and feminine characteristics, so that pure mas-culinity and femininity remain theoretical constructions of uncertain con-tent.

I am inclined to set some value on the considerations I have brought forward upon the psychological consequences of the anatomical distinction between the sexes. I am aware, however, that this opinion can only be maintained if my findings, which are based on a handful of cases, turn out to have general validity and to be typical. If not, they would remain no more than a contribution to our knowledge of the different paths along which sexual life develops.

In the valuable and comprehensive studies upon the masculinity and castration complex in women by Abraham (1921), Horney (1923) and Helene Deutsch (1925) there is much that touches closely upon what I have written but nothing that coincides with it completely, so that here again I feel jus-tified in publishing this paper.

NOTES

1. This is an opportunity for correcting a statement which I made many years ago. [Freud, 1905*b* (English Translation, 1949, 72).] I believed that the sexual interest of children, unlike

that of pubescents, was aroused, not by the difference between the sexes, but by the problem of where babies come from. We now see that, at all events with girls, this is certainly not the case. With boys it may no doubt happen sometimes one way and sometimes the other; or with both sexes chance experiences may determine the event.

2. In my first critical account of the 'History of the Psycho-Analytic Movement', written in 1914 (*Collected Papers*, 1, 287), I recognized that this fact represents the core of truth contained in Adler's theory. That theory has no hesitation in explaining the whole world by this single point ('organ inferiority', 'the masculine protest', breaking away from 'the feminine line') and prides itself upon having in this way robbed sexuality of its importance and put the desire for power in its place. Thus the only organ which could claim to be called 'inferior' without any ambiguity would be the clitoris. On the other hand, one hears of analysts who boast that, though they have worked for dozens of years, they have never found a sign of the existence of a castration complex. We must bow our heads in recognition of the greatness of this achievement, even though it is only a negative one, a piece of virtuosity in the art of overlooking and mistaking. The two theories form an interesting pair of opposites—in one of them not a trace of a castration complex, in the other nothing at all but its effects.

6

The Problem
of Feminine Masochism

Karen Horney

Interest in the problem of feminine masochism extends far beyond the
merely medical and psychological spheres, for to students of the Western
culture at least, it touches on the very roots for evaluating woman in her
cultural definition. The facts appear to be that in our cultural areas, masochistic phenomena are more frequent in women than in men. Two ways of
approaching an explanation of this observation have appeared. By one,
there is an attempt to discover if masochistic trends are inherent in, or akin
to, the very essence of female nature. By the other, one undertakes to evaluate the weight of social conditionings in the genesis of any sex-limited peculiarities in the distribution of masochistic trends.

In psychoanalytic literature . . . the problem has been tackled only
from the viewpoint of regarding feminine masochism as one psychic consequence of anatomical sex differences. Psychoanalysis thus has lent its scientific tools to support the theory of a given kinship between masochism and
female biology. The possibility of social conditioning has as yet not been
considered from the psychoanalytical side.

The task of this paper is to contribute to the efforts of determining the
weight of biological and cultural factors in this problem; to review carefully
the validity of the psychoanalytical data given in this direction; and to raise
the question of whether psychoanalytical knowledge can be utilized for an
investigation of a possible connection with social conditionings.

One may summarize the psychoanalytic views thus far presented
somewhat as follows:

"The Problem of Feminine Masochism" by Karen Horney. *The Psychoanalytic Review*, Vol. 22
(1935), through the courtesy of the Editors and the Publisher, National Psychological Association for Psychoanalysis, New York, N.Y.

The specific satisfactions sought and found in female sex life and motherhood are of a masochistic nature. The content of the early sexual wishes and fantasies concerning the father is the desire to be mutilated, that is, castrated by him. Menstruation has the hidden connotation of a masochistic experience. What the woman secretly desires in intercourse is rape and violence, or in the mental sphere, humiliation. The process of childbirth gives her an unconscious masochistic satisfaction, as is also the case with the maternal relation to the child. Furthermore, as far as men indulge in masochistic fantasies or performances, these represent an expression of their desire to play the female role. . . .

It is assumed at least implicitly that masochistic character trends of all kinds also are much more frequent in women than in men. This conclusion is inevitable when one holds the basic psychoanalytic theory that general behavior in life is modeled on the sexual behavior pattern, which in women is deemed masochistic. It then follows that if most or all women are masochistic in their attitude toward sex and reproduction, they would indubitably reveal masochistic trends in their nonsexual attitude toward life more frequently than would men. . . .

The foregoing observations are sufficient to build a working hypothesis to the effect that wishes for masculinity of some origin or other, play a role in female sex life, and this hypothesis may be used in seeking explanations for certain neurotic phenomena in women. It must be realized, however, that this is an hypothesis, not a fact; and that it is not even indisputably useful as an hypothesis. When it is claimed, moreover, that the desire for masculinity is not only a dynamic factor of primary order in neurotic females, but in every human female, independent of individual or cultural conditions, one cannot but remark that there are no data to substantiate this claim. Unfortunately little or nothing is known of psychically healthy women, or of women under different cultural conditions, due to limitations of historical and ethnological knowledge.

Therefore, as there are no data about frequency, conditioning, and weight of the observed reactions of the little girl to the discovery of the penis, the assumption that this is a turning point in female development is stimulating, but can scarcely be used in a chain of proof. Why, indeed, should the girl turn masochistic when she realizes the lack of a penis? . . .

Let us ask again: What are the data? As far as I can see, only the fact that there may exist in small children early sadistic fantasies. This is partly elicited by direct psychoanalytic observation of neurotic children (M. Klein), and partly by reconstruction out of analysis of neurotic adults. There is no evidence for the ubiquity of these early sadistic fantasies, and I wonder, for instance, whether little American Indian girls, or little Trobriand girls have them. However, even taking for granted that this occurrence was in fact ubiquitous, there still remain three further assumptions necessary for completion of the picture:

(1) That these sadistic fantasies are generated by the active-sadistic libido cathexis of the clitoris.

(2) That the girl renounces her clitoris-masturbation in consequence of the narcissistic injury of having no penis.

(3) That the hitherto active-sadistic libido turns automatically inward and becomes masochistic.

All three assumptions seem highly speculative. It is known that people can become frightened of their hostile aggressions and subsequently prefer the suffering role, but how a libido-cathexis of an organ can be sadistic and then turn inward, seems mysterious. . . .

As the evidence has not yet been presented, one looks around for analogous reactions that might lend plausibility to the assumption. A correspondent example would have to fulfill the same preconditions given in the case of the little girl: a sudden interruption of customary sexual outlets by the occurrence of some painful event. Consider, for example, the case of a man who has led a hitherto satisfactory sex life, and is then jailed and placed under such close supervision that all sexual outlets are barred. Will such a man become masochistic? That is, will he become sexually incited by witnessing beatings, by imagining beatings, or receiving actual beatings and maltreatment? Will he indulge in fantasies of persecution and inflicted suffering? No doubt such masochistic reactions may occur. But no doubt also this represents only one of several possible reactions, and such masochistic reactions will occur only in a man who *previously* had masochistic tendencies. Other examples lead to the same conclusion. A woman deserted by her husband, and without any immediate sexual outlet or the anticipation of one, may react masochistically; but the more poised she is, the better able she will be to renounce sexuality temporarily and find some satisfaction in friends, children, work, or pleasure. Again, a woman in such a situation will react masochistically only if she already had an established pattern of masochistic trends. . . .

Masochistic phenomena in women can be detected as a result of directed and sharpened observation, where they might otherwise have passed unnoticed, as in social rencontres with women (entirely outside the field of psychoanalytic practice), in feminine character portrayals in literature, or in examination of women of somewhat foreign mores, such as the Russian peasant woman who does not feel she is loved by her husband unless he beats her. In the face of this evidence, the psychoanalyst concludes that he is here confronted with an ubiquitous phenomenon, functioning on a psychobiological basis with the regularity of a law of nature.

The onesidedness or positive errors in the results obtained by a partial examination of the picture are due to a neglect of cultural or social factors—an exclusion from the picture of women living under civilizations with different customs. The Russian peasant woman of the Tsaristic and patriarchal regime was invariably cited in discussions aimed at proving how deeply masochism is ingrained in female nature. Yet this peasant woman has emerged into the self-assertive Soviet woman of today who would doubtless be astonished if beatings were administered as a token of affection. The change has occurred in the patterns of culture rather than in the particular women. . . .

For sociological and ethnological approaches, data concerning the following questions would be pertinent:

1—What is the frequency of occurrence of masochistic attitudes towards female functions under various social and cultural conditions?

II—What is the frequency of general masochistic attitudes or manifestations in women, as compared with men, under various social and cultural conditions?

If both these inquiries gave color to the view that under all social conditions there is a masochistic conception of the female role, and if equally there is a decided preponderance of general masochistic phenomena among women as compared with men, then, and only then, would one be justified in seeking further psychologic reasons for this phenomenon. If, however, such an ubiquitous feminine masochism did not appear, one would wish of the sociological-ethnological research the answer to the further questions:

(1) What are the special social conditions under which masochism connected with female functions is frequent?

(2) What are the special social conditions under which general masochistic attitudes are more frequent in women than in men?

The task of psychoanalysis in such an investigation would be to supply the anthropologist with psychological data. With the exception of perversions and masturbatory fantasies, masochistic tendencies and gratifications are unconscious. The anthropologist cannot explore these. What he needs are criteria by which he can identify and observe the manifestations that in high probability indicate the existence of masochistic drives.

To give these data is comparatively simple as in question (1), concerning masochistic manifestations in female functions. On the basis of psychoanalytic experience it is reasonably safe to assume masochistic tendencies:

(1) When there is a great frequency of functional menstrual disorders, such as dysmenorrhea and menorrhagia.

(2) When there is great frequency of psychogenic disturbance in pregnancy and childbirth, such as fear of childbirth, fuss about it, pains, or elaborate means to avoid pain.

(3) When there is a frequency of such attitudes toward sexual relations as to imply that it is debasing for, or an exploitation of, women.

These indications are not to be taken as absolute, but rather with the following two restricting considerations:

(a) It seems to have become habitual in psychoanalytic thinking to assume that pain, suffering, or fear of suffering are prompted by masochistic drives, or result in masochistic gratification. It is therefore necessary to point out that such assumptions require evidence. Alexander, for instance, assumes that people climbing mountains with heavy knapsacks are masochistic, particularly if there is a car or railway by which they might get to the top of a mountain more easily. This may be true, but more frequently the reasons for carrying heavy knapsacks are very realistic ones.

(b) Suffering, or even self-inflicted pain, in more primitive tribes, may be an expression of magical thinking meant to ward off danger, and may have nothing to do with individual masochism. Therefore, one can only interpret such data in connection with a basic knowledge of the entire structure of the tribal history concerned.

The task of psychoanalysis in regard to question (2), data concerning indications for general masochistic attitudes, is much more difficult, because understanding of the whole phenomenon is still limited. In fact, it has not advanced much beyond Freud's statement that it has something to do with sexuality and with morality. There are, however, these open questions: Is it a primarily sexual phenomenon that extends also into the moral sphere, or a moral phenomenon extending also into the sexual sphere? Are the moral and the erogenic masochism two separate processes, or only two sets of manifestations arising from a common underlying process? Or is masochism perhaps a collective term for very complex phenomena?

One feels justified in using the same term for widely discrepant manifestations because all of them have some trends in common: tendencies to arrange in fantasies, dreams, or in the real world, situations that imply suffering; or to feel suffering in situations that would not have this concomitant for the average person. The suffering may concern the physical or the mental sphere. There is some gratification or relief of tension connected with it, and that is why it is striven for. The gratification or relief of tension may be conscious or unconscious, sexual or nonsexual. The nonsexual functions may be very different: reassurances against fears, atonements for committed sins, permission to commit new ones, strategy in reference to goals otherwise unattainable, indirect forms of hostility.

The realization of this wide range of masochistic phenomena is more bewildering and challenging than encouraging, and these general statements certainly cannot be of much help to the anthropologist. More concrete data are at his disposal, however, if all scientific worries about conditions and functions are swept aside, and only those surface attitudes that have been observable in patients with distinct and widespread masochistic tendencies within the psychoanalytic situation are made the basis of his investigations. For this purpose, therefore, it may suffice to enumerate these attitudes without tracing them back in detail to their individual conditions. Needless to say, they are not all present in every patient belonging to this category; yet the whole syndrome is so typical (as every analyst will recognize), that if some of these trends are apparent at the beginning of a treatment, one can safely predict the entire picture, though of course the details vary. The details concern sequence of appearance, distribution of weight among the single trends, and particularly form and intensity of defenses built up for protection against these tendencies.

Let us consider what observable data there are in patients with widespread masochistic trends. As I see it, the main lines of the surface structure in such personalities are somewhat as follows:

There are several ways in which one can find reassurance against deep fears. Renunciation is one way; inhibition, another; denying the fear and becoming optimistic, a third one; and so on. Being loved is the particular means of reassurance used by a masochistic person. As he has a rather free-floating anxiety, he needs constant signs of attention and affection, and as he never believes in these signs except momentarily, he has an excessive need for attention and affection. He is therefore, generally speaking, very emotional in his relations with people; easily attached because he expects them to give him the necessary reassurance; easily disappointed because he never gets, and never can get, what he expects. The expectation or illusion of the "great love" often plays an important role. Sexuality being one of the most common ways of getting affection, he also tends to overvalue it and clings to the illusion that it holds the solution of all life's problems. How far this is conscious, or how easily he has actual sexual relations, depends on his inhibitions on this score. Where he has had sexual relations, or attempts at such, his history shows a frequency of "unhappy loves"; he has been deserted, disappointed, humiliated, badly treated. In nonsexual relations, the same tendency appears in all gradations from being or feeling incompetent, self-sacrificing, and submissive, to playing the martyr role and feeling or actually being humiliated, abused, and exploited. While he otherwise feels it as a given fact that he *is* incompetent or that life *is* brutal, one can see in the psychoanalytic situation that it is not facts, but an obstinate tendency, which makes him insist upon seeing or arranging it this way. This tendency, moreover, is revealed in the psychoanalytic situation as an unconscious arrangement motivating him to provoke attacks, to feel ruined, damaged, ill-treated, humiliated, without any real cause.

Because other people's affection and sympathy are of vital importance to him, he easily becomes extremely dependent, and this hyperdependency also shows clearly in relations with the analyst.

The next observable reason he never believes in any form of affection he may actually receive (instead of clinging to it as representing the coveted reassurance) lies in his greatly diminished self-esteem; he feels inferior, absolutely unlovable and unworthy of love. On the other hand, just this lack of self-confidence makes him feel that appealing to pity by having and displaying inferiority feelings, weakness, and suffering is the only means by which he can win the affection he needs. One sees that the deterioration of his self-esteem lies rooted in his paralysis of what may be termed "adequate aggressiveness." By this I mean the capacities for work, including the following attributes: taking initiative; making efforts; carrying things through to completion; attaining success; insisting upon one's rights; defending oneself when attacked; forming and expressing autonomous views; recognizing one's goals and being able to plan one's life according to them.[1] In masochistic persons one usually finds widespread inhibitions on this score, which in their entirety account for the feeling of insecurity, or even helplessness, in the life struggle, and explain the subsequent dependency on other people, and a predisposition to look to them for support or help.

Psychoanalysis reveals the tendency to recoil from competition of any kind as the next observable reason for their incapacity to be self-assertive. Their inhibitions thus result from efforts to check themselves in order to avoid the risk of competition.

The hostile feelings inevitably generated on the basis of such self-defeating tendencies, also cannot be expressed freely because they are conceived as jeopardizing the reassurance attendant on being loved, which is the mainspring of protection against anxieties. Weakness and suffering, therefore, already serving many functions, now also act as a vehicle for the indirect expression of hostility.

The use of this syndrome of observable attitudes for anthropologic investigation is subject to one source of possible major error; namely, masochistic attitudes are not always apparent as such because they are frequently concealed by defenses, often appearing clearly only after the latter have been removed. As an analysis of these defenses clearly is beyond the sphere of such an investigation, the defenses must be taken at face value, with the result that these instances of masochistic attitudes must escape observation.

Reviewing then, the observable masochistic attitudes, regardless of their deeper motivation, I suggest that the anthropologist seek data concerning questions like these: under what social or cultural conditions do we find more frequently in women than in men

(1) the manifesting of inhibitions in the direct expression of demands and aggressions;

(2) a regarding of oneself as weak, helpless, or inferior and implicitly or explicitly demanding considerations and advantages on this basis;

(3) a becoming emotionally dependent on the other sex;

(4) a showing of tendencies to be self-sacrificing, to be submissive, to feel used or to be exploited, to put responsibilities on the other sex;

(5) a using of weakness and helplessness as a means of wooing and subduing the other sex.[2]

Besides these formulations, which are direct generalizations of the psychoanalytic experience with masochistic women, I may also present certain generalizations as to the causative factors that predispose to the appearance of masochism in women. I should expect these phenomena to appear in any culture-complex that included one or more of the following factors:

(1) Blocking of outlets for expansiveness and sexuality.

(2) Restriction in the number of children, inasmuch as having and rearing children supplies the woman with various gratifying outlets (tenderness, achievement, self-esteem), and this becomes all the more important when having and rearing children is the measuring rod of social evaluation.

(3) Estimation of women as beings who are, on the whole, inferior to men (insofar as it leads to a deterioration of female self-confidence).

(4) Economic dependence of women on men or on family, inasmuch as it fosters an emotional adaptation in the way of emotional dependence.

(5) Restriction of women to spheres of life that are built chiefly upon emotional bonds, such as family life, religion, or charity work.

(6) Surplus of marriageable women, particularly when marriage offers the principal opportunity for sexual gratification, children, security, and social recognition.[3] This condition is relevant inasmuch as it favors [as do also (3) and (4)] emotional dependence on men, and generally speaking, a development that is not autonomous but fashioned and molded by existing male ideologies. It is pertinent also insofar as it creates among women a particularly strong competition from which recoil is an important factor in precipitating masochistic phenomena.

All the factors enumerated overlap; for example, strong sexual competition among women will be more potent if other outlets for competitive strivings (as for professional eminence) are concurrently blocked. It would seem that no one factor is ever solely responsible for the deviating development, but rather a concatenation of factors.

In particular one must consider the fact that when some or all of the suggested elements are present in the culture-complex, there may appear certain fixed ideologies concerning the "nature" of woman; such as doctrines that woman is innately weak, emotional, enjoys dependence, is limited in capacities for independent work and autonomous thinking. One is tempted to include in this category the psychoanalytic belief that woman is masochistic by nature. It is fairly obvious that these ideologies function not only to reconcile women to their subordinate role by presenting it as an unalterable one, but also to plant the belief that it represents a fulfillment they crave, or an ideal for which it is commendable and desirable to strive. The influence that these ideologies exert on women is materially strengthened by the fact that women presenting the specified traits are more frequently chosen by men. This implies that women's erotic possibilities depend on their conformity to the image of that which constitutes their "true nature." It therefore seems no exaggeration to say that in such social organizations, masochistic attitudes (or rather, milder expressions of masochism) are favored in women while they are discouraged in men. Qualities like emotional dependence on the other sex (clinging vine), absorption in "love," inhibition of expansive, autonomous development, etc., are regarded as quite desirable in women but are treated with opprobrium and ridicule when found in men.

One sees that these cultural factors exert a powerful influence on women; so much so, in fact, that in our culture it is hard to see how any woman can escape becoming masochistic to some degree, from the effects of the culture alone, without any appeal to contributory factors in the anatomical-physiological characteristics of woman, and their psychic effects.

Certain writers, however, . . . have generalized from psychoanalytical experience with neurotic women, and have held that the culture complexes to which I have referred are themselves the very effect of these anatomical-physiological characteristics. It is useless to argue this overgeneralization until the type of anthropological investigation suggested has been made. Let us look, however, at the factors in the somatic organization of women, which actually contribute to their acceptance of a masochistic role. The anatomical-physiological factors in women that may prepare the soil for the growth of masochistic phenomena, seem to me to be the following:

(a) Greater average physical strength in men than in women. According to ethnologists this is an acquired sex difference. Nevertheless it exists nowadays. Though weakness is not identical with masochism, the realization of an inferior physical strength may fertilize an emotional conception of a masochistic female role.

(b) The possibility of rape similarly may give rise in women to the fantasy of being attacked, subdued, and injured.

(c) Menstruation, defloration, and childbirth, insofar as they are bloody or even painful processes, may readily serve as outlets for masochistic strivings.

(d) The biologic differences in intercourse also serve for masochistic formulation. Sadism and masochism have fundamentally nothing whatsoever to do with intercourse, but the female role in intercourse (being penetrated) *lends* itself more readily to a personal misinterpretation (when needed) of masochistic performance; and the male role, to one of sadistic activity.

These biological functions have in themselves no masochistic connotation for women, and do not lead to masochistic reactions; but if masochistic needs of other origin[4] are present, they may easily be involved in masochistic fantasies, which in turn causes them to furnish masochistic gratifications. Beyond admitting the possibility of a certain preparedness in women for a masochistic conception of their role, every additional assertion as to the relation of their constitution to masochism is hypothetical; and such facts as the disappearance of all masochistic tendencies after a successful psychoanalysis, and the observations of nonmasochistic women (which, after all, exist), warn us not to overrate even this element of preparedness.

In summary: The problem of feminine masochism cannot be related to factors inherent in the anatomical-physiological-psychic characteristics of woman alone, but must be considered as importantly conditioned by the culture-complex or social organization in which the particular masochistic woman has developed. The precise weight of these two groups of factors cannot be assessed until we have the results of anthropological investigations using valid psychoanalytical criteria in several culture areas significantly different from ours. It is clear, however, that the importance of anatomical-psychological-psychic factors has been greatly overestimated by some writers on this subject.

NOTES

1. In the field of psychoanalytic literature Schultz-Hencke, "Schicksal und Neurose," has particularly emphasized the pathogenic importance of these inhibitions.
2. It may strike the psychoanalytic reader that in the enumeration of factors, I have not restricted myself to those that are influential in childhood only. One has to consider, however, that (1) the child is bound to feel the influence of those factors indirectly through the medium of the family, and particularly through the influence they have exerted on the women in her surroundings; and (2) though masochistic attitudes (like other neurotic attitudes) generate primarily in childhood, the conditions of later life determine for the average case (that is, cases in which childhood conditions have not been so severe that they alone definitely shape the characteristics).
3. It must be borne in mind, however, that social regulations, such as marriage arrangement by families, would greatly reduce the effectiveness of this factor. This consideration also throws a light on Freud's assumption that women generally are more jealous than men. The statement probably is correct so far as the present German and Austrian cultures are concerned. To deduce this, however, from more purely individual anatomical-physiological sources (penis envy) is not convincing. While it may be so in individual cases, the generalization—independent of consideration of the social conditions—is subject to the same fundamental objection as previously mentioned.
4. What I have in mind as the sources of masochistic attitudes, I shall present in a later communication.

7

Cultural Pressures in the Psychology of Women

Clara Thompson

In my study of The Role of Women in this Culture *I presented a survey of the present status of women in the United States. I pointed out the basic situation and the changes which are going on. Although the paper was chiefly concerned with the positive aspects of woman's evolution, I spoke also of the problems still remaining, and the new problems arising in the new situations.*

It is this problem aspect of woman's present cultural situation which I shall now discuss. I shall approach this through a consideration of Freud's theories about women, viewing these in the light of cultural factors.

The importance of cultural influences in personality problems has become more and more significant in psychoanalytic work. A given culture tends to produce certain types of character. In *The Neurotic Personality of Our Time* Karen Horney has well described certain trends found in this culture. Most of these neurotic trends are found working similarly in both sexes. Thus, for example, the so-called masochistic character is by no means an exclusively feminine phenomenon. Likewise the neurotic need to be loved is often found dominating the life of men as well as women. The neurotic need of power, and insatiable amibition drives are not only found in men, but also in women.

Nevertheless, in some respects the problems of women are basically different from those of men. These fundamental differences are due to two things. First, woman has a different biological function and because of this her position in society necessarily differs in some respects from that of the man. Secondly, the cultural attitude towards women differs significantly from that towards men for reasons quite apart from biological necessity. These two differences present women with certain problems which men do not have to face.

The biological problems of a woman's life cannot be ignored although it would seem that in most cases biology becomes a problem chiefly when it produces a situation which is unsatisfactory in the cultural setup. Menstruation, pregnancy and the menopause can bring to a woman certain hazards of which there is no comparable difficulty in the male biology. Freud was so impressed with the biological difficulties of woman that, as is well known, he believed all inferiority feelings of woman had their root in her biological inadequacies. To say that a woman has to encounter certain hazards that a man does not, does not seem to be the same thing as saying woman is biologically inferior, as Freud implies.

According to his theory woman has a lasting feeling of inferiority because she has no penis. The discovery of this fact at about the age of three is considered sufficiently traumatic not only to lay the foundation for later neurosis but also to have decisive influence on woman's character. She must go through life from that time with the feeling either that she was "born short" or that something terrible had happened to her; possibly as a punishment. This feeling of biological lack, Freud feels, so overshadows all other details in the picture that he is constrained to express a note of complete pessimism about the cure of women. In his paper *Analysis Terminable and Interminable*, published in English in 1937, he says the following: "The feminine wish for a penis . . . is the source of acute attacks of depression . . . because . . . they (women) feel analysis will avail them nothing. We can only agree when we discover that their strongest motive in coming for treatment was the hope that they might somehow still obtain a male organ." Such pessimism would only be warranted if it were assumed that it is the actual physical male organ which women are demanding from analysis, whereas it seems to me that when such a wish is expressed the woman is but demanding in this symbolic way some form of equality with mem.

According to Freud, because of the little girl's discovery that she has no penis she enters the Œdipus complex with castration already an accomplished fact, while in the little boy the threat of castration arises as a result of the Œdipus complex and brings about its repression. Out of this situation in the little boy Freud believes much that is important in the superego takes its origin. Since the little girl, feeling herself already castrated, need fear no further threat she has less tendency to repress her Œdipus complex and less tendency to develop a superego.

Furthermore, according to Freud, one fact which reinforces the high evaluation of the penis by the little girl is that she is at the time of its discovery unaware that she has a vagina. She therefore considers her clitoris her sole sexual apparatus and is exclusively interested in it throughout childhood. Since she believes this is all she has in place of a penis this emphasizes her inferiority. In addition, the ignorance of the vagina makes for her a special hazard at puberty because the onset of menstruation brings awareness of her female role and requires her to give up her interest in the clitoris and henceforth to seek sexual satisfaction by way of the vagina. With this comes a change in her character. She gives up her boyish aggressiveness and becomes femininely passive.

These are the highlights of the more strictly biological aspects of Freud's theory of the development of women. I shall touch presently on some other details, but now I wish to review the gross outline in the light of my first consideration, the problem aspect of the biology of woman. The question must be asked: is this the true story of the biological sexual development of women? Penis envy dating from an experience in early childhood is sometimes recalled by women patients. In my experience, however, this memory is not recalled by all patients—not even by all of those who present in other respects the clinical picture of penis envy. While a negative finding is not conclusive it suggests that other factors may also contribute to envy of the male. Also, quite frequently, one finds women patients who were not aware of the clitoris as a separate organ and learned it only later in studying biology. This was true even though they had exploited the pleasurable sensations in the region of the clitoris. Although ignorance of the vagina, sometimes until far into adolescence, has been observed especially in hysterics, equally often one finds knowledge of the vagina from an early age and often a history of vaginal masturbation. These facts certainly cast doubt on the idea that the clitoris is always the center of the little girl's interest. It seems that one is in fact entitled to question whether there is, even now, any adequate information concerning the innate sexual interests of women.

However, Freud was usually a keen clinical observer and it may therefore be assumed that his theory was based upon certain facts which he observed. The probable nature of these facts and the principal sources of error in his interpretation of the observations may be considered.

Of the latter, there seem to have been two. In the first place, he saw the problem entirely from a masculine point of view. Horney draws attention to this in her paper *Flight from Womanhood,* published in 1926. In it she marshalls data to show that the attitude prevalent in the male about his own genitals was accepted by Freud as the attitude of both sexes on the matter. She indicates that Freud based his theory on the assumption that the penis is the sexual organ most highly valued by both sexes and at no point in his work showed any recognition of the possibility of their being a female biological function in its own right. He saw the woman primarily as the negative of the male. The most extreme example of this appears in his theory that woman accepts her ability to produce a child as a compensation for her lack of a penis. Childbearing is a sufficiently important biological function to have value for its own sake. Surely, only a man could have thought of it in terms of compensation or consolation.

The second source of error in Freud's thinking is the fact that he studied only women in his own or closely related cultures, that because he had no comparative study of other cultures he believed that what he observed was universal woman. Current studies show that this is clearly not the case.

The women observed by psychoanalysts are distinctly women living in a particular culture, the Western culture, a patriarchal culture in a state of transition. It is impossible to separate from the total picture something which one can safely call biological woman. It is assumed that she exists, that she has her reactions to her particular organic makeup, but it is increasingly clear that not all that seems biological is biological. That women behave differently in different types of culture is now beginning to be known, although intensive analyses of women in other cultures have not yet been made. Freud, ignoring these considerations thought the attitudes, interests and ambitions of the middle and upper class women whom he analyzed to be the characteristic attitudes, interests and ambitions of women in general.

Today one realizes that much which even woman herself may attribute to the fact of her sex can be explained as the result of cultural pressures.

At the same time, the fact that bearing children must influence women's personality development cannot be denied. Also the type of sexual response characteristic of a woman conceivably has its influence on her character.

For example, it seems probable that the very fact that the male must achieve an erection in order to carry out the sexual act, and that any failure in this attempt cannot be hidden, while the female can much more readily hide her success or nonsuccess in intercourse, may well have an effect in the basic character patterns of both. Even here, however, more complete understanding of the cultural pressures is necessary before it can be stated in what way or to what extent biology plays a part. But one thing seems fairly certain; namely, that to the extent to which a woman is biologically fulfilled—whatever that may mean—to that extent she has no tendency to envy man's biology, or to feel inferior about her biological makeup.

In certain cultures women can meet with difficulties which would make her biological makeup appear to be a handicap. This would be true when her drives are denied expression or when fulfillment of the role of woman puts her at a disadvantage. Both of these situations are true in many respects in the United States today. This is essentially a patriarchal culture and although many values are changing and these changes on the whole are working to the advantage of women, the patriarchal situation still presents limitations to a woman's free development of her interests. Also, the newer situations have their hazards in that they usually throw women into unequal competition with men. By unequal, the reference is not to biological inequality, but an inequality resulting from prejudice and the greater advantages offered the male.

The official attitude of the culture towards women has been and still is to the effect that woman is not the equal of man. This has led to the following things: until very recently woman was not offered education even approximately equal to that given a man; when she did secure reasonably adequate education, she found more limited opportunities for using the training than did a man; woman was considered helpless, partly because she was not given an opportunity to work, and partly because she had no choice but to be economically dependent on some man; and social restrictions were placed on her, especially in connection with her sex life. These restrictions seemed to work to the advantage of the man.

The assumption of woman's inferiority was a part of the prevalent attitude of society and until very recently was accepted by both sexes as a biological fact. Since there is obvious advantage to the male in believing this, he has proved much more resistant to a new point of view on the matter than have women. Women, at the same time, have had difficulty in freeing themselves from an idea which was a part of their life training. Thus it has come about that even when a woman has become consciously convinced of her value she still has to contend with the unconscious effects of training, discrimination against her and traumatic experiences which keep alive the attitude of inferiority.

The women whom Freud observed were women in this situation and it was easy for him to generalize the effects of the attitude of the culture as a fact of biology.

It seems justifiable therefore not only to consider Freud's theory in the light of his masculine bias but to examine closely the particular cultural pressures which may have produced the picture of woman as he saw her.

He found that the central problem in the neurotic difficulties of most women was penis envy. If this is interpreted symbolically it will be agreed that in this culture where the advantages go to the possessor of the penis women often find themselves in situations which arouse their envy of men, and so, in their relations to men, they show an attitude which can be called "penis envy."

An awareness of the advantage of a penis might be vaguely conscious in a little girl's mind at the age of three—for already at that age evidences that the son is more privileged are apparent in many middle class families. Before one can settle the question of whether this early experience takes place in terms of actual envy of the penis, or whether the boy is envied in a more general way, it must be noticed that until very recently the average girl at puberty was made decidedly aware of the disadvantages of being female. In the Victorian era the transition from the freedom of childhood to the restrictions of adolescence must have been especially conducive of unhappiness. An experience of a patient as recently as fifteen years ago shows vividly the still existing cultural situation. Two children, a boy and a girl, the boy a year and a half older than the girl grew up in a family where freedom of development was encouraged. They were both very fond of outdoor life, and went on long hikes together, often camping out overnight. At the age of twelve suddenly a great change was introduced into the girl's life. She was told that now since she was about to become a woman she could no longer go away with her brother on overnight trips. This was only one evidence, but one very important to her, of the beginning limitation of her activities. She was filled with bitterness and envy of her brother and for several reasons centered her whole resentment on the fact of menstruation. This seemed to her to be the sign of her disgrace, the sign that she had no right to be a person. She became withdrawn and depressed. Her one strong feeling was that she hated to be a woman and did not want to grow up. The condition developed decisively because of the restrictions of adolescence, restrictions which actually changed her whole way of life. I do not wish to imply that this pathological reaction to the situation at puberty developed in a hitherto healthy girl. Envy of her brother had existed in childhood because of her mother's marked preference for him, but a long period of equality with him had done much to restore her self-esteem. The situation at puberty reestablished the idea that he was the more favored person.

The changes brought about by cultural restrictions at the girl's puberty are not of a superficial nature. At this time in the Victorian picture a girl passed from a position of relative equality with boys to one of inferiority. This inferiority was shown in several ways. An outstanding point of the picture was the inhibition of natural aggression. A girl might no longer make demands and go about freely. If she was interested in a boy she must not show it directly. She must never expose herself to possible rejection. This would mean she had been unwomanly. She might no longer pursue her own interests with the same freedom as a boy. Obstacles were placed in the way of her education, her play and social life. But especially in her sexual life her freedom of development was curbed. The punishment for spontaneous expression of sexual interests was very great. One impulsive act resulting in pregnancy could ruin a girl's whole life. Her training was in the direction of insincerity about her sexual interests. She was taught to be ashamed of menstruation. It was something to be concealed and any accident leading to its discovery was especially humiliating. In short womanhood began with much unpleasantness. It was characterized by feelings of body shame, loss of freedom, loss of equality with boys and loss of the right to be aggressive. The training in insincerity especially about her sexual being and sexual interests has undoubtedly contributed much to a woman's diminished sense of self. When something so vitally a part of her must be denied it is not a great step further to deny the whole self. The fact that much of this has noticeably changed in the last fifty years seems sufficient proof that this situation was due to a cultural attitude and had nothing to do with innate femininity. Freud, observing this cultural change in the girl's status at puberty, attributed it to the necessity of accepting her feminine passivity, which as he said she could not do without a struggle. Is it not more accurate to say that at puberty it became necessary for the girl to accept the restrictions placed on women, and that this was usually unwelcome. In a word, the difficulties of adjustment found in the girl at puberty are the results of social pressures and do not arise from the difficulty of giving up the clitoris in favor of the vagina.

The cultural attitude about the sexual life of women has been one of denial. In former years there was denial almost of its very existence. Today there is still some tendency to deny that it is as important or urgent as the sexual life of men. Passivity and masochism are usually considered essential characteristics of a woman's sexual drive. Passivity was clearly forced upon her by the inhibition of the right to aggression. Her masochism also often proves to be a form of adaptation to an unsatisfactory and circumscribed life.

Not only in her sexual life has the woman had reason to envy the man. The circumscribing of her intellectual development and the discouragement of personal initiative have been frustrating. Partly from lack of training and partly because of man's desire for ownership woman has had to accept a position of economic dependence on man, and this is still the rule.

Out of this situation come several personality traits which are generally considered typically feminine and which have even been described in psychoanalytic literature as the outcome of woman's biological makeup. Women are supposed to be more narcissistic than men, to have a greater need to be loved than men, to be more rigid than men, and to have weaker superegos than men, these in addition to the already mentioned attitudes of passivity and masochism.

A review of the actual position of economic helplessness of women of the recent past and the relative economic helplessness of many women today leads one to question the innateness of these personality traits. The function of childbearing cannot but have some effect on the personality of woman but when this function is accompanied by the necessity to legalize the process by marriage and economic dependency—with the only alternative social ostracism and added difficulties in the economic sphere, if she does not marry—one cannot help thinking that woman's greater need to be loved and to have one meaningful sexual relation rather than the more casual sexual life of the man comes about chiefly because she lives in a culture which provides no security for her except in a permanent so-called love relationship. It is known that the neurotic need of love is a mechanism for establishing security in a dependency relation. In the same way to the extent that a woman has a greater need of love than a man it is also to be interpreted as a device for establishing security in a cultural situation producing dependency. Being loved not only is part of woman's natural life in the same way as it is part of man's but it also becomes of necessity her profession. Making her body sexually attractive and her personality seductive is imperative for purposes of security. In the past centuries she could feel safe after she had married and could then risk neglecting her charms, but today, with the present ease of divorce the woman who depends on a man for her means of support and social position must continue to devote a great deal of her time to what may be called narcissistic pursuits, that is, body culture and concern about clothes. One sees that woman's alleged narcissism and greater need to be loved may be entirely the result of economic necessity.

The idea that women must have weaker superegos than men, as stated by Freud, derives from the notion that in the little girl the Œdipus complex is usually not repressed. Because she enters the Œdipus phase after accepting the fact of castration she has no fear to drive her to repression and the formation of a superego. Not only Freud but other writers, notably Sachs, have pointed out that women therefore often lack strong convictions, strong consciences, but rather tend to take on convictions and standards of any men on whom they become dependent in the course of their lives. This is said to be especially noticeable in women who have loved several men. Such a woman is supposed to adopt in succession the attitudes of the various men.

Undoubtedly there are many women who answer this description, but the character trait of having no strong beliefs or convictions is not found universally in women and also occurs frequently in men in this culture.

It is an attitude typical of people who have found that their security depends on approval of some powerful person or group. It is relatively easy to become converted to any ideology which will bring one advantage, especially if one has never for neurotic or reality reasons been able to achieve sufficient independence to be able to know one's own mind. This could scarcely but be the case with the Victorian girl who was not permitted to free herself from her father until she was safely entrusted to the protection of another man. For cultural reasons, the girl had to continue to be dependent on her father and emancipation from the child tie was not encouraged. Such a situation is not conducive to the development of independent standards. That some women despite this became independent is remarkable.

One other statement of Freud's requires consideration: the idea that women are more rigid than men and lose their capacity for intellectual and emotional growth earlier. He points to the fact that a woman of thirty often seems already incapable of further development while a man of the same age is at the beginning of his best period of achievement. Although he does not explain just how this is the result of a woman's sex, the implication is that it is the outcome of the difficulties of her sexual development. To quote him: "It is as though the whole process had been gone through and remained inaccessible to influence for the future; as though in fact the difficult development which leads to femininity had exhausted all the possibilities of the individual." One might be tempted to believe that because a woman's period of sexual attractiveness is shorter than that of a man she grows old mentally and emotionally earlier. However, here too the cultural factors so dominate the picture that it is hard to see anything else. As long as a woman's sole opportunity for success in life was in making a successful marriage her career was made or lost by the age of thirty. A woman of thirty in the Victorian era and even in some situations today has no future. It is well known in psychoanalytic therapy that for successful outcome of treatment an actual opportunity for further development of the person must exist. This consideration would seem to offer an adequate explanation of the greater rigidity of women, if in fact any such greater rigidity can be demonstrated. I believe that there is no dearth of inflexible personalities among men who have reached the height of their development by the age of thirty, whether because of inferior mental equipment, unfortunate early training or lack of opportunity. Moreover, today there are many examples of women not dependent on their sexual value for security who remain flexible and capable of development. All that may be said with certainty is that woman's lack of opportunity and economic dependence on men can lead to early rigidity and a narrowed outlook on life, as can any situation which curbs spontaneous development in either sex.

What I have said thus far shows that the characteristics of women which Freud has explained as the result of her biological vicissitudes beginning with the discovery that she has no penis can be quite as satisfactorily explained in terms of the cultural pressures to which she is subjected. The latter hypothesis must certainly be entertained—if only for economy's sake—before separating the female of man from the realm of general biological principles and making her something biologically unprecedented.

It is clear that Freud's theories were originally developed about Victorian women. Let me now discuss in contrast the woman of today. The position of women has changed greatly and if the cultural factors are important she is no longer as sexually inhibited and restricted, her opportunities for self-development are greatly increased and marriage is no longer the only means of economic security. These facts have undoubtedly influenced the character of women. So much so that a new type of woman is emerging, a woman capable of independence and whose characteristics differ from those described by Freud. However, the present is still a situation of transition. It takes a long time for a cultural change to come about especially in its psychological implications for nondependent persons. Something of the Victorian attitude still persists in the psychology of most women. One finds several remnants of it, for example, the notion that it is more womanly for a woman to marry and let a man support her. The majority of women still accept this idea, to be sure not as early in their lives as their grandmothers did. They often have a few years of independence first. For some the alternative of marriage with economic dependence, or independence with or without marriage, presents a serious conflict. Also under the influence of tradition and prejudice many women are convinced that their adequate sexual fulfillment, including children, and an adequate self development are not to be reconciled. Men have no such tradition and with them the two interests usually reinforce each other. In this, certainly, women still have real grounds for envying men.

In this specific, limited sense Freud's idea that women have envy because they have no penis is symbolically true in this culture. The woman envies the greater freedom of the man, his greater opportunities and his relative lack of conflict about his fundamental drives. The penis as a symbol of aggression stands for the freedom to be, to force one's way, to get what one wants. These are the characteristics which a woman envies in a man. When this envy is carried to a more pathological degree the woman thinks of the man as hostile to her and the penis becomes symbolically a weapon which he uses against her. In the pathological picture called penis envy by Freud the woman wishes to have the destructive qualities she attributes to the man and she wishes to use this destructiveness against him.

There remains to be dealt with the ways in which women have met the problem of feeling inferior to and hating men, or to use the Freudian language, have dealt with their penis envy. Freud outlined three solutions: a woman may accept her feminine role; she may develop neurosis; or her character may develop in the direction of a "masculinity complex." The first of these seemed to him to be the normal solution.

Here again the problem arises as to what is biological woman and what is cultural woman. Certainly biologically woman can only find her fulfillment as a woman and to the extent to which she denies this she must be frustrated. However, there are other implications in the idea of accepting the feminine role—it may include the acceptance of the whole group of attitudes considered feminine by the culture at the time. In such a sense acceptance of the feminine role may not be an affirmative attitude at all but an expression of submission and resignation. It may mean choosing the path of least resistance with the sacrifice of important parts of the self for security.

The solution of envy of the male by way of neurosis may be considered a solution by evasion, and although many interesting facts could be considered here the influence of the cultural pressures does not differ greatly from that found in the next type of situation.

The solution by way of developing a masculinity complex deserves careful consideration. One significant difference of neurotic character structure from neurosis arises from the fact that the character pattern is in many ways acceptable to the culture. It represents not only a working compromise of the person's conflicting trends, but also takes its pattern directly from the culture. The culture invites masculinity in women. With the passing of the old sheltered life, with the increasing competition with men growing out of the industrial revolution as well as out of women's restlessness, it is not strange that her first steps towards equality would be in the direction of trying to be like men. Having no path of their own to follow women have tended to copy men. Imitating of a person superior to one is by no means unusual. The working man seeking to move up the social and economic scale not only tries to copy the middle class way of life but may try to adopt the middle class way of thinking. He may try so hard that he becomes a caricature of the thing he wishes to be, with loss of sight of his real goals in the process.

In the same way women, by aping men, may develop a caricature situation and lose sight of their own interests. Thus, one must consider to what extent it is profitable for a woman to adopt the ways of a man. To what extent can she do it without losing sight of her own goals. This leads inevitably to a consideration of what characteristics are biologically male and what have developed secondarily as a result of his way of life. Here, as in the consideration of femininity, the same difficulty in separating biological and cultural factors is found. Not many years ago a woman's decision to follow a profession—medicine, for example—was considered even by some analysts to be evidence of a masculinity complex. This rose from the belief that all work outside the home, especially if it called for the exercise of leadership, was masculine, and anyone attempting it therefore was trying to be a man.

It is true, practically speaking, that in the business and professional world it often paid to act like a man. Women were entering a domain which had been in the possession of men, in which the so-called masculine traits of decisiveness, daring and aggression were usually far more effective than the customarily ascribed traits such as gentleness, and submissiveness. In adaptation to this new way of life, women could not but tend to change the personality traits acquired from their former cultural setting. The freedom which economic independence brought to women also had its influence in developing characteristics hitherto found only in men. It seems clear, however, that such changes are not in themselves in any fundamental sense in the direction of masculinity. It is not useful to confuse the picture of the independent woman with that of an essentially pathological character structure, the masculinity complex.

By this, I mean that the culture now favors a woman's developing certain characteristics which have been considered typical of men; but that in addition she may be neurotic and may exploit the cultural situation to protect herself from certain anxieties which have arisen in part from her difficulties of self development because she is a woman and in part from other privations and traumata. Obviously, if a woman develops characteristics which indicate that she unconsciously considers herself a man, she is discontent with being a woman. It would be fruitful to inquire what this "being a woman" means to her. I have suggested the possibility of several unpleasant meanings. Being a woman may mean to her being inferior, being restricted, and being in the power of someone. In short being a woman may mean negation of her feeling of self, a denial of the chance to be an independent person. Refusal to be a woman therefore could mean the opposite, an attempt to assert that one is an independent person. The woman with a masculinity complex shows an exaggerated need for "freedom" and a fear of losing her identity in any intimacy.

It has become clear in the treatment of some related situations that the development of this character pattern is not solely the result of conditioning against being a woman. More basic may be a threat to the personality integrity from an early dependency, a domineering selfish mother, for example, or from the undermining of self esteem by a destructive mother.

In short, many of the forces which make for the development of neurotic mechanisms in general can contribute to this one. These women fear dependency because dependency has been a serious threat to them. Such women are often unable to have any intimate relationship with men; and if they marry, show a hostile revengeful attitude towards the husband. The marriage relationship is sometimes, however, quite successful when circumstances leave them free to work and at least partially support themselves after marriage. Pregnancy is apt to be a special difficulty because of its at least temporary threat to this independence. And they are always afraid of getting into someone's clutches and losing control of the situation.

If the masculinity complex is not developed primarily as a defense against a feeling of biological lack, if the feeling of cultural inferiority at being a woman is not the sole cause of its development, but on the other hand any difficulty in any important dependency relation can contribute to its formation, why then does it take the particular form of wishing to be or pretending to be a man with associated hatred of men?

Two things in the situation encourage this type of character defense. First, because of the general cultural trend there is secondary gain in such an attitude. It looks like progress and gives the woman the illusion of going along in the direction of the freedom of her time. Second, it offers a means of avoiding the most important intimacy in life, that with a man. This relationship because of its frequent implication of dependency and subordination of the woman's interests especially reactivates all of the dangers of earlier dependencies. The struggle for some form of superiority to men is then an attempt to keep from being destroyed. Men are punished for all that women have been suffering in all sorts of dependency situations.

So it would seem that solution of envy of the male by the development of the masculinity complex does not have a simple origin and that sources not simply relating to sexual comparisons are important in it.

In conclusion, let me say that psychoanalysis thus far has secured extensive acquaintance with the psychology of women in only one type of culture. Facts observed in a particular part of the Western world have been interpreted by Freud as an adequate basis for an understanding of female psychology in general and as evidence for a particular theory about specific biological factors in the nature of woman. I have pointed out that characteristics and inferiority feelings which Freud considered to be specifically female and biologically determined can be explained as developments arising in and growing out of Western woman's historic situation of underprivilege, restriction of development, insincere attitude toward the sexual nature, and social and economic dependency. The basic nature of woman is still unknown.

PART III
Biology and Behavior

A central issue in the development of ideas about female personality and behavior has always been, and still is, the degree to which they are biologically or environmentally determined. The papers in Part I reflect strongly held beliefs in the biologically determined inevitability of woman's roles and behaviors based on anatomical differences. In Part II, we see a similar line of argument in Freud's article. But other writers in Part II, the neo-Freudians, introduced balance into the discussion by their attention to the social context of women's lives. During the 1970s, feminist writers wanted to focus on the universal facts of sex discrimination and oppression of women as determinants of "feminine" behavior and women's inferior status. For these writers, biological explanations became politically suspect.

The intellectual climate today seems receptive to explanations of gender dimorphic behavior that partake of both environmental and biological contributions. Observations of biological influences on some gender-related behaviors do not inevitably lead to pejorative interpretations for women. For example, the often-observed finding that, among human children, the higher level of aggression among boys is related to exposure to testosterone *in utero* does not of necessity have positive value for boys and negative value for girls. In a society that devalued aggression, the interpretation would be the opposite. Feminists, however, have had good reason to resist arguments that hold sexual dimorphism primarily responsible for social roles and for the relegation of women to lower status.

The papers in this section look at some research bearing on the biological fact of sexual dimorphism and, more important, its *meaning* in our lives. Susan Baker, in "Biological Influences on Human Sex and Gender," reviews research on environmental and biological influences in gender identity, gender dimorphic behavior, and sexual object choice. Following an explanation of the dimorphism of biological development that differentiates females from males, she looks at six groups of individuals whose biosocial development is "discordant"—that is, there is some degree of discordance among the sexual determinants of genes, hormones, internal reproductive structures, and genitalia. Each of these groups reflects a different interaction between the three sexually dimorphic variables of gender identity, gender dimorphic behavior, and sexual object choice, and the effects of biological and environmental factors upon them. Her analysis permits some important conclusions to be drawn about the relative influences of biology and environment on each of these sexually differentiated characteristics.

The menarche, or first menstruation, is a vivid event in the lives of most girls. Coming when the girl is already experiencing body changes accompanying puberty, it is symbolic of emerging sexual identity and the status of change from child to woman. Sharon Golub's paper, "Menarche: The Beginning of Menstrual Life," looks at the spectrum of issues involved in this developmental milestone of a woman's life. Discussion of the physiological aspects of menarche includes pubertal development, hypotheses of triggering mechanisms, the role of hormones, and the effects of other factors, such as genetics, nutrition, exercise, and climatic conditions. In addition, Golub reviews the research on the psychosocial aspects of menarche. Some premenarcheal girls equate menstruation with growing up and being normal. Some expect it to be embarrassing and a nuisance. When the event itself occurs, reactions are mixed. "Excited but scared" or "happy and embarrassed" are common. Changes occur in body image, with the postmenarcheal girl seeing herself as more grownup, more womanly, than she did a few months earlier. Too, effects are found in relationships with parents and on sexual behavior. The suggestion emerges that not only daughters but mothers also need preparation for menarche; many mothers are themselves not prepared to fill the role of informed and understanding parent. Even so, there are signs that attitudes toward this once-in-a-lifetime event are becoming more liberated and even celebratory.

Menstruation and its attendant phenomena have always been invested with great significance and with special meanings for women and for men as well. Perhaps more than any of the biological events of woman's body, the menstrual cycle has been held to have important effects on woman's behavior, effects that would diminish her functional abilities, restrict her activities, and disrupt her emotional equilibrium. Especially during the premenstruum females are expected to manifest a variety of symptoms that are incapacitating to some degree. In "Behavior and the Menstrual Cycle," Richard Friedman et al. review studies bearing on the relation between menstruation and behavior. Of interest is the research on mood and on task and sexual performance fluctuation during the cycles of normal women. Another section of this paper deals with findings on the interaction of menstrual cycle phases and neuroses and personality disorders in disturbed women. The authors conclude, once again, that it is a mistake to look for the single cause in menstrual symptomatology: "In many cases, intrapsychic-psychosocial-cognitive interactions could certainly determine or greatly influence intensity, while in others biological factors could predominate."

Conclusions about the effects of woman's biology on her behavior are not possible at the present time; contemporary research and theory substantially support interactive contributions of environment, experience, and the body. It is a basic tenet of scientific methodology that the effect of a variable, such as biology, can only be observed when other relevant variables, such as sociocultural influences, are controlled. As long as these latter determinants mediate such different experiences for females and males in our society, we are not able to see with clarity how powerful are our genes and hormones as shapers of gender-linked behavior.

8

Biological Influences on Human Sex and Gender

Susan W. Baker

The central question of this review essay is the degree to which sex dimorphic behaviors are environmentally or biologically determined. Asking such a question need not, nor should it, compromise the search for equality between men and women. The term "sex dimorphic behaviors" need clarification, for they comprise not one, but three groupings of behavioral or psychic phenomena: (1) gender identity, generally defined as the unified and persistent experience of one's self as male, female, or ambivalent; (2) gender-role behavior, the actions and activities that indicate to the self or others the degree to which one is male, female, or ambivalent; and (3) sexual object choice, usually heterosexual, homosexual, or bisexual. (For reasons of space, this review will take up neither transsexualism nor sex differences in cognition.)[1] Researchers in the field of psychoendocrinology investigate to what extent, and in what ways, biology or rearing influences each of these different phenomena.

Despite the fact that this field of inquiry is relatively new, a certain amount of knowledge is commonly held to be true. First, dimorphic biological development, which differentiates females from males, follows certain patterns in animals and humans. Except for the brain, which has yet to be studied in humans, a striking concordance seems to exist between animal and human development in this area. Next, these unfolding sequences consist of particular stages. They are: (a) The genetic, a female pattern of XX sex chromosomes or a male pattern of XY chromosomes. Later, we will deal with another genetic variant, XO, in Turner's syndrome. (b) Gonadal differentiation, from the primordial gonad in the fetus to ovaries in the female and testes in the male. *(c)* The prenatal hormonal environment. The male in utero is exposed to a high level of virilizing hormones, androgens, and testosterones, while the female is not. *(d)* The anatomical. The fetus, which has had the potential for both female (Müllerian) and male (Wolffian) internal reproductive systems, develops one of them. An absence of high levels of androgens leads to the Müllerian system; the presence of them in quantity to the Wolffian. Normally, external genitalia next appear from a structure, with a dimorphic capacity, called the genital tubercle. Again, the absence of androgens results in a development along female lines; a presence of androgens in development along male lines (see fig. 1). However, as we shall see below, in some clinical syndromes the anatomy of the external genitalia is ambiguous. Accordingly, sex anatomy itself becomes one of parameters along which we are usually forced to make the distinction between female and male. *(e)* The postnatal hormonal environment. The biological importance of this becomes especially clear during adolescence, where elevated levels of specific female and male hormones are responsible for secondary sex characteristics. This is also the time during which the gonads assume their mature reproductive capacity.

As the individual, both before and after birth, goes through these five stages, he or she normally has "concordance." That is, the chromosomes, the gonads, the prenatal hormonal environment, the reproductive systems, and the postnatal secondary sex characteristics all line up consistently in female, or male, patterns. However, some individuals are "discordant." That is, at some stages they receive female, at other male, biological influences. The data base for the literature that we will survey has been these discor-

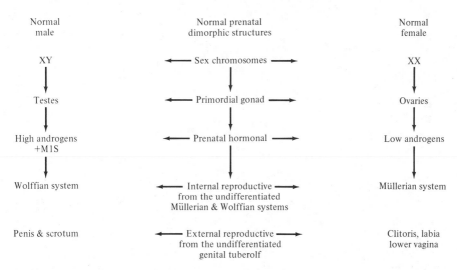

Figure 1   Prenatal sex dimorphic development in normal males. The androgen produced by the testes which cause the undifferentiated reproductive systems to differentiate along male lines is testosterone. The testes also make a Müllerian Inhibiting Substance (MIS), which causes regression of the Müllerian system in males.

dant individuals. Contemporary psychoendocrinology has focused on those who break, rather than represent, the statistical average. In other words, nature has contrived errors in the usual human development that in some ways mimic the experiments animal researchers have devised in their laboratories.

Six categories of discordancy, or six special human populations, emerge from a study of the literature. Four represent diagnosed, clinical syndromes of some genetic or endogenous, that is, internal, disorder of prenatal development: congenital, adrenal hyperplasia (CAH); complete androgen insensitivity, or testicular feminization (TF); partial androgen insensitivity, or Reifenstein's syndrome; and Turner's syndrome, or gonadal dygenesis (see fig. 2). The other two have disorders of the prenatal environment, which may never have been diagnosed and which the exogenous (i.e., external) administration of feminizing or virilizing hormones during the mother's pregnancy has induced. Each population reflects a different interaction between the three sex dimorphic behaviors and the influence of biological or environmental factors upon them. Moreover, each population has contributed data that have allowed various hypotheses to be generated about human sex and gender and about the importance of biological and environmental variables.

Before our presentation of the data and discussion, we wish to note that sex dimorphic behaviors are only those generally found to be more descriptive than not, more often than not for *groups* of normal males and females. The range of individual variation, and the overlap between the behavioral modes, is enormous among those persons with no known "abnormality" of prenatal environment. The "dimorphic" behaviors are those tendencies that differentiate large groups of females and males adequately enough to be labeled.

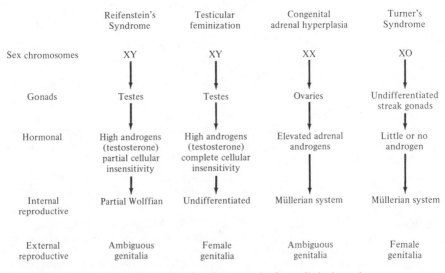

	Reifenstein's Syndrome	Testicular feminization	Congenital adrenal hyperplasia	Turner's Syndrome
Sex chromosomes	XY	XY	XX	XO
Gonads	Testes	Testes	Ovaries	Undifferentiated streak gonads
Hormonal	High androgens (testosterone) partial cellular insensitivity	High androgens (testosterone) complete cellular insensitivity	Elevated adrenal androgens	Little or no androgen
Internal reproductive	Partial Wolffian	Undifferentiated	Müllerian system	Müllerian system
External reproductive	Ambiguous genitalia	Female genitalia	Ambiguous genitalia	Female genitalia

Figure 2 Prenatal sex dimorphic development in four clinical syndromes

Hypotheses

Psychoendocrinologists have been working with three major hypotheses:

1. Gender identity is *not* determined by chromosomes or by gonadal or prenatal hormonal influence but by rearing. Further, there is a critical period, between eighteen months and two years of life, after which successful sex reassignment will be difficult, if not impossible. However, it is not known if this irreversibility after two years is determined by the child's experience or by the parents' needs. Gender identity is essentially consolidated by three to four years of age.

2. In contrast, gender-role behavior is influenced by prenatal hormonal environment. This difference in biological influence may be related to the fact that gender identity, unlike gender-role behaviors, requires a psychic state of self-awareness, for which there is no known analogue in the nonhuman animal world and for which there may be no biological etiology.

3. Sexual orientation is generally subsumed under gender role. For our purposes now, it is better considered separately as a dimorphic behavior of sexual object choice that usually appears in adolescence, with obscure relationships to antecedents or influences in earlier behavior.[2] Most researchers in this field think that rearing (i.e., social and environmental factors) determines sexual orientation more than chromosomal, gonadal, or hormonal factors.

Evidence from Clinical Studies

Evidence from the six discordant populations has led to these hypotheses. Let us summarize the evidence from each population in turn.

1. *Children and adolescents with a history of elevated prenatal androgens.* The only clinical population that has been systematically studied with a history of endogenous prenatal virilization in genetic females is CAH, which is a genetically transmitted condition. The adrenal cortex, unable to produce normal amounts of cortisol from early in fetal life, is therefore overstimulated by the brain to produce elevated amounts of adrenal androgens. The condition occurs in both males and females, but males look normal at birth. In contrast, the elevated levels of adrenal androgens have prenatally acted on the genital tubercle in females, who are then born with ambiguous genitalia. Thus females are usually identified at birth and require early surgical correction of the external genitalia for a normal female appearance. All affected individuals require lifelong management with cortisone replacement to avoid continued postnatal virilization. The internal reproductive system that differentiates (in females) is female, implying that affected girls do not have sufficient androgens during the earlier prenatal critical period for Wolffian reproductive systems to develop.

The relevant evidence from this population for the hypotheses we have outlined follows. Two clinical follow-up studies used semistructured interviews with mothers and affected female children to assess long-term (current and retrospective) behavior patterns in affected children versus experimental controls.[3] Both studies found that gender identity was female in all cases, and that affected children differed significantly from the controls in various areas of gender-role behaviors, with highly increased incidence of tomboyism, elevated activity level, preference for boys as playmates, little interest in doll play, and generally low interest in infants, etc. Sexual orientation was not examined, because the children were too young; only a very few were adolescents in either sample. However, Ehrhardt and Baker reported an adolescent follow-up of the same sample of affected children, now with a mean age of sixteen years.[4] The general pattern of findings was that both interest in and experience with such heterosexual activities as dating, necking, petting and intercourse was delayed. Of the five girls who were not interested, four were the four youngest included in the study. The fifth was a twenty-year-old socially withdrawn girl who avoided close relationships with both men and women. Only one woman reported homosexual fantasies or experiences. She had had both heterosexual and homosexual relationships. It was interesting that while in childhood most of the affected children had reported little interest in their appearance and devoted minimal effort in self-grooming and dressing attractively, this had changed in about half the girls at the time of the follow-up.

Money and Schwartz also reported findings in an adolescent follow-up study of CAH girls.[5] Their findings were quite similar overall, but with a slightly higher incidence of homosexual relationships. However, the incidence remained quite low, and it cannot be concluded that the incidence is significantly greater than would be found in a nonrandom appropriate control of equal size. Neither study used a control group, but both demonstrated nonetheless that the affected children's histories of generally tomboyish behavior in no way determined a homosexual object choice in adolescence. Most girls were heterosexual in orientation.

The CAH girls in the above studies were all reared as females. What happens to such girls if the syndrome is not accurately diagnosed in early life and they are mistakenly reared as males? The virilization of the external genitalia can be sufficient at times for this to occur. Money and Daley reported findings on a sample of CAH females unambiguously reared as males.[6] They all had a male gender identity, appropriate male gender-role behaviors, and a heterosexual (for gender identity and rearing) sexual object choice.

Thus, from clinical studies on fetally virilized genetic females gender identity was concordant with sex of rearing, gender-role behaviors appeared to be influenced by prenatal environment but were within the range of normal tomboyish girls' behaviors and in no way bizarre, and sexual orientation in most cases was heterosexual to rearing and gender identity.

2. *Children and adolescents with a history of androgen insensitivity.* Two clinical populations that have been studied fall into this category: the syndrome of complete androgen insensitivity or testicular feminization (TF) and partial androgen insensitivity (Reifenstein's syndrome). Testicular feminization is a quite rare genetically transmitted condition. Individuals with it have (see fig. 2) normal male chromosomes, gonads, and prenatal hormonal levels. However, the cells of their bodies are unable to respond to the elevated gonadal androgens prenatally, and as a result they do not virilize. The testes in normal males make an additional substance called the

Müllerian Inhibiting Substance (MIS), produced normally in TF individuals, which is responsible for the lack of differentiation of the Müllerian system. Thus, these individuals in later life do not have reproductive capacity but can have a normal sexual relationship (as the external genitalia are female) and adopt their babies. Masica, Money, and Ehrhardt studied a clinical sample of ten TF girls reared as females.[7] On follow up, gender identity was female in all cases; gender-role behaviors were female, that is, not characterized by the "virilized"[8] behavior patterns reported in the CAH-affected individuals. Sexual orientation was heterosexual (by sex of rearing and gender identity) in all cases. Many went on to marry and adopt babies.

3. *Reifenstein's syndrome.* These individuals have a genetically transmitted syndrome of partial androgen insensitivity. These individuals, like the CAH females, are identified at birth because of abnormal (ambiguous) genitalia. Genetic and gonadal males who were incompletely virilized prenatally, they have been raised as either males or females. Ideally the decision as to rearing would depend upon the viability of the development of the external genitalia for future sexual functioning. However they have been raised, they generally require some surgical correction of the genitalia. Money and Ogunro interviewed ten subjects with partial androgen insensitivity, eight reared as males and two as females.[9] Nine of the ten subjects' gender identity was concordant with sex of rearing, in spite of severe functional genital difficulties, with four of those raised as males having a "clitoral-sized phallus." One female reported herself as ambivalent about her gender identity. She had three affected siblings who had publically renounced their gender identity from female to male in adulthood. The authors speculated that this may have contributed to her ambivalence. Gender-role behaviors were gender appropriate to sex of rearing in all cases. Sexual orientation was exclusively heterosexual in eight of the nine subjects with any sexual experience. Several subjects were married and were parents by adoption. One subject, who had one lesbian experience of brief duration early in her teen years, expressed no interest in having another lesbian experience, but she also had severe doubts about being accepted coitally as a woman.

4. *Turner's syndrome, or gonadal dysgenesis.* This is the last of the clinical populations with a genetic or endogenous disorder that we will discuss. Turner's-syndrome individuals represent something of a special case compared with the other clinical groups; these individuals are missing the second sex chromosome completely, or are genetically mosaic (i.e., some cells are missing the second sex chromosome, some cells may have a normal chromosomal complement, and some have other combinations of normal or abnormal sex chromosomal complements). Individuals with this clinical condition are also not necessarily identified at birth. There is no abnormality of the external genitalia, but there are other associated features which may lead to an early diagnosis and always lead to a diagnosis by early adolescence. The associated features can include kidney and heart abnormalities and other dysmorphic features such as a webbed neck and moderate short stature. The degree to which an affected child displays any or all of these features varies widely. The chromosomal abnormality leads to undifferentiated or poorly differentiated gonads prenatally. Thus these children do not have reproductive capacity and do not develop secondary sex char-

acteristics or menstruate without hormone replacement. It is for this reason the condition is recognized in early adolescence.

Ehrhardt, Greenberg, and Money evaluated developmental behavior patterns in fifteen Turner's-syndrome girls, using matched controls.[10] All subjects were unambiguously reared as females, and all had a female gender identity. If prenatal hormonal environment plays a predispositional influencing role in later preferred gender-role behaviors (hypothesis 2), one would assume that Turner's girls would be the least "defeminized," as they are the most likely to have the lowest amounts of prenatal gonadal hormones that could have any defeminizing effect on the brain. In this study, gender-role behaviors of affected subjects differed significantly from controls in the areas of an elevated interest in appearance, a lower frequency of active outdoor play, and decreased fighting. The nonsignificant trends in gender-role behaviors were all in the expected direction of a lower frequency of being labeled a tomboy, preferring or content to be a girl, a higher interest in "frilly dresses," extensive preference for girls rather than boys as playmates, play with only dolls versus boys' toys, and a strong, actively expressed interest in infant care. Although the sample was young, among those who were adolescents there were no reports of homosexual fantasies or experiences in either affected children or controls.

5. *Children exposed to exogenous feminizing hormones prenatally.* In certain animal species, in both males and females, progesterone can antagonize androgen action under certain circumstances.[11] Therefore, it was hypothesized that progesterone might have a similar effect in humans. Yalom, Green, and Fisk, in a double-blind study of the offspring of diabetic mothers treated with diethylbestrol plus progesterone during pregnancy, reported findings that seem to support the hypotheses of an antiandrogenizing effect of progesterone upon some aspects of human gender-role behavior.[12] The twenty hormone-exposed males (aged sixteen to seventeen) were compared with a matched control group. The treated males were reported to be somewhat less assertive and aggressive and had decreased athletic coordination, decreased overall "masculine" interests, and less heterosexual experience compared with controls.

There were similar findings in a second study.[13] Here the subjects had been exposed to progesterone prenatally in mothers with preeclamptic toxemia. The authors reported findings on both males and females with a matched control group: male subjects had a significantly decreased interest in dating and marriage, females a decreased interest in tomboyish behavior and an increased interest in appearance. The most recent study in this area was reported by Meyer-Bahlburg, Grisanti, and Ehrhardt and Ehrhardt, Grisanti, and Meyer-Bahlburg.[14] The authors looked at males ($N = 13$) and females ($N = 15$) exposed prenatally to medroxy-progesterone acetate (MPA) in a double-blind study with matched controls. Because the subjects were eight to fourteen years of age, data on sexual orientation were not available. As in previous studies, gender identity was not affected, but there were some apparent treatment effects associated with gender-role behaviors in girls. Treated girls showed a lower incidence than the controls of being labeled a tomboy and a greater preference for feminine clothing styles. Hormone-exposed boys did not differ from controls.

6. *Children exposed to exogenous virilizing hormones prenatally.* Ehrhardt

and Money reported findings on ten genetic females exposed prenatally to exogenously administered synthetic progestins.[15] The hormones were given to the mothers during pregnancy because of threatened miscarriages. Some of the children evidenced signs of the prenatal virilization at birth, having an enlarged clitoris. Those who required surgery had it within the first year of life. There was no question of postnatal virilization, and these girls did not require medical follow-up or management. Subjects were matched with controls; the age range at followup was four to fourteen years. All girls had a female gender identity. The gender-role findings were similar to those in the populations of CAH girls, with a significant tendency in the subject population, as opposed to controls, toward a higher activity level, long-term tomboyish behavior, etc.

This study is important in that it decreases the possibility that postnatal virilization or long-term medical management, with the consequent parental anxiety, is responsible in any way for the gender-role findings in the CAH children. The genital ambiguity at birth was also less severe and more easily correctable with one procedure in those cases requiring surgery. Thus, the parents were less likely to have long-term lurking fears regarding their daughters as being in any way "at risk" for later problems.

Reinisch and Karow, using the Cattell Personality Inventory, studied twenty-six boys and forty-five girls aged five to seventeen who had been exposed prenatally to various combinations of synthetic progestogens and estrogens.[16] They used untreated siblings as controls. No treated children evidenced any sign of a genital anomaly. Many of the mothers did not recall having taken any drugs during pregnancy. The authors found significant treatment effects: male and female subjects *mainly* exposed to progestogens were more "independent," "sensitive," "self-assured," "individualistic," and "self-sufficient," while male and female subjects exposed primarily to estrogens were more "group oriented" and "group dependent." The authors did not report findings on gender identity or gender-role behaviors. However, the reported findings are of interest in that they indicate a behavioral consequence to prenatal hormone exposure in areas not generally considered sex dimorphic. This study raises the possibility that general temperamental predispositions in human behavior may be influenced by aspects of the prenatal hormonal environment.

The 5 α-reductase deficit of male pseudohermaphroditism. The "state of the art" was at the point we have described when the Imperato-McGinley et al. study of a new population of male pseudohermaphrodites was published.[17] The controversial study has been widely publicized, with accompanying distortions and misrepresentations in the popular press. This is not that surprising, for the authors offered findings and proposed conclusions that challenged the basic tenets of the field and leaned very far toward "biological determinism," a view with important sociopolitical implications that prior psychoendocrine findings had never supported. For these reasons, the study merits a separate and detailed treatment here.

Imperato-McGinley and their co-workers identified a group of thirty-eight male pseudohermaphrodites from twenty-three interrelated families in the Dominican Republic whose condition is genetically transmitted as an autosomal recessive trait. Affected males are born with a clitoris-like phallus and a bifid (incompletely developed) scrotum, with the testes either descended or not. Their enzymatic defect (the 5 α-reductase deficit) affects the conversion of the normal amounts of testosterone that the gonads make prenatally into another androgen, dihydrotestosterone, which is meant to act directly on the prenatal genital tubercle and to cause differentiation along male lines. The authors were able to interview thirty-three affected subjects and obtained retrospective data in two villages by interviewing subjects and other men and boys from those villages as controls. Other family members, wives, and girl friends were interviewed whenever possible.

The major findings from their interview data were: (1) Nineteen out of thirty-three subjects from the two villages had been "unambiguously reared" as females. (2) Adequate interview data were available on eighteen of the nineteen subjects. Of these eighteen, seventeen had successfully changed to a male gender identity and sixteen to a male gender role. (3) The seventeen subjects who changed gender identity recalled awareness of being different from other girls from age seven to twelve. (4) This awareness was usually associated in their minds with some incontrovertible evidence of body differences, for example, testes descending, lack of breast development, virilization of the body with the onset of adolescence. (5) The change in gender role to a male pattern generally took place either during puberty or in the postpubertal period. (6) The change in gender identity had an earlier onset, was more gradual, and spanned a longer period of time as the affected individual's body underwent the progressive development of male rather than female secondary sex characteristics of adolescence. (7) The age of onset of sexual behaviors, masturbation, morning erections, intercourse, etc., was not different between those subjects raised as girls and those raised as boys and not appreciably different from normal male controls. (8) Only one subject maintained a female gender identity. (9) All but two subjects displayed "heterosexual" sexual behavior, that is, attraction to and sexual relationships with women, following the change in gender identity to male.

The authors concluded from these findings: (1) In man, the relative influences of hormonal factors and environmental factors in the determination of gender identity remains unanswered. (2) In a laissez-faire environment, when sex of rearing is contrary to the testosterone-induced biologic sex, the biologic sex prevails if the normal testosterone-induced activation of puberty is permitted to occur. (3) The extent of androgen exposure of the brain in utero, during the early postnatal period, and at puberty has more effect in determining male gender identity than does sex of rearing. (4) Gender identity is not unilaterally fixed in early childhood but evolves until stabilized with the events of puberty.

The first question this provocative study raises is, "Are these affected children truly unambiguously reared?" It is necessary to establish firmly that they are if the data are conclusively to challenge the "critical period" hypothesis which delineates an age, the outside limits of which are widely believed not to extend beyond three to four years of life, within which gender identity is firmly and irrevocably fixed if rearing has been unambivalent. Other discussions of these data have pointed out that the 5 α-reductase affected subjects are not genitally normal as females at birth.[18] All have clitoromegaly (an enlarged clitoris) and a bifid scrotum with a urogenital sinus. In a retrospective study, it is impossible to assess clearly how the parents and extended family encompass or explain the observable facts of abnormal genital morphology at birth. Further, in a highly sex-stereotyped culture where girls marry early (often by the age of thirteen) and have a relatively rigid role definition of bearing children and taking care of the home, what fantasies of the future for these children do the parents have where the affected children lack a vagina, obviously making them incapable of normal intercourse and childbearing?

The authors note that after enough affected children had undergone puberty, the dramatic transitions of virilization rather than feminization, the culture labeled the affected children both retrospectively and at birth as "guevedoce" (eggs at twelve), "guevote" (penis at twelve), or "machi-hembra" (first woman, then man). Where no treatment or medical intervention is available, cultures must encompass and explain deviant individuals. Over some period of time, this apparently happened in the Dominican Republic. The question, however, as to whether the affected children were actually experienced from infancy on as completely normal females by family and peers, and reared as such prior to this labeling, appears unanswerable using the methods available in this study of human subjects. Even if it were possible to do the requisite prospective study, we have very little idea of how the self-sense of gender identity is conveyed to children. For example, babies, by seven months of life, are able to distinguish male faces from female faces.[19] We do not know, however, whether this perceptual feat is learned in some way or represents a behavioral expression of some biologically given internal schemata.

In summary, it appears unlikely that the genital malformation was completely unnoticed by the surrounding culture. The affected children were not normal girls until they were affected by the male hormonal activation of puberty. Next, we can assume that the affected children in early childhood most likely did not behave like most girls in that culture. The authors report that girls and boys play together until the age of about seven, at which point girls are expected to begin doing some prescribed female domestic tasks. If the affected children behave according to the gender-role patterns in childhood of other fetally virilized children, we would expect these children to be somewhat resistant to the change other girls experienced and also to be engaged in active early play more typical of male playmates than female playmates. In fact, the two 5 α-reductase children followed at The New York Hospital by New and Levine had exactly this pattern of early and long-term tomboyish, active, rough-and-tumble play, in spite of the fact that both had their testes removed early in life. These data would seem to indicate that whatever the parents' experience of their affected child's genital appearance, their reactions and questions, even if largely repressed or unconscious, could be exacerbated by the child's behavioral proclivities throughout childhood.

As is true in the study of any clinical population, there are issues regarding the interpretations and generalizations of these data for the accurate understanding of the affected individuals and their families. Since these data come from another culture, there may be relevant factors and issues that will not come to light without the inclusion of anthropological studies. Moreover, it has been of less importance to have all the data to be able to make appropriate medical decisions, as long as medical management is unavailable to these affected individuals in other cultures. However, as more of these individuals have access to medical facilities and are diagnosed early, having full information is critical since the medical decisions that might be made will have enormous implications for the individuals' lives. For example, if the authors are correct in regarding the "prescriptive" role of biology in these affected individuals, one would have to recommend to parents that the children be reared as males, in spite of the fact that they would grow up with an obvious irreparable severe genital anomaly and would not be able to have normal intercourse or reproductive capacity in adulthood.

The other major issue pertaining to the 5 α-reductase individuals is that of the interpretations and generalizations made from these data and applied within the field of psychoendocrine studies and more broadly by other researchers interested in the nature/nurture controversy. This research represents the first time that a biological "prescription" for later dimorphic behavior in humans has been proposed as a scientific fact based on a study of humans. This study has been related to discussions of nature and nurture for unaffected individuals by many individuals both in and outside of the scientific community, and many proponents of this view draw heavily on evidence from the animal studies, which the human studies in some ways parallel. However, it is far from clear that what we learn from human studies can be translated easily to animal studies or vice versa. For example (1) we do not know yet if there are morphologic sex differences in human brains (or the implications of such differences if they exist) as have been found in nonhuman animals; (2) as previously mentioned, many of the "dimorphic" behaviors studied in humans have no known analogies in other species, such as gender identity and some gender-role behaviors.

In the process of making theories one always hopes to be able to compare animal findings with findings from human studies in order to utilize the carefully controlled, methodologically sophisticated animal work. For example, the data from animal studies indicating differences in female and male brains raise the question as to whether this is true for humans, etc. It is critically important to keep in mind that although we study individuals who have clinical conditions that in some ways resemble some features of the carefully controlled studies in other mammals, we do *not* know (1) how or if data from nonhuman mammals relate to human beings; (2) to what extent the human data accurately parallel features of the animal studies (as we are unable to use biologic controls to limit compounding effects of biological and environmental factors in humans); or (3) the degree to which our observations, mostly retrospective of "deviant" behavior patterns in humans, represent "pure biologic" influences, or possibly relatively mild biological predispositional factors that then are inextricably confounded by the subsequent interrelationship of child's disposition and parental and other environmental reactions.

While it is appropriate to make hypotheses and attempt to generate principles from these data, psychoendocrinology is a relatively young science. It would be a mistake to overgeneralize these hypotheses to rules or laws that apply to unaffected individuals, or to overgeneralize from an affected group with one hormonal history to another group with a different hormonal history. One of the immediate incalculable benefits of this research, instigated by John Money at Johns Hopkins over two decades ago, has been for these affected individuals themselves. Money's pioneering research provided the data base for appropriate clinical decisions to be made early in life in various groups of hormonally and genitally deviant infants.

For example, physicians were no longer required to advise parents of a chromosomally male child, born with genitals that would never be sexually functional for a normal sexual relationship, that the genetic makeup required that the child be raised as a male. One repercussion of the study on 5 α-reductase individuals has been the uncertainty not only as to what the findings may mean about biological influences on normal development, but also whether this study in some way mitigates the findings from other clinical samples. For example, are these data adequate to revise our prior understanding regarding the central importance of rearing on the formation of gender identity? (That is, the assumption that in cases of ambiguous sexual morphology, clinical decisions as to sex assignment or reassignment can be made successfully based purely on the decision that will allow the affected child the most normal life. As long as the child is "unambiguously" reared, gender identity will be concordant with rearing regardless of the chromosomal, gonadal, or prenatal hormonal situation.) This principle is so well established from clinical experience that it should not be in jeopardy as applied to these populations.

The data from the Imperato-McGinley study do not apply to the biological constraints on gender identity formation in normal males and females in any sense unless one is absolutely certain these children were viewed as completely normal girls. As previously discussed, this is unlikely. There is ample evidence from clinical cases that ambivalently reared individuals often consolidate their gender identity around the time of adolescence. In the study of the 5 α-reductase individuals the authors concluded that the gender identity decision in adolescence was not only a reversal but also the result of the biological "activation" of the brain responding to androgens, the male hormones. An animal model for the "activation" principle in lower mammals exists; that is, adult female animals given testosterone exhibit a greater frequency of mounting behaviors than control females, and male castrate animals given estrogens exhibit more frequent lordosis (female receptive) behaviors than control males. It is clearly acceptable to hypothesize that humans may have the potential for a similar activation and on that basis attempt to formulate studies that would support or disconfirm the hypothesis.

However, much of the real value of the Imperato-McGinley study is lost if other hypotheses are not also considered and evaluated. It is quite possible, for example, that the high androgens of prenatal hormonal environment did, in some way, decrease biologic vulnerability to the impact of environmental factors that contribute to gender identity, either through extending the critical period or, more likely, creating a greater "predisposition" toward "maleness" in gender role and gender identity. The predispositional hypothesis has support in terms of biological influences on preferred gender-role behaviors but has never been demonstrated as a factor in gender identity formation. Examination of this hypothesis could lead to data that might illuminate other conditions of gender identity confusion that presently lack a known biological association.

We would agree with Imperato-McGinley that their study raises provocative questions regarding a possible role of prenatal (and/or postnatal) hormonal environment in reducing, under some circumstances, a later plasticity of the brain, which could manifest itself as decreased vulnerability of the affected individuals to environmental prescriptions in the area of gender identity. This is related to the authors' conclusion that gender identity is continually evolving. We would agree that one's experience of oneself as male or female evolves over time, throughout childhood, and certainly to adolescence with its integration of a new awareness of one's self as a sexual being. We do not feel, however, that the Imperato-McGinley study proves that those changes in self-awareness are biologically programmed rather than consequences of the bringing together of environmental influences with maturation, including increased cognitive awareness.

Discussion

In general, the studies of clinical populations indicate a rather consistent picture. In females, prenatal exposure to abnormally high levels of androgens or other virilizing hormones results in some behavioral-temperamental consequences, particularly those dimorphic behaviors generally subsumed under the category of gender-role behaviors. In males, androgen insensitivity or prenatal exposure to sufficient levels of hormones that antagonize androgen action results also in behavioral temperamental consequences.

The bulk of the evidence from human studies does *not* support the thesis that prenatal environment is responsible for choice of sex object in adolescence. In fact, with the better controlled, more elaborate studies in nonhuman mammals, where much higher amounts of hormones are given throughout the various critical periods, no one has yet succeeded in producing "homosexual" animals. In those human studies where any subjects in the sample had bisexual or homosexual experiences, no control groups were used, and it is not known, but is unlikely, that the frequency was higher than it would be in other nonrandom appropriate control groups.

In the area of gender identity formation, in all systematic studies of human populations except one, gender identity was concordant for sex of rearing regardless of the chromosomal, gonadal, or prenatal hormonal situation. The exception, reporting findings of a gender identity "reversal" in male pseudohermaphrodites and postulating a purely biological explanation, did *not* demonstrate unambivalent rearing in their subjects. In fact, no study to date has been able to exclude confounding environmental factors where there was any visible abnormality at birth. Furthermore, such "proof" would require anthropological and sophisticated prospective studies (which have not been done), and knowledge of the operational environmental variables responsible for formation or imposition upon the infant of a sense of self that is gender-specific. To date we do not know how this information is either communicated by the parents (presumably) or processed by the infant.

There are many difficulties with the human studies, among them the confounding effects of medical condition, frequent use of retrospective interview data, the difficulty of providing adequate controls, and small sample sizes. However, acting within the constraints of ethical human investigation requires many of these limitations. Low subject availability in rare genetic syndromes or other hormonally exposed individuals is also an expectable limitation. In future studies, we hope, a greater range of more sophisticated methodologies may mitigate some of the other limitations in human research.

In spite of the problems, psychoendocrine research has provided a foundation of data that indicates that biological factors, such as hormonal environment before birth, can be a real influence on at least some behavioral and/or temperamental proclivities throughout life. Future research ought to define more clearly the range and limitations of these biological influences. It will probably also investigate the human brain. A wealth of *animal* data indicates differences between male and female brains—in cell nuclear size in specific areas of the brain, and axonal and dendritic growth, both of which are hormonally sensitive during early critical periods and later in life.[20] We also know that the brain has specific receptors for dissimilar hormones, with concentrations of the various receptors in functionally different parts of the brain.[21] It is relatively parsimonious to assume that many of these biologic facts in nonhuman species are probably also true for humans,[22] although to date there are no human data in any of these areas of research. When we have elucidated some of these issues of dimorphic brain structure in humans, we may then be able to approach the issues of the association between structure and function in humans and the roles of biology and environment in shaping both.

NOTES

1. Obviously, this review essay cannot cover every aspect of a complex field. Instead, it attempts to outline some central issues and present some important data concerning them.
2. F. Whitam. "Child Indicators of Male Homosexuality," *Archives of Sexual Behavior* 6 (1977): 89–96.
3. A. Ehrhardt, R. Epstein, and J. Money, "Fetal Androgens and Female Gender Identity in the Early Treated Andrenogenital Syndrome," *Johns Hopkins Medical Journal* 123, no. 3 (1968): 160–67; A. A. Ehrhardt and S. W. Baker, "Fetal Androgens, Human Central Nervous Differentiation, and Behavioral Sex Differences," in *Sex Differences in Behavior*, ed. R. C. Friedman, R. M. Richart, and R. L. Vande Wiele (New York: John Wiley & Sons, 1974).
4. A. A. Ehrhardt and S. W. Baker, "Prenatal Androgen Exposure and Future Adolescent Behavior" (paper presented at the International Congress of Sexology. Montreal, 1976).
5. J. Money and M. Schwartz, "Dating, Romantic and Nonromantic Friendships, and Sexuality in 17 Early-treated Adrenogenital Females, Aged 16–25," in *Congenital Adrenal Hyperplasia*, ed. P. A. Lee et al. (Baltimore: University Park Press, 1977), pp. 419–31.
6. J. Money and J. Daley, "Hyperadrenocortical 46 XX Hermaphroditism with Penile Urethra: Psychological Studies in Seven Cases, Three Reared as Boys, Four as Girls," in Lee et al., pp. 433–46.
7. D. Masica, J. Money, and A. A. Ehrhardt, "Fetal Feminization and Female Gender Iden-

tity in the Testicular Feminizing Syndrome of Androgen Insensitivity," *Archives of Sexual Behavior* 1, no. 2 (1971): 131–42.

8. The term "virilization" is generally used in the animal and human literature for those hormonally responsive behaviors that are generally assumed to be most characteristic of males (such as a high degree of rough-and-tumble play in childhood in nonhuman primate males). Defeminization is used to describe a situation where behaviors generally assumed to be more characteristic of females are decreased in frequency by a hormonal manipulation. Most of the human dimorphic behavioral changes we refer to seem to fall most appropriately into the nomenclature of virilization rather than defeminization. An example in humans of defeminization rather than virilization would be if fetally virilized females had loss or severe impairment of menstrual cyclicity.

9. J. Money and B. Ogunro, "Behavioral Sexology: Ten Cases of Genetic Male Intersexuality with Impaired Prenatal and Pubertal Androgenization," *Archives of Sexual Behavior* 3, no. 3 (1974): 181–205.

10. A. Ehrhardt, N. Greenberg, and J. Money, "Female Gender Identity and Absence of Fetal Gonadal Hormones: Turner's Syndrome," *Johns Hopkins Medical Journal* 126, no. 5 (1970): 237–48.

11. J. A. Resko, "Fetal Hormones and Their Effect on the Differentiation of the Central Nervous System in Primate, Federation Proceedings 34 (1975): 1650–55.

12. I. Yalom, R. Green, and N. Fisk, "Prenatal Exposures to Female Hormones: Effect on Psychosexual Development in Boys," *Archives of General Psychiatry* 28 (1973): 554–61.

13. J. U. Zussman, P. P. Zussman, and K. Dalton, "Post-pubertal Effects of Prenatal Administration of Progesterone" (paper presented at the meeting of the Society for Research in Child Development, Denver, 1975).

14. H. F. L. Meyer-Bahlburg, G. C. Grisanti, and A. A. Ehrhardt, "Prenatal Effects of Sex Hormones on Human Male Behavior: Medroxyprogesterone Acetate (MPA)," *Psychoneuroendocrinology* 2 (1977): 381–90; A. A. Ehrhardt, G. C. Grisanti, and H. F. L. Meyer-Bahlburg, "Prenatal Exposure to Medroxyprogesterone Acetate (MPA) in Girls," ibid., pp. 391–98.

15. A. A. Ehrhardt and J. Money, "Progestin-induced Hermaphroditism: IQ and Psychosexual Identity in a Study of Ten Girls," *Journal of Sexual Research* 3 (1967): 83–100.

16. J. M. Reinsch and W. G. Karow, "Prenatal Exposure to Synthetic Progestins and Estrogens: Effects on Human Development," *Archives of Sexual Behavior* 6 (1977): 89–96.

17. J. Imperato-McGinley et al., "Androgens and the Evolution of Male-Gender Identity among Male Pseudohermaphrodites with 5 α-Reductase Deficiency," *New England Journal of Medicine* 300, no. 22 (1979): 1233–70.

18. J. Wilson, "Sex Hormones and Sexual Behavior," *New England Journal of Medicine* 300, no. 22 (1979): 1269–70.

19. J. F. Fagan, "Infants' Recognition of Invariant Features of Faces," *Child Development* 47 (1976): 627–38.

20. R. A. Gorski, "Long-Term Hormonal Modulation of Neuronal Structure and Function," in *The Neurosciences: 4th Study Program*, ed. F. O. Schmidt and F. Worden (Cambridge, Mass.: M.I.T. Press, 1979), pp. 969–82.

21. B. McEwen, "Gonadal Steroids and Brain Development," *Biology of Reproduction* 22 (1980): 43–48.

22. R. W. Goy and P. A. Goldfoot, "Neuroendocrinology: Animal Models and Problems of Human Sexuality," *Archives of Sexual Behavior* 4 (1975): 405–20.

9

Menarche
The Beginning of Menstrual Life

Sharon Golub

Menarche represents a developmental milestone in a woman's life. This paper reviews current knowledge about the physiological aspects of menarche and its place in the sequence of pubertal development. Hypotheses regarding the mechanisms that trigger menarche are presented, as is our current understanding of the influence of hormones, genetic factors, nutrition, exercise, and illness. Also discussed are the ways in which the changes of puberty and menarche affect the adolescent girl's psychosocial development, the unique problems of the early maturing girl, and the kind of preparation for menarche that is needed.

In "The Curse of an Aching Heart," playwright William Alfred captures the significance of menarche in a woman's life. One of the characters, a woman in her sixties, recalls being frightened and embarrassed when she got her first period. She awoke with stained bed clothes and sheets and didn't understand what was happening to her. Confused, she ran out of the house and after walking for awhile she happened upon a neighbor who recognized that she was upset and invited her in for a cup of tea. The neighbor explained menstruation to the girl and then, in honor of the occasion, the woman gave the girl a brooch. In the play, memory of this event was poignantly related to another woman more than forty years later.

Is this vignette a fluke, a bit of sentimental whimsy? Probably not. Psychological research confirms the dramatist's intuition that menarche is an important developmental event. In a study of recollections of menarche, Golub and Catalano (1983) found that almost all of the 137 women studied, ranging in age from 18 to 45, remembered their first menstruation. And a majority could describe in detail where they were when it happened, what they were doing, and whom they told. How many events in our lives are so vividly recalled?

It is surprising, therefore, that menarche has received so little research attention until quite recently. Now scientists have begun to look at both the physical and psychological aspects of menarche and at the ways in which they are inextricably linked. It is acknowledged that the changes of puberty do not occur in a psychosocial vacuum. Body changes affect a person psychologically and socially, and the person's life experiences influence the biological processes as well. Nowhere is this seen more clearly than at menarche. For example, what is the relationship between exercise and the onset of menarche? Do menarcheal experiences affect the later development of menstrual distress? What determines whether menarche is a stressful time for girls? What does the menarcheal experience mean to the pubertal girl? How does it affect the way she sees herself? Is there a relationship between menarche and sexual activity? And how soon after menarche is a young woman fertile? Although there is a great deal that we still do not know, this paper will address these questions and will review the highlights of what is known about the physiological and psychosocial aspects of menarche.

Physiological Aspects of Menarche

Sequence of Pubertal Development

Menarche is preceded by characteristic body changes that occur some time between the ages of 9 and 16. Breast development usually, but not always, occurs first. There is an increase in body hair and there is also a weight gain, growth spurt, and a change in body proportions with the hips becoming fuller. Sweat glands become more active and a body odor develops that is thought to be related to an increase in sex hormone secretions from the adrenal gland. The skin becomes oilier, sometimes giving rise to skin problems. And while these external changes are going on there are concomitant changes occurring within the body: the uterus and vagina are growing (Grumbach, Grave, & Mayer, 1974; Katchadourian, 1977).

As noted above, breast development is usually the first sign of puberty with breast buds beginning to form around the age of 11. Breast development is influenced by the secretion of estrogen, particularly estradiol from the ovary, and probably by the secretion of prolactin from the anterior pituitary gland as well (Warren, 1983). There is a slight enlargement of the areolar and elevation of the breast as a small mound. Soon after, pubic hair begins to develop, usually at about age 11½. Axillary hair generally appears about two years after the beginning of pubic hair development. On the average, menarche occurs between 12.8 and 13.2 years. (For photographs and a detailed description of the stages of breast and pubic hair growth during puberty see Tanner, 1978.)

Pubertal development may be fast or slow. Some girls pass rapidly through the stages of breast and pubic hair development while others move slowly. On the average, the total time for the overall process of physical transformation from child to adult is about four years (Tanner, 1978). However, some girls may take only 1½ years to pass through all the stages while the slower developers may take as long as five years to do so. For those working or living with girls in this age group it is important to keep in mind that there can be great variation in the normal time of onset and completion of pubertal development. It is perfectly normal for a girl to begin to menstruate any time between the ages of 9 and 16 and age mates may be at very different stages of sexual maturation—one 12 year old can look like a woman, another very much like a child.

There is a close relationship between menarche and the pubertal spurt in height. Girls start to menstruate after the growth spurt has peaked, when the rate of increase in height (height velocity) is falling. The growth spurt is nearly over at the time of menarche, with girls on the average growing only about two more inches after the onset of menstruation. However, some girls do grow as much as four inches more (Tanner, 1978).

Menarche marks a mature stage of uterine development but not reproductive maturity. Early cycles are often irregular and between 55 and 82 percent of menstrual cycles during the first two postmenarcheal years are anovulatory. Regular menstruation may not occur for several years. However, it is important to remember that despite the apparent absence of regular monthly ovulation, any individual cycle may be ovulatory and is potentially fertile (Brennock, 1982) as indicated by the fact that there were 30,000 pregnancies among girls under the age of 15 in the United States between 1973 and 1978. These teenagers are at high risk for pregnancy complications such as low birthweight, high infant mortality, and pregnancy induced hypertension (Leppert, 1983), in addition to the stressful social and psychological consequences of having a baby at 13 or 14 years of age.

What Triggers Menarche?

There is some controversy about what triggers menarche. Currently there are two hypotheses which relate menarcheal age to physical growth: one focusing on skeletal growth and the other on the accumulation of fat. The skeletal growth hypothesis is based on the idea that the premenarcheal girl must reach an appropriate stage of skeletal development in order to reproduce and, therefore, the age at which she reaches this structural status (mature height and pelvic dimensions) is closely correlated with menarcheal age (Tanner, 1978). The importance of skeletal maturity is related to the need for a body, specifically a pelvis, that is adequate in size to bear a child. And there is some data to support the idea that pelvic dimensions—an average biiliac diameter of 26.2 cms.—are significantly correlated with menarcheal age (Ellison, 1982). Thus menarcheal age is closely related to skeletal development and bone age can be used as an appropriate measure of developmental age in predicting when menarche will occur (Tanner, 1978). This view attributes the decline in average age at menarche during the last century (referred to in the literature as the secular trend) to the acceleration of skeletal growth during this time, presumably related to better nutrition and health. In contrast, slow skeletal growth, resulting from poor nutrition or high altitude, leads to delay in the onset of menstruation.

An alternative hypothesis, proposed by Frisch (1980), suggests that the onset of menstruation is contingent upon the accumulation of fat and that a critical minimum weight for height is necessary to trigger and maintain ovulation and menstruation. Frisch's explanation of the secular trend in menarcheal age is that girls reach 101 to 103 pounds, the average weight at menarche, sooner now, and therefore menstruation begins earlier. She points out that a late menarche is associated with slower increases in body weight such as that seen in cases of malnutrition, or among twins, because they grow more slowly. Frisch notes that the greatest change during the adolescent growth spurt up to the time of menarche is a 120 percent increase in body fat. At menarche, girls' bodies average about 24 percent fat, not much different from the 28 percent fat found in the average 18 year old woman. In contrast, boys at about 18 years of age are much leaner with 14 percent fat. Frisch theorizes that reproduction requires energy and the function of the stored fat is to provide readily accessible energy should it be needed for pregnancy and lactation.

In a recent study entitled, "Skeletal Growth, Fatness, and Menarcheal Age," Ellison (1982) compared the two hypotheses using factor analysis of longitudinal growth data on 67 middle-class white girls born in 1928 and 1919 and drawn from the Berkeley Guidance Study. Ellison found that height velocity prior to menarche was the strongest independent correlate of menarcheal age, accounting for over 50 percent of the variance. The weight factor made the second largest contribution, accounting for 18 percent of the variance in menarcheal age. Thus while there seems to be a strong relationship between adolescent weight and menarcheal age, its effect is apparently less than that of the skeletal development. Ellison makes the point that since skeletal growth tends to cease soon after menarche, natural selection would delay menarche until the pelvis could handle reproduction.

Hormones

Although incompletely understood, significant hormonal changes occur at puberty. The gonadal, adrenal, and hypothalamic-hypophyseal hormones are of major importance. It is the interrelationship of these hormones that later controls the female reproductive cycle. However, endocrinologists now believe that the hormonal changes associated with sexual maturation actually begin at the time of conception. By the third trimester of pregnancy, the negative feedback system is established. (See Figure 1.) During infancy the hypothalamic gonadotropin regulating mechanism is "set" at a low level and remains there until around the time of puberty when there is an increase in the secretion of follicle stimulating hormone (FSH) and luteinizing hormone (LH) and a decrease in hypothalamic sensitivity. Put another way, the hypothalamic set point increases inducing a subsequent increase in the secretion of FSH, LH, and gonadal hormones (Petersen & Taylor, 1980).

The adolescent growth spurt is a result of the joint action of androgens and growth hormone (Tanner, 1978). A progressive increase in plasma dehydroepiandosterone and dehydroepiandosterone sulfate, which are weak androgens, begins at about eight years of age and continues through ages 13 to 15. These hormones, thought to originate from the adrenal gland, are the earliest hormonal changes to take place at puberty (Warren, 1983). They and the more potent androgens—testosterone and dihydrotestosterone—increase significantly as pubertal development progresses (Dupon & Bingel, 1980). Increased secretion of gonadotropins from the pituitary (FSH and LH) and sex steroids from the gonads follow (Warren, 1983).

The main female sex hormone secreted by the ovaries is estradiol which is present in relatively small amounts in the blood until about age eight or nine when it begins to rise. This increase in blood levels of estradiol causes growth of the breasts, uterus, vagina, and parts of the pelvis. When menstruation begins, estradiol levels fluctuate with the various phases of the cycle and are controlled by pituitary FSH (Tanner, 1978).

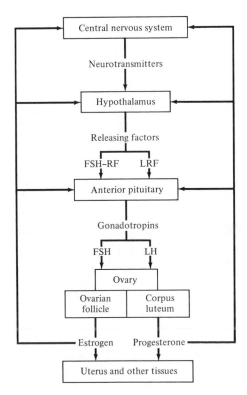

Figure 1   Menstrual cycle hormone feedback system

The two pituitary gonadotropins, follicle stimulating hormone (FSH) and luteinizing hormone (LH), are both secreted in small amounts during childhood and increase at puberty. The pubertal rise is first seen as pulses of LH that are released during sleep. This sleep-associated rise in LH is not seen in either the prepubertal child or the adult (Warren, 1983). Gradually LH is released during the daytime too.

Menstruation, as well as earlier pubertal development, is thought to begin with a signal to the hypothalamus from the central nervous system. As noted above, a hypothalamic feedback system does exist before puberty, but the hypothalamus is responsive to low levels of LH in the prepubertal girl. Then around the time of menarche, a gradual change occurs making the hypothalamus less sensitive. Higher levels of estrogen are needed. The hypothalamus then secretes more FSH-releasing hormone. This neurohormone stimulates the pituitary gland to release FSH, which, in turn, triggers the growth of the ovarian follicle. As the follicles grow they secrete estrogen which causes growth of the cells lining the uterus (the endometrium). Increasing levels of estrogen in the blood also signal the pituitary to reduce FSH and secrete LH. LH triggers the release of the ovum from the follicle which then evolves into the corpus luteum and secretes progesterone and a little estrogen. If the ovum is not fertilized, the pituitary stops production of LH, levels of both estrogen and progesterone drop, menstruation begins, and the cycle starts again. (See Figure 1.)

Other Factors Affecting Pubertal Development

Genetics. Genetic factors play an important role in determining rate of growth, pubertal development, and age at menarche. Studies of monozygotic twin sisters growing up together indicate that they reach menarche about two months apart, with the first born twin—for some unknown reason—more likely to menstruate first (Shields, 1962). Dizygotic twins differ by about 12 months (Tanner, 1978). Mother-daughter and sister-sister correlations have also been reported to be significant (Chern, Gatewood, & Anderson, 1980). Kantero and Widholm (1971) found other menstrual similarities between mothers and daughters: significant correlations were found between mothers' and daughters' length of cycle, duration of menstrual flow, and symptoms of dysmenorrhea and premenstrual tension. It is thought that both mother and father exert an equal influence on rate of growth and maturation. Thus a late-maturing girl is as likely to have a late-maturing father as a later-maturing mother (Tanner, 1978).

Nutrition. There is a well documented link between nutrition and fertility. Famine amenorrhea was reported in both world wars (Menkin, Watkins, & Trussell, Note 1). Young women who are undernourished because of excessive dieting or those with anorexia nervosa often do not have menstrual periods. And it is well known that malnutrition retards growth and will delay menarche (Tanner, 1978). The fall in age at menarche that has occurred between 1830 and 1960 coincides with the increased availability of protein in the diet of developed countries during this time. In some countries, where nutrition has remained inadequate, age of menarche is comparatively high. For example, in contrast with the average age of menarche in the United States, which is now 12.8 years, in Bangladesh it is just under 16, and among certain New Guinea tribes, it is about 18 (Menkin, Watkins, & Trussell, Note 1). A recent study by Goodman, Grove, and Gilbert (1983) in which no differences in age at menarche were found among Caucasian, Japanese, and Chinese women living in Hawaii, suggests that nutrition and environmental factors are responsible for population differences. Tanner (1978) has noted that children in urban, as opposed to rural, areas are more likely to have more rapid growth and an earlier menarche that is probably attributable to better nutrition, health, and sanitation.

Exercise. Exercise also affects menstruation. Women who experience high energy outputs, such as ballet dancers and athletes who train intensively, have a later age at menarche and a high incidence of amenorrhea. This is particularly true when intensive training begins at an early premenarcheal age (Fisch, 1980; Frisch et al., 1981; Frisch, 1983). It is not known whether an altered lean-fat ratio is responsible for the delay in menarche in young athletes, as proposed by Frisch, or if the delay occurs through the direct effects of exercise on hormonal secretion and metabolism (Rebar & Cumming, 1981). Some investigators have questioned whether delays in the age of menarche in athletes occur at all (Malina, 1982). Others have expressed concern about the short-term and long-term effects of exercise on reproductive function (Rebar & Cumming, 1981). Also at this time it is not known whether it is disadvantageous to have a later menarche rather than an early one. However, the consensus seems to be that exercise-related alterations in reproductive function are not serious and are readily reversible.

Climatic and seasonal effects. Climate has no more than a very minor effect on age at menarche. In fact, contrary to earlier beliefs, people who live in tropical countries are somewhat more likely to have a *late* menarche. This is thought to be related to nutrition rather than a climate because children in the higher socioeconomic groups in these countries experience menarche at about the same time as children living in temperate zones.

Season of the year does influence growth velocity, with peak growth seen between March and July, and girls are most likely to have their first menstruation in the late fall or early winter (Science News, 1980; Tanner, 1978).

Acute and chronic illness. There are some conditions where menstruation will not occur. For example, a child with Turner's Syndrome, a chromosomal anomaly in which the second X chromosome is absent, will not menstruate because she lacks ovaries. Ehrhardt and Meyer-Bahlberg (1975) advise that sex hormone administration is crucial in order for these girls to attain psychosocial and psychosexual maturity. Administration of estrogen will cause the breasts to grow and an artificial menstrual cycle may be produced by giving estrogen for three weeks followed by a week without treatment. This is important because these girls want to look, develop, and be treated like normal female adolescents.

Other illnesses can delay menarche, probably because of their effects on nutrition. This is most likely to be true in cases of uremia, regional enteritis, ulcerative colitis, congenital heart disease, cystic fibrosis, and diabetes mellitus. The timing of the onset of the illness as well as the illness per se seem to be important. For example, if diabetes develops during the initial pubertal period, menarche is delayed, whereas if it develops later, menarche may be unaffected (Warren, 1983).

Conversely, some conditions will advance the age of menarche. These include hypothyroidism, central nervous system tumors, encephalitis, head trauma, and some virilizing disorders. Inactive, retarded, or bedridden children also reach menarche at an earlier age than their more active counterparts. And blind children have a younger age at menarche that may be related in part to their limited activity (Warren, 1983).

Thus menarche occurs after a series of changes in hormone secretion and somatic growth. These processes are in turn influenced by genetic and environmental factors such as nutrition, exercise, and illness which may accelerate or retard the onset of menstruation. We now turn to the psychosocial aspects of menarche and its meaning to the adolescent girl and those around her.

Psychosocial Aspects of Menarche

Effects of Menarche on the Early Adolescent Girl

Much of the early writing about the psychology of menarche presented it as a traumatic experience. For example, early psychoanalytic theory postulated a marked increase in sex drive at puberty and an inevitable period of anxiety, worry about impulse control, and increased lability as "a relatively strong id confronts a relatively weak ego" (A. Freud, 1946). Benedek (1959) believed that menarche might evoke fears associated with the anticipation of pain during intercourse and childbirth. Current psychoanalytic views are much more positive. Notman (1983) and others suggest that meeting the developmental tasks of adolescence need not be as tumultuous as was previously believed. True, the early adolescent needs to modify her attachment to her parents and develop the capacity to form relationships with peers; and eventually she must establish her identity as a woman and develop the capacity for intimacy with another person. However, this need not happen overnight and the process should not cause turmoil or disintegration.

Menarche can have an organizing effect for the adolescent girl, helping her to clarify her perception of her own genitals, particularly confirming the existence of the vagina and correcting the confusion she may have had about the female genitalia. Kestenberg (1965) suggests that menarche may serve as a reference point around which girls can organize their pubertal experiences; it is a landmark for feminine identification. This is in keeping with the greater awareness of sexual differentiation between males and females among postmenarcheal girls demonstrated by Koff, Rierdan, and Silverstone (1978).

Knowledge, Attitudes, and Expectations in Anticipation of Menarche

What do the girls themselves say? Whisnant and Zegans (1975) interviewed 35 white middle class pre- and postmenarcheal girls at a summer camp. The girls had learned about menstruation from friends, commercial booklets, school, and their parents—especially their mothers. They perceived themselves as being knowledgeable about menstruation and used the appropriate terms. However, when questioned further the interviewer found that they really did not have a good conception of what the internal organs were like or how they functioned and they were even more inept at describing the external genitalia. Thus, despite their access to information about menstruation, they had not assimilated it particularly well. The girls were most concerned about what to do when they got their periods and many had mentally rehearsed what they would do in a variety of situations.

Brooks-Gunn and Ruble (1980) found that both boys and girls in the seventh and eighth grades have similar and mostly negative beliefs about menstruation. For example, most believed that menstruation is accompanied by physical discomfort, increased emotionality, and a disruption of activities. Only a third thought that the onset of menstruation was something to be happy about.

Williams (1983) found more positive attitudes toward menstruation in a group of 9 to 12 year old girls, most of whom were premenarcheal. These girls generally equated menstruation with growing up and being normal. However, about a third of these subjects also believed menstruation to be embarassing, 28 percent thought it a nuisance, 27 percent found it disgusting, and 23 percent disliked the idea that it is not controllable. The girls in this sample also believed some of the popular menstrual taboos. About half the subjects thought a girl should not swim when menstruating and 22 percent believed she should not be active in sports. Many were influenced by concealment taboos with a majority expressing concern about concealing sanitary pads and menstrual odor. A striking 85 percent thought that a girl should not talk about menstruation to boys and 40 percent did not even think that it was all right to discuss menstruation with their fathers. And, as in the Brooks-Gunn and Ruble study noted above, most believed that girls are more emotional when they menstruate.

Reactions to Menarche

What do girls actually experience at the time of menarche? In several studies menarche has been found to be an anxiety producing or negative event (Brooks-Gunn & Ruble, 1980; Golub & Catalano, 1983; Koff, Rierdan, & Jacobson, 1981; Whisnant & Zegans, 1975) and mixed feelings such as being "excited but scared" or "happy and embarrassed" are common (Petersen, 1983; Woods, Dery, & Most, 1983). Most of these data were collected using interviews and questionnaires, and sometimes were based on recollections of older subjects.

Petersen (1983) in looking at menarche as one part of her study of 400 middle-class suburban boys and girls in the 6th, 7th, and 8th grades, found that the adolescents were remarkably inarticulate in describing their feelings about their changing bodies. Therefore, she decided that projective measures might be more useful than direct questions in exploring girls' feelings about menstruation. The girls were presented with an incomplete story about menarche adapted from Judy Blume's book, *Are You There, God? It's Me, Margaret.* For example:

> "Mom—hey, Mom—come quick!" When Nancy's mother got to the bathroom she said: "What is it? What's the matter?" "I got it," Nancy told her. "Got what?" said her mother.

The girls were then asked, "What happened next?" Some of the girls responded that, "She told her Mom that she had gotten her period;" others said that Mom explained or helped. They were then asked "How did Nancy feel?" About a third gave negative or fearful responses, about half were positive or pleased, and another five percent were ambivalent.

Maxine Kumin (1982) in a short story entitled "Facts of Life" differentiates between the expectations about menarche and its actual occurrence. She describes a group of twelve-year-old girls as longing to begin to menstruate. "An eager band of little girls, itchy with the work of sprouting, sits expectant. The old reticences, embarrassments, and complaints have given way to progress. Now we have sex education, cartoon films of the reproductive tract, a beltless sanitary napkin, a slender, virginal tampon" (p. 11). Yet, when the first blood does indeed come the girl is described as both terribly happy and terribly sad as mother and daughter celebrate together.

Changes in Body Image

Changes in body image are among the most dramatic reactions to menarche. Although the body changes associated with puberty occur gradually, girls do expect to act differently after menarche and they also see themselves differently. In a clever study of seventh grade girls, Koff (1983) asked the subjects to draw male and female human figures on two occasions, approximately six months apart. Of the 87 girls sampled, 34 were premenarcheal on both test occasions, 23 were postmenarcheal, and 30 changed menarcheal status between the two test sessions. The findings were striking. Postmenarcheal girls produced drawings that were significantly more sexually differentiated than those of their premenarcheal peers and a greater percentage of the postmenarcheal girls drew their own sex first. Most notable was the difference in the drawings done by the girls whose menarcheal status changed during the course of the study. There was a significant increase in the sexual differentiation of their drawings at the time of the second testing with the postmenarcheal girls drawing womanly females with breasts and curves in contrast to their earlier, more childlike, premenarcheal drawings. (Examples of these drawings may be seen in Koff, 1983.)

To further explore girls' beliefs about the change menarche world have on them, Koff, Rierdan, and Jacobson (1981) gave a sentence completion task to seventh and eighth grade girls. In response to the cue sentence "Ann just got her period for the first time," the girls said such things as, "She saw herself in a different way," and "She felt very grown up." In response to another item, "Ann regarded her body as . . . ," postmenarcheal girls were more likely than premenarcheal girls to describe a change in body image. For example, Ann's body was "a woman's body" and "more mature than it was."

These studies clearly demonstrate that girls do experience menarche as a turning point in their development and they apparently reorganize their body images in the direction of "greater sexual maturity and feminine differentiation" (Koff, 1983). Postmenarcheal girls are more aware of sexual differentiation between males and females and of themselves as women than are premenarcheal girls of the same age.

The Early Maturing Girl

The age at which a girl experiences menarche does seem to affect her reaction to it. Peterson (1983) found that girls who experience menarche early, in the sixth grade or before, seem to have more difficulty with it. Some of the girls denied that they had begun to menstruate and when Petersen questioned the mothers of her early maturing subjects, over 70 percent of the mothers reported that menarche was very difficult for their daughters. The mothers of five of the six girls who denied having gotten their periods reported the negative aspects of the experience for them. Notman (1983) has suggested that the denial of menstruation may be related to conflicts about accepting the female role or to an attempt to delay adulthood. Certainly one of the girls in Petersen's sample who denied menstruating lends support to that view. In response to a Thematic Apperception Test card showing a middle-aged woman with a girl holding a doll, this subject described the girl in the picture as scared about growing up and asking her mother when she was going to get her period.

Unlike boys who are eager for their growth spurt and physical signs of maturity, girls would prefer to mature at the same time as everyone else. This may be because of the age difference between the sexes in the onset of puberty—boys normally start later than girls. Girls' attitudes about early development may also be related to the changes in their lives that occur when they develop the breasts and curves characteristic of a woman. There is some evidence that sixth and seventh grade girls who are already pubertal are more likely to be dating and, somewhat paradoxically, these girls also have lower self-esteem, lower school achievement, and more behavioral problems than comparable boys and non-pubertal girls (Simmons, Blyth, Van Cleave, & Bush, 1979). In this study pubertal development per se had little effect on the girls' self-esteem. However, the early maturing girls who had also begun dating were most likely to indicate low self-esteem (50 percent as opposed to 36-40 percent of the other girls). It is interesting that while early dating behavior is disadvantageous for girls, it has no statistically significant impact on boys.

Thus girls' self-esteem was negatively affected by their own physiology (early menarche) and social relationships, while boys' self-esteem was not. Simons et al. (1979) suggest some reason why this may be so. First, the sexes develop different value systems at this age. For girls, appearance and sociability assume priority, while for boys these values remain secondary. When asked to rank the importance of popularity, competence, and independence, seventh grade girls were more likely to rank popularity first. This places a great deal of importance on other peoples' opinions of oneself. These girls also placed a high value on looks. Moreover, the changes in body image may be qualitatively different for girls than for boys. Pubertal boys are generally happy with their new height and muscle development. Pubertal girls are not sure whether their new figures make them better or worse looking than their peers. Further, pubertal girls' negative reactions to dating may be a result of sexual pressures from their male partners for which these girls are not prepared. In interviews with some of these girls the researchers found them likely to express dislike for "guys trying to touch me." One subject said, "I don't really like to be kissed." It looks as if some of these girls were vulnerable, with their emotional maturity lagging well behind their physical development, causing confusion and contributing to their feelings of low self-esteem. This is in keeping with data from the California Adolescent Study which show that it is the girl with accelerated growth and maturation who is at a disadvantage (Jones, 1958; Jones & Mussen, 1959). However, social class may also play a role. Clausen (1975) found that for middle-class girls early maturation was positively related to self-confidence, whereas working class girls experienced a negative effect. In contrast to early maturation, late maturation, although quite disturbing for boys, does not seem to have the same degree of negative consequences for girls, perhaps because a childlike appearance is part of femininity for some adult women (Friedman, Note 2).

Relationships with Parents

In view of the changes that go on in girls' perceptions of themselves it seems reasonable to ask if menarche affects girls' relationships with other people, particularly family members. On the basis of limited data, the answer seems to be a qualified yes. Danza (1983) compared 48 pre- and postmenarcheal girls in the sixth and seventh grades. She found that although they were no different in age than their premenarcheal peers, the postmenarcheal girls were more likely to wear make-up or a bra, to shave their legs, and to date. They also slept less on school nights, moving from nine or more hours a night toward the more usual adult eight hour sleep cycle. The postmenarcheal girls were also significantly more uncomfortable in discussing emotionally charged topics such as love, sex, drugs, and alcohol with their parents, and they reported having more conflict with their parents than the premenarcheal girls did.

Effects on Sexual Behavior

Because it marks the onset of reproductive potential, menarche is important to a girl's family and community as well as to herself. This is seen in other cultures when one looks at the different tribal rituals celebrating menarche and at customs, such as purdah, veiling, and virginity tests, which guard girls' reproductive potential. Economics comes into play too. Paige (1983) has suggested that there is a relationship between various methods of controlling girls' chastity and the economic resources of a particular culture. In societies where marriage bargains are important, chastity is crucial to the girl's marriageability and is rigorously controlled.

This is not seen in our culture today. Rather, in the United States the physical transformation from girl to woman and the onset of menstruation are accompanied by changes in social and sexual behavior. And the timing of menarche is important. Several researchers have reported that girls with an early menarche were more likely to date and pet at an earlier age than their later maturing peers (Gagnon, 1983; Presser, 1978; Simons et al., 1979; Udry, 1979). And there is data indicating that women with early menarche begin premarital coitus earlier as well (Gagnon, 1983; Presser, 1978; Udry, 1979). In an extensive study of black and white low income women in 16 American cities, Udry (1979) found that girls with early menarche, as compared to those with late menarche, were more than twice as likely to have had intercourse by age 16. Udry and Cliquet (1982) also examined the relationship between ages at menarche, marriage, and first birth among women in four widely diverse countries (United States, Malay, Belgium, and Pakistan) and concluded that there was a clear behavioral sequence relating age at menarche to age at first intercourse and first birth. Menarche seems to initiate a chain of events. In the United States the pattern is one of dating and other sexual behavior that increase the probability of early intercourse and early childbearing.

Whether this sequence is more readily attributable to hormonal or sociocultural factors is a difficult question to answer. Gagnon (1983) found no significant relationship between the onset of menarche and masturbatory experience. Similarly, in their studies of children with the problem of precocious puberty (beginning at six to eight years of age), Ehrhardt and Meyer-Bahlberg (1975) have found that early puberty does not automatically trigger an early sex life. Masturbation and sex play in childhood did not appear to be enhanced and premarital intercourse did not occur earlier than normally expected. Thus at this time it seems reasonable to conclude that the timing of puberty influences when the girl, her parents, and her peers perceive of her as being someone for whom dating and heterosexual relationships are appropriate and this in turn affects her socio-sexual behavior.

Preparation of Menarche

In view of the ambivalent feelings about menarche expressed by so many adolescent girls and the difficulties experienced by the early maturing girl, it seems reasonable to ask if adequate preparation makes any difference? It probably does. Both Rierdan (1983) and Golub and Catalano (1983) found that subjects who report being adequately prepared have a more positive initial experience with menstruation. There are other studies indicating a need for more and better menstrual education. For example, Logan (1980), in a study of 95 women from 23 foreign countries, found that 28 percent complained about not having enough information. Similarly, in a large study of American women, 39 percent reported that their preparation was inadequate (Weideger, 1976). and Brooks-Gunn and Ruble (1980) reported that the adolescent girls they tested said they had sufficient prior knowledge about menstruation but still felt unprepared for menarche.

What do girls want to know? Rierdan (1983), in a study of 97 college women's recollections of menarche, found that the young women wanted to know about menstrual physiology and menstrual hygiene—the facts that are usually included in menstrual education materials—but they also wanted information about menstruation as a personal event. Subjects said that girls need to know about the normality of menstruation and it must be distinguished from disease, injury, and uncleanliness. They suggested that the feelings of fright and embarrassment girls experience at menarche be acknowledged as normal and the negative aspects of the menstrual experience need to be discussed in order to provide a balanced view of menstruation. The college women emphasized that girls need support and reassurance at the time of menarche and Rierdan says, "Many referred specifically to the importance of an informed, understanding, accepting mother" (Rierdan, 1983). Unfortunately, however, interviews with mothers of adolescent girls indicate that the mothers themselves are not prepared to fill this role, suggesting a need to prepare mothers as well as daughters for menarche.

In Support of a New Tradition

Some researchers have suggested that we need a "contemporary tradition for menarche" in order to overcome some of the negative connotations associated with it (Logan, Calder, & Cohen, 1980). They believe that currently we address the physical needs of the menarcheal girl, teaching her how to take care of herself, but leaving her without the social and emotional support that she needs at this time. In order to explore what the appropriate ritual might be, Logan et al. designed five short stories describing possible responses to a girl's first period and gave them to girls between the ages of eight and seventeen, mothers of girls in this age group, and women psychologists. The most popular response of the mothers and daughters to being told about the onset of menstruation was "Congratulations, our little girl is growing up." However, the psychologists preferred, "Something special has happened," apparently acknowledging the ambivalent and even negative emotions that a girl may have about the beginning

108   Sharon Golub

of menstruation. As for symbolic gestures, the most popular among the mothers was a toast to the girl from her mother and father, or a meal in her honor. But the daughters had reservations about this, fearing an invasion of privacy and reinforcing feelings that "everyone is watching her." The daughters preferred a hug or a kiss and a material token such as a gift or flowers. It seems dramatists often capture in a few lines what scientists seek in reams of data: William Alfred was right on target with the gift of a brooch.

REFERENCE NOTES

1. Menkin, J., Watkins, S. C., & Trussell, J. Nutrition, health, and fertility. Report prepared for The Ford Foundation. December 1980.
2. Freedman, R. Personal Communication. December 1983.

REFERENCES

BENEDEK, T. Sexual functions in women and their disturbance. In S. Arieti (Ed.) *American handbook of psychiatry.* New York: Basic Books, 1959.
BLUME, J. *Are you there, God? It's me, Margaret.* New York: Dell, 1970.
BRENNOCK, W. E. Fertility at menarche. *Medical Aspects of Human Sexuality,* 1982, *16,* 21–30.
BROOKS-GUNN, J., & RUBLE, D. Menarche. In A. J. Dan, E. A. Graham, & C. P. Beecher (Eds.) *The menstrual cycle, Vol. 1.* New York: Springer, 1980.
CHERN, M. M., GATEWOOD, L. C., & ANDERSON, V. E. The inheritance of menstrual traits. In A. J. Dan, E. A. Graham, & C. P. Beecher (Eds.) *The menstrual cycle, Vol. 1.* New York: Springer, 1980.
CLAUSEN, J. A. The social meaning of differential physical and sexual maturation. In S. E. Dragastin, & G. H. Elder, Jr. (Eds.) *Adolescence in the life cycle.* New York: Halsted, 1975.
DANZA, R. Menarche: Its effects on mother-daughter and father-daughter interactions. In S. Golub (Ed.) *Menarche.* Lexington, Massachusetts: D. C. Heath, 1983.
DUPON, C. & BINGEL, A. S. Endocrinologic changes associated with puberty in girls. In A. J. Dan, E. A. Gramham, & C. P. Beecher (Eds.) *The menstrual cycle. Vol. 1* New York: Springer, 1980.
EHRHARDT, A. E., & MEYER-BAHLBERG, H. F. I., Psychological correlates of abnormal pubertal development. *Clinics in Endocrinology and Metabolism.* 1975, *4,* 207–222.
ELLISON, P. T. Skeletal growth, fatness, and menarcheal age: A comparison of two hypotheses. *Human Biology,* 1982, *54,* 269–281.
FREUD, A. *The ego and the mechanisms of defense.* New York: International Universities Press, 1946.
FRISCH, R. E. Fatness, puberty and fertility. *Natural History,* 1980, *89,* 16–27.
FRISCH, R. E. What's below the surface. *New England Journal of Medicine,* 1981, *305,* 1019–1020.
FRISCH, R. E., GOTZ-WELBERGON, A. V., MCARTHUR, J. W., ALBRIGHT, T., WITSCHT, J., BULLEN, B., BIRNHOLZ, J., REED, R. B., & HERMANN, H. Delayed menarche and amenorrhea of college athletes in relation to age of onset of training. *Journal of the American Medical Association,* 1981, *246,* 1559–1563.
FRISCH, R. E. Fatness, menarche, and fertility. In S. Golub (Ed.) *Menarche,* Lexington, Massachusetts: D. C. Heath, 1983.
GAGNON, J. H. Age at menarche and sexual conduct in adolescence and young adulthood. In S. Golub (Ed.) *Menarche.* Lexington, Massachusetts: D. C. Heath, 1983.
GOLUB, S., & CATALANO, J. Recollections of menarche and women's subsequent experiences with menstruation. *Women & Health,* 1983, *8,* 49–61.
GOODMAN, M. J., GROVE, J. S., & GILBERT, R. I. Age at menarche and year of birth in relation to adult height and weight among Caucasian, Japanese and Chinese women living in Hawaii. In S. Golub (Ed.) *Menarche.* Lexington, Massachusetts, D. C. Heath, 1983.
GRUMBACH, M. M., GRAVE, G. D., & MAYER, F. E. (Eds.) *Control of the onset of puberty.* New York: Wiley, 1974.

JONES, M. C. A study of socialization patterns at the high school level. *Journal of Genetic Psychology*, 1958, *93*, 87–111.

JONES, M. C., & MUSSEN, P. H. Self conceptions, motivations, and interpersonal attitudes of early and late maturing girls. *Child Development*, 1958, *29*, 491–501.

KANTERO, R. L., & WIDHELM, O. Correlation of menstrual traits between adolescent girls and their mothers. *Acta Obstetricia et Gynecologica Scandinavica, Supplement*, 1971, *14*, 30–36.

KATCHADOURIAN, H. The biology of adolescence. San Francisco: W. H. Freeman & Co., 1977.

KESTENBERG, J. S. Menarche. In S. Lorand, & H. Schneer (Eds.) *Adolescents*. New York: Dell, 1965.

KOFF, E., RIERDAN, J., & SILVERSTONE, E. Changes in representation of body image as a function of menarcheal status. *Developmental Psychology*, 1978, *14*, 635–642.

KOFF, E., RIERDAN, J., & JACOBSON, S. The personal and interpersonal significance of menarche. *Journal of the American Academy of Child Psychiatry*, 1981, *20*, 148–158.

KOFF, E. Through the looking glass of menarche: What the adolescent girl sees. In S. Golub (Ed.) *Menarche*. Lexington, Massachusetts, D. C. Heath, 1983.

KUMIN, M. *Why can't we live together like civilized human beings?* New York: Viking Press, 1982.

LEPPERT, P. Menarche and adolescent pregnancy. In S. Golub (Ed.) *Menarche*. Lexington, Massachusetts: D. C. Heath, 1983.

LOGAN, D. D. The menarche experience in twenty-three foreign countries. *Adolescence*, 1980, *15*, 247–256.

MALINA, R. M. Delayed age of menarche of athletes. *Journal of the American Medical Association*, 1982, *247*, 3312.

NOTMAN, M. Menarche: A psychoanalytic perspective. In S. Golub (Ed.) *Menarche*. Lexington, Massachusetts: D. C. Heath, 1983.

PAIGE, K. E. Virginity rituals and chastity control during puberty: Cross-cultural patterns. In S. Golub (Ed.) *Menarche*. Lexington, Massachusetts: D. C. Heath, 1983.

PETERSEN, A. C., & TAYLOR, B. The biological approach to adolescence. In J. Adelson (Ed.) *Handbook of adolescent psychology*. New York: Wiley, 1980.

PETERSEN, A. E. Menarche: Meaning of measures and measuring meaning. In S. Golub (Ed.) *Menarche*. Lexington, Massachusetts: D. C. Heath, 1983.

PRESSER, H. B. Age at menarche, socio-sexual behavior, and fertility. *Social Biology*, 1978, *25*, 94–101.

REBAR, R. W., & CUMMING, D. C. Reproductive function in women athletes. *Journal of the American Medical Association*, 1981, *246*, 1590.

RIERDAN, J. Variations in the experience of menarche as a function of preparedness. In S. Golub (Ed.) *Menarche*. Lexington, Massachusetts: D. C. Heath, 1983.

ROSENBAUM, M. B. The changing body image of the adolescent girl. In M. Sugar (Ed.) *Female adolescent development*. New York: Brunner/Mazel, 1979.

SHIELDS, J. *Monozygotic twins*. London: Oxford University Press, 1962.

SIMMONS, R. G., BLYTH, D. A., VAN CLEAVE, E. F., & BUSH, D. M. Entry into early adolescence: The impact of school structure, puberty, and early dating on self esteem. *American Sociological Review*, 1979, *44*, 948–967.

TANNER, J. M. *Foetus into man*. Cambridge, Massachusetts: Harvard University Press, 1978. To everything there is a season. *Science News*, 1980, *118*, 150.

UDRY, J. R. Age at menarche, at first intercourse, and at first pregnancy. *Journal of Biosocial Science*, 1979, *11*, 433–441.

UDRY, J. R., & CLIQUET, R. L. A cross-cultural examination of the relationship between ages at menarche, marriage, and first birth. *Demography*, 1982, *19*, 53–63.

WARREN, M. P. Clinical aspects of menarche: Normal variations and common disorders. In S. Golub (Ed.) *Menarche*. Lexington, Massachusetts: D. C. Heath, 1983.

WEIDEGER, P. *Menstruation and menopause*. New York: Knopf, 1976.

WHISNANT, L., & ZEGANS, L. A study of attitudes toward menarche in white middle class American adolescent girls. *American Journal of Psychiatry*, 1975, *132*, 809–814.

WILLIAMS, L. R. Beliefs and attitudes of young girls regarding menstruation. In S. Golub (Ed.) *Menarche*. Lexington, Massachusetts: D. C. Heath, 1983.

WOODS, N. F., DERY, G. K., & MOST, A. Recollections of menarche, current menstrual attitudes, and perimenstrual symptoms. In S. Golub (Ed.) *Menarche*. Lexington, Massachusetts: D. C. Heath, 1983.

10

Behavior and the Menstrual Cycle

Richard C. Friedman, Stephen W. Hurt, Michael S. Arnoff, and John Clarkin

Because of the existence of multiple individual and environmental factors influencing a person's behavior, no one study can provide a complete analysis of the complex relationships that exist between behavior and the menstrual cycle. In studying that we must focus on influences on the individual arising from biological, psychological, and sociocultural factors. All three have the capacity to modify an individual woman's responses, and some factors may be more important than others in accounting for any one woman's behavioral changes. Thus dramatic biological changes, perhaps in nerve-cell receptor response to changing hormone levels, may be of such importance in the case of one individual that personality and sociocultural features may be relatively inconsequential. Alternatively, constellations of psychopathological syndromes may be primarily responsible for magnifying the effects of normal variations in hormone levels or receptor sensitivities.

In this review, we will focus on selected research studies that have attempted to explore the relationship between behavior and the menstrual cycle. Our purpose is to give an overview of the spectrum of information available. Further resource material will be noted throughout the text for those readers with a particular interest in any of the topics discussed. In considering each study, we shall devote some attention to the kind of individuals studied, the techniques employed in gathering the data, and the context in which the study took place. Our review focuses first on studies of women without demonstrable physical or mental illness; that is, "normal" women. Here we examine three types of behavior: (1) mood, (2) task performance, and (3) sexual performance. Later we turn our attention to studies of women suffering from what are considered mental health problems, that is, "abnormal" women.

Findings in "Normal" Women

Fluctuations in Mood

Fluctuations in women's emotional state at different points in the menstrual cycle received the earliest systematic research attention. Clinical reports of mood disturbances related to the menstrual cycle suggested that irritability, depression, anxiety, and hostility were most prominent during the premenstrual (two to seven days prior to menstruation) and menstrual (from onset to cessation of the menstrual flow) phases of the cycle. Research in this area has demonstrated that most women experience at least some increase in "negative" feeling states during these two phases of the menstrual cycle. A complete bibliography of studies on this topic would include data on several thousand women from many different cultural groups. These studies have employed a number of research techniques, including retrospective self-reports and periodic, objective assessments of speech samples in both structured and unstructured settings. As a point of reference, the eight-day interval, from four days prior to onset of menstruation to four days following its onset, has been termed the "paramenstruum." Substantial evidence exists that mood tends to be more "positive" in some sense during the intermenstrual interval than during this paramenstrual interval.

Contemporary interest in menstrual-cycle symptomatology has resulted in the development of several self-report questionnaires, the most widely used of which is the Menstrual Distress Questionnaire (MDQ) developed by Moos and his collaborators.[1] The questionnaire includes forty-seven descriptive items thought to fluctuate with the menstrual cycle. These items include physical symptoms such as headache and cramps, emotional symptoms such as irritability and depression, and changes in behavior such as napping, decreased efficiency, and difficulty concentrating. Women were asked to "rate their experience of each of the 47 symptoms on the MDQ on a six-point scale ranging from no experience of the symptoms to an acute or partially disabling experience of the symptoms." Ratings are made separately for "the menstrual (during menstrual flow), premenstrual (the week before the beginning of menstrual flow), and intermenstrual (remainder of cycle) phases of her most recent menstrual cycle and for her worst menstrual cycle."

Moos's original report on 839 wives of graduate students at a large university in the western United States showed that scores for negative affect (a combination of the scores for crying, loneliness, anxiety, restlessness, irritability, mood swings, depression, and tension) differed significantly from their intermenstrual level during both the premenstrual and menstrual phases. Because the women filled out the questionnaire at different points in their menstrual cycle, the possibility that there existed a systematic effect of this variable on report of symptom severity was tested and rejected. Moos also reported that these retrospective accounts of symptom severity were not affected by the amount of time that elapsed between their occurrence and their report. These two findings, taken together, lend credence to the use of retrospective accounts to gather data on menstruation and behavior.

Other investigators have focused on the development of non–self-report measures of negative affects. In the early 1960s, Gottschalk devised a method for measuring anxiety based on the analysis of tape-recorded transcripts of verbal narratives.[2] Subjects spoke freely on a topic of their own choosing for five minutes, and the material was scored according to a scale of established reliability and validity. In a small investigation involving six women (two women studied over three cycles, two women studied over two cycles, and two women studied over one cycle), a tendency was noted for anxiety to decrease during ovulation. Ivey and Bardwick subsequently investigated a larger sample using the Gottschalk technique as well as additional questionnaires.[3] Twenty-six college students were studied at ovulation and premenstrually for two cycles. The average anxiety scores for all subjects were higher premenstrually than at ovulation. Moreover, in three of five cases in which anxiety was unexpectedly higher at ovulation, it was felt that this was attributable to coincidental psychosocial stress. An analysis of thematic content revealed that these women's self-perceptions of their adequacy fluctuated with the cycle. All subjects felt less able to cope with the problems of daily living during the premenstrual period compared with the ovulatory period.

In suggesting that affective changes during the menstrual cycle may be related to coincident events, the Ivey and Bardwick study represents recent trends in menstrual-cycle research. Perhaps because much of this research had been conducted by biologically oriented investigators, one hypothesis has been that periodic, negative emotional fluctuations might be determined primarily by fluctuations in the activity of female sex hormones. While biological factors clearly play a role in affective changes during the menstrual cycle, recent studies have attempted to determine the degree to which nonhormonal events modify affective changes during the menstrual cycle. These investigations have focused on such factors as the quantity and quality of environmental events, attitudes about menstruation, and personality traits.

A convincing demonstration of the influence of external events on one's interpretation of physiological change is the elegant study reported by Schachter and Singer.[4] Although not specifically directed at menstrual-related emotional changes, this study is relevant to the larger issue of understanding individual perception of physiological events. These researchers were able to demonstrate that, after inducing a state of physiological arousal with an injection of adrenalin, subjects' subsequent evaluations of their emotional state depended on the explanation of the state that the subject adopted rather than the degree of physiological arousal per se.

Demonstrations of the influence of external events on the self-report of negative affects during different phases of the menstrual cycle have recently appeared. Wilcoxon and her co-workers studied thirty-three undergraduates who filled out daily self-reports on pleasant activities, stressful events, moods, and somatic changes for thirty-five days.[5] Subjects included eleven males, eleven females taking oral contraceptives, and eleven females not taking oral contraceptives. Males were randomly assigned a "premenstrual" day from among the thirty-five study days. This day and the next three days following this interval were assigned to the "menstrual" phase. Data from the males showed no fluctuations related to menstrual cycle "phase." Among the women, negative affects were found to be more intense during the paramenstruum, with the peak for no-pill women occurring during menstruation and that for pill women occurring during the premenstrual phase. However, Wilcoxon et al. found that for both groups of women, the experience of negative affects was more responsive to the presence of stressful external events than to the specific timing of the menstrual-cycle phase. They also noted that differences among women in the amount of negative affect experienced were still large despite their attempts to explain them on the basis of cycle phase, contraceptive status, or amount of stress experienced. Further research regarding the influence of situational factors on reports of mood fluctuations during the menstrual cycle should enhance our understanding.

This also appears to be the case with studies of the experience of menstruation and attitudes and beliefs related to menstruation itself. Paige studied 102 women, some taking oral contraceptives, using the content-analysis technique of Gottschalk et al.[6] Her data indicate that, regardless of contraceptive status, premenstrual increases in anxiety were characteristic of women with normally heavy menstrual flow but were less pronounced in women with reduced flow. This relationship could not be explained by differences in physical symptoms of distress which were of equal magnitude in the reduced-flow and normal-flow groups. In another study, Brooks, Ruble, and Clark collected self-report questionnaire data from 232 undergraduate women at a private university in the eastern United States.[7] Subjects were asked to complete the MDQ twice, once "as if" they were in the premenstrual phase and once "as if" they were in the intermenstrual phase. They also completed an attitude survey in which they were asked to agree or disagree with forty-six statements constructed to represent "beliefs about physiological and psychological concomitants of menstruation, style of dealing with menstruation, menstrual-related effects on performance, and general evaluations of menstruation." As expected, differences in negative affect were recorded, with subjects responding with higher scores for the "as if" premenstrual period. Analysis of the attitudinal variables in relation to the differences between premenstrual- and intermenstrual-symptom scores revealed that reports of increased negative affect during the menstrual phase were associated with the view of menstruation as a debilitating and predictable event.

A statistical association between two sets of data, in this case attitudes and expectations related to menstruation and reports of an increase in negative affect during the premenstrual phase, does not imply causation. This association can be explained in one of three ways: (1) because women expect to have more difficulty premenstrually, they are more aware of and more likely to report such difficulties; (2) prior experience of difficulty during the premenstrual phase has produced a negative change in attitudes regarding this phase of the menstrual cycle; or (3) attitudes about the premenstrual phase and the increase in negative affect reported during this phase are both related to a third factor which is responsible for their association with one another (e.g., personality or biological factors). Data from the Brooks et al. study do not permit us to determine which of these three possibilities is responsible for the observed association. Because the possibilities are not mutually exclusive, one or all of them may contribute to the association.

Fluctuations in mood during the menstrual cycle have also been studied in relation to personality factors. A large-scale study was conducted in 1963 by two British researchers. Coppen and Kessel, who found that mood changes during the premenstruum were associated to a moderate degree with the Maudsley Personality Inventory factor of "neuroticism."[8] This factor is described as tapping the personality traits of emotional overreactivity and a tendency to develop various neurotic symptoms generally. Subsequent studies of menstruation using the Maudsley Personality Inventory have tended to confirm the findings of Coppen and Kessel. Similar personality traits measured by other instruments and using American samples have also shown a moderate association with negative mood changes during the premenstrual or menstrual phase.[9] These studies, in general, characterize those women who report the largest mood changes as high strung, sensitive, concerned about bodily functioning, emotionally labile, and having difficulty understanding human motivations. These personality traits have been found to be more closely associated with mood changes during the paramenstruum than with physical changes during this phase such as water retention, swelling of the breasts, or pain.

These have been studies of moderate to large-sized samples of women. Consequently, the personality variations within each sample are large. Generally, care is taken to see that the range of scores spans the entire range of normal personality variation. Across the entire range, it is the women with the extreme, but not abnormal, scores on the personality traits described above that report the largest negative mood changes during the paramenstruum. An alternative strategy was employed by Golub.[10] She studied fifty parous women between thirty and forty-five years of age who were not using oral contraceptives. A battery of psychological tests was administered to each woman four days prior to the next expected period and again two weeks after the onset of menstruation. Half the women were tested first premenstrually, half were tested first intermenstrually. The women chosen for the study were selected on the basis of demonstrated capacity to function at above-average levels of psychosocial competence. In addition, the instruments in the test battery were chosen carefully and included two instruments for measuring anxiety. One of these has been shown to reflect anxiety proneness, a stable, dispositional feature of an individual's personality makeup. The second anxiety measure reflects the degree of anxiety currently experienced. An individual's scores on the first test show a good degree of similarity across time, while scores on the second test fluctuate in response to life events. Both instruments have been used to test men and women under a wide variety of circumstances and across a wide range of personality styles. This means that normative data for both tests are available and the scores of the women with different psychopathological diagnoses and with women tested under differing environmental conditions. Golub found that the amount of anxiety experienced by the women premenstrually was greater than that experienced intermenstrually. The level of premenstrual anxiety reported was found to be on a par with that reported by female college students experiencing mild situational stress. The degree of "anxiety proneness" in these women was found to be lower than that reported for the general population and was not significantly associated with the degree of "transient premenstrual anxiety" reported.

These selected findings illustrate the influence of psychological and sociocultural factors on affective changes during the menstrual cycle. While these factors play a significant role for some women, the results of these studies cannot be generalized to exclude the potential influence of hormonal factors. Beumont et al. gathered data on twenty-five women (nineteen to forty-six years old; mean age twenty-eight) with regular periods and compared them with data from seven women (twenty-six to forty-seven years old; mean age thirty-five) who had undergone hysterectomy with conservation of the ovaries one to five years previously.[11] These latter women continued to exhibit characteristic hormone fluctuations but did not menstruate. Data collected from all women included daily ratings of depression and associated symptoms, other psychological and emotional states, and physical symptoms. For the menstruating women, Beumont et al. reported significant symptomatic changes in all three areas during the menstrual cycle with a paramenstrual increase in symptoms reported. In the hysterectomized women, Beumont et al. report the same trend for the data on depression and other psychological and emotional states but not for physical symptoms. A comparison of the paramenstrual and intermenstrual scores of the hysterectomized women shows roughly the same proportion of change for depression and other psychological symptoms but, interestingly enough, not for physical symptoms. In addition, the mean symptoms scores for the hysterectomized sample tend to be higher than those of menstruating women during both the paramenstruum and the intermenstruum. These data are suggestive of hormonal influences on mood and other psychological characteristics in women *regardless of menstruation* but clearly require additional study and replication before being widely accepted.

With respect, then, to the relationship between fluctuations in mood and the menstrual cycle, the following conclusions seem warranted. Almost all women experience some increase in negative affects during the premenstrual or menstrual phase of the cycles. Furthermore, the amount of change in negative affects during the premenstrual or menstrual phase in comparison with the intermenstrual phase appears to be related to some degree to a woman's current psychosocial experience and more enduring features of her psychological makeup such as attitudes about menstruation and personality factors as well as menstrual-cycle-related hormonal changes.[12]

Task Performance

As a general rule, people's performance is influenced by the way they feel. It seems hardly surprising, then, that investigators have explored the relationship between menstruation and task performance. Sommer's recent review of the area summarizes the findings to date.[13] The research shows a consistent trend. Studies utilizing objective performance measures generally fail to demonstrate menstrual-cycle-related changes. Studies based on performance measures, including academic examinations, simple reaction-time measures, and quantity and quality of factory production all fail to demonstrate menstrual effects.

In reviewing this area, however, Sommer noted that there appeared to be a difference between women's subjective reports of their ability to perform either premenstrually or menstrually and objective measures of their performance. Some women feel that their performance paramenstrually is worse than their performance intermenstrually. Unfortunately, none of the studies cited included both subjective reports and objective data on performance. We know of no demonstration of a relationship between paramenstrual changes in self-perceived performance capacity and changes in objective task performance during the same phase. Sommer's conclusion is, however, consistent with both retrospective and daily self-report data from several other studies which report impaired concentration and decreased cognitive arousal, two factors which presumably affect a person's subjective estimate of her ability to perform.

The relationship between self-perception of performance ability during the paramenstruum and objective evaluation of performance deserves more careful research attention. The discrepancy between subjective evaluation and objective performance may be related to sociocultural attitudes and expectations. If so, such attitudes appear to have limited impact on actual performance, but this possibility requires experimental investigation before it can be claimed as a fact.

Sexual Performance

Sexual behavior appears to be influenced by menstrual-cycle changes. Although there is some inconsistency in the findings of various investigators, the major changes in sexual behavior are located in the midcycle, ovulatory phase and the paramenstrual phase. In general, there is an increase in both sexual feelings and frequency of intercourse at both points in the cycle. During the ovulatory phase, these changes are an obvious reproductive advantage and in nonhuman, mammalian species, are associated with externally observable, physical signs of the presence of estrus that are hormonally based. Investigators who have noted a peak in human sexual activity during the paramenstruum have speculated that this peak may be related to cognitive rather than hormonal factors. Coital frequency may increase because of the absence of impregnation fears and because of sexual abstinence during menstruation.

Early studies of human sexual activity, which focused on changes in coital frequency, were not methodologically sophisticated. Their reliance on retrospective accounts and their focus on coital frequency as an adequate measure of sexual activity made it difficult to detect nontrivial, but nonetheless small, changes in sexual activity. Later studies, particularly those that have used daily self-reports and have included autoerotic and fantasy activity in addition to reports of coitus, have more consistently demonstrated menstrual-cycle-related changes. The postmenstrual peak in coital frequency seems to be the most firmly established alteration noted in both early and more contemporary studies. Changes in sexual behavior during the ovulatory phase have been shown, although less frequently; more often confirmed are increases in sexual feelings during this phase of the menstrual cycle. However, more recent studies which have cataloged sexual activity in detail have been able to demonstrate small but statistically significant increases during the ovulatory phase.

Adams, Gold, and Burt felt that the inability of previous investigators to demonstrate a midcycle elevation in sexual activity was a result of their focus on predominantly male-partner initiation as the measure of female sexual activity.[14] Adams et al. studied thirty-five white, college-educated women between twenty-one and thirty-seven years of age. All women filled out daily questionnaires on their sexual experiences, including information on the initiator of each sexual episode and whether the advance was rejected. Type of sexual behaviors recorded were intercourse, caressing, masturbation, fantasy, and sexual arousal from books, films, magazines, or dreams. The thirty-five subjects provided data on 171 cycles with a median of 4.2 cycles studied per subject. The data from this study show a midcycle ovulatory peak in female- plus mutually initiated heterosexual behavior but not in male-initiated sexual behavior. Autosexual activity was increased during the midcycle phase as well. These elevations were characteristic of those women in the study whose method of contraception was not hormonal regulation but were absent in women who used oral contraceptives.

Data from the Adams et al. study suggest that female-initiated sexual activity is most pronounced during the ovulatory phase of the menstrual cycle and appears to be under some degree of biological control. They speculated that the important biological factors were changes in female sex hormones, particularly estrogen, as it is this hormonal system that is modulated by the use of oral contraceptives. Other hormonal systems, however, also appear to play a role in human sexual activity as well.

Eleven couples aged twenty-one to thirty-one years and married for at least one year were studied over three menstrual cycles by Persky.[15] Subjects were interviewed individually twice weekly and blood samples were taken and assayed for plasma levels of testosterone and cortisol in both husbands and wives and for progesterone and estradiol in wives only. The interviews were rated independently by two psychiatrists for degree of sexual initiation, avoidance, couple interaction, and mood. Wives also rated themselves for degree of sexual gratification. They found that both the husbands' and wives' initiation sources were related to their spouses' responsivity scores, as might be expected. When these relationships were studied in association with the hormonal data, however, it appeared that testosterone levels played a greater role in explaining the strength of the association between initiation and clinically rated responsivity than did either estradiol or progesterone levels. In addition, intercourse frequency was related to wives' testosterone levels at their ovulatory peak, and wives' testosterone levels correlated significantly with their self-ratings of sexual gratification.

Conclusions: Findings in Normal Women

Studies of menstruation and behavior in normal women have revealed a complex set of relationships. That the menstrual cycle is capable of altering behavior patterns in regular ways appears to be an incontrovertible fact. Women may experience increases in feelings of sexual desire as ovulation approaches. Female-initiated heterosexual activity and autosexual activity appear to increase at this point. There are some data suggesting that this might be related to midcycle androgen effects, but further studies are needed in this area.

As women approach the paramenstruum, they generally report increases in negative feeling states such as anxiety, irritability, depression, and tension as well as changes in their self-perception of performance capacity and ability. Interestingly, the intensity of negative affect experienced by women who are psychologically normal tends, as a rule, to be mild. Despite the fact that self-perception of performance might fluctuate, no objective fluctuation in menstrual task performance has been established. Despite these general tendencies, there remains a good deal of individual variability in response, across women within a menstrual cycle and across menstrual cycles for a single woman.

Findings in "Abnormal" Women

The term "premenstrual tension" was introduced in the 1930s by Frank and emphasizes one component of a painful-feeling picture.[16] Subsequent literature in the field refers either to "premenstrual tension syndrome" or "premenstrual affective syndrome." We favor the latter term, which is more inclusive and refers to a quantitative, significant difference in the severity of observable mood changes during the paramenstruum from that observed in "normal" women. For reasons that are unclear, the premenstrual affective syndrome appears to be most common and most severe roughly between ages twenty-five and forty.[17] Some investigators have suggested that this syndrome may be present in at least 25 percent of the menstruating population, and others have speculated that it is even more common.[18] Although data characterizing the population of women who are prone to suffer from extreme emotional distress during the cycle are limited, they suggest that such women are likely to suffer from other psychopathology *not* in itself specifically linked to the menstrual cycle.[19] This must be qualified, however, because other studies suggest that some women, not well characterized to date, may manifest cyclical, recurrent, extremely painful moods at certain points in the cycle and not suffer from additional global forms of pathology.[20]

In moving on to a more detailed discussion of psychopathology and the menstrual cycle, we stress that there may well be qualitative differences between subgroups of pathological individuals and normals. We emphasize, however, the necessity for caution in generalizing from data on normal women to pathological subgroups and vice versa. Psychopathology is a rapidly changing field. Strict criteria for diagnosing psychiatric illnesses have been specified relatively recently. The types of behavioral conditions considered diagnosable illnesses have also changed as knowledge has accumulated. The clinical literature in any area of psychiatry contains articles about conditions similar in name but different in form and reports from investigators using different methods to study a variety of populations. Given these limitations of a rapidly growing area of knowledge, it is perhaps surprising that a trend has emerged.

Many studies suggest that depression-anxiety-irritability-tension often covary together and become more severe premenstrually. When fluctuations in intensity are repetitive and severe, these feelings constitute the "premenstrual affective syndrome" and may be associated with significant distress and impairment of functioning. Interestingly, the mood changes reported in the clinical literature seem to account for some but not all of the variance in behavioral symptomatology. Other types of behavioral symptoms (such as decreased impulse control, multiple somatic complaints, or psychotic symptoms) also appear to be linked to the menstrual cycle in some subgroups of subjects.

A number of investigators have noted a relationship between psychopathology linked to the menstrual cycle and neurotic character structure. Perhaps the most dramatic observations dealing with this relationship were made by Benedek and Rubenstein.[21] They were able to predict cycle phase by analyzing the content of therapy sessions of fifteen patients in psychoanalysis. The investigators described a pattern in which the first part of the cycle, prior to ovulation, was a period of increased self-esteem and desire for erotic activity during which the individual's self-image was active. Following a period when active and passive-receptive tendencies were optimally fused at ovulation, the luteal phase of the cycle was characterized by passivity and more procreational interest in sex. During the few days immediately preceding menstruation, the investigators observed that regression occurred, and ego defensive strength decreased. The overall orientation of the patients tended to be more primitive. Painful feelings such as irritability, anxiety, and depression increased and tended to remit with the onset of menstruation.

Benedek and Rubenstein went beyond merely concluding that women's psychological state changes with the cycle to propose that the specific characteristics of a woman's sexual fantasy life are regulated by the same biological forces that control fertility and thereby maximize the synchrony between mind and body. Unfortunately, this 1939 study has never been replicated. The findings raise the question whether there might not be a relationship between the dramatic and often marked behavioral fluctuations noted by Benedek and Rubenstein and neurosis itself. Until this investigation is replicated, the question of whether the specific fantasies that motivate sexual behavior are in fact correlated with the hormonal events of the menstrual cycle, even in neurosis, must be considered open.

Other investigators have also noted that a correlation between psychopathological *traits*, particularly neurotic character structure, and psychopathological *states* that fluctuate with the cycle might exist. An important task for future research is to clarify this relationship from both descriptive and etiological perspectives.

In addition to the study by Coppen and Kessel mentioned above, in which the relationship between psychological symptoms, character structure, and the phases of the menstrual cycle were studied, Kramp conducted psychiatric interviews with 131 women who had applied for abortion. Sixty-six had a well-characterized "premenstrual tension syndrome" (PMT), 52 percent of whom had specific neurotic symptoms in childhood. Only 26 percent of the sixty-five patients without PMT had such symptoms.[22] Rees observed that in 145 neurotic patients with the premenstrual syndrome, there was a positive correlation between severity of neurosis and severity of cyclic affect distress. Rees suggested, however, that severe premenstrual tension could exist in normal women "of stable personality," and he noted that many severely neurotic women did not suffer from it.[23] This finding has been emphasized by others as well.

This conclusion is compatible with an observation of Cullberg's.[24] In a study he conducted, 320 women received varying doses of one type of sex steroid, "gestagen," in combination with a fixed dose of estrogen, or placebo, in a controlled study of the effect of sex steroids on behavior. The prevalance of cyclic premenstrual complaints prior to ingestion of medication was high. Forty percent of the subjects were felt to have the premenstrual syndrome. Of these, approximately 26 percent had high scores for neuroticism on personality tests. Cullberg suggested that these individuals were "high reactors" who easily experience symptoms and who might constitute a majority of cases of premenstrual syndrome that are seen clinically. It is noteworthy that the remaining 74 percent had a clinically detectable premenstrual syndrome despite low scores for neuroticism on psychological tests.

Moos et al.'s investigation of fluctuations of symptoms and moods during the menstrual cycle illustrates the importance of describing the intermenstrual behavioral state of women with premenstrual difficulties.[25] Of fifteen married nulliparous women, seven complained of high premenstrual tension and eight stated they had low premenstrual tension on a questionnaire. The subjects completed self-rating scales during nine days in each of two consecutive cycles. The results were generally consistent with the observations of Benedek and Rubenstein for all women. Feelings of pleasantness, activation, and sexual arousal increased during the first half of the cycle. Fear, tension, and general discomfort were greatest premenstrually. Relative consistency existed from cycle to cycle. Importantly, it was observed that intermenstrual differences between the two groups of women existed. Anxiety, depression, and negative affect generally were higher intermenstrually for women with high premenstrual tension than for women with low premenstrual tension. These data support the argument that psychological-state differences between women must be interpreted in the context of more stable psychological-trait characterization.

The preceding studies suggest that neurotic women may be particularly *prone* to develop behavioral symptoms correlated with the menstrual cycle. However, many neurotic women do not experience such cyclical symptom occurrence. The features that might discriminate these two neurotic populations are not clear at present. The percentage of neurotic women who could be expected to fall into each subgroup is also not certain. O'Conner, Shelly, and Stern have observed that character typology has never really been studied by interview methods to determine whether women with certain types of character defenses (such as hysterical) might differ in their emotional responsivities during the cycle from women with different types of character defenses (such as obsessions).[26] This is an intriguing area for future research, as is the systematic description of psychopathology among individuals who behave in clearly deviant ways during the paramenstruum.

Many investigators interested in the relationship between illness and the menstrual cycle have counted the frequency of certain types of behavior in relation to each woman's phase of the cycle. It can then be determined whether such behaviors cluster at particular phases of the cycle or are distributed randomly across all phases. This technique can be applied to any behavior of interest to an investigator.

When a wide variety of behaviors are looked at systematically, there seems to be a relationship between the occurrence of deviant acts and cycle phase. That is, of a population of women who commit a clearly pathological act, more are likely to be in the paramenstrual phase of the cycle than can be expected by chance. This has been shown to be true for calls to a suicide prevention center, suicide attempts, successful suicide acts, commission of nonviolent and violent crimes, disorderly conduct in schools and prisons, requests for psychiatric assistance, admission to a hospital with a psychiatric illness, and accidents.[27] As Parlee has noted, these correlations say nothing about the probability of normal women committing pathological acts as a consequence of cyclicity of psychohormonal functioning.[28] This clinical literature, taken in total, says nothing about what "women in general" are likely to be like paramenstrually. The samples studied aberrant and probably psychopathological subgroups. This is an important distinction to emphasize, in view of the evidence that the performance of normal women, at a variety of tasks, has not been shown to fluctuate with the cycle. Data garnered from deviant subgroups can be used in a biased and even a prejudicial fashion, if they are inappropriately applied. Given this reservation, however, there seems little doubt that, within the universe of potential pathological-act committers, the paramenstrual period is a time of relatively high expectancy for the occurrence of the act in question.

Parlee has also appropriately emphasized that there are no comparable studies correlating cycle phase with unusually positive behaviors, such as acts of heroism or great creativity. It is possible that data about behavioral events and cycle phase reflect a bias since investigators in this area have tended to be clinicians interested in psychopathology per se. This possible bias should not obscure the fact that data on behavioral abnormality and cycle phase has, in our view, added a helpful perspective toward understanding psychopathology. However, in the studies referred to above, the individuals who have committed the deviant acts often have not been well diagnosed or examined with standard psychological tests. This dimension will no doubt be added in future studies.

Intriguing questions are open in the area of psychopathology and the menstrual cycle. Given the present state of the field, we think it will be helpful to present our own, often speculative, point of view. We refer the reader who wishes additional discussion to recent reviews in the scientific literature.[29]

From the psychodynamic point of view, if Benedek and Rubenstein's observations that the luteal phase is associated with increased interest in maternalism are accurate, it follows that women with neurotic conflicts about maternalism and pathological identifications with their mothers would have periodic exacerbations of intrapsychic conflicts during the luteal phase. Such women would be likely to suffer from severe neurotic symptoms as a result of cyclical fluctuations in the intensity of intrapsychic conflict. One hallmark of neurosis is the presence of unresolved oedipal conflicts. If intensity of sexual desire fluctuated with the cycle, so, presumably, would symptoms resulting from unconscious anxiety mobilized by desire. The same type of cyclical fluctuation could be expected to result from aggressive urges, stemming from unresolved oedipal conflicts and resulting in cyclical anxiety and symptom formation. If the hypotheses above are valid, one would expect that waxing and waning of symptoms would be triggered by physiological changes during the cycle, but the choice of particular symptoms would be determined by the form of the patient's neurosis.

Recovery time is a confounding issue when one assumes that behavioral symptoms wax and wane on a monthly basis. Chaotic and painful social interactions could begin paramenstrually, but their consequences could extend into the intermenstrual period. From the clinician's point of view, it would take an unusual woman, in an unusual social network, to manifest severe premenstrual behavioral symptoms regularly and yet function intermenstrually in a way that was comparable to normal control subjects.

Another area that warrants attention in our view is the relationship between a psychopathological diagnostic category known as the "borderline syndrome" and the menstrual cycle. By way of explanation, the preceding discussion has referred to patients with character pathology and/or neurosis. One type of character disorder is that in which certain personality traits are hypertrophied and rigid to the point where they become maladaptive; another is that in which certain healthy traits (such as the capacity to be empathic, to feel guilt, to restrain antisocial impulses) are deficient or even absent. In either case, although the person's optimal functioning may be severely impaired, mental mechanisms responsible for reality testing continue to function adequately. Neurosis, a term of much recent controversy, traditionally has referred to conditions in which distress and impaired functioning result from unconscious irrational anxiety in such a way, however, that the individual's ability to test and evaluate reality adequately is maintained.

Only recently have patients been described who seem to fluctuate widely with regard to the effectiveness and maturity of their characterological defenses. These patients appear to have well-integrated personality structures at some times and at other times appear to function at an extremely primitive level. They often suffer from transient affective dysphoria, identity diffusion, and perceptual difficulties and might manifest loss of reality testing for brief periods.[30] Criteria for defining this borderline syndrome have been agreed upon so recently that its relationship to the menstrual cycle remains to be systematically investigated. We speculate that many borderline individuals might be unusually sensitive to the normal physiological changes of the menstrual cycle and might manifest a wide variety of symptoms, even transient psychotic symptoms, during the cycle as a consequence. Thus the character defenses of borderline individuals do not appear to function smoothly over time. Hormones and neurotransmitters that fluctuate with the menstrual cycle theoretically have the capacity to impose a strain on behavioral homeostatic mechanisms. It is possible that some borderline individuals are unable adaptively to buffer against this strain. Such individuals might manifest unusual behavioral sensitivity to alterations in physiological state. Furthermore, clinical experience suggests that borderline individuals are often quite sensitive to the effects of psychoactive drugs. Whether they are equally sensitive to endogenous fluctuations of substances possessing behavioral activity remains to be seen. It should be noted that women with character neuroses and those with the borderline syndrome constitute a potentially large number of patients, particularly in outpatient treatment.

We have thus far presented two models for conceptualizing the relationship between psychopathology and the menstrual cycle. Both our "cyclical neurosis" model and our "nonspecific overreaction" model are compatible with a modified version of Schachter and Singer's well known model for the determinants of emotional state. Schachter and Singer noted that similar physiological changes often occur in different emotional states. They suggested that the relationship between a state of physiological arousal and a cognition, appropriate to that state of arousal, resulted in a specific emotional state.[31] According to this model, individuals provide meaning to physiological change by interpreting it within its psychosocial context.

We suggest that for most women, *the fact* that fluctuation in the intensity of affect states occur is a direct result of primary (although unknown) biological determinants. We hypothesize that fluctuations in irritability, tension, depression, possibly in sexual desire, and other affects as well occur because of cyclical fluctuation in the biological activities of substances that impact on those parts of the central nervous system that regulate affect states. However, the psychosocial and intrapsychic consequences of such fluctuations all depend on cognitive state, itself a product of social context and psychobiographical determinants. We emphasize that with regard to the etiology of *intensity* of affect (i.e., how much change, how depressed in relation to controls), we see no reason to think in terms of single causes. In many cases, intrapsychic-psychosocial-cognitive interactions could certainly determine or greatly influence intensity, while in others biological factors could predominate.

We hypothesize that the subgroups may be even further subdivided with regard to the intensity of fluctuations in depression in comparison with fluctuations in other dysphoric affect states. Fluctuations in neurotic or borderline symptoms might theoretically occur as a result of fluctuations in a number of affect states other than depression (such as irritability or sexual desire). Some investigators have suggested, however, that a relatively specific relationship might exist between women who suffer from premenstrual affective symptoms and women who suffer from depression generally. In one study of headache patients at a neurology clinic, Kashiwagi, McClure, and Wetzel found a significant association between history of depression and premenstrual affective syndrome.[32] Other studies have found that not only are individuals with premenstrual affective syndrome more likely to have a history of depression in general, but their family members were also more likely to have histories of depression.[33] The number of studies in this area is still rather limited. Nonetheless, these data, as well as data on the relationship between suicide and the cycle, support the hypothesis that such a relationship might exist. This hypothesis is intriguing since it may lead to research on the basis for depression itself and on the reasons for sex differences in depression.

There is suggestive evidence that some schizophrenic patients may be prone potentially to relapse paramenstrually.[34] However, schizophrenics have not been shown to suffer from a high increase of paramenstrual affective syndrome. It is possible, of course, that paramenstrual affective symptomatic manifestations are distorted in their expression because of schizophrenia. Despite some suggestive case reports, manic-depressive illness has not been shown to fluctuate in severity during the menstrual cycle.[35] However, there has been relatively little systematic study of this area. We suspect that the absence of positive correlations reflects lack of detailed attention rather than a negative finding.

Researchers have suggested that various pathophysiological mechanisms have etiological significance in producing fluctuations in psychological symptoms associated with the menstrual cycle. These have recently been reviewed by Smith, who emphasized, as we have, that the behavioral changes associated with the cycle do not represent a unitary phenomenon.[36] Since women may develop cyclic psychic distress for a variety of reasons, no single "cause" is likely to be of unique importance. Etiological factors frequently cited in the literature are: relative excess of estrogen in relation to progesterone, endogenous sensitivity to estrogen occurring premenstrually, increased body water, increased capillary permeability, activation of the renin-angiotensin-aldosterone system, hypoglycemia, sex-steroid withdrawal effects, and cyclical fluctuations in brain neurotransmitters, particularly catecholamines.

In an extensive review, Steiner and Carroll have also emphasized that the etiology of premenstrual dysphoria is not known, and no single method of treatment has proved effective. Investigators summarize work on the possible role of prolactin, a pituitary hormone, in producing the premenstrual syndrome and the role of a dopamine agonist and prolactin-suppressing agent, bromoergocryptine, in its treatment. As Steiner and Carroll note, clinical trials of the treatment of premenstrual syndrome with bromoergocryptine have been promising. Nonetheless, data collection is still in preliminary stages. The role of prolactin in producing the syndrome and of bromoergocryptine in treating it remain important areas for future research.[37]

In reviewing the literature on psychopathology and the menstrual cycle, we see an analogy between this field and the more general area of depression. Like fleeting feelings of depression which are virtually universal, paramenstrual dysphoric affects may be minimal and unassociated with other symptoms. Feelings of depression may be severe enough to be quite painful and may lead to impaired social effectiveness. Similarly, the dysphoric feelings of the paramenstrual affective syndrome may be repetitively so severe that they warrant designation as symptoms. Depression may be associated with somatic symptoms, as may paramenstrual affective syndrome.

Depression is not a unitary concept. Different subgroups of depression have different etiologies and often have different treatments. The relationship between known biological determinants of depression and psychosocial determinants is a complex one. Thus some groups of depression result from primary biochemical lesions in the central nervous system, others result primarily from psychosocial determinants. In many, perhaps most, cases, interactions between physiological predisposition and psychosocial stress determines the form of the resultant psychopathology. We suspect that a similar matrix of complete etiologies of premenstrual affective syndrome will one day be identified. Future study of this interesting and important area should enhance our understanding of affect disorders, and perhaps even more important, of the mechanisms regulating affects in general.

NOTES

1. R. H. Moos, "The Development of a Menstrual Distress Questionnaire," *Psychosomatic Medicine* 30 (1968): 853–66.
2. L. Gottschalk et al., "Variations in Magnitude of Emotion: A Method Applied to Anxiety and Hostility during Phases of the Menstrual Cycle," *Psychosomatic Medicine* 24 (1962): 300–311.
3. M. Ivey and J. Bardwick, "Patterns of Affective Fluctuation in the Menstrual Cycle," *Psychosomatic Medicine* 30 (1968): 336–45.
4. S. Schachter and J. E. Singer, "Cognitive Social and Physiological Determinants of Emotional State," *Psychological Review* 69 (1962): 379–99.
5. L. A. Wilcoxon, S. L. Schrader, and C. W. Sherif, "Daily Self-Reports on Activities, Life Events, Moods and Somatic Changes during the Menstrual Cycle," *Psychosomatic Medicine* 38 (1976): 399–417.
6. K. Paige, "Effects of Oral Contraceptives on Affective Fluctuations Associated with the Menstrual Cycle," *Psychosomatic Medicine* 33 (1971): 515–37.
7. J. Brooks, D. Ruble, and A. Clark, "College Women's Attitudes and Expectations concerning Menstrual-related Changes," *Psychosomatic Medicine* 39 (1977): 288–98.
8. A. Coppen and N. Kessel, "Menstruation and Personality," *British Journal of Psychiatry* 109 (1963): 711–21.
9. G. H. Gruba and M. Rohrbaugh, "MMPI Correlates of Menstrual Distress," *Psychosomatic Medicine* 37 (1975): 265–72; E. E. Levitt and B. Lubin, "Some Personality Factors Associated with Menstrual Complaints and Menstrual Attitudes," *Journal of Psychosomatic Research* 11 (1967): 267–70.
10. S. Golub, "The Effects of Premenstrual Anxiety and Depression on Cognitive Function," *Journal of Personality and Social Psychology* 34 (1976): 99–105.
11. P. J. V. Beumont, D. H. Richards, and M. G. Gelder, "A Study of Psychiatric and Physical Symptoms during the Menstrual Cycle," *British Journal of Psychiatry* 126 (1975): 431–34.
12. See Wilcoxon et al., Paige, Brooks et al., Coppen and Kessel, Gruba and Rohrbaugh, Levitt and Lubin, and Golub.
13. B. Sommer, "The Effect of Menstruation on Cognitive and Perceptual Motor Behavior: A Review," *Psychosomatic Medicine* 35 (1973): 515–34.
14. D. B. Adams, A. R. Gold, and A. D. Burt, "Rise in Female-initiated Sexual Activity at Ovulation and Its Suppression by Oral Contraceptives," *New England Journal of Medicine* 229 (November 23, 1978): 1145–50.
15. H. Persky et al., "Plasma Testosterone Level and Sexual Behavior of Couples," *Archives of Sexual Behavior* 7 (1978): 157–73.
16. R. T. Frank, "The Hormonal Causes of Premenstrual Tension," *Archives of Neurology and Psychiatry* 26 (1931): 1053–57.
17. J. L. Kramp, "Studies on the Premenstrual Syndrome in Relation to Psychiatry," *Acta Psychiatrica Scandinavica* 203 (suppl.; 1968): 261–67.
18. L. Rees, "Premenstrual Tension Syndrome in Relation to Personality, Neurosis, Certain Psychosomatic Disorders and Psychotic States," in *Psychoendocrinology*, ed. M. Reiss (London: Grune & Stratton. 1958).
19. Coppen and Kessel.
20. J. Cullberg, "Mood Changes and Menstrual Symptoms with Different Gestagen/Estrogen Combinations: A Double-Blind Comparison with a Placebo," *Acta Psychiatrica Scandinavica* 236 (suppl.; 1972): 1–86; R. F. Haskett et al., "Severe Premenstrual Tension: Delineation of the Syndrome (paper presented at the Thirty-Fourth Annual Scientific Program, Society of Biological Psychiatry, Chicago, May 12, 1979).
21. T. Benedek and B. B. Rubenstein, "Correlations between Ovarian Activity and Psychodynamic Processes. 1. The Ovulative Phase," *Psychosomatic Medicine* 1 (1939): 245–70; see also pt. 2, "The Menstrual Phase," ibid., pp. 461–85. This work is also summarized in T. Benedek, *Studies in Psychosomatic Medicine: Psychosexual Functions in Women* (New York: Ronald Press, 1952).

22. Kramp.
23. L. Rees, "Psychosomatic Aspects of the Premenstrual Syndrome," *Journal of Mental Science* 99 (1953): 62–73, and "The Premenstrual Syndrome and Its Treatment," *British Medical Journal* 1 (1953): 1014–16.
24. Cullberg.
25. R. B. Moos et al., "Fluctuations in Symptoms and Moods during the Menstrual Cycle," *Journal of Psychosomatic Research* 13 (1963): 37–44.
26. J. F. O'Conner, E. M. Shelly, and L. O. Stern, "Behavioral Rhythms Related to the Menstrual Cycle," in *Biorhythms and Human Reproduction,* ed. M. Fern et al. (New York: John Wiley & Sons, 1974).
27. S. L. Smith, "Mood and the Menstrual Cycle," in *Topics in Psychoendocrinology,* ed. E. J. Sachar (New York: Grune & Stratton, 1975); and O'Connor et al. Also of interest is K. Dalton, *The Premenstrual Syndrome* (London: William Heinemann, 1964). The O'Conner study summarizes studies on a total of 1,339 women.
28. M. B. Parlee, "The Premenstrual Syndrome," *Psychological Bulletin* 80 (1973): 454–65.
29. Smith; Parlee; O'Connor et al.; M. Steiner and B. J. Carroll, "The Psychobiology of Premenstrual Dysphoria: Review of Theories and Treatments," *Psychoneuroendocrinology* 2 (1977): 321–35; R. H. Moos, *The Menstrual Distress Questionnaire Manual* (Stanford, Calif.: Stanford University, 1977), and Sommer (n. 13 above).
30. R. L. Spitzer, J. Endicott, and M. Gibbon, "Crossing the Border into Borderline Personality and Borderline Schizophrenia," *Archives of General Psychiatry* 36 (1979): 17–25; J. G. Gunderson and J. E. Kolb, "Discriminating Features of Borderline Patients," *American Journal of Psychiatry* 135 (1978): 792–97.
31. Schachter and Singer (n. 4 above).
32. T. Kashiwagi, J. M. McClure, and R. B. Wetzel, "Premenstrual Affective Syndrome in Psychiatric Disorders," *Diseases of the Nervous System* 37 (1976): 116–19.
33. M. A. Schuckit et al., "Premenstrual Symptoms in Depression in a University Population," *Diseases of the Nervous System* 36 (1975): 516–17; R. D. Wetzel et al., "Premenstrual Affective Syndrome and Affective Disorder," *British Journal of Psychiatry* 127 (1975): 219–21.
34. A. Coppen, "The Prevalence of Menstrual Disorders in Psychiatric Patients," *British Journal of Psychiatry* 111 (1965): 115–67; I. D. Glick, personal communication.
35. S. B. Diamond et al., "Menstrual Problems in Women with Primary Affective Illness," *Comprehensive Psychiatry* 17 (1976): 541–48.
36. Smith (n. 27 above).
37. Steiner and Caroll (n. 29 above.)

PART IV

Gender Differences

Between 1910 and 1919, the *Psychological Bulletin*, a journal of the American Psychological Association, published five reviews of the current literature on sex differences in "mental traits." The first two were written by Helen Thompson Woolley, the last three by Leta S. Hollingworth. In the last of these, Hollingworth concluded her review by saying:

> The year's work yields nothing consistent as a result of the comparison of the sexes in mental traits. In this respect it resembles the work of other years. Pressey finds that girls excel boys in mental tests at all ages, from 8 to 16 years, inclusive; Porteus finds that boys excel girls at nearly all ages. Pressey finds that boys are more variable than girls; Frasier finds that there are no sex differences in variability. In group after group of superior children, the highest intelligence is found now in a boy, now in a girl. Perhaps the logical conclusion to be reached on the basis of these findings is that the custom of perpetuating this review is no longer profitable, and may as well be abandoned (Hollingworth, 1919).

Hollingworth's frustration with the ambiguity of research findings on sex differences in cognitive abilities did nothing to dampen the enthusiasm of her colleagues and those who came after her. Few topics in psychology have a longer history of sustained interest and research. And almost no topic has resulted in more confusion than that of the psychological differences between females and males.

Beliefs about such differences abound in the popular culture. That both scientists and laypersons are interested in the matter implies that unequivocal answers would settle an old human issue. Following the question of what are the differences, if any, is another: Is there a biological substratum that makes them inevitable, or do they appear because of massive doses

of cultural conditioning? Or do environmental factors interact with biological givens to enhance some gender differences, while at the same time
producing that enormous diversity among humans that is independent of
sex category?

Based on the research currently available, the answer to the first question is yes, there are behavioral differences between males and females,
some of which appear during childhood. The answer to the second question is by no means resolved, but we do know from anthropological studies
that human behavior is enormously malleable, and that learning accounts
for much more of our behavior than it does for the behavior of individuals
in any other species. At the present time, it seems most probable that the
environment interacts with biology to product some gender-linked behaviors, so that the performance of groups of males and females on some
variables will differ from each other; it is most important to point out,
however, that differences within such groups are always greater than are
differences between them. In other words, females vary more among
themselves with regard to psychological variables than they differ as a group
from males.

The question of gender differences has become political in recent years,
with adherents of the women's movement and promoters of equality for
women insisting that there is no basis for discrimination against women on
the grounds that women are systematically different from men. Still, there
persists in the minds of many the idea that women and men can never be
behaviorally similar, that behavioral differences are real and natural, and
that socialization practices that treat the sexes differently are reflections of
biological givens.

The papers in this section are examples of contemporary theoretical
and empirical work that demonstrates an awareness of the meaning of sex
as a variable in psychological research and as a categorical assignment whose
consequences for the person it would be difficult to exaggerate. Since humans
are sexually dimorphic and, with rare exceptions, can be readily categorized as male or female, it is not surprising that statements about psychological characteristics often seem to imply that these, too, are sexually
dimorphic. Such statements as "boys are aggressive," or "girls are emotional," imply that these characteristics are categorically descriptive of the
members of one sex and not the other. Therefore, in any discussion of
gender differences, it is important to keep certain points in mind. The first
is that the two sexes overlap greatly on all psychological characteristics.
Differences among the members of one sex are much greater than is the
difference between the sexes. If a difference is shown to exist, it merely
means that the average score on the characteristic is somewhat higher for
one sex than for the other. Some persons in the lower group will score
higher on a measure of the characteristic than will some persons in the
higher group. This makes generalizing about the probable strength of a
psychological characteristic on the basis of a person's sex category very risky.
For example, the mean performance of girls on tests of verbal ability is
higher than the mean performance of boys. But obviously there are some
boys who score higher in verbal ability than most girls do. Knowing the sex
category of a person does not help one reliably to predict what the person's
verbal ability is.

Another problem in interpreting reports of gender differences is that girls and boys are widely observed to differ in maturity at given ages. Newborn girls are four to six weeks "older" developmentally than are newborn boys, a difference that increases to about one year by age six. Some of the differences are in physical indices, such as skeletal and dental development, and others, which may be more important for behavior, involve brain lateralization and cerebral dominance, which seem to occur earlier in girls. Girls also reach puberty a year or so before boys do. Given these developmental differences in maturity, then, the problem of making meaningful observations about gender differences at a given age becomes more complicated.

In the first paper in this section, "Toward a Redefinition of Sex and Gender," Rhoda Unger discusses issues related to the study of sex differences. She argues that the term "sex differences" implies biological mechanisms underlying psychological characteristics of females and males and proposes the use of that term to mean those differences that are in fact biological. The term "gender," then, is applied to those characteristics and traits that are defined by the culture as appropriate to females and males. This distinction would move us away from the assumption that psychological differences between females and males are the result of biological sex.

Problems exist, as Unger points out, with hypotheses of biological determinism as causative of certain gender differences. If certain behaviors are believed to have a large biological component, such as the effects of cerebral lateralization, then researchers are less likely to look at the possible effects of environmental factors on the behaviors. Yet there is some evidence that lateralization, for example, is related to the kinds of toys and play experiences that children have. Unger suggests moving away from a focus on sex differences toward the study of gender. She comments that persons with the same psychological structure often function the same way regardless of their sex category. Thus, knowing what a person's gender variables are might predict his or her behavior better than would knowing what the person's sex is.

The question of psychological sex differences among very young infants has not been finally resolved as yet, though the evidence strongly suggests that such differences have not been demonstrated. An observer of diaper-clad occupants of a nursery for newborns could not do much better than chance if he or she attempted to identify the sex of the infants by either their appearance or their behavior. Yet the baby's sex has very strong stimulus value for others, especially for its parents. That parents perceive boys and girls differently from birth, in accordance with sex role stereotypes, is demonstrated in "The Eye of The Beholder: Parents' Views on Sex of Newborns," by Jeffery Z. Rubin and others. The parents of thirty firstborn boys and girls were asked to describe their infants and to rate them on questionnaire within twenty-four hours after birth. The male and female babies did not differ in weight, height, or condition at birth. In describing their infants, parents were more likely to use "big" for their sons and "little" for their daughters. They rated boys as more firm, better coordinated, stronger, and hardier, and girls as softer, weaker, and more delicate. Fathers were more likely to stereotype their babies, seeing greater differences between boys and girls than mothers did. Since the babies did not in fact differ by sex, the study demonstrates the attribution to them of characteristics that were based entirely on parental beliefs, as they affected parents perceptions. If we assume that perception affects behavior, it is reasonable to predict that parents' behavior toward their infants will be influenced by their stereotypic perceptions. If parents respond differentially to their infants from birth on the basis of sex, thus exposing them to different contingencies and expectations, then the problem of evaluating the relative contributions of socialization and biology to later observed gender differences becomes difficult indeed.

Janet Ann DiPietro's study "Rough and Tumble Play: A Function of Gender" provides a closer look at what it is that boys do that gets them in trouble in the classroom. Rough and tumble play (R & T) describes a set of behaviors including pushing, pulling, hitting, chasing, and wrestling without inflicting injury; it mimics more intentionally aggressive actions. Many observers have reported sex differences across cultures and species, with boys, of course, being much more likely than girls to engage in it. In this study, same-sex triads of preschoolers were observed for R & T, and a robust sex difference was found in both quantitative and qualitative aspects. The boys were much more likely to engage in playful assault, hitting and wrestling. Girls, on the other hand, were more likely to play with toys in nonviolent ways, suggest responsible rules, and await their turns with toys in an orderly fashion. And, once again, it is suggested that an interaction of social and biological factors may facilitate the emission by males of more signals for such play and perhaps give them greater readiness to respond to these signals.

Finally, Camilla Benbow and Julian Stanley present the latest report from the Study of Mathematically Precocious Youth, conducted by Johns Hopkins University. In "Sex Differences in Mathematical Reasoning Ability: More Facts," they describe findings on very large samples of seventh-grade students who took the College Board Scholastic Apitude Test (SAT), which is normally administered to college-bound eleventh and twelfth graders. While the mean difference in the scores of the boys and the girls was not large, a very large sex difference appeared among the highest scorers, with boys outnumbering girls by about thirteen to one. The authors discuss "environmental" hypotheses as explanations for the differences found, as well as the variability hypothesis discussed by Shields in her paper in Part 1. While such a large sex difference, appearing at the extreme upper end of the distribution of mathematical ability, does not generalize to the majority of students, it is a phenomenon that clearly requires explanation. The reasons behind it, as the authors say, are unclear.

We have seen that the scientific study of sex and gender differences began in the early years of the twentieth century and has continued unabated ever since, suggesting that the area continues to be interesting to researchers and that few questions have been definitively answered. We have also seen evidence of a recurring problem: science is not value free. The questions asked, the methodologies used, the interpretations of the results—all have been held, at one time or another, suspect. In the area of sex differences, most of the suspicion has been voiced by women, with good reason. In the past, when differences have been found, they have too often been interpreted as supportive of the social order, with its special rules and roles for women, or as evidence of prevailing beliefs about female inferiority.

The early sex differences research, as reflected in the papers in Part I, arose from assumptions about the importance of biological sex differences and from the fact of woman's inferior status in society, which followed from her biological imperatives. As the psychology of women became an important discipline in the 1970s feminist psychologists began focusing on the sociocultural environment as a source of explanatory constructs for the observable differences between women and men. As the ancient argument of nature versus nurture has become more and more sophisticated, the old dichotomy does not serve us anymore. What is important is the interaction between them. Increasingly, we look to both these potent sources of our behavior. And let us do it, not with fear, but with curiosity and excitement.

REFERENCE

HOLLINGWORTH, LETA S. Comparison of the Sexes in Mental Traits. *Psychological Bulletin*, 1919, *16*, 371–373.

11

Toward a Redefinition of Sex and Gender

Rhoda Kesler Unger

This article discusses issues associated with the study of sex differences by psychologists. The author discusses definitions of sex as a subject variable and as a stimulus variable. The term gender *is introduced for those characteristics and traits socioculturally considered appropriate to males and females. The rationale for this addition to the psychological vocabulary is that the term sex implies biological mechanisms. Differences between females and males that are merely descriptive are frequently assumed to have biological origins. The present terminology facilitates biologically determinist models of sex differences which make it less likely that environmental sources of such differences will be explored. The author examines the area of sex differences in cerebral laterality to illustrate this process. In contrast, research on gender is more concerned with the sociocultural factors that contribute to sex differences. The author suggests that differential use of the term sex indicates different paradigms for the examination of sex differences and that psychological terminology should reflect this distinction.*

Although the study of sex differences has been with us for many years, only recently has anyone paid serious attention to what is being studied. The question of what is being studied would be of only academic interest except for the political and social implications of the results of research in this area. Although researchers have usually had neither the interest nor the confidence to use sex as a major (or the only) variable (Grady, 1979), a body of findings has accumulated that relates sex tangentially to every conceivable phenomenon. Such sex differences are usually discussed briefly if they are found and are dismissed (often unnoted) if they are not. There is no parallel field of sex similarities integrating the numerous studies in which no difference between males and females has been found.

As with another organismic variable, race, it is by no means clear just what is meant by the term *sex*. Psychologists have tended to use the term interchangeably as both an independent and a dependent variable (Unger & Denmark, 1975). As the former, it is implied that sex is built into the organism by chromosomes, genes, and hormones. As the latter, it is assumed that sex is derived (except for physical structure) from the individual's postnatal experiences as defined by the sociocultural matrix. Those who consider sex as a mainly biological variable tend to assume that psychological differences between males and females are the result of sex. Those who consider sex as a mostly social phenomenon tend to assume that the sex of males and females is a result of their different experience. It appears, therefore, that a reconsideration of terminology in this area would assist conceptualization here.

It is important to reconsider not only what is meant by the term *sex* but also what is meant by the term *sex differences*. If fewer and fewer sex differences can be unequivocally demonstrated, which seems to be the conclusion of an important book by Maccoby and Jacklin (1974), will the area cease to be an interesting one? This question relates to another that is equally difficult to answer: What is the relationship between the psychology of sex differences and the psychology of gender? Since there now exist a number of psychologists who stress that they study one or the other to the relative exclusion of the seemingly related field, this question, too, appears to be of more than academic interest.

A major problem in this area appears to be the too inclusive use of the term *sex*. In various contexts, *sex* can be used to describe the chromosomal composition of individuals, the reproductive apparatus and secondary characteristics that are usually associated with these chromosomal differences, the intrapsychic characteristics presumed to be possessed by males and females, and in the case of sex roles, any and all behaviors differentially expected for and appropriate to people on the basis of membership in these various sexual categories. It is the contention of this article that many issues can be resolved and more fruitful questions generated by re-evaluating some of the ways that psychologists have defined the terms frequently used in this area.

Some Definitions of Terms

Sex as a Subject Variable

One of the reasons for the apparent confusion between the biological and social properties of sex is that psychology has traditionally viewed sex in terms of individual differences. The most common methods of study were either self-reports of personality characteristics or preferred behaviors, or observations of subject differences in a variety of experimental contexts. Sex differences, however, often appear inconsistently. Some of the variables that affect whether or not subject sex differences are found include the size of the sample, the age of the subjects (Block, 1976), the social class and/or the culture of the subjects (Nadelman, 1974), and the sex of the experimenters (Holmes & Jorgenson, 1971). In fact, female experimenters have been found to be more likely to look for, or at least publish, a given sex difference than are males (McKenna & Kessler, 1977). A variable with this much variability would seem to be an unlikely candidate for one with much biological basis.

Sex as a Stimulus Variable

There appear to be two kinds of sex differences: one located within the individual and one existing within other persons with whom the individual interacts. The latter kind of sex difference may be termed a *stimulus sex difference* (Grady, 1979). In many of the areas in which hypothesized subject sex differences have not been substantiated by empirical research, stimulus sex differences have been found (O'Leary, 1977). In fact, men and women are especially alike in their beliefs about their own differences. To the extent that males and females share expectations regarding intrapsychic and behavioral differences between the sexes, the expression of such differences constitutes a sex similarity.

Gender

The term *gender* may be used to describe those nonphysiological components of sex that are culturally regarded as appropriate to males or to females. *Gender* may be used for those traits for which sex acts as a stimulus variable, independently of whether those traits have their origin within the subject or not. It refers to a social label by which we distinguish two groups of people. There is evidence that various components of gender-based categories are learned relatively independently of the biological information that underlies them. Thus, 2-year-olds can reliably sort photographs into male and female categories, but they are unable to sort their own pictures consistently in accordance with sex or to answer correctly traditional direct questions about their sex classification (Thompson, 1975).

The use of the term *gender* serves to reduce assumed parallels between biological and psychological sex or at least to make explicit any assumptions of such parallels. *Gender* may be broadened to include both attributions made by others and assumptions and suppositions about one's own properties (gender identity). Societies prescribe particular characteristics for males and females on the basis of assigned sex (Vaughter, 1976). Indeed, such masculine or feminine qualities may even be assigned to inanimate objects on the basis of their designated sex (Tobach, 1971). Gender identity refers to those characteristics an individual develops and internalizes in response to the stimulus functions of biological sex. As such, gender identity may be a more important predictor of behavior than is biological sex. These distinctions have not been made, however, because psychologists have traditionally assumed a close correspondence between maleness and masculinity and femaleness and femininity. This assumption is now being questioned.

Physiologically, there is some suggestion that even the dichotomy between maleness and femaleness may not be as distinct as was once believed. For example, Money's extensive studies of humans with discrepancies among chromosomal, hormonal, and morphological indicators of sex suggest that the degree of correlation among such indicators may be lower than was previously suspected (Money & Ehrhardt, 1972). Despite the evidence of a large number of people with ambiguous sexual identities, investigators of psychosexual identification have been unwilling to tolerate the presence of more than two categories—male and female. This two-category system is most commonly based on the presence or absence of anything that can be defined as a penis. If a penis is present, most people categorize the individual as a male, even in the presence of such contradictory evidence as breasts or feminine hips (Kessler & McKenna, 1978).

The Study of Sex Differences

Historical Considerations

Despite evidence that biological sex is not an either-or category and the lack of clarity regarding biologists' definition of sex, psychologists do believe that sex differences exist. Stephanie Shields (1975a) traced the history of the study of sex differences by psychologists from the mid-19th century and found that this field has never been completely free of social bias. Thus, we were told, apparent structural differences in the brains of females and males implied differences in their intelligence and temperament; hypothetically greater male variability in traits, which related to intellectuality and creativity, had implications for different educational and social structures; and assumptions about a "unique female nature" produced such psychological realities as the maternal instinct and female sexual passivity. As Shields noted, "When issues faded in importance, it was not because they were resolved but because they ceased to serve as viable scientific 'myths' in the changing social and scientific milieu" (p. 740).

Following her line of reasoning, it is plausible to suggest that issues involving sex differences cannot be resolved. Shields, for example, noted that when it was believed that the frontal lobe was the repository of the higher mental capacities, the male frontal lobes were seen as larger. When the parietal lobes came to be seen as more important, a bit of historical revisionism took place. Females were now seen as having equal or larger frontal lobes than males, but smaller parietal lobes. Widespread beliefs about sex differences in brain weight, brain contours, perceptual-motor abilities, emotionality, and intelligence were prevalent during the 19th and early 20th century. Shields (1975b) pointed out that Leta Hollingworth and Helen Montague laboriously examined the hospital records of 2,000 neonates (1,000 of each sex) for birth weight and length in order to test the hypothesis of greater male variability. Other early feminist psychologists struggled to validate empirically beliefs about greater male variability in more psychological characteristics, such as intelligence or emotionality. Despite this amount of effort, few if any differences were found.

When an assumed sex difference is investigated and found to be nonexistent, the argument simply shifts to another ground. This leads to a question the understanding and answering of which is central to the whole area of sex and gender. What does finding a given sex difference in behavior tell us? What are the mechanisms that produce such differences?

Maccoby and Jacklin (1974) provided an interesting point in this regard:

> We invite the reader to imagine a situation in which all psychological researchers routinely divide their subjects into two groups at random, and perform their data analyses separately for the two halves of the sample. Whenever a difference in findings emerges between the two groups (and this would of course sometimes happen by chance even when no difference exists that would

replicate with further samples), our imaginary researcher tests the difference for significance, and any significant differences are included in the published report of the study. If we are not told that the original subdivision has been made at random, we might misspend a great deal of time attempting to explain the differences. (pp. 3–4)

Their book attempts to determine whether assigning cases to groups by sex is any more meaningful for understanding behavior than assigning them at random. We should keep in mind, however, that selection of groups to study is not made at random. From the large number of subject or organismic variables by which humans could be grouped only a few such as sex or race are chosen.

Biological Assumptions Underlying Research on Sex Differences

There is no denying that males and females may be different in some ways, just as tall people differ from short, fat people from thin and even people with Type O blood from those with Type A. The major problem seems to be the use of sex differences as an explanatory rather than as a description suggests strong underlying (and unexamined) assumptions about the biological causality of sex differences. The source of these differences is still being sought in the central nervous system, and psychological theory in this area continues to suggest a direct hookup between the gonads and the brain. Aside from the fact that such simplistic assumptions are inappropriate given the inconsistent and variable nature of evidence about sex differences, such assumptions limit the range of research hypotheses investigated solely to the unidirectional subset implying causality only from biological to psychological phenomena.

Cerebral Laterality: A New Red Herring?

The Politicization of a Research Hypothesis

The area that most recently exemplifies the development and maintenance of ideas about the biological inevitability of differences between the sexes is that of cerebral dominance or laterality. Lateral dominance refers to the tendency for a person to favor one side of the body over the other in performing certain tasks. One of the most noted examples of lateral dominance is handedness. In right-handed people the left hemisphere of the brain is usually dominant. Studies of people with various kinds of brain damage also indicate that this half of the brain is usually dominant for verbal functions and that the right half of the brain is more important in tasks involving spatial configurations.

A variety of studies of brain-damaged people (Lansdell, 1962; McGlone & Kertesz, 1973) have suggested that females show fewer specific impairments following damage to either hemisphere than do males with a comparable degree of cerebral damage. This finding has led researchers to conjecture that as adults, at least, females appear to be less lateralized than males (Lake & Bryden, 1976). The hypothesis appears to contradict findings that girls are verbally fluent at an earlier age than boys and hence, more lateralized for verbal functions at an earlier age (Kimura, 1973). It is females' early advantage itself that is used by some researchers to explain their later degree of reduced laterality (Buffery & Gray, 1972). Somehow, the female brain specializes too early and is not able to "advance" further.

Sex differences in cerebral laterality are significant as an illustration of thinking that defines female biological processes as inferior. One could argue that the greater ability to recover from a stroke would define an area of female strength. Being lateralized, however, is in the process of being defined as good for people. The major basis for this contention appears to be evidence that children who have minimal brain dysfunction, dyslexia, or specific learning problems (however variously defined) are more likely to have ambiguous cerebral dominance than are those children who show no such impairments (Dimond, 1977). These children are also more likely than children in the general population to be left-handed, and left-handedness has been associated with less cerebral lateralization in some normal populations (Gilbert & Bakan, 1973). These hypotheses appear to represent a clear case of reasoning from effect to cause. In addition, they ignore those large numbers of left-handed individuals and even those with mixed dominance who appear to function effectively in the intellectual arena. These anomalous individuals, apparently unaware of the handicaps they have conquered, rarely come to the attention of the psychologist.

Differential laterality has also been used to explain sex differences in mathematical and spatial analytic skills. The kinship of sinistral and female in terms of brain function is all the more questionable because there is no evidence that left-handed individuals who show no evidence of neural impairment have any more difficulty in acquiring mathematical skills than do right-handed people about whom the same statement can be made. In a large-scale study of over 3,000 individuals from an unselected population, Kocel (1977) found no significant differences in any cognitive factor between right- and left-handed males or between right- and left-handed females. Variations in cerebral laterality appear to affect females and males in different ways that are too complex to be discussed in this context. Kocel noted that environmental factors may contribute to these effects:

> The fact that men and women and the right- and left-handed are usually easily differentiated, and that women and left-handers have often been discriminated against historically, raises important questions about the contribution of sociocultural factors to the relationships discovered. (p. 240)

The Limitation of a Research Hypothesis

Biologically determinist hypotheses such as those involving cerebral laterality carry with them the assumption of relatively equal social environments. Such hypotheses reduce the probability that any researcher will examine the effect of environmental factors on behaviors that are defined as having a large biological component. Nevertheless, environmental characteristics may play a larger role than is usually assumed. A student of mine, Caroline Mossip (Note 1), examined spatial lateralization in girls and boys aged 3–11. Consistent with recent hypotheses about other forms of lateralization, girls showed lateralization at an earlier age than boys did.

But boys' lateralization showed increasing development so that by the age of 9, their degree of lateralization surpassed that of girls. There was some suggestive evidence, however, that degree of lateralization was related to environmental factors, in particular, the kinds of toys that the children possessed. At every age, boys owned significantly more spatial toys (vehicles, sports equipment, construction sets, etc.) than girls did. Most interesting was the finding that the number of such toys owned was increasingly positively correlated with spatial lateralization in boys as they grew older. No such relationship was found in girls.

There are several interpretations possible from these data. Children's play preferences may reflect their developing laterality just as much as they may cause it. Girls may not have enough biological potential for spatial laterality to permit the environment to have an effect. However, we know that differential toy selection for boys and girls begins as early as the second year of life (Rheingold & Cook, 1975). Thus, we cannot assume that the psychosocial environment of females and males is an identical one in which purely biological effects can manifest themselves. Sharon Nash's (1975) studies which show that sex differences in spatial visualization in children are present only between boys and girls who prefer the sex role appropriate to their own sex also provide support for the position that social variables can affect supposedly biological ones.

Another major limitation of biologically determined hypotheses that I discuss only briefly here is their assumed irreversibility. It is strange that biological explanations are used to account for differences between males and females in verbal and mathematical skills, since most major differences between the sexes in these areas do not appear until adolescence and early adulthood (Maccoby & Jacklin, 1974). Any effects of differential maturation of the central nervous system would seem to have long disappeared by this time. For example, in discussing more major social differences between groups in early life—the cognitive development of normal South American Indian children who have been malnourished and isolated during the first few years of life—Jerome Kagan (1976) suggested that effects are reversible so that the group subjected to physiological insult reaches the cognitive level of American children by age 18. A number of studies (Hoffman & Maier, 1966; Witkin, cited by Parlee, Note 2) have indicated "improvements" in female problem solving and perceptual faculties in the direction of the male following short-term practice or instruction procedures. The evidence that sex differences do not usually decrease but increase with further socialization should suggest that biological explanations are masking more important (because they are more explanatory) social ones.

It is difficult to avoid confounding sex and gender. It is noteworthy, however, that one study of individuals with similar biological characteristics who were assigned different sexes at birth and raised in accordance with those assignments found differences based more on gender than on sex. Males suffering from testosterone insensitivity, who were therefore born with apparently female external genitalia, showed a typically feminine pattern of cognitive abilities on the Wechsler Intelligence Scale for Children when they were raised as girls (higher verbal than spatial scores) and a more masculine pattern when reared as boys (slightly higher spatial than verbal scores; Masica, Money, Ehrhardt, & Levis, 1969). It is important to remember, of course, that this finding is based on a small population with ambiguous sexuality. Nash's study does indicate that similar effects can operate in a more normal population.

Should We Study Sex Differences?

Problems with the Focus on Sex Differences

It may be valuable to summarize the reasons why some of those who are interested in gender do not concentrate on sex differences as an area of research.

1. The questions of sex differences are someone else's questions—They do not, of themselves, illuminate the mechanisms that create such differences. In fact, they may obscure the origin of such differences by leading us to believe that biological explanations are sufficient for understanding these behaviors. It is also important to remember that biological determinants which are used to distinguish between groups are sometimes chosen for other than objective, scientific reasons.

2. One cannot prove the null hypothesis, and anyway, the argument can just shift to another phenomenon.

3. Examination of sex differences obscures the examination of sex similarities. Sex similarities are not as dramatic and are less likely to be published than are differences. The fact that the sexes are similar in far more ways than they are different is not considered startling psychological news.

4. Analyses based on sex differences tend to imply a trait view of psychology that obscures the situational determinants of behavior. Under many conditions the constraints of the situation play a larger role in determining the individual's behavior in that context than do the psychological characteristics the individual brings to that situation (Wicker, 1969).

5. Studies of sex differences do not examine behaviors in which the rate is virtually zero for one sex. Thus, we do not find studies in sex differences in rape, and until recently, there was no comparison of periodic male and female cycles. In a sense, therefore, studies of sex differences concentrate on those areas in which males and females are least different.

Some of these arguments could be used against the development of a field of gender differences if such a field were to come into existence. Researchers interested in gender, however, have tended to focus more on one or the other sex rather than on differences between them. Gender, like sex, may produce problems of its own for researchers, but it does have the advantage of possessing conceptual newness—requiring a reexamination of what is assumed to be true.

What Do We Study Instead of Sex Differences?

It is always easier to criticize a particular position than to state positive alternatives. Nevertheless, researchers interested in the psychology of gender have made a number of conceptual advances in recent years. One such advance is related to the concept of androgyny, although it is not identical to the way androgyny is often used in research. Androgyny, as postulated by Sandra Bem (1974, 1975), is the simultaneous possession by an individual of an equal number of traits identified in our culture as strongly masculine and strongly feminine. Bem noted that this kind of personality constellation may facilitate effective behavior in a variety of social situations, rather than causing deficits in behavior due to confusion about sex role identity. What is important about this construct in the context of this article is the idea of independence between biological sex and the psychological components of sexual identity (gender). Although some main effects for biological sex have been found, males and females with the same psychological structure often function in similar ways. Thus, self-reports about gender may predict a person's behavior better than the person's biological sex does.

The Effect of Sex as a Stimulus

Research in this area requires that we develop methods for contrasting sex and gender. There is a generalized belief that sex differences exist, and this phenomenon has been extensively investigated under the topic of sex role stereotyping. Using no stimulus materials other than the label *male* or *female*, investigators have found that the sex of the stimulus person alters people's criteria for mental health, affects their evaluation of the goodness and badness of performance, leads them to make differential attributions about the causes of someone's behavior, and induces differential perceptions about the values of others (Broverman, Broverman, Clarkson, Rosenkrantz, & Vogel, 1970; Deaux & Emswiller, 1974; Pheterson, Kiesler, & Goldberg, 1971; Unger & Siiter, 1976). These illusions about sex differences are held by both males and females and thus, in themselves, constitute a sex similarity rather than a sex difference.

Sex may also serve as a stimulus for the evaluation and appraisal of one's own behavior. Gender identity may be the major influence in producing sex differences in performance. The greatest number of sex differences are found in studies that use self-ratings as the measure of behavior in which the investigators are interested (Frodi, Macaulay, & Thome, 1977). Gender identity may also account for the fact that many more sex differences are found in field than in laboratory studies (Unger, in press). Assumptions about the social desirability and normality of one's behavior may be more salient outside the laboratory.

It might be more valuable for the understanding of psychological processes associated with gender to examine those individuals who rate themselves as high or low in traits considered characteristic of a particular sex rather than looking at group differences between the sexes. Such a procedure would test the assumption that on any given characteristic, males and females usually form two overlapping distributions with a minority of people of either sex at the extremes. It would also permit us to determine whether sex or gender is the more important predictor of a given behavior. The degree of influence of biological and social factors will probably vary for different behaviors, but it is well to remember that even in behaviors considered highly specific to reproduction and even among more biologically determined lower mammals, no behavior unique to one sex has been found (Bermant & Davidson, 1974).

It is possible to trace the development of the concept of sex as a stimulus variable during the short history of the field presently defined as the psychology of women. First, researchers noted that psychologists studied women less frequently than they studied men (Carlson & Carlson, 1961). Next, they recognized that the sex of the experimenter or other evaluator of the subject's performance can affect that performance (S. Harris, 1971). The sex of the experimenter and the sex of the subjects may influence research in subtle ways. For example, some areas (e.g., aggression vs. attraction) have been considered more appropriate for research on males than on females (McKenna & Kessler, 1977). Some procedures (e.g., those that involve the measurement of active aggression in subjects) are considered more appropriate for males (Frodi et al., 1977). Aggression in females, in contrast, is more likely to be measured by pencil-and-paper methods. When queried on the subject, some researchers in the area of aggression have made statements about not wishing to use procedures that could be physically harmful to female subjects (Prescott & Foster, Note 3). It is also noteworthy that areas in which males are defined as the most relevant subjects are also those that have until recently received the most attention by psychologists. One can cite as examples the relative number of studies on achievement versus those on nurturance, on aggression versus cooperation, or on the acquisition of mathematical versus reading skills.

Interest in sex as a stimulus variable has been stimulated by the demonstration of persistent evaluation biases in our society. The studies of Kay Deaux and her associates (Deaux, 1976) amply support the proposition that there is no such thing as identical male and female behaviors. Perhaps more important in its implications is the finding that women are evaluated on a narrower continuum than men (Deaux & Taynor, 1973). Women not only receive less credit when they excel but also receive less blame when they fail.

Evaluation biases are particularly difficult to eliminate because they are often subtle and show up only as interactions with other variables. A recent study, for example, analyzed the relationship between the ratings given by students to actual faculty members of either sex and their evaluations of the level of difficulty of that teacher (Unger, Note 4). Although there were no significant sex differences in perceived difficulty and though sex differences in perceived effectiveness of instructor failed to reach significance, the relationship between perceived effectiveness and difficulty was radically different for the two sexes. The two dimensions were independent for ratings of male teachers ($r = .05$), but they were negatively related for females ($r = -.49$). This negative correlation indicated that women who were perceived as difficult graders received lower teacher-effectiveness evaluations relative to other women, whereas those who were perceived as easy graders received higher evaluations. The relationship appeared to be most marked for those women who were viewed as exceptionally difficult or exceptionally easy relative to the entire department. A more controlled laboratory study by M. B. Harris (1976) also revealed that instructors of either sex who were perceived as masculine in style were evaluated differently from those who were more feminine. Thus, taken together, these results suggest that suppositions involving gender may invade objective evaluation instruments, and these may measure social biases rather than subject biases.

Toward a New Definition of Biosocial Variables

The problem of viewing sex as a stimulus or social variable appears to be compounded by the fact that the stimulus aspects of sex appear to be inevitably confounded with the biological aspects of sex differences. It is difficult to find a male control group who manifest some of the biological properties unique to females. Thus, male and female subjects alike infer that a woman's bad mood during the premenstrual and menstrual phases of her cycle is more attributable to her biology than are similar behaviors during the midcycle that are assumed to have a more situational cause (Koeske & Koeske, 1975). Males, nonetheless, are no less likely to attribute their moods to biological causes than are females (Garcia, Note 5). It is also noteworthy that the five-day work week, two-day weekend sequence produces larger and more predictable cyclic variations in female behavior than does the periodicity of the menstrual cycle (Parlee, Note 6), although this finding is not widely reported.

The menstrual cycle represents an excellent avenue of analysis of the way assumptions are made about the causal relationship between sex-characteristic behavior and the central nervous system. Parlee (1978) has clearly analyzed the nature of scientific thinking and lack of objectivity in this area. It is possible to argue that psychological change is a reflection of the social response to biological factors rather than a direct result of the biological variables themselves. Thus, Paige (1973) found that women who were heavy bleeders were more likely to manifest anxiety during the premenstrual phase of the cycle, no matter what their hormonal constitution, than were women with equivalent biochemical states who bled more lightly. Paige suggested that their negative affect represented fears about the social consequences of bleeding visibly and the discomfort and inconvenience that accompanied such heavy bleeding. Behaviorally, such women were more likely to abstain from sexual intercourse during this phase than were women who bled less.

It is possible that we have underestimated the effects of social judgments about physiological conditions unique to women. In a recent, novel experiment in this regard, Taylor and Langer (1977) found that both men and women (although men more than women) stand farther away from a pregnant woman, although they stare at her more than at a nonpregnant woman. Subjects also indicated that they liked a pregnant woman more when she was passive than when she was assertive. At the same time, they rejected the pregnant woman as a companion. The authors suggested that these unacknowledged social rejection mechanisms may be an important source of stigmatizing pregnancy. Internalization of behaviors considered appropriate for this state could then account for many behaviors considered characteristic of pregnancy that are usually attributed to high levels of female hormones.

Psychologists are beginning to recognize that some variables which mediate individual differences may also mediate social differences. Physical attractiveness is one such variable that has received considerable attention. Judgments based on physical attractiveness are considered more salient for females than for males. Size and strength may be more specific mediators of sex differences (Unger, 1976). In fact, one could offer a new definition of a biosocial variable—not one that is the result of biological and social causes, but one that produces effects because of generalized sociocultural assumptions about universal biological processes. Many biological processes are evident to an observer and may be the subject of his or her social judgments. A consideration of this kind of variable may help to explain why some sex differences in psychological function seem to appear universally. After all, the biological states on which the attributions are based are themselves universal.

New hypotheses may be generated by a redefinition of biosocial processes. Questions might include the following: To what extent may greater female concern with weight be due to periodic weight instabilities generated by the menstrual cycle? Is social responsiveness in females enhanced by their designation as the physically attractive sex? Within a sex, do larger children make more attempts to influence others, and are they more overtly aggressive than smaller ones? In other words, what is the association between external bodily characteristics and gender? This position does not deny that biological differences between the sexes may exist, but explanations based on them may lie elsewhere than in direct physiological influences on the central nervous system. Social processes can, of course, of themselves differentially affect the behavior of people of different sexes. There are, for example, considerable data that there are fewer positive connections between behavior and rewards for females than for males (Unger, 1979).

Presumed sex differences, by this analysis, cannot be used to justify differential treatment of the sexes. Group data can never legitimately justify treatment of individuals, and characterization of behaviors as sex specific is particularly questionable in view of the abundant evidence that the social judgment process almost always results in the equations, *male = superior, female = inferior*. In sex, as in race, there are no separate but equal social categories.

The Scientific Value of Redefinition

In sum, this article makes a case for partitioning sex in terms of the various ways it can function biologically and socially. The distinction between sex and gender can assist in the generation of research hypotheses that do not assume the former is necessarily the basis for the latter. The use of the term *gender* makes it less likely that psychological differences between males and females will be considered explicable mainly in terms of physiological differences between them. Those who study the psychology of women are often concerned with the stimulus functions of sex—the fact that the label *male* or *female* with no additional information provided greatly alters people's view of the stimulus person described. Gender refers to the traits and behaviors considered characteristic of and appropriate to members of each sexual category. Gender identity is more appropriately used when these attributions are made with oneself as the stimulus person. These terms, however, do not imply that we have any information on the origin of gender-characteristic effects. It is likely, in fact, that a number of factors—physiological, biosocial, and environmental—contribute to differences between females and males.

Consider a rainbow. Given the full spectrum of color, we perceive red and magenta as being similar. If, however, we eliminate all other hues, red and magenta are now perceived as being different. But the price of emphasizing this difference is the loss of the rest of the spectrum. Similarly, relationships relevant to both sexes have been obscured by the limitation of research to the difference between them. Many so-called sex differences may actually be gender differences. However, the substitution of gender for sex is not the solution to this problem. Both terms—appropriately defined—are necessary parts of our psychological vocabularies. I hope that gender will provide a useful tool for our ultimate understanding of people—sex unspecified.

REFERENCE NOTES

1. Mossip, C. E. *Hemispheric specialization as seen in children's perception of faces.* Paper presented at the meeting of the Eastern Psychological Association, Boston, April 1977.
2. Parlee, M. B. *Sex differences in perceptual field dependence: A look at some data embedded in theory.* Manuscript submitted for publication, 1976.
3. Prescott, S., & Foster, K. *Why researchers don't study women.* Paper presented at the meeting of the American Psychological Association, New Orleans, August 1974.
4. Unger, R. K. *The student teacher evaluation form as an instrument of sexism.* Paper presented at the meeting of the American Psychological Association, San Francisco, August 1977.
5. Garcia, M. *Fluctuations of mood in the menstrual cycle not confirmed.* Paper presented at the meeting of the Eastern Psychological Association, New York, April 1975.
6. Parlee, M. B. *From the known into the unknown: Sexual politics becomes science.* Paper presented at the meeting of the New York Academy of Sciences, New York, November 15, 1976.

REFERENCES

BEM, S. L. The measurement of psychological androgyny. *Journal of Consulting and Clinical Psychology*, 1974, *42*, 155–162.

BEM, S. L. Sex role adaptability: One consequence of psychological androgyny. *Journal of Personality and Social Psychology*, 1975, *31*, 634–643.

BERMANT, G., & DAVIDSON, J. M. *Biological bases of sexual behavior.* New York: Harper & Row, 1974.

BLOCK, J. H. Debatable conclusions about sex differences (Review of *The psychology of sex differences* by E. E. Maccoby & C. N. Jacklin). *Contemporary Psychology*, 1976, *21*, 517–522.

BROVERMAN, I. K., BROVERMAN, D. M., CLARKSON, F. E., ROSENKRANTZ, P. S., & VOGEL, S. R. Sex-role stereotypes and clinical judgments of mental health. *Journal of Consulting and Clinical Psychology*, 1970, *34*, 1–7.

BUFFERY, A. W. H., & GRAY, J. A. Sex differences in the development of spatial and linguistic skills. In C. Ounsted & D. C. Taylor (Eds.), *Gender differences: Their ontogeny and significance.* London: Churchill Livingstone, 1972.

CARLSON, E. R., & CARLSON, R. Male and female subjects in personality research. *Journal of Abnormal and Social Psychology*, 1961, *61*, 482–483.

DEAUX, K. *The behavior of women and men.* Belmont, Calif.: Brooks/Cole, 1976.

DEAUX, K., & EMSWILLER, T. Explanations of successful performance on sex-linked tasks: What is skill for the male is luck for the female. *Journal of Personality and Social Psychology*, 1974, *29*, 80–85.

DEAUX, K., & TAYNOR, J. Evaluation of male and female ability: Bias works both ways. *Psychological Reports*, 1973, *32*, 261–262.

DIMOND, S. J. Evolution and lateralization of the brain: Concluding remarks. *Annals of the New York Academy of Sciences*, 1977, *299*, 477–501.

FRODI, A., MACAULAY, J., & THOME, P. A. Are women always less aggressive than men? *Psychological Bulletin*, 1977, *84*, 634–660.

GILBERT, C., & BAKAN, P. Visual asymmetry in the perception of faces. *Neuropsychologia*, 1973, *11*, 355–362.

GRADY, K. *Androgyny reconsidered. In J. H. Williams (Ed.), Psychology of women: Selected readings.* New York: Norton, 1979. (Originally a paper presented at the meeting of the Eastern Psychological Association, New York, April 1975.)

HARRIS, M. B. The effects of sex, sex-stereotyped descriptions, and institution on evaluation of teachers. *Sex Roles*, 1976, *2*, 15–21.

HARRIS, S. Influence of subject and experimenter sex in psychological research. *Journal of Consulting and Clinical Psychology*, 1971, *37*, 291–294.

HOFFMAN, L. R., & MAIER, N. R. F. Social factors influencing problem solving in women. *Journal of Personality and Social Psychology*, 1966, *4*, 382–390.

HOLMES, D. S., & JORGENSON, B. W. Do personality and social psychologists study men more than women? *Representative Research in Social Psychology*, 1971, *2*, 71–76.

KAGAN, J. Emergent themes in human development. *American Scientist*, 1976, *64*, 186–196.

KESSLER, S. J., & MCKENNA, W. *Gender: An ethnomethodological approach.* New York: Wiley, 1978.

KIMURA, D. The asymmetry of the human brain. *Scientific American*, 1973, *228*(3), 70–78.

KOCEL, K. M. Cognitive abilities: Handedness, familial sinistrality, and sex. *Annals of the New York Academy of Sciences*, 1977, *299*, 233–243.

KOESKE, R. K., & KOESKE, G. F. An attributional approach to moods and the menstrual cycle. *Journal of Personality and Social Psychology*, 1975, *31*, 473–478.

LAKE, D. A., & BRYDEN, M. P. Handedness and sex differences in hemispheric asymmetry. *Brain and Language*, 1976, *3*, 266–282.

LANSDELL, H. A sex difference in the effect of temporal lobe neurosurgery on design preference. *Nature*, 1962, *194*, 852–854.

MACCOBY, E. E., & JACKLIN, C. N. *The psychology of sex differences.* Stanford, Calif.: Stanford University Press, 1974.

MASICA, D. N., MONEY, J., EHRHARDT, A. A., & LEVIS, V. S. IQ, fetal sex hormones and cognitive patterns: Studies in the testicular feminizing syndrome of androgen insensitivity. *Johns Hopkins Medical Journal*, 1969, *124*, 34–43.

MCGLONE, J., & KERTESZ, A. Sex differences in cerebral processing of visuo-spatial tasks. *Cortex*, 1973, *9*, 313–320.

MCKENNA, W., & KESSLER, S. J. Experimental design as a source of sex bias in social psychology. *Sex Roles*, 1977, *3*, 117–128.

MONEY, J., & EHRHARDT, A. A. *Man and woman, boy and girl.* Baltimore, Md.: Johns Hopkins University Press, 1972.

NADELMAN, L. Sex identity in American children: Memory, knowledge, and preference tests. *Developmental Psychology*, 1974, *10*, 413–417.

NASH, S. C. The relationship among sex-role stereotyping, sex-role preference, and the sex difference in spatial visualization. *Sex Roles*, 1975, *1*, 15–32.

O'LEARY, V. E. *Toward understanding women.* Monterey, Calif.: Brooks/Cole, 1977.

PAIGE, K. E. Women learn to sing the menstrual blues. *Psychology Today*, September 1973, pp. 41–46.

PARLEE, M. B. Psychological aspects of menstruation, childbirth, and menopause. In J. Sherman & F. Denmark (Eds.), *Psychology of women: Future directions of research.* New York: Psychological Dimensions, 1978.

PHETERSON, G. I., KIESLER, S. B., & GOLDBERG, P. A. Evaluation of the performance of women as a function of their sex, achievement, and personal history. *Journal of Personality and Social Psychology*, 1971, *19*, 114–118.

RHEINGOLD, H. L., & COOK, K. V. The contents of boys' and girls' rooms as an index of parents' behavior. *Child Development*, 1975, *46*, 459–463.

SHIELDS, S. A. Functionalism, Darwinism, and the psychology of women: A study of social myth. *American Psychologist*, 1975, *30*, 739–754. (a)

SHIELDS, S. A. Ms. Pilgrim's progress: The contribution of Leta Stetter Hollingworth to the psychology of women. *American Psychologist*, 1975, *30*, 852–857. (b)

TAYLOR, S. E., & LANGER, E. J. Pregnancy: A social stigma? *Sex Roles*, 1977, *3*, 27–35.

THOMPSON, S. K. Gender labels and early sex role development. *Child Development*, 1975, *46*, 339–347.

TOBACH, E. Some evolutionary aspects of human gender. *American Journal of Orthopsychiatry*, 1971, *41*, 710–715.

UNGER, R. K. Male is greater than female: The socialization of status inequality. *Counseling Psychologist*, 1976, *6*, 2–9.

UNGER, R. K. *Female and male: Psychological perspectives.* New York: Harper & Row, 1979.

UNGER, R. K. Sex as a social reality: Field and laboratory research. *Psychology of Women Quarterly*, in press.

UNGER, R. K., & DENMARK, F. *Woman: Dependent or independent variable?* New York: Psychological Dimensions, 1975.

UNGER, R. K., & SIITER, R. Sex-role stereotypes: The weight of a "grain of truth." In B. B. Watson (Ed.), *Women's studies: The social realities.* New York: Harper & Row, 1976. (Originally a paper presented at the meeting of the Eastern Psychological Association, Philadelphia, April 1974.)

VAUGHTER, R. M. Review essay: Psychology. *Signs*, 1976, *2*, 120–146.

WICKER, A. W. Attitudes versus actions: The relationship of verbal and overt behavioral responses to attitude objects. *Journal of Social Issues*, 1969, *25*, 41–78.

12

The Eye of the Beholder
Parents' Views on Sex of Newborns

Jeffrey Z. Rubin, Frank J. Provenzano, and Zella Luria

Thirty pairs of primiparous parents, fifteen with sons and fifteen with daughters, were interviewed within the first 24 hours postpartum. Although male and female infants did not differ in birth length, weight, or Apgar scores, daughters were significantly more likely than sons to be described as little, beautiful, pretty, and cute, and as resembling their mothers. Fathers made more extreme and stereotyped rating judgments of their newborns than did mothers. Findings suggest that sex-typing and sex-role socialization *have already begun at birth.*

As Schaffer[10] has observed, the infant at birth is essentially an asocial, largely undifferentiated creature. It appears to be little more than a tiny ball of hair, fingers, toes, cries, gasps, and gurgles. However, while it may seem that "if you've seen one, you've seen them all," babies are *not* all alike— a fact that is of special importance to their parents, who want, and appear to need, to view their newborn child as a creature that is special. Hence, much of early parental interaction with the infant may be focused on a search for distinctive features. Once the fact that the baby is normal has been established, questions such as, "Who does the baby look like?" and "How much does it weigh?" are asked.

Of all the questions parents ask themselves and each other about their infant, one seems to have priority: "Is it a boy or a girl?" The reasons for and consequences of posing this simple question are by no means trivial. The answer, "boy" or "girl," may result in the parents' organizing their perception of the infant with respect to a wide variety of attributes—ranging from its size to its activity, attractiveness, even its future potential. It is the purpose of the present study to examine the kind of verbal picture parents form of the newborn infant, as a function both of their own and their infant's gender.

"The Eye of the Beholder: Parents Views on Sex of Newborns" by Jeffrey Z. Rubin, Frank J. Provenzano, and Zella Luria. *American Journal of Orthopsychiatry*, 44, 4 (1974). Copyright © 1974 by the American Orthopsychiatric Association, Inc. Reprinted by permission.

As Asch[2] observed years ago, in forming our impressions of others, we each tend to develop a *Gestalt*—a global picture of what others are like, which permits us to organize our perceptions of the often discrepant, contradictory aspects of their behavior and manner into a unified whole. The awareness of another's status,[13] the belief that he is "warm" or "cold,"[2,5] "extroverted" or "introverted,"[6] even the apparently trivial knowledge of another's name[4]—each of these cues predisposes us to develop a stereotypic view of that other, his underlying nature, and how he is likely to behave. How much more profound, then, may be the consequences of a cue as prominent in parents' minds as the gender of their own precious, newborn infant.

The study reported here is addressed to parental perceptions of their infants at the point when these infants first emerge into the world. If it can be demonstrated that parental sex-typing has already begun its course at this earliest of moments in the life of the child, it may be possible to understand better one of the important antecedents of the complex process by which the growing child comes to view itself as boy-ish or girl-ish.

Based on our review of the literature, two forms of parental sex-typing may be expected to occur at the time of the infant's birth. First, it appears likely that parents will view and label their newborn child differentially, as a simple function of the infant's gender. Aberle and Naegele[1] and Tasch,[12] using only fathers as subjects, found that they had different expectations for sons and daughters: sons were expected to be aggressive and athletic, daughters were expected to be pretty, sweet, fragile, and delicate. Rebelsky and Hanks[9] found that fathers spent more time talking to their daughters than their sons during the first three months of life. While the sample size was too small for the finding to be significant, they suggest that the role of father-of-daughter may be perceived as requiring greater nurturance. Similarly, Pedersen and Robson[8] reported that the fathers of infant daughters exhibited more behavior labeled (by the authors) as "apprehension over well being" than did the fathers of sons.

A comparable pattern emerges in research using mothers as subjects. Sears, Maccoby and Levin,[11] for example, found that the mothers of kindergartners reported tolerating more aggression from sons than daughters, when it was directed toward parents and peers. In addition, maternal nurturance was seen as more important for the daughter's than the son's development. Taken together, the findings in this body of research lead us to expect parents (regardless of their gender) to view their newborn infants differentially—labeling daughters as weaker, softer, and therefore in greater need of nurturance, than sons.

The second form of parental sextyping we expect to occur at birth is a function both of the infant's gender *and* the parent's own gender. Goodenough[3] interviewed the parents of nursery school children, and found that mothers were less concerned with sex-typing their child's behavior than were fathers. More recently, Meyer and Sobieszek[7] presented adults with videotapes of two seventeen-month-old children (each of whom was sometimes described as a boy and sometimes as a girl), and asked their subjects to describe and interpret the children's behavior. They found that male subjects, as well as those having little contact with small children, were more likely (although not always significantly so) to rate the children in sex-stereotypic fashion—attributing "male qualities" such as independence, aggressiveness, activity, and alertness to the child presented as a boy, and qualities such as cuddliness, passivity, and delicacy of the "girl." We expect, therefore, that sex of infant and sex of parent will interact, such that it is fathers, rather than mothers, who emerge as the greater sex-typers of their newborn.

In order to investigate parental sex-typing of their newborn infants, and in order, more specifically, to test the predictions that sex-typing is a function of the infant's gender, as well as the gender of both infant and parent, parents of newborn boys and girls were studied in the maternity ward of a hospital, within the first 24 hours postpartum, to uncover their perceptions of the characteristics of their newborn infants.

Method

Subjects

The subjects consisted of 30 pairs of primiparous parents, fifteen of whom had sons, and fifteen of whom had daughters. The subjects were drawn from the available population of expecting parents at a suburban Boston hospital serving local, predominantly lower-middle-class families. Using a list of primiparous expectant mothers obtained from the hospital, the experimenter made contact with families by mail several months prior to delivery, and requested the subjects' assistance in "a study of social relations among parents and their first child." Approximately one week after the initial contact by mail, the experimenter telephoned each family, in order to answer any questions the prospective parents might have about the study, and to obtain their consent. Of the 43 families reached by phone, eleven refused to take part in the study. In addition, one consenting mother subsequently gave birth to a low birth weight infant (a 74-ounce girl), while another delivered an unusually large son (166 ounces). Because these two infants were at the two ends of the distribution of birth weights, and because they might have biased the data in support of our hypotheses, the responses of their parents were eliminated from the sample.

All subjects participated in the study within the first 24 hours post-partum—the fathers almost immediately after delivery, and the mothers (who were often under sedation at the time of delivery) up to but not later than 24 hours later. The mothers typically had spoken with their husbands at least once during this 24 hour period.

There were no reports of medical problems during any of the pregnancies or deliveries, and all infants in the sample were full-term at time of birth. Deliveries were made under general anesthesia, and the fathers were not allowed in the delivery room. The fathers were not permitted to handle their babies during the first 24 hours, but could view them through display windows in the hospital nursery. The mothers, on the other hand, were allowed to hold and feed their infants. The subject participated individually in the study. The fathers were met in a small, quiet waiting room used exclusively by the maternity ward, while the mothers were met in their hospital rooms. Every precaution was taken not to upset the parents or interfere with hospital procedure.

Procedure

After introducing himself to the subjects, and after congratulatory amenities, the experimenter (FJP) asked the parents: "Describe your baby as you would to a close friend or relative." The responses were tape-recorded and subsequently coded.

The experimenter then asked the subjects to take a few minutes to complete a short questionnaire. The instructions for completion of the questionnaire were as follows:

On the following page there are 18 pairs of opposite words. You are asked to rate your baby in relation to these words, placing an "x" or a checkmark in the space that best describes your baby. The more a word describes your baby, the closer your "x" should be to that word.

Example: Imagine you were asked to rate Trees.

Good   :__:__:__:__:__:__:__:__:__:__:__:__:__:__:__:__:__: Bad
Strong :__:__:__:__:__:__:__:__:__:__:__:__:__:__:__:__:__: Weak

If you cannot decide or your feelings are mixed, place your "x" in the center space. Remember, the more you think a word is a good description of your baby, the closer you should place you "x" to that word. If there are no questions, please begin. Remember, you are rating your baby. Don't spend too much time thinking about your answers. First impressions are usually the best.

Having been presented with these instructions, the subjects then proceeded to rate their baby on each of the eighteen following, eleven-point, bipolar adjective scales: firm-soft; large featured-fine featured; big-little; relaxed-nervous; cuddly-not cuddly; easy going-fussy; cheerful-cranky; good eater-poor eater; excitable-calm; active-inactive; beautiful-plain; sociable-unsociable; well coordinated-awkward; noisy-quiet; alert-inattentive; strong-weak; friendly-unfriendly; hardy-delicate.

Upon completion of the questionnaire, the subjects were thanked individually, and when both parents of an infant had completed their participation, the underlying purposes of the study were fully explained.

Hospital Data

In order to acquire a more objective picture of the infants whose characteristics were being judged by the subjects, data were obtained from hospital records concerning each infant's birth weight, birth length, and Apgar scores. Apgar scores are typically assigned at five and ten minutes postpartum, and represent the physician's ratings of the infant's color, muscle tonicity, reflex irritability, and heart and respiratory rates. No significant differences between the male and female infants were found for birth weight, birth length, or Apgar scores at five and ten minutes postpartum.*

* Birth weight ($\overline{X}_{Sons} = 114.43$ ounces, $\overline{X}_{Daughters} = 110.00$, t (28) = 1.04); Birth length ($\overline{X}_{Sons} = 19.80$ inches, $\overline{X}_{Daughters} = 19.96$, t (28) = 0.52); 5 minute Apgar score ($\overline{X}_{Sons} = 9.07$, $\overline{X}_{Daughters} = 9.33$, t (28) = 0.69); and 10 minute Apgar score ($\overline{X}_{Sons} = 10.00$, $\overline{X}_{Daughters} = 10.00$).

Results

In Table 1, the subjects' mean ratings of their infant, by condition, for each of the eighteen bipolar adjective scales, are presented. The right-extreme column of Table 1 shows means for each scale, which have been averaged across conditions. Infant stimuli, overall, were characterized closer to the scale anchors of soft, fine featured, little, relaxed, cuddly, easy going, cheerful, good eater, calm, active, beautiful, sociable, well coordinated, quiet, alert, strong, friendly, and hardy. Our parent-subjects, in other words, appear to have felt on Day 1 of their babies' lives that their newborn infants represented delightful, competent new additions to the world!

Analysis of variance of the subjects' questionnaire responses (1 and 56 degrees of freedom) yielded a number of interesting findings. There were *no* rating differences on the eighteen scales as a simple function of Sex of Parent: parents appear to agree with one another, on the average. As a function of Sex of Infant, however, several significant effects emerged: Daughters, in contrast to sons, were rated as significantly softer ($F = 10.67$, $p < .005$), finer featured ($F = 9.27, p < .005$), littler ($F = 28.83, p < .001$), and more inattentive ($F = 4.44, p < .05$). In addition, significant interaction effects emerged for seven of the eighteen scales: firm-soft ($F = 11.22$, $p < .005$), large featured-fine featured ($F = 6.78$, $p < .025$), cuddly-not cuddly ($F = 4.18, p < .05$), well coordinated-awkward ($F = 12.52, p < .001$), alert-inattentive ($F = 5.10, p < .05$), strong-weak ($F = 10.67, p < .005$), and hardy-delicate ($F = 5.32, p < .025$).

The meaning of these interactions becomes clear in Table 1, in which it

Table 1   Mean rating on the 18 adjective scales, as a function of sex of parent *(Mother vs. Father)* and sex of infant *(Son vs. Daughter)*[a]

Scale	Experimental condition				
(I)–(II)	M–S	M–D	F–S	F–D	X̄
Firm–Soft	7.47	7.40	3.60	8.93	6.85
Large featured–Fine featured	7.20	7.53	4.93	9.20	7.22
Big–Little	4.73	8.40	4.13	8.53	6.45
Relaxed–Nervous	3.20	4.07	3.80	4.47	3.88
Cuddly–Not cuddly	1.40	2.20	2.20	1.47	1.82
Easy going–Fussy	3.20	4.13	3.73	4.60	3.92
Cheerful–Cranky	3.93	3.73	4.27	3.60	3.88
Good eater–Poor eater	3.73	3.80	4.60	4.53	4.16
Excitable–Calm	6.20	6.53	5.47	6.40	6.15
Active–Inactive	2.80	2.73	3.33	4.60	3.36
Beautiful–Plain	2.13	2.93	1.87	2.87	2.45
Sociable–Unsociable	4.80	3.80	3.73	4.07	4.10
Well coordinated–Awkward	3.27	2.27	2.07	4.27	2.97
Noisy–Quiet	6.87	7.00	5.67	7.73	6.82
Alert–Inattentive	2.47	2.40	1.47	3.40	2.44
Strong–Weak	3.13	2.20	1.73	4.20	2.82
Friendly–Unfriendly	3.33	3.40	3.67	3.73	3.53
Hardy–Delicate	5.20	4.67	3.27	6.93	5.02

[a]The larger the mean, the greater the rated presence of the attribute denoted by the second (right-hand) adjective in each pair.

can be seen that six of these significant interactions display a comparable pattern: fathers were more extreme in their ratings of *both* sons and daughters than were mothers. Thus, sons were rated as firmer, larger featured, better coordinated, more alert, stronger, and hardier—and daughters as softer, fine featured, more awkward, more inattentive, weaker, and more delicate—by their fathers than by their mothers. Finally, with respect to the other significant interaction effect (cuddly-not cuddly), a rather different pattern was found. In this case, mothers rated sons as cuddlier than daughters, while fathers rated daughters as cuddlier than sons—a finding we have dubbed the "oedipal" effect.

Responses to the interview question were coded in terms of adjectives used and references to resemblance. Given the open-ended nature of the question, many adjectives were used—healthy, for example, being a high frequency response cutting across sex of babies and parents. Parental responses were pooled, and recurrent adjectives were analyzed by X^2 analysis for sex of child. Sons were described as big more frequently than were daughters (X^2 (1) = 4.26, $p < .05$); daughters were called little more often than were sons (X^2 (1) = 4.28, $p < .05$). The "feminine" cluster—beautiful, pretty, and cute—was used significantly more often to describe daughters than sons (X^2 (1) = 5.40, $p < .05$). Finally, daughters were said to resemble mothers more frequently than were sons (X^2 (1) = 3.87, $p < .05$).

Discussion

The data indicate that parents—especially fathers—differentially label their infants, as a function of the infant's gender. These results are particularly striking in light of the fact that our sample of male and female infants did *not* differ in birth length, weight, or Apgar scores. Thus, the results appear to be a pure case of parental labeling—what a colleague has described as "nature's first projective test" (personal communication, Leon Eisenberg). Given the importance parents attach to the birth of their first child, it is not surprising that such ascriptions are made.

But why should posing the simple question, "Is it a boy or a girl?", be so salient in parents' minds, and have such important consequences? For one thing, an infant's gender represents a truly *distinctive* characteristic. The baby is either a boy or a girl—there are no ifs, ands, or buts about it. A baby may be active sometimes, and quiet at others, for example, but it can always be assigned to one of two distinct classes: boy or girl. Secondly, an infant's gender tends to assume the properties of a *definitive* characteristic. It permits parents to organize their questions and answers about the infant's appearance and behavior into an integrated *Gestalt*. Finally, an infant's gender is often a *normative* characteristic. It is a property that seems to be of special importance not only to the infant's parents, but to relatives, friends, neighbors, and even casual passersby in the street. For each of these reasons, an infant's gender is a property of considerable importance to its parents, and is therefore one that is likely to lead to labeling and the investment of surplus meaning.

The results of the present study are, of course, not unequivocal. Although it was found, as expected, that the sex-typing of infants varied as a function of the infant's gender, as well as the gender of both infant and parent, significant differences did not emerge for all eighteen of the adjective scales employed. Two explanations for this suggest themselves. First, it may simply be that we have overestimated the importance of sex-typing at birth. A second possibility, however, is that sex-typing is more likely to emerge with respect to certain classes of attributes—namely, those which denote physical or constitutional, rather than "internal," dispositional, factors. Of the eight different adjective pairs for which significant main or interaction effects emerged, six (75%) clearly refer to external attributes of the infant. Conversely, of the ten adjective pairs for which no significant differences were found, only three (30%) clearly denote external attributes. This suggests that it is physical and constitutional factors that specially lend themselves to sex-typing at birth, at least in our culture.

Another finding of interest is the lack of significant effects, as a simple function of sex of parent. Although we predicted no such effects, and were therefore not particularly surprised by the emergence of "non-findings," the implication of these results is by no means trivial. If we had omitted the sex of the infant as a factor in the present study, we might have been led to conclude (on the basis of simply varying the sex of the parent) that *no* differences exist in parental descriptions of newborn infants—a patently erroneous conclusion! It is only when the infant's and the parent's gender are considered together, in interaction, that the lack of differences between overall parental mean ratings can be seen to reflect the true differences between the parents. Mothers rate both sexes closer together on the adjective pairs than do fathers (who are the stronger sex-typers), but *both* parents agree on the direction of sex differences.

An issue of considerable concern, in interpreting the findings of the present study appropriately, stems from the fact that fathers were not permitted to handle their babies, while mothers were. The question then becomes: is it possible that the greater sex-typing by fathers is simply attributable to their lesser exposure to their infants? This, indeed, may have been the case. However it seems worthwhile to consider some of the alternative possibilities. Might not the lesser exposure of fathers to their infants have led not to greater sex-typing, but to a data "wash out"—with no differences emerging in paternal ratings? After all, given no opportunity to handle their babies, and therefore deprived of the opportunity to obtain certain first-hand information about them, the fathers might have been expected to make a series of neutral ratings—hovering around the middle of each adjective scale. The fact that they did not do this suggests that they brought with them a variety of sex stereotypes that they then imposed upon their infant. Moreover, the fact that mothers, who were allowed to hold and feed their babies, made distinctions between males and females that were in keeping with cultural sex-stereotypes (see Table 1), suggests that even if fathers had had the opportunity of holding their infants, similar results might have been obtained. We should also not lose sight of the fact that father-mother differences in exposure to infants continue well into later years. Finally, one must question the very importance of the subjects' differential exposure on the grounds that none of the typical "exposure" effects reported in the social psychological literature[14] were observed. In particular, one might have expected mothers to have come to rate their infants more favorably than fathers, simply as a result of greater exposure. Yet such was not the case.

The central implication of the study, then, is that sex-typing and sex-role socialization appear to have already begun their course at the time of the infant's birth, when information about the infant is minimal. The *Gestalt* parents develop, and the labels they ascribe to their newborn infant, may well affect subsequent expectations about the manner in which their infant ought to behave, as well as parental behavior itself. This parental behavior, moreover, when considered in conjunction with the rapid unfolding of the infant's own behavioral repertoire, may well lead to a modification of the very labeling that affected parental behavior in the first place. What began as a one-way street now bears traffic in two directions. In order to understand the full importance and implications of our findings, therefore, research clearly needs to be conducted in which delivery room stereotypes are traced in the family during the first several months after birth, and their impact upon parental behavior is considered. In addition, further research is clearly in order if we are to understand fully the importance of early paternal sex-typing in the socialization of sex-roles.

REFERENCES

1. ABERLE, D. AND NAEGELE, K. 1952. Middleclass fathers' occupational role and attitudes toward children. Amer. J. Orthopsychiat. 22(2):366–378.
2. ASCH, S. 1946. Forming impressions of personality. J. Abnorm. Soc. Psychol. 41:258–290.
3. GOODENOUGH, E. 1957. Interest in persons as an aspect of sex differences in the early years. Genet. Psychol. Monogr. 55:287–323.
4. HARARI, H. AND MC DAVID, J. Name stereotypes and teachers' expectations. J. Educ. Psychol. (in press)
5. KELLEY, H. 1950. The warm-cold variable in first impressions of persons. J. Pers. 18:431–439.
6. LUCHINS, A. 1957. Experimental attempts to minimize the impact of first impressions. *In* The Order of Presentation in Persuasion, C. Hovland, ed. Yale University Press, New Haven, Conn.
7. MEYER, J. AND SOBIESZEK, B. 1972. Effect of a child's sex on adult interpretations of its behavior. Developm. Psychol. 6:42–48.
8. PEDERSEN, F. AND ROBSON, K. 1969. Father participation in infancy. Amer. J. Orthopsychiat. 39(3):466–472.
9. REBELSKY, F. AND HANKS, C. 1971. Fathers' verbal interaction with infants in the first three months of life. Child Develpm. 42:63–68.
10. SCHAFFER, H. 1971. The Growth of Sociability. Penguin Books, Baltimore.
11. SEARS, R., MACCOBY, E. AND LEVIN, H. 1957. Patterns of Child Rearing. Row, Peterson, Evanston, Ill.
12. TASCH, R. 1952. The role of the father in the family. J. Exper. Ed. 20:319–361.
13. WILSON, P. 1968. The perceptual distortion of height as a function of ascribed academic status. J. Soc. Psychol. 74:97–102.
14. ZAJONC, R. 1968. Attitudinal effects of mere exposure. J. Pers. Soc. Psychol. Monogr. Supplement 9:1–27.

13

Rough and Tumble Play
A Function of Gender

Janet Ann DiPietro

Rough and tumble play, a prosocial behavior whose expression and purpose varies as a function of gender, is investigated in the present study. Subjects were 43 preschoolers, who are part of a longitudinal sample (targets), and 86 playmates (partners). A "playroom on wheels" was designed to maximize the amount of rough and tumble displayed in same-sex triads. Observational coding techniques were devised to record various active and verbal behaviors, including a measure of activity level. Results indicate both quantitative and qualitative differences in the behaviors of the male and female triadic groups. Further, a robust sex difference in the amount and intensity of rough and tumble play was observed for both targets and partners. Analyses of the behavioral components indicate that rough and tumble is distinct from other dominance-oriented or aggressive behaviors in this age group. A hypothesis concerning differential salience of interpersonal cues is presented to account for these findings, and speculations are made concerning the influence of rough and tumble play on subsequent development.

The term *rough and tumble* (hereafter R & T) has been used to designate the set of play behaviors that are displayed during exuberant arousal and that mimic more intentionally aggressive actions. Substantial and consistent sex differences have been reported across a variety of species and cultures. This gender dimorphism appears early in development, with young males being more likely to engage in R&T. In infant and juvenile monkeys, R&T generally involves chasing, hitting, wrestling, and biting. Further, these patterns are not associated with injury in infancy (Dolhinow & Bishop, 1972). Similarly, human children display motor patterns described as "pushing, pulling, hitting, chasing, and wrestling" (Hamburg & van Lawick-Goodall, Note 1, p. 9) almost always without hurting one another. In an extensive cross-cultural investigation by Whiting and Edwards (1973), boys were found to engage in more R&T than girls across a variety of cultures reflecting divergent stages of technological development. In that study, R&T was operationally defined as aggression, which has a strong sociable component, as opposed to assaulting with the intent to injure. No sex difference

"Rough and Tumble Play: A Function of Gender" by Janet Ann DiPietro in *Developmental Psychology*, 1981, 17, 50–58. Copyright © 1981 by the American Psychological Association. Reprinted by permission.

was observed in injurious assaulting due to its low frequency of display by either sex.

Hartup (1974) considered the possible role of juvenile R & T as direct training in an array of aggressive skills and mechanisms for coping with the affective and physical outcomes that accompany an aggressive encounter. With respect to nonhuman primates, it has also been suggested that R&T contact with peers accounts for much of the variance between individuals in subsequent aggression by providing opportunities for escalation into serious fighting (Harlow & Harlow, 1965). Suomi (1977) proposed that the development of peer attachments in monkeys permits the rehearsal of an aggressive behavioral repertoire in the context of social play and that aggression emerges predominantly in the presence of strangers.

The search for differential socialization practices that are predictive of childhood sex differences in aggression has been remarkably unfruitful (see Maccoby & Jacklin, 1974, chap. 9). However, it has been reported that male infants are "roughed up" by adults or subjected to gross motor manipulations more often than females, particularly at the hands of their fathers (Yarrow, Rubenstein, & Pedersen, Note 2). Recent work has also demonstrated that mothers are more likely to verbally and physically encourage gross motor activities in an "actor" child who is believed to be a boy than when the same child is thought to be female (Smith & Lloyd, 1978). However, it remains unclear whether mothers are acting differently on the basis of cultural stereotypes alone or if their behavior is shaped by actual experience with their own children of either sex. Reports of similar differential treatment by monkey mothers based on infant gender (Mitchell & Brandt, 1970) seem to cast doubt on the determinance of cognitive expectations alone and suggest differences in reactivity to such stimulation based on the infant's gender.

It is evident that males of all ages are not only the instigators but also the recipients of both mock and serious fighting. This pattern is evidenced as early as nursery school (Langlois, Gottfried, & Seay, 1973) as well as in nonhuman primates. Further, this is the case even though males are more likely to retaliate by counterattack than females, a contingency that is demonstrably more aversive (Patterson, Littman, & Brickner, 1967). It also appears that males stimulate motoric activity in other males by their presence alone. Again, this is true of juvenile monkeys as well as human children (Halverson & Waldrop, 1973). Although research findings on activity level per se are equivocal with respect to sex differences, males are the more active sex in certain situations and on certain measures. However, this does not preclude the possibility that qualitatively different activity patterns exist between the sexes that are obscured by quantitative measures alone. Recent findings (Jacklin & Maccoby, 1978) suggest that boys' and girls' reactions to potentially disturbing behavior by another child are largely predicated on the other child's gender. Briefly, it was found that dyads of same-sex partners displayed similar levels of social behavior at 33 months of age. In mixed pairs, however, girls tended to withdraw from male-initiated active play.

The present study was designed to assess the components involved in patterns of active and R&T play by providing a situation conducive to the maximization of these behaviors. Further, the relationship of R&T to both aggression and activity level, which may vary both qualitatively and quantitatively as a function of gender, was investigated.

Method

Subjects

Subjects were 30 male and 22 female preschoolers between the ages of 4 years 1 month and 4 years 10 months (M = 4 years 7 months). These children comprise the first two cohorts of the Stanford Longitudinal Project, being conducted by E. E. Maccoby and C. N. Jacklin, and have been observed periodically throughout infancy and early childhood. Children selected for the present study were those who were attending a nursery school or day-care center in the San Francisco Bay area beginning in September 1977. In all, a total of 43 nursery schools were visited over a period of 11 months. Familial socioeconomic status for the majority of subjects ranged from lower middle to upper middle class. In addition to the longitudinal sample's "target" subjects, two same-sex peers were observed in the experimental situation and were incorporated anonymously into some data analyses.

Materials

A converted mini-mobile home, a 22-foot (6.6-m) Winnebago, served as our "playroom on wheels." An unfurnished and thickly carpeted play area was separated from the driver's area by an opaque vinyl curtain and was illuminated by two side windows. This room measured $7.5 \times 10.5 \times 6$ feet ($2.3 \times 3.1. \times 1.8$ m). A 3×2 foot ($.90 \times .60$ m) one-way observation window was imbedded in a door on the rear wall. Toy materials included a 4-foot (1.2-m) tall inflated Bobo punching doll (presented during only the latter half of the session), a canvas mat stretched across a large inner tube serving as a "jump-o-leen," a medium-sized plastic ball, and a small stuffed pillow.

Equipment utilized by the observers consisted of adjustable interval beeper boxes, earphones, a stopwatch, and standard stenographer notebooks.

Procedure

This study consisted of three types of observations—those occurring during indoor play, outdoor play, and the trailer session. Since only minimal attention will be given to the results of the first two observation domains at this time, their procedure will be discussed only briefly. Each target child was observed during free-play time, that is, when the child had some choice of his or her activities. Behavioral coding took place during three 7-minute intervals each of indoor and outdoor free play, for a total time of 42 minutes. The observers, all female students, were introduced to the class as visitors and remained unobtrusive throughout.

The major body of data was collected in the trailer playroom. Most nursery schools were visited at least twice within 1 week, and the trailer session usually took place on the second day, interspersed among the second day's indoor and outdoor observations. Due to variable nursery schedules, it was impossible to standardize the order of the observation sequence. This was not considered to be a confounding circumstance, however, as no ordering effects were observed in preliminary data.

The procedure for the trailer session was as follows: the target child and two same-sex peers were escorted to the trailer by one of the observers, who remained seated in the playroom throughout the session. The selection of the peer playmates was based on the target child's preference if one existed, otherwise on the teacher's judgement of compatibility. Once inside, the visible observer instructed the triad that they could play any way they liked in this room and explained that while they were playing, she would be doing some work. At this point she began her coding duties, signaling the hidden observer, positioned behind the observation window, to do the same. Efforts at interaction with the visible observer were discouraged, and intervention occurred only when the observer judged the play to be getting too active. In such cases, play resumed after a brief break. There was only one premature termination of a play session. Six minutes after the initiation of the session, the Bobo doll was introduced, and play continued for an additional 6 minutes. At the end of the 12-minute session, a brief quieting period was allowed before the children returned to the classroom.

Coding and Reliability

The observational coding method utilized in the present study by the hidden observer was based on one developed by Clarke-Stewart (1973). This technique utilizes fixed interval units of measurement resulting in tallies of behavioral frequency. The occurrence of any of 14 target behaviors was recorded in a shorthand code by the hidden observer on the left side of a standard stenographer's note pad. A list of these behaviors and their operational definitions is presented in Table 1. Only those behaviors of the partners' that elicited a response from our target subject were recorded in the right-hand column, on the line preceding the response. These partner behaviors, recorded only to provide a context for the target's response, included verbal suggestions and demands and physical assaults. Intervals were demarcated by slashes in the middle of the page. Interval length was set at 6 sec in the trailer and 10 sec in the free-play observations. A behavior was recorded as occurring only once within each interval unless it was interrupted and then resumed within that same period. Also, a rating of activity level was developed on an interval scale of 1 (low activity) to 7 (high activity) for the target child alone. This rating was made at the end of each 6-sec interval and represents the observer's subjective averaging of the energy expenditure accompanying the behaviors in that period. Activity level was used to refer to the vigor of behavior, not just its form, although the two are obviously correlated.

The development of the codes and observer training took place during the 2 months prior to testing. Interjudge agreement was determined from a total of 10 pretest and experimental sessions in which two hidden observers coded for the target child. Final reliabilities, calculated by intraclass correlation, ranged from .94 to .99 (M reliability $r = .98$). Reliabilities were

Table 1 Summary list of coded behaviors

Behavior variable	Observational definition
Playful physical assault	Discrete action consisting of hitting other child with body part or object; grabbing clothing or appendage; pushing; tripping. Facial features of both actor and recipient must convey excitement or positive affect. Accompanying vocalizations of actor must be nonthreatening and verbal response of recipient, nonprohibitive. Outcome must not be accidentally injurious or distressing.
Aggressive physical assault	Includes same motor actions described for playful assault. Distinguished as aggressive on basis of facial features of actor (conveying anger or malice) and recipient (fear, anger, distress). Accompanying vocalizations of actor may include insults and threats, and those of recipient may be prohibitive ("Stop that!") or distressed ("That hurt!"). Outcome may be physically or emotionally distressing.
Physical assault on object	Hitting, biting, kicking, or throwing Bobo doll or trampoline.
Wrestling	Continuous, overall body contact that can take the form of piling on top of one another, tumbling together on the floor, dragging one another down.
Jumping	Jumping or bouncing on trampoline in standing or sitting position; jumping on floor.
Egoistic demanding	Verbal attempt to change the behavior of another child to satisfy one's own desires, in the form of a command (e.g., "Give me that!").
Responsible suggesting	Proposal of rules, activities, and behaviors that contribute to the cooperative functioning of the group (e.g., "Let's take turns.") or an individual.
Taking	Attempt to remove a toy or other object from another's possession through physical force.
Awaits turn	Momentary lull in activity while waiting for a turn to play with a given toy. Used only when the group is taking turns in an orderly, systematic fashion.
Novel play	Uses the toys in ways not usually ascribed to them (i.e., the behaviors are not accounted for by physical assault on object or jumping). Includes riding on Bobo, using the trampoline as a spaceship, and other fantasy activities that do not involve the provided toys.
Social approach to adult	Addresses, questions, approaches, or otherwise tries to initiate interaction with the visible observer.
Observing	Passively watching the behavior of other children or the visible observer; looking out the trailer window; staring into the one-way observation mirror.
Comply/noncomply	Behavioral acceptance or rejection of another's verbal demand or suggestion.
Yield/nonyield	Response to another's playful or aggressive assault (submission/retaliation), or take attempt (relinquishment/retention of object).
Activity level	Subjective averaging of the activity level displayed in the preceding 6-sec (trailer) or 10-sec (indoor/outdoor) interval. Ranges from 1, representing low energy expenditure (sitting, standing, observing for most of the interval with no locomotion), to 7, highly energetic behavior (roughhousing, vigorous running, excited play).

based on final individual behavioral rates averaged over an entire observation session, with the same parameter utilized in all analyses. Although a more microscopic interval-to-interval agreement measure may have been a more desirable index of reliability, it was not feasible due to slight discrepancies in interval length measured by the timing devices and occasional "lags" by coders. Reliability for the 7-point activity scale, also averaged across each of the 10 observation sessions, yielded an intraclass correlation of .98. These high levels of interobserver agreement were maintained through extensive training and frequent monitoring by the principal investigator. Unfortunately, no reliability estimate for the distinction between aggressive and playful assaults is available due to the infrequent occurrence of the former. However, there is indirect evidence that this distinction is viable, since during reliability testing, no two observers ever disagreed on the attribution of a playful physical assault.

A second source of trailer data is a record of selected partner activities, distinct from those instigative behaviors recorded by the hidden observer. This information can be used to provide a baseline picture of the amount of physically arousing behavior occurring in the triad as a whole. A checklist was devised for the visible observer on which she recorded the occurrence of designated behaviors in each 6-sec interval. A category was checked if one or both of the two partners were engaging in the behavior. The level of distractions for this observer was high, so it was necessary to keep this checklist minimally complex. Four behaviors considered to be most indicative of high energy expenditure were used: partner assaults on another child, assaults on objects, jumping, and wrestling. Interjudge reliability was calculated by the addition of a third coder and was determined to be .94, .97, .98, and .94, respectively (M interjudge reliability = .96).

Results

All data analyses were performed on transformations of the raw scores derived by dividing the number of times each behavior was recorded by the total amount of 6-sec intervals in the observation period. Thus, final scores for each variable represent the proportion of intervals in which a given behavior occurred. This transformation was necessary due to discrepancies in the total number of observation intervals for each subject, resulting from occasional termination of the play session by the visible experimenter before the hidden observer had completed her coding duties. Similarly, final ratings of activity level, based on the 7-point scale, represent the target's mean activity level across all intervals for that session. Those measures that were also recorded for the partners were analyzed both separately and in conjunction with the target's scores to yield an overall group measure.

A list of the measures that demonstrated sex differences in occurrence is presented in Table 2. Male targets and their partners were significantly more likely to playfully assault one another, wrestle, and hit Bobo. A combination variable called rough and tumble was derived from adding wrestling and playful assault scores. The incorporation of these scores into a single unit was based on the fact that they both involved bodily contact and

Table 2   Mean and *t*-value comparisons of male and female trailer play
behaviors and activity level

Variable	Sex	M^a	df^b	t
Trailer play behaviors				
Playful physical assault				
Target	Male	5.34	35	2.80**
	Female	1.21		
Partners	Male	6.67	30	3.66***
	Female	1.19		
Aggressive physical assault				
Target	Male	.08	29	1.79
	Female	.00		
Wrestling				
Target	Male	9.01	46	2.36*
	Female	3.49		
Partners	Male	18.10	45	3.37**
	Female	6.06		
Rough and tumble				
Target	Male	14.43	43	3.32**
	Female	4.70		
Partners	Male	24.77	42	4.12***
	Female	7.25		
Physical assault on object				
Target	Male	20.36	48	3.04**
	Female	10.79		
Partners	Male	30.35	47	3.37**
	Female	17.51		
Jumping				
Target	Male	9.21	50	−1.88
	Female	15.16		
Partners	Male	15.00	48	−.39
	Female	16.50		
Egoistic demanding				
Target	Male	2.94	38	1.84
	Female	1.36		
Responsible suggesting				
Target	Male	2.49	32	−3.22**
	Female	5.76		
Await turn in line				
Target	Male	.85	29	−1.99*
	Female	3.00		
Novel play				
Target	Male	17.64	50	−2.20*
	Female	27.78		
Activity level				
Trailer	Male	2.98^c	50	1.99*
	Female	2.60		
Outdoor	Male	2.86	46	.58
	Female	2.75		
Indoor	Male	2.16	45	1.53
	Female	2.02		

[a] Represents frequency (percentage) of behavior in observation period.
[b] Based on separate variance estimates when necessary.
[c] This column represents rating on 1–7 activity level scale.
*$p < .05$. **$p < .01$. ***$p < .001$.

can be considered alternate forms of expression. Note the low frequency and subsequent lack of sex differences in aggressive assaulting. In over 30 hours of total child observation in the trailer, only five instances of clearly aggressive actions were recorded. Aggressive actions were distinguished from playful ones on the basis of their perceived intent to inflict injury, as well as the recipient's perception of the intent. This judgement was based on the facial qualities of both children (as suggested by Blurton-Jones, 1972) and their verbalizations (see Table 1 for elaboration).

Jumping, the final high-energy behavior, was exhibited more often by girls, although the tendency did not reach the .05 level. Female targets, however, were significantly more likely to play with the toys in novel (i.e., nonviolent) ways, suggest responsible rules, and await their turns with the toys in an orderly fashion. Although this latter behavior did not occur very frequently in either sex, it refers to self-generated queuing in front of the Bobo doll or trampoline.

With respect to activity level, information is provided from the indoor and outdoor free-play periods as well as the the trailer session. No sex differences in activity level were demonstrated in either nursery setting. In the trailer, males tended to be somewhat more active, but this difference was of only borderline significance. Activity ratings from both indoor and outdoor free-play settings were significantly and positively correlated with trailer ratings for the sexes combined, indicating internal validity of the 7-point rating scale. When analysis is performed on the sexes separately, indoor activity is significantly predictive of trailer activity, as well as other active trailer behaviors, for males alone. This finding may suggest that females are more influenced by situational constraints imposed by classroom structure and that their individual differences are more likely to become obscured. Correlations of the three activity ratings with energetic behaviors in the trailer are presented in Table 3.

The report of significant sex differences alone often obscures important aspects of behavioral distribution between the sexes. Figures 1 and 2

Table 3 Correlations of activity levels and energetic behaviors for sexes combined and alone

Activity	Activity Indoor	Outdoor	Energetic behaviors Rough and tumble	Playful assaults	Wrestling	Jumping
Trailer						
Both sexes	.39**	.45***	.63***	.51***	.48***	.33**
Males	.37*	.48**	.58***	.51**	.39*	.32
Females	.35	.40	.68***	.30	.67***	.66***
Indoor						
Both sexes		.25	.40**	.34**	.30*	.16
Males		.26	.52***	.39*	.38*	.26
Females		.20	−.15	−.02	−.17	.22
Outdoor						
Both sexes			.35**	.22	.29*	.00
Males			.41**	.24	.34	.02
Females			.20	.16	.17	.02

$*p<.05.$ $**p<.01.$ $***p<.001.$

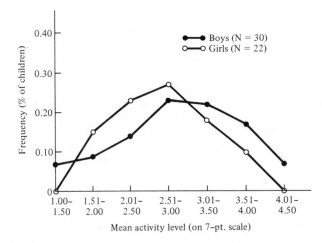

Figure 1   Activity level in triadic play by sex

show distributions of trailer activity level and R&T, respectively, by sex. Both of these behaviors demonstrated a significance level of at least .05, but it can be argued that the data presented in Figure 2 depict a more "meaningful" difference. Figure 1 shows overlapping distributions of activity level with a difference in means of .38, roughly half of a standard deviation. In Figure 2, there is a mean difference in R&T frequency of 9.7%, or just over three-quarters of a standard deviation. More importantly, it becomes apparent that male and female targets displayed identical amounts of R&T in the lowest frequency ranges, although there were differences in the

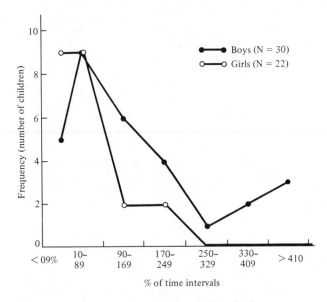

Figure 2   Rough and tumble in triadic play by sex

number of boys and girls who did not R&T at all. Further, there is no overlap between the sexes in the display of R&T in the upper frequency ranges. Similar distributions were evidenced for many of the other behaviors that demonstrated a sex difference, but space limits their presentation.

Within the group of behaviors involved in verbal dominance assertion, rates of suggesting and demanding were positively correlated for girls, $r(20)$ = .51, $p<.01$, but not for boys. For both males and females, attempts to take a toy from another child was correlated with demanding egoistically, $r(28)$ = .51, $p<.004$, and $r(20)$ = .58, $p<.005$, respectively, but not with suggesting. No significant correlations of any of these behaviors were found with any high-energy behavior, with the exception of R&T and take for males alone, $r(28)$ = .49, $p<.005$.

Discussion

The results of this study support the general proposition that given identical environmental situations, girls and boys will react in qualitatively different patterns of play and social interaction. Male sessions were more often characterized by a good deal of exuberant physical contact with one another and with the stimulus toys. The dynamics of the interaction were less likely to involve verbal structuring and were more prone to unrestrained roughhousing. Girls more often attempted to structure the session through self-generated rules and suggestions, and their play was likely to center around novel interactions with the toys. Contact with one another tended to be verbal and not physical for the girls.

Although a small quantitative difference in activity level was demonstrated, it appears to be a by-product of a specific behavioral quality—the increased propensity of males to engage in R&T play. This conclusion is based on the null findings on activity level in both nursery school settings and on the fact that when it comes to other energetic behaviors like jumping on the trampoline, girls jumped as frequently and vigorously as boys. Recent work by Tauber (Note 3) has also failed to find a sex difference in activity level when intrinsic interest in available play options is controlled.

Since activity in both nursery settings correlated strongly with R&T for males but not females, this suggests that our trailer situation elicits a kind of play in males that is similar to their free-play activities. As mentioned, males seem to stimulate activity in other males across a variety of species and age groups. However, this observation does not quite account for our findings, since even in nursery school play tends to be sex-segregated (Serbin, Tonick, & Sternglanz, 1977), and there we observed no difference. It appears to be critical that the mobile playroom was designed to elicit roughhousing and that this body contact play is more likely to be witnessed in male groups. The highly active boy on the playground is the more active in the trailer, since it was designed, so to speak, with him in mind. Girls' activity levels in nursery school situations, however, are not so clearly reflected, since the most active girl in the playroom was playing in ways that are qualitatively different from typical female patterns in nursery school.

Turning next to the complex issue of the relationship between R&T and aggression, the perspective that R&T is conducive to social development is compatible with work by Emmerich (1964) and Yarrow and Waxler (1976), who have reported prosocial correlates of aggression in young children. R&T is an activity done with consenting, or at least tolerant, partners, and it necessitates a good deal of cooperation. Children, particularly same-sex partners, seem to have no trouble discriminating mock fighting from more threatening exchanges. A problem arises when adult observers misinterpret children's interactions by attending to the behavior alone and not the context in which it is performed. Thus, the high interjudge validities often reported in studies of childhood aggression may be illusory correlations. If R&T is considered to be prosocial interaction, this may partially account for the fact that the search for cross-situational and developmental predictors of aggression has been a frustrating endeavor.

Other investigators have also reported that individual differences in aggressiveness do not predict R&T (Blurton-Jones, 1972) or agonistic dominance (Strayer, 1977) within individuals. However the relationship between these factors may emerge indirectly. First, there is a greater chance of accidental injury in a R&T interaction to the physically smaller of the contenders, which may have repercussions for subsequent dominance hierarchy formation. Also, given the highly aroused state involved in R&T play, accidental mishaps may precede rapid escalations to angry physical retaliation. From a developmental perspective, R&T provides experience in the outcomes—physical, instrumental, and affective—of a turbulent physical exchange. Since young males engage in these behaviors more often, they may have more experiential access to information concerning social interactions that may become seriously aggressive in subsequent years. Further, they may also acquire increased sensitivity to the salience of threatening aspects of environmental stimuli. These factors in turn may contribute to the consistent and cross-cultural sex differences in adult aggression.

Studies with rhesus monkeys have demonstrated that juvenile males are more likely to initiate R&T play than females, and they direct their initiations mainly toward other males. Further, males are more likely to respond to another male's play bid than to a female's. Females, however, do not discriminate either their play initiations or responses to either sex (Suomi, 1977). With respect to human children in the present study, although there are large individual differences within sexes, and some groups of girls played as roughly as some male groups, it must be stressed that to have a successful R&T interaction there must be two consenting partners. It is suggested that an interaction of social and biological factors act to sensitize males to differential emission rates of interpersonal signals and possibly differential readiness to respond to these cues in certain ways. That is, males may not only emit more cues that are invitations to roughhouse but may be more likely to respond to such signals as playful instigations, whereas females might perceive the identical cue as threatening. For example, the positive relationship between attempts to take a toy from another child and R&T play for males alone may suggest that this behavior can serve as a physical instigation to roughhouse. In female groups, where no such relationship was observed, taking may be more accurately regarded as a potentially threatening dominance bid than as an invitation to social interaction. The concept of behavioral compatibility as an instrument for maintaining sex segregation even in preschool children may be regarded as a function of this signal-response "meshing."

REFERENCE NOTES

1. Hamburg, D. A., & van Lawick-Goodall, J. *Factors mediating development of aggressive behavior in chimpanzees and humans.* Unpublished manuscript, Stanford University School of Medicine, 1977.
2. Yarrow, L. J., Rubenstein, J. F., & Pedersen, F. A. *Dimensions of early stimulation: Differential effects on infant development.* Paper presented at the meeting of the Society for Research in Child Development, Minneapolis, Minnesota, April 1971.
3. Tauber, M. *Girls' physically active play and parental behavior.* Paper presented at the meeting of the Society for Research in Child Development, San Francisco, March 1979.

REFERENCES

BLURTON-JONES, N. Categories of child-child interaction. In N. B. Jones (Ed.), *Ethological studies of child behavior.* London, England: Cambridge University Press, 1972.

CLARKE-STEWART, A. Interactions between mothers and their young children: Characteristics and consequences. *Monographs of the Society for Research in Child Development,* 1973, *38*(6–7, Serial No. 153).

DOLHINOW, P., & BISHOP, N. The development of motor skills and social relationships among primates through play. In P. Dolhinow (Ed.), *Primate patterns.* New York: Holt, Rinehart & Winston, 1972.

EMMERICH, W. Continuity and stability in early social development. *Child Development,* 1964, *35*, 311–332.

HALVERSON, C. F., & WALDROP, M. F. The relations of mechanically recorded activity level to varieties of preschool play behavior. *Child Development,* 1973, *44*, 678–681.

HARLOW, H. F., & HARLOW, M. K. The affectional systems. In A. M. Schrier, H. F. Harlow, & F. Stollitz (Eds.), *The behavior of non-human primates* (Vol. 2). New York: Academic Press, 1965.

HARTUP, W. W. Aggression in childhood: Developmental perspectives. *American Psychologist,* 1974, *29*, 336–341.

JACKLIN, C. N., & MACCOBY, E. E. Social behavior at 33 months in same sex and mixed sex dyads. *Child Development,* 1978, *49*, 552–569.

LANGLOIS, J. H., GOTTFRIED, N. W., & SEAY, B. The influence of sex of peer on the social behavior of preschool children. *Developmental Psychology,* 1973, *8*, 93–98.

MACCOBY, E. E., & JACKLIN, C. N. *The psychology of sex differences.* Stanford, Calif.: Stanford University Press, 1974.

MITCHELL, G., & BRANDT, E. M. Behavioral differences related to experience of mother and sex of infant in the rhesus monkey. *Developmental Psychology,* 1970, *3*, 149.

PATTERSON, G. R., LITTMAN, R. A., & BRICKNER, W. Assertive behavior in children: A step toward a theory of aggression. *Monographs of the Society for Research in Child Development,* 1967, *32*(5, Serial No. 113).

SERBIN, L. A., TONICK, I. J., & STERNGLANZ, S. H. Shaping cooperative cross-sex play. *Child Development,* 1977, *48*, 924–929.

SMITH, C., & LLOYD, B. Maternal behavior and perceived sex of infant: Revisited. *Child Development,* 1978, *49*, 1263–1265.

STRAYER, J. Social conflict and peer-group status. In F. F. Strayer (Ed.), *Ethological perspectives on preschool social organization.* Memo de recherche Department of Psychology, University of Quebec, Canada, April 1977.

SUOMI, S. J. Development of attachment and other social behaviors in rhesus monkeys. In T. Alloway, P. Pliner, & L. Kranes (Eds.), *Attachment behavior* (Vol. 3). New York: Plenum Press, 1977.

WHITING, B., & EDWARDS, C. A cross-cultural analysis of sex differences in the behavior of children aged three through eleven. *Journal of Social Psychology,* 1973, *91*, 177–188.

YARROW, L. J., & WAXLER, C. Z. Dimensions and correlations of prosocial behavior in young children. *Child Development,* 1976, *47*, 118–125.

14

Sex Differences in Mathematical Reasoning Ability
More Facts

Camilla Persson Benbow and Julian C. Stanley

Almost 40,000 selected seventh-grade students from the Middle Atlantic region of the United States took the College Board Scholastic Aptitude Test as part of the Johns Hopkins regional talent search in 1980, 1981, and 1982. A separate nationwide talent search was conducted in which any student under age 13 who was willing to take the test was eligible. The results obtained by both procedures establish that by age 13 a large sex difference in mathematical reasoning ability exists and that it is especially pronounced at the high end of the distribution: among students who scored ≥ 700, boys outnumbered girls 13 to 1. Some hypothesized explanations of such differences were not supported by the data.

In 1980 we reported large sex differences in mean scores on a test of mathematical reasoning ability for 9927 mathematically talented seventh and eighth graders who entered the Johns Hopkins regional talent search from 1972 through 1979 (1, 2). One prediction from those results was that there would be a preponderance of males at the high end of the distribution of mathematical reasoning ability. In this report we investigate sex differences at the highest levels of that ability. New groups of students under age 13 with exceptional mathematical aptitude were identified by means of two separate procedures. In the first, the John Hopkins regional talent searches in 1980, 1981, and 1982 (3), 39,820 seventh graders from the Middle Atlantic region of the United States who were selected for high intellectual ability were given the College Board Scholastic Apitude Test (SAT). In the second, a nationwide talent search was conducted for which any student under 13 years of age who was willing to take the SAT was eligible. The results of both procedures substantiated our prediction that before age 13 far more males than females would score extremely high on SAT–M, the mathematical part of SAT.

The test items of SAT–M require numerical judgment, relational thinking, or insightful and logical reasoning. This test is designed to measure the developed mathematical reasoning ability of 11th and 12th graders *(4)*. Most students in our study were in the middle of the seventh grade. Few had had formal opportunities to study algebra and beyond *(5, 6)*. Our rationale is that most of these students were unfamiliar with mathematics from algebra onward, and that most who scored high did so because of extraordinary reasoning ability *(7)*.

In 1980, 1981, and 1982, as in the earlier study *(1)*, participants in the John Hopkins talent search were seventh graders, or boys and girls of typical seventh-grade age in a higher grade, in the Middle Atlantic area. Before 1980, applicants had been required to be in the top 3 percent nationally on the mathematics section of any standardized achievement test. Beginning in 1980, students in the top 3 percent in verbal or overall intellectual ability were also eligible. During that and the next 2 years 19,883 boys and 19,937 girls applied and were tested. Even though this sample was more general and had equal representation by sex, the mean sex difference on SAT–M remained constant at 30 points favoring males (males' $\overline{X} = 416$, S.D. $= 87$; females' $\overline{X} = 386$, S.D. $= 74$; $t = 37$; $P > 0.001$). No important difference in verbal ability as measured by SAT–V was found (males' $\overline{X} = 367$, females' $\overline{X} = 365$).

The major point, however, is not the mean difference in SAT–M scores but the ratios of boys to girls among the high scorers (Table 1). The ratio of boys to girls scoring above the mean of talent-search males was 1.5:1. The ratio among those who scored ≥ 500 (493 was the mean of 1981–82 college-bound 12th-grade males) was 2.1:1. Among those who scored ≥ 600 (600 was the 79th percentile of the 12th-grade males) the ratio was 4.1:1. These ratios are similar to those previously reported *(1)* but are derived from a broader and much larger data base.

Scoring 700 or more on the SAT–M before age 13 is rare. We estimate that students who reach this criterion (the 95th percentile of college-bound 12th-grade males) before their 13th birthday represent the top one in 10,000 of their age group. It was because of their rarity that the nationwide talent search was created in November 1980 in order to locate such students who were born after 1967 and facilitate their education *(8)*. In that talent search applicants could take the SAT at any time and place at which it was administered by the Educational Testing Service or through one of five regional talent searches that cover the United States *(9)*. Extensive nationwide efforts were made to inform school personnel and parents about our search. The new procedure (unrestricted by geography or previous ability) was successful in obtaining a large national sample of this exceedingly rare population. As of September 1983, the number of such boys identified was 260 and the number of girls 20, a ratio of 13.0:1 *(10)*. This ratio is remarkable in view of the fact that the available evidence suggests there was essentially equal participation of boys and girls in the talent searches.

The total number of students tested in the Johns Hopkins regional annual talent searches and reported so far is 49,747 (9,927 in the initial study and 39,820 in the present study). Preliminary reports from the 1983 talent search based on some 15,000 cases yield essentially identical results. In the ten Middle Atlantic regional talent searches from 1972 through 1983 we have therefore tested about 65,000 students. It is abundantly clear that

Table 1 Number of high scorers on SAT—M among selected
seventh graders—19.883 boys and 19,937 girls—tested in
the Johns Hopkins regional talent search in 1980, 1981,
and 1982, and of scorers of ≥ 700 prior to age 13 in the
national search (9).

Score	Number	Percent	Ratio of boys to girls
Johns Hopkins regional search			
420 or more*			
Boys	9119	45.9	1.5:1
Girls	6220	31.2	
500 or more			
Boys	3618	18.2	2.1:1
Girls	1707	8.6	
600 or more			
Boys	648	3.3	4.1:1
Girls	158	0.8	
National search In Johns Hopkins talent search region			
700 or more			
Boys	113	†	12.6:1
Girls	9	†	
Outside Johns Hopkins talent search region			
700 or more			
Boys	147	†	13.4:1
Girls	11	†	

*Mean score of the boys was 416. The highest possible score is 800.
†Total number tested is unknown (9).

far more boys than girls (chiefly 12-year-olds) scored in the highest ranges
on SAT–M, even though girls were matched with boys by intellectual ability, age, grade, and voluntary participation. In the original study (1) students were required to meet a qualifying mathematics criterion. Since we
observed the same sex difference then as now, the current results cannot
be explained solely on the grounds that the girls may have qualified by the
verbal criterion. Moreover, if that were the case, we should expect the girls
to have scored higher than the boys on SAT–V. They did not.

Several "environmental" hypotheses have been proposed to account
for sex differences in mathematical ability. Fox *et al.* and Meece *et al.* (11)
have found support for a social-reinforcement hypothesis which, in essence,
states that sex-related differences in mathematical achievement are due to
differences in social conditioning and expectations for boys and girls. The
validity of this hypothesis has been evaluated for the population we studied
earlier (1) and for a subsample of the students in this study. Substantial
differences between boys' and girls' attitudes or backgrounds were not found
(5, 6, 12). Admittedly, some of the measures used were broadly defined
and may not have been able to detect subtle social influences that affect a
child from birth. But it is not obvious how social conditioning could affect
mathematical reasoning ability so adversely and significantly, yet have little
detectable effect on stated interest in mathematics, the taking of mathe-

matics courses during the high school years before the SAT's are normally taken, and mathematics-course grades *(5,6)*.

An alternative hypothesis, that sex differences in mathematical reasoning ability arise mainly from differential course-taking *(13)*, was also not validated, either by the data in our 1980 study *(1)* or by the data in the present study. In both studies the boys and girls were shown to have had similar formal training in mathematics *(5, 6)*.

It is also of interest that sex differences in mean SAT–M scores observed in our early talent searches became only slightly larger during high school. In the selected subsample of participants studied, males improved their scores an average of 10 points more than females (the mean difference went from 40 to 50 points). They also increased their scores on the SAT–V by at least 10 points more than females *(6)*. Previously, other researchers have postulated that profound differences in socialization during adolescence caused the well-documented sex differences in 11th- and 12th-grade SAT–M scores *(11)*, but that idea is not supported in our data. For socialization to account for our results, it would seem necessary to postulate (ad hoc) that chiefly early socialization pressures significantly influence the sex difference in SAT–M scores—that is, that the intensive social pressures during adolescence have little such effect.

It is important to emphasize that we are dealing with intellectually highly able students and that these findings may not generalize to average students. Moreover, these results are of course not generalizable to particular individuals. Finally, it should be noted that the boys' SAT–M scores had a larger variance than the girls'. This is obviously related to the fact that more mathematically talented boys than girls were found *(14)*. Nonetheless, the environmental hypotheses outlined above attempt to explain mean differences, not differences in variability. Thus, even if one concludes that our findings result primarily from greater male variability, one must still explain why.

Our principal conclusion is that males dominate the highest ranges of mathematical reasoning ability before they enter adolescence. Reasons for this sex difference are unclear *(15)*.

REFERENCES AND NOTES

1. C. BENBOW AND J. STANLEY, *Science* **210,** 1262 (1980).
2. Also see letters by C. Tomizuka and S. Tobias; E. Stage and R. Karplus; S. Chipman; E. Egelman *et al.;* D. Moran; E. Luchins and A. Luchins; A. Kelly; C. Benbow and J. Stanley, *ibid.* **212,** 114 (1981).
3. The Johns Hopkins Center for the Advancement of Academically Talented Youth (CTY) conducts talent searches during January in Delaware, the District of Columbia, Maryland, New Jersey (added in 1980), Pennsylvania, Virginia, and West Virginia. In 1983 coverage expanded northeast to include Connecticut, Maine, Massachusetts, New Hampshire, Rhode Island, and Vermont.
4. T. DONLON AND W. ANGOFF, in *The College Board Admissions Testing Program,* W. Angoff, Ed. (College Board, Princeton, N.J., 1971), pp. 24–25; S. Messick and A. Jungeblut, *Psychol. Bull.* **89,** 191 (1982).
5. C. BENBOW AND J. STANLEY, *Gifted Child Q.* **26,** 82 (1982).
6. ———, *Am. Educ. Res. J.* **19,** 598 (1982).
7. We have found that among the top 10 percent of these students (who are eligible for our

fast-paced summer programs in mathematics) a majority do not know even first-year algebra well.

8. J. STANLEY, "Searches under way for youths *exceptionally* talented mathematically or verbally," *Roeper Rev.*, in press.

9. The regional talent searches are conducted by Johns Hopkins (begun in 1972), Duke (1981), Arizona State-Tempe (1981), Northwestern (1982), and the University of Denver (1982). Because there was no logical way to separate students who entered through the regional programs from those who entered through the national channel, results were combined. Most students fit into both categories but at different time points, since the SAT could be taken more than once to qualify or could be retaken in the regional talent search programs. The SAT is not administered by the Educational Testing Service between June and October or November of each year. Therefore, entrants who had passed their 13th birthday before taking the test were included if they scored 10 additional points for each excess month or a fraction of a month.

10. There is a remarkably high incidence of left-handedness or ambidexterity (20 percent), immune disorders (55 percent), and myopia (55 percent) in this group (manuscript in preparation).

11. L. FOX, D. TOBIN, L. BRODY, in *Sex-Related Differences in Cognitive Functioning*, M. Wittig and A. Petersen, Eds. (Academic Press, New York, 1979); J. Meece, J. Parsons, C. Kaczala, S. Goff, R. Futterman, *Psychol. Bull.* **91,** 324 (1982).

12. L. FOX, L. BRODY, D. TOBIN, *The Study of Social Processes that Inhibit or Enhance the Development of Competence and Interest in Mathematics Among Highly Able Young Women* (National Institute of Education, Washington, D.C., 1982): C. Benbow and J. Stanley, in *Women in Science*, M. Steinkamp and M. Maehr, Eds. (JAI Press, Greenwich, Conn.; in press); L. Fox, C. Benbow, S. Perkins, in *Academic Precocity*, C. Benbow and J. Stanley, Eds. (Johns Hopkins Univ. Press, Baltimore, 1983).

13. For example, E. Fennema and J. Sherman, *Am. Educ. Res. J.* **14,** 51 (1977).

14. Why boys are generally more variable has been addressed by H. Eysenck and L. Kamin [*The Intelligence Controversy* (Wiley, New York, 1981)] and others.

15. For possible endogenous influences see, for example, R. Goy and B. McEwen, *Sexual Differentiation of the Brain* (MIT Press, Cambridge, Mass., 1980); J. Levy, *The Sciences* **21** (No. 3), 20 (1981); T. Bouchard and M. McGue, *Science* **212,** 1055 (1981). D. Hier and W. Crawley, Jr., *N. Eng. J. Med.* **306,** 1202 (1982); C. De Lacoste-Utamsing and R. Holloway, *Science* **216,** 1431 (1982); L. Harris, in *Asymmetrical Function of the Brain*, M. Kinsbourne, Ed. (Cambridge Univ. Press, London, 1978); M. McGee *Psychol. Bull.* **86,** 1979); S. Witelsen, *Science* **193,** 425 (1976); J. McGlone, *Behav. Brain Sci.* **3,** 215 (1980); D. McGuiness, *Hum. Nat.* **2** (No. 2), 82 (1979); R. Meisel and I. Ward, *Science* **213,** 239 (1981); F. Naftolin, *ibid.* **211,** 1263 (1981); A. Ehrhardt and H. Meyer-Bahlburg, *ibid.*, p. 1312; J. Inglis and J. Lawson, *ibid.*, **212,** 693 (1981); M. Wittig and A. Petersen, Eds., *Sex-Related Differences in Cognitive Functioning* (Academic Press, New York, 1979).

16. We thank K. Alexander, L. Barnett, R. Benbow, R. Gordon, P. Hines, J. Minor, B. Person, B. Polkes, D. Powers, B. Stanley, Z. Usiskin, and P. Zak. This study was supported by grants from the Spencer and Donner Foundations.

PART V

Growing Up Female

All societies structure the rearing of children and the social experiences of childhood in accordance with their values and their beliefs and attitudes about what constitutes a good citizen and how people should live their lives. Thus it has traditionally been assumed that girls will mature to become wives and mothers, and boys to become workers and economic providers. This assumption of the desirability of different outcomes for males and females has led to differential treatment from birth, first by family, later by school and the other institutions of society.

In recent years, the socialization of girls and its effects on their education, their aspirations, their achievements, and their self-concepts, as well as their status and the evaluation of them in society, have come under close scrutiny by researchers and by feminist theorists. Styles and practices of childrearing and the availability of options to young women have been identified as profoundly influencing their subsequent lives, their mental health, and their happiness.

The gender stereotyping of social and work roles and the prescription for almost all females of domestic, expressive, and nurturant roles have resulted in a waste of female potential. For example, Stanford psychologist Lewis Terman's classic study of gifted children showed that the girls in the sample were more gifted artistically and that the seven most talented writers were girls. But when these gifted children grew up, all the eminent artists and writers among them were men. Only 11 percent of the women were in professions, mostly teaching, whereas nearly half the men were professionals in high-level occupations.

Thus the differential socialization of girls and boys has important determinants for their lives. First, it constrains them by restricting the range of choices they have for living their lives. Second, since the role of provider conveys power on him who is in it, that women rarely hold that role assures that they will have less power than men have. And third, by a negative halo effect, women are inevitably seen as less valuable, and their work, their talents, their customs, and the whole of what makes the female style are trivialized. Too, when it is found that women and men differ in some way, the male behavior or characteristic is taken as the norm, the standard, whereby the way of the female can only appear as lesser and deviant.

In "Woman's Place in Man's Life Cycle," Carol Gilligan explores just such an effect in her analysis of life cycle theories in psychology. "The fascination with point of view and the corresponding recognition of the relativity of truth . . . begin to infuse our scientific understanding as well when we begin to notice how accustomed we have become to seeing life through men's eyes." Freud's theory of psychosexual development is the most striking example of this. But Gilligan shows how contemporary theorists view the world from a male vantage point. Both Erik Erikson, whose psychosocial stages trace development from infancy to old age, and Lawrence Kohlberg, who contributed a model for stages of moral development, took the male as the prototype. For them, when the female could not fit into the system, or when she appeared to be different from the model's prediction, her performance was seen as less mature.

Drawing on literary as well as psychological sources, Gilligan shows how such influential theories have failed to account for the life experience of women. Their evaluative bias has promoted a concern with such male values as autonomy and achievement, to the neglect of such female values as attachment and intimacy. Gilligan urges that more systematic attention to women's lives and the integration of these concerns will help to balance our conceptions of human development.

Attention to the experience of growing up female has focused largely on white populations, neglecting other groups whose young lives might be different from those in the mainstream culture. The socialization of black children, for example, is different from that of white children in our society because of differences in sociocultural traditions, values, and beliefs, as well as because of economic conditions and the effects of racial discrimination. Young black people suffer more from unemployment, low wages, lack of education, and, in the case of girls, higher rates of teenage pregnancy than their white peers. In the next paper in this section, Elsie J. Smith reviews the educational, career, and psychological literature dealing with the black female adolescent.

Although the literature on young black women is not large, the author is able to develop several conclusions, some of which are at variance with widely held beliefs about the experience of daughters in black families. For example, available studies do not support the "farmer's daughter" effect, whereby girls are thought to have a favored position in the family and are encouraged to aspire to higher achievement in education and careers than are their brothers. Black high school girls, however, do have higher scholastic achievement than black males, and they also have higher aspirations than both black males and white females.

Anticipating the world of work, young black women are motivated more by economic reality factors than by wishes for self-fulfillment, more characteristic of young white women. Their aspirations are affected by sex-role stereotyping, and, like their white counterparts, they tend to make career choices in traditional woman-associated occupations. On the average, though, black females tend to have positive self-concepts and are consistently reported to have a low fear of success.

Along the northern fringe of the Kalahari Desert in southern Africa lives a nomadic group called the !Kung, who have had considerable attention from anthropologists as their numbers dwindle and their lifestyle gives way to agrarian settlements. With no written language, the !Kung are eloquent storytellers. Marjorie Shostak, in "Memories of a !Kung Girlhood," relates the autobiographical narrative of Nisa, who tells of her life as child, young woman, and wife. Most striking are the similarities between her feelings and experiences and those of young girls in our own culture: her jealousy when her baby brother took her place at her mother's breast, her rivalrous spats with him as he got older, her conflicts with her mother, and the deep feelings of family love and solidarity; then her developing maturity, her introduction to sex, her struggle for independence from marriage, and her ambivalence, finally turning to love, in the role of wife. Reading Nisa's story, we are impressed again by the basic commonalities among members of the human community, across vastly different cultures.

Across the world from the Kalahari Desert is Smith College in Massachusetts. A private, elite institution for women, its students were chosen by Barbara Grizzuti Harrison to help illuminate for today's society the old question of "What Do Women Want?"—the title of the essay, itself an investigation of feminism and its future as perceived by this select and thoughtful group.

It would be difficult to find a segment of the population more affected by feminism and the women's movement than these young women at Smith. All are intelligent, highly motivated, achievement-oriented. In the class of 1960, 61 percent of all graduates said they wished to be homemakers. In the class of 1970, 15 percent chose that vocation. By 1980, fewer than 1 percent of the graduates chose domesticity. Yet these women want to have marriage and motherhood, too. "Having it all" seems to be the goal—yet how to do that eludes them, when they consider the demands of careers in law, medicine, and international banking. Discussing the validity of women's studies on campus, lesbian separatism, the effects of the absence of male students, and new visions of the family, these young women take us into their hopes and fantasies for the future and tell us, though variously, what it is that women want.

During the last decade, researchers have become more and more aware of and interested in the development of young women in our society. No longer are the different tracks that promote one kind of outcome for girls and another for boys taken for granted. While the limitations of those tracks are now widely recognized, they are still the subject of examination, since it is necessary to understand the problem before the problem itself can be addressed and strategies developed to mitigate its effects. Awareness of the limitations and degradations that have characterized scenarios for the lives of girls and women in our society may give rise to feelings of anger and regret for potential and promise unfulfilled. But it also awakens us to the possibility of new ways of being, of a better set of life chances with broader horizons for ourselves and our daughters.

15

Woman's Place in Man's Life Cycle

Carol Gilligan

Drawing on literary and psychological sources, Carol Gilligan documents the way in which theories of the life cycle, by taking for their model the lives of men, have failed to account for the experience of women. Arguing that this bias has promoted a concern with autonomy and achievement at the expense of attachment and intimacy, she suggests that systematic attention to women's lives, in both theory and research, will allow an integration of these concerns into a more balanced conception of human development.

In the second act of *The Cherry Orchard,* Lopakhin, the young merchant, describes his life of hard work and success. Failing to convince Madame Ranevskaya to cut down the cherry orchard to save her estate, he will go on, in the next act, to buy it himself. He is the self-made man, who, in purchasing "the estate where grandfather and father were slaves," seeks to eradicate the "awkward, unhappy life" of the past, replacing the cherry orchard with summer cottages where coming generations "will see a new life" (Act III). Elaborating this developmental vision, he describes the image of man that underlies and supports this activity: "At times when I can't go to sleep, I think: Lord, thou gavest us immense forests, unbounded fields and the widest horizons, and living in the midst of them we should indeed be giants." At which point, Madame Ranevskaya interrupts him, saying, "You feel the need for giants—They are good only in fairy tales, anywhere else they only frighten us" (Act II).

Conceptions of the life cycle represent attempts to order and make coherent the unfolding experiences and perceptions, the changing wishes and realities of everyday life. But the truth of such conceptions depends in part on the position of the observer. The brief excerpt from Chekhov's play (1904/1956) suggests that when the observer is a woman, the truth may be of a different sort. This discrepancy in judgment between men and women is the center of my consideration.

This essay traces the extent to which psychological theories of human development, theories that have informed both educational philosophy and

"Woman's Place in Man's Life Cycle" by Carol Gilligan in the *Harvard Educational Review,* 1979, 49, 4, 431–446. Copyright © 1979 by the President and Fellows of Harvard College. Reprinted by permission.

classroom practice, have enshrined a view of human life similar to Lopak-hin's while dismissing the ironic commentary in which Chekhov embeds this view. The specific issue I address is that of sex differences, and my focus is on the observation and assessment of sex differences by life-cycle theorists. In talking about sex differences, however, I risk the criticism which such generalization invariably invites. As Virginia Woolf said, when embarking on a similar endeavor: "When a subject is highly controversial—and any question about sex is that—one cannot hope to tell the truth. One can only show how one came to hold whatever opinion one does hold" (1929, p. 4).

At a time when efforts are being made to eradicate discrimination between the sexes in the search for equality and justice, the differences between the sexes are being rediscovered in the social sciences. This discovery occurs when theories formerly considered to be sexually neutral in their scientific objectivity are found instead to reflect a consistent observational and evaluative bias. Then the presumed neutrality of science, like that of language itself, gives way to the recognition that the categories of knowledge are human constructions. The fascination with point of view and the corresponding recognition of the relativity of truth that has informed the fiction of the twentieth century begin to infuse our scientific understanding as well when we begin to notice how accustomed we have become to seeing life through men's eyes.

A recent discovery of this sort pertains to the apparently innocent classic by Strunk and White (1959), *The Elements of Style.* The Supreme Court ruling on the subject of discrimination in classroom texts led one teacher of English to notice that the elementary rules of English usage were being taught through examples which counterposed the birth of Napoleon, the writings of Coleridge, and statements such as, "He was an interesting talker, a man who had traveled all over the world and lived in half a dozen countries" (p. 7) with "Well, Susan, this is a fine mess you are in" (p.3) or, less drastically, "He saw a woman, accompanied by two children, walking slowly down the road" (p. 8).

Psychological theorists have fallen as innocently as Strunk and White into the same observational bias. Implicitly adopting the male life as the norm, they have tried to fashion women out of a masculine cloth. It all goes back, of course, to Adam and Eve, a story which shows, among other things, that, if you make a woman out of a man you are bound to get into trouble. In the life cycle, as in the Garden of Eden, it is the woman who has been the deviant.

The penchant of developmental theorists to project a masculine image, and one that appears frightening to women, goes back at least to Freud (1905 / 1961), who built his theory of psychosexual development around the experiences of the male child that culminate in the Oedipus complex. In the 1920s, Freud struggled to resolve the contradictions posed for his theory by the different configuration of female sexuality and the different dynamics of the young girl's early family relationships. After trying to fit women into his masculine conception, seeing them as envying that which they missed, he came instead to acknowledge, in the strength and persistence of women's pre-Oedipal attachments to their mothers, a developmental difference. However, he considered this difference in women's development to be responsible for what he saw as women's developmental failure.

Deprived by nature of the impetus for a clear-cut Oedipal resolution, women's superego, the heir to the Oedipus complex, consequently was compromised. It was never, Freud observed, "so inexorable, so impersonal, so independent of its emotional origins as we require it to be in men" (1925 / 1961, p. 257). From this observation of difference, "that for women the level of what is ethically normal is different from what it is in men" (p. 257), Freud concluded that "women have less sense of justice than men, that they are less ready to submit to the great exigencies of life, that they are more often influenced in their judgments by feelings of affection and hostility" (pp. 257–258).

Chodorow (1974, 1978) addresses this evaluative bias in the assessment of sex differences in her attempt to account for "the reproduction within each generation of certain general and nearly universal differences that characterize masculine and feminine personality and roles" (1974, p. 43). Writing from a psychoanalytic perspective, she attributes these continuing differences between the sexes not to anatomy but rather to "the fact that women, universally, are largely responsible for early child care and for (at least) later female socialization" (1974, p. 43). Because this early social environment differs for and is experienced differently by male and female children, basic sex differences recur in personality development. As a result, "in any given society, feminine personality comes to define itself in relation and connection to other people more than masculine personality does. (In psychoanalytic terms, women are less individuated than men; they have more flexible ego boundaries.)" (1974, p. 44)

In her analysis Chodorow relies primarily on Stoller's research on the development of gender identity and gender-identity disturbances. Stoller's work indicates that male and female identity, the unchanging core of personality formation, is "with rare exception firmly and irreversibly established for both sexes by the time a child is around three" (Chodorow, 1978, p. 150). Given that for both sexes the primary caretaker in the first three years of life is typically female, the interpersonal dynamics of gender identity formation are different for boys and girls. Female identity formation takes place in a context of ongoing relationship as "mothers tend to experience their daughters as more like, and continous with, themselves. Correspondingly, girls tend to remain part of the dyadic primary mother-child relationship itself. This means that a girl continues to experience herself as involved in issues of merging and separation, and in an attachment characterized by primary identification and the fusion of identification and object choice" (1978, p. 166).

In contrast, "mothers experience their sons as a male opposite" and, as a result, "boys are likely to have been pushed out of the preoedipal relationship and to have had to curtail their primary love and sense of empathic tie with their mother" (1978, p. 166). Consequently, boys' development entails a "more emphatic individuation and a more defensive firming of ego boundaries." For boys, but not for girls, "issues of differentiation have become intertwined with sexual issues" (1978, p. 167).

Thus Chodorow refutes the masculine bias of psychoanalytic theory, claiming that the existence of sex differences in the early experiences of individuation and relationship "does not mean that women have 'weaker ego boundaries' than men or are more prone to psychosis" (1978, p. 167). What it means instead is that "the earliest mode of individuation, the primary construction of the ego and its inner object-world, the earliest conflicts and the earliest unconscious definitions of self, the earliest threats to individuation, and the earliest anxieties which call up defenses, all differ for boys and girls because of differences in the character of the early mother-child relationship for each" (1978, p. 167). Because of these differences, "girls emerge from this period with a basis for 'empathy' built into their primary definition of self in a way that boys do not" (1978, p. 167). Chodorow thus replaces Freud's negative and derivative description of female psychology with a more positive and direct account of her own:

> Girls emerge with a stronger basis for experiencing another's needs and feelings as one's own (or of thinking that one is so experiencing another's needs and feelings). Furthermore, girls do not define themselves in terms of the denial of preoedipal relational modes to the same extent as do boys. Therefore, regression to these modes tends not to feel as much a basic threat to their ego. From very early, then, because they are parented by a person of the same gender . . . girls come to experience themselves as less differentiated than boys, as more continuous with and related to the external object world, and as differently oriented to their inner object-world as well. (1978, p. 167)

Consequently, "issues of dependency, in particular, are handled and experienced differently by men and women" (Chodorow, 1974, p. 44). For boys and men, separation and individuation are critically tied to gender identity since separation from the mother is essential for the development of masculinity. "For girls and women, by contrast, issues of femininity or feminine identity are not problematic in the same way" (1974, p. 44); they do not depend on the achievement of separation from the mother or on the progress of individuation. Since, in Chodorow's analysis, masculinity is defined through separation while femininity is defined through attachment, male gender identity will be threatened by intimacy while female gender identity will be threatened by individuation. Thus males will tend to have difficulty with relationships while females will tend to have problems with separation. The quality of embeddedness in social interaction and personal relationships that characterizes women's lives in contrast to men's, however, becomes not only a descriptive difference but also a developmental liability when the milestones of childhood and adolescent development are described by markers of increasing separation. Then women's failure to separate becomes by definition a failure to develop.

The sex differences in personality formation that Chodorow delineates in her analysis of early childhood relationships as well as the bias she points out in the evaluation of these differences, reappear in the middle childhood years in the studies of children's games. Children's games have been considered by Mead (1934) and Piaget (1932/1965) as the crucible of social development during the school years. In games children learn to take the role of the other and come to see themselves through another's eyes. In games they learn respect for rules and come to understand the ways rules can be made and changed.

Lever (1976), considering the peer group to be the agent of socialization during the elementary school years and play to be a major activity of socialization at that time, set out to discover whether there were sex differences in the games that children play. Studying 181 fifth-grade, white, middle-class, Connecticut children, ages 10 and 11, she observed the organization and structure of their playtime activities. She watched the children as they played during the school recess, lunch, and in physical education class, and, in addition, kept diaries of their accounts as to how they spent their out-of-school time.

From this study, Lever reports the following sex differences: boys play more out of doors than girls do; boys more often play in large and age-heterogeneous groups; they play competitive games more often than girls do, and their games last longer than girls' games (Lever, 1976). The last is in some ways the most interesting finding. Boys' games appeared to last longer not only because they required a higher level of skill and were thus less likely to become boring, but also because when disputes arose in the course of a game, the boys were able to resolve the disputes more effectively than the girls: "During the course of this study, boys were seen quarrelling all the time, but not once was a game terminated because of a quarrel and no game was interrupted for more than seven minutes. In the gravest debates, the final word was always to 'repeat the play,' generally followed by a chorus of 'cheater's proof' " (1976, p. 482). In fact, it seemed that the boys enjoyed the legal debates as much as they did the game itself, and even marginal players of lesser size or skill participated equally in these recurrent squabbles. In contrast, the eruption of disputes among girls tended to end the game.

Thus Lever extends and corroborates the observations reported by Piaget (1932 / 1965) in his naturalistic study of the rules of the game, where he found boys becoming increasingly fascinated with the legal elaboration of rules and the development of fair procedures for adjudicating conflicts, a fascination that, he noted, did not hold for girls. Girls, Piaget observed, had a more "pragmatic" attitude toward rules, "regarding a rule as good as long as the game repaid it" (1934 / 1965, p. 83). As a result, he considered girls to be more tolerant in their attitudes toward rules, more willing to make exceptions, and more easily reconciled to innovations. However, and presumably as a result, he concluded that the legal sense which he considered essential to moral development "is far less developed in little girls than in boys" (1932 / 1954, p.77).

This same bias that led Piaget to equate male development with child development also colors Lever's work. The assumption that shapes her discussion of results is that the male model is the better one. It seems, in any case, more adaptive since as Lever points out it fits the requirements Riesman (1961) describes for success in modern corporate life. In contrast, the sensitivity and care for the feelings of others that girls develop through their primarily dyadic play relationships have little market value and can even impede professional success. Lever clearly implies that, given the realities of adult life, if a girl does not want to be dependent on men, she will have to learn to play like a boy.

Since Piaget argues that children learn the respect for rules necessary for moral development by playing rule-bound games, and Kohlberg (1971) adds that these lessons are most effectively learned through the opportunities for role-taking that arise in the course of resolving disputes, the moral lessons inherent in girls' play appear to be fewer than for boys. Traditional girls' games like jump rope and hopscotch are turn-taking games where competition is indirect in that one person's success does not necessarily signify another's failure. Consequently, disputes requiring adjudication are less likely to occur. In fact, most of the girls whom Lever interviewed claimed that when a quarrel broke out, they ended the game. Rather than elaborating a system of rules for resolving disputes, girls directed their efforts instead toward sustaining affective ties.

Lever concludes that from the games they play boys learn both independence and the organizational skills necessary for coordinating the activities of large and diverse groups of people. By participating in controlled and socially approved competitive situations, they learn to deal with competition in a relatively forthright manner—to play with their enemies and compete with their friends, all in accordance with the rules of the game. In contrast, girls' play tends to occur in smaller, more intimate groups, often the best-friend dyad, and in private places. This play replicates the social pattern of primary human relationships in that its organization is more cooperative and points less toward learning to take the role of the generalized other than it does toward the development of the empathy and sensitivity necessary for taking the role of the particular other.

Chodorow's analysis of sex differences in personality formation in early childhood is thus extended by Lever's observations of sex differences in the play activities of middle childhood. Together these accounts suggest that boys and girls arrive at puberty with a different interpersonal orientation and a different range of social experiences. While Sullivan (1953), tracing the sequence of male development, posits the experience of a close same-sex friendship in preadolescence as necessary for the subsequent integration of sexuality and intimacy, no corresponding account is available to describe girls' development at this critical juncture. Instead, since adolescence is considered a crucial time for separation and individuation, the period of "the second individuation process" (Blos, 1967), it has been in adolescence that female development has appeared most divergent and thus most problematic.

"Puberty," Freud said, "which brings about so great an accession of libido in boys, is marked in girls by a fresh wave of repression" (1905 / 1961, p. 220) necessary for the transformation of the young girls' "masculine sexuality" into the "specifically feminine" sexuality of her adulthood. Freud posits this transformation on the girl's acknowledgement and acceptance of "the fact of her castration." In his account puberty brings for girls a new awareness of "the wound to her narcissism" and leads her to develop, "like a scar, a sense of inferiority" (Freud, 1925 / 1961, p. 253). Since adolescence is, in Erikson's expansion of Freud's psychoanalytic account, the time when the ego takes on an identity which confirms the individual in relation to society, the girl arrives at this juncture in development either psychologically at risk or with a different agenda.

The problem that female adolescence presents for psychologists of human development is apparent in Erikson's account. Erikson (1950) charts eight stages of psychosocial development in which adolescence is the fifth. The task of this stage is to forge a coherent sense of self, to verify an identity that can span the discontinuity of puberty and make possible the adult capacity to love and to work. The preparation for the successful resolution of the adolescent identity crisis is delineated in Erikson's description of the preceding four stages. If in infancy the initial crisis of trust vs. mistrust generates enough hope to sustain the child through the ardous life cycle that lies ahead, the task at hand clearly becomes one of individuation. Erikson's second state centers on the crisis of autonomy versus shame and doubt, the walking child's emerging sense of separateness and agency. From there, development goes on to the crisis of initiative versus guilt, successful resolution of which represents a further move in the direction of autonomy. Next, following the inevitable disappointment of the magical wishes of the oedipal period, the child realizes with respect to his parents that to beat them he must first join them and learn to do what they do so well. Thus in the middle childhood years, development comes to hinge on the crisis of industry versus inferiority, as the demonstration of competence becomes critical to the child's developing self-esteem. This is the time when children strive to learn and master the technology of their culture in order to recognize themselves and be recognized as capable of becoming adults. Next comes adolescence, the celebration of the autonomous, initiating, industrious self through the forging of an identity based on an ideology that can support and justify adult commitments. But about whom is Erikson talking?

Once again it turns out to be the male child—the coming generation of men like George Bernard Shaw, William James, Martin Luther, and Mahatma Gandhi—who provide Erikson with his most vivid illustrations. For the woman, Erikson (1968) says, the sequence is a bit different. She holds her identity in abeyance as she prepares to attract the man by whose name she will be known, by whose status she will be defined, the man who will rescue her from emptiness and loneliness by filling "the inner space" (Erikson, 1968). While for men, identity precedes intimacy and generativity in the optimal cycle of human separation and attachment, for women these tasks seem instead to be fused. Intimacy precedes, or rather goes along with, identity as the female comes to know herself as she is known, through her relationships with others.

Two things are essential to note at this point. The first is that, despite Erikson's observation of sex differences, his chart of life-cycle stages remains unchanged: identity continues to precede intimacy as the male diagonal continues to define his life-cycle conception. The second is that in the male life cycle there is little preparation for the intimacy of the first adult stage. Only the initial stage of trust versus mistrust suggests the type of mutuality that Erikson means by intimacy and generativity and Freud by genitality: The rest is separateness, with the result that development itself comes to be identified with separation and attachments appear as developmental impediments, as we have repeatedly found to be the case in the assessment of women.

Erikson's description of male identity as forged in relation to the world and of female identity as awakened in a relationship of intimacy with another person, however controversial, is hardly new. In Bettelheim's discussion of fairy tales in *The Uses of Enchantment* (1976) an identical portrayal appears. While Bettelheim argues, in refutation of those critics who see in fairy tales a sexist literature, that opposite models exist and could readily be found, nevertheless the ones upon which he focuses his discussion of adolescence conform to the pattern we have begun to observe.

The dynamics of male adolescence are illustrated archetypically by the conflict between father and son in "The Three Languages" (Bettelheim, 1976). Here a son, considered hopelessly stupid by his father, is given one last chance at education and sent for a year to study with a famous master. But when he returns, all he has learned is "what the dogs bark" (1976, p. 97). After two further attempts of this sort, the father gives up in disgust and orders his servants to take the child into the forest and kill him. The servants, however, those perpetual rescuers of disowned and abandoned children, take pity on the child and decide simply to leave him in the forest. From there, his wanderings take him to a land beset by furious dogs whose barking permits nobody to rest and who periodically devour one of the inhabitants. Now it turns out that our hero has learned just the right thing: he can talk with the dogs and is able to quiet them, thus restoring peace to the land. The other knowledge he acquires serves him equally well, and he emerges triumphant from his adolescent confrontation with his father, a giant of the life-cycle conception.

In contrast, the dynamics of female adolescence are depicted through the telling of a very different story. In the world of the fairy tale, the girl's first bleeding is followed by a period of intense passivity in which nothing seems to be happening. Yet in the deep sleep of Snow White and Sleeping Beauty, Bettelheim sees that inner concentration which he considers to be the necessary counterpart to the activity of adventure. The adolescent heroines awaken from their sleep not to conquer the world but to marry the prince. Their feminine identity is inwardly and interpersonally defined. As in Erikson's observation, for women, identity and intimacy are more intricately conjoined. The sex differences depicted in the world of the fairy tales, like the fantasy of the woman warrior of Maxine Hong Kingston's (1977) recent autobiographical novel (which in turn echoes the old stories of Troilus and Cressida and Tancred and Chlorinda) indicate repeatedly that active adventure is a male activity, and if women are to embark on such endeavors, they must at least dress like men.

These observations about sex difference support the conclusion reached by McClelland that "sex role turns out to be one of the most important determinants of human behavior. Psychologists have found sex differences in their studies from the moment they started doing empirical research" (1975, p. 81). But since it is difficult to say "different" without saying "better" or "worse," and since there is a tendency to construct a single scale of measurement, and since that scale has been derived and standardized on the basis of men's observations and interpretations of research data predominantly or exclusively drawn from studies of males, psychologists have tended, in McClelland's words, "to regard male behavior as the 'norm' and female behavior as some kind of deviation from that norm" (1975, p. 81). Thus when women do not conform to the standards of psychological expectation, the conclusion has generally been that something is wrong with the women.

What Horner (1972) found to be wrong with women was the anxiety they showed about competitive achievement. From the beginning, research on human motivation using the Thematic Apperception Test (TAT) was plagued by evidence of sex differences which appeared to confuse and complicate data analysis. The TAT presents for interpretation an ambiguous cue—a picture about which a story is to be written or a brief story stem to be completed. Such stories in reflecting projective imagination are considered to reveal the ways in which people construe what they perceive—that is, the concepts and interpretations they bring to their experience and thus presumably the kind of sense that they make of their lives. Prior to Horner's work, it was clear that women made a different kind of sense than men of situations of competitive achievement, that in some way they saw the situation differently or the situation aroused in them some different response.

On the basis of his studies of men, McClelland (1961) had divided the concept of achievement motivation into what appeared to be its two logical components, a motive to approach success ("hope success") and a motive to avoid failure ("fear failure"). When Horner (1972) began to analyze the problematic projective data on female achievement motivation, she identified as a third category the unlikely motivation to avoid success ("fear success"). Women appeared to have a problem with competitive achievement, and that problem seemed, in Horner's interpretation, to emanate from a perceived conflict between femininity and success, the dilemma of the female adolescent who struggles to integrate her feminine aspirations and the identifications of her early childhood with the more masculine competence she has acquired at school. Thus Horner reports, "When success is likely or possible, threatened by the negative consequences they expect to follow success, young women become anxious and their positive achievement strivings become thwarted" (1972, p. 171). She concludes that this fear exists because for most women, the anticipation of success in competitive achievement activity, especially against men, produced anticipation of certain negative consequences, for example, threat of social rejection and loss of femininity.

It is, however, possible to view such conflicts about success in a different light. Sassen (forthcoming), on the basis of her reanalysis of the data presented in Horner's thesis, suggests that the conflicts expressed by the women might instead indicate "a heightened perception of the 'other side' of competitive success, that is, the great emotional costs of success achieved through competition, or an understanding which, while confused, indicates an awareness that something is rotten in the state in which success is defined as having better grades than everyone else" (Sassen, forthcoming). Sassen points out that Horner found success anxiety to be present in women only when achievement was directly competitive, that is, where one person's success was at the expense of another's failure.

From Horner's examples of fear of success, it is impossible to differentiate between neurotic or realistic anxiety about the consequences of achievement, the questioning of conventional definitions of success, or the discovery of personal goals other than conventional success. The construction of the problem posed by success as a problem of identity and ideology that appears in Horner's illustrations, if taken at face value rather than assumed to be derivative, suggests Erikson's distinction between a conventional and neohumanist identity, or, in cognitive terms, the distinction between conventional and postconventional thought (Loevinger, 1970; Inhelder & Piaget, 1958; Kohlberg, 1971; Perry, 1968).

In his elaboration of the identity crisis, Erikson discusses the life of George Bernard Shaw to illustrate the young person's sense of being co-opted prematurely by success in a career he cannot wholeheartedly endorse. Shaw at seventy, reflecting upon his life, describes his crisis at the age of twenty as one caused not by lack of success or the absence of recognition, but by too much of both:

> I made good in spite of myself, and found, to my dismay, that Business, instead of expelling me as the worthless imposter I was, was fastening upon me with no intention of letting me go. Behold me, therefore, in my twentieth year, with a business training, in an occupation which I detested as cordially as any sane person lets himself detest anything he cannot escape from. In March, 1876, I broke loose. (Erikson, 1968, p. 143)

At which point Shaw settled down to study and to write as he pleased. Hardly interpreted as evidence of developmental difficulty, of neurotic anxiety about achievement and competition, Shaw's refusal suggested to Erikson, "the extraordinary workings of an extraordinary personality coming to the fore" (1968, p. 144).

We might on these grounds begin to ask not why women have conflicts about succeeding but why men show such readiness to adopt and celebrate a rather narrow vision of success. Remembering Piaget's observation, corroborated by Lever, that boys in their games are concerned more with rules while girls are more concerned with relationships, often at the expense of the game itself; remembering also that, in Chodorow's analysis, men's social orientation is positional and women's orientation is personal, we begin to understand why, when Anne becomes John in Horner's tale of competitive success and the stories are written by men, fear of success tends to disappear. John is considered by other men to have played by the rules and won. He has the *right* to feel good about his success. Confirmed in his sense of his own identity as separate from those who, compared to him, are less competent, his positional sense of self is affirmed. For Anne, it is possible that the position she could obtain by being at the top of her medical school class may not, in fact, be what she wants.

"It is obvious," Virginia Woolf said, "that the values of women differ very often from the values which have been made by the other sex" (1929, p. 76). Yet, she adds, it is the masculine values that prevail. As a result, women come to question the "normality" of their feelings and to alter their judgments in deference to the opinion of others. In the nineteenth-century novels written by women, Woolf sees at work "a mind slightly pulled from the straight, altering its clear vision in the anger and confusion of deference to external authority" (1929, p. 77). The same deference that Woolf identifies in nineteenth-century fiction can be seen as well in the judgments of twentieth-century women. Women's reluctance to make moral judgments, the difficulty they experience in finding or speaking publicly in their own voice, emerge repeatedly in the form of qualification and self-doubt, in intimations of a divided judgment, a public and private assessment which are fundamentally at odds (Gilligan, 1977).

Yet the deference and confusion that Woolf criticizes in women derive from the values she sees as their strength. Women's deference is rooted not only in their social circumstances but also in the substance of their moral concern. Sensitivity to the needs of others and the assumption of responsibility for taking care lead women to attend to voices other than their own and to include in their judgment other points of view. Women's moral weakness, manifest in an apparent diffusion and confusion of judgment, is thus inseparable from women's moral strength, an overriding concern with relationships and responsibilities. The reluctance to judge can itself be indicative of the same care and concern for others that infuses the psychology of women's development and is responsible for what is characteristically seen as problematic in its nature.

Thus women not only define themselves in a context of human relationship but also judge themselves in terms of their ability to care. Woman's place in man's life cycle has been that of nurturer, caretaker, and helpmate, the weaver of those networks of relationships on which she in turn relies. While women have thus taken care of men, however, men have in their theories of psychological development tended either to assume or devalue that care. The focus on individuation and individual achievement that has dominated the description of child and adolescent development has recently been extended to the depiction of adult development as well. Levinson in his study, *The Seasons of a Man's Life* (1978), elaborates a view of adult development in which relationships are portrayed as a means to an end of individual achievement and success. In the critical relationships of early adulthood, the "Mentor" and the "Special Woman" are defined by the role they play in facilitating the man's realization of his "Dream." Along similar lines Vaillant (1977), in his study of men, considers altruism a defense, characteristic of mature ego functioning and associated with successful "adaptation to life," but conceived as derivative rather than primary in contrast to Chodorow's analysis, in which empathy is considered "built-in" to the woman's primary definition of self.

The discovery now being celebrated by men in mid-life of the importance of intimacy, relationships, and care is something that women have known from the beginning. However, because that knowledge has been considered "intuitive" or "instinctive," a function of anatomy coupled with destiny, psychologists have neglected to describe its development. In my research, I have found that women's moral development centers on the elaboration of that knowledge. Women's moral development thus delineates a critical line of psychological development whose importance for both sexes becomes apparent in the intergenerational framework of a life-cycle perspective. While the subject of moral development provides the final illustration of the reiterative pattern in the observation and assessment of sex differences in the literature on human development, it also indicates more particularly why the nature and significance of women's development has for so long been obscured and considered shrouded in mystery.

The criticism that Freud (1961) makes of women's sense of justice, seeing it as compromised in its refusal of blind impartiality, reappears not only in the work of Piaget (1934) but also in that of Kohlberg (1958). While girls are an aside in Piaget's account of *The Moral Judgment of the Child* (1934), an odd curiosity to whom he devotes four brief entries in an index that omits "boys" altogether because "the child" is assumed to be male, in Kohlberg's research on moral development, females simply do not exist. Kohlberg's six stages that describe the development of moral judgment from childhood to adulthood were derived empirically from a longitudinal study of eighty-four boys from the United States. While Kohlberg (1973) claims universality for his stage sequence and considers his conception of justice as fairness to have been naturalistically derived, those groups not included in his original sample rarely reach his higher stages (Edwards, 1975; Gilligan, 1977). Prominent among those found to be deficient in moral development when measured by Kohlberg's scale are women whose judgments on his scale seemed to exemplify the third stage in his six-stage sequence. At this stage morality is conceived in terms of relationships, and goodness is equated with helping and pleasing others. This concept of goodness was considered by Kohlberg and Kramer (1969) to be functional in the lives of mature women insofar as those lives took place in the home and thus were relationally bound. Only if women were to go out of the house to enter the arena of male activity would they realize the inadequacy of their Stage Three perspective and progress like men toward higher stages where morality is societally or universally defined in accordance with a conception of justice as fairness.

In this version of human development, however, a particular conception of maturity is assumed, based on the study of men's lives and reflecting the importance of individuation in their development. When one begins instead with women and derives developmental constructs from their lives, then a different conception of development emerges the expansion and elaboration of which can also be traced through stages that compromise a developmental sequence. In Loevinger's (1966) test for measuring ego development that was drawn from studies of females, fifteen of the thirty-six sentence stems to complete begin with the subject of human relationships (for example, "Raising a family. . . . ; If my mother. . . . ; Being with other people. . . . ; When I am with a man. . . . ; When a child won't join in group activities. . . .") (Loevinger & Wessler, 1970, p. 141). Thus ego development is described and measured by Loevinger through conception of relationships as well as by the concept of identity that measures the progress of individuation.

Research on moral judgment has shown that when the categories of women's thinking are examined in detail (Gilligan, 1977) the outline of a moral conception different from that described by Freud, Piaget, or Kohlberg begins to emerge and to inform a different description of moral development. In this conception, the moral problem is seen to arise from conflicting responsibilities rather than from competing rights and to require for its resolution a mode of thinking that is contextual and inductive rather than formal and abstract.

This conception of morality as fundamentally concerned with the capacity for understanding and care also develops through a structural progression of increasing differentiation and integration. This progression witnesses the shift from an egocentric through a societal to the universal moral perspective that Kohlberg described in his research on men, but it does so in different terms. The shift in women's judgment from an egocentric to a conventional to a principled ethical understanding is articulated through their use of a distinct moral language, in which the terms "selfishness" and "responsibility" define the moral problem as one of care. Moral development then consists of the progressive reconstruction of this understanding toward a more adequate conception of care.

The concern with caring centers moral development around the progressive differentiation and integration that characterize the evolution of the understanding of relationships just as the conception of fairness delineates the progressive differentiation and balancing of individual rights. Within the responsibility orientation, the infliction of hurt is the center of moral concern and is considered immoral whether or not it can otherwise be construed as fair or unfair. The reiterative use of the language of selfishness and responsibility to define the moral problem as a problem of care sets women apart from the men whom Kohlberg studied and from whose thinking he derived his six stages. This different construction of the moral problem by women may be seen as the critical reason for their failure to develop within the constraints of Kohlberg's system.

Regarding all constructions of responsibility as evidence of a conventional moral understanding, Kohlberg defines the highest stages of moral development as deriving from a reflective understanding of human rights. That the morality of rights differs from the morality of responsibility in its emphasis on separation rather than attachment, in its consideration of the individual rather than the relationship as primary, is illustrated by two quotations that exemplify these different orientations. The first comes from a twenty-five-year-old man who participated in Kohlberg's longitudinal study. The quotation itself is cited by Kohlberg to illustrate the principled conception of morality that he scores as "integrated [Stage] Five judgment, possibly moving to Stage Six."

> [What does the word morality mean to you?] Nobody in the world knows the answer. I think it is recognizing the right of the individual, the rights of other individuals, not interfering with those rights. Act as fairly as you would have them treat you. I think it is basically to preserve the human being's right to existence. I think that is the most important. Secondly, the human being's right to do as he pleases, again without interfering with somebody else's rights.
>
> [How have your views on morality changed since the last interview?] I think I am more aware of an individual's rights now. I used to be looking at it strictly from my point of view, just for me. Now I think I am more aware of what the individual has a right to. (Note 1, p. 29)

"Clearly," Kohlberg states,

> these responses represent attainment of the third level of moral theory. Moving to a perspective outside of that of his society, he identifies morality with justice (fairness, rights, the Golden Rule), with recognition of the rights of others as these are defined naturally or intrinsically. The human's right to do as he pleases without interfering with somebody else's rights is a formula defining rights prior to social legislation and opinion which defines what society may expect rather than being defined by it. (Note 1, pp. 29–30)

The second quotation comes from my interview with a woman, also twenty-five years old and at the time of the interview a third-year student at Harvard Law School. She described her conception of morality as follows:

> [Is there really some correct solution to moral problems or is everybody's opinion equally right?] No, I don't think everybody's opinion is equally right. I think that in some situations . . . there may be opinions that are equally valid and one could conscientiously adopt one of several courses of action. But there are other situations which I think there are right and wrong answers, that sort of inhere in the nature of existence, of all individuals here who need to live with each other to live. We need to depend on each other and hopefully it is not only a physical need but a need of fulfillment in ourselves, that a person's life is enriched by cooperating with other people and striving to live in harmony with everybody else, and to that end, there are right and wrong, there are things which promote that end and that move away from it, and in that way, it is possible to choose in certain cases among different courses of action, that obviously promote or harm that goal.
>
> [Is there a time in the past when you would have thought about these things differently?] Oh, yah. I think that I went through a time when I thought that things were pretty relative, that I can't tell you what to do and you can't tell me what to do, because you've got your conscience and I've got mine. . . .
>
> [When was that?] When I was in high school, I guess that it just sort of dawned on me that my own ideas changed and because my own judgments changed, I felt I couldn't judge another person's judgment . . . but now I think even when it is only the person himself who is going to be affected, I say it is wrong to the extent it doesn't cohere with what I know about human nature and what I know about you, and just from what I think is true about the operation of the universe, I could say I think you are making a mistake.
>
> [What led you to change, do you think?] Just seeing more of life, just recognizing that there are an awful lot of things that are common among people . . . there are certain things that you come to learn promote a better life and better relationships and more personal fulfillment than other things that in general tend to do the opposite and the things that promote these things, you would call morally right.

These responses also represent a reflective reconstruction of morality following a period of relativistic questioning and doubt, but the reconstruction of moral understanding is based not on the primary and universality of individual rights, but rather on what she herself describes as a "very strong sense of being responsible to the world." Within this construction, the moral dilemma changes from how to exercise one's rights without interfering with the rights of others to how "to lead a moral life which includes obligations to myself and my family and people in general." The problem then becomes one of limiting responsibilities without abandoning moral concern. When asked to describe herself, this woman says that she values

> having other people that I am tied to and also having people that I am responsible to. I have a very strong sense of being responsible to the world, that I can't just live for my enjoyment, but just the fact of being in the world gives me an obligation to do what I can to make the world a better place to live in, no matter how small a scale that may be on.

Thus while Kohlberg's subject worries about people interfering with one another's rights, this woman worries about "the possibility of omission, of your not helping others when you could help them."

The issue this law student raises is addressed by Loveinger's fifth "autonomous" stage of ego development. The terms of its resolution lie in achieving partial autonomy from an excessive sense of responsibility by recognizing that other people have responsibility for their own destiny (Loevinger, 1968). The autonomous stage in Loevinger's account witnesses a relinquishing of moral dichotomies and their replacement with "a feeling for the complexity and multifaceted character of real people and real situations" (1970, p. 6).

Whereas the rights conception of morality that informs Kohlberg's principled level [Stages Five and Six] is geared to arriving at an objectively fair or just resolution to the moral dilemmas to which "all rational men can agree" (Kohlberg, 1976), the responsibility conception focuses instead on the limitations of any particular resolution and describes the conflicts that remain. This limitation of moral judgment and choice is described by a woman in her thirties when she says that her guiding principle in making moral decisions has to do with "responsibility and caring about yourself and others, not just a principle that once you take hold of, you settle [the moral problem]. The principle put into practice is still going to leave you with conflict."

Given the substance and orientation of these women's judgments, it becomes clear why a morality of rights and noninterference may appear to women as frightening in its potential justification of indifference and unconcern. At the same time, however, it also becomes clear why, from a male perspective, women's judgments appear inconclusive and diffuse, given their insistent contextual relativism. Women's moral judgments thus elucidate the pattern that we have observed in the differences between the sexes, but provide an alternative conception of maturity by which these differences can be developmentally considered. The psychology of women that has consistently been described as distinctive in its greater orientation toward relationships of interdependence implies a more contextual mode of judgment and a different moral understanding. Given the differences in women's conceptions of self and morality, it is not surprising that women bring to the life cycle a different point of view and that they order human experience in terms of different priorities.

The myth of Demeter and Persephone, which McClelland cites as exemplifying the feminine attitude toward power, was associated with the Eleusinian Mysteries celebrated in ancient Greece for over two thousand years (1975, p. 96). As told in the Homeric *Hymn to Demeter* (1971), the story of Persephone indicates the strengths of "interdependence, building up resources and giving" (McClelland, 1975, p. 96) that McClelland found in his research on power motivation to characterize the mature feminine style. Although, McClelland says, "it is fashionable to conclude that no one knows what went on in the Mysteries, it is known that they were probably the most important religious ceremonies, even partly on the historical record, which were organized by and for women, especially at the onset before men by means of the cult of Dionysus began to take them over" (1975, p. 96). Thus McClelland regards the myth as "a special presentation of feminine psychology" (1975). It is, as well, a life-cycle story par excellence.

Persephone, the daughter of Demeter, while out playing in the meadows with her girl friends, sees a beautiful narcissus which she runs to pick. As she does so, the earth opens and she is snatched away by Pluto, who takes her to his underworld kingdom. Demeter, goddess of the earth, so mourns the loss of her daughter that she refuses to allow anything to grow. The crops that sustain life on earth shrivel and dry up, killing men and animals alike, until Zeus takes pity on man's suffering and persuades his brother to return Persephone to her mother. But before she leaves. Persephone eats some pomegranate seeds which insures that she will spend six months of every year in the underworld.

The elusive mystery of women's development lies in its recognition of the continuing importance of attachment in the human life cycle. Woman's place in man's life cycle has been to protect this recognition while the developmental litany intones the celebration of separation, autonomy, individuation, and natural rights. The myth of Persephone speaks directly to the distortion in this view by reminding us that narcissism leads to death, that the fertility of the earth is in some mysterious way tied to the continuation of the mother-daughter relationship, and that the life cycle itself arises from an alternation between the world of women and that of men. My intention in this essay has been to suggest that only when life-cycle theorists equally divide their attention and begin to live with women as they have lived with men will their vision encompass the experience of both sexes and their theories become correspondingly more fertile.

REFERENCE NOTES

1. KOHLBERG, L. *Continuities and discontinuities in childhood and adult moral development revisited.* Unpublished manuscript, Harvard University, 1973.

REFERENCES

BETTELHEIM, B. *The uses of enchantment.* New York: Knopf, 1976.
BLOS, P. The second individuation process of adolescence. In A. Freud (Ed.), *The psychoanalytic study of the child* (Vol. 22). New York: International Universities Press, 1967.
CHEKHOV, A. *The cherry orchard.* (Stark Young, trans.) New York: Modern Library, 1956. (Originally published, 1904).
CHODOROW, N. Family structure and feminine personality. In M. Rosaldo & L. Lamphere (Eds.), *Women, culture and society.* Stanford, Calif.: Stanford University Press, 1974.
CHODOROW, N. *The reproduction of mothering.* Berkeley: University of California Press, 1978.
EDWARDS, C. P. Societal complexity and moral development: A. Kenyan study. *Ethos,* 1975, **3,** 505–527.
ERIKSON, E. *Identity: Youth and crisis.* New York: Norton, 1968.
FREUD, S. Female sexuality. In J. Strachey (Ed.), *The standard edition of the complete psychological works of Sigmund Freud* (Vol. 21). London: Hogarth Press, 1961. (Originally published, 1931.)
FREUD, S. Some psychical consequences of the anatomical distinction between the sexes. In J. Strachey (Ed.), *The standard edition of the complete psychological works of Sigmund Freud* (Vol. 10). London: Hogarth Press, 1961. (Originally published, 1925.)
FREUD, S. Three essays on sexuality. In J. Strachey (Ed.), *The standard edition of the complete psychological works of Sigmund Freud* (Vol. 7). London: Hogarth Press, 1961. (Originally published, 1905.)
GILLIGAN, C. In a different voice: Women's conceptions of the self and of morality. *Harvard Educational Review,* 1977, **47,** 481–517.

The Homeric Hymn (C. Boer, trans.). Chicago: Swallow Press, 1971.

HORNER, M. Toward an understanding of achievement-related conflicts in women. *Journal of Social Issues,* 1972, **28** (2), 157–174.

INHELDER, B., & PIAGET, J. *The growth of logical thinking from childhood to adolescence.* New York: Basic Books, 1958.

KINGSTON, M. H. *The woman warrior.* New York: Vintage Books, 1977.

KOHLBERG, L., & KRAMER, R. Continuities and discontinuities in childhood and adult moral development. *Human Development,* 1969, **12,** 93–120.

KOHLBERG, L. From is to ought: How to commit the naturalistic fallacy and get away with it in the stufy of moral development. In T. Mischel (Ed.), *Cognitive development and epistemology.* New York: Academic Press, 1971.

LEVER, J. Sex differences in the games children play. *Social Problems,* 1976, **23,** 478–487.

LEVINSON, D. *The seasons of a man's life.* New York: Knopf, 1978.

LOEVINGER, J., & WESSLER, R. *The meaning and measurement of ego development.* San Francisco: Jossey-Bass, 1970.

MCCLELLAND, D. *The achieving society.* New York: Van Nostrand, 1961.

MCCLELLAND, D. *Power: The inner experience.* New York: Irvington Publishers, 1975.

MEAD, G. H. *Mind, self and society.* Chicago: University of Chicago Press, 1934.

PERRY, W. *Forms of intellectual and ethical development in the college years.* New York: Holt, Rinehart & Winston, 1968.

PIAGET, J. *The moral judgment of the child.* New York: Free Press, 1965. (Originally published, 1932).

RIESMAN, D. *The lonely crowd.* New Haven: Yale University Press, 1961.

SASSEN, G. Success-anxiety in women: A constructivist theory of its sources and its significance. *Harvard Educational Review,* forthcoming.

STRUNK, W., & WHITE, E. B. *The elements of style.* New York: Macmillan, 1959.

SULLIVAN, H. S. *The interpersonal theory of psychiatry.* New York: Norton, 1953.

VAILLANT, G. *Adaptation to life.* Boston: Little, Brown, 1977.

WOOLF, V. *A room of one's own.* New York: Harcourt, Brace & World, 1929.

16

The Black Female Adolescent
A Review of the Educational, Career and Psychological Literature

Elsie J. Smith

This article presents a basic overview of the literature on the educational, career, and psychological development of black female adolescents. Adolescence is defined primarily in terms of individuals' attempts to deal effectively with life developmental tasks. As such, adolescence is viewed as that broad period covering the ages of 12 to 21. Emphasis is placed, however, on the early and mid-stages of adolescent development. Comparisons and contrasts are made regarding the development of black female, black male, white male, and white female adolescents.

Generally speaking, the black female adolescent has been underrepresented in educational, psychological, and career literature. Consequently, much of what we know about young black females consists of bits and pieces of fragmented knowledge. More attention has usually been placed on studying black males, white female adolescents, or black and white women. For instance, Psychological Abstracts for 1977 cited only fourteen sources relating to black female adolescents. A similar ERIC search for approximately the same time period yielded fifteen references pertaining to black female adolescents and college women. Only a few of these sources were, however, articles which related to the career development of members of this racial and age group. As Lightfoot (1976) has stated: "Young black girls are an ignored and invisible population" (p. 239).

This situation may be attributed to a number of factors. Compared to their male counterparts, black female adolescents have a tendency to exhibit fewer behavioral difficulties (Pettigrew, 1964). An analogous situation exists with black women. Moreover, as forerunners in the women's movement, white women have tended to research themselves and white female adolescents. The prevailing assumption has been that many of the educational and socialization problems facing white girls apply uniformly to black females

"The Black Female Adolescent: A Review of the Educational, Career and Psychological Literature" by Elsie J. Smith in the *Psychology of Women Quarterly*, 1982, 6, 3, 261–288. Copyright © 1982 by Human Sciences Press, Inc.

as well. While the socialization processes for these two groups may be similar, there are important cultural and historical differences between them. The net result has been, however, that little attention has been given to either how a black girl perceives herself as a female or how she is perceived by others as a female.

This article presents a review of the literature on the black female adolescent's educational, psychological, and career development. Because of the apparent paucity of available empirical studies, it will be, admittedly, a limited review. Several questions are raised: What are the early socialization practices which affect the career and educational development of black female adolescents? What is the current educational and occupational status of young black females? Is there a discernible pattern to their development in these two areas? How do such young women react to traditional sex roles delineated in the broader society? Where appropriate, comparisons and contrasts are made in the development of white female, white male, and black male adolescents. Issues are also raised regarding adult role models for black female adolescents.

The Many Meanings of Adolescence

The black female adolescent provides the developmental link between childhood and black womanhood. Within her lie many of the answers for understanding the black woman. In examining the black female adolescent, it is important that we understand not only the broad American context in which adolescence takes place but also the influence of black culture.

The term adolescence is derived from the Latin verb *adolescere*, which means "to grow up" or "to grow into maturity." Depending upon one's professional affiliation, however, the term may take on different connotations. For instance, sociologists have tended to describe adolescence as the transitional period that occurs from dependent childhood to self-sufficient adulthood (Muuss, 1968). Psychologists have usually portrayed it as a period during which an individual strives for independence from parents and for sexual and career adjustment. From a legal and chronological perspective, adolescence is defined as the time span that occurs from twelve to the early twenties. The actual time span for adolescence varies within cultures and socioeconomic groups (Muuss, 1968). Differences may be observed regarding the time at which a female is considered to be ready to take on the responsibilities and freedoms of womanhood (Ladner, 1971).

Within the lower socioeconomic black culture, adolescence is usually conceived of as ending at about age 18. As Ladner (1971) has maintained: "Becoming a woman in the low-income black community is somewhat different from the routes followed by the white middle class girl. The poor Black girl reaches her status of womanhood at an earlier age because of the different prescriptions and expectations of her culture" (pp. 424–425).

This situation may be attributed in part to the overall conditions that lower socioeconomic class black female adolescents face. In poor homes, adolescent girls tend to assume adult responsibilities at an early age. Compared to their white middle-class counterparts, they are more likely to have direct experience in taking care of younger siblings and household responsibilities (Lewis, 1967; Riessman, 1965; and Lightfoot, 1976). Such experiences are inclined to give young black girls a sense of both competency and independence which may not be internalized by middle class white girls until much later in life. According to some researchers, the economic and cultural climate in which some middle class whites are raised may foster a sense of learned helplessness and, consequently, an extended period of adolescence (Bird, 1975).

There are also other broad sociocultural and racial factors which have a bearing on the meaning of adolescence for black females. For instance, the majority of black female adolescents grow up realizing that they will assume the dual roles of mother and worker when they enter adulthood. This view is usually based on three central factors: (1) economic need or their perceptions of future economic needs; (2) their historical exposure to female work role models in the home; and (3) the relative egalitarian relationship between the sexes within the black race (Pettigrew, 1964; Billingsley, 1968; Turner & Turner, 1975).

Despite these observations, there is no single set of experiences that characterize the lives of black female adolescents. Each girl is affected by a number of influences, including family background, socioeconomic status, available role models and opportunities, and the extent to which she incorporates the values of both mainstream and black culture. Moreover, depending upon the type of environment to which she is exposed and the developmental life tasks that she has mastered (i.e., independence from parents, self-definition, and career adjustment), the black female adolescent may fall within a broad age group. For the lower class black female, this age range is likely to be from 12 to 18; for middle class black adolescents, from 12 to 21. These figures correspond to similar approximations made for white females within these respective socioeconomic groups (Rainwater, 1966; Lerner, 1972).

The Educational Status of Black Female Adolescents

The educational status of black female adolescents has been analyzed traditionally in terms of: (1) early socialization practices within black families; (2) white society's preferential treatment or greater acceptance of black females over black males; (3) black females' ability to acculturate or to adjust themselves more easily than black males to the demands of white society; and (4) the tendency of females in general to receive better high school grades than boys (Bernard, 1966).

Family Socialization and Education

According to Bock (1969), black parents tend to have higher educational and career aspirations for their daughters than for their sons. In his opinion, such higher educational aspirations may be attributed to the purported matrifocal nature of black families; black parents' belief that their daughters have greater chances for survival and can be more successful at school than their sons; and the higher school enrollment of females over that of males. Whereas it is believed that black mothers are inclined to cultivate within their sons a "surrendered identity" that teaches them how to coexist within a dominant white society, black female adolescents are believed to be taught just the opposite (Erikson, 1966). These conditions have led to what Bock (1969) calls "the farmer's daughter effect," that is, the tendency of farmers to encourage within their daughters rather than their sons a conscious value of education. As Bock (1969) has stated: "Similar to farm parents, the Negro parents seem to have made the assumption that daughters will be more successful than sons in attending school, acquiring occupational training, obtaining a job equal to their education, and generally improving themselves" (p. 19).

Bock's (1969) thesis concerning "the farmer's daughter effect" and Bernard's (1966) theory of the "unnatural superiority" of black women in both education and work have received conflicting support in the literature. For instance, an early study by Rosen (1959) indicated that in comparison with mothers of Jews, Protestants, and Greeks, more than 80% of black mothers said that they intended their sons to go to college. However, black mothers' vocational and educational aspirations for their sons were lower than all except one of the seven studied ethnic-religious groups.

Mulvihill (1974) studied the relationship of sex, matriarchy (or influence of family structure), and academic achievement of eleventh and twelfth grade black students. Of the 173 students who constituted the sample, 20 males and 16 females reported that their mothers were the primary breadwinners or heads of household in their families. Students were analyzed in terms of their: (1) academic achievement—total grade point average; (2) self-concept of academic ability; and (3) perceived parental evaluation of academic ability. Mulvihill reported no significant differences between black males and females whose mothers were the primary breadwinners on any of these three variables. He did find, however, that the grade point averages of males in female-headed household were significantly lower than those for males living in intact families wherein fathers were the primary breadwinners. Mulvihill (1974) concluded that: "males whose families are matriarchal do suffer some ill effects, at least in comparison with other males, but the cause does not seem to be linked to parental evaluation of ability" (p. 3916-A). It should be noted that the term matrifocal rather than matriarchy may have been more appropriate for Mulvihill to have used.

Kelly and Wingrove (1975) also tested the theory that black mothers perpetuated the higher achievement of black females than males by taking a greater interest in their daughters than in their sons. Kelly and Wingrove administered questionnaires to 1,344 white students and 361 black students in grades six through twelve in a primarily rural public school system in Georgia. Their findings revealed that according to black students' perceptions, "black mothers not only have higher educational aspirations for their children than do black fathers," but also the mothers have higher aspirations for their daughters than for their sons (Kelly & Wingrove, 1975, p. 54).

One of the more interesting studies regarding the black matriarchy theory and parental influences of black females' educational and career achievements was conducted by Heaston (1976). Using a focused, in-depth personal interview technique, Heaston asked a selected group of black women in the "elite" professions of law and medicine to cite the major influences on their educational and career developments during adolescence and early adulthood. The majority of the women responded that they had been influenced either to continue their education or to pursue their professional aspirations by their fathers. The theory regarding the powerful role of the black mother on their daughters' educational and professional achievements was not supported.

It should be pointed out, however, that much of the extant research on parental influence on both black male and female adolescents has a built-in bias. The influence of black fathers on the educational development of black female adolescents was seldom raised as a research question. In fact, of the available empirical studies completed on the educational development of black female adolescents, none specifically investigated the role of black fathers. Only two studies, one of which (above) was completed on black women in elite professions, even sought to assess the influence of fathers on young black girls' development. This situation does not seem to exist with white female girls. Recent research has indicated, for example, that white fathers may have a great bearing on their daughters' educational and career progress. Conversely, much of the research on both black female and male adolescents has examined maternal rather than paternal influence.

The effect of family socialization on the education of black female adolescents is complex. With the exception of Kelly and Wingrove (1975), there are little or no empirical or self-report survey data to indicate that black females have been socialized by their mothers or families to achieve at a higher educational rate than black males. There may be other factors, operating in the society at large, which contribute to the black female's early success.

Educational Achievement and Status of Black Females

As noted previously, black female adolescents tend to have higher academic achievement and intellective development than black males. For example, in a study of the relationship of IQ and age of white boys, white girls, black boys, and black girls in North Carolina, Baughman and Dahlstrom (1968) report that the mean IQ of black males dropped after age 10. The authors noted that this situation is also true for white boys and girls, but interestingly enough, it is not the case for black girls. At age 14, the mean IQ of black females was slightly higher than that for black males. When the authors combined the eight grade levels for black males and females, they found this difference was less than two IQ points, which, for all practical purposes was not significant.

Baughman and Dahlstrom (1968) also investigated the scholastic performance of youngsters of both races and sexes. The mean scores of both male and female black adolescents were lower than those of their white peers. The overall scholastic performance of black girls was consistently better than that of 13- and 14-year-old black boys. When scholastic achievement was examined in specific academic areas, the findings were even more revealing. Beginning at age 13, the spelling scores for black females on the Scholastic Achievement subtest were higher than those for both white and black male adolescents. Similar results were reported for the Language subtest of the Scholastic Achievement Test. In contrast, white female adolescents manifested greater academic achievement than black females, regardless of whether overall or specific performance was considered on the Scholastic Achievement Test.

The educational status of black female adolescents is also reflected in their modal grade of school enrollment. The modal grade is defined as the grade in which the greatest number of students of that age are enrolled. In 1970, 51.8% of 14-year-old black females were in their modal grade. By 1974, this figure had increased to 59.7% for this age group (United States Department of Commerce, 1976). For black females 17 years of age, 58.6% were in their modal high school grade in 1970 and 61.9% in 1974. White female adolescents for the same ages and time periods manifested a higher percentage of modal grade enrollment, approximately 72% for the 14-year-olds and 76% for the 17-year-olds in 1972 and 1974.

Likewise, more white male adolescents were in their modal grades than black females; however, the discrepancy was less than that observed between white and black females. In 1974, 68.9% of white males as compared with 61.9% of 17-year-old black females were in their modal high school grade. On the other hand, black males demonstrated lower modal grade school enrollment than any of the other mentioned groups. Again, the fact appears to be that the longer black female adolescents remain in school, the more clearly their enrollment and achievement approximate that of white males in selected areas.

The more recent 1978 report on *Social Indicators of Equality for Minorities and Women* (United States Commission on Civil Rights) analyzed black female adolescents' educational achievements in terms of their delayed education rate. For the purposes of this study, students were considered behind in school if their grade was two years or more below their modal grade. The report calculated the measure of delay for persons 15 to 17 years, since these are the ages at which accumulated delays tend to be the longest and most evident. Black females evidenced steady progress in reducing their delayed education rate. For example, in 1960, 25% of 15- to 17-year-old black females were at least two years behind the schooling process for their age; in 1970, 17% were, and in 1976, 15% were.

These figures can be compared with those for black male and white female adolescents within the same age range. In 1960, 36% of the black male adolescents were two or more years behind in school; in 1970, 26% were; and in 1976, 23% were. For white female adolescents, the delayed education rate was 10% for 1960, 6% for 1970, and 7% for 1976. White females averaged lower delayed education rates than did white males. For white males, the figures were 18% in 1960, 12% in 1970, and 10% in 1976.

To obtain an index of educational equality for black male and female adolescents, a ratio was computed for each of these groups in comparison to white males. The delayed education rate for black females was 1.50 times greater than the rate of majority males in 1976. For black males in 1976, the delayed education rate was 2.30 times greater than that for white males (United States Commission on Civil Rights, 1978). The report concluded:

> Although virtually every group showed improvement (i.e., a decrease in the
> percentage of those educationally delayed) . . . most of the improvements were

proportionately less than that exhibited by majority males. That is, the *relative* delayed rates for minority males and females increased from 1970 to 1976. (p. 8)

The educational achievement, enrollment, and delayed education rates of black female adolescents raise some interesting questions. For instance, to what extent does their academic performance affect their educational and career aspirations? How do their aspirations in these areas compare with those of other youth? Whether it can be attributed to early socialization patterns or not, black female adolescents seem better able than black males to cope with the middle class demands of school.

Educational and Career Aspirations of Black Female Adolescents

The quality and amount of education that individuals obtain are important factors in helping to shape their positions in American society. As Turner (1964) has pointed out, adolescents formulate personal and educational goals to acquire future status and recognition within social structures. Generally speaking, the concept of aspiration implies individuals' striving toward some kind of desired goal. That is, aspirations can be conceptualized as statuses that are desired (Finn, 1972). Conversely, expectations carry with them some notions of individuals' estimation of reality factors that may affect aspirations.

Basically, researchers have presented conflicting points of view on the aspirations of black youth. While some investigators have reported that black youth have aspirations similar to those of youth of other racial backgrounds, others have declared just the opposite. According to Stephenson (1957), black youth of American society have the common cultural value of high achievement, but when faced with the obstacles of racial barriers or prejudice, they reduce their aspirations to what they consider realistic levels.

Essentially, black adolescents are caught in a paradox: They are torn between the culturally ordained common success goals and their relatively limited access to the socially structured avenues for realizing them. This conflict may give birth to the disparity between their aspirations and their expectations.

Sexual differences have at times been found to affect the aspirations and expectations of both black and white adolescents. Middleton and Grigg (1959) analyzed racial and sexual differences in educational aspirations of rural youth in Florida. These investigators found that proportionally more black than white high school seniors of both sexes planned to attend college. The investigators reported that the differences between the sexes for each race were small and much less significant than the racial differences.

An early study by Antonovsky and Lerner (1959) revealed that males tend to reflect slightly higher job aspirations. Again, the hypothesized "farmer's daughter effect," the "unnatural superiority" of black women, and the purported preferential treatment of black females within the black family are called into question. A clear understanding of the interaction of sex and race for black female adolescents would profit from more recent studies on educational and career aspirations.

In contrast, Youmans (Note 1) found in another study of Florida adolescents that greater percentages of black female adolescents than white planned to attend college, but just the reverse held true for male adolescents. Black male adolescents were least likely to plan further education after high school, whereas black females were the most likely to do so.

Ohlendorf and Kuvlesky's (1968) investigation of rural southern adolescents yielded different findings. The educational aspirations of black and white boys were generally higher than those for girls of both races. Although the vast majority of both black and white males demonstrated high levels of educational aspiration, there were some important differences evidenced between them. Proportionally more black males indicated that they wanted to complete graduate study, while a large percentage of white males said that they wanted to terminate their education after graduation from a college or university. Likewise, more white than black males desired to terminate their education with high school graduation.

Ohlendorf and Kuvlesky's (1968) findings indicated that the educational aspiration profiles of black and white girls were similar to each other. Nearly one-half of each grouping reported that they wanted to take technical training after graduation from high school. The significant racial difference between these two groups was that a much larger proportion of black females than white females desired to complete graduate study. Hence, in general, the data show that rural black male and female adolescents have higher educational aspirations and expectations than rural white youth of both sexes.

Kuvlesky and Thomas (1971) explored social ambitions in a large metropolitan ghetto area. Overall, more black males than females held high educational goals. More than three-fourths of the males gave "very high" or "high level" goals, while only a small number of black females did so. These results did not, therefore, support some of the findings of other studies, which indicated that among black metropolitan youth, female adolescents tend to have slightly higher educational and occupational goals than males.

More recently, Dole and Passons (1972) compared 66 black male and female graduating high school seniors with 276 white high school seniors in terms of post-high school plans and goals. In comparison with white students, black seniors demonstrated higher altruistic values and the influence of school and science on their plans. In a related study, Dole (1973) assessed the aspirations of white and black parents for their children. As with the earlier research on the black family. Dole concluded that interpersonal dynamics in black homes may have an influence on the aspirational plans of adolescents. Black homes were seen to have a different set of dynamics from those of white homes, which affected adolescents' occupational aspirations differently. More specifically, Dole established that among the parents who perceived that their children had a good deal of freedom in educational and career planning, black daughters were more inclined to be at work, while white daughters were more likely to be in college. Dole (1973) concluded that: "Conformity, in the sense of parents' reporting that intimates were important influences upon the child's planning, was significantly associated with work only for the black females, whereas black females whose parents believed in the control of the child's planning were likely to attend college" (p. 28).

Moreover, national surveys of black high school seniors conducted in 1971 and in 1974 (NSSFNS—National Scholarship Service and Fund for Negro Students, 1972) yielded data regarding sex differences in degree aspirations. Of the total number of high school students sampled in 1974 who desired a bachelor's degree or less, black women were more likely (16%) to aspire to technical certificates or associate degrees than black men (12%), but less inclined to seek bachelor's degrees. In contrast, black women were more predisposed (28%) to seek master's degrees than black men (26%) but less likely (22%) to aspire to doctoral or professional degrees (24%). The statistics also point to a general increase in black women's level of aspiration from 1971 to 1974.

Moerk (1974) combined a cross-sectional and longitudinal approach to investigate the educational-vocational aspirations of white, Mexican-American, and black adolescents. During the initial measurement in 1964, Mexican-Americans showed the lowest expectations, while white adolescents manifested the highest. By 1970, the aspirations and expectations of the minority groups studied had increased, while those of the whites had decreased. The longitudinal aspect of the study revealed that sex differences existed among the groups. Black female adolescents obtained higher scores than both white and Mexican-American females.

Analyzing black and white adolescents from the sixth to the twelfth grade, Kelly and Wingrove (1975) also found that except for the ninth grade, a greater proportion of black females not only tended to have higher educational aspirations than black males, but also had greater expectations of completing their educational goals. Black females were (again with the exception of the ninth grade—the period in which drop-outs frequently take place) "consistently equal to or above whites in expectations" (Kelly & Wingrove, 1975, p. 54). The authors observed that black females did, however, demonstrate a discrepancy between aspirations and expectations beginning in the tenth and lasting through the senior year. Except for the twelfth grade, no similar pattern was noted for white male and female adolescents.

Teahan (1974) studied the influence of sex and school climate on the expectations of black female and male adolescents. Students were sampled from five predominantly black schools in a Catholic school system of a large industrial Midwestern city. Of the five schools involved, two were categorized as lower socioeconomic, two as predominantly middle class, and one an all black male, predominantly middle class high school. Teahan's findings indicated that socioeconomic status did affect students' occupational aspirations. All students showed the same level of desire for success, but they differed in terms of their expectations of reaching that desired level. Higher socioeconomic students expressed greater expectations of attaining their goals. Teahan reported female adolescents tended to be "depressed in terms of expectations of success whether they are of lower or higher socioeconomic status and regardless of whether they are students in primarily low or high socioeconomic settings" (p. 252).

The same was not true for black males. Lower socioeconomic males in higher socioeconomic surroundings gave more positive statements concerning their goals. According to Teahan (1974): "Perhaps the most important conclusion of the present study may be that the only condition as bad as being a lower socioeconomic black male in a predominantly lower socioeconomic school is to be a black female in any school" (pp. 254–255).

In an investigation of the relationship of school desegregation to the aspirations of 324 southern black high school seniors, White and Knight (1973) found that black females seemed to be much more affected by attending desegregated schools. In contrast, black males attending segregated and desegregated schools did not reflect this pattern. In interpreting their findings, White and Knight hypothesized that either black females were more influenced by the predominant white culture of the desegregated high school and the presumed undervaluation of college for females, or that attending a segregating school resulted in unrealistically high aspirations for females rather than males.

Although there was conflicting evidence for the belief that black female adolescents (like their younger and adult sex counterparts) have higher aspirations than black males, the majority of the studies reviewed indicated that such is the case. That is, black female adolescents generally have not only higher aspirations but also greater expectations of completing their goals. Some support for this conclusion is provided by the data concerning the college enrollment of black students. For instance, Bayer's (1972) national study of black and nonblack students entering all U.S. institutions in 1971 revealed that the majority of black students (53%) were women, while less than half of the nonblack students were women. Similar racial and sex differences were found in the Baughman and Dahlstrom 1968 national study. Apparently, black female adolescents do follow through on their educational aspirations.

These facts raise some interesting questions regarding the socialization of black girls. For instance, why do black females tend to have higher educational and occupational aspirations than black males? Why isn't the black female adolescent more similar to her white female counterpart? What factors contribute to black females' aspirations' being more similar to those of white male adolescents than other comparable age and racial groups? What role do black women have in the formalization of young black girls' educational and occupational aspirations?

For the most part, none of the studies reviewed provided any definitive answers to these questions. The general tendency was simply to compare the educational and occupational aspirations among black females, black males, white males, and white females. Emphasis was placed on varying such factors as socioeconomic class, grade level, and residency (rural or urban location). More studies are needed regarding black female adolescents' educational achievement and residency and the desegregation process.

To understand better black female adolescents' development of educational and occupational aspirations, more attention should be placed on analyzing the role of family structure and parental figures. It is one matter to state, for instance, that black female adolescents inherit or are socialized into favorite positions within the black family and quite another to base such conclusions upon empirical evidence. The finding that black female adolescents have higher aspirations than males does not necessarily indicate that females occupy a favorite position in the black family. On the contrary, to take such a stance may confuse effects with causes. A rival hypothesis might be that black female adolescents' higher strivings are, in reality, attempts to compensate for their devalued sexual status—not only in white American society but in black society as well. As Beale (1970) has pointed out, to be Black and female is "double jeopardy," and in order to render this double jeopardy into what Epstein (1973) calls the "positive effects of the multiple negative," the black female has to work very hard indeed.

Some of this work involves being able to convert aspirations into reality, making occupational choices, mastering career maturity tasks, dealing with one's sexuality—in short, taking all the steps that occur between adolescence and adulthood. As with adolescents in general, and females in particular, these are no easy tasks. For the black female, the difficulties entail coming to terms with their inner and outer selves, their sexuality and relationships with men, and their eventual work roles and multiple statuses within the broader society and the black community.

The Career Development of Black Female Adolescents and College Women

Research on the career development of black female adolescents is scanty at best. Most of the studies concerning work and work values, for instance, have been conducted on either college populations or adult men and women. Some of the reasons for this situation are often an issue of simple availability of college students and the belief that understanding work values is more critical for adult than younger people.

Concept of Work and Career Adjustment

According to some individuals, work values are well developed by the fifth grade. In fact, Hales and Fenner (1972) found that fifth and eighth grade students differed only slightly from eleventh grade students in terms of their work values.

On the average, blacks have been said to have a low concept of work and work values. A recent review of the studies on the attitudes of black workers demonstrated conflicting support for this theory (Smith, 1977b). Some of the studies not only revealed that blacks had similar work values to whites but that in some instances, blacks evidenced higher work values than whites.

Thomas (1974), however, examined the relationship of social position, race, and sex on the work values of ninth grade students. White students expressed a significantly greater value for each of the work value constructs outlined by Super and Bohn (1970). Whereas low social position black girls placed low value on the various scales of Super's and Bohn's (1970) Work Values Inventory, high position black girls placed high value on the work values of the different subscales. The investigator concluded that black female adolescents' work values are influenced by their socio-economic position.

Occupational awareness is one index of an individual's career progress. In a study of young black male and female adolescents, Amos (1960) found that black females were more aware of the occupational opportunity structure for members of their race than were males.

More recent studies on young black females' occupational awareness indicate that knowledge of the occupational system falls far beyond that of young white females. For example, the Ohio State University's Center for Human Resource Research (cited in Stevenson, 1975) conducted a five-year study of the work experiences of a sample of over 5,000 women who were 14 to 24 years of age when first surveyed in 1968. The results of the study indicated that young black women are less knowledgeable about the work world than young white women. Black females scored lower on the occupational information test than white women. Women who scored high on the information test were more likely to be employed than those who scored low. High scorers on the test were also more often found in white collar positions and higher paying jobs than low scorers. Although these patterns prevailed for young women of both races, the differences were more pronounced for black women than for white.

A study conducted by the Metropolitan Applied Research Center, Inc. (MARC) of New York City (cited in Stevenson, 1977) supported the findings of Ohio State's five-year study. The MARC study focused on the economic, psychological, and sociological aspects of unemployment among 18 black teenage girls between 15 and 19 years old who lived in poverty neighborhoods in New York. Because of its limited number of subjects, the findings cannot be generalized to all black female adolescents. Nevertheless, the findings are instructive and do have some support in the literature.

The MARC study reported that when given a wide range of professional, skilled, and semiskilled job positions and titles, the girls had difficulty explaining the duties of the workers. Instead, they demonstrated little familiarity with job titles, duties, and salaries listed in newspaper want ad sections. Black teen-age females also manifested little appreciation of the hierarchy of work organizations or status differences associated with various jobs and had little information about the necessary education, training, and lines of progression which led to job advancement.

According to the MARC study, black teen-age girls' lack of knowledge about the work world resulted largely from the limited scope of their contacts with successful adult workers. Most of the adult work role models in their lives were employed in menial and / or unskilled jobs. The fact that young black women did not make long-range career plans seemed to be influenced by family expectations. Generally, their families did little to encourage them to work, but instead expected them to care for younger children or to assume major household responsibilities. Families considered these activities far more important than their daughters working for low wages. Moreover, the girls seemed to be poignantly aware of racial prejudice in hiring and promotion, and anticipated exploitative and sexual advances from male supervisors if employed.

The lack of readily available adult women role models in the professional areas has also been cited by other researchers. As Shaw (1977) has stated:

The public image of black women as professional persons is almost non-existent. This lack of public visibility contributes to societal myths and keeps professional women from serving as role models for black youth. How many film strips, videotapes or other media used for educational purposes, include black women physicians, lawyers, or nurses? How many pictures in textbooks portray black women as professionals? (pp. 77–78)

Career Maturity, Race, and Sex

Career maturity is a construct used to denote the rate and level of individuals' mastery of vocational tasks and vocational progress. Only a few studies have analyzed the relationship of sex differences to black youth's career maturity. Lawrence and Brown (1976) explored the relationship of black youth's self-concept, intelligence, socioeconomic status and sex, as measured by Crites's (1973) Career Maturity Inventory. The results of the study suggested that when predicting career maturity a separate equation using different predictors, based on race and sex of subjects, should be considered. The authors conjectured that Super's (1953) self-concept theory may be more applicable to white males than to females, or to blacks in general.

In a study of twelfth grade black seniors, Smith (1976) likewise reported no significant sex differences. The investigation revealed, however, that vocational maturity was correlated positively with middle class reference group perspectives or outlooks on life. Smith theorized that the Career Maturity Inventory was measuring middle class values rather than career maturity and that the previously ascribed career development advantages of black females over black males may be eroding.

Career Interests and Choices

Sprey (1962) was one of the first to study sex differences in the occupational choice patterns of black adolescents. Sprey reported that black females tended to show less occupational choice indecision than black males. Black girls wished to become white collar workers to the same degree as whites; however, sons of black skilled workers were more likely to desire a skilled manual job than white boys within the same social class.

Hall (1974) explored some of the social psychological determinants of urban high school seniors' occupational decision-making. Her findings evidenced that low socioeconomic black males and high socioeconomic white males manifested the highest percentages of occupational indecision when compared to white and black girls. Black females exceeded white in aspiring to and expecting to achieve high status positions, even when social class and curricula enrollment were controlled. Both groups of girls selected the traditional careers of school teacher, nurse, social worker, etc., and both groups perceived more potential obstacles to career goals than did males.

In a study of the expressed and tested career interests of black inner-city adolescents, Omvig and Darley (1972) maintained that sex is another variable to be considered for black male and female adolescents. The data showed that expressed interests were more useful in conducting career counseling with black males than with black females. Black females' expressed interests correlated significantly with only 13 of the 24 Ohio Vocational Interest Survey work areas, with the highest correlation in the areas of Nursing / Technical Services, Medical, and Music.

Gurin and Gaylord have raised serious questions regarding the findings of studies stating that black women have unusual "motivational assets for the world of work" (1976, p. 10). In two surveys conducted in 1964 and in 1970 at historically black colleges, the investigators found that black women held lower educational expectations and aspired to jobs with lower prestige and ability requirements than did black men. Compared to women freshmen, women seniors were less sure than men that they would go to graduate or professional school. Whereas more women than men viewed the master's degree as terminal, more men than women said that the Ph.D. was their goal.

Moreover, Gurin and Gaylord (1976) found that although the men and women surveyed had the same opinions regarding which occupations held the greatest prestige, demanded the most ability, and were the most difficult for blacks to enter because of racial discrimination, black women tended to choose occupations that they themselves had said were not very demanding in terms of ability. Black women not only consistently selected traditionally feminine occupations, but also were inclined to choose occupations that were less racially discriminatory and more likely to be traditional rather than nontraditional for blacks. Gurin and Gaylord concluded that the major sex differences that were observed in aspirations, expectations, and career choices reflected sex role effects on motivation and women's perceptions of the opportunity structure rather than early childhood socialization of different needs and values. The authors based their conclusion on the fact that both men and women in the study demonstrated no significant differences in motives, values, and self-confidence. According to Gurin and Gaylord (1976):

> The finding that the black women we studied differed from the black men primarily in their aspirations and expectations, not in their need for achievement or in their anxieties or basic values, suggests that early socialization may be far less important than has been suggested in some of the analyses of achievement among women. These black women were motivated, but they chose to direct their motivation into conventional roles, at least partly because they did not as often expect to fulfill more challenging goals (p. 15).

Research by Turner and Turner (1975b) has supported some of Gurin and Gaylord's (1976) contentions. Turner and Turner found that race and sex are important factors in first year college students' perception of the opportunity structure. Although black students of both sexes perceived more racial discrimination against members of their race than did white students, black females and white males perceived significantly more occupational discrimination against women than did white females. Only the black males did not see significantly more discrimination toward females than did the white college women. Apparently, black women, having participated more than white women in the labor force, may be more sensitized than white females to sexual discrimination in the occupational world.

It seems that whatever advantages young black females had over black males in educational and career aspirations and expectations, they begin to erode in college. The environmental press of the college or reassessment of the career opportunity structure appear to lead to traditional career goals for black college females.

Employment Status of Black Female Adolescents

Statistics indicate that black female adolescents' unemployment is higher than that of black male, white male, or white female adolescents. According to the U.S. Commission on Civil Rights (1978), 18.8% of the black females in the 16-to-19 age range were unemployed in 1960, as were 24.6% in 1970 and 51.3% in 1976. These figures were accurate only for those who were out of work and actively seeking work. The percentage of unemployment may be even higher for those who have given up looking for work.

White females have encountered considerably less unemployment than black females. Unemployment figures for white females in the 16-to-19 age bracket were 2.9% in 1960, 10.9% in 1970, and 19.2% in 1976. Black female unemployment in 1976 was 32.1% higher than that for white females of comparable age.

A similar situation can be said to exist when black female youth are compared with black males and white males within the 16-to-19 year range. Black males had an unemployment rate of 12.1% in 1960, 20.5% in 1970, and 47.8% in 1976. Although the figures for black males and females more nearly resemble each other, the black female still has a higher unemployment rate.

White adolescent males have experienced the lowest overall unemployment rate. In 1960, 4.7% were unemployed, in 1970, 3.6%, and in 1976, 5.9%. The black female teenage unemployment rate in 1976 was 8.69 times the majority male total unemployment rate. It seems clear that among teenagers, the white male enjoys a favorable position in the labor market. In contrast, the unemployment figures of black female adolescents hardly indicate they have escaped sexual or racial discrimination.

Black girls who find work may end up in routine and dead-end jobs. A survey conducted by the Bureau of the Census in 1973 revealed that slightly over half of all employed black female adolescents from 16 to 19 hold factory jobs, work in private households, or are in "nondomestic service occupations (food service, personal service, and other jobs where pay is generally low and unemployment rates relatively high")" (cited in Stevenson, 1975, p. 5).

There are a number of possible explanations for the unemployment rate and the labor force participation of young black women. Black women have traditionally faced discrimination in the labor force and in society at large. As pointed out by the Ohio State Survey cited earlier (cited in Stevenson, 1975), black female adolescents tend to acquire fewer skills than white female adolescents. They are also more likely to be enrolled in the general curriculum rather than in a vocational, college preparatory, or commercial program. Black girls are inclined to obtain fewer years of total education than white and to have higher dropout rates. Early motherhood is another factor which has affected the employment of young black women.

All of these factors point to the need for greater educational, career, and personal counseling for young black girls.

Self-Concept, Sex Role, and the Psychological Development of Black Females

Individuals' self-concept and sex role attitudes have been related to their educational, career, and psychological development (Coleman et al., 1966). The term self-concept generally refers to how individuals perceive themselves and how they feel that they are perceived by others. Basically, researchers have theorized that positive self-concepts lead to a healthy educational, career, and psychological development, while negative self-concepts foster stunted growth in these areas (Ausubel & Ausubel, 1963).

Literature regarding the self-concepts of black youth has yielded conflicting findings. While some investigators have found that black youth tend to have lower self-concepts than their white peers, others have reported that black youth have either the same or higher levels of positive self-concepts than white youth (Zirkel, 1971; Smith, 1977a). The self-concept of black female adolescents has received, however, little attention in the literature.

In a national study on the self-image of girls aged 9 to 17, Prendergast, Zdep, and Sepulveda (1974) found that social class, age, and urbanicity were not related to black and white girls' self-image, but that race was. Black girls rated themselves higher on all of the following six studied dimensions; (1) being quick to learn; (2) being good in sports; (3) being well dressed; (4) being good looking; (5) having the teacher like you; and (6) having many friends.

Samuel and Laird (1974) explored the self-concepts of black female college students at a predominantly white and at a predominantly black southern college. The findings showed no significant difference between the two samples of black females on seven selected dimensions of the Tennessee Self Concept Scale. A comparison of the mean scores of females at the predominantly white campus with normative scores did suggest a significant departure from the normative group in the Concepts of Physical Self Scale. A similar comparison of the black females at the predominantly black campus did indicate that this group was significantly below the normative group in concepts of Family Self and Total Positive Scores. The authors conjectured that the lower physical self-image of black females on a predominantly white campus may have resulted from constant comparisons with white females.

Scott and Horhn's (Note 2) pilot study of 25 black female undergraduate majors in nontraditional curricula (engineering, business, natural science, communications, and agriculture) at a University of Tennessee campus revealed that the majority of the women felt that white women and black men were better accepted by both students and faculty from these curricular areas. Despite the fact that black females in the study manifested feelings of isolation and alienation in their classroom experiences, most "perceived themselves as independent, planned to marry, and believed that they would devote a lifetime to their careers" (Scott, 1977, p. 8).

Sterling (1975) explored the experience of black identity among black female adolescents between the ages of 16 and 18 in terms of being-me and not-being-me. She reported that black adolescents experience the process of identity on two levels simultaneously—one that is common to all adolescents and another that is unique to the black experience. Results of the study showed that black female adolescents like and feel good about themselves as people. Most of the situations in which subjects said that they were being-me or being-themselves tended to take place within the black community. On the other hand, subjects were inclined to state that they were not-being-themselves in settings that were predominantly white. According to Sterling, none of the adolescents in either situation expressed any sort of self-hate feeling. "In situations where they felt they were not-being-themselves, the dislike seemed to be more of a situational dislike rather than a dislike for self" (1975, p. 5040-A).

The findings of these studies tend to concur with those on black female children and older black women (Watson, 1974; Henderson, 1974). That is, despite the evidence that black girls and women are faced with the prospects of being devalued by both blacks and the general white society in favor of white women, black females have been able to maintain a positive sense of self against what appear to be overwhelming odds. It seems plausible that the positive self-concepts of black females may have been instrumental in their academic, career, and psychological development.

Sex Role Factors

Whether or not black girls experience the same sex role development as do white girls has been an object of much debate. As noted previously it has generally been presumed that by advocating an egalitarian family structure, the black family may inculcate fewer sex role stereotypes than does the white family. Such attitudes have been related to African concepts of male and female sexuality and the economic needs of black families for dual husband and wife workers in American society.

Davis (1977) investigated the degree to which traditional women's role orientation inhibits eleventh and twelfth grade black females' career preferences and aspirations. Davis's findings suggested that students' preferences for traditional occupations were unrelated to femininity measures but were related to belief in the traditional women's role. She concluded that preferences for traditional and non-traditional careers are developed differently among black female adolescents.

Harris (1975) reported that white college females' grid responses to George Kelly's Role Repertory Test were significantly more structured than the responses of black females. That is, white females structured their perceptions of males and females who occupied roles varying from traditional to innovative more in terms of sex role stereotypes than did black females.

Gump (1975) has reported that young black college women are more traditional in sex-role attitudes than white college women. Although both groups believed in the importance of maximizing their own potential, black women were more inclined to state that a woman's identity was derived primarily from marriage, that a mother should stay at home with her children, and that a woman should be submissive to men. This study does not support the belief that young black women are more nontraditional in their sex role attitudes.

Young women's approaches to work and family responsibilities have been two primary areas of investigation in sex role literature. Generally, researchers have pointed to the differences in approaches that young black and white women take concerning these two areas (Gurin & Epps, 1975). It has been theorized, for example, that young black women are less traditional than whites in their approaches to work and family responsibilities. Recent data have indicated, however, that the plans of both black and white young women to work and assume family responsibilities are becoming more similar than dissimilar to each other (Gurin & Epps, 1975).

Gump and Rivers (1975) have noted that young black women's decision to work should not necessarily be construed to mean that they hold non-traditional sex role attitudes for women. The investigators pointed out that black and white young women's expectations for work depend on different motivations. Whereas black young women formulated their work commitments on a socialized sense of family economic responsibility, white women more often indicated that they desired to work for self-fulfillment. That is, black women's decision to work is often based on their recognition of the social forces that limit black men's earning power. The black female is socialized into a sense of family economic responsibility from early adolescence and throughout her adult life.

Fear of success has often been related to sex role socialization of young girls. In spite of this observation, this investigator could find no available studies on fear of success with black high school girls. Several studies have been completed, however, on young college—usually first-year—women. Mednick (1973) and Mednick and Puryear (1975) have reported that the overall level of fear of success imagery expressed by black college women is relatively low when compared to that of white college women.

Research on the self-concept and sex role perceptions of black female adolescents and college women has produced some conflicting results. On the average, black females tend to have positive self-concepts. It is unclear to what extent being in a predominantly white educational setting may influence the self-concept development of black females. It appears that the sex role orientation of black females is both similar to and different from that of white females. Black females may be socialized early into a sense of family economic responsibility that results in a greater commitment for them to combine work and family responsibility. Black females' overall low fear of success imagery has been reported as a consistent finding in the literature.

Early Womanhood Experiences

Early womanhood experiences constitute an important element in young black females' psychological development. Such experiences form the basis of how black women perceive themselves in relationship to men of their race. Do black females have, for example, a different set of young womanhood experiences than white females?

Johnson (1977) conducted a study concerning the womanhood experiences of young black and white females, ranging from 17 years of age to the twenties. White subjects gave a significantly greater number of womanhood experiences that involved successful interpersonal relationships than did black subjects. Black young women not only reported many more instances of mistreatment than did white women, but they also reported a greater number of womanhood experiences entailing situational defeat.

A study by Turner and Turner (1975a) revealed that black females rated men as more unreliable than other racial groups in response to such questions as "most men are like . . ." on a semantic differential scale. In contrast, white females' responses to the phrase "most men are like . . ." were more positive and idealized than those of black females. Turner and Turner hypothesized that black females may have a different set of socializing womanhood experiences than white women.

It is difficult to formulate any definitive conclusions regarding black females' early womanhood experiences on the basis of the limited research. Concern has been expressed in the literature that the popular but inaccurate view that black females have fared better both educationally and economically than black males has influenced negatively the male and female relationships between members of this racial group (Jackson, 1973).

Summary of Findings

As a result of the review of the literature, a number of statements can be made regarding young black females' educational, psychological, and career development. Admittedly, some of the statements are based on limited data. The following findings seemed to have the most significance and/or support in the literature:

1. There are few empirical or survey data to support the theory that young black females are socialized within their families to achieve at or aspire to a higher educational and career level than that for black men. In fact, the influence of the mother on the young black female has been inadequately assessed.
2. Black females tend to have higher scholastic achievement than black males at the high school level, although it is difficult to determine just what leads to this greater success.
3. White female adolescents have higher scholastic achievement and performance than black females throughout high school.
4. The educational attainment of black females at the high school level (as measured by their modal grade enrollment and delayed education rates) is lower than that for white female and male adolescents but higher than that for black males.
5. Black female adolescents tend to have higher educational and career aspirations than both black males and white females at the high school level. There is some evidence that regional differences may assume an important role in the aspiration rates of black and white females and of white males.
6. The educational and occupational aspirations of black females appear to decline in college. Black females have lower educational and career aspirations at the college level than black males.

7. School desegregation tends to be associated more adversely with the educational and career aspirations of black females than with those of black males.

8. Attending a predominantly white college institution may have a negative influence on black females' physical self-concept and on their feelings of acceptance by college instructors and students.

9. Young black females tend to have less knowledge of the world of work than white females within the 16-to-early twenty age-group. They have greater difficulty in identifying job titles and related duties, the work organization, and status among various occupational groupings. Moreover, young black women are not inclined to make long-range career plans.

10. Black females manifest the effects of sex-role stereotyping in their educational/occupational aspirations and career choices.

11. Black females are similar to whites in that both groups tend to make career choices in traditional women-associated occupations.

12. Within the 16-to-19 year-old age bracket, black females experience a higher rate of unemployment than black males and white female and male adolescents.

13. The sex role attitudes of black young women in college are similar to those of white women.

14. Black females seem to have different work motivations from those of white females. The work motivations of black females are more oriented toward economic reality factors affecting black male employment rather than toward self-fulfillment, as is the case for white females. Black girls may be socialized into a sense of family economic responsibility in their decision to work.

15. The early womanhood experiences of black females may be negative.

16. Young black females have not escaped sexual and racial discrimination.

Discussion and Conclusions

Literature on the educational, career, and psychological development of black female adolescents and college students has been reviewed. Developmentally speaking, there are gaps between the black female child, the adolescent, and the black woman. For instance, we know painfully little about how young black females feel about themselves as emerging adults and women—about the kinds of "growing up" experiences that they encounter with the male members of their racial group, with white females, and with young white males. For instance, do young black females tend to view themselves in terms of the stereotypes that are traditionally associated with older black women? How do the stereotypes of adult black women affect the development of young girls?

A review of the literature indicates that the young black female is inundated with both negative research and popular misconceptions about her educational and career progress. Not only did much of the literature on the young black female begin on a negative tone, but also it tended to be geared toward explaining whatever educational and career successes she has achieved in terms of the supposed pathology of the black family—that is, the black matriarchy, the "unnatural superiority" of black women, the "farmer's daughter effect," the emasculation of the black male, and white society's preferential treatment of her over black males. Yet, as Ladner (1971) has pointed out, much of the literature on the strong black mother figure has tended to confuse strength with dominance and to ignore the fact that strong mother figures have assumed an important role throughout American history—from the early pioneering and immigrant periods to present day American society.

To provide some of the answers in the developmental gaps between the black female child, the adolescent, and the black woman, more research is needed on the role of the father in young black females' educational, psychological, and career development. Self-report or survey questions might center on black females' perceptions of their fathers' influences on their lives. Moreover, case studies might be conducted on the early womanhood experiences of black female adolescents and their views regarding their own sexuality. Models or approaches for the career counseling of black female adolescents also need to be developed to help such adolescents become more knowledgeable about the world of work and to assist them in making informed, long-range career plans.

REFERENCE NOTES

1. Youmans, F., *After high school what? Highlights of a study of career plans of Negro and white youth in three Florida counties.* Gainesville: University of Florida. Cooperative Extension Service, 1965.
2. Scott, P., & Horhn, M. *A pilot study of black female undergraduates enrolled as majors in nontraditional curricula at the University of Tennessee. Knoxville.* Unpublished study, 1975.

REFERENCES

AMOS, W. E. A study of the occupational awareness of a selected group of ninth grade Negro students. *Journal of Negro Education,* 1960, *29,* 4, 500–503.

ANTONOVSKY, A., & LERNER, M. J. Occupational aspirations of lower class Negro and white male youth. *Social Problems,* 1959, *7,* 132–138.

AUSUBEL, D. P., & AUSUBEL, P. Ego development among segregated Negro children. In H. A. Passow (Ed.), *Education in depressed areas.* New York: Bureau of Publications, Teachers College, Columbia University, 1963.

BAUGHMAN, E. E., & DAHLSTROM, W. G. *Negro and white children: A psychological study in the rural South.* New York: Academic Press, 1968.

BAYER, A. E. *The black college freshman: Characteristics and recent trends.* Washington, D.C.: American Council on Education, 1972.

BEALE, F. Double jeopardy: To be black and female. In T. Cade (Ed.), *The black woman: An anthology.* New York: New American Library, 1970, 90–100.

BERNARD J. *Marriage and family among Negroes.* Englewood Cliffs, N.J. Prentice-Halll, Inc.,1966.

BILLINGSLEY, A. *Black families in white america.* Englewood Cliffs, N.J.: Prentice-Hall, Inc., 1968.

BIRD, C. *The case against college.* New York: David McKay Co., Inc., 1975.

BOCK, W. E. Farmer's daughter effect: The case of the Negro female professionals. *Phylon,* 1969, *30,* 17–26.

COLEMAN, J. S., and others. *Equality of educational opportunity.* Washington, D.C.: U.S. Government Printing Office, 1966.

CRITES, J. O. *Career maturity manual.* California: McGraw-Hill, 1973.

DAVIS, M. S. Sex-role factors in the career development of black female high school students (Doctoral dissertation, University of Cincinnati, 1977). *Dissertation Abstracts International,* 1977, *38,* 1874-B. (University Microfilms No. 77-21, 704).

DOLE, A. A. Aspirations of blacks and whites for their children. *Vocational Guidance Quarterly,* 1973, *23,* 24–31.

DOLE, A. A., & PASSONS, W. R. Life goals and plans determinants reported by black and white high school seniors. *Journal of Vocational Behavior,* 1972, *2,* 209–222.

EPSTEIN, C. F. Positive effects of the multiple negative: Explaining the success of black professional women. In J. Huber (Ed.), *Changing women in a changing society.* Chicago: University of Chicago Press, 1973.

ERIKSON, E. The concept of identity in race relations: Notes and queries. In T. Parsons & K. B. Clark (Eds.), *The Negro American.* Boston: Houghton Mifflin, 1966.

FINN, J. D. Expectations and the educational environment. *Review of Educational Research,* 1972, *42,* 387–410.

GUMP, J. P. Comparative analysis of black women's and white women's sex-role attitudes. *Journal of Consulting and Clinical Psychology,* 1975, *43* 858–863.

GUMP, J. P., & RIVERS, L. W. A consideration of race in efforts to end sex bias. In Esther E. Diamond (Ed.), *Issues of sex bias and sex fairness in career interest measurement.* Washington, D.C.: Department of Health, Education and Welfare, National Institute of Education, 1975.

GURIN, P. & EPPS, E. *Black consciousness, identity, and achievement.* New York: Wiley, 1975.

GURIN, P., & GAYLORD, C. Educational and occupational goals of men and women at black colleges. *Monthly Labor Review,* June 1976, *99,* 10–16.

HALES, L. W., & FENNER, B. Work values of 5th, 8th, and 11th grade students. *Vocational Guidance Quarterly,* 1972, *20,* 199–203.

HALL, J. G. An examination of some social psychological determinants of the occupation decision-making of urban high school seniors (Doctoral dissertation, University of Pennsylvania, 1973). *Dissertation Abstracts International,* 1974, *34,* 5331A–5332A. (University Microfilms No. 74-2418)

HARRIS, M. M. Personal constructions of sex-typed roles and need achievement among black and white women (Doctoral dissertation, University of Pittsburgh, 1974). *Dissertation Abstracts International,* 1975, *36,* 973B–974B. (University Microfilms No. 75-18,238)

CHEASTON, &. Y. W. An analysis of selected role perceptions among successful black women in the professions (Doctoral dissertation, Northwestern University, 1975). *Dissertation Abstracts International,* 1976, *36,* 4352-A. (University of Microfilms No. 75-29,651)

HENDERSON, G. G. The academic self-concept of black female children within differential school settings. *Journal of Afro-American Issues,* 1974, *2,* 248–266.

JACKSON, J. J. Black women in a racist society. In Charles V. Willie, B. M. Kramer, & B. S. Brown (Eds.), *Racism and mental health.* Pittsburgh: University of Pittsburgh Press, 1973.

JOHNSON, L. J., SR. A comparative study of the womanhood experiences of black young adult females and white young adult females (Doctoral dissertation, University of South Carolina, 1976). *Dissertation Abstracts International,* 1977, *38,* 177-A. (University Microfilms No. 77-13,890)

KELLY, P. E., WINGROVE, C. R. Educational and occupational choices of black and white, male and female students in a rural Georgia community. *Journal of Research and Development in Education,* 1975, *9,* 45–56.

KUVLESKY, W. P. & THOMAS, K. A. Social ambitions of Negro boys and girls from a metropolitan ghetto. *Journal of Vocational Behavior,* 1971, *1,* 177–187.

LADNER, J. A. *Tomorrow's tomorrow.* New York: Doubleday, 1971.

LAWRENCE, W., & BROWN, D. An investigation of intelligence, self-concept, socioeconomic status, race, and sex as predictors of career maturity. *Journal of Vocational Behavior,* 1976, *9,* 43–52.

LERNER, G. *Black women in white America.* New York: Vintage Books, 1972.

LEWIS, H. Culture, class, and family life among low income urban Negroes. In M. Ross and H. Hill (Eds.), *Employment, race and poverty.* New York: Harcourt, Brace and World, 1967.

LIGHTFOOT, S. L. Socialization and education of young black girls in school. *Teachers College Record,* 1976, *78,* 239–262.

MEDNICK, M. T. *Motivational and personality factors related to career goals of black college women.* Washington, D.C.: U.S. Department of Labor, Manpower Administration, 1973. (NTIS No. PB218 969).

MEDNICK, M. T. S., & PURYEAR, G. Motivational and personality factors related to career goals of black college women. *Journal of Social and Behavioral Science*, 1975, *21*, 1–30.

MIDDLETON, R., & GRIGG, C. M. Rural-urban differences in aspirations. *Rural Sociology*, 1959, *24*, 347–354.

MOERK, E. L. Age and epogenic influences on aspirations of minority group children. *Journal of Counseling Psychology*, 1974, *21*, 294–298.

MULVIHILL, F. X. Sex, matriarchy and academic achievement of black students (Doctoral dissertation, Michigan State University, 1974). *Dissertation Abstracts International*, 1974, *35*, 3916-A. (University Microfilm No. 74-27,460).

MUUSS, R. E. *Theories of adolescence.* (2nd ed.) New York: Random House, 1968. National Scholarship Service and Fund for Negro Students (NSSFNS). A national profile of black youth: The class of 1971. *NSSFNS Research Reports*, 1972, *1(1)*.

OHLENDORF, G. W., & KUVLESKY, W. P. Racial differences in the educational orientations of rural youths. *Social Science Quarterly*, 1968, *49*, 274–283.

OMVIG, C. P.,& DARLEY, L. K. Expressed and tested vocational interests of black inner-city youth. *Vocational Guidance Quarterly*, 1972, *21*, 109–114.

PETTIGREW, T. F. *Profile of the Negro American.* Princeton, N.J.: Van Nostrand, 1964.

PRENDERGAST, P., ZDEP, S.M., & SEPULVEDA, P. Self image among a national probability sample of girls. *Child Study Journal*, 1974, *4*, 103–114.

RAINWATER, L. Crucible of identity: The Negro lower-class family. In T. Parsons and K. B. Clark (Eds.), *The Negro American.* Boston: Houghton Mifflin, 1966.

RIESSMAN, F. The overlooked positives of disadvantaged groups. *Journal of Negro Education*, 1965, *34*, 160–166.

ROSEN, B. C. Race, ethnicity, and the achievement syndrome. *American Sociological Review*, 1959, *24*, 47–60.

SAMUEL, N., & LAIRD, D. S. The self concepts of two groups of black female college students. *Journal of Negro Education*, 1974, *43*, 228–233.

SCOTT, P. B. Preparing black women for nontraditional professions: Some considerations for career counseling. *Journal of National Association of Women Deans, Administrators, and Counselors*, 1977, *40*, 135–139.

SHAW, E. Professional schools and their impact on black women. In *Conference on the educational and occupational needs of black women, Vol. 2: Research papers.* United States Department of Health, Education and Welfare. Washington, D.C.: National Institute of Education, 1977.

SMITH, E. J. Reference group perspectives and the vocational maturity of lower socioeconomic black youth. *Journal of Vocational Behavior*, 1976, *8*, 321–336.

SMITH, E. J. Counseling black individuals: Some stereotypes. *Personnel and Guidance Journal*, 1977, *55*, 390–396. (a)

SMITH, E. J. Work attitudes and the job satisfaction of black workers. *Vocational Guidance Quarterly*, 1977, *25*, 252–263. (b)

SPREY, J. Sex differences in occupational choice patterns among Negro adolescents. *Social Problems*, 1962, *10*, 11–23.

STEPHENSON, R. M. Mobility orientation and stratification of 1000 ninth graders. *American Sociological Review*, 1957, *22*, 204–212.

STERLING, D. H. The experience of being-me for black adolescent females: A phenomenological investigation of black identity (Doctoral dissertation, University of Pittsburgh, 1974). *Dissertation Abstracts International*, 1975, *35*, 5039A–5040A. (University Microfilms No. 75-4083).

STEVENSON, G. Counseling black teenage girls. *Occupational Outlook Quarterly*, 1975 *19*, (2), 2–13.

SUPER, D. E. A theory of vocational development. *American Psychologist*, 1953, *8*, 185–190.

SUPER, D. E., & BOHN, M. *Occupational Psychology.* Belmont, California: Wadsworth, 1970.

TEAHAN, J. E. The effect of sex and predominant socioeconomic class school climate on expectations of success among black students. *Journal of Negro Education*, 1974, *43*, 245–255.

THOMAS, H. B. The effects of social position, race, and sex on work values of ninth-grade students. *Journal of Vocational Behavior*, 1974, *4*, 357–364.

TURNER, B. F., & TURNER, C. B. The political implications of social stereotyping of women and men among black and white college students. *Sociology and Social Research*, 1975a, *15*, 155–162.

TURNER, B. F., & TURNER, C. B. Race, sex, and perception of the opportunity structure among college students. *Sociological Quarterly*, 1975b, *16*, 345–360.

TURNER, R. H. *The social context of ambition.* San Francisco: Chandler, 1964.

United States Commission on Civil Rights. *Social indicators of equality for minorities and women.* Washington, D.C.: GPO 1978.

United States Department of Commerce, Bureau of the Census. *Current Population Reports,* Series P-20, Nos. 222 and 286, Education and Training / Enrollment and Attainment. Washington, D.C.: GPO, 1976.

WATSON, V. Self-concept formation and the Afro-American woman. *Journal of Afro-American Issues,* 1974, *2,* 226–235.

WHITE, K., & KNIGHT, G. School desegregation, socioeconomic status, sex and the aspirations of southern Negro adolescents. *Journal of Negro Education,* 1973, *42,* 71–77.

ZIRKEL, P.A. Self-concept and the "disadvantage" of ethnic group membership and mixture. *Review of Educational Research,* 1971, *41,* 211–225.

17

Memories of a !Kung Girlhood

Marjorie Shostak

I remember when my mother was pregnant with Kumsa. I was still small and I asked, "Mommy, that baby inside you . . . when that baby is born, will it come out from your belly button? Will the baby grow and grow until Daddy breaks open your stomach with a knife and takes my little sibling out?" She said, "No, it won't come out that way. When you give birth, a baby comes from here," and she pointed to her genitals. Then she said, "And after he is born, you can carry your little sibling around." I said, "Yes, I'll carry him!"

I wanted the milk she had in her breasts, and when she nursed him, my eyes watched as the milk spilled out. I'd cry all night, cry and cry until dawn broke. Some mornings I just stayed around and my tears fell and I cried and refused all food. That was because I saw him nursing. I saw with my eyes the milk spilling out, the milk *I* wanted. I thought it was mine.

Another day, my mother was lying down asleep with Kumsa, and I quietly sneaked up on them. I took Kumsa away from her, put him down on the other side of the hut, and came back and lay down beside her. While she slept, I took her nipple, put it in my mouth and began to nurse. I nursed and nursed and nursed. Maybe she thought it was my little brother. But he was still lying where I left him, while I stole hi~ ᴍilk. I had already begun to feel wonderfully full when she woke up. She saw me and cried, "Where . . . tell me . . . what did you do with Kumsa? Where is he?" At that moment, he started to cry. I said, "He's over there."

She grabbed me and pushed me, hard, away from her. I lay there and

"Memories of a !Kung Girlhood" by Marjorie Shostak from *Nisa: The Life and Words of a !Kung Woman* by Marjorie Shostak. Cambridge, Massachusetts: Harvard University Press, 1981. Reprinted by permission of the publisher.

cried. She went to Kumsa, picked him up, and laid him down beside her. She insulted me, cursing my genitals, "Have you gone crazy? Nisa-Big-Genitals, what's the matter with you? What craziness grabbed you that you took Kumsa, put him somewhere else, then lay down and nursed? Nisa-Big-Genitals! You must be crazy! I thought it was Kumsa nursing!" I lay there, crying. Then I said, "I've already nursed. I'm full. Let your baby nurse now. Go, feed him. I'm going to play." I got up and went and played. Later, I came back and stayed with my mother and her son. We stayed around together the rest of the day.

Later, when my father came back from the bush, she said, "Do you see what kind of mind your daughter has? Go, hit her! Hit her after you hear what she's done. Your daughter almost killed Kumsa! This tiny little baby, this tiny little thing, she took from beside me and dropped somewhere else. I was lying down, holding him, and fell asleep. That's when she took him from me and left him by himself. She came back, lay down, and started to nurse. Now, hit your daughter!"

I lied, "What? She's lying! Me . . . Daddy, I didn't nurse. I didn't take Kumsa and leave him by himself. Truly, I didn't. She's tricking you. She's lying. I didn't nurse. I don't even want her milk anymore." My father said, "If I ever hear of this again, I'll beat you! Don't ever do something like that again!" I said, "Yes, he's my little brother, isn't he? My brother, my little baby brother, and I *love* him. I won't do that again. He can nurse all by himself. Daddy, even if you're not here, I won't steal mommy's breasts. They belong to my brother."

We lived and lived, and as I kept growing, I started to carry my little brother around on my shoulders. My heart was happy then; I had grown to love him and carried him everywhere. I'd play with him for a while and whenever he would start to cry, I'd take him to Mother so he could nurse. Then I'd take him back with me and we'd play together again.

That was when Kumsa was little. But once he was older and started to talk and then to run around, that's when we were mean to each other and hit and fought all the time. Because that's how children play. One child does mean things and the other children do mean things back. If your father goes out hunting one day, you think, "Won't Daddy bring home meat? Then I can eat it, but I can also *stinge* it!" When your father does come home with meat, you say, "My daddy brought back meat and I won't let you have *any* of it!" The other children say, "How come we play together yet you always treat us so badly?"

When Kumsa was bigger, we were like that all the time. Sometimes we'd hit each other. Other times, I'd grab him and bite him and said, "Oooo . . . what is this thing that has such a horrible face and no brains and is so mean? How come it is so mean to me when I'm not doing anything to it?" Then he'd say, "I'm going to *hit* you! What's protecting you that I shouldn't?" And I'd say, "You're just a baby! I, *I* am the one who's going to hit *you!* Why are you so miserable to me?" I'd insult him and he'd insult me and I'd insult him back. We'd just stay together and play like that.

Once, when our father came back carrying meat, we both called out, "Ho, ho, Daddy! Ho, ho, Daddy!" When I heard him say, "Daddy, Daddy," I said, "Why are you greeting my father? He's *my* father, isn't he? Now, you can only say, 'Oh, hello, Father.' " But he called out, "Ho, ho . . . Daddy!" I yelled, "Be quiet! Why are you saying hello to my father? When I say, 'Daddy . . . Daddy . . .' you be quiet. Only *I* will greet him. Is he your father? I'm going to hit you!" We fought and argued until mother finally stopped us. Then we just sat around while she cooked the meat.

This was also when I used to steal food, although it only happened once in a while. Some days I wouldn't steal anything and would just stay around playing, without doing any mischief. But other times, when they left me in the village, I'd steal and ruin their things. That's what they said when they yelled at me and hit me. They said I had no sense.

It happened over all types of food: sweet nin berries or klaru bulbs, other times it was mongongo nuts. I'd think, "Uhn, uhn, they won't give me any of that. But if I steal it, they'll hit me." Sometimes, before my mother went gathering, she'd leave food inside a leather pouch and hang it high on one of the branches inside the hut. If it was klaru, she'd peel off the skins before putting them inside.

But as soon as she left, I'd steal whatever was left in the bag. I'd find the biggest bulbs and take them. I'd hang the bag back on the branch and go sit somewhere to eat. When my mother came back, she'd say, "Oh! Nisa was in here and stole all the bulbs!" She'd hit me and yell, "Don't steal! What's the matter with you that inside you there is so much stealing? Stop taking things! Why are you so full of something like that?"

One day, right after they left, I climbed the tree where she had hung the pouch, took out some bulbs, put the pouch back, and mashed them with water in a mortar. I put the paste in a pot and cooked it. When it was ready, I ate and finished everything I had stolen.

Another time, I took some klaru and kept the bulbs beside me, eating them very slowly. That's when mother came back and caught me. She grabbed me and hit me, "Nisa, stop stealing! Are you the only one who wants to eat klaru? Now, let me take what's left and cook them for all of us to eat. Did you really think you were the only one who was going to eat them all?" I didn't answer and started to cry. She roasted the rest of the klaru and the whole family ate. I sat there, crying. She said, "Oh, this one has no sense, finishing all those klaru like that. Those are the ones I had peeled and had left in the pouch. Has she no sense at all?" I cried, "Mommy, don't talk like that." She wanted to hit me, but my father wouldn't let her.

Another time, I was out gathering with my mother, my father, and my older brother. After a while, I said, "Mommy, give me some klaru." She said, "I still have to peel these. As soon as I do, we'll go back to the village and eat them." I had also been digging klaru to take back to the village, but I ate all I could dig. My mother said, "Are you going to eat all your klaru right now? What will you eat when you get back to the village?" I started to cry. My father told me the same, "Don't eat all your klaru here. Leave them in your pouch and soon your pouch will be full." But I didn't want that, "If I put all my klaru in my pouch, which ones am I going to eat now?"

Later, I sat down in the shade of a tree while they gathered nearby. As soon as they had moved far enough away, I climbed the tree where they had left a pouch hanging, full of klaru, and stole the bulbs. I had my little pouch, the one my father had made me, and as I took the bulbs, I put them in it. I took out more and more and put them all in together. Then I climbed down and sat, waiting for them to return.

They came back, "Nisa, you ate the klaru! What do you have to say for yourself?" I said, "Uhn, uhn, I didn't take them." My mother said, "So, you're afraid of your skin hurting, afraid of being hit?" I said, "Uhn, uhn, I didn't eat those klaru." She said, "You *ate* them. You certainly did. Now, don't do that again! What's making you keep on stealing?"

My older brother said, "Mother, don't punish her today. You've already hit her too many times. Just leave her alone.

We can see. She says she didn't steal the klaru. Well then, what did eat them? Who else was here?"

I started to cry. Mother broke off a branch and hit me, "Don't steal! Can't you understand! I tell you, but you don't listen. Don't your ears hear when I talk to you?" I said, "Uhn, uhn. Mommy's been making me feel bad for too long now. I'm going to go stay with Grandma. Mommy keeps saying I steal things and hits me so that my skin hurts. I'm going to go stay with Grandma. I'll go where she goes and sleep beside her wherever she sleeps. And when she goes out digging klaru, I'll eat what she brings back."

But when I went to my grandmother, she said, "No, I can't take care of you this time. If you stay with me, you'll be hungry. I'm old and only go gathering one day in many. Most mornings I just stay around. We'll sit together and hunger will kill you. Now, go back and sit beside your mother and father." I said, "No, Daddy will hit me. Mommy will hit me. My skin hurts from being hit. I want to stay with you."

I lived with her for a while. But I was still full of tears. I just cried and cried and cried. I sat with her and no matter if the sun was setting or was high in the sky, I just cried. One month, when the nearly full moon rose just after sunset, I went back to my mother's hut. I said, "Mommy, you hate me. You always hit me. I'm going to stay on with Grandma. You hate me and hit me until I can't stand it any more. I'm tired."

Another time when I went to my grandmother, we lived in another village, nearby. While I was there, my father said to my mother, "Go, go bring Nisa back. Get her so she can be with me. What did she do that you chased her away from here?" When I was told they wanted me to come back I said, "No, I won't go back. I'm not going to do what he said. I don't want to live with Mother. I want to stay with Grandma; my skin still hurts. Today, yes, this very day here, I'm going to just continue to sleep beside Grandma."

So, I stayed with her. Then, one day she said, "I'm going to take you back to your mother and father." She took me to them, saying, "Today, I'm giving Nisa back to you. But isn't there someone here who will take good care of her? You don't just hit and hit a child like this one. She likes food and likes to eat. All of you are lazy. You've just left her so she hasn't grown well. If there were still plenty of food around, I'd continue to take care of her. She'd just continue to grow up beside me. Only after she had grown up, would she leave. Because all of you have killed this child with hunger. With your own fingers you've beaten her, beaten her as though she weren't a Zhun/twa. She was always crying. Look at her now, how small she still is." But my mother said, "No, listen to me. Your little grand-daughter . . . whenever she saw food with her eyes, she'd just start crying."

Oh, but my heart was happy! Grandmother was scolding Mother! I held so much happiness in my heart that I laughed and laughed. But when

Grandmother went home and left me there I cried and cried. My father yelled at me, but he didn't hit me. His anger usually came out only from his mouth. "You're so senseless! Don't you realize that after you left, everything felt less important? We wanted you to be with us. Yes, even your mother wanted you and missed you. Today, everything will be all right when you stay with us. Your mother will take you where she goes; the two of you will do things together and go gathering together. Why do you refuse to leave your grandmother now?"

But I cried and cried. I didn't want to leave her. "Mommy, let me go back and stay with Grandma, let me follow after her." But my father said, "That's enough. No more talk like that. There's nothing here that will hit you. Now, be quiet." And I was quiet. After that, when my father dug klaru bulbs, I ate them, and when he dug chon bulbs, I ate them. I ate everything they gave me, and I wasn't yelled at any more.

Mother and I often went to the bush together. The two of us would walk until we arrived at a place where she collected food. She'd set me down in the shade of a tree and dig roots or gather nuts nearby.

One time I left the tree and played in the shade of another tree. Hidden in the grass and among the leaves, I saw a tiny steenbok, one that had just been born. It was lying there, its little eye staring out at me. I thought, "What should I do?" I shouted, "Mommy!" I just stood there and it just lay there, looking at me. Suddenly I knew what to do—I lunged at it and tried to grab it. But it jumped up and ran away, and I started to chase it. It was running and I was running and it was crying as it ran. Finally, I got close enough to put my foot in its way and it fell down. I grabbed its legs and started carrying it back. It was crying, "Ehn . . . ehn . . . ehn . . ."

Its mother had been close by, and when she heard it call, she came running. As soon as I saw her, I started to run again, still carrying the baby steenbok. I wouldn't give it back to its mother! As I ran I called out, "Mommy! Come! Help me with this steenbok! Mommy! The steenbok's mother is coming for me! Run! Come! Take this steenbok from me." But then the mother steenbok was no longer following so I took the baby, held its feet together, and banged it hard against the sand until I had killed it. Then it no longer was crying; it was dead. I was very happy. My mother came running and I gave it to her to carry.

The two of us spent the rest of the day walking in the bush. While my mother gathered, I sat in the shade of a tree, waiting, and played with the dead steenbok. I picked it up; I tried to make it sit up; I tried to open its eyes; I looked at them. When my mother had dug enough sha roots, she came back. We left and returned home.

My father had been out hunting that day and had shot a large steenbok with his arrows. He had skinned it and brought it back hanging on a branch. "Ho, ho, Daddy killed a steenbok!" Then I said, "Mommy! Daddy! I'm not going to share *my* steenbok. Now *don't* give it to anyone this time. After you cook it, just my little brother and I will eat it, just the two of us."

I remember another time when we were traveling from one place to another, and the sun was burning. It was the hot, dry season and there was no water anywhere. The sun was *burning!* Kumsa had already been born and I was still small. We had been walking a long time and then my older brother saw a beehive. We stopped while he and my father chopped open the tree. All of us helped collect the honey. I filled my own little container until it was completely full. We stayed there, eating the honey, and I started to get very thirsty. Carrying my honey and my digging stick, I got up and we continued to walk. The heat was killing us and we were all dying of thirst. I started to cry because I wanted water so badly.

After a while, we sat down again in the shade of a baobab tree. There was no water anywhere. We just sat in the shade like that. Finally, my father said, "Dau, the rest of the family will stay here under this boabab. But you, take the water containers and get us some water. There's a well not too far away." Dau collected the empty ostrich eggshell containers, took the large clay pot, and left. I lay there, dead from thirst. I thought, "If I stay here, I'll surely die of thirst. Why don't I follow my big brother and go drink water with him?" I jumped up and started to run after him, I ran and ran, crying out to him and following his tracks, but he didn't hear me. I kept running, crying and calling out. Finally, he heard something and turned to see what it was. "Oh, no! Nisa's followed me. What can I do with her now that she's here?" He stood, waiting for me to catch up. When I was beside him, he picked me up and carried me high up on his shoulder, and along we went.

The two of us went on together like that. We walked and walked and walked until finally we reached the well. I ran to the water and drank and soon my heart was happy again. We filled the containers and put them in a twine mesh sack that my brother carried on his back. He took me and put me once again on his shoulder.

We started to walk back, Dau carrying the water and carrying me. After a while, he set me down and I ran along beside him. Soon I began to cry. He said, "Nisa, I'm going to hit you! I'm carrying these water containers and they're very heavy. So, just run along beside me and we'll take back this water to our parents. Thirst must have killed them by now. What are you crying about? Have you no sense?" I cried, "No, carry me. Dau, pick me up and carry me on your shoulder." He refused and I ran along beside him, crying, running and crying. After a while he said, "All right, I'll carry you again," and he picked me up. We went a long way before he set me down again. We had gone very far! I ran along with him until I tired again and he carried me again. That's how we were when we arrived at the baobab, where our parents were waiting for us.

They drank the water, drank and drank, more and more. "How well our children have done, bringing us this water! We are alive once again!" We rested in the shade of the baobab. Then we left and traveled to another water hole, and even though it was a long walk, I didn't cry. I just carried my container full of honey and walked. When we finally arrived, we settled there for a while. My heart was happy, eating honey and just living.

We lived there and after some time passed we saw the rain clouds. One came near, but just hung in the sky. It stayed hanging, just like that. Then another day, more rain clouds came over and they, too, just stood. Then the rain started to spill itself and it came pouring down.

The rainy season had finally come. The sun rose and set and the rain spilled itself. It fell and kept falling. It fell tirelessly, without ceasing. Soon the water pans were full. And my heart! My heart within me was happy. We lived and ate meat and mongongo nuts and more meat and it was all delicious.

My heart was so happy I moved about like a little dog, wagging my tail and running around. Really! I was so happy, I shouted out what I saw: "The rainy season has come today! Yea! Yea!"

There were caterpillars to eat, those little things that crawl along going, "Mmm . . . mmmm . . . mmmm . . ." And people dug roots and collected food and brought home more and more food. There was plenty of meat and people kept bringing more back, hanging on sticks, and they hung it up in the trees where we were camped. My heart was bursting and I ate lots of food and my tail kept wagging, wagging about like a little dog. And I'd laugh with my little tail, laugh a little donkey's laugh, a tiny thing that is. I'd wag my tail one way and the other, shouting, "Today I'm going to eat caterpillars . . . cat—er—pillars!" Some people gave me meat broth to drink and others prepared the skins of caterpillars and roasted them for me to eat and I ate and ate and ate! Then I lay down to sleep.

But that night, after everyone was dead asleep, I urinated right in my sleeping place. In the morning, when the others got up, I just lay there, lay there in the same place where I had urinated. The sun rose and was already high in the sky, and I was still lying there. I was afraid of people shaming me. Mother said, "Why is Nisa acting like this, refusing to leave her blankets when the sun is sitting up in the sky? Oh . . . she probably wet herself!"

When I did get up, I stood looking at my little pubic apron. *Wet!* "Ooh! I peed on myself!" And my heart felt miserable. I thought "I've peed on myself and now everyone's going to laugh at me." I asked one of my friends, "How come, after I ate all those caterpillars, when I went to sleep I peed in my bed?" Then I thought, "When this day finishes, I'm going to lie down separate from the others. If I wet my bed again, won't Mother and Father hit me?"

At night, when a child lies beside her mother, in front, and her father lies down behind and her mother and father make love, the child watches. Her parents don't worry about her, a small child, and her father just has sex with her mother. Because, even if the child sees, even if she hears her parents doing their work at night, she is unaware of what it *is* her parents are doing; she is still young, without sense. She just watches and doesn't have any thoughts about it.

But when she grows and is bigger and begins to walk, she has many thoughts. She sits and starts to think about things, and to think about her work—sexual play. Because when children play, that is what they do. Little boys play at sex and teach themselves, just as baby roosters teach themselves. Little girls also learn it with one another in the same way.

Little boys are the first to know the sweetness of sexual games. That's why they do that when they play. Yes. A girl, while she is still young, doesn't know about sex. Her thoughts don't really understand. But a little boy has a penis and perhaps, while he is still inside his mother's belly, he already knows about sex.

Once when there was a lot of rain and the water pans were full, we played in the water.

When we left, we went back to play in the bush, in our little village. We entered our huts and stayed there, playing. The boys pretended they were men, that they were tracking an animal and that they struck it with their poisoned arrows. They took some leaves and hung them over a stick, carrying them as though they were strips of meat. The girls stayed in the village, and when the boys came back, we pretended we were living there and eating—until all the meat was gone. On the next hunt, the boys took the girls and we followed along. After we found another animal and killed it, we all carried the meat back: the girls, in their karosses, and the boys, hanging it on sticks. We played in the bush like that, pretending we were living there, getting water and eating meat.

Sometimes the boys would ask each other, "When you play at sex, what do you do?" and they would ask us. We would say, "We don't know how to play that kind of play. You're the ones always talking about it. But we, we don't know. Anyway, however you play it, we won't do it. Why can't we just play?" That's when the boys would say, "Isn't having sex what playing is all about?"

When adults talked to me, I listened. When I was still a young girl with no breasts, they told me that when a young woman grows up, her parents give her a husband and she continues to grow up next to him.

When they first talked to me about it, I said, "What kind of thing am I that I should take a husband? When I grow up, I won't marry. I'll just lie by myself. If I married, what would I be doing it for?"

My father said, "You don't know what you're saying. I, I am your father and am old; your mother is old, too. When you marry, you will gather food and give it to your husband to eat. He also will do things for you. If you refuse, who will give you food? Who will give you things to wear?"

I said, "There's no question about it, I won't take a husband. Why should I? As I am now, I'm still a child and won't marry." I said to my mother, "You say you have a man for me to marry? Why don't you take him and set him beside Daddy? You marry him and let them be co-husbands. What have I done that you're telling me I should marry?"

My mother said, "Nonsense. When I tell you I'm going to give you a husband, why do you say you want me to marry him? Why are you talking to me like this?"

Long ago, my parents traveled far, to a distant water hole. There we met Old Kantla and his son Tashay, who had also come to live near the well.

One day soon after we had arrived, I went with my friend Nukha to get water at the well. That's when Tashay saw me. He thought, "That woman . . . that's the young woman I'm going to marry." He called Nukha over to him and asked, "Nukha, that young woman, that beautiful young woman . . . what is her name?" Nukha told him, "Her name is Nisa." He said, "Mmmm . . . that young woman . . . I'm going to tell my mother and father about her. I'm going to ask them if I can marry her."

Nukha came back and we finished filling the water containers. We left and walked the long way back to our village. When Nukha saw my mother, she said, "Nisa and I were getting water and while we were there, some other people came to the well and began filling their water containers. That's when a young man saw Nisa and said he would ask his parents to ask for her in marriage."

I didn't say anything. Because when you are a child and someone wants to marry you, you don't talk. But when they first talked about it, my heart didn't agree. Later, I did agree, just a little; he was, after all, very handsome.

The next night there was a dance at our village. We were already singing and dancing when Tashay and his family came. They joined us and we danced and sang into the night. I was sitting with Nukha when Tashay came over to me. He touched my hand. I said, "What? What is the matter with this person? What is he doing? This person . . . how come I was just sitting here and he came and took hold of me?" Nukha said, "That's your husband . . . your husband has taken hold of you. Is that not so?" I said, "Won't he take you? You're older. Let him marry you." But she said, "He's my uncle. I won't marry my uncle. Anyway, he, himself, wants to marry you."

Later his mother and father went to my mother and father. His father said, "We came here and joined the dance, but now that the dancing is finished, I've come to speak to you, to Gau and Chuko. Give me your child, the one you both gave birth to. Give her to me and I will give her to my son. Yesterday, while he was at the well, he saw your child. When he returned, he told me that in the name of what he felt, I should today ask for her. Then I can give her to him. He said he wants to marry her."

My mother said, "Eh, but I didn't give birth to a woman, I gave birth to a child. She doesn't think about marriage, she just doesn't think about the inside of a marriage hut." Then my father said, "Eh, it's true. The child I gave birth to is still a child. She doesn't think about her marriage hut. When she marries a man, she just drops him. Then she gets up, marries another, and drops him, too. She's already refused two men."

My father continued, "There is even another man, Dem, his hut stands over there. He is also asking to marry her. Dem's first wife wants Nisa to sit beside her as a co-wife. She goes out and collects food for Nisa. When she comes back, she gives Nisa food to cook so Nisa can give it to her husband. But when the woman unties the ends of her kaross and leaves it full of food beside Nisa, Nisa throws the food down, ruins it in the sand and kicks the kaross away. When I see that, I say that perhaps Nisa is not yet a woman."

Tashay's father answered, "I have listened to what you have said. That, of course, is the way of a child; it is a child's custom to do that. When she first marries, she stays with her husband for a while, then she refuses him. Then she goes to another. But one day, she stays with one man. That is also a child's way."

They talked about the marriage and agreed to it. I was in my aunt's hut and couldn't see them, but I could hear their voices. Later, I went and joined them in my father's hut. When I got there, Tashay was looking at me. I sat down and he just kept looking at me.

When Tashay's mother saw me, she said, "Ohhh! How beautiful this person is! You are certainly a young woman already. Why do they say that you don't want to get married?" Tashay said, "Yes, there she is. I want you to give me the one who just arrived."

The day of the wedding, everyone was there. All of Tashay's friends were sitting around, laughing and laughing. His younger brother said, "Tashay, you're too old. Get out of the way so I can marry her. Give her to me." And his nephew said, "Uncle, you're already old. Now, let *me* marry her." They were all sitting around, talking like that. They all wanted me.

I went to my mother's hut and sat there. I was wearing lots of beads and my hair was completely covered and full with ornaments.

That night there was another dance. We danced, and some people fell asleep and others kept dancing. In the early morning, Tashay and his relatives went back to their camp; we went into our huts to sleep. When morning was late in the sky, they came back. They stayed around and then his parents said, "Because we are only staying a short while—tomorrow, let's start building the marriage hut."

The next day they started. There were lots of people there—Tashay's mother, my mother, and my aunt worked on the hut; everyone else sat around, talking. Late in the day, the young men went and brought Tashay to the finished hut. They set him down beside it and stayed there with him, sitting around the fire.

I was still at my mother's hut. I heard them tell two of my friends to go and bring me to the hut. I thought, "Oohh . . . I'll run away." When they came for me, they couldn't find me. They said, "Where did Nisa go? Did she run away? It's getting dark. Doesn't she know that things may bite and kill her?" My father said, "Go tell Nisa that if this is what she's going to do, I'll hit her and she won't run away again. What made her want to run away, anyway?"

I was already far off in the bush. They came looking for me. I heard them calling, "Nisa . . . Nisa . . ." I sat down at the base of a tree. Then I heard Nukha, "Nisa . . . Nisao . . . my friend . . . a hyena's out there . . . things will bite and kill you . . . come back . . . Nisa . . . Nisao . . ."

When Nukha finally saw me, I started to run. She ran after me, chasing me and finally caught me. She called out to the others, "Hey! Nisa's here! Everyone, come! Help me! Take Nisa, she's here!"

They came and brought me back. Then they laid me down inside the hut. I cried and cried. People told me, "A man is not something that kills you; he is someone who marries you, who becomes like your father or your older brother. He kills animals and gives you things to eat. Even tomorrow, while you are crying, Tashay may kill an animal. But when he returns, he won't give you any meat; only he will eat. Beads, too. He will get beads but he won't give them to you. Why are you so afraid of your husband and what are you crying about?"

I listened and was quiet. Later, we went to sleep. Tashay lay down beside the opening of the hut, near the fire, and I lay down inside; he thought I might try and run away again. He covered himself with a blanket and slept.

While it was dark, I woke up. I sat up. I thought, "How am I going to jump over him? How can I get out and go to mother's hut to sleep beside her?" I looked at him sleeping. Then came other thoughts, other thoughts in the middle of the night, "Eh . . . this person has just married me . . ."

and I lay down again. But I kept thinking, "Why did people give me this man in marriage? The older people say he is a good person, yet . . ."

I lay there and didn't move. The rain came beating down. It fell steadily and kept falling. Finally, I slept. Much later dawn broke.

In the morning, Tashay got up and sat by the fire. I was so frightened I just lay there, waiting for him to leave.

After Tashay and I had been living together for a long time, we started to like each other with our hearts and began living nicely together. It was really only after we had lived together for a long time that he touched my genitals. By then, my breasts were already big.

We were staying in my parents' village the night he first had sex with me and I didn't really refuse. I agreed, just a little, and he lay with me. But the next morning, I was sore. I took some leaves and wound them around my waist, but I continued to feel pain. I thought, "Ooo . . . what has he done to my insides that they feel this way?"

That evening, we lay down again. But this time, before he came in, I took a leather strap, held my leather apron tightly against my legs, tied the strap around my genitals, and then tied it to the hut's frame. I was afraid he'd tear me open and I didn't want him to take me again.

The two of us lay there and after a long time, he touched me. When he touched my stomach, he felt the leather strap. He felt around to see what it was. He said, "What is this woman doing? Last night she lay with me so nicely when I came to her. Why has she tied her genitals up this way? What is she refusing to give me?"

He sat me up and said, "Nisa . . . Nisa . . . what happened? Why are you doing this?" I didn't answer. He said, "What are you so afraid of that you had to tie up your genitals?" I said, "Uhn, uhn. I'm not afraid of anything." He said, "No, now tell me. In the name of what you did, I'm asking you."

Then he said, "What do you think you're doing when you do something like this? When you lie down with me, a Zhun/twa like yourself, it's as though you were lying with another, a stranger. We are both Zhun/twasi, yet you tied yourself up!"

I said, "I refuse to lie down with anyone who wants to take my genitals. Last night you had sex with me and today my insides hurt. That's why I've tied myself up and that's why you won't take me again."

He said, "Untie the strap. Do you see me as someone who kills people? Am I going to eat you? No, I'm not going to kill you, but I have married you and want to make love to you. Do you think I married you thinking I wouldn't make love to you? Did you think we would just live beside each other? Do you know any man who has married a woman and who just lives beside her without having sex with her?"

I said, "I don't care. I don't want sex. Today my insides hurt and I refuse." He said, "Mm, today you will just lie there, but tomorrow, I will take you. If you refuse, I'll pry your legs open and take you by force."

He untied the strap and said, "If this is what use you put this to, I'm going to destroy it." He took his knife and cut it into small pieces. Then he put me down beside him. He didn't touch me; he knew I was afraid. Then we went to sleep.

The next day we got up, did things and ate things. When we returned to our hut that night, we lay down again. That's when he forced himself on me. He held my legs and I struggled against him. But I knew he would have sex with me and I thought, "This isn't helping me at all. This man, if he takes me by force, he'll really hurt me. So I'll just lie here, lie still and let him look for the food he wants. But I still don't know what kind of food I have because even if he eats he won't be full."

So I stopped fighting and just lay there. He did his work and that time it didn't hurt so much. Then he lay down and slept.

After that, we just lived. I began to like him and he didn't bother me again, he didn't try to have sex with me. Many months passed—those of the rainy season, those of the winter season, and those of the hot season. He just left me alone and I grew up and started to understand about things. Because before that, I hadn't really known about men.

But I started to learn. People told me, "A man is someone who has sex with you. He doesn't marry you and just keep you there, like a string of beads. No, a man marries you and makes love to you." They told me more, "A man, when he marries you, he doesn't marry you for your face, he doesn't marry you for your beauty, he marries you so he can have sex with you."

And more. My mother told me, "When a woman marries a man, he doesn't just touch her body, he touches her genitals and has sex with her." And my aunt, "A man marries you and has sex with you. Why are you holding that back from him? What's the matter with your genitals, the ones right there?" And even Tashay talked about it. I used to watch other couples who were together and he'd say, "The old people told you that people make love to one another, didn't they? That's what people do, they make love."

I listened to what everyone said and then I understood, my thoughts finally understood.

We were living in his parents' village again when my breasts began to swell. They grew bigger and bigger and then they were huge. I thought, "why are my breasts hurting me?" Because they were tender and painful.

Some days, I would tell Tashay that I wanted to go gathering with the other women. But often, he refused, "We two, just the two of us will go about together." He'd refuse to let me go. He was jealous; he said that when I followed along with the women, a man might come and make love to me.

He didn't want me to leave him, and we were always together: when he went to gather food, it was the two of us that went; when we went to get water, it was the two of us that went. Even to collect firewood, that's the way we went—together.

One day, my breasts felt especially sore and painful. Earlier that morning, the women had said, "Tashay, won't you lend Nisa to us so we can take her gathering? You take the springhare hook and go with your younger brother Twi to look for springhare. Nisa will go with us to gather things and to collect dcha fruits; we'll go to the well before we return."

Tashay refused, "Nisa's not going to do that. She's going to go with Twi and me. I'll take them both with me. If you find food that Nisa would have gathered, collect it for yourself. Nisa will go kill springhare with us and help carry back the meat."

I was unhappy. I wanted to go with the women, but I followed along instead with the two men. There wasn't another woman, only the two of them and myself. We walked for a long time and then came to a springhare burrow. They trapped the animal and killed it. They gave it to me and I carried it in my kaross. We walked and walked and walked. They were a little ahead of me. I was walking behind and stopped to urinate. I saw something red. I thought, "Is it the urine that's red or am I menstruating?" I took something and wiped my genitals. I looked at it, "Oh, I'm menstruating! I have followed along with the men and now I'm menstruating, way out here! What am I going to do?"

Because when you first menstruate, you don't tell anyone. A child who begins to menstruate isn't supposed to talk. I was stunned. I started to shake; I was trembling. I took my digging stick and threw it aside, because whatever a young girl was supposed to do, that's what I did. I took off my kaross and lay down on a part of it and covered myself with the rest.

My heart was miserable. I thought how I was still a child and how I didn't want to menstruate yet. I don't know why I was so afraid. Perhaps, of the days of hunger during the menstrual ceremony; I really don't know.

Tashay and his brother had walked on ahead and had reached the next group of trees. Tashay called to me, "Nisa . . . he—ey! Nisa . . . he—ey!" But I didn't call back. I was silent.

Tashay said to his brother, "Twi, Nisa's breasts are very big. Maybe she has begun to menstruate. Or, maybe she just ran away, following those other people whose tracks we passed. Go look for her. Call out to her and see if you can find her tracks. If she ran away with those other people, just leave her. But if she started to menstruate, come back to me."

Twi followed back along their tracks, calling out to me as he went. I lay still. When he came near to where I was lying, he saw the digging stick. He acted respectfully, as custom dictates, because a man isn't supposed to be there when a woman first menstruates. He stood there, then took the digging stick back to Tashay.

He said, "Here's your wife's digging stick. Just this morning Mother said, 'Your wife's a child. Now leave her and let the women take her with them.' But you refused to let her go. Now, she has begun the moon. I found her lying down at the base of a tree."

Tashay walked and walked, following the tracks, until he saw me lying there. He thought, "Oh, there's my wife. She has started to menstruate, but there are no other women around!" He stayed with me while Twi went to bring back the others. He told them, "Tashay and I went with Nisa today and while she was way out in the bush, she started to menstruate. We two men didn't know what to do."

All the women came to me. They took their beads and ornaments and tied them in my hair; they rubbed oil on my skin. Then Tashay's younger sister, my friend, picked me up and carried me back to the village. They made a place for me to lie down, then made the hut. After they put grass on it, they laid me down inside and started to dance and sing. I lay there and listened. They sang like this:

Ouh -- eh ---- ouh, ouh - eh,   ouh - eh,   eh - hi -- hi.

They sang and talked and danced and danced. I thought, "Mm . . . I don't see my mother . . . I'm living with Tashay's people . . ." Then I thought, "When am I going to be like the others again. I'm feeling terrible. When are they going to give me food to eat?"

Because they didn't give me much food to eat or water to drink. I just got up in the morning and stayed there, resting in the hut. I hardly ate or drank. I just lay there. I started getting thin, thin to death. The third day, my husband said, "What is this? My wife is only a child. It was days ago that she started to menstruate but she has hardly eaten food or drunk water. Why is that?"

He got up and went out to get some food. He dug for sha roots and cooked a springhare. He roasted and peeled the roots and gave them to his younger sister and said, "Go, give this to my wife. A child doesn't live for days with hunger." She came and gave it to me and I ate, but only very little. Wouldn't my stomach have hurt otherwise? I ate just a little and gave the rest to the others. His sister also gave me water to drink.

They danced every day until it was finished. Then they washed me, and we continued to live.

One day, soon after that, Tashay asked, "Do you want to go to your mother's?" I said yes, so we traveled the long distance to my mother's village. I was, of course, very beautiful then, young and beautiful. Not drawn and lined like a horse's face, as I am now.

When we finally arrived at my mother's village, my mother saw me. She asked, "What young woman has just arrived and is sitting over there? Whose daughter is that?" My father said, "It's Nisa and her husband." My mother cried out, "My daughter . . . little Nisa . . . my daughter . . . my little Nisa!"

I sat at a distance from her hut, by another hut, out of respect and due to custom. My husband got up and went and sat with them. Then my mother and my aunt came and brought me back to their hut. My mother asked, "The way you are sitting . . . the way you are acting . . . because you were sitting over there by that hut, does that mean you started to menstruate?" I said, "Mm." She cried, "Oh, my daughter! Is it right for a little girl like yourself to have menstruated for the first time in someone else's village, without your relatives? Could they possibly have taken care of you well?"

I stayed with her for a while. Tashay left me there and I just stayed with my mother. I thought, "Today, I'm happy. I've come to my mother and I'm happy. All the time I was living at Tashay's village, I wasn't. But now I am."

Tashay left me to spend time with my mother for a while. Then he came back and brought me again to his village. We lived on and then I menstruated again. Both of my ceremonial months occurred in Tashay's village and not in my mother's. The women danced for me again during the days of the flow, and then it was over. I left the hut and the women washed me.

We continued to live and it was as if I was already an adult. Because, beginning to menstruate makes you think about things. Only then did I bring myself to understand, only then did I begin to be a woman.

When Tashay wanted to lie with me, I no longer refused. We just had sex together, one day and then another. In the morning, I'd get up and sit beside our hut and I wouldn't tell. I'd think, "My husband is indeed my husband now. What people told me, that my husband is mine, is true."

We lived and lived, the two of us, together, and after a while I started to really like him and then, to love him. I had finally grown up and had learned how to love. I thought, "A man has sex with you. Yes, that's what a man does. I had thought that perhaps he didn't."

We lived on and I loved him and he loved me. I loved him the way a young adult knows how to love; I just *loved* him. Whenever he went away and I stayed behind, I'd miss him. I'd think, "Oh, when is my husband ever coming home? How come he's been gone so long?" I'd miss him and want him. When he'd come back my heart would be happy, "Eh, hey! My husband left and once again has come back."

We lived and when he wanted me, I didn't refuse; he just lay with me. I thought, "Why had I been so concerned about my genitals? They aren't that important, after all. So why was I refusing them?"

I thought that and gave myself to him, gave and gave. We lay with each other and my breasts were very large. I was becoming a woman.

18

What Do Women Want?
Feminism and Its Future

Barbara Grizzuti Harrison

When the Women's Liberation Movement began to be felt as a social force in the late 1960s, it was called exactly that—the Women's *Liberation* Movement. There was something fierce and flamboyant about that, something heady and gallant, tough, energizing, and also something perhaps in the best sense naïve, and something brave-new-world as well, banners unfurled. It is no accident—it was not simply for the sake of brevity—that the name of the movement soon became truncated: the women's movement, we say, or, even more modestly, the feminist movement. When we say the "feminist movement," we sound elegiac and muted: implicit in those words is a recognition (in equal parts heartening and disheartening) that we are not so new, after all; we are tied to the past, part of a continuum—the struggle for women's rights was not born with us; trumpets have sounded before.

More to the point, the word "liberation" is a vexing one; it accommodates a host of meanings, and it cannot possibly mean the same thing to everyone who gives it utterance.

To be a female is not to be a lesser human being; women are fully human—on that ground all feminists (all responsible human beings) stand firm.

Having said that, we are obliged to recognize that nothing yields to simplicity. What does it mean to be "liberated"? Does it mean to part radically with all the forms of the past, all traditions? Do we want altogether to smash the family as we have known it? Do we mean to alter and reconstruct the family? (We certainly can't *ignore* the family.) Does to be liberated mean to rediscover and reenact (or to invent and enact) forms of religion peculiar to a matriarchal past, amazons and witches? (*Was* there ever a true matriarchy? Is matriarchy by definition superior to patriarchy?) Is our vision an egalitarian one? Will our desires be satisfied if women wrest corporate and political positions from men? Will we have achieved liberation when there is a full complement of women in the boardroom and in the war room?

Questions in the wake of questions: Can any woman be said to be liberated in a capitalist society? Is socialism a prerequisite for liberation . . . ?

What Do Women Want?

Who does the real work of the world? What *is* the real work of the world? If the real work of the world is that which extends into the future, that which is not ephemeral, and that which sustains life, we are talking about poetry and bread and babies, not (one supposes) about finance and guns.

Can women play in the sandbox *and* in the corporate world? Should men be dividing their time between the sandbox and the corporate world? How? How, in the real world, does this work? Does being liberated mean doing it all—making babies (and love) and poetry, and forming social policy? Can we have it all? How? Is it right, fair, or reasonable to expect to have it all?

That "a woman has a right to control her own body" has become a cliché. While not exactly opposed in meaning to the words of the traditional marriage vows in *The Book of Common Prayer* ("with my body I thee worship"), the phrase encapsulates an entirely different world view. Does one world view have to be sacrificed to the other?

In talking about women's liberation, are we talking about a separatist culture? about romping androgynes free of all sexual restraint and constraint?

It may seem unfair to raise these questions at a time when the Supreme Court has made it easier to justify distinctions based on gender, and proponents of women's rights feel themselves to be more than ever beleaguered. But hard times demand hard questions.

I wanted to see how a small part of the world addressed these questions. More than that, I wanted to understand on what assumptions a relatively small number of women—and their mentors—based their hopes and plans for the future. The part of the world I chose was Smith College. It is arguably unfair to use a small, private, elite institution as a microcosm of the women's movement. Nevertheless, the questions are being asked at Smith; and the assumptions that are being acted on tell us a great deal about the women's movement today—and about what is meant by "liberation."

Nothing that happened during the turbulent 1960s at Smith—the largest privately endowed liberal-arts college for women in America and one of the largest women's colleges in the world—did much to disturb the image of that institution as a sheltered and genteel haven, an oasis of civility and cloistered scholarship. Smith functioned with every appearance of harmony: there were no sit-ins and few visible disruptions; there was no apparent rancor between students and faculty or between students and administrators. All normal college activities were suspended for four days as a protest (such a polite protest) against America's bombing of Cambodia; by Thursday-night candlelight suppers and Friday afternoon teas continued to be held—as they had been for 106 years—during that decade of civil-rights protests, antiwar protests, and student uprisings. While students at other northeastern colleges and universities formed militant caucuses and noisy alliances, Smith women skated on Paradise Pond (named by Jenny Lind when she was in the area on her honeymoon), continued to indulge their appetite for eighteenth-century Spanish literature and cranberry muffins, and made ritual pilgrimages to Emily Dickinson's house in the neighboring town of Amherst. Smith, true to its traditions, was ladylike.

Smith is no longer quite so ladylike. A combination of forces—a recessionary economy and the women's movement—has altered Smith in ways both subtle and profound. There are still Friday-afternoon teas; but few people are shocked—and even fewer surprised—when they become the occasion for "lesbian workshops." There are still Thursday-night candlelight suppers; but abortion rights, two-family paychecks, "flexitime," child-care sharing, and the inducements of corporate recruiters are as likely to be discussed as the merits of Amherst men and weekend "road tripping" to nearby coeducational institutions.

Smith remains, on the surface, almost overwhelmingly polite—"civilized," faculty and students call it, with resignation, smugness, or bravado, depending on their temperaments and on the struggles in which they are embroiled. But the last decade has wrought changes, in students' expectations of themselves, in their plans for the future, and in what students are being taught and the way in which they are being taught.

A case can be made that every important social movement obliges pedagogues to take a hard look at their teaching. This is certainly true of Smith: whether or not women's studies, like American studies, ought to be a separate department appears to have stirred up more controversy than the invasion of Cambodia.

The question, refined, is whether women's studies are a legitimate field of scholarship at all. The issue of tenure has become a thorny one, not unrelated to women's studies and the very definition of liberal arts: Smith has been charged with denying tenure on the basis of sex. According to feminist faculty members, male and female (none of whom will speak for attribution), one of the determinants of the decision to grant tenure is the degree of allegiance a scholar has to traditionalists who regard women's studies as trendy, peripheral, subjective, parochial.

Change can be measured in small ways, too. In seven days on campus, not once did I see a woman wearing an engagement ring. (I say "woman" deliberately: one calls a Smith student a girl only if one wishes to invite unpleasantness.) "You'd have to wear mittens if you owned an engagement ring," one young woman said. She was stitching a needlework sampler for her Harvard lover at the time ("For you I pine"), at the Women's Resource Center, the hub of feminist activity on campus, where civility, once again, prevailed. She was gently ragged by other students, made to feel as if she were engaging in a mildly subversive activity, but, blushingly defiant, she stitched away.

And: "I'm so uninteresting," Serena, a freshman, said to me. "All I really care about is Jane Austen." She said it self-deprecatingly, but not without her own measure of defiance. Privilege—the right to pursue personal happiness (and wisdom)—is something people are defensive about at Smith. The charge of elitism has been leveled against the college so often, students hardly know whether to feel burdened, pleased, or abashed by their special place in society. Not infrequently, they manage to feel that they are all three at once.

And: the bulbs were in bloom at Smith's Botanical Gardens when I visited. Every day, Ann Shanahan, Smith's director of public relations, urged me to see them, but I never did. Nor did I find time to attend ecumenical services at Helen Hills Chapel, where Smith women design the liturgy. This was an activity urged upon me by Dr. Jill Ker Conway, Smith's president, who thought it might make for a pleasant change of pace. Indeed, as delightful as I found most Smith women, I could have done with flowers and prayers after seven days of entertaining clamorous voices, voices that told me how the women's movement had—or had not—affected their lives and their perceptions of themselves.

Smith College is located eighty-five miles west of Boston, in Northampton, a town with a population of 30,000 that invariably calls to mind the adjective "charming." Pleasantly situated in the Connecticut River Valley, framed by the Holyoke mountains, Northampton, with its eclectic mix of wood-and-shingle early-Victorian houses, gothic masonry mansions, and chaste and severe Colonial architecture, looks sleepy—but is not.

In the center of town, on a side street abutting a parking lot, is a huge mural that gives some indication of organized women's activities in the Valley. Painted by the five-woman Hestia Art Collective on a wall of the New England Telephone and Telegraph building, the mural—busy, vivid, energetic—is a visual representation of the history of women in the Valley from Colonial to modern times: a woman field-worker harvests tobacco plants; a native American woman demonstrates the medicinal properties of herbs to a Colonial woman; directly below them (chronology, in an oddly exhilarating way, is made nonsense of), are women engaged in a family-planning session; contemporary women play volleyball; nineteenth-century women toil at the looms of the Northampton Woolen Manufacturing Company, cheek by jowl with women holding ERA signs, with suffragists, and with women protesting violence against women (TAKE BACK THE NIGHT, their signs read). The mural is executed in a self-consciously primitive style: it is vibrant with color, delightful. The gates to Smith College figure prominently in it, as does Sophia Smith, founder of the college.

Diagonal to the mural, which is a source of pride to every woman I spoke with, is a bookstore: Womon Fyre Books (Specializing in Wimmin's culture / Books by and about Wimmin in all fields). The bookstore serves as a gathering place for women who are strongly disposed to alter language to suit their politics or their sexual preference, which many of them consider to be the same thing. For reasons no one claims to understand, the area surrounding Northampton has become a gathering place for lesbian-separatist collectivists, and for self-declared radical feminists, among whom are Mary Daly (author of *Beyond God the Father*, and *Gyn/Ecology: The Metaethics of Radical Feminism*) and Adrienne Rich.

It is a short drive from Womon Fyre to the chic boutiques that encircle the 125-acre Smith campus, but one feels as if one is in a different world. (The point at which these worlds intersect is part of the story of Smith today.)

The entire campus is an arboretum. Even on a gray, misty day, the quadrangle is inviting, both womblike and expansive. House loyalties are very strong. (Smith's 2,600 undergraduates live in forty-eight "houses.") Students eat in house dining rooms rather than in a central cafeteria. There are no plastic trays at Smith—the painted china may be cracked and faded, but it is pretty. Pretty, too, to see young women flock to dining rooms in bathrobes and slippers, looking rather other-worldly—drowsy, perhaps from predinner naps, or still immersed in classroom concerns.

("When was the shah elected president of Iran?" one bemused woman asked at dinner on the eve of a visit by George McGovern. I must have looked startled. Smith, after all, is a highly competitive school, and to hear most people tell it, there are no limits to what "the Smith Woman" can do. "She's really very smart," somebody else at table whispered. "She knows everything there is to know about caliphs and stuff. She just hasn't read a newspaper in three years." Someone asked the woman who knew all about caliphs whether she was going to hear George McGovern. "George who?" she said. "Quite right," another student said, saluting her with her teacup. "He didn't do nearly enough for reproductive rights.")

Smith women are cosseted, but they are also, willy-nilly or by choice, embroiled in the ferment of a powerful social movement. And they are not isolated. Smith is part of a five-college consortium: Amherst, Mount Holyoke, Hampshire, and the University of Massachusetts are all within a fifteen-mile radius. Many teachers "float" among the five colleges, comparing— for the benefit of the students and one another—the degree of feminist activity at each. Smith students are both protected in their own immediate environment and exposed to the travails of neighboring institutions. And this probably accounts for the sense of disequilibrium one feels emanating from all directions. It probably accounts, as well, for the number of students—and faculty—who knocked on the door of my guest room at unpredictable hours of the day and night to give me the "lowdown" on Smith, to talk to me about women's studies, to ask me how one juggled a career with marriage and children—or to tell me that they had no doubt they could have it all . . . no *real* doubt . . . well, perhaps a few doubts.

Small colleges tend to breed intense loyalty and intense criticism, even within one individual, I am thinking this while I listen to Julie, a sophomore who presents herself at my door one morning before breakfast, fixes her large, beautiful blue eyes on me, and, without regard for my early-morning grogginess, delivers herself of an impassioned monologue. Julie is a Gold Key Guide, one of two hundred young women who escort visitors around campus.

"I love it," she says. "I haven't met anyone yet who isn't proud of being here. But it's really difficult to have a social life at Smith. The administration glosses over that. We've structured our whole lives on male approval, and there are no men. When I first came here, I missed boys an awful lot. I went to frat parties, which were a bad joke. None of those guys want solid, permanent relationships. I'd come back from the parties and think, What's wrong with me?

"Boys in high school were loyal to one another, and bosomy. I noticed that. Girls were gossipy and bitchy. And that's why Smith is wonderful, because we're learning how we feel about ourselves without having to compete with men. If I'd gone to a coed school, I'd never be a whole person.

"In Lamont House, where I live, there used to be a a lot of lesbian radicals. It was a wonderful house, no cliques and no 'road tripping,' and no feeling that women were inferior to men. I'm not a lesbian; but they raised my consciousness. But they didn't understand my need to meet men. And then I realized, my God, for years I've been training myself to think that I need men around to make myself feel good. When I realized that I'd just been brainwashed, I didn't care that there were no men.

"If I meet someone tomorrow from Amherst who's wonderful, that's great. But I won't die if I don't. I want to get married and have kids very much, and I want to be a writer. But first I want to work for a world where nobody ever has to have an abortion. I want to get birth-right organizations established, you know, like day-care centers. Society doesn't make room for unwanted children, so women have to kill them. I hate that so much. I see abortion as a symptom of women's oppression. Gosh, I'm afraid to tell the feminists at the Women's Resource Center that I think that.

"Smith made me a feminist, but the college has refused to have a women's studies program—and I want a women's studies major. What Smith says is that being a woman here is secondary. What's first is your education. But we're taught from a male point of view.

"Oh, but it's like a magic kingdom here. I just love it so much. A magic kingdom."

Jennifer, a sophomore, is a late-night visitor. We chat in a living room of Gillette Hall, a large house where I am ensconced in a prim but comfortable guest room. Jennifer, with whom I have talked earlier at the Women's Resource Center, wants to talk with me about the brochure. Smith sends prospective applicants. She doesn't like it. She calls it "a lie." On the cover of the brochure is a picture of a spacious room, bow windows looking out on mountains and sky. In the foreground of the photograph is a wholesome-looking young woman with a stylish hairdo, wearing a casually elegant dress, reading an art book.

"That's *my* room at Tyler House," Jennifer says. "They yanked me and my roommate out of the room and put in the president of the Gold Key Guides because she looks like a perfect corporate type. A real 'Smithie.' Or what they'd like people to think Smithies are, feminine and corporate bound. When they took the photograph, they pulled down my Women's Resource Center posters and substituted a Monet poster and a Toulouse-Lautrec poster. I made a stink at the Publications Department, but they just fended me off with kindness—hostility clothed in gentility. My real protest was to put a copy of *Praxis*—a femininist newspaper—on the bookcase. I wanted that to show in the picture." In the photograph, *Praxis* is invisible to the naked eye.

Jennifer is one of only five students at Smith who have so far managed to steer their way through the appropriate advisers and committees to win college approval for an "interdisciplinary" women's studies major. It was an enterprise that consumed almost a year of her time, and her success makes her something of an anomaly on campus. On the other hand, Serena, whose interest in Pablo Neruda and Jane Austen exceeds her devotion to contemporary women's issues, also feels herself to be anomalous, as does Julie, whose convictions, especially concerning abortion, are idiosyncratic and unpopular. Perhaps this private, slippery feeling that one is painfully different from one's peers is also an inevitable characteristic of undergraduate life. But the feeling is exaggerated when, as now, social change is in the air, and everyone is obliged to define herself in relation to the women's movement.

Jill Ker Conway, Smith's seventh president, and the first to be a woman, is nothing if not politic when she talks about the women's movement. Implicit in what she says is the idea that women aspire to have it all—everything— and that if they are Smith women they are likely to get it. She holds an honors degree from the University of Sydney, a doctorate from Harvard. Although she is far too reticent to volunteer so frontal a statement about her personal life, it is widely assumed that Mrs. Conway and her husband, historian John Conway, take turns at high-prestige appointments. It is her turn now; her husband teaches Canadian studies at UMass.

We met in Mrs. Conway's office in College Hall. The outer office, with its gothic arches, leaded windows, rich Persian carpet, mirrorlike oak floors, evokes images of a private chapel in the house of an affluent Victorian, reminding one that Sophia Smith, the sole inheritor of a large fortune who founded the college in 1871, had in mind a "Christian education" for women:

"It is my opinion," her will stated, "that by the higher and more thorough Christian education of women, what are called their 'wrongs' will be redressed, their wages adjusted, their weight of influence in reforming the evils of society will be greatly increased, as teachers, as writers, as mothers, as members of society, their power for good will be incalculably enlarged. . . . It is not my design to render my sex any the less feminine, but to develop as fully as may be the powers of womanhood, and furnish women with the means of usefulness, happiness and honor, now withheld from them."

These words, bittersweet, redolent of an era when everyone believed in progress, were very much on my mind when I spoke with Mrs. Conway. I had yet to meet a student who thought of motherhood as a vocation, or one who thought of teaching as a means of achieving either status or economic rewards. What would Sophia Smith have thought of this generation of Smith students?

Mrs. Conway spoke to me from across a polished conference table in her airy, uncluttered office. I had to strain to hear her. She speaks with long pauses punctuating considered, measured sentences. Her hands clasp and unclasp in the attitude of prayer, fingertips meeting. Her light-brown hair is tightly curled; her features are delicate—large, slightly hyperthyroid green eyes in a fine-boned patrician face. She looks more ethereal than stereotypically feminine (pictured jogging in the Smith brochure, she looks as incongruous as a bishop on a skateboard), yet there is about this forty-seven-year-old woman an ineffable managerial aura. Little wonder that she has been able to get money and internships from IBM and Gulf Oil.

Except that Smith has no ties to institutionalized religion, "the mission of the college," Mrs. Conway says, "has remained basically unchanged since Sophia Smith's day: to provide the very best liberal-arts education for an all-female student body, to educate leaders who will serve as spokeswomen for women's needs and issues nationally."

Have "women's needs" been articulated by the women's movement? I ask.

"There were men and women doing great scholarship in this country and in Europe relating to the history of women—to social theory as it explains the behavior of gender groups—before the women's movement," she says. "The resurgence of feminism affects the interests of students, but I don't believe that the scholarly enterprise goes on because of it. The effect of the feminist movement on students has been to make it clearly acceptable to be identified with a women's college," she goes on to say. "It is now seen as dignified and strong to share in the lives of other women." (I am thinking of something a Smith alumna, class of 1959, told me: "When I went to Smith, friends who were at coed schools thought of my choice as one of extreme docility or as an act of belligerence. Whether they thought I was a 'lady' or a rebel, they all had the same question: How are you going to find a husband?")

"Feminism," Mrs. Conway says, "has changed students' goals—to what extent compared with the effects of inflation on the lives of the American middle class I cannot say. The middle-class lifestyle is maintained today by a two-career family, and had that economic change not come along I'm less sure how strong the redefinition of students' goals would have been."

Jill Conway talks of the students' "internalizing" strong and positive models of "femininity." The ratio of male to female faculty is sixty-forty in the senior ranks; in the junior ranks it is fifty-fifty. She is quick to deny that feminists find it difficult to get tenure: "People are entitled to their own opinions, and one should be free to advocate any change in the curriculum. What is important is how one stacks up as a scholar. The college has had a long history of support for women in senior administrative positions, and of distinguished women deans. Although it has had male presidents, the chairman of the board has traditionally been a woman, reversing the pattern of other women's colleges."

She does not view her own appointment as a victory for feminism: "I don't believe that sex was a precondition for the search, because the board saw equal numbers of female and male candidates." ("How better to damn the board!" a senior faculty member said when I repeated this remark to him. "The thing is, one doesn't know if Jill's truckling to them or if she's a consummate game player. Unspeakable even to think of having a male president at this point in history!" "Whatever happened to the idea that the best person for the job—male or female—ought to get the job?" I asked. "The best person for the presidency of a woman's college is a female person," he said firmly, "to say nothing of the fact that the female heads of boards she spoke of were figureheads, nothing more.")

Mrs. Conway has her own agenda: "The college is seen by the corporate world as a resource for providing absolutely first-rate management trainees. That is true of the legal and financial world, as well. Women entering highly selective women's colleges score out as much less interested in service careers and much more interested in the high-status, high-achieving careers. I'm not inclined to be overly sad about this. I'd like to see a higher proportion of males doing social work. What is of some concern to me is that young women may be so hell-bent to succeed in one of the very highly pressured careers that they don't early find time for serving others."

This is all very well, except that there is nothing to indicate that men are flocking to the helping professions. And—in spite of her avowed concern for introducing women to a life of service—Mrs. Conway, as I am later to learn, is not urgently propelling women in that direction. She is pragmatic; whether or not she is shortsighted is arguable.

Only once did Mrs. Conway not have a ready response to a question. I asked her whether the reportedly large number of "women-identified women" in the Valley, and their claim to an exclusive culture, had any effect on the Smith population. She paused for what was, even for her, an extraordinarily long time, and said, falteringly: "I would say that there's the same proportion of people with homosexual orientation in the population here as there is in the society at large. I don't define it as a problem because I think it's a private and personal preference with which the college should have no prying concern . . . Have you been to the Helen Hills Hills Chapel yet? It's very lovely . . . " This signaled an end to our conversation. Without knowing why, I asked Mrs. Conway if *Gaudy Night,* Dorothy Sayer's mystery novel about a women's college at Oxford, was one of her favorite books.

"Oh, yes," she said. "Yes, yes," beaming.

Well, of course. One could see the appeal for Mrs. Conway, of the amiable and uncompromising dons about whom Sayers wrote, not one of whom placed personal loyalties above professional honor. Their sole allegiance was to fact; they enjoyed the narrow serenity of academic pursuits.

"That was a long time ago," Mrs. Conway said, "a very long time ago." She removed her glasses, on which her name is stamped in raised letters (one gets the feeling that Jill Conway leaves little to happenstance). "A long time ago . . . But quite lovely to think of, don't you agree?"

I am having lunch at the Faculty Club with Philip Green, an advocate of women's studies programs, and with Catherine Portuges, a professor of comparative literature. Cathy, who has taught at Smith, is director of the women's studies program at the University of Massachusetts, and is also involved in the national task force for women's studies. In the last ten years, 350 women's studies programs have been established across the country. According to their proponents, the aim of these programs is to include the experiences and achievements of women—traditionally neglected—in the teaching of subjects ranging from history and literature to economics and biology.

"There's no argument against a women's studies program, as far as I can see, that isn't also valid against an American studies program," Phil says. "It's a totally arbitrary slice of the field. If you take history, government, sociology, literature, and the English language seriously, you must address yourself to the American versions of them, and you shouldn't have to have a separate program to get you to do that. It would be absurd to study parliamentary government without studying the American Congress; why do you need an American studies program with a concentration on American politics? Nevertheless, American studies are regarded as essential; women's studies are not.

"We have a real problem here: I personally don't feel that there *are* any women in the canon of political theory; if you told me to integrate my nineteenth- and twentieth-century political theory course with women's studies, I would be hard put to do it. I might assign John Stuart Mill's *On the Subjection of Women*, but I wouldn't, and couldn't assign anything by a woman. In Cathy's field, comparative literature, that particular problem doesn't exist. Women's studies developed out of fields in which there were women—English literature, for example."

Cathy: "Yes; but it's not only a question of 'works by' women but ways of *treating* women. That's part of the difficulty of making the case for women's studies. Part of my job is to go to departments and talk about how they can integrate women's studies into their curriculum. I remember one botanist saying, 'But *plants?* Plants don't have a sex!' I said, 'That may be so, but it doesn't mean that you can't be aware of the needs of womens students, not enough of whom feel they're capable of doing work in the sciences.' "

"Of course," Phil says, "it's fair to say that since Jill Conway's been president, Smith has moved away from its parochial, medieval view of liberal arts. Jill's reached out to the business world. But Smith remains immobilized when it comes to breaking away from the disciplinary view of knowledge.

"Sometimes, I'm inclined to believe that power—a kind of power—resides more with the students than with the faculty. Students will ask their teachers if they can do a project related to women in the context of the class; this then shifts the locus of investigation, and widens it for everyone's benefit.

"My own research has been changed by students' concerns. I wrote a book—*The Pursuit of Inequality*—that began out of articles about race, and then I felt obliged to widen that to take in gender discrimination. The book is, as a result, as much about women as it is about blacks and minorities. The subject was in the air—you couldn't avoid it. People do find themselves changing their research as a result of the women's movement—and not just because of pressure. They simply get interested . . . if they're not so defensive that they can't hear new ideas. Amazing how things have changed."

"Not enough," Cathy says.

In 1978, Smith solicited and received a $350,000 grant from the Mellon Foundation for a research project called "Women and Social Change." In 1976, an idea for a research program on women had been informally circulated throughout the college. Some faculty members, female as well as male, expressed their "misgivings" in an open letter to the administration:

Nowhere in her will did Sophia Smith state that the educational excellence she had in mind would best be achieved by a curricular and scholarly emphasis on women. . . .

The intellectual history of this College suggests quite powerfully that women's minds, like men's, are most apt to flourish when they are encouraged to range widely. . . . It would be a mistake to suggest to students or to faculty members that any one set of research topics or techniques has a special place in the "unique responsibility" of the College. . . . No amount of ideological zeal can make research on women more significant than it already is as a legitimate field of scholarly interest. This kind of zeal . . . can create a bias that tends to constrain the wide range of inquiry and freedom to dissent that we consider vital to an institution of higher learning. . . .

The 1976 idea was then modified, and Jill Conway, who had originated it, also gave the 1978 proposal her full support. ("Jill," one of the women active in the project says, her tongue loosened by three Bloody Marys, "is perceived by the conservative faculty as a threat to Western civilization on this campus.") There are nine principal "investigators" involved in the Women and Social Change project, who, with their sixteen undergraduate research assistants, function as a collective in summer workshops. I have lunch one day with four of them in a quiche-and-cider restaurant just off campus.

Donna Devine is researching the social history of Jerusalem's upper-class Palestinian Arabs between World War I and World War II. "When I started to look closely at women in this culture," she says, "everything else seemed superficial by comparison. I started forging new connections: it was no longer possible, for example, to look at the role of Islam in independence movements without looking at the social, political, and historical implication of purdah."

Marilyn Schuster is working on the problems of narrative in French fiction by contemporary women, from Colette to Monique Wittig. She is trying to discover "what is unique to women writers and what they are able to do that conventional narratives or male-dominated narratives are unable to do."

Marilyn believes that whatever distinguishes women's voices from men's is owing to biology—to a woman's experience of herself as a physical being. Susan Van Dyne, who is studying American women poets, believes, on the other hand, that these differences are socially derived and determined. This is a question that vexes most feminists.

When we ask what women want, we must ask this prior question: Are gender differences biologically or socially determined? And nothing like a consensus exists. Which is probably why many women echo the words of earlier feminists: never mind what *women* want; ask me what *I* want. In some quarters this is seen as a "retreat" from politics and a return to personal solutions.

The participants in the project—divided on key issues—take umbrage when they are seen as an undifferentiated mass: "I've had letters from my own department," Susan Van Dyne says, "expressing the fear that my work will be unthinking, uncritical advocacy of women poets—that I will confuse intention with accomplishment, and make the mistake of assuming anything written by a woman is good. In other words, because I am—we are—politically committed to feminism, it is assumed that our zeal will pervert our judgment."

"We're accused of being sloppy and of having no methodology because our work isn't rooted in one discipline," Martha Acklesberg says. (She is studying the anarchist collectives in Spain during the Civil War, especially women's roles in them.) "They think we're a consciousness-raising group because we share our ideas and papers. The idea of a support group—of people not jealously preserving their own academic turf—is alien to them."

"And leads," says Marilyn Schuster, "to people saying that our lectures and conferences are 'just like revival meetings, where you sit around and pay homage to your speaker.' Whereas, in fact, we've had fierce fights."

Susan Van Dyne says: "I'm happy to tell my classes that my criteria are subjective, and that I am presenting only one way of analyzing a problem. Students learn to love it. They understand that a passionate political commitment to feminism can coexist with a love for facts, even when the facts upset your theories. To be tentative is to be human."

Serena, a freshman who is my daughter's friend and therefore mine, has invited me to dinner at her house, Martha Wilson. This greatly pleases public-relations director Ann Shanahan, who is afraid that I will spend an inordiante amount of time with special-interest groups, like the Lesbian Alliance, and that, as a consequence, the "typical" Smith student will elude me, though Ann herself is hard put to assemble a group that she would define as "typical."

Student elections are being held. Posters—orange, blue, green, yellow—enliven Martha Wilson's chintz and mahogany expanses. Everywhere there are signs advising students to conserve electricity (a cause far more popular, if one is to judge from the weight of paper devoted to it, than El Salvador, disarmament, or ERA). Graffiti in the public telephone booth reveals a fondly intimate knowledge of male anatomy. As I enter the house, I hear a woman chanting, "I am *madly* in love . . . madly . . . He is wonderful . . . wonderful . . ."

Serena introduces me to Page Kelley, head resident of Martha Wilson, a senior who functions as liaison between students and deans. Page says that in order to become head resident, she had to reassure the administration that she had no "personal grudge" against lesbians, and that she could handle tensions that might arise in a house where there was lesbian activity. The tensions arise from the fact that "heterosexuals worry that homosexuals will scare men off. And they have done. Lesbians have gotten hostile when men visited."

Fair-minded, Page says she understands the source of lesbians' hostility: "It's hard to be homosexual in a heterosexual world. Actually, someone who plays a phonograph too loud is more trouble to me than a lesbian who minds her own business." Page is looking forward to a workshop in which lesbians will discuss the "political implications of homosexuality." ("What are the political implications of heterosexuality?" I ask. "Oh. I guess I've never had to think about that," Page answers. "Should I?")

Because the women don't compete for men on campus, Smith promotes intense friendships; in the view of many, emotional intimacy, in turn, gets confused with sex. "I'm not sure people know what they're doing," says Meredith, a freshman. "I have to tell myself to take it easy when I see displays of affection between women." "The thing that shocked me," Serena adds, "is that when I saw . . . cuddling . . . I *was* shocked. I thought I was so open-minded."

It is interesting how a minority population can become a major concern on campus—a major concern, but not *the* major concern. Page and Serena's friends are much more concerned with their Smith education than with homosexual activity. Kirsten, a freshman, speaks for all the women when she says she is convinced Smith will uniquely prepare her for the executive position she expects to take: "My father, who's an insurance executive, says that women graduates are much more finished and polished and mature than men of the same age. And Smith women are more poised and graceful—more classy—than other college women."

All of these women expect to work. Some of them expect to take time off to have children, others—somewhat naïvely, perhaps—expect that corporations will provide the flexible work schedules that will enable them to be wives, mothers, and career women. All of them are, I think, a little scared that there may be a gap between their expectations and reality. Not all of them admit they're scared. Page does.

"I'm going through this horrible crisis right now," she says, "because I've been going out with somebody for two years, and I love him. It wouldn't be a problem if I didn't love him. It would be very easy for me to get a job and work in New York, where he works. But the thing is, I've passed the Foreign Service exam. And on top of that, I've had two years of Chinese here, and I've enrolled in a school in Taiwan. I'd need to stay there for at least two years to become fluent in the language. He doesn't want to give up his job; why should he? I could compromise and work for a bank or go to law school, but I don't want to.

"So right now my relationship with my boyfriend is just falling apart. We're hardly speaking to each other.

"If I do pursue a career in the Foreign Service, I would have to marry someone in the service and then worry all my life about getting transferred every two years, or I would have to marry somebody who would not mind being a 'househusband.' And, as much as I like to think of myself as liberated, I'm not sure, since working is so important to me, that I could respect somebody who did the housework, or was my dependent.

"I love the idea of having children. Ask any woman in this house how much I like bossing people around and telling them how to run their lives. I'd enjoy taking care of kids.

"A doctor in our infirmary here has the perfect situation: she gets up at six in the morning, dresses the children, gives them breakfast, plays with them for an hour, and then leaves home and arrives here by eight or nine. Then her husband plays with the kids till eleven, when the housekeeper comes in. At four the doctor comes home from work . . . something tells me I'm sounding silly."

Well, not silly, exactly. Listening to herself talk, Page almost immediately sees the problem: the situation she describes (which sounds, she admits, a little bit like musical chairs) takes enormous luck and discipline—and it takes money. Page falls back on an unexamined cliché: "The quality of time you spend with children counts, not the quantity."

"No," says Kirsten, "it doesn't. My best friend's mother went off to work when she was in the first grade, and it was terrible to see how all the values of the family changed from affection and cooperation to an emphasis on monetary things: if you were going to the dentist you'd get two Matchbox cars or a doll or something. The house started working like a corporation. The mother was paying her family off." And yet Kirsten wants a career, preferably one with a corporation for which she can travel. She is visibly troubled by the sacrifices and compromises this may entail: "I don't want to think about it. I can't."

Not one of the women present did not think of children as a form of social security: "I get the feeling," Page says, "that a lot of women here who are interested in finance and corporate work are going to discover—and I'm afraid of it for myself—that they're going to be lonely. I really get depressed when I think about a future where I don't have someone to come home to."

All the women believed that by virtue of being Smith women, they could automatically accede to high-entry jobs when they graduated; they are, they say (as unselfconsciously as possible), "leaders." ("Vassar's reputation dropped fifteen notches when it went coed.") "We're not going to have to fight our way to the top," Meredith says. "If a company wants a token woman, chances are it'll be a Smith woman."

Kirsten says: "Sometimes I get the feeling that everyone at Smith is telling us, Look what you've broken out of! Your mothers weren't considered good women unless they were wonderful mothers and kissed their kids and their husbands goodbye after a perfect breakfast and cleaned the whole house and had wonderful lunch waiting and then had wonderful dinner waiting. Now the message we're getting from Smith is that if you're not the head of a corporation, you're not a successful woman."

Page looks defiant. "Why *can't* we have it all?"

A report from the Office of Career Development: in 1959, there were four Smith alumnae in teaching for every one in business; in 1979, there were four Smith alumnae in business for every one in teaching. In the class of 1960, 61 percent of all graduates said they wished to be homemakers; in the class of 1970, 15 percent said they would be homemakers. In the class of 1980, not even one percent chose domesticity.

Nancy Steeper is a career and program counselor in the Office of Career Development. She is distressed: "A large number of students have mothers who have not worked. They're getting very mixed messages. Their parents are pushing hard: 'Choose! Find something out there in the world! Surely you'll be going on to law school?'

"All this at the same time as they admire the mother who stayed home. They want to have a family, and they want to have it the way she had it. Those who've thought hard enough about it know it's economically not feasible.

"I don't think there's any question that the women's movement has raised our sights and our opportunities. At the same time, it's putting us in a tremendous double bind. These young women feel they have to be superwomen, and there really isn't much for them to model themselves on. It's no accident that the magazine I see most around campus is *Savvy* [subtitled: *The Magazine for the Executive Woman*].

"When the head of the career development office came here from Radcliffe in 1972, her task was to place people in jobs in education and the social services. Now the emphasis has changed. The head of the career development office now oversees the on-campus recruiting program for corporations. She feels very keenly that *that* is her mission. We're talking very heavy banking, we're talking investment houses, we're talking IBM, Digital, Procter & Gamble, marketing and sales positions.

"I have to tell you that I believe the women's movement has failed us completely. Whose interest does it serve for a visionary feminist to present a fantasy of a world where people easily share responsibility for child rearing, where corporations are sensitive to these issues? It's just not happening in the real world at all."

Nancy Steeper invites me to look at the March 1981 issue of *The New Current,* a college magazine. I see this cartoon: four young women stand in line outside the career development office. They are dressed in various styles of attire—funky, preppy, casual, and punk. The same four women exit from the career development office. They are dressed exactly alike: all four are wearing three-piece business suits—the executive woman's uniform.

I am thinking: Who among Smith's famous alumnae might serve as "role models"? It goes without saying that nobody wants to emulate Jean Harris, or, for that matter, Sylvia Plath. Gloria Steinem and Betty Friedan do not come equipped with husbands and children. Nancy Reagan won't do either; she is perceived by most students as having no life of her own.

It is perhaps a paradox that one has to reach further back in time—before the resurgence of feminism—to find a woman who did manage to have a husband, children, and a career: Anne Morrow Lindbergh. To the young, of course, Anne Morrow Lindbergh is part of ancient history; since people under thirty tend to telescope time, Mrs. Lindbergh might have been a contemporary of Cleopatra. To say nothing of the fact that economic circumstances did not oblige her to work for a living. One can't imagine Anne Morrow Lindbergh talking about two-paycheck families.

I am spending an evening at the Davis Student Center, with students from the Women's Resource Center and the Lesbian Alliance. (On this night, I like Davis—maybe I have had an overdose of good taste. I like the molded day-glo hot-orange panels that line the walls, the vending machines, the sound of a Diana Ross record pounding in the background, the thumping of a piano: "Heart and Soul," a song I haven't heard since the Fifties.)

There is real reluctance on the part of many Smith students who define themselves as feminists to ally themselves with the Women's Resource Center. They are afraid that if they do so they will become identified as lesbians. The actual number of lesbians on campus is of course, impossible to determine. Seventy-five are associated with the Alliance; three times as many women, from both the college and the local community, came to a lesbian dance held last year.

Some lesbians have contrived to create their own mini-environments at Smith: they live in two co-op houses, Hover and Tenney, which are small and, according to the lesbians, predominantly homosexual. The administration prefers to act as if this were not so; the lesbian women insist that it is so. Somebody is engaged in wishful thinking. Sorting fact from fiction, I draw rumors the way a magnet draws filings: one student, at an earlier meeting, made a point of telling me that Tyler House is a lesbian house. "How absurd," an assistant dean says. "Tyler is full of theater students who keep erratic hours. Your informant was making a quantum leap from thespianism to lesbianism." And, in fact, my "informant" was confusing Tyler with Tenney.

"Bliss to live in a co-op," the lesbians say. "We have the best food—we cook our own, and do our own cleaning, too—and the best dinner-table conversations, and the best parties. And we have very little to do with the administration." (So far, they seem to be making a better case for their exclusivity than for their oppression.)

Allison, a junior, says, "The administration knows it has a lot to preserve and a lot to gain by minimizing and even hiding the lesbian presence on campus. Smith gets its money from the men that alumnae marry. We are ignored—which is a subtle form of oppression."

"How's this for oppression?" a young women demands: "I wrote a paper on biblical criticism, and I attacked current interpretations of the Bible because they were misogynist—and I got a C+. I always get A's. So I went to the man. He said my criticism was defensive, and that I was trying to change the Bible. Imagine.

"And another time, I spoke up in class and said that the 'holes and slime' section of Sartre's *Being and Nothingness* was offensive and compromised his entire philosophy. I got no support from the other feminists in class. They were afraid of getting bad grades."

Of course it's impossible to evaluate these charges, although I see their point. It is difficult for me to believe, however, that they will ever find an environment *less* inhospitable than Smith. This makes me feel both glad for them and sad: the shocks they will encounter in what they call the real world are, I think, going to be a far ruder than they expect.

While most of the women reject lesbian separatism as "static" and "unrealistic," some of the women see a separatist environment as the only one in which they will be able to flourish.

"There's a debate among separatists," one woman says, "about whether a male child who is over five years old can be admitted into a separatist collective." I am as chilled by this remark as they are amused by my asking them how they expect to have children at all if they refuse to consort with men.

"Why do you see that as a problem?"

"It would be if you regarded sex as an act of love," I say. Silence. "For that matter, it would be a problem even if you divorced sex from love, wouldn't it? If it isn't love, it's lust . . . "

Laughter. Most of them seem to think I am hopelessly old-fashioned— possibly Catholic?—because I make a distinction between lust and love. I admit to confusion: these women have made it very clear that they don't wish to be regarded as "breeders"; how will they regard the men who sow the seeds for their children? And what man would wish to be chosen for so peculiar a task? More laughter. The "obvious" solutions have escaped me: adoption, artifical insemination, and . . . parthenogenesis. *Parthenogenesis?* Yes. "Mary Daly says male scientists conspire to keep information from us; we really don't need men at all." I have no trouble believing that Mary Daly has said this; in *Gyn/Ecology*, she talks about being able to have "nonverbal conversations" with animals, a privilege denied men.

"Mary Daly is gaga," a woman from the Resource Center says. She is knitting socks for her lover (male).

"It takes a lot of imagination nowadays to find something besides going to graduate school, getting married, or going corporate," a senior says, "and those are options I entirely reject. My political commitment coincides completely with my personal aversion to marriage and corporations. So, maybe I'll travel across the country till I get to San Francisco—look into alternative educational systems, maybe, or alternative health-care systems."

One would-be separatist suggests to me that the perfect job is driving a bus—you can look straight ahead and avoid eye contact with men.

But most of the women in this room are no different from their peers in wishing to enter high-status professions, politics, and the corporate world. Berry, a junior, says she is "aiming at graduate school in business and planning to test out the corporate world—you know, work for a multinational or some horrid thing like that. I know the arguments against it. I can understand it when my friends—most of whom are socialists or socialist-feminists or whatever they call themselves—say to me, How can you be a capitalist and a token? But what I find myself doing is taking a look at what I can do that will leave me the most options five or ten years from now. It's easy to talk about the patriarchal structure and how messed up it is; I want to experience it. I want to see just what's wrong with it and then move away from it. Unless I do that, I won't know what it is I really have to do. I think the corporate structure will serve me; it may help me to evolve."

One woman announces her intention to do "grass-roots organizing around feminist issues—abortion, in particular"; another is interested in a "career in films—documentaries about women's lives." Joy, a sophomore, is an athlete who wants, in some way, to change the National Collegiate Athletic Association, which is "very male-oriented and money-oriented—the NCAA will take over women's sports and just kill them." She seems—this is hardly uncommon among people who want to work "outside the system"—to have a love-hate relationship with money: "I'm convinced now that what my parents have always told me is true—without money you can do a lot on a small scale, but you really get dumped on. I just want to *demolish* football."

The notion of separatist communities disturbs me profoundly. Utopianism dies hard; while the idea is durable, no exclusive sectarian community has endured the test of time in America. Lesbian-separatist communities are a permutation of an idea that continues to excite the imagination to visions of a perfect world, and that continues, in practice, to fail. I can't forget the words I heard at Smith: "Once a male child is over five years old, it becomes questionable as to whether he should remain in the community."

I have come, with these words sounding discordantly in my head, to Jean Bethke Elshtain, professor of political science at UMass, who does little to soothe me. She tells me of a student who, after her divorce, began to associate exclusively with "women-identified women." After a few months in a lesbian commune, she declared she couldn't deal with a male child—her own. So she gave the child over to her ex-husband, whom she despised, forfeiting her right ever to see him again. The little boy was two and a half years old.

Jean Elshtain—who has taught at Smith—has an arsenal of such stories: "Three or four years ago I had a student in one of my courses who was very bright but obviously quite disturbed. Her papers were cogently argued, but ruined by spurts of gratuitous, idiot rhetoric: 'Freud was a cancer-ridden pig.' She finally did well in the course, after a lot of give and take, and then she disappeared from campus for six months. She came into my office one afternoon, toward the end of the day; she had been crying, and she was holding a puppy in her arms. She'd been living in Northampton, in a home with a group of women, and the women had held a group meeting about the puppy. It was the consensus that she had to get rid of the puppy because it was male, and nothing male was allowed in the household. She was told that either the puppy had to go or she had to go. Of course this is—I hope—an extreme example of separatist life; still, it shows what the logical consequences of a certain kind of thinking—if you can call it thinking—are. She asked for my advice. I said, 'Keep the puppy and find a different place to live.' I don't know what became of her; I never saw her again."

Jean points out that Western political thought, from, Plato and Aristotle on, has been imbued with the notion that there are two realms: the realm of necessity and the realm of freedom. "The realm of necessity—the daily renewal of life, which includes everything from washing the dishes to giving birth and caring for a senile aunt—was despised; it was the work of women and of slaves. The realm of freedom has, in practice, consisted of adult males contracting together to do politics, make policy. One of the major contributions of Christianity, with its emphasis on the goodness of the material world, was to enable us to understand that the 'despised' is sacred. The realm of necessity has its own dignity and its own integrity: it's the realm in which people live and die and find meaning."

The trouble is, of course, that the profoundly revolutionary idea that the realm of necessity is sacred has been more honored in word than in deed. We still have adult males contracting to do what is considered the important work of the world. When feminists started arguing—frivolously, many of us thought—about who was going to wash the dishes and take out the garbage, they were, in part, and with justification, reacting against being excluded from the realm of freedom. But they were also, in part, refusing to accept the idea that no work that sustains human life is dirty work. That is why one feminist at Smith was able to say that "both Mother Teresa of Calcutta and Dorothy Day are nothing but super housekeepers."

(A Marxist feminist from Smith tells Jean that to raise a child is to "reproduce a future commodity for the labor force." Jean says: "Is that why I'm scared when my son goes bike riding? Because capitalism may be losing a wage earner? Tell me another.")

When women at Smith talk of "flexitime," child-care sharing, and two-career families, they are talking about a new model for the family, one that would allow them to exist in the realm of necessity and in the realm of freedom. When lesbian separatists talk about communes in which men will have no part—or in which men will be so denatured as not to be recognizable as men at all—they are talking about dismantling the family, which they no longer see as a functioning unit.

Whether Smith women honor the family or wish to overthrow it, they are almost without exception in favor of abortion on demand, which is seen not as a terrible necessity but as an absolutely moral act. To say that "we have the absolute right to control our own bodies" is to express the wish for absolute freedom, and to deny that we live *in relation to* other people. I have trouble squaring their position on abortion with their position on ERA.

Many of the same women who believe absolutely in every woman's right to abort are not in favor of ERA or are to some extent ambivalent about it. This is due in part to ignorance: few women know its exact wording. It may also be a consequence of their being privileged women: they simply don't expect to be discriminated against. I keep thinking of one sentence I heard at Smith, and of the worlds of meaning it contains: "I want the right to an abortion if I need one; but I want men to open the door for me, too."

The women's movement originated the slogan "the personal is political." If that were altogether true, it would also be true that the political is (always) personal; and if *that* were true, it would be very nearly impossible to form friendships across gender, class, or race lines. Any slogan, no matter how resonant, is only a slogan, simplistic, and not expressive of layered, complex realities, of profound truths.

A Passage to India ends, as nobody needs to be reminded, with an Indian saying to a member of the Raj: we can be friends only when we are equals. And yet it was also Forster who said, "Only connect." Both sentiments can exist in one human heart. And if no way is found to reconcile these apparently opposing ideas—muddle, waste, and tragedy.

Toward the end of my visit, I grow tired of "sexual politics" (hateful phrase). I retreat into the past.

In the Sophia Smith Collection, I come across this passage from a diary written in 1786: "I almost wished for some memorable event to begin this little volume with, but my life flows in a smooth stream . . . tho insignificant as it is, me thinks I would not like to forget it all together."

The life of this anonymous woman—births, deaths, marriage days—is neatly contained in one of the thousands of gray filing boxes in the Sophia Smith Collection, amassed by Margaret Storrs Grierson, college archivist from 1942 to 1965. The collection attracts scholars from all over the world who wish to do research on women and the labor movement, women and peace movements, birth control, property rights, suffrage. Manuscripts and photographs document the achievements, and celebrate the daily lives, of women famous and unknown. In happy hours at the Collection, I find myself moved by the letters, photographs, even recipes, of dead, ordinary women.

Once I bought an early-American jam cupboard from the Salvation Army. After my son had stripped it of seven layers of paint and peeled off the yellow newspapers that lined its pine shelves, we found written, in faded, spidery letters: *Peaches, Put Up June 1801; Plums, July.* I felt as if I were entering a dead woman's life; to say that I felt a surge of love for her is not to exaggerate. (Love calls us back to the things of this world: peaches, plums.)

I experience that same sense of linkage to the past (the thrill, not at all morbid, one sometimes feels in an old graveyard, which speaks eloquently of life as a continuum, and of death as a part of life) at the Sophia Smith Collection: leather-bound daguerrotypes held together by frayed ribbons, buttons from the early twentieth-century British suffrage movement, suffrage Valentine's Day cards, recipes written in fine copperplate, yellow ribbons of watered silk, "for the Amendment." Lovely, after hearing so many many words at Smith, to be able to touch, feel, hold the past in one's hands.

An elaborate fold-out suffrage Valentine's Day card, hand-lettered and painted:

With wisdom, dauntless will, or gold or
*   grace or just sheer grit,*
Some special part is yours to play
So come and help us win the Day!
For woman's sake, oh don't Decline
To be
*   A Suffrage Valentine*

A suffrage postcard: "WOMAN should not condemn MAN . . . rather condemn parents for having trained their sons since the beginning of time, in the belief that MAN only is competent to vote." (The terms of the dialectic remain the same: Is MAN the enemy? Are we the victims of societally imposed roles? Will these questions ever be resolved? [Does it matter? Silver thimbles marked VOTES FOR WOMEN; silver hooks and eyes in packets marked UNITE! These things are real.])

In her diary, Clara Barton writes from Gettysburg in a large, sprawling hand (she was by this time almost blind): "I wonder if a solder [sic] ever does mend a bullet hole in his coat."

Shoulder to shoulder, English women marched in freezing weather, calling for suffrage and a fifty-hour work week. They marched from Carlisle to London; near Watling Street, police trained fire hoses on them. I am reading an anonymous woman's account. It is phlegmatic, but underlined with the joy of collective action:

One shopkeeper was heard to remark with great surprise and credulity in her tone, "They looks quite respectable." . . . Every now and then some man would raise his hat to us, as we marched past, and if only they could have realised how encouraging a simple action like that was to us, I am sure it might have happened oftener. . . . I was sorry to think that our visit to Oxford was over, but I had to keep reminding myself that we were not out for pleasure.

A handwritten cookbook, 1832: "To Make a Bridal Cake." Recipes for Cream Flummery, Quince Marmalade, Orange Wine. "A Sidedish—Boil a calve's head until half-done," "Funeral Meats . . ."

I am not a scholar; I will never do research here. It does not take a scholar's appetite for facts to see the irony implicit in a 1919 poster: EQUAL PAY FOR EQUAL WORK.

I leave the college with hope and sorrow so intimately braided I cannot tell them apart.

And I leave asking myself the only question that seems immediately answerable: not, What do women want? but, What do I want most? (and Is it good? and Can I have it?) I know I cannot have it all. Nor can my daughter. Nor can my son. Nobody.

PART VI

Sexuality

The sexual behavior and experience of woman, their meaning for her and their effects on others, have been the subject of writers for most of the history of Western civilization. Beliefs about her sexuality and its effects on men have caused her to be seen as dangerous and polluting and have inspired punitive attempts to prohibit or control its expression. The demeanor of her sexual behavior has been viewed as evidence of her goodness or badness as a person; she might be modestly asexual and virtuous, or seductive, lustful, and wicked. Traditionally woman's highest praise has been awarded her in the role of mother, made possible by her sexual submission in the bonds of marriage. But the traditional wisdom of our society has not sanctioned expression of her sexuality for its own sake. Young men's sowing of wild oats might be viewed with indulgence, and even married men might occasionally stray, or keep a mistress. But young women must be virginal at marriage and faithfully submissive thereafter.

The truth about female sexuality has historically eluded its commentators, be they priests or philosophers. Reasons for this have included the unacceptability of sex as a subject for research, a moral climate wherein openness was impossible, and the constraints upon women as investigators or as writers on the subject. Until recently, then, most of the writings on female sexuality have been by males, speaking from personal experience or strongly held beliefs, unembarrassed by the lack of both empirical data and validation from women themselves.

Beliefs about female sexuality have generally been of two kinds: that woman's lust is insatiable and dangerous to man; or that she has little or no sex drive at all, being primarily the passive recipient of man's desire, to which she submits in the service of her potential motherhood. The first of these beliefs is exemplified by the witch persecutions that swept over Europe during the Middle Ages and later, causing millions of women to be tortured or put to death because of their suspected sexual liaisons with the Devil. The second became a modal belief during the Victorian era, with its rigid codes of morality and decency that held physical passion to be immoral and unladylike. These coexisting beliefs are incarnated respectively in the prostitute and the virtuous wife.

Though Freud's theories of female sexuality have been shown to be reflections of both a patriarchal society and the Victorian ideal, his writings on this and other areas of sexuality eventually helped to convey respectability on it as a topic for further study by scientists. From midcentury on, the works of Alfred Kinsey, William Masters and Virginia Johnson, Mary Jane Sherfey, and many others have greatly illuminated the area. There are now scholarly journals and professional conferences devoted to research on sexual behavior, and courses on sexuality are offered in many colleges and universities. Recent investigations have included such methods as interviews, questionnaires, and direct observation of sexual responses under controlled conditions. From all these have emerged better understandings of the impressive diversity and variability of female sexuality. The inadequacy of explanations based solely on woman's biology or social condition is now realized. New research and theories are helping us to sample the range and variety of female sexuality, its development, its course, and its many experiential qualities.

The first paper in this section, John Haller's "From Maidenhood to Menopause: Sex Education for Women in Victorian America," fittingly describes the "manners and morals" teachings that informed American women about sex and prescribed its expression. Steeped in piety and sentimentality, the sex-in-life manuals of the time dealt with the proper training of girls, the problem of masturbation, the vices of novel reading and dancing, and sexual relations in marriage. Girls should be ideal models of proper behavior, refraining from talk of romance, letter writing, affectionate displays with other girls, and, above all, from any stimulus that might inflame their senses. Advised always to be passive, women were taught that courtship, proposals, and marital sex were to be instigated by the male. The wife was responsible for keeping her husband's lust in check, by separate bedrooms and avoidance of any provocative behavior. Orgasms might make a woman barren, and sex during pregnancy could result in unhealthy, short-lived offspring. As Haller points out, the manuals acted as moral judges of society, documenting middle-class myths about the role of sexuality in life. Though they seem utterly out of touch with reality as we know it today, one wonders how many women were made anxious and even damaged by them; and one sees, too, their tracings in some contemporary attitudes and policies concerning, for example, birth control and sex education.

Communication between mothers and daughters about intimate matters such as sexuality is open and valued for some, problematic or nonexistent for others. In "Changes in Female Sexuality: A Study of Mother/Daughter Communication and Generational Differences," Marilyn Yalom and her colleagues describe a recent study of mothers and daughters, their sexual behavior in high school and college, their sexual attitudes and values, and the communication between them on sexual subjects. Using questionnaires, the authors collected data on these subjects from women who had graduated from college in 1954 and who had college-age daughters, and from college women of the class of 1980. As one might expect, significantly different patterns of behavior emerged from the class of 1954 than from the class of 1980, with the latter reporting earlier and more frequent sexual activity in high school and college. The shift in norms, however, was not reflected in the quality of communication between the younger group and their own mothers, and the older group and their own daughters. Interestingly, the older group were both more comfortable and more satisfied with discussions of sexuality with their daughters than were the younger group with such discussions with their mothers. The daughters seemed to feel there was more of a problem than the mothers did, perhaps identifying their mothers as more conservative in their values or more fragile or easily shocked than in fact they are. Some subjects are easier to talk about than others, however. Menstruation, marriage, and abortion are more likely to be discussed; open communication about masturbation, orgasm, and love with another woman is less common.

Marriage has been the only universally approved relationship within which women can experience their sexuality. While sex outside of marriage is common today among both the unmarried and the married, the shift is rather recent historically, and such conduct, for women especially, has had many negative consequences. This differential treatment, plus the attitudes described in Haller's paper above, means that marriage is the most typical setting for women's sexual activities. In "Sexuality in Marriage," I examine the historical setting for marital sexuality, including early research on marital sex, and survey some variables of sexual behavior in marriage today.

Contemporary research on frequency of sex, on foreplay and techniques of intercourse, and on the experience of orgasm for married women is reviewed. These studies support observations that today's women are experiencing sex more frequently and enjoying it more than did their counterparts of earlier times. Masturbation and sex during pregnancy have shed their old taboos, and a majority of married women now report being satisfied with their sex lives.

Patterns of sexual behavior are part of society and culture; they reflect sex roles, beliefs about men and women, notions of modesty, and socialization practices. Prior to the 1970s, however, little was known about sexual practices in other cultures, as anthropologists seemed to share the Victorian ideal of reticence. Recent studies are developing a knowledge base for the subject, and "Sexuality in Marriage" surveys some findings about marital sex practices in non-Western societies. This work reminds us once again of the diversity, in this area as in others, among earth's people.

If the study of female sexuality in general was slow to emerge from the shadows, the study of lesbians has been even more neglected. Defining a lesbian as a woman who prefers another woman as a sexual partner, Del Martin and Phyllis Lyon in "The Realities of Lesbianism" proceed to dispel the most common myths and misconceptions about lesbianism: that lesbians can be identified by their attempts to dress, look, and act like males, that lesbians are psychologically disturbed because they are frustrating their "nature" by not having children, and that lesbians frequently try to seduce heterosexual women. The authors describe in particular the problems faced by the woman who is trying to accept her lesbianism, but who has to deal with her own old attitudes, guilts, and values, as well as with those of her family and of society. The young woman, especially, faces self-doubt and feelings of isolation as she strives to reconcile her sexuality with her still developing personal identity.

The only difference between the sexuality of lesbians and all other women is in their choice of partner. This paper promotes understanding and acceptance of women who have suffered dual discrimination, as women and as lesbians.

The papers in this section are unified by their respect for the sexuality of women, its meanings, diversity, and importance within the contexts of women's lives. Variously regarded as unimportant, dangerous, or non-existent, the sexual life of women can now be appreciated as a significant part of human behavior and as a legitimate area of inquiry and study. While the openness and interest that have emerged in the past two decades are part of the general climate of greater freedom and permissiveness growing out of the counterculture movement of the 1960s, the research itself, its content and style, partake of feminism and the women's movement, as they gave women permission to be sexual persons and to investigate with respect and with pleasure the phenomena of their own bodies.

19

From Maidenhood to Menopause
Sex Education for Women in Victorian America

John S. Haller, Jr.

The "twilight talks" for American women during the Victorian era, concealed in manuals of hygiene and ethics, religious pamphlets, medical articles, and etiquette books, reflected the late nineteenth century's conspicuous mask of prudery. Sex, like nature, proceeded according to an established set of laws or principles which, when carefully observed, would prevent women from yielding to the lower passions. Sex had a certain order and harmony which manifested the infinite wisdom of the Deity, but seldom did the concept include the words beauty and goodness. The sex-in-life manuals were calculated to impress the feminine mind with sentiments of virtue and chastity, and the notion that sex had somehow interfered with the realization of those objectives. Intelligent discussion of sex predisposed the Victorian woman to an assortment of inferences in which sex was somehow at variance with the search for morality and the proper definition of virtue. The same Providence that watched over America in its victories and peace was similarly engaged in the management of the American woman and her capacity as preserver of the species. In this fashion, American manners and morals became the darlings of religious and medical tracts which found in sex the pernicious spectre of Satan and the engine of immorality. Deeply Protestant in tone, with a strong undercurrent of Old Testament vengeance, nineteenth century manuals protrayed sex as the basest of human tendencies, the aberrations of which were invariably detected and punished through disease and mental anguish. Sex as described in the manuals became middle-class, with all the marks of sobriety, propriety, modesty, and conformity, and provided for rural America much the same function it provided for urban America looking across the Atlantic for cues for correct behavior. American sexual morality consisted of—and reflected— middle class prejudices, sentimentality, romanticized expectations, the working of Divine Providence, and pseudo-scientific sophistication.

From another point of view, the sex-in-life manuals were a carry-over from the dabblers of the mid-nineteenth century society in the area of pseudo-science, liberal Christianity, Transcendentalism, and perfectionist tendencies. It was with the sex manuals that the clergy, who were declining in their function as medical advisors, and the physicians, who were attempting to widen their function as spiritual as well as physical healer, met to reform both medicine and morals. Strands of Thomsonianism, sentimentalism, Swedenborgianism, homeopathy, phrenology, and animal magnetism converged to create a congenial atmosphere for reconciling the spiritual affectations of middle class morality with matters of the flesh.[1]

The sex-in-life manuals gave to the American woman a common body of ideals to be taken seriously, out of which she was to shape the manner and morals of her class. Here was a pedagogical apparatus molded to direct her duties as maiden and anxious parent in the area of personal conduct. The empirical data from which the manuals drew their social and moral fabric came from a body of middle-class fictions—myths which sought to explain the discrepancy between middle-class principles and the reality of sin, disease, poverty and immorality. A sense of pretention, along with a very real sense of educational, ethical, and economic superiority to the rawness of working-class America, combined to create a thinly concealed romantic moral code, steeped in fictitious parables and impossible ideals, struggling to assert a new and imaginative perspective for the American class structure. The aspirations of the middle class form a vital link in a proper understanding of sexual attitudes of the late nineteenth century.

The proper training of girls, their personal hygiene, their relations with other children, their reading habits, and the embarrassing problem of masturbation (variously called the "solitary vice," "self-pollution," or "the "soul-and-body-destroyer") dominated a major portion of the sex manuals of the day. Girls were cautioned never to handle their sexual organs, for, while it gave a temporary pleasure, the habit left "its mark upon the face so that those who are wise may know what the girl is doing."[2] The misuse of the sexual organs brought an inevitable threat of disease and severe complications in later life. "The infliction of the penalty may be somewhat delayed," wrote one physician, "but it will surely come, sooner or later." The young girl who practiced the solitary vice would never escape the consequences of her indiscretion. All through life, "the penalty of unlawful transgression [would] be visited upon her," and when she became a wife and mother, her earlier abuse would make the "perils incident to [her present role] be vastly increased."[3] She would become subject to a multitude of disorders such as backaches, tenderness of the spine, nervousness, indolence, pale cheeks, hollow eyes and a generally "languid manner." Her attitude, once pure and innocent, would turn peevish, irritable, morose, and disobedient; furthermore, she would suffer loss of memory, appear "bold in her manner instead of being modest," and manifest unnatural appetites for mustard, pepper, vinegar, cloves, clay, salt, chalk, and charcoal.[4] One writer conjectured that her eyes became dull (with bluish rings), that she would have difficulty in concentration and in study, and that blindness, stupidity, and even idiocy could occur.[5]

Nearly all manuals condemned the romantic novel as the villain behind the increased evidence of sexual neurasthenia, hysteria, and generally poor health in American women. Not only did sentimental literature tempt them to impurity, but the emotional stimulation that accompanied novel reading tended "to develop the passions prematurely, and turn the thoughts into a channel which leads in the direction of the formation of vicious habits."[6] Whatever stimulated emotions in the young girl caused a corresponding development in her sexual organs. Overindulgence in romantic stories produced a flow of blood to certain body organs causing "excessive excitement" and finally disease.[7] For this reason, children's parties, staying up late, puppy love, hot drinks, "boarding-school fooleries," loose conversation, "the drama of the ballroom," talk of beaux, of a "strange pleasure" in her constitution—her pulse fluttered, her cheeks glowed with the approach of her partner, and she "could not look him in the eye with the same frank gayety as before." Acoording to Sylvanus Stall in *What a Young Husband Ought to Know*, the male transferred his physical emotions to the woman through animal magnetism. It was not the dance itself, nor even the intentions of the male dance partner; rather, the female absorbed the male's more domineering and passionate nature through the magnetic contact. Thus, wrote a ruined and repentant girl, "I became abnormally developed in my lowest nature."[8]

The manuals passed hurriedly over another nasty habit—the display of unnatural affection of girls for other girls. The custom of holding each other's hands, of kissing and caressing "should be kept for . . . hours of privacy, and never indulged in before gentlemen." The reasons for this admonition "readily suggest themselves," and there were other motives "known to those well acquainted with the world."[9]

In one of her more important functions, the young lady was to provide a constant source of idealism to her brothers. "So many temptations beset young men of which young women know nothing," wrote the author of *The Young Lady's Friend* (1860), that it was of utmost concern that the sister tend to her brothers' needs. Her evenings should be devoted to their happiness, encouraging them to spend more time at home, and to make their friends her own friends; furthermore, she should encourage "innocent amusements" within the family circle for their benefit. In this manner, brothers could pass "unharmed through the temptations of youth," and would owe their purity to the "intimate companionship of affectionate and pure-minded sisters." Once having enjoyed the influence of "home engagement," brothers would refrain from "mixing with the unpure." Because of the loving attentions of sisters, many a brother would lay aside the wine-cup and even stronger tonics "because they would not profane with their fumes the holy kiss, with which they were accustomed to bid their sisters good-night."[10]

In her relations with the male of the species, girls were advised constantly to play a passive role. "The safest and happiest way for women," wrote one author, was "to leave the matter [of courtship] entirely in his hands." Though matrimony was a great and noble vocation, it was "an incident in life, which, if it comes at all, must come without any contrivance of [the woman]."[11] And in all relations with the wooer, the girl must maintain a strict modesty in order to guard against all personal familiarity. She was never to participate in any "rude plays" that would make her vulnerable to a kiss. She was not to permit men to squeeze or hold her hands "without showing that it displeases [her], by instantly withdrawing it." Accept no unnecessary assistance, the author cautioned, "sit not with another in a place that is too narrow; read not out of the same book; let not your eagerness to see anything induce you to place your head close to another person's."[12]

Girls were to carefully guard themselves from strangers. More important, they were to have little confidence in men. "Watch them, and be ever on your guard," wrote Henry S. Cunningham in his *Lectures on the Physiological Laws of Life* (1882), "never give them ANY chance to abuse your confidence."[13] According to Dr. H. N. Guernsey, author of *Plain Talks on Avoided Subjects* (1882), young women should have no "sexual propensity, or amorous thoughts or feelings." If properly educated, he wrote, women would live through the years before marriage "perfect strangers to any sensations" and would develop such feelings only when a suitable gentleman proclaimed his intentions.

> After this acquaintance has ripened into love, and when she has become convinced of the purity of his heart, [the woman] enjoys being with him, in sitting by his side, and is unhappy in his absence. When betrothed, owing to her great and pure love for him, she takes pleasure in receiving such marks of affection from him as are shown by a tender father or brother, but nothing more. After marriage, she feels that she is really his and that he has become a part of herself—that they are no more twain but one flesh. All this has transpired without her hardly suspecting such a quality in herself as an amorous affection.[14]

Women were to passively await the male's declaration of matrimonial intentions before expressing even the slightest evidence of reciprocating love. To allow even a "partially animal basis" to appear, or to fall prey to the evils of blighted love, fomented horrible physical and mental deterioration. Blighted love weakened not only the charms of the girl but also her most important organs. Trifling with a woman's love was unethical if not wholly damaging to the physical and mental balance of her delicate structure. "It may be sport to your fiendish soul," wrote O. S. Fowler to the man, "but it is death to her and her prospective issue, or at least an essential damage to both, and if not literal death, no thanks to you." In recognition of this, many manuals addressed themselves to the young man:

> Engage her affections, and you thereby quicken the action of all the organs, all the functions of her sex proper; and thereby enhance her every female charm and virtue . . . : Then break that love, AND YOU CRIPPLE ALL THE FEMALE FUNCTIONS AND ORGANS, and of course break down the very elements of female attractiveness, because of the perfect reciprocity which exists between the mental and physical sexuality. This reciprocity compels you, when you blight her love, thereby and therein to impair the PHYSICAL organs of her sex.[15]

Young girls were also to avoid the hazards of early marriage. Premature love robbed the nerve and brain of their natural needs and blighted the organs of sex. It was consummate folly, wrote one author, for girls to "rush into the hymenial embrace" since it would only encourage exhaustion of the life powers, disease, and an early grave. In order to prevent this from occurring, young women should place themselves "on high ground" apart from "gushing affections." They should hold their love as the "choicest treasure" and not confer even the smallest degree of affection to the male wooer. This etiquette would promote in the male a higher understanding of love, expressing "upon the bended knees of confession and solicitation" only the purest form of veneration. Girls became "dog-cheap" when they yielded to the feelings of the male.[16]

While it was not the purpose of nineteenth century manuals to make the woman unaware of the differences between male and female, they did little to inform her, in other than derisive terms, of the sexual relations in married life. A large number of women entered marriage ignorant of sex; indeed, one writer said that there were some women "into whose minds the thought of coition has never once entered.[17] The honeymoon, therefore, was the focus of much of the marriage counselor's attention. Many marriages which would normally have developed into lasting relationships, wrote Dr. Emma Drake, professor of obstetrics at the Denver Homeopathic Medical School and Hospital, were ruined in the very first days of married life due to the thoughtless passions of the male. "Frightened and timid, and filled with a vague unrest at the mysteries of marriage which await their revelation," innocent brides not infrequently put their lives in the possession of husbands who "thought that every right is theirs immediately." Their "rapacious passion" wrecked whatever love and honor the young bride had developed for her husband. Manuals advised young brides to avoid these problems by introducing, through the intervention of a friend, such books that the bridegroom might wisely read for the good of the marriage.[18]

Because of the aggressive nature of the male, it was necessary and natural for women to remain cold, passive, and indifferent to the husband's sexual impulses. Careless and amative acts by the female destroyed the "innate dignity" of the wifely role and led to the misuse of the sexual function in irresponsible and immodest responses in the male.[19] It was part of nature's plan that women "have comparatively little sexual passion." Though women loved, and while they gladly embraced their husbands, they did so "without a particle of sex desire." For Mrs. Mary Wood-Allen, national superintendent of the Purity Department of the Woman's Christian Temperance Union, the most genuine sort of love between man and wife existed in the lofty beauty of platonic embrace.[20]

It should also be pointed out that the woman was not advised to experience the same pleasures as the male in the sexual union. As a passive creature, she was to endure the attentions of her husband in a negative sense, if only to deter the greater weakening of the "vital forces" in the male. Writers also believed that if women experienced "any spasmodic convulsion" in coition it would interfere with the possibility of conception—the primary function of the marriage act. "Voluptuous spasms," wrote one author of a manual in 1850, caused a weakness and relaxation in the woman which tended to make her barren.[21]

Reflecting the efforts of urban Americans to imitate Britain's Victorian mood, the sex-in-life manuals pointed out that the English people had the most reasonable understanding of marriage. It was the custom in English homes to have separate bedrooms for the husband and wife. Though "freedom-loving" Americans might think it a rather "cold custom," separate bedrooms provided the perfect environment when "proper self-control seems difficult," and when too much freedom "degenerates into license."[22] According to Dr. Mary Wood-Allen in *Marriage: Its Duties and Privileges* (1901), if the husband found sleeping with his wife a source of great temptation, then, for the sake of chastity, he must take a bed to himself.[23] While the doors separating the two rooms should "seldom be shut," nonetheless, the custom relieved the married couple of temptation and "prevent[ed] the familiarity, which even in married life, breeds contempt."[24] Furthermore, the exposure to undressing in one another's presence caused excessive emotion that harmed lasting marital relations. "If the husband cannot properly control his amorous propensities," wrote one author, "they had better by all means occupy separate beds and different apartments, with a lock on the communicating door, the key in the wife's possession."[25] The man's body, wrote Sylvanus Stall in *What a Young Man Ought to Know* is "like a cage that encloses a beast, an angel and a devil, and no young man can afford to arouse the beast."[26] Part of the pseudo-scientific reasoning behind separate beds (like the dance) grew out of speculation regarding animal-magnetism and the belief that the vital forces of both the husband and wife would change from too frequent intimacy—the wife becoming masculine in her cravings, and the husband showing signs of peevishness, fretfulness and faultfinding.[27]

The separation of bedrooms was an important goal of late nineteenth century sex-in-life manuals. It represented a major effort to contain the evils of man's appetites. The double bed, wrote physician J. H. Greer, was a relic of a primitive age. "No matter who else might sleep together," he wrote, "husband and wife should not."[28]

> [The bed] is the most ingenious of all possible devices to stimulate and inflame the carnal passion. No bed is large enough for two persons. If brides only knew the great risk they run of losing the most precious of all earthly possessions—the love of their husbands—they would struggle as resolutely to secure extreme temperance after marriage as they do to maintain complete abstinence before the ceremony. The best means to this end is the separate bed.[29]

Since the husband was seldom strong-willed enough to master his appetites, this custom encouraged him to subordinate the bestial nature and allow his thoughts to "soar above the earth, even unto the region of the heavens."[30]

Since the sex manuals stated that conception could result at any time, they advised coition only when there was a desire for parenthood. There was to be "no pandering to sexual indulgence" or "gratification of the lower nature" as long as the slightest unwillingness for parenthood existed. Those not wishing to have children had to have a "proper manly and womanly Christian temperance in those things." Too many marriages were nothing more than licensed prostitution where the lower natures of both man and wife were "petted and indulged at the expense of the higher."[31] Since the sexual act caused an expenditure of vital force in the male body, the release of seminal fluid which was "prostituted to the simple gratification of fleshy desire" weakened the husband and endangered the well being of his physical and mental state. The husband should conserve his seminal fluid for only limited coition—the implication being that the vital energy expended in the sexual act could be better diverted to the "mental and moral force of the man." According to Dr. J. H. Greer, author of *Woman Know Thyself; Female Diseases, Their Prevention and Cure* (1902), the conservation of sperm by the male caused its assimilation by the brain, where it was expended in thought.[32]

Many manuals expressed the hope that married couples would accept strict continence as the standard in marital relations. If parents would assure their children that sexual powers in the human species were properly used only for reproduction, then "the whole veil of mystery would be blown away and the subject would then be presented in a beautiful and ennobling light." There would be no further need of prostitution; no need for "governmental regulation of vice," no white slave traffic, nor any further reason for the degradation of women. The world would be safe from the greatest social evil of life, and men and women would meet "upon the basis of intellectual congeniality" without the perplexing issue of sex, and for the first time, "the delight of friendship, now practically unknown, could be enjoyed to the fullest extent." If sexual continence prevailed in marriage, the husband and wife would not have to live as "comparative strangers" in separate bedrooms, in constant fear of inflammatory desires. "If the human body were always held in thought as a sacred temple," wrote Dr. Wood-Allen, "its outlines would be suggestive of nothing but the purest and holiest feelings." The acceptance of marital continence would eliminate forever the thought that the woman was "the means of gratifying desire," and her figure would cease to inflame the passions of the opposite sex.[33]

Nineteenth century manuals quoted extensively from ministers on the subject of sexual relations. "I firmly believe," wrote one minister, "that the purpose of the Creator in the institution of the marital relation can be fulfilled only when the two parties in the relation are agreed to *make no provision for the flesh* in thought, desire or practice." It was his belief that true marital bliss could only be achieved by perfect marital continence. There was a loss of dignity of both husband and wife if either thought of the other as a "sexual being." No matter what "pet names" be given to the sexual appetite, it was none other than lust of the basest sort. Any use of the sexual act other than for the expressed purpose of procreation was "a waste of vital energy," deteriorating the conservation of necessary forces in the body and depriving the system of its "legitimate demands." Perfect continence in marriage did not mean mere moderation in sexual relations; moderation was a casuist rationalization for the gratification of the physical appetites.[34] Sex, argued Wood-Allen, was not located entirely in the sexual organs, but permeated the entire body. Hence, a "social mingling of men and women without a thought of sex in their minds" could be a valid and proper substitute for physical pleasure.[35]

In 1900, Delos F. Wilcox wrote *Ethical Marriage*, which he dedicated to youths and maidens "who do what they think they ought to do, admitting no ideal that is impractical, and omitting no duty that is seen." Using a

Spencerian formula, he argued that the institution of marriage had undergone an evolution from brute savagery to nomadic marriage, and finally
into ethical marriage. The new ethical family was founded on the principles of love, intelligence, and duty, and intended to perpetuate only those
traits which it considered of "superior social value."[36] According to Wilcox,
nature ruled that sexual intercourse "should be had at long intervals and
during a limited portion of adult life." Any sexual union other than for the
expressed desire for procreation was contrary to nature's laws. In practice,
this meant that married couples ought to be "loyally affectionate" until they
chose to have children, at which time "they should have a single complete
sexual congress."

> Time should then be given to ascertain whether or not conception has taken
> place. Normally menstruation ceases during pregnancy. If the menses are not
> interrupted, the probabilities are strong that conception has not taken place,
> and then another copulation will be necessary. Intercourse may take place
> once a month until there is reason to believe that the woman is pregnant, or
> until the season favorable to reproduction has passed. After impregnation has
> been secured there should be no more intercourse until another child is desired.[37]

Wilcox believed that continence was a practical answer to the sexual
passions in marriage. Speaking from his own experience, he argued that
the desire for sexual continence alone was not sufficient. Married couples
needed to take specific steps to prevent the unleashing of passions. These
steps included an understanding that marriage "should make no more
immediate difference in their lives than the taking of a roommate does to
a student," the avoidance of a honeymoon, the use of separate beds or
sleeping quarters, the avoidance of stimulants, the emphasis upon exercise,
and finally the education of children to prevent sexual curiosity or abnormal habits.[38] The benefits from marital continence were self-evident—the
abandonment of habits that encouraged passion, the conservation of vital
energies in the male, increased love and respect, and fewer doctor's bills.[39]
Women would be freed from the "taxes of lust," they would develop a
higher sense of social responsibility, marriage "would no longer be to [them]
the bartering of [their] freedom for a mess of pottage," and they could
enjoy a far greater freedom in dress. If men accepted the ideal of continence women could wear shorter skirts "without the sensuous desires of
men being aroused." Women whose clothes had been styled in order to
prevent the "prurient curiosity of men" from creating a sense of shame in
the virtuous woman, could now cast off the oppressive garments of defensive purity.[40]

In marriage, wrote Gustavus Cohen in his *Helps and Hints to Mothers
and Young Wives*, "principle should be the controlling power of every
thought and action." The law of continence was one of the more important
principles that governed every relationship. Cohen urged every husband
to permit his wife to decide when to have intercourse. A horrible blight to
the marriage contract could be removed if women had the right "to deny
all approaches, save and only when [they] desired maternity."[41]

Manuals for men also suggested the use of strict continence in married
life. Sylvanus Stall's book, *What a Young Husband Ought to Know*, pointed out
that many married couples who had chosen strict continence secured "not

only greater strength and better health, but greater happiness also."[42] The passions, "the controlling organ of which lies at the very bottom and lowest part of the brain," degraded both the mind and morals of the individual. Stall advised the young husband not to eat foods such as eggs and oysters, pepper and condiments, to avoid theater-going, the reading of "salacious books," viewing nude statuary and pictures, and to "avoid such bodily exposure and postures as mar the modesty of both man and woman."[43] Dr. J. H. Kellogg, famous for his health foods and rest homes for the century's neurasthenics in Battle Creek, Michigan, suggested that many of the problems of intemperance in sex habits grew out of an improper diet, and particularly, from the use of meats and stimulating foods. The too liberal use of animal foods had encouraged "unrestrained indulgence of the passions" in both men and women. It is not too surprising that Kellogg recommended a diet of his own cereals.[44]

Physician J. H. Greer, in his *Woman Know Thyself* advocated two interesting alternatives to marital continence, called "Dianism" or love-union, and "Zugassent's Discovery." In Dianism, the husband and wife embraced each other in a state of nudity with only an "interchange of magnetic elements" which tranquilized the husband and strengthened the wife. In Zugassent's Discovery, the husband and wife united as in intercourse but refrained from orgasm. The intention here was, again, to exchange only magnetic currents and achieve a "magnetic harmony." Since complete intercourse expended a large amount of vital force in both husband and wife, Greer suggested Dianism and Zugassent's Discovery as acts which would help to replenish the waning vitality without gratification of the animal instinct.[45]

While not all manuals subscribed fully to strict marital continence, the majority certainly sanctioned it as the ideal marriage relationship. Many were content to accept a moderate sexual indulgence, after first establishing certain restrictions. For example, nearly all manuals restricted sexual relations during pregnancy. The very fundamentals of science ruled against this practice. "The submission of an unwilling wife or the sexual irritability that may be engendered through the mother who gives herself up to the indulgence of desire" might jeopardize the physical and moral future of the child. The upheaval of the child's embryonic home "through gusts of passion," left an indelible mark on the child's character.[46] Coition during pregnancy, according to one physician, predisposed children to epilepsy. "The natural excitement of the nervous system in the mother by such a cause," he wrote, "cannot operate otherwise than inflicting injury upon the tender germ in the womb." Dr. Kellogg believed that the mental and nervous sensations of the mother molded the brain of the prenatal-child, and that when the mother indulged in sexual relations with her husband, she increased the chance of the child's developing an abnormal sexual instinct. "Here is the key to the origin of much of the sexual precocity and depravity which curse humanity," wrote Kellogg.[47] Every pang of grief [or passion] you feel," added O. S. Fowler in *Maternity*, "will leave its painful scar on the forming disk of their souls."[48]

The child's future depended upon the proper conduct of the mother during pregnancy, a conduct that concerned not only her diet, but also her reading material, relations with her husband, and her most private thoughts.

Dr. Holbrook, in his book *Stirpiculture*, explained why some children were more virtuous and beautiful than others. The child's character, morals, and even physical appearance, he wrote, depended largely upon the manner in which his parents conducted themselves during the pregnancy.

> In my early married life [confessed one mother] my husband and I learned how to live in holy relations, after God's ordinance. My husband lovingly consented to let me live apart from him during the time I carried this little daughter under my heart, and also while I was nursing her. These were the happiest days of my life. . . . My husband and I were never so tenderly, so harmoniously, or so happily related to each other, and I never loved him more deeply than during these blessed months.

As a result of the parents' relationship, the child born at this time was beautifully formed, and grew to be virtuous, healthy, and extremely happy. Several years later, wrote Holbrook, the same mother became pregnant with her second child, but during that pregnancy, her husband "had become contaminated with the popular idea that even more frequent relations were permissible during pregnancy." Yielding to her husband's rapacious demands, the wife became "nervous and almost despairing." The child was born sickly and nervous, and after five years of constant difficulty, died "leaving [them] sadder and wiser."[49]

A woman during her pregnancy was a "soul-gardener." The beauty and virtue of her children depended ultimately upon the manner in which she acted during her nine months of pregnancy. Since she had the duty of providing the "good soil" in which the child grew during its prenatal life, the pregnant woman was to direct herself to the single goal of creating the best possible child. She must change her dress, allowing no weight to hang around her hips. "The union suit of underclothing, the union skirt and waist combined, and the gown," wrote Dr. Drake, "are all that should be worn throughout the entire period."[50] Most important, however, the expectant mother must cultivate her mind with only the highest thoughts. Mind engendered physiological and psychological character upon the unborn child. It was common knowledge, wrote Drake, that Italian children bore "a striking resemblance to the pictures of the child Jesus, from the veneration which the mothers give to the Madonnas." From this, Drake concluded that "we not only become like what we most love, and think most about, but that we may transmit this likeness to our little ones." In order to ensure beautiful and vigorous children, the woman was to observe beautiful pictures, study statuary, yet "forbid as far as possible the contemplation of unsightly and imperfect models."[51] In particular, wives were warned to avoid the alcoholic and tobacco breath of their husbands during this period.

> Many wives are struggling alone in ill health that is directly traceable to the inhaling, night after night, of the breath of the husband, poisoned with nicotine. Many a little one is wailing through its infancy, and if it have strength sufficient, inherited from its remote ancestors, to pull it through, yet will it all its life suffer from its antenatal and postnatal poisoning; and the chances are that as soon as it is old enough it will take up the habit which is already acquired, to pass down along the line a more enfeebled heritage.[52]

Some manuals advised only the presence of a midwife in the delivery of children. The reason for this, as O. S. Fowler wrote, was to prevent the possibility of the mother's relaxing the "bars of virtue" by disclosing her particular female complaints to the male physician. Besides, there was always the added possibility that such talks and examinations by the male physician would "excite impure desires" in either of the two parties.[53]

Just as the mothers' emotions during pregnancy went into the making of the child's emotional system, so the nursing period was extremely important to the child's mental development. For this reason, sexual intercourse was also restricted during the time of nursing. There was no doubt in Kellogg's mind, for example, that the gratification of passions during the nursing period would cause "the transmission of libidinous tendencies to the child."[54] For the same reasons, mothers were continually warned of the evils of the wet-nurse. Too often, mothers employed wet-nurses with bad habits, women who drank or carried on affairs in secret. (Invariably, the examples listed in the manuals were of Irish wet-nurses.) In any case, the child suffered irreparable harm in that the mentality as well as the emotional deficiencies of the wet-nurse transferred to the child in feeding.[55] Physician Gustavus Cohen believed that mothers who neglected this important function would invite disease and any number of constitutional disorders. The failure of women to nurse their own babies, he wrote, caused eventual barrenness, premature aging, and even early death.[56]

Although the manuals strongly denounced the practice of birth control, there were indications that the practice was accepted in extreme cases where the life of the woman was in peril. But before even broaching the subject, authors were insistent upon censuring those with sordid intentions. In *The Married Woman's Private Medical Companion* (1847), for example, the author publicly rebuked a segment of his audience.

> Libertines and debauchees! these pages are not for you. You have nothing to do with the subject of which they treat. Bringing to its discussion, as you do, a distrust or contempt of the human race—accustomed as you are to confound liberty with license, and pleasure with debauchery, it is not for your palled feelings and brutalized senses to distinguish moral truth in its purity and simplicity. I never discuss this subject with such as you.

Just as readily as the author refused to enlighten the libertines of society with contraceptive knowledge, so he also restricted it verbally from those "prudes and hypocrites" which Christ had likened to "whited sepulchres," and who "at dinner, ask to be helped to the bosom of a duck, lest by mention of the word breast, [they] call up improper associations."[57] After these proper restrictions, the author then offered to his reader packages of contraceptives that could be obtained from his New York office at prices ranging from five to ten dollars, and which included, so he advertised, the baudruche, or "French secret."[58]

Manual writers advised endlessly on the dangers attendant to the woman's change of life. Physicians invariably characterized menopause as the "Rubicon" in a woman's life, and they measured the extent of discomfort and disease by the degree of abuse women had allowed their constitutions to suffer. In typically Calvinistic terms, manuals blamed the frequency and seriousness of disease upon the "indiscretions" of earlier life. Excesses of any kind, whether in sexual passion, dress, reckless use of stimulating foods, prurient reading, contraception, or solitary vice, accentuated the hardships of this period of change. The woman who transgressed nature's laws, wrote Kellogg, "will find this period a veritable 'Pandora's box' of ills, and may well look forward to it with apprehension and foreboding."[59] "Many things that have been laid to our ancestors remotely distant," wrote Dr. Drake, "are really the results of wrong-doing and living in the first decade and a half of our lives."[60] Dr. Charles D. Meigs, for example, in his *Females and Their Diseases* (1848), a book which was extensively quoted in the manuals of the time, described a young woman's efforts to prevent her monthly period in order that she might go to a ball. To achieve this, she accepted the advice of her "confidential servant" and took a hip-bath in cold water. While she succeeded in stopping the flow, she suffered an attack of "brain fever" and in her later years "felt the effects of the dereliction of duty." As a result of that single breach of nature's law, her life "was rendered a scene of bitterness, of vapours, of caprices."[61] "Nature," wrote Drake, "rebels and compels the payment of her violated laws." Usually, nature accomplished this through malignant disease, or "failing in this, a slow and dangerous change is likely to be experienced, followed by years of discomfort or invalidism."[62]

There seemed to be a certain status-suffix to every aspiring view of the role of sex. In a sense, the manuals attempted to interpret and grapple with the lack of tradition in the urban life, and to reach for an understanding of sexual relationships in a way that would give added relevance to the aspiring urban society of America. The sex-in-life manuals were an arena for imaginative writing in this period, and seem, at times, to shroud the urban middle class in a romantic arcadia set apart from the lusty vernacular of urban immigrants and city slums. The manuals were choice caricatures of subjective prejudices and assumptions concerning middle-class values. In a sense, the romantization of family and marriage portrayed in the manuals was not so much a plea for re-shaping the marriage relationship as it was a technique for explaining the incongruity that existed between middle-class "principles" and reality. The middle class measured their greatness not by their achievements but by their principles—a situation which allowed them to blame the discrepancy upon a gallery of villains. Manual writers sought out the victims of sexual deviation in the empirical reality of the city slums where sex, disease, poverty and depravity seemed to spawn the nations's problems. Acting as moral judges of society, the sex-in-life manuals became documentaries of middle-class myths seeking not only to justify their own social and moral fabric, but to explain, without the sense of personal guilt, the survival of a less imaginative reality.

NOTES

1. For an excellent treatment of medicine, pseudo-science, and the perfectionist tendencies of 19th century American society, see Joseph F. Kett, *The Formation of the American Medical Profession, The Role of Institutions 1780–1860* (New Haven, 1968), chaps. 4, 5, and 6.
2. Mary Wood-Allen, *What a Young Girl Ought to Know* (Philadelphia, 1897), 106; S. B. Wood-

ward, *Hints for the Young in Relation to the Health of Body and Mind* (Boston, 1856); E. B. Lowry, *Herself; Talks with Women Concerning Themselves* (Chicago, 1911), 137–48.

3. J. H. Kellogg, *Ladies Guide in Health and Disease. Girlhood, Maidenhood, Wifehood, Motherhood* (Iowa, 1883), 146–47, 154; Catherine Ester Beecher, *Letters to the People on Health and Happiness* (New York, 1855), 12–13; Alexander Walker, *Intermarriage: or the Mode in Which, and the Causes Why, Beauty, Health, and Intellect Result from Certain Unions, and Deformity, Disease, and Insanity from Others* (n.p., 1850), 35.

4. Wood-Allen, *What a Young Girl Ought to Know*, 106–107; Kellogg, *Ladies Guide in Health and Disease*, 152; Lowry, *Herself; Talks with Women Concerning Themselves*, 140–41.

5. Henry S. Cunningham, *Lectures on the Physiological Laws of Life, Hygiene and a General Outline of Diseases Peculiar to Females, Embracing a Revival of the Rights and Wrongs of Women, and a Treatise on Disease in General, with Explicit Directions How to Nurse, Nourish and Administer Remedies to the Sick* (Indianapolis, 1882), 98.

6. Kellogg, *Ladies Guide in Health and Disease*, 208–209. See also John S. Haller, Jr., "Neurasthenia: The Medical Profession and the 'Urban Blahs' of the 19th Century," *New York Journal of Medicine*, LXX (Oct. 1970), 2489–2497.

7. Beecher, *Letters to the People on Health and Happiness*, 45; J. H. Greer, *Woman Know Thyself; Female Diseases, Their Prevention and Cure* (Chicago, 1902), 90–92.

8. Sylvanus Stall, *What a Young Husband Ought to Know* (Philadelphia, 1807), 244–45; Stall, *What a Young Man Ought to Know* (Philadelphia, 1897), 243; Beecher, *Letters to the People on Health and Happiness*, 18–19; Fowler, *Maternity*, 130–32.

9. Mrs. John Farrar, *The Young Lady's Friend* (New York, 1860), 241–42; Wood-Allen, *What a Young Girl Ought to Know*, 173.

10. Farrar, *The Young Lady's Friend*, 201–04; [WCTU], *Physiology for Young People* (New York, 1884), 13–17.

11. Farrar, *The Young Lady's Friend*, 258–59.

12. *Ibid.*, 263.

13. Cunningham, *Lectures on the Physiological Laws of Life*, 100–101.

14. H. N. Guernsey, *Plain Talks on Avoided Subjects* (Philadelphia, 1882), 78–79.

15. Fowler, *Maternity*, 75–79; Lowry, *Herself; Talks with Women Concerning Themselves*, 157–62.

16. Fowler, *Maternity*, 78–79; Lowry, *Herself; Talks with Women Concerning Themselves*, 155.

17. Stall, *What a Young Husband Ought to Know*, 126.

18. Emma F. Angell Drake, *What a Young Wife Ought to Know* (Philadelphia, 1908), 54.

19. *Ibid.*, 85.

20. Wood-Allen, *Marriage; Its Duties and Privileges* (Chicago, 1901), 194.

21. Walker, *Intermarriage*, 256; William M. Capp, *The Daughter: Her Health, Education and Wedlock* (Philadelphia, 1891), 94.

22. Drake, *What a Young Wife Ought to Know*, 85; Greer, *Woman Know Thyself; Female Diseases, Their Prevention and Cure*, 67.

23. Wood-Allen, *Marriage; Its Duties and Privileges*, 49.

24. Drake, *What a Young Wife Ought to Know*, 85.

25. Stall, *What a Young Husband Ought to Know*, 94–96.

26. Stall, *What a Young Man Ought to Know*, 241.

27. Gustavus Cohen, *Helps and Hints to Mothers and Young Wives*, (London, 1880), 88.

28. Greer, *Woman Know Thyself; Female Diseases, Their Prevention and Cure*, 186.

29. Dio Lewis, quoted in Stall, *What a Young Husband Ought to Know*, 95; Dio Lewis, *Our Girls* (New York, 1871).

30. Drake, *What a Young Wife Ought to Know*, 86.

31. *Ibid.*, 87–88.

32. *Ibid.*, 88–89; Greer, *Woman Know Thyself; Female Diseases, Their Prevention and Cure*, 110–13, 153–54.

33. Wood-Allen, *Marriage; Its Duties and Privileges*, 196–97.

34. *Ibid.*, 201–03.

35. *Ibid.*, 208–09. One of the few exceptions to this interpretation is found in Dr. A. J. Ingersoll, *In Health* (New York, 1884). While strongly religious, Ingersoll blamed most marital problems on the "fear" of the sexual appetite—the woman's fear of having desires and her efforts to thwart natural inclinations.

36. Delos F. Wilcox, *Ethical Marriage* (Michigan, 1900), 56–57.

37. *Ibid.*, 82–84. Because the child's character was greatly influenced by the intentions of the

parents at the moment of conception, physician J. H. Greer advised intercourse in the morning, since "The best qualities of each parent . . . have been refreshed by rest." Greer, *Woman Know Thyself; Female Diseases, Their Prevention and Cure*, 194.

38. Wilcox, *Ethical Marriage*, 124–25.
39. *Ibid.*, 133–34.
40. *Ibid.*, 137–39.
41. Cohen, *Helps and Hints to Mothers and Young Wives*, 83; Greer, *Woman Know Thyself; Female Diseases, Their Prevention and Cure*, 206–08.
42. Stall, *What a Young Husband Ought to Know*, 81.
43. *Ibid.*, 93–94.
44. Kellogg, *Ladies Guide in Health and Disease*, 142, 342–43.
45. Greer, *Woman Know Thyself; Female Diseases, Their Prevention and Cure*, 188–89.
46. Wood-Allen, *Marriage; Its Duties and Privileges*, 207.
47. Stall, *What a Young Husband Ought to Know*, 200–01; Kellogg, *Ladies Guide in Health and Disease*, 425–26.
48. Fowler, *Maternity*, 16, 124; Aimée Raymond Schroeder, *Health Notes for Young Wives* (New York, 1895), 31.
49. Holbrook quoted in Drake, *What a Young Wife Ought to Know*, 91–93; Greer, *Woman Know Thyself; Female Diseases, Their Prevention and Cure*, 182–83.
50. Drake, *What a Young Wife Ought to Know*, 101–02; Kellogg, *Ladies Guide in Health and Disease*, 294–95.
51. Drake, *What a Young Wife Ought to Know*, 105–109; Lowry, *Herself; Talks with Women Concerning Themselves*, 98–100.
52. Drake, *What a Young Wife Ought to Know*, 118; Kellogg, *Ladies Guide in Health and Disease*, 309.
53. Fowler, *Maternity*, 183; Beecher, *Letters to the People on Health and Happiness*, 160.
54. Kellogg, *Ladies Guide in Health and Disease*, 425–26.
55. Harland, *Eve's Daughters*, 22–35.
56. Cohen, *Helps and Hints to Mothers and Young Wives*, 57.
57. A. M. Mauriceau, *The Married Women's Medical Companion* (New York, 1847), 110–12.
58. *Ibid.*, 143–44.
59. Kellogg, *Ladies Guide in Health and Disease*, 372–73.
60. Drake, *What a Woman of Forty-Five Ought to Know*, (Philadelphia, 1902), 39, 137.
61. Meigs quoted in Cohen, *Helps and Hints to Mothers and Young Wives*, 6; Edward H. Dixon, *Woman and Her Diseases, From the Cradle to the Grave* (Philadelphia, 1860), 156.
62. Drake, *What a Woman of Forty-Five Ought to Know*, 55.

20

Changes in Female Sexuality
A Study of Mother/Daughter Communication and Generational Differences

Marilyn Yalom, Suzanne Estler, and Wenda Brewster

Questionnaires on various aspects of female sexuality (including sexual activity in high school and college, sexual attitudes and values, and communication between mothers and daughters on sexual subjects) were completed by 141 women who graduated from college in 1954 and had college-age daughters and by 184 women who were sophomores at Stanford University in 1977–78. The present article reports (1) similarities and differences in sexual behavior between college-age women of the early 1950s and late 1970s, (2) communication between mothers and daughters on the subject of sex, and (3) the effects of generational change in sexual behavior and attitudes on the overall mother-daughter relationship.

Teen-age pregnancy, abortion, and homosexuality are common enough subjects in our daily newspapers. Contraception, cohabitation and venereal disease get regular coverage in the women's magazines. Lovemaking between women and men, between women and women, between men and men, even "solitary pleasures" are openly depicted on the contemporary screen and stage. Compared to the delicate, if not silent, treatment of sex by the media some twenty-five years ago, a sexual revolution has undoubtedly occurred.

Revolution, however, is a word of many meanings. While communication regarding sex has clearly changed, are we witnessing a true revolution in sexual behavior? Are young people today acting differently from their parents at a similar age? Do they possess a radically new set of attitudes and values that conflict with parental injunctions? Has the traditional generation gap widened into an unbridgeable chasm between parent and off-spring? These are some of the questions that led Stanford University's Center for Research on Women (CROW) to undertake a study of female sexuality.

A number of researchers present evidence to support the view that a radical change in sexual attitudes and behavior has indeed taken place, particularly with regard to women. Reiss (1960) suggested that American youths were in a period of transition from premarital sexual abstinence and the double standard to a single standard of permissiveness for both sexes. In support of this position, Robinson, King, and Balswick (1972), comparing data gathered in 1965 and in 1970, found that while both sex-ual attitudes and behavior had remained approximately the same for col-lege males, there had been a dramatic liberalization in premarital sexual attitudes and behavior for college females. In a 1975 replication of the earlier study, King, Balswick, and Robinson (1977) reported an accelera-tion of the trend toward more liberal sexuality for college-age women.

Hunt (1974), reporting the results of a survey of 982 men and 1044 women, concluded that

> during the past generation the sexual attitudes of Americans in general have shifted considerably in the direction of permissiveness, and among younger adults this shift has been so pronounced as to markedly diminish the attitudi-nal dissimilarities previously associated with differences in social class, educa-tional attainments, religious feelings and political orientation, (p. 31)

He also reported a similar trend in the area of sexual behavior. For exam-ple, while one-third of the females in Kinsey's sample had premarital inter-course by the age of 25 (Kinsey, 1953, p. 333), the figure had risen to over two-thirds in Hunt's female sample.

Communications between Mothers and Daughters

These apparent changes in behavior over the past 25 years mark a shift in norms related to sexuality. We hypothesized that mothers would have difficulty contending with their daughters' new sexual mores. One might expect mutual discomfort between mothers and daughters which would be reflected in the quality of their communication. Our study, how-ever, does not support this hypothesis.

Comfort Level.   A number of pieces of evidence suggest, instead, some degree of comfort between mothers and daughters in discussing sexual matters. The most relevant evidence was derived from a series of questions concerning the degree of comfort both mothers and daughters experi-enced in discussing sexual topics with various individuals.

The majority of mothers (70%) rated themselves as "comfortable" or "very comfortable" in discussing sexuality with their college-aged daugh-ters. Only their husbands or lovers ranked higher than their college-aged daughters in a list of fifteen persons or groups of persons (which also included male and female friends and groups of friends, sisters, brothers, and daughters and sons of various ages ranging from pre-adolescent to mar-ried). Their present comfort in discussing sex with their daughters can be understood within the context of an overall improved sexual self-image, reported by the majority of mothers, in contrast to their memories of sexual inexperience and lack of assurance when they themselves were in college.[1]

Sexual Behavior in College Women of the 1950s and 1970s

Changes in sexual behavior are the most obvious indication of some form of sexual revolution. Our data, derived from responses to direct questions and inferences from less direct questions, present a picture of significantly different patterns of sexual behavior in the high school and early college years for the two generations of women.

The class of 1980 reported considerably more sexual activity than the class of 1954 both in high school and in college. Table 1 compares the responses of the class of 1954 with those of the class of 1980 regarding *high school* sexual experience. They suggest greater activity among the younger group in every area of activity: kissing, petting and intercourse. The majority of both groups were reportedly virgins upon graduation from high school, but the group of non-virgins had grown from 6% in the class of 1954 to 32% in the class of 1980.[2] As points of reference: related to the 1980 group, Zelnik and Kantner (1978) report that 41% of teenagers between 15 and 19 currently have sexual intercourse before marriage; and related to the 1954 group, Kinsey et al. (1953, p. 288) reported 20% of women in the 16–20 age group had experienced premarital intercourse.

Regarding sexual experience *in college,* we have no statistics comparable to Table 1 for the 1954 graduates. Written comments, however, suggest that most of the older women probably remained virgins until marriage. "Losing your virginity" ranked second in a list of fourteen possible sex-related fears experienced during the college years—a finding which adds more systematic support to the conclusion suggested by the written comments.

According to our data, two thirds of Stanford women of the class of 1980 entered as virgins. However, there appears to have been a notable increase in their sexual activity between the end of high school and the sophomore year in college, which suggests a departure from the apparent behavior of their mothers. In response to a group of three questions about their current behavior and attitudes, 76% of the 1980 students stated that their sexual behavior had changed since they had entered college; 74% of the students said they did not anticipate marrying as virgins; and 58% of the students reported that they had used contraceptives.

Table 1 Classes of 1954 and 1980 high school experience: Percent of mothers and daughters who engaged in kissing, petting and intercourse in high school

	Kissing		*Petting*		*Intercourse*	
	1954	*1980*	*1954*	*1980*	*1954*	*1980*
	n = 140	*n = 183*	*n = 139*	*n = 183*	*n = 140*	*n = 183*
Never	4%	4%	29%	17%	94%	68%
Rarely	11	12	19	21	0	14
Sometimes	34	25	30	30	4	9
Frequently	51	59	22	32	2	9

Movement toward more liberal attitudes about female sexual behavior has been supported in studies by Croake and James (1973), Smigel and Seiden (1969), and Tolone et al. (cited in Ferrell, Tolone, & Walsh, 1977). Somewhat more qualified results have been obtained by Kaats and Davis (1970), Christensen (1971), and Ferrell et al. (1977).

Wilson (1975) provides further evidence of changes in sexual practices. In a cross-sectional survey of a national probability sample of 2486 adults, the younger people in the sample reported earlier ages for the initiation of masturbation and sexual intercourse. Wilson also found that college students in the early seventies had earlier sexual experiences than college students of a previous generation.

In a survey of 1442 married Australian women, Bell (1974) reported some of the subtler changes between younger and older women. Not only do younger women have earlier sexual initiation and higher rates of premarital and extramarital coitus, but they also have a greater number of sexual partners and a greater incidence of orgasm than older women. However, in spite of these generational differences from which Bell concludes that a sexual revolution has indeed occurred, women of all ages still held more liberal views towards premarital sex for their sons than for their daughters.

Rubin (1971) argues that while the changes in sexual attitudes and behavior can hardly be called a revolution, there has clearly been an evolution in female sexuality since World War I toward "greater sexual equality with the female being regarded both by males and by herself less as a sexual object to be exploited and more as a fellow human with her own needs, expectations and rights" (p. 38).

A few researchers, however, argue against a sexual revolution by attributing any apparent change to the increased openness about sexual topics in the media. For example, in an eight-year longitudinal study of 1500 middle-class teenagers, Offer (1972) reported no change in teenagers' attitudes from 1962 to 1970. Gottheil and Freedman (1970), in a study of single male medical students, also report that "little change has occurred in sexual behavior and attitudes since Kinsey."

While the literature reveals considerable research on the subject of changing sexual attitudes, behavior, and values, the effects of these changes on family interactions have received scant attention.[3]

The CROW study focused primarily on the communication process between mothers and college-age daughters on the subject of sex. We hypothesized that, if there had been a revolution in sexual mores during the sixties and seventies, it would affect the relationship between mothers raised in a pre-revolutionary period and their post-pubertal daughters. Mothers socialized in the thirties and forties and attending college in the early fifties might have difficulty accepting their daughters' more liberal attitudes and freer sexual behavior. Daughters would be uneasy in revealing to their mothers a set of values and lifestyles which their mothers might not condone. The potential for conflict between them was assumed to be very high.

Specifically, the study sought to determine: (1) the level of comfort mothers and college-age daughters experienced in discussing sex; (2) the sexual subjects most frequently discussed and avoided; (3) mothers' concerns about their daughters' practices; and (4) daughters' concerns about their mothers' attitudes. More generally, it examined similarities and differences in sexual attitudes and behavior between mothers and daughters and the effect of these comparative factors on the mother/daughter relationship.

The present article will report the findings of two surveys, one representing a cohort of mothers and the other a cohort of daughters, concerning: (1) similarities and differences in sexual behavior between college-age females of the early 1950s and late 1970s, (2) communication between mothers and daughters on the subject of sex; and (3) mother/daughter relationships from the vantage point of their common or differing sexual attitudes and values. The study involved college-educated mothers and daughters tending to be from maritally stable and prosperous homes. Thus, its value lay in the identification of patterns of mother-daughter communication regarding sexuality which emerge under optional conditions of education, family stability and economic stability.

Method

Subjects

Three hundred twenty-five college-educated women completed one of two questionnaires. The first questionnaire, designed to address mothers of college-age daughters, was completed by 141 women from the class of 1954 at Stanford University (percent of respondents = 70%) and Wellesley College (percent of respondents = 45%). The second questionnaire, containing parallel questions for college-age daughters, was completed by 184 women who were Stanford University sophomores in the class of 1980. (The Stanford students were self-selected for dormitory "questionnaire parties.") Since the class of 1954 "mothers" and the class of 1980 "daughters" were not matched, we do not refer to communication between these specific groups. We can, however, consider the communication between the "mothers" in the class of 1954 and their daughters and that between the "daughters" in the class of 1980 and their mothers.[4] In that the two samples (class of 1954, class of 1980) represent similar populations separated, most notably, by time, the study also provides information about generational changes in sexual attitudes and behavior that have taken place in college-educated women within the past quarter century.

Instruments

The two sets of questionnaires used included three distinctive sections: one seeking demographic information, a second seeking information about communication in general and attitudes related to sexuality, and a third seeking information about sexual behavior and mother/daughter communication on the subject of sex. Most questions provided a range of specific answers. The answers were subjected to appropriate non-parametric techniques to test apparent differences in responses between the two samples. In addition, there were a number of open-ended questions to provide a more qualitative understanding of the data.

Results and Discussion

The results can be viewed from two perspectives: comparisons in sexual behavior between two generations of women and communication about sexuality between mothers and daughters.

In comparison with the mothers' comfort level, nearly half of the 1980 students (46%) reported that they were "comfortable" or "very comfortable" in discussing sex with their mothers. Only sexual or romantic partners rated higher than mothers in a list of ten possible communicants (including male and female friends and groups of friends, sister(s), brother(s), father, and surrogate mother).

In response to another "comfort" question, the majority of mothers expressed satisfaction with the current communication about sexuality between themselves and their daughters, with 65% responding positively, 28% responding neutrally, and 7% responding negatively. To a lesser extent, the 1980 students expressed qualified satisfaction with the sexual communication between themselves and their mothers, with 48% evaluating it positively, 24% neutrally, and 28% negatively. It is noteworthy that the size of the group expressing dissatisfaction with sexual communication was 7% in the mothers' sample compared to 28% in the daughters' sample—a fourfold increase. Clearly, the daughters are identifying the problem of poor sexual communication more readily than the mothers. Daughters who rate their communication as poor frequently stated that they could not be "open" or "honest" with their mothers because mother and daughter had different ideas as to what was acceptable behavior for a non-married woman of college age; many indicated that they avoided discussing personal situations that might lead to conflict. For the most part, the poor communicators seemed to believe that silence was the best policy. This is not to say that they were not frustrated by the poor communication with their mothers: when asked if they would change this communication in any way, 65.8% of the poor communicators said yes.

Although more than a fourth of the daughters rated their sexual communication with their mothers as poor, the majority of older and younger women appeared to be relatively comfortable in discussing sexual topics with their respective daughters and mothers. We find a similarity in the content of these discussions, as reported by older and younger women, but some differences in the frequency of specific topics.

Topics Discussed.   The respondents in both groups were asked to identify topics in a list of 14 related to sexuality that had been discussed in mother-daughter conversations. Table 2 shows the order of the topics for each group, determined by ranking the percentage of the group reporting discussion of each topic. The close parallel in the order of the rankings is indicated by a rank-correlation coefficient of .88. Both groups reported *menstruation, marriage, abortion, pregnancy,* and *love relationship with a male* as the most frequently discussed sexual topics in mother-daughter conversations. *Masturbation, orgasm, multiple sexual relations,* and *love relations with a female* ranked as the least frequently discussed subjects for both groups.

Despite the similarity in the rank orders, some differences emerge from comparing the proportion of each group responding to specific topics. For

Table 2 Subjects discussed by mothers and daughters: Percent of mothers and daughters who report discussing the following subjects and rank order of subjects according to frequency

	Mothers		Daughters	
Subject	Percent	Rank	Percent	Rank
Menstruation	99%	1	97%	1
Marriage	88%	2	92%	2
Abortion	81%*	3	62%*	6
Pregnancy	80%	4	75%	5
Love Relationship with a Male	78%	5	77%	4
Contraception	76%*	6	58%*	7
Virginity	69%*	7	54%*	8
Cohabitation	68%	8	78%	3
Sexual Intercourse	66%*	9	53%*	9
Venereal Disease	64%**	10	32%**	10
Masturbation	26%*	11	9%*	14
Orgasm	24%	12	13%	12
Multiple Sexual Relations	23%	13	20%	11
Love Relations with a Female	21%	14	12%	13

*Significant at .05 level (χ^2)
**Significant at .01 level (χ^2)
Rank correlation = .88

12 of the 14 topics, a greater percentage of older women reported discussing the subject with their daughters than did younger women with their mothers. Six of these percentage differences reflect statistical significance (χ^2) at the .05 level: the topics of abortion, contraception, virginity, sexual intercourse, venereal disease, and masturbation. Three possible explanations for this difference in the response levels of "mothers" and "daughters" are: (1) these reflect topics closer to the awareness and/or concern of the mothers' group, (2) these responses are based on conversations from the past, remembered by the mothers from a time when the nature of the subjects discussed may have been beyond the level of sophistication or comprehension of a younger daughter, or (3) these differences are in fact simply an artifact of unrelated samples.

These findings suggest that while most mothers and daughters feel free to discuss a variety of sexual subjects ranging from such benign ones as menstruation and marriage to more controversial ones like contraception, abortion, and venereal disease, there are still several topics which most mothers and daughters shy away from. Additional data suggest that such avoidance may reflect a kind of societal taboo. For example, 90% of the mothers said they would feel negative or very negative if their daughters established a homosexual relationship. This compared to 78% of the daughters who expressed comparable sentiments for themselves. The relatively less negative feelings on the part of the daughters are probably related to some change in the public treatment of homosexuality, but it nevertheless remains a sensitive topic for the younger group.

The subject of masturbation may also be considered taboo given long-standing injunctions against it in the Western world, though in recent years the American view of masturbation has become more indulgent. Although statistics indicate that the majority of females, like the majority of males, masturbate (Kinsey, 1953, pp. 153–158), there is probably sufficient confusion, hesitation, or even shame surrounding the practice to prevent discussion of it between mother and daughter—and most other dyads, for that matter.

It is equally likely, however, that masturbation, like orgasm, is not discussed because it is considered an eminently private act which does not lend itself to interpersonal communication. Throughout both sets of questionnaires mothers and daughters emphasized the importance of privacy. Both mothers and daughters, without being asked, wrote over and over, "It's private," indicating that there were some subjects deemed too personal to share with someone else, especially if that person is not the sexual or romantic partner.

Daughters' concern for their mothers' feelings was reflected in the many instances where daughters wrote that they did not ask their mothers to help them obtain contraception or did not tell their mothers about their sexual relations because they were afraid of hurting them. Daughters expressed concern about hurting or shocking their mothers, as well as about the possibility of censure or reprisal.

Attitudes and Values

Overall, the data generally suggest a similarity in attitudes between the groups representing mothers and daughters, with a slightly more traditional tendency on the part of the mothers' sample (though less so than predicted by daughters). One extreme example of the discrepancy between the "mothers'" more traditional values and the "daughters'" greater liberalism was found in answers to a question concerning virginity. A greater percentage of the mothers' sample expected their daughters to remain virgins until marriage (51%) while a smaller percentage of the daughters' sample (27%) expected to do so. Another example of similar attitudes with greater liberalism on the part of the daughters was found in a question concerning abortion. In an open-ended question, 50% of the mothers stated they would counsel abortion for their daughters if they knew their daughters were pregnant and unmarried, as compared to 74% of the daughters who stated that they would have or would seriously consider having an abortion if they were pregnant and unmarried.

The relative traditionalism of mothers and daughters was also evident in each group's response to questions asking how they would feel if: (1) the daughter were involved in a homosexual relationship; (2) the daughter never married; and (3) the daughter never had children. The daughters were also asked to give their perceptions of their own mothers' views. The reactions to the possibility of involvement in a homosexual relationship showed that while mothers were clearly less liberal than daughters on this subject, they were not quite so traditional as the daughters perceived their own mothers to be: 91% of the mothers *vs* 78% of daughters gave "negative" or "very negative" responses, and 94% of daughters anticipated a "negative" or "very negative" response from their own mothers.

The remaining two questions, regarding marriage and children, however, elicited more apparently traditional reactions from the daughters than from the mothers. Daughters felt more keenly the desire for marriage and children than their mothers expressed for them: 57% of the daughters reacted negatively to the thought of never marrying, as compared to 34% of the mothers who expressed similar feelings for them. Similarly, 51% of the daughters reacted negatively to the thought of never having children, as compared to 30% of the mothers. In both instances, daughters overestimated their mothers' conservatism in these areas (49% of daughters anticipated a negative response from their mothers if they never married; 33% anticipated a negative response if they had no children). This might suggest a general tendency on the part of the daughters to see their mothers as more traditional than they really are. It might also reflect less a difference in values than a difference in intensity between what one hopes for oneself and what one hopes for another, even someone as close as offspring.

Another misperception of the daughters is their appraisal of the degree to which they have influenced their mothers' sexual attitudes: daughters appear to underestimate their influence on their mothers. While 55% of mothers report that their college-aged daughters have influenced their sexual attitudes, only 30% of daughters think they have influenced them. Daughters who report having poor sexual communication with their mothers are especially prone to underestimate their influence on their mothers' views; yet mothers seem to be affected by their daughters, whether or not they have good sexual communication.

Implications

It is probably impossible to find a period in history when the change in sexual behavior for women has been more dramatic.[5] Mothers have had to deal with the suspicion or knowledge that their daughters were sexually active in their teen years, vulnerable to pregnancy, venereal disease, psychological injury, and the disapproval of parents and parental friends. While they may have been able to exercise some control while the daughters were still under the parental roof, sending daughters off to college has become tantamount to sexual initiation for about a third of the female students. Most of the mothers and daughters in our study indicated that these problems have not torn the family apart.

Granted, the women in our study are skewed in favor of middle- and upper-class families with close, stable relationships. We would need data from different socio-economic levels in order to make generalizations that would apply to the overall national population. Nonetheless, our findings offer certain insights into the nature of this change in sexual mores.

First, major changes in sexual behavior have occurred within affluent and well-educated families. There is no evidence of a backlash by mothers in this class against the greater sexual freedom of their daughters, at least as far as heterosexuality is concerned.

Second, the difference in college sexual behavior between the older and younger women is not accompanied by an equal difference in current attitudes and values. These mothers and daughters expressed largely similar attitudes toward sex, though the daughters tended to be somewhat more liberal than their mothers. Perhaps we are witnessing less a sexual revolution than an evolution where the behavior of the younger women has caught up with attitudes of the older women. The psychologist Wardell Pomeroy states that "changes in behavior usually lag at least a generation behind changes in attitude" (Friday, 1977, p. 7). Our data suggest that, despite their own traditional sexual behavior in the fifties, women were prepared to be influenced by the newer sexual mores that began to emerge in the sixties and became more prevalent in the seventies.

Finally, the communication between mothers and daughters on the subject of sex seems to have improved during the last twenty-five years. The large majority of mothers reported that verbal communications with their own mothers about sex had been either nonexistent or distinctly uncomfortable, as compared to verbal communication with their daughters, which was generally reported by the 1954 and 1980 samples as comfortable. The responses of 325 mothers and daughters indicate that they are talking to each other with a certain measure of ease on a variety of highly-charged, even explosive, sexual topics.

NOTES

1. There was a high rate of non-response (11%) to this question by the 1954 sample. Such a high rate cannot be ignored and, for this reason, the non-responses on this question for both samples are included in the base figures used to assess the differences between the two groups of women and to calculate percentages, making them relative rather than adjusted frequencies. Adjusted frequencies were: Mother—78% "comfortable" or "very comfortable," Daughters—46% "comfortable" or "very comfortable."

2. All percentages reported are adjusted frequencies, that is, they represent the percent of women responding to the question. For any given question, the percent of women who did not respond was generally between one and three percent.

3. For one such study, however, see Bell & Buerkle (1970).

4. Comparison of the 1954 respondents and the mothers described by class of 1980 respondents: On the whole, the similarities between the mothers of the Stanford students and the respondents to the mothers' questionnaire are more striking than the dissimilarities. There were, however, some differences, in educational attainment, age, and occupation. The mothers sampled from the Wellesley and Stanford classes of 1954 by definition had at least some college education and all but 11% graduated. Among the mothers of the current Stanford students, 59% had a B.A. or higher degree, 25% had some college but did not graduate, and 16% had no college. Since the class of 1954 mothers represented a specific age cohort, they tended to be 44 or 45 years old with few exceptions. The mothers of the Stanford students, on the other hand, ranged from 38 to 61 years of age. The average age was 47. While occupational patterns are generally similar between both sets of mothers and fathers, there is a higher proportion of homemakers among the mothers of the current Stanford students (47% as compared with 34% of the class of 1954 respondents).

    Comparison of the class of 1980 respondents and the daughters described by the class of 1954 respondents: The most notable differences between the two groups are birth order and educational attainment. While mothers were asked to respond to their questionnaire in relation to their eldest daughters, only 69% of the class of 1980 sample were eldest daughters. The educational level of the class of 1980 sample was controlled by seeking responses only from those in their second year at Stanford. The daughters described by the mothers' sample, while generally of college age, varied in their educational pursuits from no college to graduate or professional school attendance.

5. The historian Edward Shorter (1975) takes another view: he argues in favor of the early nineteenth century as the crucial revolutionary period in Western sexual mores.

REFERENCES

BELL, R. R. *The Sex Survey of Australian Women*. Melbourne, Australia: Sun Books, 1974.

BELL, R. R., & BUERKLE, J. V. Mother and daughter attitudes to premarital sexual behavior. In A. Shiloh (Ed.), *Studies in Human Sexual Behavior*. Springfield, Ill.: Charles C Thomas, 1970.

CHRISTENSEN, H. T. Scandinavian vs. American sex patterns. *Sexual Behavior*, September 1971, *1*, 4–10.

CROAKE, J. W., & JAMES, B. A four-year comparison of premarital sexual attitudes. *Journal of Sex Research*, 1973, *9*, 91–96.

FERRELL, M. Z., TOLONE, W. L., & WALSH, R. H. Maturational and societal changes in the sexual double-standard: A panel analysis (1967–1971; 1970–1974). *Journal of Marriage and the Family*, 1977, *39*, 255–271.

FRIDAY, N. *My mother / my self*. New York: Delacorte Press, 1977.

GOTTHEIL, E., & FREEDMAN, A. Sexual beliefs and behaviors of single, male medical students. *Journal of the American Medical Association*, 1970, *212*, 1327–1332.

HUNT, M. *Sexual behavior in the 1970's*. Chicago: Playboy Press, 1974.

KAATS, G. R., & DAVIS, K. E. The dynamics of sexual behavior of college students. *Journal of Marriage and the Family*, 1970, *32*, 390–399.

KING, K., BALSWICK, J. O., & ROBINSON, I. E. The continuing premarital sexual revolution among college females, *Journal of Marriage and the Family*, 1977, *39*, 455–459.

KINSEY, A. C., POMEROY, W. B., MARTIN, C. E., & GEBHARD, P. H. *Sexual behavior in the human female*. Philadelphia: W. B. Saunders, 1953.

OFFER, D. Attitudes toward sexuality in a group of 1500 middle class teen-agers. *Journal of Youth and Adolescence*, 1972, *1*, 81–90.

REISS, I. L. *Premarital sexual standards in America*. New York: Macmillan Free Press, 1960.

ROBINSON, I. E., KING, K., & BALSWICK, J. O. The premarital sexual revolution among college students. *The Family Coordinator*, 1972, *21*, 189–194.

RUBIN, I. New sex findings: Some trends and implications. In H.A. Otto (Ed.), *The new sexuality*. Palo Alto, Calif.: Science and Behavior Books, 1971.

SHORTER, E. *The making of the modern family*. New York: Basic Books, 1975.

SMIGEL, E. D., & SEIDEN, R. The decline and fall of the double standard. In J. Hodden & M. L. Borgatta (Eds.), *Marriage and the family*. Itasca, Ill.: F. E. Peacock, 1969.

WILSON, W. C. The distribution of selected sexual attitudes and behaviors among the adult population of the United States. *Journal of Sex Research*, 1975, *11*, 46–64.

ZELNICK, M., & KANTNER, J. F. Contraceptive patterns and premarital pregnancy among women ages 15–19 in 1976. *Family Planning Perspectives*, 1978, *10*, 135–142.

21

Sexuality in Marriage

Juanita H. Williams

The sexual behavior of women and men in the marriage relationship probably has just as much variety as any other behaviors. Affected by deeply ingrained attitudes, themselves determined by cultural and idiosyncratic histories, sexual behavior also reflects the quality of the relationship, situational variables, and personal characteristics such as age, health, and parity. Biological, psychological, cultural, and historical determinants interact to produce similarities and differences, fascinating mosaics within which patterns can be discerned, some stronger and more pervasive than others.

Currently, both marriage and sexuality are the subjects of examination, commentary, and criticism by social scientists and those in a variety of other disciplines. Sexual permissiveness, along with other contemporary phenomena such as the availability of birth control and abortion, declining birth rates, and the increasing incidence of divorce, is seen by some as threatening the survival of marriage. At the same time the new permissiveness is seen to encourage marital happiness by disavowing old inhibitions and taboos and by stimulating new practices to banish boredom, expand experiment, and enhance consciousness.

Sexual behavior in marriage today can be observed, studied, and understood by the conventional methods of social science. But to fully appreciate its importance, its relation to its sociocultural context at any given time, and its sensitivity to sex roles and the power relationship of women and men, historical beliefs, attitudes, and practices must be studied.

The discussion will begin by reviewing sexuality and marriage historically, examining normative attitudes and values as they were formulated, promoted, and supported by religious and secular leaders.

During the first half of the twentieth century, sexual behavior first was studied seriously by investigators in such disciplines as anthropology, medicine, and psychology. For the first time, objective studies using interviews, questionnaires, and direct observation began to appear. These data required the conventional wisdom to be modified and sanctioned the emergence of more open attitudes toward and greater freedom in sex in and out of marriage.

Publication of such scholarly studies as those of Kinsey and later of Masters and Johnson, facilitated subsequent inquiry, and sex research became a respectable discipline. At the same time, other social movements, such as the counter-culture movement of the sixties and the women's liberation movement, demanded freedom from authoritarian teachings about role and place. There was a serious examination of the old institution of marriage and its place in the new society. Sexual behavior in marriage, its norms and variety, emerged from the Victorian shadows as a topic fit for science and the public media.

Sexual activity outside of marriage always has been legally and morally proscribed in our society. Sexual activity outside of marriage always has had vastly different meanings for women and men, a double standard which persists today. Even so, the heterosexual monogamous pattern is being eroded by experiments in group marriage, communal living arrangements, and casual physical exchanges. The long-term effects of these as competitors with conventional sexual monogamy are not yet known.

The renaissance of the feminist movement of the past decade has had a significant impact on all the institutions of our society, including marriage. As the old power relationships in which man was dominant and woman submissive began to shift, so did the sexual relationships, and women began to express their needs and to make their demands in this most private encounter between the sexes. Reports of the effects of the new female consciousness on marital sexuality are just beginning to appear, and while so far unsystematic, they suggest a new pattern of expectations, especially for the educated young.

There is human diversity in this area of behavior as in all others. Variability is the rule, and what is normative in one culture is deviant in another. It is both healthful and humbling to realize, as Havelock Ellis pointed out long ago, that not everyone is like us.

Historical Perspective

Marriage is older than recorded history, and its origins are unknown, though the question has stimulated several theories. These include the sexual promiscuity-matriarchy theory (Bachofen, 1967); the theory that monogamy has always been characteristic of human groups, as it is of other primates with whom we share common ancestors (Westermarck, 1921); and theories of ubiquitous patriarchy, in which the formal institution of marriage arose from the reciprocal exchange of women (e.g., Levi-Strauss, 1969). Although each of these has had its supporters and detractors (Murstein, note 1), the last is the most influential today and is worth a closer look because of its implications for the history of relations between women and men and of the development of attitudes about sexuality.

It is Levi-Strauss's contention that the universally observed incest taboo served to promote exogamy, whose functional value was the formation of alliances between groups through the elaboration of kinship systems. Such alliances were based on reciprocity, the ceremonial exchange of gifts, property, and especially women.

> Such is the case with exchange. Its role in primitive society is essential because it embraces material objects, social values and women. But while in the case of merchandise this role has progressively diminished in importance . . . as far as women are concerned, reciprocity has maintained its fundamental function, on the one hand because women are the most precious possession . . . but above all because women are not primarily a sign of social value, but a natural stimulant; and the stimulant of the only instinct the satisfaction of which can be deferred, and consequently the only one for which, in the act of exchange, and through the awareness of reciprocity, the transformation from the stimulant to the sign can take place, and defining by this fundamental process the transformation from nature to culture, assume the character of an institution (Levi-Strauss, 1969, pp. 62–63.)

The systematic exchange of women greatly strengthened the original family, bringing it into a cultural kinship system, and ensuring its existence as a group. The giving away of sisters and daughters became an insurance against extinction.

The significance of this theory for our discussion is that an important sex difference is made: it is men who are exchanging women. The opposite, as far as we know, has never occurred in any human society (Mitchell, 1974). Levi-Strauss wrote: "The reciprocal bond basic to marriage is not set up between men and women, but between men and men by means of women, who are only the principal occasion for it" (cited in Mitchell, 1974, p. 373).

Marriage, then, was an important link between kinship groups and permitted the establishment of kin lines through which property and power were transmitted from one generation to the next. This being the case, marriages had to be arranged carefully to provide the maximum advantage to all parties. Such a serious matter could not be left to the young, and arranged marriages were the norm until recent times. Such marriages included the payment of a bride price to the bride's father or, in some cases, the custom of the dowry, valuable goods, which went with the bride to her new home.

Attitudes toward sex and marriage revealed in the Old Testament indicate a sensual and earthy consciousness of sex with an accompanying double standard and devaluation of women. The Song of Solomon is essentially a hymn of appreciation for the sexual potential of the human body. Women as sexual beings were, however, regarded as property, and there were strict sanctions against such trespasses as violating a virgin and adultery. The unchaste maid was no longer marriageable, thus worthless to her father; the violator had to marry her and pay money to her father (Exodus 22: 17). Adulterers could be put to death (Leviticus 20: 10), the woman for her sin, the man for violating the property of another man. The sexual behavior of women was carefully prescribed and guarded in order to ensure that legal offspring would inherit property. Women were unclean and required ritual purification in connection with the natural events of their bodies, such as menstruation and childbirth. If a woman gave birth to a son, the period required for her purification was thirty-three days. If the child was a daughter, the time required was sixty-six days (Leviticus 12: 4–5).

Although sexual behavior was carefully regulated, especially for women, and fornication and adultery were serious crimes, marriage itself was an important institution, and everyone was expected to marry and produce children (Kennett, 1931). The good wife, described in the Book of Proverbs, had a price "above rubies," and the impression in that account is that she was a respected companion in the marital enterprise, though subservient (Proverbs 31: 10–26). Sexual desire was an accepted characteristic of humans, and chastity was valued only before marriage.

With the advent of Christianity, beliefs and values about marriage and sexuality began to change. Chastity and asceticism became synonomous with holiness; marriage was a sorry state, to be contracted only in direct need or for procreation, and the status of women declined accordingly. At best, the woman was a silent submissive wife; at worst, she was the instrument of damnation, exciting lust and luring man from his holy mission. Paul wished that all men could be celibate as he was. "But if they cannot contain, let them marry; for it is better to marry than to burn" (I Corinthians 7: 7–9). The man was not made for the woman, but the woman for the man. "Wives, submit yourselves unto your own husbands, . . . as unto the Lord. For the husband is the head of the wife, even as Christ is the head of the church" (Ephesians 6: 22–23). "Let the woman learn in silence with all subjection . . . I suffer not a woman to teach, nor to usurp authority over the man, but to be in silence" (I Timothy 2: 11–12).

The doctrine of asceticism was largely responsible for the low esteem to which marriage fell during this period:

> "It would be difficult to conceive of anything more coarse or more repulsive than the manner in which (the ascetics) regarded it. . . . Even when the bond had been formed, the ascetic passion retained its sting. . . . Whenever any strong religious fervor fell upon a husband or wife, its first effect was to make a happy union impossible. The more religious partner desired to live a life of solitary asceticism, or at least, if no ostensible separation took place, an unnatural life of separation in marriage" (Lecky, 1905, vol. 2, 117–18).

During the Middle Ages the equation of chastity and abstinence with sanctity and superior virtue continued to be prominent in the writings of the theologians. The Penitentials of Theodore, seventh-century archbishop of Canterbury, described various punishments for transgressions. A man who had intercourse with his wife must take a bath before entering the church. Newly married persons or women who had given birth were likewise barred from the church for a period, followed by a set penance. Even the more liberal St. Thomas Aquinas thought that marriage was inferior to virginity. Sexual intercourse, even in marriage, partook of the profane connotations of the body. One who indulged would never be as high on the ladder of sanctity as one who abjured the devilments of the flesh in favor of the spiritual life and its promised rewards.

If this was the approved model, however, it appears that in many cases practices in real life were less elevated and more corporeal. Between the sixth and the eleventh centuries the clergy were noted for their sexual excesses and license. Consort with women as wives or concubines was common, and friars, monks, and priests were the main clientele of prostitutes. Suggestions that some women appreciated the pleasures of sex appear in the love letters of Héloise to Abelard, and in the frank sensuality of Chaucer's Wife of Bath. In general, however, women and their sexuality continued to be devalued, and there is little evidence that sexual gratification and emotional satisfaction were normally expected to be part of marriage (Murstein, 1974).

Attitudes toward marriage and sex became somewhat more positive during the Reformation, even though women, their bodies, minds, and functions continued to be denigrated. Martin Luther in his *Table Talk* (Luther, 1890) said that women had narrow chests and broad hips because they were destined to "remain at home, sit still, keep house, and bear and bring up children" (p. 299). Even so, he was a strong advocate of marriage; knowing that celibacy was an elusive goal for most, including the clergy, he saw it as a gift approved by God and a prevention of graver sins. His contemporary, John Calvin, also favored marriage over its inevitable alternatives. He thought that one should refrain from marriage in favor of celibacy as long as possible, however, and recommended restraint and modesty in this activity as in all others. The renunciation of pleasure and worldliness was a strong theme of his, and their equation with sin and the evocation of guilt continued to permeate Western ideas about sex and morality until recent times (Rugoff, 1971).

During the eighteenth and nineteenth centuries, the romantic movement began, with its emphases on nature, freedom, defiance of traditional mores, and the ascendancy of the invididual. Sexual love was imbued with divinity; and emotion, rather than cool reason, was the guide to truth and happiness. Romanticism was the antithesis of conventional bourgeois marriage, arranged for practical reasons of family and patrimony. The romantic might marry, but only for love and its passion. Leaders of the romantic movement were such literary figures as Shelley, Byron, and Keats, who themselves exemplified this life style. George Sand, though married, had many lovers, and her public flouting of conventional norms provided an unusual model of assumed sexual equality. The romantic tradition waned with the influence of the Victorian era, but its thematic ideas of the relationships among love, sex, and marriage continue to be important, and its rejection of traditional values echoed through the Victorian counter-culture, the bohemian ethos, and the emergence of the widespread acceptance of sexual freedom in modern times.

The arrival of the Victorian era with its attitudes toward sexuality and marriage linked many of these antecedent themes and integrated a system of morals and values which became a powerful arbiter of behavior for our society. Abolition of slavery, woman suffrage, and labor unions were among the reforms reflecting ideological change as the political and social environment became more and more complex. As Strong (1973) observed, "The comforting security derived from a sense of hierarchy and order appeared to be crumbling with the advent of the new democracy" (p. 457). Opposing this was the vision of the family, united in the sacred and secular bonds of love and marriage, as a refuge from the swirling uncertainties of the world and as a conservatory of traditional values.

The Victorian model of the family relied upon rigid role segregation of the sexes, the husband as head of the household and economic provider and the wife as keeper of the home, maintaining domestic serenity and inculcating spiritual and moral values in the young—the "angel in the house." The idealized notion of the moral superiority of women in this role meant that she was to regulate the display of human passions, including sex. The repressive control of sexual passions was the major motif of Victorian morality, and physicians, preachers, and moralists of all persuasions, male and female, inveighed against the horrors of its abuse, citing disease, mania, and death. (For a detailed review of this literature, see Haller and Haller, 1974.)

Chastity until marriage was valued by both sexes, but its loss for women had far more sinister implications: "Preeminence has its perils—those who fall from it fall farthest, and a female who lost her virtue was, if anything, more reprehensible than a male who did; she went against her nature, while he only obeyed his" (Walter, 1974, p. 68). Marriage was seen as a means for containing and restraining the sexual urges of men, even more the victims of their power than women were. It was part of nature's plan that women have little sexual passion and that to restrain man's ardor, it was both necessary and natural for her to be passive and indifferent to his sexual impulses.

> It should also be pointed out that woman was not advised to experience the same pleasures as the male in the sexual union. As a passive creature, she was to endure the attentions of her husband in a negative sense, if only to deter the greater weakening of the "vital forces" in the male. Writers also believed that if women experienced "any spasmodic convulsion" in coition it would interfere with the possibility of conception—the primary function of the marriage act (Haller, 1972, p. 56).

Married couples were advised to avoid undressing in each others' presence and to sleep in separate beds if possible. The ideal was continence in the marital relationship, the principle being that indulgence of the sexual impulses was not only debilitating and degrading but ran counter to the development and strengthening of character, will, and social responsibility (Haller, 1972).

Given the Victorian status of the parameters of male hegemony, sex role segregation, differential valuing of male and female sexuality, and the role of sex in human arrangements, it was inevitable that sex in marriage was paradoxical, loaded with conflicts and contradictions, and at the same time, invested with feelings of love and responsibility.

Expectations for marriage and the sexual relationship had to be based on the obscure and highly sentimentalized teachings of the times. It was not uncommon for a bride to experience her wedding night totally unprepared for the realities of sexual intercourse, her first experience with sex being closer to rape than to her romantic dreams of sanctioned closeness. What she knew was fiction, gathered from casual talk, overheard conversations, romantic stories and novels, sermons, what her parents and teachers taught her, and her own integration of all these resulting in an utterly unrealistic expectation of what her future as a wife and a sexual partner would be like.

Advice on sexual matters for the married couple was plentiful (Walters, 1974; Haller and Haller, 1974). Unlike the contemporary emphases on both quantity and quality of sexual experience, nineteenth-century authorities, almost to a man, laid down spartan rules for permissible frequency of intercourse and discussed its quality not at all. Dr. Sylvester Graham, for example, thought that once a month was just about right, and Dr. John Cowan advised complete abstinence during pregnancy, lactation, and for an additional year after weaning. "This may not be required in a perfectly healthy woman, but healthy women being an exception, the rule holds good" (in Walter, 1974, p. 89). Since women were held to be asexual (except in rare and pathological cases), there was no obligation to arouse her or to be concerned for her satisfaction.

Because a pretentious and repressive morality was the official position of family, school, and church it is still not possible to know the extent of its influence on married couples. That even the educated were often ignorant and uninformed about sex is doubtless true. When one considers the hold that fear, guilt, and shame of sex continues to have, it seems likely that most conventional marriages of the time were affected by the prevalent attitudes.

It is worthwhile to note, however, that the Victorian era had another side, less often mentioned in chronicles of the times. Prostitution flourished as did the institution of the mistress, at least in Europe (Pearsall, 1969). Pornography, the organized sexual use of children, and ritual flagellation all were common. There existed, too, a free love movement which flourished briefly toward the end of the century, a harbinger of the loosening of restraints which would appear again in the 1920s. Finally, the era brought forth the most scholarly and progressive work on sex yet to appear, the classic six-volume *Studies in the Psychology of Sex,* by Havelock Ellis. Appearing between 1898 and 1910, this monumental work covered a panorama of human sexuality and demolished most of the myths cherished by the proper Victorians. Ellis's work will be discussed in a later section.

Nineteenth-century Experiments in Sex and Marriage

Although the family, founded in monogamous marriage, was considered the basis of society in the nineteenth century, its sanctity and its assumption of sexual exclusivity of husband and wife were not unchallenged. Utopian communities, with missions of economic, religious, or social reform, sought to change or exclude marriage as antagonistic to the communal spirit. Some of these were celibate, some adopted polygyny, and some had a system of "complex marriage," in which every man was married to every woman, and vice versa (Muncy, 1973). The most important of these was the Oneida community in New York, founded by John Humphrey Noyes in 1848.

Exclusive attachments were not permitted at Oneida. Any man could approach any woman, but she was under no obligation to accept his proposal, even if he were her legal husband. The young did not mate exclusively with the young but were introduced into the system of complex marriage by older persons of the opposite sex. Thus, virgins learned about sex from the skilled attentions of older men, and boys were taught to give and receive pleasure by experienced women. Noyes regarded the amative function of sex as superior to the procreative function, knowing that children were expensive and childbirth dangerous. He developed the art of what he called "male continence," the restraint of ejaculation through self-control. The female orgasm was the objective, and when the male became skilled at the technique, intercourse could last for an hour or more and pregnancy could be avoided. Though not foolproof male continence was highly regarded at Oneida, and careless or unskilled men were avoided by the women of the community (Muncy, 1973).

Early Research on Marital Sex

The intellectual climate which made sex research possible appeared during the 1890s with the work of Freud and Ellis. A major contribution of theirs was to remove sexuality from its status of alienation and discontinuity in other areas of life, bringing it into the cultural consciousness of the late nineteenth-century—an act of inclusion, as Gagnon (1975) described it.

> They exposed and brought forward deeply held cultural beliefs about sexuality. The act of including the sexual into life not only as a pathological manifestation but also as it informed and shaped conventional lives was a profound challenge to that elite for whom the sexual existed outside the normal social order (Gagnon, 1975, p. 116).

Although sexuality was a central concern for both Freud and Ellis,* neither gave marital sex a special place separate from sex in general. Freud was more interested in psychosexual development and its effect on personality than he was in the sexual lives of married people. Ellis, less interested in distinctions between pathologies and normal behavior, was an unsparing and exhaustive observer of sex in natural settings—what real people really do, all over the world.

Although Freud himself had a conventional marriage in the patriarchal tradition, he was quite aware of its typical constraints, particularly as they affected women. In a 1908 paper, " 'Civilized' Sexual Morality and Modern Nervousness," he showed how the double standard of morality, the Victorian ideal of abstinence, and women's sexual frustrations in marriage brought about neurosis:

> Marriage under the present cultural standard has long since ceased to be a panacea for the nervous sufferings of women; even if we physicians in such cases still advise matrimony, we are nevertheless aware that a girl must be very

---

*The two, however, were utterly different in their cultural backgrounds, approaches and appreciations, and in intellectual and research styles.

healthy to "stand" marriage. . . . Marital unfaithfulness would . . . be a much more probable cure for the neurosis resulting from marriage; the more strictly a wife has been brought up, the more earnestly she has submitted to the demands of civilization, the more does she fear this way of escape, and in conflict between her desires and her sense of duty she again will seek refuge in a neurosis (p. 177).

Ellis was highly progressive in his attitudes about sexuality. He favored sex education, birth control, trial marriage, and lifting legal and social restrictions against sexual acts of all kinds between consenting adults, and opposed the rigid and narrow definition of marriage in his time. His studies, drawing on anthropological data, case histories and correspondence with friends and other scholars, and his own observations and enormous erudition are unmatched examples of the cultural relativism of sexual behavior and sexual standards. The first essay in the *Studies*, "The Evolution of Modesty," was named by Brecher (1971) as "the best introduction I have found to the scientific study of sex" (p. 26).

Ellis (1937) had no illusions about the state of sexual knowledge and of the art of love in his society. "At times one feels hopeless at the thought that civilization in this supremely intimate field of life has achieved so little" (p. 121). In an essay on "The Play-Function of Sex" (1937), he wrote that the average man had two ideals regarding sex: his wish to prove himself a man, to experience his virility, and to enjoy the pleasurable relief from sexual tension. Both of these, said Ellis, are essentially self-regarding. But "love is not primarily self-regarding. It is the intimate, harmonious, combined play . . . of two personalities" (p. 123–24). Because of these male values, the woman typically attains neither pride in her womanliness nor physical satisfaction. Though she may appear in her role as wife and mother to be playing her proper part in the home and in the world, she remains as emotionally immature and virginal as a schoolgirl (Ellis, 1937).

The influence of Freud's and Ellis's ideas interacted with other cultural phenomena, setting the stage for a new kind of research on sexuality which adopted the quantitative methods and techniques of the natural sciences. (For a detailed analysis of this evolution, see Gagnon, 1975.) Before the publication of *Sexual Behavior in the Human Male* (Kinsey and others, 1948), however, only a few such studies had appeared, dealing mostly with students and patients. Of the few whose samples were normal married persons, three deserve mention: *Factors in the Sex Life of 2200 Women*, (Davis, 1929); *A Research in Marriage* (Hamilton, 1929); and *One Thousand Marriages* (Dickinson and Beam, 1932). The first two were based on questionnaire data, and the last relied on cases in Dickinson's files on his gynecological patients.

It becomes clear from these early studies that ignorance and frustration among married persons was commonplace, as they tried to work out their sexual lives in an era when accurate information was not readily available and when the prevailing mores and attitudes still reflected what Brecher (1972) called the debilitating disease of Victorianism. Dickinson, for example, reported that eighteen of his one thousand patients remained virgins for an average of four years after marriage, because neither the husband nor the wife knew how to have intercourse. Characteristically, he said, the marital coitus of his patients was brief and male-oriented, the wife remaining passive and unaroused. Intercourse occurred once or twice a week, usually without foreplay. Intromission lasted about five minutes, after which the husband had an orgasm and the wife did not.

Hamilton, in his study of one hundred married persons of each sex, felt that the institution of marriage had "fared rather better than had been expected" (p. 553), when 48% of his sample had been rated as reasonably satisfied with their marriage. Of the one hundred women, only thirty-six had had orgasm during the first year of their marriages, though this number had increased to fifty-four by the time of the study. Hamilton thought that his study gave evidence that in many families the children "are so affected by their parents that when adult life is reached no conceivable mode of prolonged and intimate relationship with a person of the opposite sex is likely to end otherwise than disastrously" (p. 554).

During the same period, there appeared a noteworthy attempt to change this dismal picture, to give to physicians and married men the knowledge they needed to introduce satisfaction and joy into marital sex for both the man and the woman, and to dispel the tedium and misery of the sexual side of marriage which seemed to be so typical of the time. *Ideal Marriage,* by Dutch gynecologist Theodoor Van de Velde (1930), was an explicit manual whose intention was to dispel ignorance, to teach men how effectively and lovingly to introduce their brides to the marriage bed, and, by describing in detail many possible variations and techniques, to help couples to keep their sex lives alive and interesting through their lives. One of Van de Velde's most important contributions was to emphasize the mutuality of sex, of the reciprocal giving and receiving of pleasure between the partners. He insisted throughout the work on the importance of the wife's satisfaction and described the typical sex act consisting of brief or no foreplay, intromission, and ejaculation as a parody of how sex could be. Though himself a Victorian who believed that sex should be expressed only within the context of marriage, Van de Velde provided a popular and knowledgeable antidote to the prevailing climate of ignorance and inhibition about sex.

Sexual Behavior in Marriage

There are few studies of sexual behavior in marriage which meet even minimal criteria for scientific acceptability. The most important attempts to get a representative picture of sexual behavior in the United States were those of Kinsey and others (1948, 1953). Two more recent large-scale surveys (Hunt, 1974; Tavris and Sadd, 1977) have looked at marital sexual behavior, and both have reported remarkable changes in the thirty years since Kinsey and his colleagues collected their data. We shall consider the nature of each of these studies as they pertain to marital sex.

The Kinsey studies consist of samples of 5,300 males and 5,940 females of a wide range of ages, educational levels, and geographical distribution, and are based on data collected in structured interviews and statistically analyzed to reveal what Gagnon (1975) called social bookkeeping: who does what with whom, how, and how often. Each of the volumes contains a chapter on marital intercourse, as well as numerous references to it throughout the books. The studies do not claim to be representative, since some groups in the population are underrepresented (e.g., less educated and rural groups) or not represented at all (e.g., blacks). Besides methodological problems in the studies, we can be sure that much of the data are now obsolete. Nevertheless, they do provide a framework for sexual behavior and a reference for comparison with later studies.

The Hunt study, *Sexual Behavior in the 1970s,* was based on a sample of 982 males and 1,044 females, supposedly representative of the adult U.S. population in such variables as race, marital status, education, occupation, and urban-rural background. The data for the statistical analyses were gathered by self-administered questionnaires; an additional sample of 100 males and 100 females were interviewed in depth for the book's narrative material. The intention was to collect data paralleling that of Kinsey's so as to compare his sample with the present generation. The study does not claim to be truly representative of the American population. One problem is that only one in five of those persons originally contacted agreed to participate. Another is that the material was presented in *Playboy* magazine (October 1973–February 1974) and in book-form (Hunt, 1974) for the general public, and the analyses are not nearly as comprehensive or detailed as Kinsey's. Even so, despite shortcomings of the data presentation, it is a study of adult sexual behavior in our society, it looks at many of the same variables that Kinsey used, and it, too, has a chapter on marital sex.

The third study by Tavris and Sadd (1977), is based on a sample of 2,278 married women, whose questionnaire responses were scientifically selected from 100,000 such responses by women readers of *Redbook* magazine. The sample was claimed to be "virtually parallel" (p. 20) to the national distribution of married women in geographical area, religious belief, and percentage who work outside the home. They are, however, younger, better educated, and more affluent than are married women in general.

The problem in discussing marital sexual behavior, then, is obvious: not enough up-to-date, reliable, methodologically sound data. Despite these limitations, this section will deal with frequency of marital intercourse, coital techniques, orgasm, masturbation, pregnancy, and satisfaction with marital sex.

Frequency

The increase in reported sexual activity over the past decade or so is reflected in the data on marital intercourse. Tables 1 and 2 show the weekly frequencies of marital intercourse reported by husbands and wives in the Kinsey and Hunt studies. There are increases for all age groups, though they are greater for males than for females. Hunt makes the interesting observation that the smaller increase for females may mean that women are perceiving the frequency of their sexual intercourse more accurately today. If frequency of intercourse were tied more to the male's desire than to the female's, so that she had to meet his needs rather than her own, she might tend to overestimate the incidence of such events. By contrast, if we assume that wives today have more control over the frequency of intercourse, then their estimates should be closer to reality. If this hypothesis is

Table 1 Marital coitus: Frequency per week as estimated by husbands, 1938–1946 and 1972[a]

1938–1946 (Kinsey)			1972 (Present Survey)		
Age	Mean	Median	Age	Mean	Median
16–25	3.3	2.3	18–24	3.7	3.5
26–35	2.5	1.9	25–34	2.8	3.0
36–45	1.8	1.4	35–44	2.2	2.0
46–55	1.3	.8	45–54	1.5	1.0
56–60	.8	.6	55 & over	1.0	1.0

[a] Reprinted from Morton Hunt, *Sexual Behavior in The 1970s*. Chicago: Playboy Press, 1974. By permission.

Table 2 Marital coitus: Frequency per week as estimated by wives, 1938–1949 and 1972[a]

1938–1949 (Kinsey)			1972 (Present Survey)		
Age	Mean	Median	Age	Mean	Median
16–25	3.2	2.6	18–24	3.3	3.0
26–35	2.5	2.0	25–34	2.6	2.1
36–45	1.9	1.4	35–44	2.0	2.0
46–55	1.3	.9	45–54	1.5	1.0
56–60	.8	.4	55 & over	1.0	1.0

[a] Reprinted from Morton Hunt, *Sexual Behavior in The 1970s*. Chicago: Playboy Press, 1974. By permission.

valid, then the smaller increase in females' reported frequency is related to subjective factors.

Frequencies reported by the *Redbook* wives are shown in Table 3. Though not directly comparable to the data from the Hunt study, the median frequency is calculated at 8.5 times per month, or about twice a week. This is nearby identical with the medians which Hunt obtained for the twenty-five to thirty-four and thirty-five to forty-four age groups. Since three out of four women in the *Redbook* sample were under thirty-five, the frequencies for the two groups appear to be very similar.

Obviously median frequencies are only one kind of indication of how often married people have intercourse. Individual variation, as one would expect, was considerable in all the studies. For example, even in Kinsey's younger groups, a few individuals had marital coitus less often than once in two weeks, while in every age group, from the youngest to age forty, some persons were having marital coitus on an average of four times a day, seven days a week (Kinsey and others, 1953).

Table 3 Frequency of intercourse per month[a]

0	1–5	6–10	11–15	16–20	20+
2%	26%	32%	21%	11%	8%

[a] Reprinted from Carol Tavris and Susan Sadd, *The Redbook Report on Female Sexuality*. New York: Delacorte Press, 1977. By permission.

Neither Kinsey nor Hunt found a relationship between frequency of coitus in marriage and either education or occupational status. Religion, however, was related to frequency in both studies. Kinsey and others (1948) reported that less religious husbands had intercourse 20% to 30% more often than did religious mates; such an effect was not found for women, however, leading Kinsey and others (1953) to remark that the wife's coital rate was more likely to be tied to her husband's desires than to her level of devotion. Hunt (1974) found the opposite effect: churchgoing females reported a lower frequency of marital coitus than did churchgoing males or non-churchgoing males and females. Hunt thought that this, too, might reflect the greater influence that wives now have over marital sexual activity. The frequency of sex for married women now might reflect more closely their own wishes than their husbands' desires.

Although intercourse with the spouse is the chief sexual outlet for married people, it falls far short of being their only outlet. Kinsey and others (1948) found an interesting relationship between social level and percent of the total outlet which the married male derived from intercourse with his spouse. For the lower group, marital intercourse accounted for 80% of the outlet during the early years of marriage, increasing to 90% by age fifty. College-educated males on the other hand derived 85% of their total outlet from their wives during the early years, but only 62% by age fifty-five. Kinsey thought that one explanation for this dramatic decline was an increasing dissatisfaction "with the relations which are had with restrained upper level wives" (p. 568).

Wives, likewise, derived only part of their sexual outlet from marital coitus. The maximum part of the sexual outlet derived from marital intercourse was 89%, reached between the ages of twenty-one and twenty-five, after which the percentage steadily dropped. By age sixty, only 72% of the total outlet of the married women was derived from marital coitus (Kinsey and others, 1953, p. 354, note 2).

A recent study (Edwards and Booth, 1976b) provides evidence that marital intercourse tends to be discontinuous for a sizeable segment of the population. Their stratified probability sample consisted of 144 men and 221 women who had been married between one and twenty years. As part of a two-hour interview, subjects were asked whether intercourse had ever stopped for any reason other than pregnancy, and if so, why and for how long. One-third of the respondents indicated that they had experienced such a cessation, the median length of which was eight weeks. Significant differences emerged between the men and women reporting such cessation: for the men, social background factors such as recent emigration from Europe, being non-Catholic, and lack of employment for the wife were important; for the women, avoidance of intercourse was related to factors in the marriage: perception of the husband as dominant, as not affectionate, or as threatening to leave home. The only common factor for the two sexes was perception of a lack of privacy. Self-reported causes, however, were the same for both men and women: surgery, illness, marital discord, and type of birth control used were some of them. The incidence of discontinuity in marital sex for this sample suggests that the phenomenon is by no means uncommon and enhances, as the authors point out, the sense of intercourse as a symbolic communication between spouses who are other-wise distant from each other's true feelings.

Intercourse, Foreplay, Duration, and Techniques

Not only has the frequency of marital intercourse increased in this generation, but its other parameters also appear to have been affected by attitudinal and behavioral changes in the direction of greater freedom and permissiveness. Both foreplay and coitus are reported to last longer and to include acceptance and use of a greater variety of techniques by more peo-ple. These increases have occurred in all age groups and across educational levels but are greatest among the young and the noncollege population.

Kinsey found that precoital activities such as mouth-breast contact, manual stimulation of the genitals, and cunnilingus and fellatio were more characteristic of the college-educated persons in his samples, and that at any educational level, they were more often reported by younger individ-uals (1948, p. 368; 1953, p. 399). For example, the percentages of males using cunnilingus in marital foreplay were 4%, 15%, and 45% for grade school, high school, and college levels respectively. Manual stimulation of the female genitalia was utilized by 95% of the under-twenty-five age group, compared to 83% of the over-forty-six group.

Hunt (1974) found striking increases in the use of certain techniques in marital foreplay. In general, the increases were greatest for those activ-ities whic had been most strongly tabooed. The increase in breast play, for example, was small, since this activity was common in Kinsey's time. The biggest changes were in oral-genital acts, which have long been not only morally tabooed but legally forbidden as well in most states. In contrast to the 15% of high school males whom Kinsey found had used cunnilingus, Hunt's study revealed that 56% of his sample at that educational level had done so. Corresponding data for college males in the two studies were 45% and 66% (p. 198). Among the *Redbook* wives, (Tavris and Sadd, 1977) 87% reported experience with cunnilingus. The fact that this group was younger and better educated fits with the observations of both Kinsey and Hunt on the greater incidence of such behavior in these populations.

Duration of foreplay has also increased, especially among the less edu-cated. Kinsey's histories for his lower-level sample suggested that precoital play in marriage was often quite perfunctory, consisting of a kiss or two, while his college men might extend such play to five minutes or more. Hunt found no difference by educational level. Foreplay averaged about fifteen minutes for both college and noncollege married men.

Married people today report using a greater variety of positions in actual intercourse than did their counterparts a generation ago. Kinsey reported that nearly all coitus in our culture occurs with the partners face-to-face and the man on top. As many as 70%, he said, had never used any other position (1948, p. 578). By contrast, Hunt found that the female-above position is used by three-fourths of all married couples at least some of the time. Likewise, rear-entry vaginal intercourse was used by only a tenth of Kinsey's sample, compared to four-tenths of Hunt's (Hunt, 1974, p. 202).

Finally, the duration of coitus has increased dramatically among married people. Kinsey reported that three-fourths of all males probably reached orgasm within two minutes after intromission. In an interesting discussion of the pros and cons of the speedy orgasm for males, Kinsey revealed his belief that the male who responded so quickly, far from being "impotent" as some had labeled him, was in fact normal or even superior, 'however inconvenient and unfortunate his qualities may be from the standpoint of the wife" (1948, p. 580). Today prolongation of the sexual act is the goal for many. Hunt found that the median duration of marital intercourse, as reported by both males and females, was ten minutes—not long, but an improvement (from the female view) over the hasty performance reported by a generation past. Moreover, differences owing to such factors as education, occupation, religious and political attitudes were either nonexistent or quite small. Younger people, however, spend more time on their marital love-making than older ones do. Given the greater urgency associated with youthful libido, this must reflect subjective differences in values as a function of age.

It is not difficult to identify at least some of the factors responsible for these changes: lifting of old sanctions against sex for nonprocreative purposes; increase in premarital sex; availability of birth control, with increasing acceptance of sterilization and abortion; disinhibiting effects of media presentations: explicit movies, books, and magazines; greater availability of information about sex, with emphasis on sex as valuable and pleasurable in and of itself; and the contemporary women's movement, which has informed women and men that the sexual needs of women are just as important as are those of men and has taught women to ask and to expect that their needs will be met in the sexual relationship. In any case, the shifts in marital sexual behavior are remarkable: "We stand convinced that a dramatic and historic change has taken place in the practice of marital coitus in America" (Hunt, 1974, p. 206).

Orgasm

The experience of orgasm by the female has been variously valued, even during the present century. Kinsey, for example, commented on the "post-Victorian" development of the idea that respectable women should enjoy marital coitus. Even so, he cited a 1951 study which found evidence in the British working class that responsiveness in the wife was hardly expected and if too marked, was disapproved (1953, p. 373). Kinsey's research suggested to him that orgasm was not nearly as important to the female as it was to the male. Without orgasm, she could still feel pleasure in the "social aspects" of a sexual relationship: "Whether or not she herself reaches orgasm, many a female finds satisfaction in knowing that her husband or other sexual partner has enjoyed the contact, and in realizing that she has contributed to the male's pleasure" (p. 371). Even so, "persistent failure of the female to reach orgasm in her marital coitus, or even to respond with fair frequency, may do considerable damage to a marriage" (p. 371).

About 36% of the married females in Kinsey's sample had never experienced orgasm from any source before marriage. By contrast, over 99% of the late adolescent male sample were responding sexually to orgasm more than twice a week. While almost all marital intercourse of his male sample resulted in orgasm, the average female reached orgasm in only 70% to 77% of her marital sexual experiences. The longer the women were married, however, the more likely they were to experience orgasm. For example, the percent of females who never had orgasm in marital coitus decreased from 25% by the end of the first year to 11% by the end of the twentieth year. Likewise, the percent of those having orgasms more than 60% of the time increased from 51% in the first year to 64% in the twentieth.

In addition to length of marriage, some factors which were strongly related to occurrence of orgasm in Kinsey's sample were decade of birth and premarital experience in orgasm, whether through coitus, petting, or masturbation. For example, 33% of women born before 1900 were unresponsive in the first year of marriage, compared to only 22% of those born after 1909. As for experience, no factor showed a higher correlation with the frequency of orgasm in marital coitus than the presence or absence of premarital experience in orgasm. Among those women with no premarital experience of orgasm, 44% failed to have orgasm during their first year of marriage. Among those with even limited experience only 19% failed to reach orgasm in the first year.

Neither the Hunt nor the *Redbook* data can be directly compared with Kinsey's figures, since neither is broken down by length of marriage. Hunt did, however, compare his females with fifteen-years-median-duration of marriage with Kinsey's females in their fifteenth year of marriage. Of the Kinsey wives, 45% reported having orgasm 90% to 100% of the time, compared to 53% of the Hunt wives who had orgasm "all or almost all of the time" (p. 212). Of the same Kinsey group, 12% never had orgasm, compared with 7% of the Hunt group.

Figures for the *Redbook* sample show that 63% of these wives have orgasm all or most of the time, 7% never. These data are more recent than Hunt's and as we have noted, the sample consists of younger, more educated individuals, all of which could account for the higher orgasmic figure.

Hunt collected some interesting data on the incidence of orgasm among married men. Contrary to Kinsey's assertion that married men achieved orgasm in nearly 100% of their marital coitus, Hunt found that 8% of the husbands aged forty-five and up did not have orgasm anywhere from occasionally to most of the time; 7% of the men between twenty-four and forty-four did not have orgasm at least a quarter of the time; and 15% of the under-twenty-five husbands failed to have orgasm a quarter or more of the time.

Kinsey's stress on the relationship between length of marriage and sexual responsiveness in his married sample was challenged in part by Clark and Wallin (1965). Proposing that women's responsiveness is influenced by the quality, not just the duration, of their marriages, they did a twenty-year longitudinal study which began with 1,000 engaged couples, 602 of whom were studied after a "few years" of marriage, and the 428 remaining couples again after sixteen or more years of marriage. They found a strong relationship across time between positive ratings of the quality of the marriage and sexual responsiveness. Sexual responsiveness increased from 65% to 91% among those wives who rated their marriages as positive, and from

61% to 69% among those rating them negative. The authors suggest that increased responsiveness does not inevitably follow as a function of length of marriage, but rather is interdependent with the perceived quality of the marital relationship.

Masturbation

Although masturbation is used less frequently by married than by unmarried people, it continues to be an outlet for many. Among Kinsey's married males between the ages of twenty-six and thirty-five, almost half masturbated occasionally, along with about one-third of the female sample in that age range (1948, p. 241; 1953, p. 178). Hunt found about 72% of his married male sample in that age range still masturbating, along with two-thirds of the wives, a quite remarkable increase (1974, p. 86).

Consistent with Hunt's data, the *Redbook* study found 68% of their sample, all married women, masturbating often or occasionally (p. 96). Reasons given included husband absent (38%), relaxation of tensions (31%), and enjoyable addition to intercourse (31%).

A recent Danish study (Hessellund, 1976) of thirty-eight couples married a mean of 10.7 years found that 60% of the men and 37% of the women masturbated at least occasionally. Analysis of the relationship between intercourse and masturbation for this sample led the authors to conclude that, since intercourse frequency was determined by the wife and was generally not more than twice a week, masturbation functioned as a supplement to the sexual activity of the men and as a substitute for the women.

Pregnancy and Sexuality

Taboos against intercourse with a pregnant woman are very common in undeveloped countries and have been observed historically as a religious rule among some people. A study of sexual behavior in sixty preliterate societies found that twenty-one of them forbade sexual intercourse during most or all of the pregnancy (Ford & Beach, 1951). Among a Ghana group, the Ashanti, the taboo begins with the discovery of the pregnancy, and husbands, tiring of abstinence, often take another wife (Saucier, 1972).

In our society the continuation of sexual activity by pregnant women is not only common practice but is generally sanctioned by physicians. For example, a study of sexual attitudes and behavior in pregnancy (Tolor and DiGrazia, 1976) noted that the subjects' physicians placed no restrictions whatever on their sexual activity from conception to delivery, unless complications such as bleeding, occurred. After delivery the women were advised to refrain from intercourse for four weeks and then to let their own preferences and comfort be their guide.

A study of 101 women revealed an increase in sexual tension and performance during the second trimester, attributed by the authors to the increased pelvic vascularity associated with pregnancy (Masters and Johnson, 1966). But other studies are in general agreement that sexual interest and activity fall off during pregnancy, especially during the last trimester (Kenny, 1973; Morris, 1975; Solberg and others, 1973). An example is a study (Tolor and DiGrazia, 1976) of a sample of 216 women who were patients of a group of obstetricians. The women comprised four groups: first trimester, second trimester, third trimester, and six weeks postpartum. The median frequency of sexual intercourse for all groups combined was 2.10 per week. Separately, the median reported frequencies for the first, second, and third trimesters and for the postpartum period were 2.25, 2.39, 1.08, and 2.65, respectively. Except for the third trimester group, about two-thirds of each group expressed satisfaction with the frequency of intercourse they were having. The third trimester group, however, had the strongest preference for less intercourse than they were having.

In a study of a large sample of Thai women, Morris (1975), reporting similar findings of marked decline in frequency of intercourse with advancing pregnancy, suggested that the cross-cultural consistency of this phenomenon raises the question of a biological reason. This would be difficult to test because of cultural norms, perhaps medical advice, and psychological factors which no doubt also play a part in such behavior.

Coital techniques and positions also are affected by the course of pregnancy. The preferred sexual practice for the first trimester women in the Tolor and DiGrazia (1976) study was vaginal stimulation, whereas the later pregnancy groups preferred breast and clitoral manipulation. These women also reported a very strong need for physical contact, for wanting to be held. Given a choice of alternatives when they did not wish to have intercourse, most of them wanted just to be held. As for positions in coitus, Solberg and others (1973) found that side-by-side or rear entry became the preferred modes as pregnancy advanced.

Women who reported a change in their sexual behavior during pregnancy gave these reasons: physical discomfort, 46%; fear of injury to the baby, 27%; and loss of interest, 23%. Less frequently reported reasons included awkwardness and loss of attractiveness (Solberg and others, 1973). Of the 260 women in this study, 29% were instructed by their physicians to abstain from coitus from two to eight weeks before the delivery date. Ten percent were advised about positions that might be more comfortable than the male superior position, and only two percent received suggestions about sexual activities that could be substituted for coitus (hand stimulation for both partners in all cases). This finding suggests a notable paucity of discussion between doctor and patient of sexuality in pregnancy.

The resumption of coitus after the woman has given birth follows no particular pattern, and its regulation and prescription vary widely from culture to culture. Ford and Beach (1951) reported postpartum taboos in sixty-six societies ranging in length of time from a few weeks to the end of lactation, sometimes three years. When there are no religious or cultural taboos against postpartum intercourse, abstention may be practiced for a few weeks for a variety of reasons relating to the woman's health and comfort (Saucier, 1972). Four out of six women in one study (Masters and Johnson, 1966) experienced erotic arousal four to five weeks after delivery, but their physiological responses—vasocongestion of the labia, lubrication, and orgasmic contractions—were reduced in degree and intensity. About half of this large sample reported a low level of sexual response; their reasons included fatigue, fear, pain, and vaginal discharge. By three months, however, most of the women had returned to their prepregnancy level of activity.

Satisfaction with Marital Sex

Because of the attention in our professional literature given to problem sexuality, its causes and treatment, it is interesting to find that significantly high percentages of married people find their sex lives to be
pleasurable and satisfying. Though Kinsey's studies did not report data on
satisfaction with marital sex, Hunt (1974) presented some findings which
indicate the extent to which his sample viewed the sexual part of their marriage as positive. Among the youngest married male cohort, 99% termed
their marital coitus "mostly" or "very" pleasurable, as did at least 94% of
the older cohorts. The married women in this sample presented a somewhat different picture. The percentage rating their marital coitus "very
pleasurable" rose from 57% for the under-twenty-five cohort to a high of
63% for the thirty-five to forty-four age group. Thereafter, the highly positive appraisal dropped, with only 45% of the forty-five to fifty-four group
and 38% of the fifty-five and over group giving their marital sex such a
rating. Adding the "mostly pleasurable" responses to these resulted in 88%
for the under-twenty-five women, 93% for those between thirty-five and
forty-four, followed by a decline to 91 and 83%, respectively, for women
in the next two decades (p. 215).

The Tavris and Sadd (1977) *Redbook* study found that happiness and
sexual satisfaction were related to religiosity and freedom of communication with husbands. The more religious the wives, the more likely they were
to report their marital sex as good or very good. Even so, two-thirds of the
nonreligious or moderately religious wives rated their sex lives good to very
good, compared with 88% of the very religious wives (p. 99).

The strongest indicator of sexual and marital satisfaction for the *Redbook* wives was the ability to discuss sex with their husbands. "The more
they talk, the better they rate their sex lives, their marriages, and their
overall happiness" (p. 106). For example, of the 47% who "always" or "often"
discuss sex with their husbands, 56% and 43%, respectively, rated their sex
lives as "very good."

Meanwhile, a survey of British wives recently reported in *Sexuality Today*
(February 27, 1978) concluded that 54% of them are contented with their
sex lives. The "average woman" in this sample of 836 wives makes love
about twice a week; more than a fourth consider themselves "pretty sexy."

Extramarital Sexual Relations

Extramarital sexual relations, sexual intercourse of a married person with
someone other than the spouse, have been considered sinful, criminal, and
immoral throughout the history of Western society. Theologians of all times
and creeds have treated adultery as a heinous act, and as late as the seventeenth century the penalty for adultery in most of the New England colo-
nies was death. Although few courts enforced such laws, whippings, fines,
and brandings were common. During the nineteenth century, adultery came
to be viewed more casually—for males—and upper-class men might have
mistresses or meet their surplus sexual needs with servants, as long as they
were discreet (Murstein, 1974).

A double standard for adultery traditionally has been recognized and rationalized. A trenchant example was provided by the British literary figure, Dr. Samuel Johnson:

Confusion of progeny constitutes the essence of the crime; and therefore a woman who breaks her marriage vows is much more criminal than a man who does it. A man, to be sure, is criminal in the sight of God; but he does not do his wife a very material injury . . . if he steals privately to her chambermaid. Sir, a wife ought not greatly to resent this (Boswell, 1956, p. 160).

The reasons for the double standard are not difficult to identify: the long tradition with legal sanction of the view of woman as property, in which a man who committed adultery with a married woman was violating the property of another man; and as noted by Dr. Johnson, the possibility of uncertain parentage, clouding matters of ownership of property and inheritance.

Although the double standard may have lost ground in recent years, condemnation of extramarital sex continues to be very strong in our society. In studies conducted during the past twenty years reviewed by Hunt (1974), all reported that the "great majority" of their respondents disapproved of extramarital sex. In Hunt's own sample, from 80% to 98% said that they or their mates would object to extramarital affairs. In a recent study of a national sample of 1,044 registered voters representing various regions, races, ages, and religious groups in the United States, 76% of the respondents said that it is "morally wrong" for a man to be unfaithful to his wife, while 79% believed that it is wrong for a woman to be unfaithful to her husband. Female respondents were somewhat more conservative than male, and both male and female were more disapproving of unfaithful wives than of unfaithful husbands (*Time,* November 21, 1977).

Our discussion here will be on a distinction proposed by Smith and Smith (1974) between conventional adultery and consensual adultery. The former is characterized by secrecy and deception, unknown and uncondoned by the spouse. The latter is characterized by openness and consent of the spouse. Consensual adultery may take the form of a spousal agreement for such activity for one or both mates.

Conventional Adultery

Comparison of the various data sources on the incidence of adultery is difficult because of differences in the collection and presentation of data. Even so, results of the few studies we do have are consistent enough to tell us something about trends and to reveal some surprises.

Kinsey and others (1948) provided an interesting essay on extramarital sex among males, but very little data. A major reason for this, explained by the authors, was the inability to get adequate representation in the male sample of older married men from upper educational and social levels: "We have every reason for believing that extramarital intercourse is the source of the hesitance of many of the individuals in such groups to cooperate" (p. 585). Frequency figures given are thus held to be a minimum, the truth perhaps being 10% to 20% higher.

From available data and allowing for the "cover-up," Kinsey estimated that about half of all married males had intercourse with women other than their wives, at some time while they were married. Age, social level, and religion were important variables for this sample, the first two, especially, introducing some interesting differences. Among lower-level males, 45% of the youngest married cohort reported having had extramarital intercourse, whereas only 27% did so by age forty and not more than 19% by age fifty. On the other hand, among college-level males, the lowest frequencies were found among the youngest group, in which only 15% to 20% had, the incidence increasing steadily to age fifty, when about 27% was having extramarital relations. Kinsey suggested that lower-level males were more likely to have a great deal of premarital intercourse, with some carry-over into marriage followed by a slowing down, which he did not attempt to explain, among the older males. By contrast, upper-level males had a history of greater restraint in the premarital years which continued to be characteristic for some years after marriage, loosening up as they grew older. Though not nearly as great as the differences among social levels, a difference was found between church and nonchurch related males, the more devout having significantly less experience with extramarital sex.

The data for Hunt's (1974) most closely comparable group revealed that only 41% of the males had ever had extramarital sex. Hunt thought that the lifetime accumulative incidence for the entire sample would be somewhat higher, but still not more than 50%, since the data showed no rise after the age of forty-four. Though Hunt found a slight increase among the youngest cohort, it was small compared to the increases in other types of sexual outlets for this group. Likewise, he found little change compared to the Kinsey data for educational level and religion.

Kinsey and others (1953) presented much more data on extramarital activity among females than in the earlier volumes on males. His female sample, however, had a much higher ratio of previously married to married women, than is the case in the general population. Since previously married women have a much higher incidence of extramarital relations than do women who have been married only once (Bohannon, 1971), this had the effect of inflating Kinsey's figures. When Hunt "rebalanced" Kinsey's figures to account for this and compared them with his own sample, he concluded that there was no difference in the accumulative incidences up to age forty-five for the two groups. By age forty-five, 20% of Kinsey's sample had had extramarital intercourse, compared to 18% of Hunt's sample. Broken down by age groups, however, a remarkable change was found in the group of women below age twenty-five. Whereas only 8% of Kinsey's group had had such experience, 24% of Hunt's had. Comparisons between the generations sampled in these two studies, then, suggest that, in spite of widespread beliefs to the contrary, the incidence of extramarital intercourse has changed little if any among male and female groups in general; it has increased slightly among under-twenty-five males, and greatly among under-twenty-five females, bringing them nearly to the level of their male cohorts. Extramarital sex is increasing in the direction of equality, with the greater increase being among females.

The figures on the *Redbook* wives who had had extramarital sex by different ages are somewhat different, as one would expect, given the nature of the sample. Twenty-nine percent of the total sample had had extramarital sex, the accumulative incidence rising from 20% of the under-twenty-five wives to 40% by age forty and over. A very important variable not mentioned in the other studies was employment of the wife. Full-time employed wives were far more likely to have had extramarital relations than were stay-at-home wives. Among wives in their late thirties, for example, 53% of those employed had had extramarital sex, compared to only 24% of the housewives. Religion was also a factor, with more than twice as many nonreligious women as devout women reporting such activity.

Other findings in these studies, which we will briefly summarize, relate to number of partners, frequency of orgasm, and overall pleasure of extramarital sex compared to marital sex, reported by those with both kinds of experience.

Kinsey did not report on any of these variables for his male sample. The data for the number of extramarital partners for both the Kinsey and the Hunt females are almost identical: about 40% in each had had only one partner, and more than 80% had had five or fewer. For the *Redbook* women, the corresponding percents are 50% and 40%.

The only data comparing marital and extramarital frequency of orgasm are from the Hunt female sample. These women who had had extramarital sex reported that they had orgasm all or almost all the time in 53% of their marital coitus, compared to only 39% of their extramarital coitus, and that they had orgasm almost none or none of the time in 7% of their marital coitus but in 35% of their extramarital coitus. These data suggest that extramarital intercourse is considerably less satisfying than marital intercourse. It is likely that factors such as guilt, haste, anxiety, and inexperience with the partner enter to some extent in these findings.

Related to the figures on orgasm are some data from Hunt's survey on overall pleasure of marital and extramarital relations. Males rated both marital and extramarital sex more pleasurable than females did, and both sexes gave their marital sex higher ratings than their extramarital experiences.

While adultery seems to be an enduring and intimate aspect of marriage, the data are skimpy, indeed, to support a conclusion that it is increasing, compared to other forms of sexual experience such as premarital or postmarital sex. The exception is its rather dramatic rise among young married women, and this may portend a trend for future observations. As for the other parameters, though one must be very cautious in generalizing from the research, it appears that women, at least, who have extramarital experiences tend to have a few partners rather than many and share with men the experience of being less orgasmic and getting less pleasure from their extramarital encounters than from their sexual relations at home.

Why do people seek sex outside of marriage? Edwards and Booth (1976a) looked for correlates of the frequency of extramarital involvement among a stratified probability sample of Toronto families among both subject-background variables and marital variables. Unlike previous research, they found no effects from education, occupation, employment of the wife, or religion. Age was the strongest predictor of the demographic variables, with reported involvement being greater among the younger members of the sample. The frequency of extramarital relations was related more to contextual variables in the marriage: the more negative was the perception of the marriage, the greater was the sexual deprivation in the marriage; as the latter increased, the more probable was extramarital sex to occur.

Although most of the studies in this area support the plausible expectation that having an unhappy marriage increases the probability of having an extramarital relationship, there still remains the observation by Tavris and Sadd (1977), Hunt (1974) and others of a stable minority of happily married persons who have other sexual partners, some of them of long duration. This suggests that variables other than marriage rating are important in some cases. In looking at female extramarital coital behavior, Bell, Turner, and Rosen (1975) were able to identify four groups of women in their sample of 2,262, to show how ratings of the marriage interacted with sexual values to predict extramarital coitus. These groups were labeled Traditional, Modern, Uptight, and Experimenting, and were characterized respectively by the following combinations of marriage ratings and sexual values: high rating, conservative values; high rating, liberal values; low rating, conservative values; and low rating, liberal values. Examination of some aspects of life styles and sexual preferences of these groups led the authors to propose that the general set most predictive of a high rate of extramarital sex for women would be a low rating of their marriage with sexually liberal views and a liberal life style. The set most predictive of a low rate would include women with highly rated marriages and with sexually conservative views and conventional life styles.

Finally, Johnson (1970) examined sixty case histories from a Family Service Agency for actual reasons given by clients for engaging in sex outside of their marriages. As one would expect, they tended to blame the spouse. He or she was: physically handicapped, unfaithful, unloving, physically unattractive or unclean, absent, or an unwilling or uninterested sex partner. Murstein (1974) added other factors, including curiosity, need for variety, uncertainty about one's sexuality, unusual opportunity, need for escape, fear of aging, and relative lack of inhibitions and guilt for unconventional behavior.

A number of writers on the subject have concluded that for many an extramarital experience or relationship can have beneficial effects on both the participant and her or his marriage. One of the strongest supporters of this view is Albert Ellis (1977), who believes that adultery has its distinct advantages even in a society such as ours, which makes it difficult and hazardous. Ellis's views include these benefits:

• Sexual variety. Humans have a biological need for sexual variety. With the emergence of alternative marriage forms and more liberal values, more people will meet their needs for sexual variety in nonmonogamous activities.

• Desire for freedom. Marriage can be confining and boring, and outside affairs can add to a feeling of freedom by breaking up the routine.

• Frustration reduction. "Exclusive" marriage leads to the limiting of one's experiences and to frustration when sexual appetites differ. Affairs can drain off these frustrations and help the person to cope with marital problems better.

• Improved marriages. Clinical evidence suggests to Ellis that married people are less resentful and more open with each other after an affair. Sex may improve because of increased knowledge and / or greater appreciation of the partner.

Ellis would like to see the removal of legal and social sanctions against adultery, the encouragement of open marriage, and moves toward educating people to cope better with feelings of jealousy and other emotional problems that accompany adultery today.

Consensual Adultery

Consensual adultery occurs with the knowledge and consent of the spouse. Smith and Smith (1974) have described three forms: adultery toleration, comarital relations, and group marriage. Adultery toleration is similar to conventional adultery except that the spouses extend to each other the freedom to engage in extramarital sex, relieving the partners of the requirement of sexual exclusivity and of the need for secrecy and deception. Such liberal arrangements are by no means new. Havelock Ellis had such an agreement with his wife, and the gynecologist, Robert L. Dickinson in 1932 described such a case among his series (Brecher, 1971). Others have been reported by Hamilton (1929) and by Lindsey and Evans (1929). On a more contemporary level, the open marriage model proposed by the O'Neills (1972) includes absence of sexual exclusivity.

Comarital relations incorporate extramarital relations into the marital relationship. Both partners participate as a dyad, both on a couple-to-couple basis and sometimes a group basis, which is popularly called mate swapping or swinging. Although such relations may be quite impersonal and transient, the Smiths (1974) say that their studies suggest that some couples "succeed in establishing basic friendship relations which yield more enduring and more rewarding social networks" (p. 89).

Group marriage does not include, strictly speaking, extramarital relations, since it consists of members of a group all of whom consider themselves married to each other. Rarer than the other two forms, it is ideologically the same as the Oneida model discussed earlier, with unrestricted sexual access of the individual members to each other.

Such forms of extramarital sex with the knowledge, consent, and sometimes the participation of the spouse are phenomena which have attracted much more attention than their prevalence in the population seems to justify. Their deviance from traditional norms in an area of behavior which more than any other has historically been rigidly defined and prescribed has attracted a high level of attention in the popular media.

Recent estimates agree that the numbers of persons participating in any of the forms of consensual adultery are quite small. No reliable data exist on adultery toleration but if they did, they would probably be higher than figures for the other two forms, simply because "toleration" is less deviant from conventional norms than is mate swapping or group marriage. Hunt found that about two percent of the husbands and wives in his sample had ever engaged in mate swapping, but Tavris and Sadd (1977) reported that four percent of the *Redbook* wives, a less representative sample, had tried swapping at least once. A stratified probability sample of 579 married adults drawn from a midwestern community of 40,000 found that less than two percent of the respondents had ever participated in swinging (Spanier and Cole, 1975). Smith and Smith (1974) state that the incidence of group marriage is far lower than either of the other forms. Ramey (1974) provides an interesting account of eighty upper-middle class couples who explored over a three-year period the various problems and possibilities of communal and group marriage arrangements. Only eighteen of these couples did, in fact, have any experience in such living arrangements.

Finally, in an analysis of some moral and social implications of infidelity, Bernard (1974) speculates that the conditions of exclusivity and permanence required in traditional marriage may now be incompatible: "It may be that we will have to choose. . . . If we insist on permanence, exclusivity is harder to enforce; if we insist on exclusivity, permanence may be endangered. The trend . . . seems to be in the direction of exclusivity at the expense of permanence in the younger years but permanence at the expense of exclusivity in the later years" (p. 138).

Bernard reveals in this same paper that she has changed her views on the signficance for women of extramarital relations. A few years ago she thought that women could not be casual about such relations. She sees now that there is a new kind of woman who can be casual about sex and can accept the idea of sex-as-fun without conflict. She believes that the increasing economic independence of women plays some part in this change. We have seen already that working women were more likely than nonworking (outside the home) women to have affairs, certainly in part because of more opportunities and contacts with men. At the same time, such a woman, less dependent on her husband for economic security, might be less fearful of the consequences of discovery. She also might be less frightened at the prospect of her husband's involvement with another woman although, as Bernard rightly pointed out, economic independence is far from the whole story. The threat to one's psychological needs can be more terrifying than the threat to one's material security.

The Woman's Movement and Marital Sex

The changing roles and status of women are rooted in the renaissance of feminism, the women's movement which re-emerged in the late 1960s. These changes generally are toward greater equality for women, through the removal of historic oppression. Shifts toward greater power and participation for women now can be seen in the personal, social, political, and economic sectors of their lives. These changes affect sexuality in marriage either directly or indirectly.

1. Availability of birth control and abortion means that women now control their reproductive functions and can limit their fertility. Birth control also frees women to participate in and to enjoy sexual experiences without the fear of pregnancy.

2. Sex research, such as that of Masters and Johnson (1966), Sherfey (1973), and Hite (1976), have brought to women a new awareness and appreciation of their own sexuality and its potential. The dissemination of such information to large numbers of the population has reduced inhibitions and changed expectations and behavior (Humphrey, 1975).

3. Opportunities for education and employment have brought women into contact with the outside world more than ever before and have provided them with the means for economic independence. Women are exposed

to a greater number and variety of possible sex partners, increasing both their level of sophistication and the probability of extramarital sex experiences. Economic independence removes one source of inequality in marriage, as well as the need to remain in an incompatible situation.

4. The availability of alternative life styles—deferred marriage, staying single, nonmarital cohabitation—again suggests options to a traditional marriage, which was until recently the most desirable and socially acceptable outcome for women.

5. The women's movement has provided an intellectual and experiential framework within which women can find self-esteem, respect for other women, and supportive relations with others, both women and men, outside the old exclusive bonds of marriage.

6. Finally, the goal of egalitarian relationships between women and men promises to free both from old power and dominance roles, with their inherent components of exploitation and deceit, and to substitute more humane and satisfying relationships.

Sexuality and Aging

The sexuality of older people has only recently begun to receive attention. The prevalent view has seemed to be that sex is the prerogative of the young, that older people do not participate in or enjoy sex and if they do, such activity is ridiculous, embarrassing, or downright obscene. In May 1974, however, the *SIECUS Report* published a policy statement on sex and aging: "Aging people are too often deprived of opportunities for sexual companionship and expression, which they need despite unscientific beliefs to the contrary. Society has an obligation to create conditions conducive to the fulfillment of these needs" (p. 1). In a recent issue of the *SIECUS Report*, Alex Comfort (1976) expanded on that statement, presenting some facts about sexuality in older people along with some suggestions for alleviating problems, many of which are the result of ignorance, superstition, and prejudice against the elderly.

Changes in sexual physiology occur with aging in both sexes. Some of these are in common and are related to the general effects of aging: strength and energy are reduced, and body responses are generally slowed and attenuated. However, both men and women continue to respond as before, though frequency and intensity of sexual response are reduced. Both remain capable of orgasm. Exceptions to this are produced by factors other than normal physiology, that is, loss of orgasmic capacity is not an inevitable part of aging.

Most studies support the idea that women have a more stable sex drive than men have and that it is less susceptible to the effects of aging. Although many men remain potent and sexually active into their eighties, impotence is a common problem after middle age. Studies of sexual inadequacy revealed that 83% of the impotent males were past forty years of age, and 75% were past fifty (Masters and Johnson, 1968). There are a number of reasons for male impotence, such as the ego-shattering "fear of failure" which sometimes leads men to seek newer or younger partners to reassure them of their virility. Since women often marry men who are older than they are, it is inevitable that some who are still as interested as ever in sex will find themselves with a husband who has withdrawn from sexual activity or is directing it elsewhere. Also, some husbands in the older age groups may have physical problems or disabilities associated with advancing age which may make their accustomed form of sexual activity impossible. Still, Comfort reports studies showing that as many as one-third of men past seventy are still sexually active. It appeared that those most active as youths continued to be active longer in their later years, but those with a low sex drive in their younger years were less likely to be having sex as they grew older.

Most important to sexual behavior in older women are the availability of a partner and the opportunity for regular sexual expression (Williams, 1977). With these, many women in their fifties and sixties have an increased interest in their sexuality for a number of reasons. The cessation of the menses beings a freedom from fear of pregnancy, so that the woman, perhaps for the first time, can abandon herself to the enjoyment of sex without apprehension. This release from "pregnancy phobia" is probably one of the most plausible reasons for increased sexual interest given by postmenopausal women who did not have effective birth control methods available to them in their reproductive years. The problems which may beset a young marriage, such as finances, in-laws, and adjustment to the marital relationship, all may be in the past. For both members of the couple the draining demands of having and rearing children, and of establishing and succeeding in a job or career, may no longer exhaust and preoccupy them, leaving more time and energy for the renewal of interest in each other.

Sviland (1976) has described a "sexual liberation" program for elderly couples with basically sound marriages who want to get rid of their inhibitions and to increase their repertoire of sexual behavior. The program focuses on attitude restructuring and relationship enhancement. The therapist gives permission for sexual curiosity and exploration, and gives exercises designed to replicate the fun of dating, such as candlelight dinners, love notes, and making love by the fireplace. She reports that the program has changed attitudes and behavior within weeks, helping couples to communicate, to increase intimacy, and to enjoy without guilt sexual pleasures usually restricted to youth.

Cross-Cultural Observations

Anthropology has shared with the other social sciences a Victorian reticence to include investigation of sexual behavior among its interests in diverse cultural groups. Little more than a decade ago, an analysis (Marshall, 1967) of ten leading anthropology textbooks concluded that sexual behavior was accorded neither space nor attention in the basic formulations of anthropological knowledge. This lack of attention in the profession did not come from lack of either interest or knowledge; indeed, Suggs and Marshall (1971) noted that researchers might be interested in and know quite a bit about the sexual behavior of "their people," without ever including such information in their scholarly books and articles. Scientists who violated the taboo on writing about sex risked their reputation, or at least the onus of being thought too interested in "pornography," or too ready to violate the privacy of their subject groups. Stimulated by the work of Masters and Johnson, however, papers and monographs have begun to appear, and there is now a knowledge base sufficient to inform us of the diversity of sexual practices among earth's people.

Patterns of sexual behavior among people do not arise independently or quixotically in some random fashion. Rather, they are part of society and culture, and reflect patterns of sex roles, beliefs about men and women, religious beliefs, notions of modesty and socialization practices, population and ecological factors, and other characteristics of a particular group. As Rostand (1961) said, in the joining of two human bodies, all society is the third presence.

An example of the interrelationship between sexual and nonsexual phenomena is an analysis by Friedl (1975) of sex roles in foraging and horticultural societies. She suggests that the universality of a degree of male dominance is the male monopoly on hunting game and their power to distribute it. If male hunting is minimal, and both sexes collect the plants which comprise most of the diet, women's status is more equal to that of men. Women have the lowest status in groups whose main food is big game hunted entirely by the men. The importance of variations in patterns of male dominance is especially noted in marital sex relations. If woman has a more equal status, because of her role in providing a large share of the food, she has considerable autonomy in sexual matters. She may initiate sex and expect satisfaction. She may divorce, and her adultery is not more serious than is the husband's. If her status is very low, the male being sole provider of all food, she may have no control over sexual relations in or out of marriage. Among the Eskimo, for example, who subsist on big game or sea mammals hunted by men only, the sexual services of women are considered a commodity that men can take at will, or give or exchange to another man. Pubertal girls are fair game for any man, and wives are freely exchanged among men who wish to make alliances with one another or to repay favors (Friedl, 1975).

Frequency

Average frequencies of marital coitus among groups vary from about two to five times per week (Gebhard, 1971). The Ecuadorian Cayapa Indians described by Altschuler (1971) thought that twice a week was an occasion for bragging by new husbands. This group has an exceptionally low level of sexuality, accompanied by avoidance of women, anxiety, inhibition about sexual matters, and much homoerotic behavior among the men. Even the more virile and forward men can go for long periods with little sexual activity. Male sexual inadequacy is the norm, resulting apparently from high-anxiety socialization practices in the weaning and toilet training of children. The Inis Beag, an Irish folk community studied by Messenger (1971) have very strict rules of modesty and separation of the sexes from childhood on. Frequency of marital coitus is not known but is probably low. Men believe that intercourse is debilitating and drains energy needed for other work. Sexual inhibitions extend to avoidance of nudity at all times and shunning of sexual innuendoes and jokes, even with the most pallid content. Asked to compare the sexual desires of men and women, a married woman said, "Men can wait a long time before wanting it, but we can wait longer" (p. 16).

Other people described by Davenport (1965), Marshall (1971), and Merriam (1971), value sex highly, frequent copulation being an important part of their life styles. The Mangaians (Marshall, 1971) of central Polynesia engage in a high level of sexual activity before marriage, valuing frequent coitus, many partners, and multiple orgasms for their women. After marriage the male wishes to copulate with his wife every night, beginning to skip nights only after a decade or so of marriage. Davenport's East Bay Melanesian group (1965) expects that sexual excitement will remain high during the early years of marriage, and it is usual for couples to have intercourse each day while they are in their garden and again at night after going to bed. Frequencies of three times in a twenty-four-hour period were not uncommon. Merriam (1971), in his study of the Bala, a people of the Congo, collected data on frequency of intercourse by asking men, each morning, how many times they had had intercourse in the preceding twenty-four hours. Although the data may be less than reliable, the average over a ten-day period ranged from 1.2 to 1.9 acts of marital coitus per day. Even the men in their fifties and sixties reported having intercourse more than seven times per week.

These examples only suggest the variability of frequency of marital coitus among human groups. Obviously, it depends on factors such as attitudes toward sex, availability (as when the men are absent for long periods), restrictions and taboos, and the woman's right of refusal. In general, if teachings are repressive with many negative sanctions and taboos, and if sex is thought to be dangerous and tinged with evil, frequency is low. But if attitudes are permissive, children's exploratory activity indulged or encouraged, and people are rewarded for sexual interest and exploits, frequency is high.

Foreplay and Coital Techniques

Foreplay, precoital sexual activity directed toward arousing the partner for intercourse, is widely observed among both literate and nonliterate groups of people. Its duration and techniques vary greatly. The puritannical Inis Beag men limit foreplay to brief kissing and some fondling of the buttocks. Underclothes are not removed. Only the male superior position is used; intercourse is quite brief, the orgasm quickly achieved for the male, after which he immediately falls asleep. Davenport's Melanesians, by contrast, consider foreplay to be the indispensable "root" of intercourse, to be prolonged until both partners are close to orgasm. Techniques include kissing, fondling the woman's breasts, and mutual manual manipulation. Mouth-genital contact does not occur. Coital positions include the male superior and side-by-side, with little or no experimenting reported. After prolonged foreplay, coitus is brief, culminating in orgasm for both partners. The male, apparently, feels a responsibility for his partner's orgasm, though it need not occur simultaneously with his. Gebhard (1971), summarizing foreplay and coital practices in groups for whom data exist, said that foreplay is usually initiated by males, with female reciprocity varying from little to great. Kissing is absent in a minority of societies. Male fondling of the female breasts and genitalia is universal, and female handling of the penis is common nearly everywhere. Cunnilingus and fellatio are similarly distributed; where the former is practiced, the other is likely to be also, although the reverse is not necessarily true. Though anthropological data are scant, mouth-genital techniques are widely used in parts of Oceania, in the higher civilizations of Asia, and in North Africa, where it is said to be an Arabic invention.

Coital positions common in one group may be quite uncommon in another. Among the Bala, the usual position is with the man on his right side and the woman on her left, facing each other. The male superior position is known, but the female superior position is considered odd. Other varieties are not practiced.

The male superior position, with the female supine and the male prone on top of her, is very common, and where it is the preferred position, other positions may not be used at all, or only when conditions of time or place require a modification. In Melanesia, Australia, and parts of India, the favored position is the female supine with the male squatting between her outspread legs (Gebhard, 1971). Side-by-side is also common, especially during the later months of pregnancy.

Orgasm

According to available data, male orgasm in marital intercourse is a universal norm. For males, the correlation between incidence of intercourse and incidence of orgasm is positive and nearly perfect. The female experience of orgasm is far more variable, not only in our own society but cross-culturally as well, and its occurrence is highly influenced by cultural values and norms, and socialization practices. As Mead (1949) pointed out, "There seems therefore to be a reasonable basis for assuming that the human female's capacity for orgasm is to be viewed much more as a potentiality that may or may not be developed by a given culture" (p. 217).

Messenger reported of the Inis Beag that "there is much evidence to indicate that the female orgasm is unknown—or at least doubted, or considered a deviant response" (p. 16). In the Tepoztlan village in Mexico, wives are not expected to be passionate, and husbands refrain from arousing their wives sexually, assuming that the passive and frigid wife will be faithful (Lewis, 1960).

Mangaian women, by contrast, have a great deal of premarital experience and develop orgasmic response as a matter of course. Female orgasm is highly valued: "The really important aspect of sexual intercourse for either the married man or the more experienced unwed male is to give pleasure to his wife or woman or girl—the pleasure of the orgasm" (Marshall, 1971, p. 123). Davenport's East Bay Melanesian group likewise took for granted the woman's experience of orgasm in marital coitus. They believed firmly that, once engaged in foreplay, there was nothing to prevent a woman from having orgasm if intercourse followed (Davenport, 1965).

The evidence suggests that, in general, young females take longer in coitus to reach orgasm than young males do. Therefore, in repressive societies, in which even marital sex is furtive and hurried, characterized by attitudes antagonistic to sensuality and pleasure, the incidence of female orgasm is predictably low. If sexuality is openly valued and enjoyed, emphasizing prolongation and satisfaction for both partners, the orgasmic potential of women is more likely to be realized.

Sexual Taboos in Marriage

Many societies forbid sexual relations between marital partners during menstruation, pregnancy, and the postpartum period. In general, these taboos reflect fear of the woman's power to contaminate at these times, though the postpartum taboos also serve as a control on fertility by spacing births. Such spacing serves as a protective health measure for both the lactating mother and the nursing child, and also assures that she will not be burdened with two children needing to be carried, an important consideration in foraging societies (Friedl, 1978).

Menstruating women historically have been held to have the power to pollute and to contaminate food, utensils, and livestock, and to harm men by weakening them or bringing them bad luck in hunting or war. Among the Baganda, for example, a menstruating wife may not touch anything belonging to her husband, nor may she cook his food. Were she to handle any article of his, he would fall ill; if she touched his weapons, he would be killed in the next battle. She also has the power to dry up wells and spoil milk (Frazer, 1951). Among the East Bay Melanesian in Davenport's group, intercourse was avoided during the woman's menstrual period because the flow was extremely repulsive. Women were not secluded during their periods, a common practice elsewhere, but they did not cook for their husbands.

Pregnancy and postpartum taboos also are very common. The Mangaians, however, can have intercourse with their wives up until the onset of labor. In East Bay, there is no postpartum taboo, although husbands are supposed to give their wives at least a month to recuperate from giving birth.

Such taboos and practices seem to be less related to attitudes toward sex than to attitudes toward women. Their prevalence is widespread among both literate and nonliterate groups, and there is much literature describing them (e.g., Delaney and others, 1976).

Attitudes Toward Marital Sex

Among groups, with few exceptions, men regard marital sex as a natural right, to be sampled regularly and enjoyed. As with orgasm, the data for women are more variable. Rainwater (1971), in his study of marital relations in four cultures of poverty, found a range of responses to questions on interest and enjoyment of marital sex by women. The gamut went from, "If God made anything better he kept it to himself," to "I would be happy if I never had to do that again; it's disgusting" (p. 188). The norm among his four groups, however, was closer to the latter attitude. Sex was generally considered to be a man's pleasure and a woman's duty. Women were believed not to have sexual desires at all or to have much weaker needs than men had. In Tepoztlan respectable women were expected also to have strong negative attitudes toward sex. Women who needed men sexually were called *loca* (crazy) and perhaps bewitched (Lewis, 1960).

Although data are scant, the women of Mangaia, Bala, and East Bay appear to have more positive attitudes toward the sexual parts of their marriages, if frequency is any indication. Even so, a high normative interest and positive regard for sex by married women is not frequently encountered in the cross-cultural literature. Reasons for this are not hard to find: emphasis on virginity for girls, with lack of premarital experience; the cultural / experiential factor in women's orgasmic response, typically observed to be more important to women than to men; the characteristic male domination of marital sex, in that males initiate sexual activity and direct it to their satisfaction (with some exceptions as previously noted); the consequences for women of pregnancy and child care; the fairly widespread regard for women as sexual property, to be used, bartered, and exchanged; and rules of modesty, religious sanctions, and taboos which are directed more against women's participation in sex than against men's.

Extramarital Sexual Relations

In most societies, marital intercourse accounts for most of the sexual activity of adults. Even so, extramarital coitus is very common and is even institutionalized and sanctioned under certain conditions and regulations. Although wives everywhere are more restricted than husbands are, it is estimated that from two-fifths to three-fifths of nonliterate societies permit some kind of extramarital coitus for wives (Gebhard, 1971). Variables include the double standard, the knowledge and / or permission of the spouse, the choice of partner, the occasion and place where intercourse may occur, and the risks and penalties involved. Often, as Gebhard (1971) noted, the concern is less with the act itself than with its social implications, such as degradation of the spouse, implications of pregnancy, and effects on kinship ties and loyalty.

A typical example of the way adultery is viewed and managed is described in Davenport's account of the East Bay people. Before marriage, control of the right of sexual access to a young woman belongs to her father. When the bride price is paid to him at her marriage, the controlling right passes to her husband and any kin who contributed to the bride price. Adultery, then, with a married woman is an offense against the husband and the other contributors. Although a wife has some of the same rights in her husband, she, as a woman, has no recourse to law. Therefore, any offense by her, as the accused or the accuser, immediately affects those close male kin who are her legal representatives. If the offense goes into litigation, it affects the men of several families and may become very complex, as all the offended ones must finally be compensated in money. Although most of the concern seems to be for the violation of the rights of the men with an investment in the woman, the moral culpability rests more heavily on the man in the adulterous relationship. In this society, in which women are trained to serve and to be obedient to the men with legitimate authority over them, it is expected that they are unable to refuse the request of a male for sexual services, especially if he offers presents.

Another widespread pattern includes the expectation that husbands will stray, but wives will be faithful. In Tepoztlan sexual promiscuity is for males only, and married men are expected to prove their masculinity by having affairs, usually with widows, unmarried women, or prostitutes. Husbands are anxious about their wives' fidelity in the early months of marriage and feel most secure when they are pregnant or caring for an infant (Lewis, 1960).

In horticultural societies there is often an option according to which adults can have sex with someone other than a spouse (Friedl, 1975). Even so, adultery is thought to be risky for both partners and may be punishable by penalties or divorce. Men have firmer entitlements to their wives' sexual services than do wives to their husbands'. An adulterous man may be required to pay a penalty to the husband of his lover or to her father if she is unmarried. A wife, however, cannot usually extract a penalty from the woman with whom her husband is involved.

Finally, Schneider (1971) described an institutionalized form of adultery among the Turu of Tanzania. The lover relationship, called *mbuya*, is compared to romantic love in the West, with the same components of courtship, mooning, and jealous, possessive behavior. Love songs are composed and gifts exchanged. The furtiveness of the relationship adds to its delights, so that its clandestine nature may be preserved even when the affair is well known to everyone and tacitly approved by the husband. A husband may forbid such a relationship but may have difficulty doing so, since others will not cooperate with him. His wife may point out to him that he, himself, has a mistress, or she may go to her father and request an annulment of her marriage on the grounds that her husband is treating her shabbily.

Summary

Marriage is the only human relationship within which sexual intercourse is universally sanctioned. We have seen, however, how variable are individuals within groups. Among some people, marital intercourse is proscribed at certain times, as during menstruation and pregnancy. Among others, provision is made routinely for extramarital liaisons, as among the Turu, and in Western countries which have institutionalized the mistress-lover relationship. Within groups data also testify to individual variation in needs, tastes, and behavior. Even within an individual's historical repertoire, changes over time may be observed as a life style evolves and new behaviors emerge.

Generalizations about sex in marriage seem possible only for carefully defined samples, the results qualified by attention to the sources of variation and their effects. Currently in our society, we can describe the scene of marital sexuality only as pluralistic, providing many models, each with adaptations and variants. From one couple's brief, once-a-week encounter, never deviating from the male superior position, to another's daily, highly sensual, experimenting adventure, to yet another's exploration of swinging and group sex, and many others closer to and farther from the norm, we gain a sense of the plasticity of human sexual experience as it occurs in the old institution of marriage.

REFERENCE NOTES

1. The theory of primitive matriarchy, in which women were family heads, bequeathing their names and goods to their children until they were finally vanquished and subdued by the physical superiority of males, is no longer considered viable by theorists of the origin of the family. B. L. Murstein, *Love, Sex, and Marriage through the Ages.* (New York: Springer, 1974).
2. All page numbers for quotations from Kinsey and others, (1953) are from the 1965 Pocket Book edition.

REFERENCES

ALTSCHULER, M. 1971. Cayapa personality and sexual motivation. In *Human sexual behavior,* ed. D. S. Marshall and R. C. Suggs. New York, Basic Books.
BACHOFEN, J. J. 1967. *Myth, religion, and mother-right,* trans. R. Manheim. Princeton, N.J.: Princeton University Press.
BELL, R. R.; TURNER, S.; and ROSEN, L. 1975. A multivariate analysis of female extramarital coitus. *Journal of Marriage and the Family* 37: 375–84.
BERNARD, J. 1972. *The future of marriage.* New York: World Publishing.
———. 1974. Infidelity: some moral and social issues. In *Beyond monogamy,* ed. J. R. Smith and L. G. Smith. Baltimore: Johns Hopkins University Press.
BOHANNON, P., ed. 1971. *Divorce and after.* Garden City N.Y.: Doubleday Anchor.
BOSWELL, J. 1956. *In search of a wife.* New York: McGraw-Hill.
BRECHER, E. M. 1971. *The sex researchers.* New York: New American Library.
CLARK, A. L., and WALLIN, P. 1965. Women's sexual responsiveness and the duration and quality of their marriages. *American Journal of Sociology* 71: 187–96.
COMFORT, A. 1976. Sexuality and aging. *SIECUS Report* 4: 7–9.
DAVENPORT, W. 1965. Sexual patterns and their regulation in a society of the Southwest Pacific. In *Sex and behavior,* ed. F. A. Beach. New York: Wiley.
DAVIS, K. 1929. *Factors in the sex life of 2200 women.* New York: Harper.
DECKARD, B. 1975. *The women's movement: political, socioeconomic, and psychological issues.* New York: Harper & Row.
DELANEY, J.; LUPTON, M. J.; and TOTH, E. 1976. *The curse: a cultural history of menstruation.* New York: Dutton.
DICKINSON, R. L., and BEAM, L. 1932. *One thousand marriages.* London: Williams and Northgate.
EDWARDS, J. N., and BOOTH, A. 1976a. The cessation of marital intercourse. *American Journal of Psychiatry* 133: 1333–36.
———. 1976b. Sexual behavior in and out of marriage: an assessment of correlates. *Journal of Marriage and the Family* 38: 73–81.
ELLIS, A. 1977. Pros and cons of extramarital sexual relations. In *the Densen-Gerber Crusade and ongoing developments in contemporary sexuality.* New York: ATCOM.
ELLIS, H. 1937. *On life and sex.* New York: Garden City Publishing Co.
FORD, C., and BEACH, F. 1951. *Patterns of sexual behavior.* New York: Perennial (Harper & Row).
FRAZER, J. G. 1951. *The golden bough.* New York: Macmillan.
FREUD, S. 1947. "Civilized" sexual morality and modern nervousness. In *On war, sex, and neurosis,* ed. S. Katz. New York: Arts and Sciences Press.
FRIEDL, E. 1975. *Women and men: an anthropologist's view.* New York: Holt, Rinehart & Winston.
———. 1978. Society and sex roles. *Human Nature* 1: 68–75.
GAGNON, J. H. 1975. Sex research and social change. *Archives of Sexual Behavior* 4: 111–41.
GEBHARD, P. 1971. Human sexual behavior: a summary statement. In *Human sexual behavior,* ed. D. S. Marshall and R. C. Suggs. New York: Basic Books.
HALLER, J. S. 1972. From maidenhood to menopause: sex education for women in Victorian America. *Journal of Popular Culture* 6: 49–69.
———, and HALLER, R. M. 1974. *The physician and sexuality in Victorian America.* Urbana, Ill.: University of Illinois Press.
HAMILTON, G. V. 1929. *A research in marriage.* New York: Lear.
HESSELLUND, H. 1976. Masturbation and sexual fantasies in married couples. *Archives of Sexual Behavior* 5: 133–47.

316 Juanita H. Williams

HITE, S. 1976. *The Hite report*. New York: Macmillan.
HUMPHREY, F. G. 1975. Changing roles for women: implications for marriage counselors. *Journal of Marriage and Family Counseling* 1: 219–27.
HUNT, M. 1974. *Sexual behavior in the 1970s*. Chicago: Playboy Press.
JOHNSON, R. E. 1970. Some correlates of extramarital coitus. *Journal of Marriage and the Family* 32: 449–56.
KATCHEDOURIAN, H. A., and LUNDE, D. T. 1975. *Fundamentals of human sexuality*, 2d ed. New York: Holt, Rinehart & Winston.
KENNETT, R. H. 1931. *Ancient Hebrew social life and custom*. London: Oxford University Press.
KENNY, J. A. 1973. Sexuality of pregnant and breastfeeding women. *Archives of Sexual Behavior* 2: 215–29.
KINSEY, A.; POMEROY, W.; and MARTIN, C. 1948. *Sexual behavior in the human male*. Philadelphia: W. B. Saunders.
———; and GEBHARD, P. H. 1965. *Sexual behavior in the human female*. New York: Pocket Books.
LECKY, W. E. H. 1905. *History of European morals*. 2 vols. New York: Appleton.
LEVI-STRAUSS, C. 1969. *The elementary structures of kinship*. London: Eyre & Spottiswoode.
LEWIS, O. 1960. *Tepoztlan: village in Mexico*. New York: Holt, Rinehart & Winston.
LINDSEY, B. B., and EVANS, W. 1929. *The companionate marriage*. New York: Garden City.
LUTHER, M. 1890. *The table talk of Martin Luther*. London: George Bell & Sons.
MARSHALL, D. S. 1967. General anthropology: strategy for a human science. *Current anthropology* 8: 61–66.
———. 1971. Sexual behavior on Mangaia. In *Human sexual behavior*, ed. D. S. Marshall and R. C. Suggs. New York: Basic Books.
MASTERS, W., and JOHNSON, V. 1966. *Human sexual response*. Boston: Little, Brown.
———. 1968. Human sexual response: the aging female and the aging male. In *Middle age and aging*, ed. B. Neugarten. Chicago: University of Chicago Press.
MEAD, M. 1949. *Male and female*. New York: William Morrow.
MERRIAM, A. P. 1971. Aspects of sexual behavior among the Bala (Basongye). In *Human sexual behavior*, ed. D. S. Marshall and R. C. Suggs. New York: Basic Books.
MESSENGER, J. C. 1971. Sex and repression in an Irish folk community. In *Human sexual behavior*, ed. D. S. Marshall and R. C. Suggs. New York: Basic Books.
MITCHELL, J. 1974. *Psychoanalysis and feminism*. New York: Pantheon.
MORRIS, N. M. 1975. The frequency of sexual intercourse during pregnancy. *Archives of Sexual Behavior* 4: 501–7.
MUNCY, R. L. 1973. *Sex and marriage in utopian communities*. Bloomington, Ind.: Indiana University Press.
MURSTEIN, B. I. 1974. *Love, sex, and marriage through the ages*. New York: Springer.
O'NEILL, G. C., and O'NEILL, N. 1972. *Open marriage: a new life style for couples*. New York: M. Evans & Co.
PEARSALL, R. 1969. *The worm in the bud: the world of Victorian sexuality*. Toronto: Macmillan.
RAINWATER, L. 1971. Marital sexuality in four "cultures of poverty." In *Human sexual behavior*, ed. D. S. Marshall and R. C. Suggs. New York: Basic Books.
RAMEY, J. W. 1974. Communes, group marriage, and the upper-middle class. In *Beyond monogamy*, ed. J. R. Smith and L. G. Smith. Baltimore: Johns Hopkins University Press.
ROSTAND, J. 1961. The evolution of the species. In *The Orion book of evolution*. New York: Orion Press.
RUGOFF, M. 1971. *Prudery and passion*. New York: Putnam.
SAUCIER, J. F. 1972. Correlates of the long postpartum taboo: a cross-cultural study. *Current Anthropology* 13: 238–49.
SCHNEIDER, H. K. 1971. Romantic love among the Turu. In *Human sexual behavior*, ed. D. S. Marshall and R. C. Suggs. New York: Basic Books.
SHERFEY, M. J. 1973. *The nature and evolution of female sexuality*. New York: Vintage Books.
SIECUS Report. 1976. Sexuality and the aging: a selective bibliography 4.
SMITH, L. G., and SMITH, J. R. 1974. Co-marital sex: the incorporation of extramarital sex into the marriage relationship. In *Beyond monogamy*, ed. J. R. Smith and L. G. Smith. Baltimore: Johns Hopkins University Press.
SOLBERG, D. A.; BUTLER, J.; and WAGNER, N. N. 1973. Sexual behavior in pregnancy. *New England Journal of Medicine* 288: 1098–103.
SPANIER, G. B., and COLE, C. L. 1975. Mate swapping: perceptions, value orientations, and participation in a midwestern community. *Archives of sexual behavior* 4: 143–59.

STRONG, B. 1973. Toward a history of the experiential family: sex and incest in the nineteenth-century family. *Journal of Marriage and the Family* 35: 457–66.

SUGGS, R. C., and MARSHALL, D. S. 1971. Anthropological perspectives on human sexual behavior. In *Human sexual behavior*, ed. D. S. Marshall and R. C. Suggs. New York: Basic Books.

SVILAND, M. A. P. 1976. Helping elderly couples attain sexual liberation and growth. *SIECUS Report* 4: 3–4.

TAVRIS, C., and SADD, S. 1977. *The Redbook report on female sexuality.* New York: Delacorte Press.

TOLOR, A., and DIGRAZIA, P. V. 1976. Sexual attitudes and behavior patterns during and following pregnancy. *Archives of Sexual Behavior* 5: 539–51.

VAN DE VELDE, T. 1930. *Ideal marriage.* New York: Random House.

WALTER, R. G. 1974. *Primers for prudery: sexual advice to Victorian America.* Englewood Cliffs, N.J.: Prentice-Hall.

WESTERMARCK, E. 1921. *The history of human marriage.* 3 vols. London: Macmillan.

WILLIAMS, J. H. 1977. *Psychology of women: behavior in a biosocial context.* New York: Norton.

22

The Realities of Lesbianism

Del Martin and Phyllis Lyon

The Lesbian minority in America, which may run as high as ten million women, is probably the least understood of all minorities and the most downtrodden. The Lesbian has two strikes on her from the start; she is a woman and she is a homosexual, a minority scorned by the vast majority of people in our country. If, in addition, she is a member of a racial minority, it is hard sometimes to understand how she survives.

A Lesbian is a woman who prefers another woman as a sexual partner; a woman who is drawn erotically to women rather than to men. This definition includes women who have never experienced overt sexual relations with a woman—the key word is "prefers." There is really no other valid way to define the Lesbian, for outside of the sexual area she is as different in her actions, dress, status and behavior as anyone else. Just as there is no typical heterosexual woman, neither is there any typical Lesbian.

However, there is a popular misconception, or stereotype, of the Lesbian. She is believed to embody all the worst masculine attributes of toughness, aggressiveness, lack of emotion, lack of sentiment, overemphasis on sex, lack of stability—the need and desire to dress as a man or, at least, as much like a man as possible.

At some time in her life the Lesbian may fit this stereotype—usually when she is very young and just finding out about herself. After all, the Lesbian is a product of her heterosexual environment, and all she has to go on, at her first awareness of Lesbian feeling in herself, is society's image. Part of the reason for her over-masculinization is the sexual identity of being attracted to women. At this point the Lesbian feels that in order to be attractive to another woman she must appear masculine. Another reason is for identification purposes. How will she meet other Lesbians? How will they know her to be one of them unless she indicates herself in her outward appearance? A third reason is one of releasing her hostility against society, of defying the mores which she finds stifling to what she considers her very being. A fourth reason is comfort. Any woman who says that girdles and high heels are comfortable is simply lying.

While it is true that occasionally a Lesbian gets trapped in this way of life (emulation of the male) and never finds her way to being a person rather than a symbol, the vast majority pass through this phase and learn to accept their femininity. As a Lesbian she comes to realize she is a human being first, a woman second, and a Lesbian only third. Unfortunately, however, society places the emphasis on the third—sexual identification—and does not acknowledge the Lesbian as a woman or a person.

But the average Lesbian (if there can be anything approaching "average" in our very complex world) is indistinguishable from other women in dress, in manner, in goals and desires, in actions and in interests. The difference lies only in that she looks to women for her emotional and sexual fulfillment. She is a member of the family—a distant cousin, or perhaps a maiden aunt. But more than likely she's closer to home—maybe a daughter, a wife and mother, a grandmother or a sister. She may work in an office, in a factory production line, in the public school system, at the corner grocery. She is not bound by lines of class distinction or educational level, race or religion.

What causes a woman to become a Lesbian? How can it be that two sisters, raised by the same parents in the same home, can turn in two different directions—one toward heterosexuality, the other toward homosexuality? Very simply, the answer is that no one knows. A great deal of research and study has been done in this country on the male homosexual, but very little has been done on the Lesbian. The reason for this, we suspect, lies in the status of women in our country. Because the male—masculinity—is so highly valued, it has been deemed to be imperative to search out the reasons for any deviation from this American norm. Also, the majority of persons working in research are men. Research on the Lesbian has, for the most part, been confined to women who were either psychiatric patients or in prison—which hasn't made for a very full or accurate picture.

Nevertheless, if you begin reading about the "causes" of homosexuality you will find that, as in the Bible, the answer you want to find will be somewhere. Each "expert" on the subject presents a different "cause." Our feeling, which is supported by a growing number of professional persons, is that homosexuality (in both men and women) is merely one dimension of the vastly complicated and varied spectrum of human sexuality. There has always been homosexuality; it has appeared in almost every culture in recorded history; it occurs in every species of animal.

Perhaps the most logical and least hysterical of all statements about homosexuality is the following made by Dr. Joel Fort, psychiatrist and public health specialist; Dr. Evelyn G. Hooker, research psychologist at the University of California at Los Angeles; Dr. Joe K. Adams, psychologist and former mental health officer in California. The statement, made in August of 1966, is as follows:

> Homosexuals, like heterosexuals, should be treated as individual human beings, not as a special group, either by law or social agencies or employers.

> Laws governing sexual behavior should be reformed to deal only with clearly antisocial behavior, such as behavior involving violence or youth. The sexual behavior of individual adults by mutual consent in private should not be a matter of public concern.

> Some homosexuals, like some heterosexuals, are ill; some homosexuals, like some heterosexuals, are preoccupied with sex as a way of life. But probably for a majority of adults their sexual orientation constitutes only one component of a much more complicated life style.

Why then, if the Lesbian is by and large indistinguishable from other women and if her sexuality is not abnormal, does she face such genuine problems in her search for self-fulfillment? For struggle she does against myriad obstacles presented to her by a hostile society. Through our work with the Daughters of Bilitis, Inc., a Lesbian organization started in San Francisco in 1955, we have talked to literally thousands of Lesbians (and almost as many male homosexuals). And, although each case is different, each person individual, through all is a searching for self-identity and self-fulfillment to the utmost of the person's ability.

Consider the stereotyped "box" most women in this country are placed in from birth: that of becoming wife and mother, nothing else. Consider then, the girl brought up in this box who finds her sexual identification to be Lesbian. How then express the "wife-and-mother" role? This conflict often starts the process of self-searching which goes on for years and which, for some, is never resolved.

Toward a Quaker View of Sex, which came out of England and is more enlightened than most religious treatises on male homosexuality, fails utterly in its chapter on the female homosexual. The only statement with which we can agree is the first sentence: "Homosexuality is probably as common in women as it is in men." The Quaker view of the Lesbian is apparently that of the wishy-washy, namby-pamby old maid who holds hands with another old maid (or preferably an adoring younger girl, if available) because she never was able to catch a man and fulfill her deep yearning for the rewards of the pangs of childbirth. At least the American stereotype of the predatory, aggressive masculine woman has a little more color!

The Quaker view indicates that woman's prime requisite is her "maternal tenderness," that her only reason for being is to have babies, and that the Lesbian is warped and frustrated because she isn't doing her fair share toward the population explosion. To this question of maternity we must point out that the mere possession of biological machinery to produce babies has no correlation whatever with the attributes of motherhood. Let's face it—many women can have babies but make lousy mothers.

The art of motherhood in the human species is not instinctual. It is learned. We have courses in the care of the baby, and there are countless books on the market to help the young mother with the problems she may encounter during the course of her child's growth and development. In some cultures, babies are taken from the mothers and raised by the community without any apparent psychically traumatic results for the biological mothers or their offspring. In other cultures it is the male who tends the young.

It simply does not follow, then, that every Lesbian is suffering untold qualms because she is frustrating her "natural" birthright for giving birth. There are many other ways for women to contribute creatively to society, and at this particular point in the history of the population of our globe, they may also be highly desirable. The Lesbian who does feel frustrated because she doesn't have any children of her own may work in the teaching profession, she may be a playground director or a social worker who comes in contact with families and children. But the majority of Lesbians we have known have not expressed in any way the "void" they feel because they have no children. To the contrary, the expression "I would prefer to lead a heterosexual life if I could," is much more apt to come from the male homosexual than from the female.

It must be said, however, that there are many Lesbians who are raising children—some successfully, some not so successfully. The rate of success is, of course, determined by the degree of self-acceptance and self-assurance of the mother, and the permanence and stability of her relationship to her Lesbian partner. It takes guts, grit and determination. For if a mother is determined to be a Lesbian the courts will assume she is an "unfit mother" on the face of it and take her children away from her. It seems children must have the protection of heterosexuals, regardless. The fact that *all homosexuals are products of heterosexuality* seems to escape those who would judge the homosexual relationship.

The teenage Lesbian has a particular problem which has not been met. Homophile organizations, like the Daughters of Bilitis, have had to refuse membership to those under 21 for fear that they will be charged with "contributing to the delinquency of a minor." The teenager has no one to turn to. Society thinks only in terms of counseling the variety that would tend toward reestablishing the sexual identity in a heterosexual vein, and the teenage Lesbian is whisked off by her parents to the family doctor or clergyman to put a stop to this nonsense. However, in the cases that have come to our attention, the teenager has no doubt about her sexual orientation. What she wants to know is what to do about it. She wants to meet others like herself; she wants to socialize and to discuss the problem she faces. She is looking for Lesbian models, those who have worked out their problems and have established long-term relationships.

When she is denied this social outlet, she very often winds up in unsavory areas of a city like the Tenderloin in San Francisco. There she may find other youth, but she also finds herself in the company of prostitutes, pimps, drug addicts and dope peddlers. There have been several attempts in various cities to set up coffee houses where there is dancing for the teenage homosexual. But they have lacked the influential backing of, say, the church, to provide protection against police harassment while creating a wholesome social fabric for the teenage homosexual.

Because of the absence of role models in working out her way of life, and because the only marriage she has known is that of Mom and Dad, the young Lesbian usually gets hung up in the "butch-femme" syndrome in her early relationships. It is only with painful experience that she learns the Lesbian is attracted to a woman—not a cheap imitation of a man. The lasting Lesbian liaison (and there are many) is one based on mutuality of concern, love, companionship, responsibility, household chores, outside interests and sex.

The successful Lesbian relationship cannot be based on society's exaggerated male-female, dominant-passive roles, as depicted in the flood of Lesbian novels on the newsstands which are, for the most part, written by men for heterosexual male consumption. It is the realization that, contrary to cultural myths, all human beings have both feminine and masculine traits and that a person has to find her own identity as a woman and as a partner in this love relationship that makes for success. The fact that Lesbian relationships are generally long-lasting without benefit of religious ceremony or legal sanction is indicative of a strong bond of love and respect which sees the couple through all the obstacles society places in their way.

Fortunately for all women, there is a growing awareness in this country that woman needs and is more openly demanding an identify for herself as a human being, an identity over and beyond the societal role of housewife and mother. This awareness, coupled with more openness about sexuality and homosexuality, is making it easier now for the young girl, newly aware of her Lesbianism, to cope with the negative sanctions of society. But it is still true that in most areas of our country she has no place to turn for counsel, no one with whom she can talk about her feelings without running the very real risk that the counselor will turn away from her with horror and revulsion.

The Quakers state: "Female homosexuality is free from the legal and, to a large extent, the social sanctions which are so important in the problems of male homosexuals." This is a myth that even the male homosexual has come to believe. It is true that in England there were never any laws pertaining to female homosexuality. But this is not true in the U.S.A. The Lesbian is just as subject to the sanctions of certain laws as the male homosexual; she is just as subject to arrest when she sets foot in a "gay bar"; she is just as subject to blackmail and police harassment. The stigma attached to homosexuality has just as much effect on the Lesbian as she tries to deal with fear and society-imposed guilt in the problem areas of employment, family relationships and religion. Just because the record of arrests is so much smaller is no indication that the Lesbian is relatively free from legal or social sanction. It only means that she is less obvious and less promiscuous. She has done a better job of covering up.

Lesbian problems we have dealt with over the years include the 20-year-old driven to thoughts of suicide because she could not resolve the conflict between her identity as a Lesbian and as a Christian. Or the 40-year-old mother who telephones Daughters of Bilitis 3,000 miles across the country to break "18 years of silence" after reading a book called *The Grapevine* by Jess Stearn. Then there was the nurse with a "perfect work record" in a federal hospital who was interrogated by a government investigator, flown from Washington, D.C., at the taxpayers' expense, because someone wrote to a Congressman accusing her of being a Lesbian.

There was the 19-year-old who was trying to find out what homosexuality was all about because she was drummed out of the armed services on

a charge she didn't understand. The daughter who receives a monthly al-
lowance from her wealthy family in the Midwest to stay on the coast lest her
district attorney father be threatened with a "family skeleton" by his political foes. And the 25-year-old who, after five years of psychiatric therapy,
decides she must make the best of herself as herself—a Lesbian.

The most serious problem a Lesbian faces in life is that of self-acceptance. Like everyone else, she has been taught the cultural folklore that a
Lesbian is something less than human—a sick, perverted, illegal, immoral
animal to be shunned and despised. Needless to say, with the first glimmer-
ing of self-knowledge, of awareness that she has Lesbian tendencies, she
becomes bogged down in doubt, fear, guilt and hostility.

Some Lesbians claim they have been aware of their Lesbianism since
early childhood. Others first become aware during adolescence. Yet there
are some women who make this discovery about themselves much later in
life—after they have been married and have had children. Still others, either by choice or lack of opportunity, never admit or act out their Lesbianism.

It isn't easy for a woman to say to herself, let alone anyone else, "I am a
Lesbian." But once the words are said, has she really changed? Isn't she still
the same person she was—the dear friend, the competent employee, the
loving sister? And yet the words become a barrier in her personal and
working relationships. To protect her family and her job, she is forced to
live a lie, to take on a dual life. No wonder many Lesbians seek out some
type of psychiatric or therapeutic help. The miracle is that so many are able
to function so well and to contribute so much to society.

The Lesbian is thus a secretive, chameleon creature. She is not easily
recognized. The old adage, "It takes one to know one," is not true. Not
being distinguishable from other women, she has difficulty meeting others
like herself. The "gay bar" is still a meeting place, but there are few such
bars which cater to women exclusively because they do not constitute a
steady clientele. Besides, a Lesbian, as a woman, has no doubt heard many
times the old saw "nice girls don't go into bars," or "no lady would ever go
into a bar alone." The Lesbian goes out on the town only occasionally and is
more apt to settle down with a partner, to build a home and a lasting relationship, and to develop a small circle of friends—usually both homosexual
and heterosexual. Another social outlet for the Lesbian can be homophile
organizations throughout the country (if she knows about them), such as
Daughters of Bilitis, which has chapters in New York and San Francisco.

The Lesbian, being a woman, comes out of the same cultural pool as
do heterosexual women. Therefore, on top of everything else, she may
have the same hang-ups and inhibitions about sex, dress, work, actions,
etc., as do her heterosexual sisters. Since women have been taught to be
passive, to shun the role of the aggressor, the Lesbian finds herself without
the slightest idea of how to approach another woman for a date, for a conversation, for sex. It is a rarity for a heterosexual woman to be approached
by a Lesbian unless she has given much indication that such advances are
welcome.

Even when the Lesbian accepts her sexual identity and herself as a person, she still faces very real discrimination from society. If she has educated
herself to a profession (a role doubly difficult for any woman), she can lose

her professional status merely because s someone points a finger. This is especially true of teachers, attorneys, doctors, social workers and other professions licensed by the state. But it can also be true for file clerks and secretaries. Very few employers are aware enough to realize that in the Lesbian he has an employee who must work, who will not get married or pregnant, who will devote her energies and capabilities to her job because she will always have to support herself.

As Rabbi Elliot Grafman has stated, "People fear that which they do not understand, and what they fear they despise." It is only through more knowledge and more personal confrontation that the stereotype of the Lesbian can be dispelled. However, to accomplish this feat is to overcome the vicious circle that now envelops the Lesbian who tries to be honest.

If she divulges her identity, she automatically becomes vulnerable. She faces loss of job, family, and friends. Yet, until she opens herself to such possibilities, no one will have the opportunity to come to know and to understand her as the whole person she is.

Through The Council on Religion and the Homosexual, which was formed in San Francisco in 1964 after a three-day retreat attended by clergymen and male and female representatives of the homophile community, such a dialogue began in earnest. Avenues of communication have been opened up not only with the religious community (seminaries and other church groups), but with governmental agencies, the police, business and professional groups, college and high school students. But the task of demythologizing, of education and redefinition of the homosexual is a long and arduous one.

PART VII

Birth Control

The development of birth control technology and the availability of abortion are of critical importance in women's lives and therefore have important implications for the psychology of women. Women have always sought control over the reproductive potential of their bodies so that they could choose when and how many children they would have. With the introduction of the oral contraceptive pill in the United States in 1960 and the legalization of abortion in 1973, the possibility of choice became a reality for many. Even so, the initial enthusiasm for the pill in its many forms has been tempered as possible undesirable side-effects have been identified. Many women are turning to more benign barrier methods or are having tubal sterilizations. Whatever the method, should it fail, some women seek abortion as an alternative to continuing the pregnancy. For the most part, birth control continues to be women's concern and responsibility.

Freedom from unwanted pregnancies plainly has a liberating effect on women's lives. A woman can enjoy her sexuality more when she is not anxious about getting pregnant. Too, freedom to choose how many children she will have gives a woman more power to design the kind of life she wants to live and opens new channels for the investment of time, energy, and other resources. As more opportunities become available, women are likewise freer than before from the old exigencies of their bodies. These two factors, freedom from unwanted pregnancies and access to opportunities in the larger world outside the home, together make the liberation of women truly possible. Without them, or with only one of them, the concept is only empty rhetoric.

The evolution of human reproduction has been characterized by the increasing dominance of choice over chance. In the first paper in this section, "Chance, Choice, and the Future of Reproduction," Warren B. Miller

325

describes some manifestations of this historic trend and discusses possible future developments and some of their implications.

As noted earlier, humans have historically tried to regulate reproduction. In preindustrial times such attempts involved primarily the regulation of sexual activity, though in some times and places infanticide and abortion were also common. With the advent of the industrial revolution and the rise of individualism, traditional authority and social control began to erode, and interest turned to the development of ways to enjoy sex without the risk of conception. Today, choice is a strong factor in U.S. childbearing; even so, Miller's studies have shown that most nonmarital pregnancies were not connected with a choice either to have or not to have a child. In other words, chance still plays a role in conception.

Such developments as amniocentesis, genetic screening, sex preselection, semen storage, ovum transfer, and in vitro fertilization further strengthen the role of choice in reproductive behavior. These techniques and others, such as the use of surrogate mothers, raise ethical and psychological questions yet to be answered. Miller also discusses the selective technique of progenesis, whereby parents may choose for or against certain characteristics in their offspring. The most obvious examples include choosing not to bear a defective child or selecting the sex of the child. Miller believes that progenesis is a natural extension of the trend in reproduction from chance to choice, and since it will increase in power and scope as technology improves, it is important to begin now to understand and to evaluate the issues it raises.

What are the attitudes of the public toward the new technologies of reproduction? The second paper in this section, addresses this important question. In "Widening Choices in Motherhood of the Future," Nan Chico and Shirley Hartley describe a survey of such attitudes among more than two thousand adults. They also look at the impact that widespread use of these new alternatives could have on the future of women in particular, and on society in general. Of particular interest in the results of the survey were the male-female differences that emerged. Women were more likely than men to give high priority to research into sperm banking, in vitro fertilization with embryo transplants, and artificial wombs. Research into cloning, the production of genetically identical people, was rejected by all racial and sex categories of respondents. Again, questions arise, and the authors point out that men, who do the research and make the laws, must not be allowed to do so without input from women, who will be affected by them.

Physicians and behavioral scientists once shared with men in general the notion that woman's mental and emotional status was intimately connected with her uterus and its functions. Thus they naturally assumed that any interference with these would have sinister consequences. Abortion, especially, was held to be followed inevitably by guilt, depression, feelings of worthlessness, and loss of femininity. No doubt such consequences did indeed occur, but they could have been equally well explained by social stigma, by the illegality of abortion, and by the conditions under which it often occurred. Since abortion has become more readily available, research on its psychological consequences has forced revisions of old assumptions about it. Lisa Shusterman's paper, "The Psychosocial Factors of the Abortion Experience: A Critical Review," looks at the research on both illegal and legal abortion for insight on what the abortion experience means to women.

Data on abortions performed before 1970, when it was illegal in all states except to save the mother's life, are not reliable, but in 1972 when legal abortion was available in some states, more than half a million legal abortions were performed in the United States. Shusterman provides some demographic data from recent studies revealing the characteristics of women who seek abortions. She also surveys the data on such questions as public opinion about abortion, motivations for unwanted pregnancies and for abortions, and the medical and psychological sequelae of abortion. It is interesting to observe that this is one area of professional concern where informed opinion has made a complete turnabout in the past few years. Shusterman concludes that the more recent research on abortion by request clearly indicates that, for most women, the psychological effects of abortion are negligible, if not actually favorable.

Issues of choice, technologies of the present and future, the effects of abortion—these topics are only a small sample of a growing literature on the complex and far-reaching subject of birth control. Woman's ability to bring forth life has been variously valued in human history, honored and encouraged in some times, disparaged in others. At the global level, there is hardly a more important problem facing humanity today than the control of reproduction. As the number of people on earth threaten to outstrip the planet's ability to support them, societies try to change people's attitudes about having children and seek to develop ever more refined techniques for controlling reproduction. But as important as birth control is to the macrocosm of the world and its cultures, it is just as important, on another level, to the microcosm of the individual. No other issue so intimately affects the lives of so many women.

23

Chance, Choice, and the Future of Reproduction

Warren B. Miller

The evolution of reproduction has been characterized by the development of complex biological and behavioral mechanisms that serve to regulate chance events. Human reproduction has been characterized by the increasing importance of individual choice. The author describes some contemporary manifestations of this broad trend and anticipates probable future developments and some of their psychological and social implications.

Futurists are those people who attempt to understand systematically what will happen in the future. However, they tend not to think in terms of *the* future, but rather in terms of *possible* futures. This is because the world is too complex and our analytic tools too limited for us to identify with any certainty what will happen a few decades, or even a few years, from the present. Therefore, futurists select the most important current trends and try to conclude which futures are possible and the relative likelihood of each one.

What are the possible reproductive futures? What patterns of reproduction will become most common among the people of the United States during the next few decades? These questions may seem surprising. After all, it might be argued that reproduction has not really changed over the millennia. However, let me suggest not only that human reproduction has been changing, but that the rate of change is accelerating. Further, we stand, so to speak, at the hinge of history, facing a whole new set of changes that will have the most profound effects yet.

Before I jump too far ahead in the story, let me discuss what I perceive to be the fundamental and most important trend in human reproduction, the progressive dominance of choice over chance. First, I will identify the origin of this trend in biological evolution and trace its development through human history. Then, having described its manifestations in the contemporary United States, I will be in a position to project its future course and thereby anticipate and describe possible reproductive futures.

It has been said that life has three primary characteristics: growth and development, self-maintenance, and reproduction. The second of these, self-maintenance, is obviously necessary if the individual organism is to survive the constant struggle against disorder and death. The first and third of these characteristics, growth from a young organism to a mature one and the reproduction of new organisms, are important not just for individual survival, but for species survival. These two characteristics remind us that life does not consist simply of individual organisms struggling to adapt and survive, but rather of a temporal succession of organisms whose adaptive strategies form a continuity. In other words, although it is the individual organism that lives by growing and maintaining itself, it does this in the context of a group of closely related and interbreeding organisms. It is this local population, or deme, and its gene pool that is the entity which ultimately must struggle against disorder in order to survive. One of the primary ways that this is accomplished is through the maintenance of a reserve adaptive capacity within the deme in the form of genetic heterogeneity. This heterogeneity facilitates the expression of new characteristics in succeeding generations of the deme, which in turn allows for the development of new adaptive strategies in individuals and groups of individuals. The potential for new adaptive strategies allows the deme, so to speak, to roll with the environmental punches, either by adjusting to changing conditions in its present locale or by expanding into slightly different conditions in adjacent locales.

In this context sexual reproduction offers a substantial advantage over asexual reproduction. Because sexual reproduction generally involves the pooling of genetic material from two distinct individuals, it can greatly increase the genetic heterogeneity of succeeding generations and thus the diversity of organisms within the local breeding population. In this way the deme's reserve adaptive capacity is increased.

But sexual reproduction has inherent risks. It means bringing together the germ cells (sperm and ova) from two separate individuals in a way and with a frequency that ensures maintenance of the deme. Whether two germ cells will unite to form a new organism and which two from among the many possible sperm and ova it will be depends on a process filled with uncertainties. In some species chance plays an enormous role. For example, the oyster releases billions of sperm cells into the ocean water, and successful reproduction depends very much on the chance union of one or more of these sperm cells with a receptive egg cell. Successful species, however, do not depend exclusively on chance. Thus, a rich variety of mechanisms have evolved to ensure that a certain level of fertilization is achieved. For example, flowering plants attract insects that carry pollen from male to female flowers. In many higher animals the adult males and females are mutually attracted. This leads to sexual behavior and, ultimately, to fertilization, which occurs within the body of one sex (usually defined as female). The mechanisms that bring this chain of events about are powerful and complex. They include anatomical, physiological, behavioral, and social factors. Especially in the higher vertebrates, all four of these factors are woven together in an intricate sequence that acts to overcome chance. Which male and female engage in this sequence depends to a great extent upon social conditions and patterns within the local interbreeding population, including such factors as proximity, the existence of pair bonds, the local group's dominance hierarchy, and the overall community social structure. The net effect is that what could be a very chancy event is, in fact, very carefully regulated to the point of ensuring species continuity.

It is worth noting that in the typical mammalian sequence there is no component that might be called a reproductive drive. The only drive is a sexual one, and reproduction follows as a result of sexual behavior. This pattern seems to be as true of the monkeys and apes as of any other mammalian orders. This is not to say that biological and other mechanisms do not support reproduction. Clearly the imprinting of newborn babies and the natural responsiveness of adults to infants have biological components. But these operate after the baby's arrival. Before the fact, the primary force that sets the chance regulating processes in motion and thereby ensures reproduction is sexual drive.

The evolutionary transition from apes to humans over three million years ago involved a radically new adaptive strategy. Although this change represented a culmination of evolutionary trends already apparent in the primate order, what emerged in humans ultimately represented a qualitative leap to a new level of evolution, one in which the individual organism, and the local group of which it was a member, no longer simply adapted passively to the environment, but rather began to actively control and regulate that environment to satisfy its own needs. Many developments contributed incrementally and interactively to this new strategy, such as the shift to bipedalism, the development of the opposable thumb, and an increase in the size of the brain. The basic adaptive strategy that emerged included living in small groups with the concomitant gathering, hunting, and sharing of food; the extensive use of tools; and the use of language. In the course of these developments, memory, learning, and decision making assumed greater importance in the determination of individual behavior, group culture increased in complexity and in its importance as a regulator of individual and group activities, and biological mechanisms lost much of their imperative force.

These developments had an important impact on human reproduction, especially in two respects: Sexual activity was further freed from basic biological regulation and the causal relationship between sexual intercourse and childbearing came to be recognized. These in turn meant that childbearing was much more susceptible to regulation by individual choice and by social custom. In other words, the biobehavioral mechanisms that heretofore in evolution had acted to overcome the chanciness of sperm meeting ovum had become appreciably subjected to the rule of a whole new set of psychosocial mechanisms.

Early in human history the regulation of reproduction appears to have been achieved primarily by the regulation of sexual activity, although abortion and infanticide were also important. Sexual activity was, in turn, regulated to a large degree by social custom. This was accomplished both through the effect of external factors such as family living arrangements, opportunities for social intercourse, the ascription of marital status, and through the socialization of individuals—as, for example, when they internalized religious and moral prescriptions.

During the industrial revolution a new social order began to develop in which less credence was given to traditional and religious authority and more emphasis was placed on rationality, scientific understanding, and technological achievement. Established lineage systems and family forms began to change, and a new emphasis was placed on individualism. Many activities became subject to greater degrees of individual choice at the expense of both general social custom and choice by family or community elders. Initially, this affected reproduction primarily as a result of individuals' exerting greater choice over spouse selection and the timing of marriage. Gradually, however, individual choice began to exert itself in the area of conception control as the application of human rationality and technology was turned increasingly to the development of ways to enjoy sex without incurring a major risk of conception. By the middle of the 20th century, methods for the prevention of conception achieved considerable reliability and safety, which assured their widespread use by individuals and societies that placed a net positive value on this particular dimension of self-regulation. Today, their widespread acceptance and use in some societies appear to be associated with a loosening of the hold of the traditional social values and practices that had earlier served to regulate reproduction. As a result, we are near the point at which individual choice, rather than chance modulated by biological imperatives and social customs, serves as the primary regulator of reproduction. With respect to reproduction, humans have moved from a passive adaptation to active regulation.

This brings us up to date, at least as far as the majority of people in the United States are concerned. Let me apply some of these historical themes to the patterns of contemporary reproduction in the United States. First, it should be pointed out that although choice is currently a strong factor in U.S. childbearing, chance continues to play a major role. Perhaps the best way to understand the complex reasons for this is to begin by considering what I like to call the intended/counterintended pregnancy continuum.

Any conception can be rated according to the degree of intention that precedes it. On the one hand, many conceptions are completely the result of planning. For example, a couple may discontinue their use of contraception for the specific purpose of having a child. This type of conception is fully intended. On the other hand, many conceptions occur completely by accident. For example, a couple may use a reliable contraceptive method correctly and conscientiously and still the woman becomes pregnant. This type of conception has no preceding intention. In fact, because the couple was trying to prevent conception with a proven, effective method, it may be said to be fully counterintended. Between these two poles fall conceptions that occur as a result of various degrees of intention and counterintention. Those that are closer to the fully intended pole result from ambivalence about having a child and inconsistent efforts to achieve conception. Those that are closer to the counterintended pole result from ambivalence about preventing conception and the inconsistent use of contraception. Right in the middle of this continuum lies an important group of conceptions—those that occur as a result of sexual activity unassociated with any intention to conceive or not to conceive.

In one of my research studies (Miller, 1981) I evaluated about 500 conceptions in a group of married and unmarried women. As might be expected, most marital conceptions (65%) were fully intended and only a small proportion (about 10%) were fully counterintended. On the other hand, most premarital conceptions (about 40%) were unassociated with either intention or counterintention; some (15%) were fully counterintended, and very few (1%) were fully intended.

It seems that this intended / counterintended pregnancy continuum fits well with the evolutionary / historical sketch presented above. The mid-point on the continuum represents the kind of conception that was common early in human history when reproduction was regulated by the biological and social mechanisms that had evolved to channel chance according to the interests of the species and the group. The two poles of the continuum represent the kinds of conceptions that occur with greater frequency as reproduction becomes more regulated by individual choice and action. The counterintended pole, of course, represents a failure to overcome chance, just as the intended pole represents the successful mastery of chance events.

The continuum I have described suggests that there are two distinct, and in certain respects very different, types of behavior that regulate conception. On the one hand, there is contraceptive behavior, and on the other hand, there is what I have called proceptive behavior (Miller, 1981; Miller & Godwin, 1977). Just as *contraception* is a contraction of the prefix *contra* meaning *against* and the word *conception,* so *proception* is derived from *pro* meaning *in favor of* and *conception.* Contraceptive behavior is oriented to the prevention of conception, and proceptive behavior is oriented to the achievement of conception. Both are instrumental behaviors, contraceptive behavior being an attempt to reduce the chance of conception to 0.0 and proceptive behavior being an attempt to increase the chance of conception to 1.0. Both behaviors are ultimately defined in terms of the individual's intention.

The analogy between proceptive and contraceptive behavior is quite striking. For example, individuals can alter the frequency or, more commonly, the timing of sexual intercourse to either achieve or prevent conception. Thus, concentrating intercourse around the time of ovulation is a type of proceptive behavior, while avoiding intercourse during that time is a type of contraceptive behavior. Similarly, identifying the timing of ovulation through the use of temperature charts or from the quality of the cervical mucus can serve either proceptive or contraceptive purposes. Finally, the use of drugs to manipulate reproductive hormones can serve either to help achieve or to prevent conception.

It should not be assumed that proceptive behavior is relatively infrequent or unimportant. In a three-year study of 1,000 women, I found that proceptive behavior was by far the most important factor predicting the occurrence of conception among married couples (Miller, 1981). The other factors studied included the couples' biological capacity to conceive (i.e., how fertile they were), how frequently they had sexual intercourse, what type of contraceptive method they used, and how effectively they used it.

My research has also revealed that it is useful to distinguish between the active and passive forms of proception. The difference is essentially the difference between the active and passive pursuit of any goal. Active pursuit involves taking the initiative by attempting to influence or control the course of events. Passive pursuit involves allowing the course of events to proceed in the direction they appear to be going and participating in them with no, or relatively little, intervention. During interviews, my research subjects tended to confirm this distinction, reporting either that they were actively trying to conceive or that they were primarily letting conception occur when it would. Certain behaviors were associated with active proception, including a planned discontinuation of contraception, the timing of sexual intercourse so that it occurred during the fertile period, and an increased frequency of sexual intercourse during that time.

Two thirds of the 489 women who tried to become pregnant during the three years of the research reported that they had procepted actively, and one third indicated that they had procepted only passively. Of course, the difference between active and passive proception was not always clear-cut, but in most cases this was because certain women seemed to be in a period of transition, either from passive to active as they grew impatient with their failure to conceive, or from active to passive as they became frustrated by a prolonged failure and backed off from "trying too hard."

These observations remind us that there are other important transitions in the practice of proceptive and contraceptive behavior. For example, although some couples who are planning to have a child move abruptly from the regular use of contraception to the concerted effort to achieve conception (i.e., from active contraception to active proception), many move gradually and in stages, first through a period of passive and more irregular contraceptive use, then through a period of no contraceptive use but without the intent to conceive, and finally to the passive pursuit of proception. Another important transition is the one that occurs at the initiation of many people's sexual careers, typically during adolescence. Although some individuals may be actively trying to conceive or to prevent conception right from the start, many begin their sexual activities without any consciously developed contraceptive or proceptive intent. Thus, contemporary individuals who are beginning their sexual careers tend to manifest conception-oriented behaviors quite comparable to what was common throughout the reproductive life span during the early periods of human history. We are in a major transition period with respect to reproduction and all the related behaviors. As a result, although sexual and reproductive practices, and to some extent, social norms, have changed, early socialization still tends to reflect the old, high-chance / low-choice system. Until a reasonably strong consensus develops regarding the content and form of early sexual and reproductive socialization that is appropriate to the new realities, the adolescent launching of sexual careers will remain an especially vulnerable transition.

The formation of intention implies some degree of prior decision making. Thus, both proceptive and contraceptive behavior are really the result of individual and couple choices. For this reason, it is important at this point to consider several issues related to making choices. For purposes of illustration, I will limit myself to a discussion of the choice-related antecedents of proception only. First, let us consider reproductive motivation. As I discussed earlier, there does not seem to be a biologically based drive to produce offspring in any of the vertebrates below homo sapiens. Even among the great apes, the choices individuals make have nothing to do with the drive or desire to bear children, but rather with mate selection and sexuality. Humans are evolutionarily unique in their ability to anticipate and therefore choose childbearing. This means that human reproductive motivation probably does not have a strong biological origin apart from the extent to which it is strengthened by such inborn traits as responsiveness to babies and the capacity to enjoy caretaking. Rather, it seems to spring primarily from a very complex set of personal, family, and cultural experiences. One wonders, therefore, if the diffuse and tenuous nature of the biological factors and the complexity of the learned factors do not, especially during periods of change like the present, play a significant role in the many different ways with which individual humans approach childbearing decisions and in the difficulties they encounter while making them.

There are at least three general strategies that people follow while making childbearing decisions: a terminating strategy, a sequencing strategy, and a preplanning strategy. In the terminating strategy, a couple makes no decision about childbearing until the number of children they have becomes enough or too much. They take what they get until they want no more, and then they decide to stop. In the sequencing strategy, decisions to have children are made one child at a time until a satisfactory limit is reached. Each child is chosen in the context of the number of children already present, but unlike the terminating strategy, a decision is made in each case. In the preplanning strategy, a plan is worked out ahead of time and this general plan is subsequently carried out. For example, a couple may agree at marriage to have four children and then build many other aspects of their partnership around that plan.

These three types form a continuum. In the order presented, they seem to follow the historical trend toward greater reproductive control that I have already described. At the extreme end of the terminating strategy are individuals and couples who exercise no control over reproduction, accepting whatever chance gives them. They may not even decide to terminate childbearing, in spite of being in a situation that seems to cry out for it. At the extreme end of the preplanning strategy are those who decide both the number and timing of their children ahead of time as part of a very thoroughly planned and controlled life course.

It should also be noted that although the movement toward greater choice in childbearing is widely supported and practiced, especially in the industrialized nations, choice is by no means universally endorsed, nor is it an unmitigated joy. Some people feel that controlling reproduction is either undesirable or inappropriate for humans. They do not feel comfortable asserting their own personal wishes in so important a matter as having a baby. In addition, many people feel that leaving matters to chance creates a certain excitement and challenge and that there is an important kind of satisfaction that comes through accepting one's fate or God's will. Related to this is a joy in facing the unknown and being part of a force larger than oneself. This philosophy, often—but not necessarily—associated with strong religiosity, seems to occur most commonly in those adopting the terminating strategy.

At the other end of the spectrum, among those using the more decision-based strategies, there are definite choice-associated problems. For example, now that childbearing has become a real option in so many people's lives, a large number of them find it extremely difficult to actually make a decision about having a child. Many cannot seem to find within themselves a real motivational basis for their decision, as though some important kernel of desire is missing; others feel extremely ambivalent, torn in a double-approach conflict (e.g., having children versus having a career) or in a double avoidance conflict (e.g., not wanting to take care of children versus not wanting to be childless). Often, these difficulties are resolved through passive decision making (i.e., failing to make a decision) or by contraceptive chance taking. Usually, this means that the outcome is determined by biology, chance, or some other person.

The great importance of childbearing decisions and the problems that many people encounter in making them mandate our developing a better understanding of how individuals and couples actually make them. To some extent people rationally evaluate the costs and benefits of childbearing and then try to maximize satisfaction through their decisions (Burch, 1980). However, there are important nonrational elements in this process. Some of these elements probably derive from the evolutionary newness of human decision making and can be related to the complex task faced by the human mind, the ego if you will, as it processes and integrates various cognitive, emotional, and motivational factors. Faced with considerable complexity, not only within the reproductive domain but also on the interface between that domain and other, potentially conflicting domains such as those having to do with sexuality, gender roles, and occupational activities, the ego is often an inconsistent and inefficient integrator (Miller & Godwin, 1977). Other nonrational elements probably derive from the historical recency of human reproductive decision making and can be related to the considerable importance of social learning in the development of reproductive motivations, attitudes, and beliefs, as well as to the growing ambiguity of social norms in the face of new reproductive technologies and changing reproductive practices.

One aspect of decision making that is uniquely human and particularly important for reproduction is decision making by couples. It adds a fundamentally new dimension to reproductive choice because in most instances integration must occur not only at the level of the individual ego but also at the level of the marital dyad. Especially important considerations affecting dyadic integration include a couple's pattern of communication, its decision role allocation (which member of the couple decides what), its usual methods of conflict resolution, and the power processes most commonly used by each member. For example, reproductive choices can be made during communication, which involves high or low empathy between partners; they can be made jointly or primarily by the woman or by the man; conflict can be resolved by a change within one partner, by the concession of one partner but without change, or by the compromise of both; and each partner can influence the other (to cite three examples) by conferring or withholding gratification, through the use of information and knowledge, or by attempting to induce guilt.

Let me now turn to a consideration of how some of the themes of reproductive chance and choice may extend out into the short-term and long-term future. Two types of future developments seem especially important for such a forecast. One is the continued, and very likely escalating, development of new reproductive technology. The other is a progressive, and perhaps radical, change in society's reproduction-related values and beliefs. These two trends are by no means independent, each seeming to be stimulated by and reinforcing of the other.

With respect to technology, the past few decades have already seen major innovations in the areas of contraception, sterilization, induced abortion, and diagnosis and treatment of infertility. We have also begun to see important developments in such areas as amniocentesis, genetic screening, sex preselection, semen storage, artificial insemination, ovum transfer, and in vitro fertilization (the so-called test-tube babies). Who knows what new technological capabilities will emerge as biologists continue to map human chromosomes and pursue their research with recombitant DNA, and as physicians continue to improve their tools and techniques for manipulating the anatomy and physiology of human reproduction? Whatever unfolds, it can almost certainly be said that the coming decades will see vast, perhaps logarithmic, increases in the human capacity to regulate all aspects of reproduction, including not only whether to have children, how many to have, and when to have them, but also how to have them and what kind of children to have.

Of course, none of these technological developments will occur except in the context of massive changes in the shared values and beliefs that are dominant in our society. The capacity to make new choices does two things: It creates conflict with the traditional value and belief systems that evolved out of the high-chance / low-choice situation, and it creates apprehension and confusion because existing values and beliefs are insufficiently clear to guide decision making and to reinforce the taking of responsibility that is associated with it. I am convinced that we are well along in one of those massive value and belief changes as a result of the contraceptive revolution. Because most of us have completely internalized the values and beliefs associated with this revolution, it is difficult now to appreciate how much change has actually taken place. It is easier to illustrate the importance of value and belief change in relation to an area where traditional values and beliefs are just beginning to be challenged. I have in mind surrogate maternity, the practice whereby a woman is inseminated and conceives by a man who is not her spouse or partner in order to provide him (and usually his infertile spouse) with a newborn child after completion of the pregnancy. Before reading further, it may be instructive to pause and consider your own "gut" reaction to the practice of surrogate maternity and the numerous issues that it raises.

Some professionals with whom I have talked feel that the practice creates unusual risks: first, the psychological strain for the birth mother of lending her body for the project and separating permanently from the offspring; and second, the "adoption" process, with possible strain and impaired bonding for the psychological parents, especially the mother. To them it exaggerates the importance of the physical and genetic aspect of parenthood over the psychological. It risks psychological impairment for the sake of what might be called "genetic vanity." These professionals ask, What would one tell the child? What if disputes arose about the "rights" of the birth mother? What if the child wanted to pursue the birth mother later on, as is sometimes allowed by adoption agencies or the courts?

However, other professionals feel differently. Philip Parker, a psychiatrist involved in the screening of surrogate maternity candidates, reports that his research on the surrogate mother's motivation has revealed three primary factors: (1) a desire for financial gain, (2) an enjoyment of being pregnant, and (3) the perception of a net advantage in giving up the baby. This third factor involves both the idea of giving the gift of a baby to a needy couple and the need for the repetition of a previously unresolved voluntary loss of a fetus or child (Parker, 1983). In another context he states that he has "so far found no evidence that surrogate motherhood, with or without a fee, leads to serious adverse psychological consequences" (Parker, Note 1). Finally, he comments on the notion that the practice of surrogate maternity will contribute to the breakdown of the traditional family: "I do not believe that the viability of our society depends upon the preservation of any particular family arrangement. . . . Society should give the greatest flexibility and choice to its members and allow them to adjust their own lifestyle and family arrangements to suit their own needs. . . . I believe that a married couple's use of a surrogate mother to bear the husband's biologic child falls into the category of a fundamental right" (Parker, Note 2).

It would be possible to elaborate much further on the important psychological and moral issues raised by this new reproductive practice and the extent to which thoughtful and sensitive individuals disagree about it. Suffice it to say here that if I surveyed my readers about the value of this practice I suspect there would be great divergences of opinion. Even though the technology necessary for surrogate maternity has been available for years, we are only now beginning as a society to talk about it openly and actually experiment with its practice. My point is that this new reproductive practice must plough through a considerable amount of resistance in the form of established values and beliefs before it becomes integrated into our culture. My own hunch is twofold: that it is now beginning to do just that, and that it will lead to the development of some meaningful and unique forms of family relationships once it becomes normatively embraced.

To cite an example of one such form, I can foresee instances of surrogate maternity in which a relationship between the receiving couple and the surrogate woman is maintained rather than terminated after the pregnancy, with the child developing some form of attenuated but meaningful attachment to the surrogate in addition to the more traditional attachment that develops with the "parental" couple. Although this prospect may seem totally without merit to many readers, I would make three brief points regarding it. First, there are probably no behavioral science data that can demonstrate convincingly that such a "family" arrangement will not work satisfactorily if it is freely chosen by all participants. Second, there are probably various instances of this arrangement already in progress. Third, we should certainly not rule out acceptance of this practice until we learn much more about how it actually works out.

This brings me to a final but very important consideration, one that seems likely to represent a whole new step in human reproductive strategy. Earlier, I projected a progressive increase in the human capacity to regulate all aspects of reproduction. I included regulation of the kind of children to be borne. Since this is a choice that potentially provides both a rich opportunity and a heavy psychological burden, it deserves special comment.

In order to influence the occurrence or nonoccurrence of characteristics in an offspring, couples may use various selective childbearing techniques. Because these techniques are intended to favor the genesis of a particular type of offspring over and above what might be produced on a chance basis, I have coined the term *progenesis*. Although this term may have elements in common with the discredited concept of eugenics, I believe it is basically a very different term, and I hope that it will survive the possibility of such an association in people's minds. I believe that the two terms are very different, because whereas eugenics emphasized the selection of genes that were presumed to be good for all humans and had extremely unpleasant racist overtones, progenesis emphasizes the process whereby individuals and couples select for or against specific characteristics in a specific offspring on the basis of their own specific needs and values. I am hopeful that the term will survive because I am convinced that individuals and couples are beginning to make progenetic decisions and exhibit progenetic behavior, that this pattern will only increase in the future, and that we very much need an appropriate term in order just to think and talk about what is going on.

Let me describe the concept in a little more detail. The goals of progenesis may be directed along either of two paths: the avoidance of an undesired characteristic in an offspring or the achievement of a desired characteristic. In contemporary U.S. society, the prevention of congenital abnormalities and genetic diseases serves as the best example of the former, and the best example of the latter is the effort to select the sex of a particular child. Although the technology that makes progenesis of this sort a reality is at best only in its infancy, it should not be concluded that progenetic psychology is of no practical and immediate importance. In fact, progenetic issues have been intimately connected to the practice of artificial insemination for many years and are inevitably becoming a part of the embryonic practice of surrogate maternity.

The methods for achieving progenesis involve selective action on the part of an individual or couple and take numerous forms. A few contemporary examples will bring home the point. There is selective marriage, in which, for example, an individual known to carry a gene for a genetic condition such as sickle-cell anemia might avoid marrying someone else carrying the same gene. There is also selective proception: An example would be the timing of sexual intercourse with respect to ovulation in order to affect the chances of having a boy or girl. There is selective abortion after amniocentesis (the medical procedure that involves drawing off small amounts of the fluid surrounding the fetus for diagnostic purposes). When such a procedure indicates the presence of Down's syndrome, the couple may elect to abort the fetus. Finally, as already mentioned, there are the selective activities that go on in connection with donor insemination. These take the form of efforts to select the donor germ cells (i.e., sperm or ova) for specific characteristics, such as racial type or subtype, hair and eye color, or intelligence. A very recent manifestation of this type of activity has been the creation of a so-called Nobel laureate sperm bank. I suspect that we will see more and more developments of this sort, with an expansion of the selectable characteristics to include ones such as athletic ability, musical talent, and mathematical ability. This is probably only the beginning. As scientists develop detailed chromosomal maps and achieve the ability to manipulate genetic units, increasing numbers of progenetic choices will become realities.

There is no doubt that progenesis raises many important and complex issues both for individuals and for society as a whole. I cannot even begin to consider these in any detail. My primary goal here is threefold. First, I would like to suggest that progenesis represents a very natural extension of the evolutionary trend in reproduction from chance to choice. Second, I wish to point out that it has been going on for some time and will probably only increase in scope and frequency as our technological capacities improve. Third, I want to emphasize how important it is that we all begin to examine, understand, and evaluate this activity as it emerges from its cultural closet and gradually becomes sanctioned throughout society.

These points can perhaps best be summarized by suggesting that progenesis, as it becomes more common in practice and diverse in form, will indeed represent a third level of evolution, beyond adapting to the environment, beyond manipulating the environment, to changing the very nature of the adapting and manipulating organism. Many of you will perhaps react to this possibility with the thought that this is playing God, interfering with matters that are best left unchanged, attempting to do what will only create many more problems than it will solve and generate much more psychological distress than satisfaction. But I wonder. Is that not the reaction that many people had yesterday to the possibility of regulating the number and timing of births, and that many have today to innovative reproductive practices such as surrogate maternity? My own hunch is that progenesis can readily be incorporated into the broad array of standard reproductive practices. If individuals and couples make progenetic decisions that are highly specific to their needs and values, and if they do so within the context of an evolving set of social values, the burdens of choice need not be substantially more troublesome than they already are with other kinds of reproductive choice. Although ultimately we may reach a point at which the aggregate effect of progenetic choices includes noticeable social outcomes in the short run and important evolutionary consequences in the long run, neither of these results should necessarily be a cause for alarm if the choices are made under free and democratic social and political conditions. For example, if the aggregate of individual, progenetic choices in one or more generations begins to make a difference in some social variable such as the sex ratio or the mean IQ and if individuals in subsequent generations are free to evaluate and respond to that difference as they make their own choices, then it seems likely that the aggregate outcome will tend to fluctuate around some median value that best represents the general interest. In this way, choice changes the choosers and becomes a major new factor in the ongoing evolution of humanity.

Summarizing briefly in conclusion, I can see the increasing dominance of choice over chance as a highly likely trend for the future of reproduction. It will certainly provide a great variety of new options, some quite unsuspected today. As with any kind of freedom, these developments will require care, caution, and responsibility. And perhaps most important for the readers of this journal, this broad trend will present psychologists with fascinating opportunities for study and exciting challenges to provide understanding and guidance.

REFERENCE NOTES

1. Parker, P. J. *Surrogate motherhood—An opinion essay*. Personal communication, 1982.
2. Parker, P. J. *Surrogate motherhood—Psychological, legal, and moral issues*. Paper presented at the meeting of the American Orthopsychiatric Association, San Francisco, March 1982.

REFERENCES

BURCH, T. K. Decision-making theories in demography: An introduction. In T. K. Burch (Ed.), *Demographic behavior: Interdisciplinary perspectives on decision-making*. Boulder, Colo.: West-view Press, 1980.

MILLER, W. B. *The psychology of reproduction*. Springfield, Va.: National Technical Information Service, 1981.

MILLER, W. B., & GODWIN, R. K. *Psyche and demos: Individual psychology and the issues of population*. New York: Oxford University Press, 1977.

PARKER, P. J. Motivation of surrogate mothers: Initial findings. *American Journal of Psychiatry*, 1983, *140*, 117–118.

24

Widening Choices in Motherhood of the Future

Nan Paulsen Chico and Shirley Foster Hartley

The new biomedical techniques of reproduction either currently available or being researched, such as sex predetermination of offspring, sperm banking, test tube conception with embryo transplant, development of artificial wombs and human cloning, allow greatly expanded choices in methods of procreation. A survey of attitudes among 2,138 adults, most of whom are in the early to middle stages of reproductive decision making, shows varying levels of acceptance towards the use of such techniques and towards priority values they would assign to ongoing research to perfect specific technologies. Male-female variation in response patterns are analyzed along with racial and religious differences. Possible and probable impacts that widespread use of these new alternatives might have on the future of women in particular and on various aspects of society in general are discussed.

In addition to having the choice of whether or not to be a mother, women in the future will also have new choices about the actual *means* of procreation. This paper reports the attitudes of adults in the early childbearing ages toward the new techniques of reproduction as a part of an ongoing research program on this topic. It explores possible reasons for the use of alternative procedures and discusses the implications of more widespread acceptance of new reproductive technologies.

It is only recently that the news media have published the claim of human cloning (Rorvik, 1978), the duplication of genetic material by transfer of the nucleus of an ordinary cell to an egg cell whose nucleus was destroyed. (A host mother would be necessary to carry the clone to birth.) The birth of Louise Brown appears to be the first well documented case of "test tube conception" followed by the implantation of the embryo in the mother, where it was successfully carried to term (All About That Baby, 1978). While these seem to be very recent developments, the "new biologists" have long been at work perfecting reproductive techniques previously discussed mainly in science fiction. The use of artificial insemination with genetic screening already would allow the selection of desired traits in offspring (such as body build and eye color). Any of several methods of sex predetermination would allow the choice of a son first and daughter next (as parental preference in this country implies, see Westoff and Rindfuss, 1974; Williamson, 1976). Prenatal diagnosis of the precise chromosomal makeup of the fetus facilitates abortion of those with gross genetic errors or undesirable genetic traits. Futuristic possibilities like cloning, parthenogenesis (the chemical transformation of an egg so that it develops into a fetus without fertilization by male sperm) and human hybrids (the combination of human with non-human genes) may be nearer at hand than many of us want to believe (Francoeur, 1971; Howard and Rifkin, 1977).

Human genetic engineering becomes possible because of Watson and Crick's initial work in breaking the genetic code (Handler, 1970) and because of extensive research in animal husbandry (Marx, 1973). The first week of human life has been reproduced entirely under laboratory conditions (Frankel, 1974). Fetal diagnosis now permits control over the sex as well as some of the physical and mental qualities of offspring. More than 60 of the 1500 genetically caused defects are now identifiable by the procedure known as amniocentesis, which involves the chromosomal analysis of amniotic-fluid cells withdrawn from the fetal sac (Milunsky, 1973). One to ten percent of all births are classified as involving very serious to moderate genetic disorder (Lubs & Lubs, 1975; National Research Council, 1975). Although social scientists tend to focus on the effects of early childhood socialization and environment in attempts to improve the quality of human life (e.g., McCandless, 1976), ethicist Charles Frankel suggests that "the day may not be that far away when genetic manipulations to improve human intelligence will be a cheaper and more effective means to get results than environmental reforms" (1974, p. 25).

There is no accurate count, but estimates indicate that there are between ten and twenty-five thousand conceptions yearly by artificial insemination in the United States alone (Taylor, 1968). Using this procedure, it becomes not only possible, but also, according to some prominent thinkers, logical to choose semen from among the most intelligent, healthy males rather than to select by chance, convenience, or, as is often the case, merely because the man is married to the woman. Geneticist Hermann Muller (1973) has been foremost among those arguing for germinal selection of the finest human attributes.

But who will decide what characteristics are most important and which persons would be allowed to avail themselves of these procedures? Encouraging public involvement in scientific decision-making, John Cobb, Professor of Preventive Medicine (1976) suggests "we must all set about trying to weigh short-term, obvious, and proven benefits (of whatever scientific research) . . . against long-term, suspected, but unproven dangers" (p. 674). Famed biologist J. D. Watson has also called for more public involvement in policy-making decisions concerning "the role genetics will play in the future of mankind" (English, 1976, p. 54; see also Etzioni, 1973).

Method

To measure attitudes toward some of the new technologies of reproduction, a 52-item questionnaire was developed and piloted. The pilot sample consisted of male and female students in two sections of Social Research Methods at the California State University at Hayward in the summer of 1976. After revising, the instrument was pretested by administering it to 540 respondents of varied ages and work statuses and analyzing the results. Following this, the instrument was finalized with a few minor changes.

In the spring of 1977 the large sample upon which this analysis is based was selected (N = 2138). Students in classes from five colleges in Northern California were asked to respond to the revised 60-item questionnaire. Stanford University and the University of California at Berkeley were chosen to represent PhD-granting universities (N = 801). California State University at Hayward (CSUH) was used to represent the State College and University system (N = 744), and Laney and Chabot Colleges were included to represent the two-year Community Colleges (N = 593).

A table of random numbers was used to sample specific classes within each of four departments on the five campuses. Biology classes were sampled from the physical sciences, sociology classes from the social sciences, business and accounting classes were tapped to represent the occupationally-oriented fields, and music and art classes were sampled from the humanities. Cooperation in responding was close to 100 percent in each class selected.

The usable response sets comprised 53.1 percent males and 46.9 percent females, sex distribution within one percent of that for enrollees in higher education in California in the fall of 1975 (most recent data). 11.6 percent identified themselves as black, 3.8 percent Latino, 10.2 percent reported themselves to be Oriental and 0.9 percent American Indian (subsequently combined with the 5.3 percent "other") and 68.3 percent classified themselves as white. (These may be compared with the San Francisco-Oakland racial distribution from the 1970 census. Although the proportions of blacks and whites were identical to those of the census, there are twice the percentage of Orientals and only one-third the proportion of Latinos among our respondents as were recorded by the census.) In terms of religious background, the sample is overrepresented by Catholics (29.4 percent) in comparison to the larger population. 18.1 percent indicated that they were Protestant fundamentalists, 20.7 percent Protestant nonfundamentalists, 5.3 percent reported themselves Jewish, 7 percent other, and 19.6 percent indicated that they had no religious backgrounds or were atheists.

While the sample cannot be considered representative of even the college population in general, much less all adults in the United States, it does have the advantage of being heavily weighted with persons in the early to middle stages of reproductive decision-making. The mean age of respondents was 23.7 years, with 53 percent between ages 20 and 24 and only 13 percent reporting themselves as over 30 years of age. College students are often thought to be opinion leaders, and thus their attitudes toward reproductive engineering should be of interest in themselves, and will serve as benchmarks to future measurement. (In fact, about one-third of the sample volunteered to participate in a follow-up study, which has already been conducted but is not yet tabulated.)

Analysis was carried out using cross tabulations of nominal variables with chi-square tests of statistical significance and using Spearman rank-order correlation coefficients for ordinal variables. (We also tested to see whether the priority items formed a Guttman scale; they did not.)

Results

Over 83 percent of our respondents agreed that "the general public should be included in discussions and decision-making regarding genetic engineering." Few respondents were willing to leave these decisions to legislators, although many would have allowed these decisions to be made by medical doctors or biological researchers. Confidence in the leaders of science and medicine was significantly related to a willingness to leave the decisions in their hands ($p<.01$) and to the priorities given to ongoing research into techniques of reproduction ($p<.001$) (see Hartley &. Pietraczyk, Note 1).

Many of our early questions assessed *attitudes* about different biomedical procedures, including sex predetermination, early or late abortion under several conditions of genetic defect, cloning in general and under five specific circumstances, and parthenogenesis. We later asked what *priority* respondents would have to research in these areas. Results are reported in Table 1. This prioritizing seemed to provide respondents with the opportunity to make more refined judgements than with the Likert-type agreement scales. For instance, about 66 percent of our respondents agreed that "if it becomes possible to predetermine the sex of offspring, such a possibility should be available to all parents." Yet only 9.7 percent would give the procedure a high research priority. In contrast, while almost 80 percent similarly agreed that early abortion might be desirable to prevent mentally retarded infants, 64 percent also gave highest research priority to this item. (In spite of the wide range in priorities suggested, see Table 1, these responses were all significantly correlated with one another, Spearman correlation coefficients ranging from 0.14 to 0.66.)

When questions focused only on those research priorities related to reproductive engineering (see Table 1), in contrast to the very large proportions of respondents (63.8 and 58.4) who gave highest priorities to minimizing mental retardation and physical deformities, only 9.7 percent gave a high priority to research on predetermining the sex of offspring, and 23.1 percent would positively support ongoing research on sperm banking. Ten percent gave a high priority to the perfection of test tube conceptions to be implanted in a host mother, while almost twice that proportion would *prohibit* that research. Indeed, the proportions of respondents willing to prohibit research increases dramatically for techniques to develop artificial wombs, with only 5.8 percent giving a high priority and 31.2 percent wanting to prohibit it. Human cloning is even less attractive as a possibility, with only two percent strongly supportive and 58.4 percent willing to prohibit the research entirely.

Table 1 Priority values assigned to ongoing biomedical research to perfect specific reproductive technologies (N = 2138) (in percentages)

Research area	High priority	Moderate priority	Low priority	No opinion	Prohibit	Total
Sex predetermination	9.7	27.5	44.5	4.8	13.5	100.0
Physical features of offspring: choice of height, hair & eye color, etc.	4.9	18.5	49.8	5.3	21.5	100.0
minimize physical deformities	58.4	23.6	8.5	3.0	6.4	99.9
Mental aspects: maximize intelligence potential	22.6	33.4	23.9	4.3	15.8	100.0
minimize mental retardation	63.8	20.7	6.4	2.4	6.6	99.9
Maximize conception capacities for those who have difficulty conceiving: e.g., with sperm banks	23.1	39.7	23.1	5.2	8.9	100.0
e.g., with test tube conceptions later implanted in host mother	10.1	30.8	33.6	5.8	19.6	99.9
e.g., develop artificial wombs	5.8	18.1	37.4	7.4	31.2	99.9
Cloning to duplicate human beings	2.0	7.7	25.3	6.7	58.4	100.1

There were few overall differences between female and male in response patterns. However, when we examined male / female responses by race, there were some pronounced differences (see Table 2). Blacks were twice as likely as any other category to give high priority to ongoing research perfecting our ability to predetermine the sex of children, and black women were much more likely than black men to do so. Black women were three times as likely as white women to give a high priority here (24% vs. 7%). Holding constant either age or church attendance on cross-tabulations made very little difference overall except to highlight the large proportion of black women, either aged 25 or over or attending church rarely, who have a high priority to research perfecting sex-predetermination. For the entire sample those who reported Catholic, Protestant, Fundamentalist or no religious background were more likely than Protestant Non-Fundamentalists or Jews to give such research high priority.

Women in all racial categories, regardless of age or amount of church attendance, were more likely than men to give high priority to research into sperm banking techniques. Female respondents of each racial category were also more likely than the males to give a high priority to research to perfect in vitro fertilization with embryo transplants. However, only among Latinos is the male / female difference a pronounced one, with these women of all ages four times as likely as their male counterparts to give a high priority here. Black, Latino, and Oriental woman were about twice as likely as their male counterparts to give a high priority to the development of artificial wombs (see Table 2). Furthermore, Latino women were almost

Table 2   Proportions giving a high research priority to reproductive technologies* by sex and race

Research area	Sex	N	White (1,363)	Black (210)	Latino (70)	Oriental (198)	Other (118)
					Race		
Sex predetermination	Males	(1,038)	8.9	18.2	10.3	10.3	13.4
	Females	(921)	7.2	24.3	9.7	12.5	11.8
Sperm Banking	Males	(1015)	21.9	21.1	25.1	12.2	21.9
	Females	(914)	29.2	29.7	30.0	30.9	14.9
Test tube conceptions implanted in mother	Males	(1006)	11.0	9.7	2.6	7.4	6.7
	Females	(894)	12.4	14.0	11.5	9.2	4.4
Artificial womb	Males	(968)	6.7	5.7	8.1	2.5	7.0
	Females	(850)	5.5	11.6	15.4	7.8	2.3
Cloning humans	Males	(1000)	3.1	6.5	5.1	0.0	1.6
	Females	(908)	.8	3.6	3.4	0.0	2.0

*Closed-ended responses allowed a choice of high, moderate, or low research priorities, prohibition of research, or no opinion.

three times as likely as Anglo women to give artificial wombs high priority.

Ongoing biomedical research into human cloning was rejected by all racial and both sex categories. Of the 188 Oriental respondents, none gave the research a high priority, and among Whites, Blacks and Latinos, women were less likely than men to give high priorities to research on cloning. Since these initial responses were gathered almost a year before the widespread publicity surrounding the Rorvik claim of an actual human clone, these responses were most often reflecting a first reaction to the possibility. In a more detailed series of questions on specific circumstances under which cloning might be acceptable (e.g. to reproduce a dead son or daughter, a genius, etc.) the lack of enthusiasm was pronounced under all circumstances mentioned, with only a slight increase acceptance in the case of cloning an individual to furnish spare parts for the respondent.

We are currently conducting a separate analysis which examines attitudinal variation by church affiliation and attentance. It is sufficient to note that when controls were introduced neither fundamentalist nor non-fundamentalist orientation nor church attendance patterns eliminated the differentials noted above. Controls for age of respondents also did not influence these response patterns.

Discussion

One of our most important findings is the degree to which our respondents felt that the general public should be involved in discussion and decision-making regarding genetic engineering (86%); such public involvement would logically take place *before* research dollars are allocated.

Some of the differences in male/female responses were surprising, particularly where females gave a higher priority than males to sperm banking research. We have thought of sperm banks as primarily advantageous to men in allowing a less fertile male to collect (and thus concentrate) sperm in order to increase the probability of conception by the female. However, women may see not only this advantage (when appropriate) but also the possible use of sperm banks with male sterilization (vasectomy) as a birth control convenience.

Also unexpected was the number of Latino women, a predominantly Catholic group, who gave artificial womb research high priority. These women, and Black women as well, have had traditionally high fertility, so perhaps they are more likely to appreciate the possibility of fetal development without the burden of pregnancy. Certainly these responses give rise to an interest in continued research on these issues.

Implications

Let's assume, for the sake of discussion, that these procedures will become reliable, inexpensive, and widely available. Why would women or men choose to use them, and what cumulative effect could individual decisions have on society as a whole? In particular, what impact could widespread use of these new alternatives have on the future of women?

Sex Preselection

Use of any one of the several techniques of sex selection would allow a person with a sex-linked hereditary defect to have a child of the no-risk sex and avoid having a child with the same defect. Couples who wanted to limit their families to two or three children, but who also wanted a sex mix, could stay within their limit by selecting the sex of the last to be born. Parents who prefer sons, as is true in many countries of the world (Williamson, 1976; Horn, 1974), could have them and not be burdened with less favored daughters. Parents who don't care too much about numbers or mix could have a first born son, as is frequently desired. Parents who might not care at all what sex their children were could still be persuaded to have a child of a particular sex by grandparents, aunts or uncles, or even older siblings of the child-to-be.

If fewer people are born who have serious sex-linked genetic defects (like hemophilia) the gene pool will be cleaner and the costs to individuals and society will be less. It should be noted, however, that while offspring actually afflicted with such hereditary diseases need not be born, the children that *are* born to such parents may still be carriers of the defect. An increase in the number of these carriers could have a long term "dirtying" effect on the gene pool.

Parents who can choose the sex of their offspring are likely to have smaller families. Past studies have shown that parents with children of the same sex are more likely to have an additional child than are those who have already achieved a sex mix (Bumpass and Westoff, 1970, p. 93). In some societies we know that parents prefer many sons but few, if any, daughters. Indeed, one reason for explosive population growth in some of these societies is a result of efforts to have a desired number of sons. By enabling such parents to have as many sons as they wish and at the same time avoid having unwanted daughters, we should expect to see smaller-sized families. Sex preselection, then, could do a great deal to alleviate the population explosion. But what happens in the next generation? Presumably, these sons will want to marry and produce sons of their own, but who will they marry? The shrewd parents who have produced a lot of daughters will be in a nice bargaining position; any commodity that becomes scarce is given a higher value. Perhaps we would see an upgrading in the status of women that would lead to a new set of values whereby daughters were more highly regarded. Meanwhile, we might expect that the excess of males would increase such problems as gang delinquency, criminality and violence. It could also lead to an increase in homosexuality as availability of female sex partners diminished.

In societies where parents already prefer a sex mix we might see more subtle implications of sex preselection. First-born children have been found to be more independent, more motivated, and more achieving. If very many parents want their first-born to be male, this could serve to reinforce and perpetuate the traditional male-female sex stereotypes.

Ideally, if children are loved, sex should not make a difference—yet we assume that parents want a sex mix because boys and girls are different from one another. The strength of the desire to use sex preselection techniques could be one indicator of the extent of the preference.

Women and men who wish true equality between the sexes must be made aware of these various possibilities if they are to make wise decisions about using such a technique.

Sperm Banking

Probably the least controversial use of the preservation of spermatozoa is when a husband of low fertility is able to have enough of his own sperm collected and stored to eventually impregnate his wife by artificial insemination (AIH). In cases of extremely low sperm count, the husband's sperm can be mixed with that of a matched donor. When the wife becomes pregnant, both may believe that the husband is the biological father.

As shelf life of spermatozoa is extended, a combination of sperm storage and vasectomy may become the preferred (as it is the least hazardous) method of birth control. Males might also choose to routinely bank their sperm simply as a form of insurance; others may bank it prior to entering jobs that deal with radiation or other mutagenic substances. Sperm banking on a widespread basis could also allow prospective mothers or couples to choose artificial insemination using the sperm of a donor (AID) for reasons not connected to fertility problems. Individual women, or lesbian couples, could avoid heterosexual intercourse yet still become mothers if they so desired. Husbands with hereditary defects might join their wives in choosing AID to avoid passing on particular genetic problems. Parents might want to use a high-IQ donor in hopes of giving their child a better intellectual potential. The sperm of donors might be chosen for a variety of other characteristics: physique, eye or hair color, particular talents, such as artistic or musical, and so forth. The choice of a specific donor might become popular (e.g., an Einstein, an Elvis). A Hitler or an Idi Amin might choose to make his sperm widely available—what better proof of patriotism than for couples to allow him to really be the father of his country? Leaders of some religious cults could also see this process as a true test of faith. In a monarchy, particularly loyal subjects could be rewarded by allowing their children to be of royal "blood."

If multiple use is made of one donor, will records have to be kept in order to avoid eventual incest? Or will such interbreeding of "superior" or "selected" stock be desired? How, by whom, and to whom will access to such sperm be made? Will economics prevail or will prospective users be chosen by lot? Many legal and ethical problems have already risen with regard to AID: questions of the child's legitimacy, child support and inheritance rights, and even the doctor's liability (see Kinney, 1977). Many more challenges may be expected as the technique expands in its applications.

Although women will have an increasingly wide choice in the use of donor sperm, the more complex technology of test tube conception and embryo transplant will be required if ova banking is to be useful. Meanwhile, current attention is given only to male donor characteristics, or the possible matching of these with characteristics of the prospective mother of her husband.

Test Tube Conception and Embryo Transplant

After many years of research this technique has successfully overcome a not uncommon fertility problem—blocked or surgically removed Fallopian tubes. The technique also opens up the possible use of a surrogate mother, one who receives the implant and carries the baby to term but who has not herself contributed any hereditary material to it. The advantages of a womb-for-rent are several: women for whom pregnancy is a real health hazard, or those who have had a series of miscarriages or stillbirths, could have their own ova combined with their husband's sperm in the laboratory—the resulting child would be a genetic offspring, even though carried to term by another woman. Another possibility arises for women who do not wish to pass on some of their own deleterious genes. They could use donor ova (perhaps from a nonaffected sister) and husband's sperm, with the resultant embryo transplanted into the wife's womb. In addition, those women who did not wish to become pregnant for career reasons (movie stars, women physicists working with radiation) could also avail themselves of the technique.

What of the woman who chooses to become a surrogate mother? She could have many reasons to enter this new role: financial reward, the pleasure of pregnancy and childbirth without the burden of raising a child, possibly a means of status (a good breeder?). Could this be a possible form of employment for the mentally retarded, or therapy for the emotionally disturbed? One can imagine what a fertile field this would be for lawyers: contracts to cover all parties and all contingencies; public health regulations, standards, and laws to be enacted. Who decides on the availability of this technique? What rights and obligations do each of the parties (including the child) have?

Artificial Wombs

The use of artificial wombs is not likely to be achieved in the near future due to both the tremendous complexity and the relative lack of data about the human placenta. If and when such a technique were to become a reality, it would remove the necessity of pregnancy for the entire gestational period. What would be the advantages? It would reduce the risk of all side effects (e.g. morning sickness) related to maternity; reduce maternal mortality; eliminate the inconvenience of being pregnant; and it would be a profound technological achievement. It would eliminate all risks to the fetus from the mother's use of cigarettes or drugs, risk from Rh incompatibility, etc. It could also possibly provide the "best" prenatal environment (optimum safety for the child, comfort, constant monitoring for distress, etc.). This technique, with the use of "superior" ova and sperm, could provide a "superior" person, or even a breed.

The financial costs of the procedure could be enormous. However, we can make a good case for putting research dollars into this area: we would learn a great deal more than we now know as to what constitutes the best possible prenatal environment—the physical (conditions of gravity, warmth, darkness), biological (chemistry of the mother, placenta; hormone interplay), psychological (mood changes, emotional states of the mother and child). An artificial womb might save the life of an extremely premature child, or it might be used to grow embryos to a larger, perhaps better, size for transplant.

Cloning

If cloning can be done, it no doubt will be done. If nothing else, better data will be generated for the never-ending heredity vs. environment debate. Future scenarios are endless: an individual could clone him or herself and raise the child as a son or daughter, even though it would really be a genetic twin. Lovers could clone each other, hoping that their perfect love would go on and on. Families could clone a favorite relative, perhaps a dying one, and perhaps even replace a dead child. A dictator could clone himself (for loyal followers) or could clone a soldier-hero (for a superior army); a king could clone himself to be his own heir, or he could clone the natural heir and have organ replacements for the original in case of accident. The idea of cloning a whole person in order to have spare parts is, or should be, unthinkable for most people. But research into cloning might show ways to clone only the parts themselves; that reason alone might make research into this area worthwhile.

Conclusion

The possibilities raised by these newly available (or about to be developed) techniques of reproduction may frighten the tradition-bound mind. Yet, just as the techniques of birth control have moved from early condemnation to widespread acceptance and abortion has become increasingly acceptable, some of these technologies, if not all, will be viewed as increasing the choices open to women and men. And, just as birth control and abortion have facilitated the gradual liberation of women, some of these technologies will aid in the liberating process over time.

Birth control allowed a movement from the accidental nature of pregnancy to planned parenthood, with "every child a wanted child." Similarly, the new technologies increase the planning potential. Yet, detailed planning of the characteristics of one's offspring may be more than human beings are psychologically ready to handle. If a choice is available as to particular characteristics of a child-to-be, those making such a choice are doing so on the basis of definite expectations. Whether or not these expectations will be met cannot be known in advance. Parents who want a child of a particular sex today, when methods of preselection are simply not reliable, often are disappointed initially when the child is born the "wrong" sex, but they generally manage to make the best of it. What if the sex, or other characteristics, of the child could be predetermined, yet the parents were still dissatisfied with the particular child? Will they still make the best of it? What of the child, who, in spite of being tailored to fit, still cannot fulfill the parents' boundless expectations and feels unwanted?

Some applications of the new techniques are quite valid, especially those that allow previously infertile couples to bear children, children who are very much wanted. Other applications may seem frivolous, and some are totally unacceptable. The question is, of course, who is going to be making the decisions about which techniques will be perfected and who will be allowed to use them? Women in particular should address themselves to this: men, who now do most of the biomedical research and pass nearly all the laws, must not be allowed to do so without input from the women who will be profoundly affected by the application of such technology.

We have just begun to explore the future possibilities in the use of the new reproductive technologies. It is important to expand the concern with, and discussion about, the new techniques before the future is upon us.

REFERENCES

All about that baby. *Newsweek,* August 7, 1978, pp. 80–83.
BUMPASS, L., & WESTOFF, C. *The later years of childbearing.* Princeton, N.J.: Princeton University Press, 1970.
COBB, J. C. Public involvement in scientific decision-making. *Science,* 1976, *194,* 674.
ENGLISH, D. S. Genetic manipulation: past, present, future. In N. C. Ostheimer & J. M. Ostheimer (Eds.), *Life or death—who controls?* New York: Springer, 1976.
ETZIONI, A. *Genetic fix.* New York: Macmillan, 1973.
FRANCOEUR, R. *Utopian motherhood.* London: George Allen & Unwin, 1971.
FRANKEL, C. The specter of eugenics. *Commentary,* March 1974, pp. 25–33.
HANDLER, P. *Biology and the future of man.* New York: Oxford University Press, 1970.
HARTLEY, S. F., & PIETRACZYK, L. M. Pre-selecting the sex of offspring: Technologies, attitudes and implications. *Social Biology* 1979, 26:232–246.
HORN, P. Parents still prefer boys. *Psychology Today,* August 1974, pp. 29–30.
HOWARD, T. and RIFKIN, J. *Who should play god?* New York: Dell, 1977.
KINNEY, L. H. Legal issues of the new reproductive technologies. *California State Bar Journal,* 1977, *52–6,* 514–519.
LUBS, H. A., & LUBS, M. Genetic disorders. In G. N. Burrow & T. S. Ferris (Eds.), *Medical complications during pregnancy,* Philadelphia: Saunders, 1975.
MARX, J. L. Embryology: Out of the womb—into the test tube. *Science,* 1973, *183,* 811–814.
MCCANDLESS, B. R. *Children: Behavior and development.* New York: Holt, Rinehart and Winston, 1976.
MILUNSKY, A. *The prenatal diagnosis of hereditary disorders.* Springfield, Ill: Charles C. Thomas, 1973.
MULLER, H. J. *Man's future birthright.* Albany: SUNY Press, 1973
National Research Council Committee for the Study of Inborn Errors of Metabolism. *Genetic*

screening: Programs, principles, and research. Washington, D.C.: National Academy of Sciences, 1975.

RORVIK, D. M. *In his image, the cloning of a man.* New York: Lippincott, 1978.

TAYLOR, G. R. *The biological time bomb.* New York: World Publishing Co., 1968.

WESTOFF, C. and RINDFUSS, R. Sex preselection in the U.S.: Some implications. *Science*, 1974, *184*, 633–636.

WILLIAMSON, N. E. *Sons or daughters.* Beverly Hills: Sage Publications, 1976.

25

The Psychosocial Factors of the Abortion Experience
A Critical Review

Lisa Roseman Shusterman

The literature on the psychosocial factors of abortion is critically reviewed. It is concluded that due to faulty methodology no general statements can be made about these factors for women receiving illegal abortions. It appears that the data showing that women receiving therapeutic abortions experienced favorable psychological consequences are stronger than the data indicating negative consequences. Studies of abortion on request, which, for the most part, have been methodologically sound, indicate that the new abortion patients are mostly young, unmarried women who are not in a social position to bear and care for a child. They tend to end their pregnancies for social and economic reasons. Further, they are either not aware of or not concerned about the possibility of getting pregnant at the time of intercourse, or they have a contraceptive failure. Finally, the psychological consequences of abortion on request appear to be mostly benign.

Abortion is the termination of pregnancy before the developing embryo or fetus can exist independently. Abortion may be either spontaneous or induced. Spontaneous abortion is the natural death of the embryo or fetus, while induced abortion is the intentional removal of the embryo or fetus. The present review deals mainly with the psychosocial factors of the induced abortion experience.

The role of women in society is in great flux and many of the greatest changes concern women's fertility. In order to understand the nature of these changes and their implications, the psychosocial aspects of abortion must be explored and charted. The woman who interrupts her pregnancy is the central figure in the abortion, and her attitudes, feelings, and behavior in regard to abortion are not well understood. Not only should the psychology of abortion be understood for the sake of knowledge itself, but also so that informed social decisions about abortion can be made.

"The Psychosocial Factors of the Abortion Experience: A Critical Review" by Lisa R. Shusterman in *The Psychology of Women Quarterly*, 1, 1 (1976), 79–106. Reprinted by permission of the Human Sciences Press.

The present paper is a comprehensive review of what has been written about the psychosocial aspects of abortion. There are several recent reviews which deal with one or two aspects of the abortion experience (Simon & Senturia, 1966; Peck & Marcus, 1966; Walter, 1970; Whitman, 1971; Osofsky, Osofsky, & Rajan, 1971), but this paper considers many abortion issues: (a) demographic characteristics of those obtaining abortion, (b) the public's opinion about abortion, (c) the reasons why aborting women have unwanted pregnancies, (d) the motivations of women seeking abortion, and (e) the medical and psychological sequelae of abortion. Since issues (b), (c), and (d) are relevant before the abortion, they can be considered antecedent variables, while (e) constitutes a consequent variable.

This review evaluates the quality of the research on the psychosocial factors of abortion. As would be expected, the more recent studies are better methodologically than the earlier studies. Much of the literature is so poor it can be dismissed on the basis of gross methodological problems, e.g., biased samples and unreliable measurements. The critical analysis here varies with the quality of the studies. More sophisticated critiques can be made of the newer research. The better studies allow for more detailed analyses and demand closer attention because their conclusions can be taken more seriously.

Demographic Characteristics of Those Obtaining Abortion

In this section a summary is presented of the demographic characteristics of the women in each of three groups (a) those who received illegal abortions, (b) those who received therapeutic abortions under restrictive laws, and (c) those who received abortions on request.

Estimates of the number of illegal abortions that occurred in the United States and descriptions of the characteristics of the women who obtained illegal abortions have been difficult to make. Estimates of the number of illegal abortions ranged from 20,000 to 1,500,000 per year prior to 1970 (Calderone, 1958; Lader, 1966; Pipel & Norwick, 1969; Chisolm, 1970). According to Steinhoff, Diamond, Palmore, and Smith (1973), most of the women getting illegal abortions were single, young, middle class, and primaparous.

Before 1970, abortion was illegal in all states except to preserve the life of the pregnant woman. Estimates of the number of therapeutic abortions performed in the United States ranged from 10,000 per year (Lee, 1969; Newman, 1973) to 18,000 per year (Hefferman, 1953; Moore-Cavar, 1974). Women who received therapeutic abortions have been said to be mostly middle-aged, wealthy, and highly educated white women with completed families (Calderone, 1958; Gebhard, Pomeroy & Martin, 1958; Gold, Erhard, & Jacobziner, 1965; Lader, 1966; Peck & Marcus, 1966; Newman, Beck, & Lewit, 1971). However, statements about the characteristics of therapeutic abortion patients are not very reliable for a number of reasons. First, since there were different indications for legal abortions in different states, composite statistics made up of women obtaining therapeutic abortions for extremely diverse reasons are difficult to interpret. Second, the records may have been falsified or distorted (Lader, 1966) so that women with less than technically legal indications could have their pregnancies ended.

Unlike data on the two previous groups of aborting women, data on the women receiving abortion on request are highly reliable. According to Moore-Čavar (1974), in 1972, with legal abortions available in several states, 586,000 abortions were legally induced in the United States. It has been concluded that, in contrast to past legal abortion patients, the recent ones are more likely to be young, single, and primaparous (Duffy, 1971; Pakter & Nelson, 1971; Rovinsky, 1971; Tietze & Lewit, 1972; Steinhoff, *et al.*, 1973). However, Steinhoff, (1973) deduced from Hawaii figures that "when both the age distribution and the probability of pregnancy are taken into consideration, it becomes apparent that women at the two ends of the fertile age range are more likely to terminate a pregnancy by abortion than those in the 25–35 age group" (p. 17). The Hawaii researchers conclude that "the women who utilize legal abortion now, but would not have sought illegal abortion, are primarily older, married women, who already have children. The rest [are] women who would have utilized illegal abortion, plus a substantial number of young women who would have married and begun their families earlier" (Steinhoff *et al.*, 1973, p. 10).

Data on the ethno-racial make-up of the population of women obtaining abortions are available by state; national statistics are unavailable. Statistics indicate that the number of legal abortions per 1000 live births was higher for blacks than for whites in California, Colorado, Delaware, Kansas, Maryland, and New York, although this was not true for Alaska, Arkansas, Georgia, North Carolina, and South Carolina (Pakter & Nelson, 1971; Tietze, 1973; Steinhoff, 1973; Moore-Čavar, 1974).

In Hawaii it has been reported that the recent patients tend to be more highly educated than women in the population at large (Steinhoff, 1973). In that state, for example, over 80 percent of the abortion patients had completed high school and more than 50 percent had been educated beyond high school (Smith, Diamond, & Palmore, 1973). Researchers in Hawaii also concluded that the upper income groups are not over-represented in the abortion population as they were reported to be in abortion populations prior to abortion on request (Smith, *et al.*, 1973; Steinhoff, 1971). Such a conclusion, of course, needs to be verified in other states and samples.

The Abortion Situation in Foreign Countries

Since many of the abortion studies have been conducted in countries other than the United States, the facts of the abortion situation in several foreign countries are presented.

In Sweden, where most of the foreign studies on the psychology of abortion have been conducted, the abortion law has been fairly liberal since 1938. Abortion during the first twenty weeks of pregnancy is legal on socio-medical, humanitarian, and eugenic grounds (Shaw, 1968), including possible strain on the pregnant woman in rearing her child (Pohlman, 1969). However, in Sweden a substantial number of women seeking legal abortions are refused, and it has been suggested that there are as many or more illegal abortions in that country than legal ones (Ekbald, 1954). Many of the women getting illegal abortions in Sweden have been said to be young, single women (Gebhard *et al.* 1958), the same type of women who, according to Steinhoff *et al.* (1973), had been getting most of the illegal abortions in the United States.

The legality of abortion and the rate of illegal abortion in Denmark is similar to that in Sweden (Gebhard *et al.*, 1958). In the Soviet Union, Hungary, Czechoslovakia, and Japan, abortion for any indication has been legal since the mid 1950's.

Antecedents of Abortion

Public Opinion

National opinion surveys of the last decade indicate that the American public generally has approved of abortion under certain circumstances (threat to the woman's life or health, incest, rape or possible fetal deformity), but has disapproved of abortion available on request (Shaw, 1968; Moore-Čavar, 1974). Moore-Čavar (1974) concluded from statistics compiled from 27 studies that in the United States more liberal attitudes are associated with higher education and single marital status. Jews and Protestants are more favorable toward abortion than are Catholics, and males more than females. Further, she states that the findings on the relationship between occupation, income, socio-economic status, race, and age are inconsistent. In a study of currently married women, Miller (1973) found that attitudes toward abortion are not related to a woman's age, the size of her family, the experience of unwanted children, or intentions to have additional children.

It is quite likely that public attitudes toward abortion affect the attitudes and behavior of women who terminate their pregnancies. For instance, it is probably more difficult for a woman to commit an act that is condemned by most of society than an act that is condoned by society. The dynamics of how and to what extent publicly held views influence the decisions and experiences of women needs to be investigated.

Why Aborting Women Have Unwanted Pregnancies

There are many possible reasons why aborting women have unwanted pregnancies. Miller (1973) assessed these reasons directly. A sample of women who were obtaining abortions on request were asked to complete Miller's Contraceptive Sexual Attitude Questionnaire (CSAQ), a list of 53 possible reasons for unwanted pregnancy derived from interviews with physicians and social workers who worked with women applying for abortion or seeking contraceptive advice. On the CSAQ each respondent was asked to check any item which may have played a role in her pregnancy. The sample were mostly young, never married, white, middle- and upper-middle class, private patients.

Miller concluded that several factors were responsible for the unwanted pregnancies of a large proportion of these women. The first factor he referred to as "retrospective rhythm," where the woman "rationalizes the safety of a particular act of sexual intercourse" after it is over. In fact, only a few of the women who reported that they thought they were in a safe period actually knew anything about ovulation and fertility cycles. At the time of conception, 54 percent of the women reported using no form of contraception, 14 percent reported using rhythm, and the rest reported using various kinds of contraceptive devices. Diamond, Steinhoff, Palmore, and Smith (1973) also reported that many of the married women seeking abortions in Hawaii said they did not use birth control because they thought they were in a safe period. Many of the young, single women in the Hawaii population expected intercourse but did not use birth control because they did not want to seem prepared for sex. In that same population, single, unattached women used birth control the least, followed by single women going steady, and then by women living with a man or married.

Another reason for unwanted pregnancy defined by Miller was contraceptive failure, which was indicated as the reason for pregnancy by one-third of the respondents. The accuracy of the women's testimony with regard to contraceptive failure was found to be quite high, as verified by interviewing a subset of 328 respondents and judging whether contraceptive failure or contraceptive misuse had actually occurred. Approximately 19 percent of the aborting women in Hawaii also attributed their pregnancy to birth control failures (Diamond *et al.*, 1973). A third factor was misuse or fear of certain contraceptives, and a fourth factor was denial or refusal to recognize the possibility of getting pregnant.

Miller also found that demographic variables were related to reasons for unwanted pregnancy. Married women, women with higher education, and women with previous induced abortions reported more contraceptive failures than other women, and women with higher education were more likely to be afraid of the side effects of certain contraceptives. In Miller's sample, Catholic women living with their parents were the most likely to get pregnant because they felt such matters as contraception were unimportant in view of their overwhelming love for their partners. High income non-Catholics, living at home, were the most accepting of abortion as a way of coping with an unwanted pregnancy. In a related study, McCormick (1973) concluded that in a group of women seeking abortion, black women are less accepting than white women of abortion as either a primary or a secondary way to control fertility.

The bulk of Miller's data came from the CSAQ responses. Miller reported that the validity of the CSAQ was substantiated by several results: the logical and easily interpretable response patterns in the regression analysis, the accuracy of the reports on contraceptive failure, and the lack of relationship between contraceptive failure and denial, rationalization, or impulsiveness. The CSAQ appears to be a fairly useful method of assessing the way in which women account for their own unwanted pregnancies and is representative of the focus on conscious reasons for unwanted pregnancy.

In much of the older literature, unconscious, psychopathological motivations have been assumed to play a significant role in unwanted pregnancy, although such reasons were endorsed infrequently in Miller's study. Traditionally, women with unwanted pregnancies were said to be manipulative, sado-masochistic, compulsive conceivers, and afraid of disapproval (Deutsch, 1945; Romm, 1954; Bolter, 1962). These conclusions were based solely on the writers' uncorroborated clinical opinion and should not be seen as scientifically founded deductions.

In more recent investigations of unconscious motives for unwanted pregnancy, Simon, Rothman, Goff, and Senturia (1969) and Ford, Castelnuevo-Tedesco, and Long (1972) concluded that women obtaining therapeutic abortions have marked emotional conflict about their female identity and reproductive role and end the pregnancy to satisfy sado-masochistic impulses. Simon *et al.* compared 46 women who obtained therapeutic abortions with 32 women who had spontaneous abortions. Ford *et al.* compared 40 women seeking therapeutic abortion with 52 pregnant women not seeking abortion. Both studies relied on pre-abortion MMPI scores. Since these conclusions were based on pre-abortion data in which women were trying to convince an abortion committee that their mental health was endangered by the pregnancy, the picture presented of women seeking abortions is probably misleading. Since these women were aware that they had to demonstrate their psychopathology as a result of the pregnancy, it appears likely that the pre-abortion assessments of the women reflect the women's attempt to appear as unstable as possible. In fact, Ford *et al.* (1972) reported that women seeking therapeutic abortions had elevated F scale scores on the MMPI which might indicate "intentional exaggeration of symptoms."

Abernathy (1973) also was interested in unconscious motives. She tested the hypothesis that a woman who aborts had assumed elements of her mother's role in the family during adolescence because her mother was alienated from her daughter. Women (N = 65, average age = 28 years) who had an abortion were compared with matched controls who were judged to be effective users of contraception. Two independent judges rated the extent of "role redefinition in the family of origin," assigning each woman a score from 1 to 6 where 1 is high role-redefinition, including an overt incestuous relationship with the father and dating the father, and 6 is normal assignment of roles within the family.

Abernathy reported several differences between the two groups. Women who had obtained induced abortions were more likely to be rated high on role redefinition. They were more likely to have assumed household and child-caring responsibilities in their teens, were more likely to be intimate with men than women, were more sexually precocious, and were more likely to recall that their parents were often hostile to one another than the controls. Abernathy concludes

> that a daughter both fosters and can be the victim of a weak parental coalition, and that because of attraction to the father and alienation from the mother she may be willing to substitute for the maternal figure in domestic spheres and in providing companionship for the father. However, her feelings may then become disturbing because of the excessive intimacy of the ensuing relationship with the father and anxiety may be augmented to the extent that the mother is not warm and supportive. This pressure together with low-self-esteem appear to be major factors in predisposing a woman to risk unwanted pregnancy. (p. 350)

There are a number of problems with Abernathy's methodology that make the conclusions of little value. First, the 1-to-6 scale assumes unidimensionality. However, there are actually two dimensions to the scale which are confounded in the measurement. The two dimensions are the sexual attraction to the father and the assumption of the instrumental mother role. The scale as it was used implies that the two components covary such that if a woman is high on one then she will be high on the other. The scale does not allow for the likely possibility of a woman who was forced by external circumstances to adopt a mother role in the family but who has a very traditional daughter relationship with the father. Second, it may be that the woman's role redefinition score was actually a measure of how disclosing she was about her early history and her feelings about her parents. It seems reasonable that women who admit to abortion are generally more open about themselves and thus revealed certain thoughts or feelings that might have led to a high role-redefinition score. On the other hand, the low role-redefinition scores of the controls may have just indicated a tendency to not reveal intimate feelings. If the controls were more likely to receive high scores, then many may have scored "5," which is "lack of information contrary to normalcy, so it is assumed." Thus an absence of overt role redefinition is classified as normal role development but may really represent nondisclosure of early history.

An additional problem with the Abernathy study is that it assumes that women have some control over unwanted pregnancy. However, given the high percentage of women who have contraceptive failure, the conclusion that adolescent experiences predict unwanted pregnancy would seem to be quite limited.

Why women have unwanted pregnancies should be studied in relation to the woman's decision to have an abortion and the consequences of the abortion procedure. It may be, for example, that women who have unwanted pregnancies because of contraceptive failure have less severe reactions to abortion than women who failed to contracept because they were afraid of how it would appear to their partner. The former may feel less responsible for the pregnancy. Further research might also explore personality correlates of unwanted pregnancy.

Why Women Have Abortions

A review of the literature indicates that the reasons for inducing abortion are different for women who obtained therapeutic abortions under restrictive laws, women who obtained illegal abortions, and women who obtain abortions on request.

Before liberalization of the abortion laws, legal "therapeutic" abortions could be performed for (a) medical indications and (b) psychiatric indications. Since 1950's, the major philosophy regarding medical indications has been that abortion is unnecessary unless pregnancy intensifies the illness (Spivak, 1967). Most sources conclude that the strictly biological reasons for abortion have been declining (Schur, 1955; Routledge, Sparling, & McFarlan 1953; Rosen, 1967; Peel & Potts, 1969). Opinion varies as to what constitutes a medical indication for termination of pregnancy. Frequently cited indications are heart disease, lung disease, kidney disease, malignancy, chorea, ostosclerosis, syphilis, abdominal emergencies, and obstetric and gynecological conditions (Peel & Potts, 1969).

Although the frequency of abortions for medical indications has been decreasing, the frequency of abortions for psychiatric indications had been increasing until psychiatric requirements were dropped with legalization of abortion on request (Schur, 1955; Christakos, 1970). Prior to the broadening of the laws, the only legal psychiatric reason for granting abortion was to prevent a pregnant woman from committing suicide. Rosen (1967) commented that although psychiatrists received many suicidal threats from pregnant women "the suicide rate among pregnant women is less than what would statistically be expected for the population as a whole" (p. 83). However, he also pointed out that "eight percent of all women who committed suicide in Sweden during the twenty-year period from 1925 through 1945 . . . were found on autopsy to be pregnant, and in each case, on investigation, their pregnancy was felt to be the precipitating factor in the suicide" (p. 83). Because of such ambiguity about the real threat of suicide in pregnant women, it had been difficult for American psychiatrists and hospital abortion committees to decide what constituted legitimate psychiatric indications for abortion (Lader, 1966; Rosen, 1967). And since there were no standarized abortion screening practices (Whitman, 1971), a woman could be refused abortion by one hospital and granted abortion by another.

Many authors have asserted that any woman who wants an abortion is necessarily, by reason of her want, emotionally ill (Galdston, 1958; Dunbar, 1954; Bolter, 1962). The only empirical support for such notions comes from an unpublished study cited by Whitman (1971) in which therapeutic abortion applicants scored higher on several MMPI scales than maternity patients. However, the differences were not statistically significant in most cases. In addition, the MMPI scores may have been affected by the abortion applicants' stressful state rather than their general psychopathology. In fact, Ford et al. (1972) and Brody, Meikle, and Gerritse (1971) offer evidence that pre-abortion psychological distress can be attributed to the woman's situation and not to any lasting emotional problems. Kane, Lacherbruch, and Lipton (1973) also found that abortion patients are no more neurotic than a comparable group of nonpregnant women, as measured by the Neuroticism Scale Questionnaire. However, the women who were ending pregnancies were reported to be more anxious than those in the comparison group. Kane et al. suggest that high anxiety is due to waiting for the procedure. In light of these writings, it appears unreasonable to conclude that women seeking abortion are emotionally unstable.

In contrast to what has been written about women seeking therapeutic abortions, women who obtained illegal abortions have been said to be concerned mostly about how a baby would affect their lives and the lives of people they cared about, and about the social stigma of being an unwed mother (Lee, 1969). Lee (1969) found that single women who had an illegal abortion terminated their pregnancies because they did not want to be forced into marriage, or because they did not want the responsibility of caring for a child. Engaged or cohabitating women aborted because they did not want to begin a marriage with pregnancy, and married women because they thought a new child would cause or add to family and marital problems, or because they felt too old to raise a baby. Finally, Lee found that divorced or separated women aborted because they felt they could not afford to raise a child. Lee's sample may have been biased since she located her respondents through personal contacts.

Recent research indicates the women receiving abortion on request are aborting for reasons similar to those reasons reported for women seeking illegal abortions before liberalization of the laws. According to the Hawaii studies, women decide to terminate their pregnancies "based on evaluation of objective factors related to the woman's perceived capacity to care for the child" (Steinhoff *et al.*, 1972; Smith *et al.*, 1973). In addition, situational and demographic variables, such as financial status, education, career plans, marital status, and age, were found to be extremely important in determining whether or not a particular pregnancy will be aborted (Steinhoff *et al.*, 1972; Smith *et al.*, 1973).

For example, according to Steinhoff *et al.* (1972), young, single women abort to delay marriage and family, while older, married women abort to prevent their existing family from getting any bigger. In comparison with maternity patients, "women who abort their first pregnancy tend to have become pregnant at an earlier age than those who carry their first pregnancy to term" (Steinhoff *et al.*, 1972). Also, since a large proportion of the Hawaii abortion population is students, while a large proportion of the maternity population is housewives, Steinhoff *et al.* (1972) concluded that "a much higher proportion of maternity patients are already in the occupational position most easily adapted to childbirth and infant care, while a higher proportion of abortion patients are committed to activities outside the home" (p. 5). Also, although over half of the aborting women in Hawaii were reportedly involved in a continuing relationship with a man, it was felt that "women who carry their pregnancy to term seem to have relatively stable family situations into which to bring children, while abortion tends to be chosen by women who do not have those family conditions." In general, the researchers of the Hawaii abortion population concluded that "at the individual level as well as in the overall group comparisons, the reason women give for choosing abortion appear to reflect a fair appraisal of their capacity to provide a satisfactory home for a child" (Steinhoff, *et al.*, 1972).

A variety of methods were used by the Hawaii Pregnancy, Birth Control, and Abortion Study group, including extensive interviews, self-administered questionnaires, and medical charts. The Hawaii studies are all methodologically sophisticated and might well be used as examples for other large scale studies of the psychology of abortion.

Consequences of Abortion

Medical Sequelae

Medical complications of abortion vary with the length of gestation of the pregnancy, the physical condition of the pregnant women, and the method of inducing abortion. The earlier the pregnancy, the better the physical condition of the woman, and the more medically appropriate the abortion procedure, the less likely there will be physical complications (Tietze, 1969; Cushner, 1971; Smith *et al.*, 1973). Also, there is a greater risk of complications for women who have had a previous abortion (Pohlman, 1969). Some of the possible complications of abortion are infection, hemorrhage, perforation, sterility, or risk to subsequent pregnancies (Peel & Potts, 1969).

Before liberalization of the laws, estimates of the mortality rates of women receiving illegal abortions were difficult to make. According to many reports, however, mortality and morbidity rates have been declining and generally there is less risk associated with abortion than with childbirth (Tietze & Lehfeldt, 1961; Lader, 1966; Peel & Potts, 1969; Pipel & Norwick, 1969; Cushner, 1971; Newman, 1973).

Psychological Sequelae

The literature on the psychological effects of induced abortion is quite contradictory: many studies conclude that there are severe psychological consequences; many conclude that there are mild or no consequences, and some conclude that the consequences vary with other factors. Some people have taken the stand that because there are so many divergent results, the after-effects of abortion remain unknown (Population Study Commission, 1966; Newman et al., 1971).

The contradictory results are attributable to methodological differences, differences in the variables investigated, sample differences, and theoretical differences. Many of the conclusions have been drawn from shoddy or nonexistent data. Investigations of the psychological sequelae must be examined separately for the therapeutic abortion population, the illegal abortion population, and the abortion on request population. Several recent reviews of the effects of abortion can be found in Peck and Marcus (1966), Simon, Senturia, and Rothman (1967), Osofsky et al. (1971), and Osofsky and Osofsky (1972).

Several investigations, based on women obtaining legal, therapeutic abortions, concluded that the psychological sequelae of abortion were unfavorable. One of the earliest investigations was conducted by Hesseltine, Adair, and Boynton (1940). Through psychiatric records they assessed the outcome of the therapeutic abortions of 82 women after a time period ranging from one to eight years. For 21 women, the outcome was judged to be "satisfactory" ("improved"), for 22 "unchanged," for 3 "unsatisfactory," and for 35 "undetermined." Although so few women actually were judged to be worse for the abortion, and despite the number of women said to be improved, the authors concluded that abortion was very rarely necessary. Further, the exact manner in which evaluations of psychiatric material were made was not reported, and the large number of "undetermined" outcomes was unexplained (Simon & Senturia, 1966). Also, the possible sample biases and the quite variable time spans between the abortion and the assessment are other problems. Therefore, this study is of little value.

The second major study in which unfavorable emotional sequelae of abortion were reported was the Ebaugh and Heuser (1947) investigation. From evaluations of 29 women, they state that feelings of guilt, self-depreciation, and hostility toward one's male partner were the after-effects of abortion. However, since so little of their methodology was presented, it is difficult to evaluate their conclusions.

Wilson and Cain (1951) set out to investigate the consequences of therapeutic abortion of the 226 women who had received them between 1930 and 1949 at a particular medical facility. However, they were able to interview only nine of these women in the follow-up. Two of the women said they felt a loss and felt guilty about the abortion. Four women complained of minor physical discomfort that they felt was related to the abortion. Wilson and Cain concluded that "abortion, regardless of how early it occurs, or whether it is spontaneous or induced, is not without lasting effects and the emotional response may be deep and lasting" (p. 22). This conclusion seems to have been based on the sequelae of two women out of a self-selected group of nine women and to have been overgeneralized to all aborting women. However, in a following study, Wilson (1952) arrived at a different evaluation of the effects of abortion. He interviewed 25 women who had had either a therapeutic, illegal, or spontaneous abortion and concluded only that the consequences of abortion vary with the period of gestation of the pregnancy and the personality of the woman. In addition, Wilson did not use an appropriate comparison group in either study. As Sherman (1975) points out, the appropriate comparison group for abortion patients is women with unwanted pregnancies who deliver at full term.

Using a different approach, Hefferman and Lynch (1953) evaluated the psychology of abortion from questionnaires received from 152 of 367 hospital administrators. Although they did not assess the psychological sequelae directly, they deduced that guilt, disgust, and negative feelings toward one's male partner are the consequences of abortion. Since the data was not gathered from primary care-takers of abortion patients and since the authors appear to have had a strong anti-abortion bias prior to data collection, the value of the study is doubtful.

In Rosen's (1954) compilation of essays on abortion, which had a major impact on the field, three articles strongly argued that abortion leads to adverse psychological reactions. Romm (1954), Dunbar (1954), and Lidz (1954) wrote that the effects of abortion are severe conscious or unconscious guilt, anger toward the male partner, reactivation of the female castration fear, reactive depression, and, in extreme cases, psychosis. The authors' conclusions were based on their own clinical experiences which are subject to reliability and validity problems and, thus, the conclusions have limited scientific worth. However, clinical opinion has constituted much of the literature on the psychology of abortion (Galdston, 1958; Bolter, 1962).

A number of studies of the psychological consequences of therapeutic abortion were conducted in other countries. Malmfors (1958) determined the effect of abortion on 84 Swedish women two years after the abortion had occurred. He concluded that 39 of the women were pleased about the abortion, 4 were unwilling to discuss it, 9 were repressing guilt about it, 22 were openly expressing guilt, and 10 were psychologically impaired because of it. Of those who were granted abortions for psychiatric indications, 12 percent were said to have deteriorated psychologically. Unfortunately the accuracy of Malmfors' interpretations is difficult to determine since the methodology is not clearly spelled out.

Arén (1958) investigated a random sample of Swedish women who had legal abortions three years prior to the interview. Twenty-three percent of the women had severe reactions, 25 percent had mild guilt, and 23 percent believed problems subsequent to the experience were punishment for the abortion.

Slightly different results were reported in a subsequent study by Arén and Åmark (1961) of a Swedish sample. Of 234 women, 21 percent were

364   Lisa Roseman Shusterman

judged to be deteriorated emotionally, 43 percent were unchanged, and 37 percent were improved. Arén and Åmark wrote that "a relatively large number of women afterwards regret the performance of the operation or feel more or less pronounced self-reproach . . . guilt and remorse . . . on account of it" (p. 207).

In each of the above studies indicating unfavorable psychological sequelae of abortion there were methodological problems. First, the methodology often is not described fully and most of the measuring devices are not scientifically rigorous, e.g., one therapist's clinical opinion and uncorroborated interviews. Second, most of the studies relied on recall or retrospective data which is always subject to witting or unwitting distortion. Women asked about their abortion might have tended to overemphasize their feelings of guilt or remorse so as not to appear callous and cold-hearted. Also, the majority of the interviews were conducted by males. According to Kummer (1963), data on a topic as sensitive as abortion may be different in nature and different in interpretation when collected by male and female researchers. Also, few of the studies indicated the type, frequence, or severity of the sequelae. Further, no studies compared the psychological effects to those of an appropriate control group—women with unwanted pregnancies who bear the child anyway. In spite of these problems, the studies conclude that since the sequelae of abortion are so much worse than full-term delivery for women with unwanted pregnancies, preservation of the mother's health or prevention of suicide are the only legitimate reasons for inducing abortion. Several authors even concluded that there were unfavorable psychological consequences when their own data are ambiguous or mixed regarding the outcome of abortion. Simon and Senturia (1966) noted that "it is sobering to observe the ease with which reports can be embedded in the literature, quoted, and requoted many times without consideration of the data in the original paper. Deeply held personal convictions frequently seem to outweigh the importance of data, especially when conclusions are drawn" (p. 187).

It also may be that a woman's emotional symptoms after the abortion are more a function of her overall mental health then of the interruption of her pregnancy. And, it has been argued that the development of negative after-effects, such as guilt or depression, is dependent upon the attitude of the medical staff and clinic toward the aborting woman. Negative effects have been said to be more likely to develop when the medical environment is not supportive (White, 1966; Walter, 1970). An additional limitation is that the samples in the studies usually have been self-selected and often included women who were sterilized simultaneously with the abortion so the consequences of both procedures could not be assessed independently (Rosen, 1958; Walter, 1970). Therefore, it appears unwarranted to conclude that therapeutic abortion produces negative psychological reactions in women. In fact, there is no high quality study which supports this conclusion.

In contrast to studies which conclude that the emotional effects of therapeutic abortion are severe, others have concluded that the effects are positive or neutral. As the following review shows, the scientific quality of the studies which have concluded that there are mild, negligible, or favorable psychological sequelae is quite varied. Some of the projects are as methodologically poor as those indicating unfavorable consequences, but many meet the standards of good scientific research.

Hamilton (1940, 1941) studied the importance of the length of time between the abortion and the assessment of its emotional outcome. In these studies, only 30 of 537 women interviewed had obtained therpeutic abortions, the rest had had spontaneous or illegal abortions. Immediately after the abortion, 46 percent felt regret, 39 percent felt relief, and 15 percent felt indifferent about the abortion. Fewer women who had therapeutic or illegal abortions felt regret than those who had had spontaneous abortions. Otherwise, no variables were reported that accounted for such different feelings. From such findings, there were no clear indications of the emotional effects of abortion, only that the effects were variable. However, Hamilton (1941) re-interviewed 100 of the women in the first study who came back for a four-week check-up. From these interviews, Hamilton concluded that with time, feelings of relief and satisfaction become more prominent than feelings of regret and guilt. However, there were problems in the two studies, i.e., a self-selected follow-up sample, no distinction made between women who had therapeutic, spontaneous, and illegal abortions, and no correlation made between pre-abortion and post-abortion psychological condition.

In 1963, Kummer (1963) attempted to validate psychiatrists' opinions of the emotional after-effects of abortion by polling 32 psychiatrists in California. According to Kummer, "75% [of the psychiatrists] had never encountered any moderate to severe psychiatric sequelae of abortion. The remaining 25% encountered such sequelae only rarely, the highest figure reported was six cases in fifteen years of practice" (p. 981). On the other hand, the psychiatrists reported treating many more women for unfavorable post-childbirth psychological problems. Kummer concluded that "apparently pregnancy and parturition exert greater stresses than does induced abortion upon women susceptible to mental illness" (p. 982). Kummer did not report how his sample of psychiatrists was selected, how the emotional condition of the women was evaluated, how standardized were the methods of evaluation, or how many and what types of women constituted the population. Further, he did not prorate the occurrence of psychological problems by the occurrence of abortion and live births.

In the same year that Kummer's study appeared, Mumford (1963) published an article that assessed the after-effects of therapeutic abortion by a totally different method. Mumford conducted an in-depth investigation of four married women with two or more children, who had one or more abortions between the ages of 25 and 35. As Mumford pointed out, the sample was quite unique because these four women had ten induced abortions among them. Throughout the entire abortion procedure and one year afterward, the women were interviewed and tested extensively. Mumford reported "no evidence in any case of significant negative ideational or emotional sequelae to the abortion experience" (p. 868). Clearly, his conclusions are quite limited given the small size and uniqueness of his sample.

An in-depth investigation of a larger sample was conducted by Peck and Marcus (1966). Fifty women were interviewed when they applied for legal abortions, and three to six months following the procedure. Demographic, personal history, obstetric and gynecological, and psychiatric data were collected in the pre-abortion interview. In the follow-up, an examination reportedly was made of the woman's psychological condition, her relationships with others, and her attitudes toward future pregnancies. Most of the women in the sample were between the ages of twenty and forty, married, Jewish, well-educated, and private patients. Half of the sample obtained abortions for psychiatric indications and half for nonpsychiatric indications. Of those in the psychiatric group, 72 were schizophrenic, 24 percent were depressed, and 4 percent were neurotic with severe character disorders.

Peck and Marcus reported no significant demographic differences between the psychiatric and nonpsychiatric groups. Only one woman in the psychiatric group had a negative reaction to the abortion, a short-lived depression. Of the nonpsychiatric, 36 percent felt a mild depression and regretted that the abortion had been necessary, but such reactions reportedly did not interfere with their everyday functioning. No woman was hospitalized for psychiatric care following the abortion. Relationships with men did not change for most of the women in the nonpsychiatric group, and improved for 36 percent and worsened for 20 percent of the women in the psychiatric group.

Peck and Marcus concluded that "there would seem to be little reason to fear that a therapeutic interruption of pregnancy will result in psychiatric illness *de novo* or that it will make pre-existing minor psychiatric illness worse . . . On the contrary, it was found to be truly therapeutic in that it alleviated acute states of depression and anxiety, which had resulted from becoming pregnant" (p. 422). While this study is better methodologically than many previous investigations, the validity of the conclusions is questionable on several grounds. First, although the authors claim that few negative consequences occurred and even though hospitalization was evaluated, the post-abortion condition was not assessed rigorously. Second, given that eligibility for abortion was at issue prior to the procedure, it may be that the diagnostic labels were used liberally. Thus, women may have been categorized as being severely disturbed, i.e., schizophrenic, in order to facilitate granting the abortion. Such a practice would make post-abortion normality look like a positive change in contrast. Third, the sample is quite select because although such a large percentage are labelled schizophrenic, they are Jewish, wealthy, private patients who are nonhospitalized—an unusual group.

Niswander and Patterson (1967) found results similar to those of Peck and Marcus (1966) although they used a questionnaire rather than an interview. From a sample of 116 women, they found that immediately after the abortion most women reported feeling better, and that as time passed more women had favorable rather than unfavorable feelings about the procedure. Women who aborted for nonpsychiatric reasons were reported to have more unfavorable responses. According to Niswander and Patterson, "the abortion is usually therapeutic in the best sense of the word—the patient feels better and therefore functions more effectively" (p. 706).

In studying abortion, Simon, Senturia, and Rothman (1967) analyzed interview, MMPI, and Loevinger Family Problem Scale data, rather than depending on only one measurement of post-abortion effects. The sample consisted of mostly white, middle-class, well-educated women. Simon *et al.* reported that 23 women felt relieved and well, 13 felt mild depression, and six felt marked depression immediately after the abortion. Of three groups—those who aborted for psychiatric (35 percent), medical (26 percent), and eugenic (19 percent) reasons—a larger proportion of the women in the psychiatric group had positive responses and a larger proportion of the women in the medical group had negative responses. Although no statistical analyses are presented, Simon *et al.* concluded that the eugenic group were more likely to become depressed and the medical group to feel guilty after the abortion than the other groups. According to Simon *et al.*, "psychiatric illness does occur after therapeutic abortion, but it is not primarily related to the abortion itself. Our study did not produce support for the frequently expressed belief that therapeutic abortion results in involuntary infertility, difficulty in sexual relations, or is a precipitant in involuntional depression" (p. 64).

One major problem with such a statement is that it is extremely difficult to determine the precipitant of any psychiatric illness and to eliminate any particular recent event from consideration as a possible contributor to emotional disturbance. However, even though Simon *et al.* do not present strong evidence that subsequent psychiatric illness is not causally related to abortion, they did find a low rate of psychopathology in women obtaining an abortion.

In the same year, an investigation by Kretzchmar and Norris (1967) also concluded that psychological sequelae of abortion are not negative. The sample consisted of mostly non-Catholic, married women who aborted for medical or eugenic reasons. Only two of the 32 women in the study aborted for psychiatric indications, and of the total, one-third were sterilized at the time of the abortion. The follow-up interviews and questionnaires were administered from one to five years after the abortion. The researchers reported that although most of the patients felt anxious and depressed before the abortion, most felt better following a short period of depression after the abortion. The only flaw with the Kretzchmar and Norris study is that a large proportion of the women were sterilized in addition to having an abortion, and so the outcome of abortion cannot be studied as an independent factor, although one would expect that psychiatric reaction to abortion plus sterilization would be more negative than the psychiatric reaction to abortion alone. Overall, the Kretzchmar and Norris investigation is particularly good.

Support for mild or negligible psychological sequelae also was reported by Patt, Rappaport, and Barglow (1969). In a one- to two-hour semi-structured interview, 35 white, middle-class, young women were asked to discuss their reasons for aborting, their feelings about the abortion, their immediate and long-term reaction to abortion, their life situations prior to and after the abortion, their parental and heterosexual relationships, their childhoods, and whether or not they had tried to present exaggerated psychiatric symptoms.

Twenty of the 35 women felt relieved and relaxed immediately after the pregnancy termination. For half of the remaining 15, whose symptoms included suicidal gestures, promiscuity, depression, and physical complaints, the immediate negative consequences were judged to be due to pre-abortion problems and not to the abortion itself. Twenty-six of the 35 felt that in the long term they had improved, four felt unchanged, and six felt worse. However, of the 15 patients who had short-term unfavorable symptoms, "ten considered their long-term emotional status or life functioning improved" (p. 412). Also, half of the women said that their sexual relations had improved. In sum, Patt *et al.* felt that therapeutic abortion generally had positive effects. However, like Simon *et al.*, Patt *et al.* do not present data to support their conclusion that the immediate negative after-effects were not attributable to the abortion. Yet, even if there were some short-term negative effects in some women, the majority of women obtaining an abortion felt that there were no long-term sequelae. A further problem might be that the study depended on recall data. Reports of past feelings, attitudes, motivations, and behaviors may be distorted, and no attempt was made to analyze the existence, direction, or strength of the distortion. In spite of any possible distortion, however, the Patt *et al.* data are important in that women report that they generally come to feel positively about the abortion in the long run.

In one of the few prospective studies of the effect of therapeutic abortion, Brody, Meikle, and Gerritse (1971) concluded that the procedure is generally very beneficial and effective in reducing psychopathological symptoms. They administered several tests to 117 abortion applicants and to 58 "control" patients who were were in the same state of pregnancy as the abortion applicants. The 94 women who received abortions were re-tested six weeks, six months, and one year after the procedure, whereas those applicants who were not granted an abortion and the control patients were retested only six weeks after the initial testing.

The MMPI scores of the abortion applicants indicated a significantly greater degree of psychological disturbance than the controls whose scores were essentially normal. Those who received the abortions had MMPI profiles approaching normalcy by six weeks after the abortion. Women who obtained tubal ligation at the time of termination did not differ in improvement from those who only aborted. The rejected applicants ($N = 23$), on the other hand, remained as disturbed as they were on the initial testing. The Borday *et al.* study is good methodologically.

Ford *et al.* (1971) conducted a study very similar in methodology and results to the Brody *et al.* study. Forty abortion applicants scored high on several MMPI scales. In a six month follow-up of 29 of the applicants, the MMPI scores showed much less psychological distress. The only after-effect reported was a short-lived depression. Only those who were initially diagnosed as psychotic did not show any improvement in emotional stability. The Ford *et al.* study also is methodologically sound.

Several studies conducted in other countries also have concluded that the psychological consequences of therapeutic abortion are negligible or favorable (Ekbald, 1954; Brekke, 1958; Gillis, 1969; Todd, 1972; Moore-Čavar, 1974). The comparability of foreign studies with American research is limited because the samples are different.

It is difficult to comment generally on the large number of studies which have indicated no severe sequelae because the studies vary along every research dimension. Several of the studies suffer because they had to rely on self-selected small samples, and others suffer because the length of time between the abortion and assessment of outcome was too variable. Often methods and criteria for evaluation were not presented, and demographic variables were not considered. Further, many of the studies of therapeutic abortion are open to question because of the unreliable use of psychiatric labels in order to enhance the granting of the abortion. Similarly, those studies which concluded that negative reactions were not connected to the abortion do not support this with data. Like studies concluding that the effects of therapeutic abortion are negative, there are few methodologically sound studies which conclude that the effects of therapeutic abortion are essentially benign. However, there are several very good studies and, overall, the evidence is stronger that therapeutic abortion is basically untraumatic than that therapeutic abortion has negative after-effects.

The illegal abortion experience is so radically different from that of therapeutic abortion that the two can hardly be compared. The illegal experience usually is clandestine, expensive, and the abortion is often performed by less than competent operators. First, a women has to find an abortionist who agrees to terminate her pregnancy. Lee (1969) and Schulder and Kennedy (1971) describe such a search as typically frustrating, dangerous, and humiliating. Lee (1969) and Schulder and Kennedy (1971) reported many cases of women who developed medical complications from illegal abortions but were too afraid to go to a hospital for treatment.

Lee (1969) reported that of those women she interviewed, eight percent had severe emotional problems resulting from the abortion, and less than half were depressed following the abortion. The most common complaint was that the women did not feel that their male partners were sufficiently supportive. Lee concluded that any negative emotional effects disappear in a few weeks. Gebhard et al. (1958) reported few unfavorable emotional sequelae of illegal abortion.

There are several problems in collecting data about any individual's experience in an illegal activity, i.e., the quality and conditions of the abortion are not standardized, the validity of the disclosed information is not substantiated, and the sample is subject to bias. Well-founded conclusions about the psychological sequelae of illegal abortions cannot yet be made.

Recent reports on the emotional effects of abortion on request concur that the majority of women do not suffer any measurable psychological trauma. In the Osofsky et al. (1971) and Osofsky and Osofsky (1972) studies, unfavorable consequences rarely occurred. The Osofsky sample consisted of 380 women, most of whom were young and white; half were single and the rest were split evenly among married, separated, or divorced women. Immediately and one month after the abortion, follow-up data were collected through individual interviews.

Osofsky et al. (1971) reported that 64 percent of the patients felt moderately or very happy about the abortion, 20 percent felt neutral, 10 percent felt moderately unhappy, and 5 percent very unhappy. Also, the majority (76 percent) experienced no guilt, although a minority experienced some (15 percent) or considerable (8 percent) guilt. More than three-fourths were satisfied with their decision to terminate the pregnancy. Consistent with the Hawaii studies, most of the women (77 percent) reported that they wanted children in the future. Osofsky *et al.* concluded that "the predominant reactions would appear to be relief and happiness" (p. 230).

In a subsequent article (Osofsky & Osofsky, 1972), intercorrelations among the psychological variables were reported. The data indicated that patients who had more difficulty in deciding to abort also had greater guilt, greater desire for future children, and would have been less likely to abort if it had been illegal. Demographic variables were also important. For example, Catholic patients had a harder time deciding to abort and experienced more guilt. Both of the Osofsky studies were better than most of the previous research. The sample characteristics and methodological procedures were clearly and thoroughly presented.

Athanasiou, Michaelson, Oppel, Unger, and Yager (1973) compared the sequelae of term birth for women with wanted pregnancies, abortion by dilation and curretage, and abortion by saline injection, matching groups on demographic variables (N = 373). The original assessment of the woman's emotional status included the Srole Anomie Scale, Rosenberg's Self-Esteem Scale, and a 90-minute structured interview. The follow-up assessment, 13 to 16 months after the delivery or the abortion, included a symptom check list, a shortened version of the MMPI, the Srole and Rosenberg scales, and another interview.

Athanasiou *et al.* found that women ending their pregnancies were not significantly different on any factors from women continuing their pregnancies. In support of the findings of the Osofsky *et al.* and Osofsky and Osofsky studies, they concluded that there were no serious physical or psychological after-effects of abortion. However, women high on scales 4 and 9 of the MMPI have a longer time to emotional recovery. The authors tentatively suggest that such women need special attention when they present themselves for either abortion or term birth. The Athanasiou *et al.* study was good in that it looked at long-term sequlae, used multiple measures of the woman's psychological condition, and compared the effects of abortion with other groups.

In another recent study, Smith (1973) obtained follow-up assessments on 80 women one to two years after their abortions. Most of the women were young, single, and in school. Medical students using very thorough, structured questionnaires interviewed the women. Follow-up interviews were conducted between one and two years later either by mail, by telephone, or in person. At follow-up, 90 percent reported no negative psychological after-effects, and 94 percent were satisfied with their decision to abort. Forty percent said that the abortion had no effect on their lives, and 40 percent said that it had a positive effect in that it was a maturing experience. Most said that their pre-abortion feelings of desperation ended when the pregnancy was terminated and that relief and satisfaction followed. Two of the 15 women who had a history of psychiatric problems sought psychiatric help after the abortion.

A small minority of the Smith (1973) sample reported having negative consequences. According to Smith, this group of women tended to be single teenagers who were ambivalent about the abortion, who had been concerned about the abortion's possible adverse effect on their fertility, were especially fond of children, and were not involved in a continuing relationship with their sexual partner. The data collection method and length of the follow-up period are strengths of the Smith study.

Still another study, Monsour and Stewart (1973), reported that in 20 randomly selected college women who had aborted, the predominant reaction was positive, not negative. Only one woman felt guilty about ending her pregnancy and her guilt attenuated after five months. The main flaws in the study are that the sample is small and select and the follow-ups ranged from as little as one month to as much as 25 months later. Other studies indicating no negative psychological after-effects for women obtaining abortion on request are Addelson (1973) and Adler (1973).

The recent studies indicate that abortion on request is a relatively benign procedure; no studies conclude negative sequelae. However, there appears to be a certain percentage of women who experience at least mild negative sequelae. These women tend to be less certain about their decision to abort, to be involved in less stable heterosexual relationships, and to be more concerned about the consequences of abortion. In general, however, negative after-effects seem to be short-lived and rarely intense.

There are several methodological limitations of many of the studies of abortion on request. The studies use small, often unrepresentative samples, and measuring devices whose reliability and validity are unclear, or at least not reported. Despite such problems, the recent studies are significantly better than earlier research. That is, the analyses are less subjective, the measures are more reliable, comparisons are made with other groups of women, and, in some cases, statistical analyses are made.

In future research there is a clear need to identify conclusively the significant interrelationships among psychosocial variables in aborting women, to identify what variables account for differences in reaction to abortion, and to cross-validate the findings in a different sample.

Conclusion

Research on the psychosocial factors of abortion has focused on therapeutic abortion, illegal abortion, and abortion on request. The quality of the studies on the first two types of abortion generally has been poor. The literature has included anecdotes, which are not solid scientific material; surveys, which often have lacked depth, particularity, and precision; and interviews, which often have been uncontrolled and retrospective. Furthermore, samples have been incomplete and insufficiently described, and statistical analyses have been almost nonexistent. Reliable information about even the most basic facts of therapeutic and illegal abortions has not yet been established firmly, and so conclusions cannot be drawn.

Studies of abortion on request, however, have been, over-all, sound methodologically, and so the findings have greater validity. Some conclusions can be made. The abortion population seems to be comprised basically of young, single women who are neither prepared for nor willing to adjust their lives to a child. In general, many of the women report that they are not consciously aware of the possibility of conceiving at the time of intercourse. The emotional stability of women who have abortions is another issue of controversy, although there is evidence that the women are no more psychopathological than women who deliver term pregnancies.

The reasons why women have abortions are significant and often ignored variables in the study of the psychology of abortion. For the new abortion patients, the reported rate of contraceptive failure is surprisingly high and, although the rate needs to be validated further, it suggests that to a large extent abortion is being used as a back-up to other means of controlling pregnancy. The data on the abortion on request samples indicate that social and economic reasons account for most abortions. Finally, it appears warranted to conclude that the effects of abortion on request are negligible, if not favorable.

Many dimensions of the psychology of abortion remain unclear. The attitudes of aborting women toward abortion, the reasons why women have unwanted pregnancies, and the reasons why women have abortions need to be clarified and validated further. In addition, the consequences of abortion should be studied further. The extent to which demographic and personality variables influence the psychology of abortion are other issues that warrant investigation. In the past few years great improvements have been made in research methodology; however, the relationships among important variables remain to be studied. In particular, a major study which investigates the relationships among the antecedent psychological variables and the consequent variables is needed to give a coherent shape to the study of the subjective experience of terminating pregnancy.

REFERENCES

ABERNATHY, V. The abortion constellation. *Archives of General Psychiatry*, 1973, *29*, 346–350.

ADDELSON, F. Induced abortion: Source of guilt or growth? *American Journal of Orthopsychiatry*, 1973, *43*, 815–823.

ADLER, N. *Dimensions underlying emotional responses of women following therapeutic abortion.* Presented at American Psychological Association meeting. Montreal, August 30, 1973.

ARÉN, P. Legal abortion in Sweden. *Acta Obstetrica et Gynecologica Scandanavica*, 1958, *36*, supplement 1.

ARÉN, P., & ÅMARK, C. The prognosis in cases in which legal abortion has been granted but not carried out. *Acta Obstetrica et Gynecologica Scandanavica*, 1961, *36*, 203–278.

ATHANASIOU, R., MICHELSON, L., OPPEL, W., UNGER, T., & YAGER, M. *A longitudinal study of sequelae to term birth and therapeutic abortions.* Paper presented at 21st Annual Clinical Meeting of the American College of Obstetricians and Gynecologists, Bal Harbour, May 23, 1973.

BOLTER, S. The psychiatrist's role in therapeutic abortion: The unwitting accomplice. *American Journal of Psychiatry*, 1962, *119*, 312–314.

BREKKE, B. Other aspects of the abortion problem. In M. Calderone (Ed.), *Abortion in the United States*, New York: Hoeber and Harper, 1958, 133–136.

BRODY, H., MEIKLE, S., & GERRITSE, R. Therapeutic abortion: A prospective study. 1. *American Journal of Obstetrics and Gynecology*, 1971, *109*, 347–352.

CALDERONE, M. (Ed.). *Abortion in the United States.* Proceedings of the conference held under the auspices of Planned Parenthood Federation of America in April & June, 1955. New York: Hoeber & Harper, 1958.

CHISOLM, S. Foreward. In D. Schulder & F. Kennedy, *Abortion rap.* New York: McGraw-Hill Book Co., 1971.

CHRISTAKOS, A. Experience at Duke Medical Center after modern legislation for therapeutic abortion. *Southern Medical Journal*, 1970, *63*, 655–661.

CUSHNER, I. Outcomes of induced abortion: Medical-clinical view. In S. Newman, M. Beck, & S. Lewit (Eds.), *Abortion obtained and denied: Research approaches.* Bridgeport, Connecticut: The Population Council, 1971, 21–36.

DEUTSCH, H. *The psychology of women.* (Vol. 2). New York: Grune & Stratton, Inc., 1945.

DIAMOND, M., STEINHOFF, P., PALMORE, J., & SMITH, R. Sexuality, birth control and abortion: A decision-making sequence. *Journal of Biosocial Science*, 1973, *5*, 347–361.

DUFFY, E. *The effect of changes in the state abortion laws.* Washington: United States Government Printing Office, 1971.

DUNBAR, F. A psychosomatic approach to abortion and the abortion habit. In H. Rosen (Ed.), *Therapeutic abortion.* New York: The Julain Press, Inc., 1954, 22–31.

EBAUGH, F., & HESUER, A. Psychiatric aspects of therapeutic abortion. *Post-graduate Medicine,* 1947, *2*, 325–332.

EKBALD, M. Induced abortion on psychiatric grounds: A follow-up study of 479 women. *Acta Psychiatrica Neurologica Scandanavica,* Supplement 99, 1954.

FORD, C., CASTELNUOVO-TEDESCO, P., & LONG, K. Abortion: Is it a therapeutic procedure in psychiatry? *Journal of the American Medical Association,* 1971, *218*, 1173–1178.

FORD, C., CASTELNUOVO-TEDESCO, P., & LONG, K. Women who seek abortion: A comparison with women who complete their pregnancies. *American Journal of Psychiatry,* 1972, *129*, 546–552.

GALDSTON, I. Other aspects of the abortion problem. In M. Calderone (Ed.), *Abortion in the United States.* New York: Hoeber & Harper, 1958, 117–121.

GEBHARD, P., POMEROY, W., & MARTIN, C. *Pregnancy, birth and abortion.* New York: John Wiley & Sons, Inc., 1958.

GILLIS, A. Follow-up after abortion. *British Medical Journal,* 1969, *1*, 506.

GOLD, E., ERHARD, C., & JACOBZINER, H. Therapeutic abortions in New York City: A twenty-year review. *American Journal of Public Health,* 1965, *55*, 964–972.

HAMILTON, V. Some sociologic and psychologic observations on abortion. *American Journal of Obstetrics and Gynecology,* 1940, *39*, 919–928.

HAMILTON, V. Medical status and psychologic attitudes of patients following abortion. *American Journal of Obstetrics and Gynecology,* 1941, *41*, 285–287.

HAMILTON, V. The clinical and laboratory differentiation of spontaneous and induced abortion. *American Journal of Obstetrics and Gynecology,* 1941, *40*, 61–69.

HEFFERMAN, R., & LYNCH, W. What is the status of therapeutic abortion in modern obstetrics? *American Journal of Obstetrics and Gynecology,* 1953, *66*, 135–145.

HESSELTINE, H., ADAIR, F., & BOYNTON, M. Limitation of human reproduction. Therapeutic abortion. *American Journal of Obstetrics and Gynecology,* 1940, *39*, 549–562.

KANE, F., LACHENBRUCH, P., & LIPTON, M. Motivational factors in abortion patients. *American Journal of Psychiatry,* 1973, *130*, 290–293.

KRETZCHMAR, R., & NORRIS, A. Psychiatric implications of therapeutic abortion. *American Journal of Obstetrics and Gynecology,* 1967, *198*, 365–370.

KUMMER, J. Post-abortion psychiatric illness—a myth? *American Journal of Psychiatry,* 1963, *119*, 980–983.

LADER, L. *Abortion.* Indianapolis: The Bobbs-Merrill Co., Inc., 1966.

LEE, N. *The search for an abortionist.* Chicago: The University of Chicago Press, 1969.

LIDZ, T. Reflections of a psychiatrist. In H. Rosen (Eds.). *Therapeutic abortion.* New York: The Julian Press, Inc., 1954, 276–283.

MCCORMICK, P. *Attitudes toward abortion among women undergoing legally induced abortions.* Paper presented at Abortions Research Workshop. New Orleans, April, 1973.

MALMFORS, K. Other aspects of the abortion problem. In M. Calderone (Ed.), *Abortion in the United States.* New York: Hoeber & Harper, 1958, 133–135.

MILLER, J. *The social determinants of women's attitudes toward abortion: 1970 analysis.* Unpublished manuscript, 1973. Available from Ms. J. Miller, Center for Demography and Ecology, University of Wisconsin, Madison, Wisconsin.

MILLER, W. *Psychological antecedents to conception in pregnancies terminated by therapeutic abortion.* Unpublished manuscript, 1973. Available from Dr. W. Miller, Department of Psychiatry, Stanford University, Stanford, California.

MOORE-ČAVAR, E. *International inventory of information on induced abortion.* Division of Social and Administrative Sciences. International Institute for the Study of Human Reproduction. Columbia University, 1974.

MONSOUR, K., & STEWART, B. Abortion and sexual behavior in college women. *American Journal of Orthopsychiatry,* 1973, *43*, 804–813.

MUMFORD, R. An interdisciplinary study of four wives who had induced abortions. *American Journal of Obstetrics and Gynecology,* 1963, *87*, 865–876.

NEWMAN, S. Personal communication, March, 1973.

NEWMAN, S., BECK, M., & LEWIT, S. (Eds.), *Abortion, obtained and denied: Research approaches.* Bridgeport, Connecticut: The Population Council, 1971.

NISWANDER, K., & PATTERSON, R. Psychologic reaction to therapeutic abortion. *Obstetrics and Gynecology,* 1967, *29*, 702–706.

OSOFSKY, J., OSOFSKY, H., & RAJAN, R. Psychological effects of legal abortion. *Clinical Obstetrics and Gynecology,* 1971, *14*, 215–234.

OSOFSKY, J., & OSOFSKY, H. The psychological reaction of patients to legalized abortion. *American Journal of Orthopsychiatry,* 1972, *42,* 48–60.

PAKTER, J., & NELSON, F. Abortion in New York City: The first nine months. *Family Planning Perspectives,* 1971, *3,* 5–12.

PATT, S., RAPPAPORT, R., & BARGLOW, P. Follow-up of therapeutic abortion. *Archives of General Psychiatry,* 1969, *20,* 408–414.

PECK, A., & MARCUS, H. Psychiatric sequelae of therapeutic interruption of pregnancy. *Journal of Nervous and Mental Disease,* 1966, *143,* 417–425.

PEEL, J., & POTTS, M. *Textbook of contraceptive practice.* London: Cambridge University Press, 1969.

PIPEL, H., & NORWICK, K. When should abortion be legal? *Public Affairs Pamphlet No. 429,* January, 1969.

POHLMAN, E. *Psychology of birth planning.* Cambridge: Schenkman Publ. Co., Inc., 1969.

Population Study Commission. State of California, Report to the Governor, 1966.

ROMM, M. Psychoanalytic considerations. In H. Rosen, (Ed.), *Therapeutic abortion.* New York: The Julian Press, Inc., 1954, 209–212.

ROSEN, H. (Ed.), *Therapeutic abortion.* New York: The Julian Press, Inc., 1954.

ROSEN, H. Other aspects of the abortion problem. In M. Calderone (Ed.), *Abortion in the United States.* New York: Hoeber & Harper, 1958, 129–131.

ROSEN, M. Psychiatric implications of abortion: A case study in social hypocrisy. In D. Smith (Ed.), *Abortion and the law.* Cleveland: The Press of Western Reserve University, 1967, 72–95.

ROUTLEDGE, F., SPARLING, A., & MACFARLAND, S. Present status of therapeutic abortion. *American Journal of Obstetrics and Gynecology,* 1953, *66,* 335–345.

ROVINSKY, J. Abortion in New York City, preliminary experience with a permissive abortion statute. *Obstetrics and Gynecology,* 1971, *38,* 333–342.

SCHULDER, D., & KENNEDY, F. *Abortion rap.* New York: McGraw-Hill Book Col., 1971.

SCHUR, E. Abortion and the social system. *Social Problems,* 1955, *3,* 94–99.

SHAW, R. *Abortion on trial.* London: Robert Hall, 1968.

SHERMAN, J. Personal communication, September, 1975.

SIMON, N., ROTHMAN, D., & GOFF, J. Psychological factors related to spontaneous and therapeutic abortion. *American Journal of Obstetrics and Gynecology,* 1969, *104,* 799–808.

SIMON, N., & SENTURIA, A. Psychiatric sequelae of abortion. *Archives of General Psychiatry,* 1966, *15,* 378–389.

SIMON, N., SENTURIA, A., & ROTHMAN, D. Psychiatric illness following therapeutic abortion. *American Journal of Psychiatry,* 1967, *124,* 97–103.

SMITH, E. A follow-up study of women who request abortion. *American Journal of Orthopsychiatry,* 1973, *43,* 574–585.

SMITH, R., DIAMOND, M., & STEINHOFF, P. Abortion in Hawaii: 1970–1971. *Hawaii Medical Journal,* 1973, *32,* 213–220.

STEINHOFF, P. *Ethnic and social class differences in the use of abortion.* Paper presented at Population Studies Seminar, East-West Center, University of Hawaii, November, 1971.

STEINHOFF, P. Background characteristics of abortion patients. In J. Osofsky & H. Osofsky (Eds.), *Abortion experience in the United States.* New York: Harper and Row, 1973, 206–231.

STEINHOFF, P., DIAMOND, D., PALMORE, J., & SMITH, R. *Who are the new abortion patients?* Paper presented at Abortion Research Workshop, New Orleans, April, 1973.

STEINHOFF, P., SMITH, R., & DIAMOND, M. The Hawaii pregnancy, birth control and abortion study: Social psychological aspects. *Conference Proceedings: Psychological Measurement in the Study of Population Problems.* Institute of Personality Assessment and Research, University of California, Berkeley, 1972, 33–40.

TIETZE, C. Mortality with contraception and induced abortion. *Studies in Family Planning,* 1969, *1,* 6–8.

TIETZE, C. Two years' experience with a liberal abortion law: Its impact on fertility trends in New York City. *Family Planning Perspectives,* 1973, *5,* 36–41.

TIETZE, C., & LEHFELDT, H. Legal abortion in Eastern Europe. *Journal of the American Medical Association,* 1961, *175,* 1149–1154.

TIETZE, C., & LEWIT, S. Joint program for the study of abortion (JPSA): Early medical complications of legal abortions. *Studies in Family Planning,* 1972, *3,* 97–122.

TODD, N. Follow-up of patients recommended for therapeutic abortion. *British Journal of Psychiatry,* 1972, *20,* 645–646.

WALTER, G. Psychologic and emotional consequences of elective abortion. *Obstetrics and Gynecology,* 1970, *36,* 482–487.

WHITE, R. Induced abortions: A survey of their psychiatric implications, complications and indications. *Texas Reports of Biological Medicine*, 1966, *24*, 528–558.

WHITMAN, III, H. *Medical and psychiatric factors in decision-making about abortion.* Unpublished manuscript, 1971. Available from Department of Psychology; Harvard University, Boston, Massachusetts.

WILSON, D., & CAINE, B. The psychiatric implications of therapeutic abortions. *Neuropsychiatry,* 1951, *1*, 22.

WILSON, D. Psychiatric indications of abortion. *Virginia Medical Monthly,* 1952, *79*, 448–451.

PART VIII
Pregnancy, Birth, and Bonding

The ephemeral dramas of pregnancy and childbirth, biological events that are exclusively in the female experience, are of great psychological significance to the woman who experiences them. The psychological importance of reproductive events lies in their meanings, meanings that have several sources whose confluence determines the psychic significance with which they are invested for a particular woman. It is useful to analyze these meanings in terms of their sources: psychodynamic, situational, and cultural. While these sources are related and overlapping, each has its own features that are important theoretically.

Psychodynamic implications of pregnancy include the woman's perceptions of herself, as woman and as potential mother. Her relationship with her own mother, her resolution of childhood problems and stages, her self-image, her feelings about her body, and her motivation for becoming pregnant all can have determining effects on her intrapsychic response to her pregnancy and her impending motherhood. Though her psychodynamic reaction to her pregnancy may be partly unconscious, it can affect the course of the pregnancy and her later response to her child.

Situational variables are identified in her immediate environment. The quality of her relationship with her mate—for example, his presence and reaction to her pregnancy—can interact with and affect her own feelings and attitudes. Her employment and educational status, the life changes necessitated by having a child, and the level and quality of emotional and financial resources available to her all enter into her adaptation to this life cycle milestone.

Cultural meanings of childbearing are those that are shared by most or all others with whom she identifies. These include beliefs about and attitudes toward pregnancy, birth, and motherhood, values attached to the reproductive functions of women, expectations for the behavior of a woman who is pregnant or mothering, and limitations that may be placed on her by any of these.

In addition to these experiential variables that affect women's reactions to pregnancy and mothering, evidence is emerging that suggests contributions from biological factors as well. As we have seen, the role of biology in gender-linked behavior has had a long and stormy history. Supporters of traditional male-female roles and biologists who want to emphasize cross-species similarities argue that biology has a closer relation to our destinies as women and men than we may wish to acknowledge. Cultural determinists, by contrast, document the great malleability of human behavior and believe that behavior that is linked to sex category is learned in a sociocultural context. Feminists in particular have, with good reason, been suspicious of and hostile to the arguments in favor of biological underpinnings for some of our role assignments. Too often the argument for biological determinants of male-female differences in behavior has led to injustice and inequality for women.

In view of this controversy, it is of particular interest to read Alice Rossi's paper, "The Biosocial Side of Parenthood." Rossi is a feminist sociologist who for more than two decades has made many scholarly contributions to women's struggle for equality and to the growth of feminist scholarship as well. In this paper, she points out that modern society is but a second in the long course of our evolution and that it is naïve to assume that our new ideas about birth control and sex-role equality can overcome millennia of custom and adaptation. "Different," she stresses, does not have to mean "unequal." That males and females are different is a biological fact, whereas equality is a political and social concept. What is needed is a better understanding of physiological influences on social behavior, rather than a denial of their existence.

Rossi points out, for example, that it makes good evolutionary sense for mothers to have "built-in" positive reponses to their infants, in that the survival of immature humans depends on prolonged care based on intense attachment of mother to baby. The dependence of infants and their reliance on such a bond have roots in the evolutionary history of our species that cannot be wished away. None of this means that fathers cannot be nurturant or that mothers need care for their own babies all the time. But attention to the biosocial side of parenting can make for a more humane environment for both parents and children. For example, childbirth practices that include anesthetizing the laboring woman and separating her from the newborn can interfere with the formation of the mother-infant bond, which, some researchers have found, facilitates maternal attachment behavior, which is related to the quality of care that the infant receives. Also, distortion or diminution of the bond may lead to such behaviors as neglect and child abuse. Rossi calls for a society better attuned to its environment and more respectful of natural body processes, one concerned for its children and for individual differences in people as well.

Looking more specifically at the course of normal pregnancy, Patsy Turrini describes in "Psychological Crises in Normal Pregnancy" certain marking events and the kinds of reactions they may provoke in the mother-to-be. The decision to become pregnant, for example, seems to be problematic for more and more young and not-so-young married people today, who have the luxury of choice and feel the need to examine their motivations. The early weeks of pregnancy, when some body changes such as breast tenderness and perhaps morning sickness occur before the baby quickens, bring anxiety about the reality of the child and its well-being. Then one copes with the reactions of friends and family to the impending new one. Later in pregnancy, time may hang heavily as the woman enters the period of waiting. The uncertainty about when labor will begin, how it will feel, and the need to make preparations for being away and for the return with the baby are matters of concern for most women. Finally, the onset of labor and the obstetrical management of the birth itself, while usually normal and problem-free, are events that are fraught with high significance for the woman, such that it is not improper to call them crises. The author suggests that even women with well-developed ego functions will be challenged by these developmental tasks of pregnancy and that less fortunate ones may experience great stress. Women, says Turrini, should be encouraged to be active participants, to learn more about their bodies, and therapists need better to appreciate the effects of pregnancy and parenting on the psychological state of women.

In the last paper in this section, "The Role of the Mother in Early Social Development," H. Rudolph Schaffer and Charles K. Crook describe recent research on the dimensions of mothering. Far from being a simple matter of responding to the infant's needs, mothering also includes a set of attitudes that underlie behavior and influence the kind of psychological environment the baby has. Mothering also includes providing the kinds of stimulation the baby needs for healthy development. Most important, the authors believe, is the reciprocal nature of the mother-infant relationship. The baby is not a lump of clay to be shaped by her or his caretaker. Rather, from the beginning, the baby is an active agent, emitting a stream of behavior, vocal and physical, into which the mother keys her responses. Thus we see two individuals, both acting and reacting, each affecting and shaping the behavior of the other. The critical variable is the mother's sensitivity to her child's behavior, and her awareness of appropriate adjustments to it. For example, the mother's language and speech patterns change as the neonate becomes the three-month-old infant, adjusting to the older baby's more complex social behavior. Socialization, then, is a process based on mutuality, a two-way relationship in which the mother's effects on her infant are balanced by the child's effects on her. The sensitive adult, then, will synchronize her mothering behavior with her perceptions of the meaning of her child's behavior at any given moment. Clearly such research is critically important to children's development and to the quality of care they receive.

The biosocial events that are the bases for the papers in this section are of great significance in human societies everywhere. Because of this they are laden with meaning, integrated into cultural patterns of ritual and belief, and celebrated in diverse ways. Only women who experience them can appreciate them fully, and even that experience has at times been distorted, attenuated, and mystified by ignorance or the desire to control.

Stimulated by research findings and by their own consciousnesses, women have begun to question some of our society's ways of dealing with childbirth and to "take back" what is really theirs. Of the many areas that affect the psychology of women, none is more deserving of scientific attention, both theoretical and empirical, than this one.

26

The Biosocial Side of Parenthood

Alice S. Rossi

When it comes to aging, no one denies the role of maturation and physiology in explaining the differences between old people and children. Learning, change, and the biological limitations of growth obviously affect the aging process. Where sex and gender are concerned, though, no such reasonable position is today acceptable. The nature-nuture debate has, if anything, rigidified in recent years. The nature camp—people such as George Gilder, Robin Fox, and Lionel Tiger—holds that sex differences arose and persist because of hormones and other biological factors. Women have evolved to be nurturant and submissive; their natural role is the bearing and rearing of the next generation. Men, so the nature camp says, have evolved to be aggressive and dominant; their natural role is to protect women and children and to provide for them. The nurture camp counters that no innate differences between the sexes exist and that raising boys and girls in the same way, without discrimination will produce androgynous adults. There is no biological basis, they argue, for the male's investment in work and the female's in family.

The reason for the bitterness of the argument comes, I think, from the tendency to confuse difference with inequality. As far as male and female are concerned, difference is a biological fact, whereas equality is a political, ethical, and social concept. No rule of nature or of social organization says that the sexes have to be the same or do the same things in order to be social, political, and economic equals.

The confusion might be cleared if we move toward a biosocial perspective, one that links the cultural, socially learned causes of behavior to the mammalian heritage we share with other primates. Modern society is a mere second in our evolutionary history, and it is naive to assume that our audacious little experiments in communal living, birth control, sexual liberation, and sex-role equality can overturn in a century, let alone a decade, millennia of custom and adaptation.

A biosocial perspective does not argue that genes determine what men and women can do. Instead, it suggests that biological factors create differences in the ease with which the sexes learn certain things. Men, who on the average are taller and stronger (particularly in the shoulders) than women, generally surpass women in construction work and military combat; women generally surpass men in forming intense emotional bonds with infants and young children. Historically and cross culturally, the organization of society has reflected this difference, and the difference has been the basis of the family system.

I think it is important to distinguish between biosocial science and sociobiology. The latter term, made popular with the publication of Edward Wilson's *Sociobiology*, heavily emphasizes common features in social organization across species. In contrast, biosocial science searches either for critical contributions of physiological factors to human behavior or for the impact of social and psychological factors on body functioning. Biosocial science restricts its analysis to a single species; sociobiology stresses cross-species analysis. I do not share Wilson's optimism that the human sciences can be readily subsumed under some overarching synthesis rooted in biology. I believe instead that we will do more to deepen our understanding of human behavior by searching for the influence of physiology on social behavior or by examining variation in biological factors within the human species than by making largely speculative leaps across the great differences that separate animal species.

Many cultural determinists now claim that the only difference between men and women is that women bear young and lactate. This use of "only" implies that pregnancy, childbirth, and nursing are insignificant activities, especially because few women breast-feed nowadays and because women are having fewer children than they once did. But the reproductive and endocrine systems that underlie childbearing and lactation function throughout the woman's life cycle. To deny their importance to female psychology or to the organization of the family devalues the woman's role in the survival of the species, ignores the findings of science, and reveals the profound degree to which many women accept masculine technocratic thinking, which places exceedingly heavy stress on rational control over nature and on purely technical solutions to human problems.

One reason that cultural determinists tend to dismiss biological factors is that their view of sex differences is based on an obsolete model of the endocrine system. From the 1920s to the 1950s, the accepted model was a closed loop involving the pituitary, the adrenal glands, and the gonads (testes and ovaries). Hormones circulated through the bloodstream, acting as chemical messengers linking the glands. The basic assumption in this early view was that the endocrine system worked independently of the external environment and was only minimally responsive to the nervous system.

Since the 1950s, new discoveries have shattered the old model. The central finding was that the hypothalamus (part of the old cortex surrounding the brain stem and kingpin of the nervous system) is intricately involved in the endocrine system. J. D. Green and G. W. Harris showed that blood flowed *from* the hypothalamus *to* the pituitary, a major new link in the chain of endocrine events. Subsequent research discovered that neurons in the hypothalamus receive electrical signals from the rest of the brain, and these neurons in turn send chemical messages to the pituitary. Unlike the closed-loop model of endocrine function, which assumed that hormones communicate only with other hormones, the new model showed that the endocrine system receives messages from nerve impulses. Neural inputs are converted to endocrine outputs.

This brain research was significant because it showed that hormones are subject to social stimuli. Behavioral and environmental influences may thus affect hormonal secretions through the nervous system. The endocrine system was demoted to the status of equal partner with the nervous system in controlling hormonal events. These findings force us to discard the idea of a one-way path between hormones and behavior. An interactive model, showing that behavior also affects hormones, is more accurate.

Unfortunately, most social scientists are unaware of the advances in endocrinology and they persist in the mistaken belief that when anyone speaks of hormonal influences, he or she is clinging to the old one-way model. This model was misused for so long—to justify prejudice, racism, and the belief that women were simply slaves to their hormones—that most psychologists and sociologists understandably spurn the notion of any physiological component to behavior. (They also had the legacy of social Darwinism to shake, a legacy that told them women's energy was so drained by reproduction that they had little left for intellectual and personal growth, and that women were unalterably quiescent and passive whereas males were just as unalterably active and aggressive.)

The ironic result is that biological scientists have gone further in incorporating social factors into their theories than social scientists have gone in incorporating biological factors into theirs. In fact, contemporary endocrinologists and primatologists are just as likely to study the influence of the environment on hormonal secretion as they are to trace the influence of hormones on behavior.

A good example comes from studies of monkeys and men. Male rhesus monkeys who suffer defeat and loss of status in their groups show an abrupt drop in their levels of testosterone. If they are put next to a seductive female rhesus, however, their testosterone level shoots up. The old view that testosterone causes aggressiveness and sexual interest must be modified. Sometimes experience and opportunity change hormone levels.

For a social scientist interested in the role of endocrine functioning in gender differences, this research gets more and more fascinating and complex. We know now that it is useless and inaccurate to call androgen the "male" hormone and estrogen the "female" hormone, if by that we mean they are exclusively male or female. Both hormones are present in both sexes, although in different proportion. And there is accumulating evidence that we can reject the notion that androgen is the "aggressive" hormone, a thesis that some people have used to explain why men are usually more combative and powerful and have higher status than women.

Instead, it appears that androgen is the "erotic" hormone, for both sexes. Males have a higher level of androgens than females, but it takes less androgen to have an effect on women. Androgen therapy enhances male sexual response only if the man's hormone level has been below normal; women who have androgen therapy almost always report an increase in sexual desire. Conversely, loss of androgen is worse for the sexual responsiveness of women than for that of men. If male animals are castrated after puberty (which removes the major source of androgen), they can continue to perform sexually with as much interest and effort as ever. If both the ovaries and adrenal glands of women are surgically removed (eliminating their major sources of androgen) the women typically report a sharp drop in clitoral sensitivity and orgasmic response.

The impact of gonadal hormones during fetal development now appears to play an important role in sex differences in adult behavior. The evidence is strong for critical periods of hormone activity that affects the organization of the brain. In the human fetus it is the presence of androgens, such as testosterone, that turns the fetus into a male. Without androgen, the fetus develops into a female.

John Money, Anke Ehrhardt, and their colleagues have done extensive research on this problem, tracing the relative contributions of hormones, genetics, and sexual labeling to a person's gender identity, i.e., the sense of self as male or female. Usually, all three components work together, but we can learn a great deal from Money and Ehrhardt's studies of nature's abnormalities: genetic females who accidentally get a dose of prenatal androgen, genetic males who lack prenatal androgen, hermaphrodites, and so on. Most sociologists have drawn two environmentalist conclusions from Money and Ehrhardt's work: first, that gender identity is fixed at an early age, no later than at two or three years; second, that the sex label the baby is given at birth has a much stronger effect on his or her gender identity than either genes or gonads.

The researchers themselves have drawn a third conclusion: that the hormonal drama played out during fetal development has long-lasting effects on the brain. In particular, they believe, fetal exposure to hormones heightens the brain's capacity to comply with the demands of learning the behavior associated with one's sex assignment. They point out that females who get an excess of male hormones during fetal life behave like tomboys despite their feminine upbringing. Obviously, powerful cultural pressures may drown out physiological propensities. Money and Ehrhardt's point, along with others, who share the biosocial view, is that the brain's predispositions affect the ease with which males and females learn socially defined, appropriate behavior for their gender.

Many sociologists, nevertheless, use Money and Ehrhardt's data to demonstrate that culture overrides physiology. On rare occasions in the prenatal development of boys the testes fail to secrete androgen during a critical phase. The result is a genetic male who has male internal gonads and also the external genitals of a female. If the infant is defined as a girl at birth and raised as one, she will have no trouble defining herself as female. It seems that social learning can turn a genetic male into a normal female. But it is not that simple. As Money and Ehrhardt note, these genetic males never had prenatal testosterone flowing through their brains. Perhaps this lack increased their ability to follow the demands of their female sex assignment.

What are these demands? I am not talking about behavior that is completely determined by cultural fad or occupational fashion—dentistry, or the ability to boil an egg or hammer a nail. I am talking about some fundamental qualities of women's and men's roles that affect the family unit, for it is in the family that the children who will be the next generation of men and women are socialized.

Psychologists and parents have long acknowledged the innate abilities of the infant to suck, grasp, and cry. But few have attended to the innate predisposition of the mother to react intensely to her infant. Studies from dozens of researchers suggest that women have many unlearned responses to infants. Physiologically, an infant's crying stimulates the secretion of oxytocin in the mother, the sex hormone that makes the uterus contract, erects the nipples for nursing, and lets down the milk. The overwhelming majority of mothers, without being aware of it, cradle their infants in their left arms (regardless of whether they themselves are right- or left-handed); from this position the infant hears and is soothed by the familiar heartbeat. Similarly, new mothers reveal a shared sequence of reactions to their babies, as films taken after delivery show. The new mother touches the baby's fingers and toes with her own fingertips, puts her palms on the baby's torso, and then wraps the baby in her arms. All the while she maintains full eye contact with the infant, and her tension mounts until the baby opens its eyes and returns the gaze. Finally, when mothers talk to their babies, they also share a set of actions: wide-open eyes, raised eyebrows, sustained facial expressions, and "baby talk"—a shift in speech that elongates the vowels.

It makes good evolutionary sense for mothers to have developed built-in positive responses to infants. Because human infants are much more immature at birth than infants of any other primate species, their survival depends on prolonged care based on intense physical and emotional attachment of mother to offspring. For most of human history, the intensity of this attachment was enhanced, even required, by the infant's need to breast-feed for several years. Human societies vary widely in the size and composition of the family group and in the number of adults who supplement maternal care, but in all societies the mother has been the primary caretaker of her infants.

The existence of a predisposition among women to develop an intense attachment to their young is different from the old, clumsy concept of a maternal instinct, which supposedly existed within each female. We know from the extraordinary diversity of styles of mothering, from the shameful examples of maternal deprivation and child abuse, and from the thousands of perfectly healthy women who have chosen not to have children that the motives for having children and treating them well are far from instinctive in every female. Nor am I saying that men cannot be or have not been excellent, loving fathers.

What I do believe is that on the average, because of their evolutionary history, men and women differ in their predispositions to care for infants, and in their ability to learn those caretaking skills. In comparison to the women's attachment to her infant, the man's attachment is socially learned.

Rhesus monkeys and human males can become good fathers if they put their minds to the task or if they are forced into it by need or proximity, but it takes them a long time, full of trial and error. Around the world, family systems register extreme diversity in roles for fathers. In some societies men play an active part in child rearing; in others they are absentee parents. But there is little or no variation in the cultural rule for the relationship of mothers and children: A close bond between them is the universal demand.

One reason for the female's bond has to do with sexual orientation and response. Biologically, men have one sexual drive—to mate. But in female physiology there is a closely woven connection between sexuality and maternalism. One link is oxytocin, the hormone that stimulates uterine contractions that move the sperm up the birth canal to the ovum; the hormone that at higher levels causes the stronger contractions of childbirth; the same hormone that causes the nipples to erect during nursing or love play.

This chemical bridge between intercourse, childbirth (undrugged), and breast-feeding, as Niles Newton of Northwestern University Medical School has often pointed out, means that all three experiences can be very sexual for women. The female reproductive system is designed to assure a woman's sexual satisfaction and her continued cooperation in species survival. Western society has never come to terms with this intimate connection, preferring to separate sex and motherhood so that women are seen either as sexy temptresses or saintly mothers. But evidence for the connection is there in female reproductive physiology. By gaining sensual pleasure from nursing, a woman is more likely to breast-feed her infant, and breast-feeding in turn hastens the return of the uterus to its prepregnancy shape and size. Pregnancy and childbirth themselves may improve the pleasures of intercourse because orgasmic intensity is related to congestion of blood vessels in the pelvic area, a condition that increases with each pregnancy.

Sexual attitudes and experiences in childbirth are apparently related, as some anthropological and psychological studies indicate. Margaret Mead and Niles Newton report that in tribes that have relaxed sexual beliefs and customs, such as the South American Siriono, childbirth is remarkably short and uncomplicated. In contrast, in tribes that are sexually inhibited—such as the Panamanian Cuna, who prevent young girls from learning anything about sex or childbirth until the marriage ceremony—birth is usually a prolonged and painful event. Western societies, needless to say, have approximated the Cuna more than the Siriono.

By ignoring the biosocial dimension of human life American society has created unprecedented stress on young mothers and impoverished relationships with children. The heavy emphasis on cultural determinism has set up unnecessary problems for women during pregnancy and childbirth and blocked the knowledge we all need on how best to organize our lives and families.

We do not know enough, for example, about the causes of stress in pregnant women. Some women are probably made anxious by working, others by not working, others by some kinds of high-pressure work. We need better guidelines to assist women in deciding whether and for how long to work during their pregnancies. Even more important, we need to know the effects of the work environments themselves. Millions of women are employed in factories that expose them to chemicals and synthetics, but we know little about the possible effects on the fetus.

We know from the hundreds of studies that have been done on the menstrual cycle that hormonal fluctuations are accompanied by changes in mood. But no one seems to care much about the effect of hormones during pregnancy, when hormone levels are many times higher.

At least we have learned how disastrous the medical management of childbirth is to mothers and infants. General anesthesia cheats the mother of consciousness at the moment of birth, when her high hormone levels and the euphoria of her accomplishment contribute to positive feelings and a deep attachment between mother and child. This early bonding appears to be important for both of them in their continuing attachment, but the first 24 hours are critical.

The typical isolation of new mothers after they have returned home from the hospital also represents a radical departure from the historical behavior of our species. In earlier stages of human history, mothers in most cultures moved in a world crowded with kin who helped them with the care of their infants. For the majority of American women today, the natural birth process is impeded by the medical distortion of spontaneous birth. The mother is separated from the baby for most of the critical first few days, the infant is fed according to a rigid schedule, and the two are sent home afterward, where the inexperienced mother is left alone to cope with her new responsibilities. And then we wonder why some women break down under this strange regimen.

Studies have found that as women have more children, their emotional stress increases. Post-partum depression gets worse with the third or fourth child. One biosocial reason may be that the short interval between births now popular ("Have all your children close together and get it over with") is relatively new in human history and contradicts the physiology developed in the course of human evolution. In earlier times, breast-feeding, together with physical activity and a diet low in carbohydrate and protein, kept body fat low enough to prevent ovulation and helped to space children at least three years apart. With the enriched diets of American women, lactation no longer works as birth control. A second child in two years taxes the mother's emotional and physical stamina and puts undue stress on her ability to give each of them the best kind of attention.

Human continuity through reproduction and child rearing is the basic function of any family system. The older sociological view of the family distorted that fact by overemphasizing women's role, and the new view ignores it. It has become fashionable to disparage the nuclear family. Some proponents of sexual liberation, gay liberation, socialism, humanism, self-actualization, and some segments of feminism are allied in a general denunciation of the traditional model—husband, wife, and children, in which the husband is breadwinner and the wife is homemaker. Such families, they say, are oppressive, sexist, bourgeois, and sick. They offer, by way of replacement, everything from open and group marriages and communal living to mate swapping, cohabitation, and the dual-career childless couple. The implicit (or explicit) premise in many of these denunciations of the family is the right of the individual to pursue private sexual pleasure and complete personal freedom. James Smith and Lynn Smith, for example, refer to monogamous marriage as "sexual monopoly," and "a form of emotional and sexual malnutrition." Similarly, Judith Lorber claims that "a feminist goal is total freedom of choice in sex partners throughout one's life."

One problem with all this freedom is that nobody is looking after the children. Researchers who study alternatives to the family tend to concentrate on the relationships between the adults, the chances for the wife's self-actualization at work, and the husband's emotional gratification at home. In a special 1972 issue of *The Family Coordinator,* subtitled "Variant Marriage Styles and Family Forms," only 5 percent of the pages in the volume dealt with any aspect of being a parent or caring for children. When children are discussed, it is generally in the same tones as the analysis of sexual liberation: The adult should be able to turn parenthood on and off, free to exchange children as well as sexual partners.

The following statement by Robert Thamm advocating communal families expresses the attitude typical of much family sociology these days: "By always having some children in our unit, we will be able to assume parental roles when and for as long as we want. . . . Our children will have an advantage [in that] from the adults they can select their own parents, brothers, sisters, friends. . . . Our social ties will not be forced nor strained by the mandates of kinship and marital obligation."

Most serious studies of such experiments find that the ideology is not that easily put into practice. Many counterculture parents are trying to rear children without being bothered by them, with tragic results for the children. In Rosabeth Kanter's studies of urban communes, the children, who ranged from four to 12 years of age, showed a considerable amount of confusion, which Kanter believes is a result of their continually facing many rapid demands or corrections made by unrelated adults at the same time. John Rothchild and Susan Wolf's book on children of the counterculture described children who were almost uniformly neglected, deprived, and tormented. Many were uneducated and disorganized. Boredom, depression, and undernourishment were prevalent. The authors concluded that communes are the best way to rear children because they do away with materialism and competitiveness.

It is hard for me to see how adults or children benefit from this new model of human liberation. So far, the standards of sexual and parental liberation have followed a male script for both sexes. Traditionally, men, not women, have been more likely to seek numerous sexual partners without emotional entanglement; men, not women, have been more likely to turn parental duties on and off as business demands or personal choice dictates. This turn of events apparently comes from confusing difference with equality.

The arguments set forth in this essay may rankle those whose version of sexual equality requires females to model their lives on male patterns, placing great emphasis on work and little emphasis on family and home. But I am no stranger to criticism. In 1964 I wrote an article in the journal *Daedalus* called "Equality between the Sexes: An Immodest Proposal." By later feminist standards my argument for equality was mild indeed, but the reaction of traditionalists in 1964 was not. I was considered by some a monster, an unnatural woman, an unfit mother. My husband, also a sociologist, received an anonymous condolence card lamenting the death of his wife.

My theme was simple enough. For the first time in known history, I wrote, motherhood had become a full-time occupation for adult women, and motherhood was not enough. For the psychological and physical health of mother and child, for the sake of the trembling family unit, and for the progress of society, equality between men and women was essential and inevitable.

Older women, who were past career choices, resented my article; younger women felt reprieved. I know for certain that my essay lowered the birth rate by at least 12 children, and increased the number of Ph.D.s accordingly.

Last year I wrote another article for *Daedalus*, one that represented an evolution of my views. I said that cultural determinism had gone too far. In the effort to debunk the wrong-headed beliefs that had debased women for so long, the environmentalists had got themselves into an untenable position. Instead of replacing outdated biological theories with new, accurate knowledge, they were forced to deny that there are any physiological differences between men and women. This view is as foolhardy as the view that sex differences are caused only by physiology.

Once again I found myself being screamed at—this time by the very people whose cause I had supported for nearly two decades. I was accused of selling out, of betraying my commitment to political and economic equality for women, of pandering to conservatives who believe in Man the Aggressor and Woman the Doormat. In this area, as in any research that has serious implications for how we run our lives, commitments are strong and tempers short.

But I believe that contemporary efforts to break up traditional family systems are doomed unless aspects of our biological heritage are acknowledged and then, if we wish, compensated for. The mother-infant relationship will continue to have greater emotional depth than the father-infant relationship because of the mother's physiological experience of pregnancy, birth, and nursing. A society that chooses to overcome the female's greater investment in children must institutionalize a program of compensatory education for boys and men that trains them in infant and child care. (Even then, women may still have the stronger bond with their offspring.) Conversely, any goal that sets women equal to men in the military or in strength-related fields will also require compensatory training for women. Any slackening of such compensatory training—for generations to come— will quickly lead to a regression to the sex-role tradition of our long past, as so many social experiments of this century have shown.

This point of view upsets environmentalists, but we cannot just toss out the physiological equipment that centuries of adaptation have created. We can live with that biological heritage or try to supersede it, but we cannot wish it away. I think we should aim for a society better attuned to its environment, more respectful of natural body processes and of the differences between individuals, more concerned for its children, and committed both to achievement in work and in personal intimacy. This version is more radical, and more human, than one of an equality between the sexes that denies differences.

ADDITIONAL READING

FRIEDMAN, RICHARD, R. M. RICHART, AND R. L. VAN DE WIELE, eds. *Sex Differences in Behavior.* John Wiley & Sons, 1974.

MONEY, JOHN, AND ANKE EHRHARDT. *Man and Woman, Boy and Girl.* Johns Hopkins University Press, 1972.

ROSSI, ALICE S. "A Biosocial Perspective on Parenting." *Daedalus,* Vol. 106, 1977, pp. 1–31.

ROSSI, ALICE S. "Equality between the Sexes: An Immodest Proposal." *Daedalus,* Vol. 93, 1964, pp. 607–652.

ROSSI, ALICE S., AND PETER E. ROSSI. "Body Time and Social Time: Mood Patterns by Menstrual Cycle Phase and Day of Week." *Social Science Research,* Vol. 6, 1977, pp. 273–308.

27

Psychological Crises in Normal Pregnancy

Patsy Turrini

This [paper] discusses psychological experience during normal pregnancies, an area sorely in need of attention and study. The ideas are based primarily upon the work of psychoanalytic theorists (e.g. Benedick, 1973; Bibring, 1959; Deutsch, 1973; Kestenberg, 1978), clinical observations and research conducted at the Mother's Center, Hicksville, New York, research in Developmental Ego Psychology (e.g. Blanck & Blanck, 1974; Hartman, 1958, Jacobsen, 1964, Mahler, 1974) and upon the work of the women's health movement. A brief review of some major contributions of each of these positions to understanding pregnancy will be presented first; a description of psychological experiences during the course of pregnancy and case examples will follow.

Bibring (1959) introduced the concept of pregnancy as a *maturational crisis*. She observed severe psychological disturbances in pregnant women who had no previous history of psychopathology or symptomatology. She concluded, and other theorists have concurred, that pregnancy represents a crisis that is resolved only after the child is born. Further, she noted, that therapeutic intervention provides rather immediate relief of the symptoms.

Research at the Mother's Center focuses on factors affecting mothers' self-esteem, self-representations, and the maternal ego ideal. The studies take place a year or more after the pregnancy. Using an exploratory study vehicle, the Post Natal Questionnaire, the events of the pregnancy are reconstructed. Evidence to date has suggested that there are traumas experienced in normal pregnancy and delivery that are laid down in memory states with affect attached to these memories. The memories reside largely in the unconscious or preconscious. The research also indicates that there are some universal psychic developmental crises in pregnancy as well as unique individual responses.

Psychoanalytic developmental ego psychology, which began with Freud, was dramatically augmented by the publication in 1939 (1958 in the United States) of Hartman's "Ego Psychology and the Problem of Adaption." Hartman proposed that the infant *arrives* into the world with a set of inborn ego apparatus of primary automomy, which then interact in the *average expectable environment.* The unfolding of the ego apparatus and the psychoanalytic study of normal development became primary foci of the ego developmentalists.

The women's movement and the women's health movement have challenged and helped in the advancement of our understanding of the developmental and health needs of the female, as well as of the male. *Our Bodies Ourselves* (Boston Women's Health Collective, 1975) noting an example of one of the best writings from the movement, has an excellent chapter on childbearing.

Ego psychology and the women's movement have in common the appreciation that people are a product of their birth and interaction with the environment. They also share the belief that a phenomenon of specific behavior should be appreciated for its adaptation to survival. Further, they both would reject labeling and prejudicial views of women's behavior.

Waelder's (1936) concept of the principle of multiple function also is relevant to understanding experiences during normal pregnancies. Waelder proposed that a "double or generally multiple conception of each psychic action is altogether necessary in the light of psychoanalysis." The principle of multiple function states that even if a psychic act is an attempted solution for one definite problem, it must also, at the same time and in some way, be an attempted solution for other problems; that is, any psychic act is to be understood as the expression of the collective function of the total organism. Pregnancy serves a multiple of psychic needs, and the specific behavior of a pregnant woman is a result of multiple determinants.

The discussion to follow is limited to crises experienced in normal pregnancies. The focus is on the "good enough mother," a term used by Winnicott (1953), in an uncomplicated pregnancy. The good enough mother is defined herein as the person with a structured ego with self-protective functions. She has the capacity for psychological parenthood; as distinguished from mothers who only have a capacity for biological motherhood. Blum (1978) highlighted this distinction in the concept of *the maternal ego ideal,* a substructure of the ego ideal, which resides in the superego. It is the ideal state of the woman's internalizations of how she would like to be as a mother. The maternal ego ideal is determined by many sources, but it is mainly organized by her experiences with her own mother and father. It is a crucial substructure within the personality that organizes the act of protective nurturing.

The following discussion considers only five of the hundreds of "crises" that the good enough mother experiences in a normal pregnancy.

The Decision to Become Pregnant

The decision to become pregnant may not be made consciously and the attempt to make this decision may in and of itself cause an intrapsychic or interpsychic crisis. The female, more often, has the stronger conscious driving force in determining the pregnancy. The male tends to follow the lead. She is more consciously determined and more in pursuit of a child. Although the following example is extreme, it highlights this hypothesis. In one of our postnatal exploratory survey groups, five out of seven women reported that they "pulled the plug" (i.e., consciously did not use the diaphragm unbeknownst to their husbands.) They suffered shame and guilt about their decisions.

As a result of greater freedom of choice in choosing childbearing, young people are thrown into a confusion of *how* to decide to become pregnant. What justifies a decision to bring a child into this world? As one woman said, "I can't just decide to have a child for my own happiness." She was acknowledging that having a child would give her pleasure and that this "too selfish" proposition did not recognize the needs of the "other" (the child and her husband). We might call this confusion a normal conflict residing in the intrasystemic conflict within the ego ideal, and an intersystemic conflict between the id and superego. To have a child is, in fact, based on the pleasure principle and the right to pleasure is not so easily attained in our culture, despite the fact that we tend to see, on the surface, pleasure-seeking adults. Being able to have pleasure *without guilt* often is quite difficult for the unanalyzed person.

Unconscious pleasures are obtained and gratified in having a child. Freud and others postulated on the psychosexual maturation line that the baby is equated with breast-feces-penis, as well as being longed for as the ultimate gift to and union with the father.

An active conscious decision to have a child, therefore, calls up unconscious determinants, sometimes producing guilt. Kohut (1971) proposed that the gleam in the mother's eye is a beacon which influences the child's perception of self and behavior. I have observed clinically that if the parents have discouraged the child from reproducing (and this does happen), it has a profound influence on the motive for nonchildbearing. The grandparents-to-be's wish for a child, a wish determined by their own generativity, has a basic positive influence on the child's freedom to have a child. Having healthy parents who can love themselves encourages the birth of the next generation.

Neugarten's (1972) study of social clocks indicates that we are influenced to adjust to a perceived timetable for life's events. So, for example, we say, we graduated on time; or we married later than most; or we had our baby earlier than some. We judge ourselves against a timetable. She cited the following facts in a paper presented at the American Psychoanalytic Conference: "In 1920, a woman left school at 14, married at 22, had her first child at 24, and her last born child at 42. Her husband died when she was 53, and her last child married when she was 55. She usually was widowed before her last child left home. Today, a woman leaves school at

18, is married at 20, has her first child before 21, and her last child at 26. At 32 her last child is in full-time school, and her last child leaves home when she is 48. Her husband will die when she is 64, and she will live to be 80." Looking at the facts, we can see that a timetable does in fact exist.

Consider another framework. A real family consists of four people. If you are a family of five or three, you are not conforming to the model, and might feel cultural pressure. You are either underpopulating or overpopulating. Our research on the mother of the only child indicated that she suffers extensively from being told she is selfish and obviously raising a spoiled child. One determinant of these remarks stems from the jealousy of those who have had siblings, and have longed for exclusivity with their parents. (Arlow, 1972).

Other people's timetables and views may not have a direct bearing on what we do but the degree to which we are unable to separate or individuate psychologically is the degree to which we may make decisions on others' timetables, or may suffer from considerable criticism if we have differed from the norm.

Does This Child Exist?

Active psychic preparation for parenthood begins with the first missed menstrual period. At this point, however, the only things that are changing in the woman's life are some body features and internal silent physiological processes. Prior to quickening there is enlargement of the breasts, fatigue, some weight gain, and perhaps some morning sickness—body signals that are signs of pregnancy. Few women report any conscious knowledge of the conception or early detection of the fetus. Questions aroused by these body changes include: What is the self and what is the baby? Am I pregnant or not? Should I begin psychological readiness for mothering? Should I announce the pregnancy? There is great fear about announcing a pregnancy and many attitudes color the decision. The superstition exists for some that to think about a healthy baby tempts the hand of fate. This message is frequently taught by the parents, but, also, resides in the harsh superego of the woman herself. The good enough mother frequently suffers from a harsh superego. A critical conflict develops: should she think about being pregnant or not. When the healthy ego, fueled by self-protective functions and ideals of the maternal ego ideal wins, the good enough mother enters into a constant monitoring of her health and of the health of the fetus. On trips to the bathroom, for example, the woman watches for staining, one signal to her of the safety of the fetus. A life and death detection process goes on in the conscious experience, privately, and alone in the bathroom.

The event of quickening brings "great relief." The first physiological response of the baby is often described as a feeling of a bubble or gas. Therefore, the obstetrician's listening with the stethoscope for the heartbeat is a most momentous dramatic event. We have recorded a common reporting of the terrible fear a woman feels while she waits, for what seems endless hours, in a deafening silence, for the physician's verdict. Is there a baby? Is the baby alive? Zimmerman et al. (1977) quotes one woman:

"Someone told me I should feel life at the end of my third month. When I went for my check-up I could hardly stand up, I was so sure I was carrying a dead baby."

At this stage a woman has a strong dependence on her obstetrician and the obstetrical equipment. Awaiting the verdict from the stethoscope reading deepens the woman's perception of the physician as critical to the life and death of her baby. The physician's knowledge of the use of the stethoscope intimidates and influences feelings of self-inadequacy that become set in motion in pregnancy. A group in San Francisco have a storefront pregnancy center where the women take their own urine and blood pressure tests, and use the stethoscope. At last report, they were planning to integrate a pregnancy check center within the local hospital where the women would use the obstetrical equipment themselves. It seems that the more active, the more knowledgeable, the more self-protective a woman can be early in the pregnancy, the more her feelings of resourcefulness and competence can be set in motion.

Decisions women will make during pregnancy by deciding on a particular doctor and hospital have grave consequences. That decision basically determines the type of prenatal care and delivery she and the child will experience. She may be in a crisis state a day, month, or years later as a result of that decision. Overcoming the memory of the psychoticlike state she was in while under the influence of scopolamine, or bearing the pain or hindsight awareness of having chosen a delivery that caused a learning disability in the child are traumas with lasting effects (Turrini, 1977). Therapeutic help to rework the memories can bring relief, but she will suffer from chronic sorrow.

The Last 6 Weeks of Pregnancy

Although the whole of pregnancy has been termed a catastrophe, the last 6 weeks of a pregnancy might be considered a disaster. Here follows a composite image of the state of things, some of which is drawn from the text in *Our Bodies Ourselves* (1975):

> The stomach is pushed up by the uterus and flattened. Indigestion is common. There is shortness of breath and pressure on the lungs from the uterus. The diaphragm may be moved up as much as an inch. There may be difficulty getting a breath. The body is heavy, and walking becomes different in order to effect the proper balance, often leaning back to counteract the heavier front. Backaches occur. Hemmorhoids, constipation, are common, as are varicose veins and stretch marks. The body is in a total state of change. Bending over is impossible, and the protruding abdomen prevents looking at the feet. The Braxton Hicks contractions are frequent, and are quite painful for some women. The baby is very active and kicks may cause bruising and disturb sleep. Activities are sorely restricted. Many women can no longer fit behind the wheel of the car.

Psychic preparation for delivery is complete prior to the last 6 weeks of pregnancy, and the woman is as ready as she ever will be to deliver at the beginning of the last 6 weeks. Completion of psychic preparation for delivery is defined as the acceptance of the reality of the coming baby, an attachment to, yet differentiation and individuation from the longed-for baby. Although there is some controversy on this point, the last 6 weeks do not seem to serve a function in psychic preparation time for delivery. The time hangs heavily. Working women have by this time left their employment, and are beginning to experience isolation, boredom, and the impact from all that it means to be suddenly unemployed. It is the time of the beginning glimmer of the "I felt like I fell off the end of the world" syndrome. In this period resides the looking and listening for the awaited signal for the beginnings of labor. The awareness that there is no way to affect the onset of labor leads to an increase in fears and peculiar thoughts. One woman reported that everytime the phone rang, she thought that she was being called to inform her that labor had begun. Although there are joyful feelings in this period, evidence indicates that there are morbid feelings, not to mention the particularly conflicting feelings about sexual behavior in this period.

We have repeatedly observed that women experience a mild depression if they do not deliver on the due date. The longer the time goes beyond the date, the greater the intensity of the depression. Fears about the babies' health increase rapidly. The delay seems to symbolize an image of a defect, or a "something has gone wrong" sensation.

The Onset of Labor

The onset of labor creates a crisis. All good childbirth preparation courses aim at reducing these fears. Such instructions as: "When you begin labor, do not panic, do not wake your husband, as he will need his sleep for later" reflect interventions to reduce fear. It is too bad that it does not work. When the first contraction hits, when the bloody mucous discharge is observed, if the water breaks, whatever the signal, the woman is on red-alert. She is internally mobilized to arrange conditions to properly deliver a healthy baby. This event needs more intensive study. Perhaps there is a species-specific, i.e., preprogrammed genetically determined behavior that is set in motion at the onset of labor. Klaus & Kennell (1976) describe it this way:

> Detailed and precise observations of many species have shown that adaptive species-specific patterns of behaviour—including *nesting*, exploring, grooming and retrieving—before, during and after parturition, have evolved to meet the needs of the young in the animal's usual environment. For example, the domestic cat, whether in Russia, the United States, or England, behaves in a characteristic way at the time of the birth of her kittens.

If, as I believe, a species-specific behavior exists, it works in combination with the healthy developed ego functions. A mother is capable of mothering as a result of a combination of these structures and forces. Consider then, that the signs in early labor stimulate instinctual "nesting" activity. What starts to go wrong is that others are not in tune with the woman's feelings in early labor. Our culture has arranged for her to be alone during the beginning of labor. Research has indicated that women do a fine job of going through the early labor process alone, putting aside their needs and fears and mounting terror about the delivery. As one woman described, "When labor began I went out to get food. I was standing in line at McDonald's buying food for the other children, when it hit me, 'This is a funny place to be.'" She suddenly became aware of her aloneness, and the inappropriate place for a delivery.

In our studies, women report feelings of extreme fright during early labor. Any time in life that one experiences strong feelings of fright or helplessness, a resulting scar image will be laid down. Therefore, psychological scars result from fears of labor.

A particular phenomenon observed repeatedly that creates more of a crisis in early labor is the assumption of certain "indisputable truisms" of the medical team. An article in the living section of *Newsday*, March 13, 1978 entitled: "Bouquets for Unlikely Midwives" reflected this phenomenon:

> Mrs. Pope, age 31, was not due to deliver for another two weeks . . . but she began having labor pains while lying on the couch. "My father," said Mrs. Pope, "called the fire department, and they were in contact with our Doctor. He (the Doctor) said it must be false labor pains. But the fire chief said, 'No way. She's giving birth right now.' They (the firemen) did all the work. The baby came out and they wrapped him up and clamped up the umbilical cord." The truth is that no one can predict the course of the labor nor the timing of the delivery. (p. 7)

Women are repeatedly told that they should enter the hospital when they have 3-minute regular contractions. The majority of women in our studies indicated there is "no such thing as a regular 3-minute contraction." A commonly reported pattern in early labor is a 10-minute, 3-minute, 12-minute, 5-minute, 10-minute contraction pattern. Women accept the myth of the regular 3-minute contraction, and become additionally confused and frightened about where to be during early labor. Furthermore, they assume that their irregularity is peculiar to them and representative of their being abnormal. We have had reports from women of being rejected from entry into the hospital because of irregular contractions. In one reported incident, the family went home, the mother tried to keep calm during increasingly intense contractions, and when she would stand it no longer, they rushed back to the hospital. Then she was required to go through the admission procedure and then placed on the stretcher in the hall. When she said she was about to deliver, the physician told her not to push. Two minutes later she delivered the child, alone in the hospital hallway. The physician screamed that she could have killed the baby and ripped her insides out by having pushed. This same woman reported having difficulty in bonding in the early period with her baby. The inhumane care she received and the accusation made, I interpret, caused her to feel a terrible sense of inadequacy. The truth is that there are irregular contractions, and that the 3-minute contraction is not an appropriate signal for entering the hospital.

The simple solution for humane care in early labor is that a woman should be with an empathic aware person who is knowledgeable and able to help her deliver. Being alone is an excessive strain. Having someone to ask questions of, and being in a place where the woman knows she can deliver comfortably, is essential to her mental health in early labor. Early labor lounges, where families can be together and move about would be better for the mental health of the husband, too.

Labor and Obstretrical Intervention

The effects of obstetric tools, e.g., fetal monitors, forceps, the strapped labor table, the intravenous bottle, on women's behavior also must be considered. Feridian's introduction to Lang's (1972) *The Birth Book* traces the history of forceps in obstetrical care:

> In 1598, the Chamberlain brothers invented the forceps, but kept them selfishly as a family secret until the latter half of the 17th Century. The forceps were of extreme value in certain deliveries, but unfortunately, when the use of this tool became popularized, it began to be used needlessly in uncomplicated cases without warrant. With the introduction of such skilled manipulations, men once again entered the profession of midwifery. It is of great significance that the attendance of male midwives followed closely upon the introduction of forceps into childbirth. In the late 1600's, Mauriceau first began to deliver his childbearing "Patients" in bed. In America, Dewees introduced the back delivery in the mid 1800's. Previously, and dating to antiquity, women had given birth squatting, seated on the obstetrical stool, or upon the lap of another woman. With Mauriceau's intervention, the woman was placed flat on her back, a position which offers a fine view to the performing physician, but is in total defiance to the active forces of gravity. Nor does this position encourage the laboring woman to utilize her own efforts in delivery.

Obstetrical teams do not exactly have a perfect track record in the use of equipment, yet many persons are in awe of machinery. Roberto Caldero-Barcia, past-President of the International Federation of Gynecologists and Obstetricians, and director of the Latin American Center for Perinatology and Human Development of the World Health Organization, has described (1975) the extreme deleterious effects to the baby of the early breaking of the amniotic sac to stimulate labor, thereby removing the protective cushion for the baby's head as it moves and bangs down the birth canal. Mehl (1976) has reported the damage to the infant's head through the use of forceps. These are but two of the frightening results of the use of obstetrical equipment during birth.

Research continues to suggest that certain birth practices may have consequences to the fetus which can cause severe organic difficulties, minimal brain dysfunction, and even death. It is the work of a few people, like Doris Haire (e.g. 1972), which has brought to public awareness, and which has begun to raise the consciousness of the community to the cataclysmic effects that can occur through the use of obstetrical equipment.

The challenge in regard to the use of obstetrical equipment is that all parties involved in pregnancy and delivery must be aware of the ramifications of its use, both psychologically and physiologically, both to the mother and to the child. The physician alone should not make all the decisions. The parents should have the opportunity to have full knowledge of the type of equipment that may be used, alternative approaches, and then be in the position to participate actively with the obstetrical team in the decision-making process. It is essential that medical and nonmedical people work together to assure the most optimal delivery possible.

Issues for the Therapist or Counselor

Critical to helping women in pregnancy is a proper diagnostic assessment. It must be appreciated that certain psychic developmental tasks of pregnancy are universal to all pregnant women. The major body changes in a short period of time and the challenge of attaching to, yet differentiating out from the developing baby are two of the critical tasks. It must be recognized that the women with well-developed ego functions (the good enough mother) will be deeply challenged by these tasks. Some denial, regression in the service of the ego, and mood states of depression, anxiety, unusual fears, and guilt can be considered normal in pregnancy. Women with less structured egos, and less self-protective functions, particularly those with out object constancy, will experience severe stress and will need even greater support and help.

It must be recognized in diagnostic assessment that external events will have a potentially damaging effect on the pregnant women's mental health, and therapists need to know what these are, and help women anticipate what will be of help to them, what will facilitate their growth, so that scars can be prevented. We must find ways to use the maturational crisis of pregnancy, the obstetrical tools, the setting in which she gives birth to promote growth, maturity, confidence, a positive body image, and a sense of well-being. Women should be encouraged to be active, to learn more about their bodies and their capacity and strength to overcome previously inhibiting fears, and to rise to their optimal capacities. Therapists must come to appreciate the cataclysmic effects of pregnancy and parenting and to have full knowledge of this subject.

Conclusion

The traumas associated with pregnancy are laid down in memory states residing largely in the unconscious and affect is attached to these memories. When a woman says everything was fine for her, she consciously believes that. The repressed memories, however, can drain energies away from more positive self-esteem within herself, and away from the interchange in bonding with her child. The Post Natal Questionnaire used at the Mother's Center is one tool which enables women to work through the pregnancy and birth trauma (Turrini, 1977). Not only does the Mothers' Center help women get relief with this hindsight experience, it is a gathering place to complement programs which will prevent trauma to the mother, father, and child.

It is hoped that the psychiatric, social work, psychological, and nursing communities will attend to the critical psychic components affecting members of the family in pregnancy and childbirth. These psychic phenomena must be researched, catalogued, and the findings disseminated. Can anyone dispute the fact that healthy children born into a healthy family is the basis for a sound sane society?

REFERENCES

ARLOW, J. The only child. *Psychoanalytic quarterly,* 1972 *61* (4,) 507–536.

BENEDEK, T. Psychological aspects of mothering. Parenting as a developmental phase, *Psychoanalytic investigations.* New York: Quandrangle / The New York Times, 1973.

BIBRING, G. Some considerations of the psychological process in pregnancy, *The Psychoanalytic study of the child, 14:* 113–121.

BLANCK, G., & BLANCK, R. *Ego psychology: Theory and practice,* New York: Columbia University Press, 1974.

BLUM, H. The maternal ego ideal, Unpublished paper. New York, March, 1978.

BOSTON WOMENS HEALTH COLLECTIVE. *Our bodies ourselves.* Boston: Simon & Schuster, 1975.

CALDEYRO-BARCIA, R. Obstetric intervention: Its effect on the fetus and newborn Part II. Paper presented at the *Obstetrical Management and Infant Outcome: Implications for Future Mental and Physical Development.* Wednesday, April 9, 1975, New York.

DEUTSCH, H. *The Psychology of Women, Volume II: Motherhood,* New York: Bantam Books, 1973.

FREUD, S. (1909) Analysis of a phobia in a five-year old boy. *The Collected works of Sigmund Freud* Vol. 10, London: Hogarth Press, 1955.

HAIRE, D. *The cultural warping of childbirth.* Seattle: International Childbirth Education Association, 1972.

HARTMAN, H. *Ego psychology and the problem of adaptation.* New York: International Universities Press, 1958.

Bouquets for unlikely midwives. *Newsday,* March 13, 1978.

JACOBSON, E. *The self and the object world.* New York: International Universities Press, 1964.

KESTENBERG, J. Regression and reintegration in pregnancy. *Journal of the American Psychoanalytic Association,* 1976, *24,* 243–250.

KLAUS, M. & KENNELL, J. *Maternal and infant bonding.* St. Louis. Mosby, 1976.

KOHUT, H. *The analysis of the self.* New York: International Universities Press, 1971.

LANG, R. Introduction. *The birth book.* Palo Alto, Cal: Genesis Press, 1972.

MAHLER, M. PINE, F. BERGMAN, A. *The Psychological Birth of the Human Infant,* Basic Books, Inc., 1975.

MEHL, L. Statistical outcome of home births in the U.S., current status *Safe alternatives in childbirth.* Chapel Hill, N.C.: National Association of Parents and Professionals for Safe Alternatives in Childbirth, (NAPSAC), 1976.

NEUGARTEN, B. Social Clocks, A paper presented at the American Psychoanalytic Association. New York, December, 1972.

TURRINI, P. A Mothers Center: Research, Service and Advocacy. *Social Work Journal,* 1977, *22,* (6), 478–483.

WAELDER, R. The principle of multiple function. *The psychoanalytic quarterly,* 1936, *5,*

WINNICOTT, D. W. Transitional objects and transitional phenomena, *International Journal of Psychoanalysis,* 1953, *34.*

ZIMMERMAN, H. TURRINI, P. WEISS, S. SLEPIAN, L. A mothers center, women work for social change. *Children Today,* 1977, 11–13. 6, (2).

28

The Role of the Mother in Early Social Development

H. Rudolph Schaffer and Charles K. Crook

The child's transformation from a biological to a social being in the space of just the first year or two of life is surely the most important aspect by far of early development. How it occurs is a matter of fascination to both the student of human nature and the practitioner wanting to improve the conditions under which children are reared.

That the particular society in which children are brought up has powerful effects on the course of their development cannot be doubted. Anthropological evidence in particular can highlight the sharply contrasting effects on personality development that different child-rearing patterns may have. Take some of Margaret Mead's (1935) descriptions of socialization practices and their outcome in different cultures: the angry rejection by the Mundugumour mother of her child from the moment of pregnancy onward and the pattern of hostility which pervades all adult behaviour; the pathological teasing that Balinese children continually experience from their mothers and the emotional bluntness that becomes the outstanding characteristic of individuals in that society; the reversal of sex-role appropriate behaviour in comparison with Western norms that Tchambuli upbringing of boys and girls induces, and so on. The same point emerges from intra-societal comparisons, albeit in a less dramatic form: the influence of social class on language acquisition and subsequent intellectual performance is one such instance.

Yet it is easy to concentrate on differences and neglect the similarities underlying the diversity. The very nature of mother and child imposes constraints that ensure a basic similarity underlying the social behaviour of all. Thus all infants are born motorically helpless and dependent and signal their needs by such species-specific responses as crying and smiling, and the manner of responding to these signals on the part of their caretakers shows remarkable similarities too—see, for example, the universal usage of adults' baby language when addressing young children (Fergusson, 1964). An account of social development ought therefore not to confine itself to explaining differences alone: it should also consider similarities.

The society that impinges on a child is, of course, not an abstract entity; it functions through particular agents. Two questions arise, namely who these agents are and how they function. Our concern in this chapter is with the latter problem; before we turn to its examination, however, let us also acknowledge the importance of the former. The identity of socialization agents varies to some extent from one culture to another: older siblings, the maternal uncle, and unrelated women have all been found to play roles in other societies that they do not play in our own. Yet in our society too there is nothing absolute about the identity of socialization agents, particularly in view of the rapid changes overtaking such institutions as the nuclear family. The increasing recognition given to the influence of the father (Lamb, 1976) and of peers (Bronfenbrenner, 1971; Hartup, 1970) is ample testimony of this fact, as is the virtual disappearance of the wet-nurse and the nanny who in former times played such important parts in certain social circles.

Nevertheless, in the first year or two of life (the period of concern to us in the present chapter) the child's care in most cases tends to be the primary responsibility of one person. That person—whether the child's biological parent or not, even whether male or female—we shall refer to as 'mother'. It is by analysing the child's interactions with that individual that we can learn how the first steps in the socialization process are taken. This [paper] will therefore examine the events that take place in these interactions, with particular reference to the part played by the mother in determining their structure.

Approaches to Socialization

Socialization is an umbrella term that refers to a wide range of topics frequently bound together in only the most tenuous manner. The very diversity of definitions given to the term is an indication of this confusion. LeVine (1969), for example, distinguishes three views of the process, namely socialization as enculturation, as the acquisition of impulse control, and as role training. The three views are said to correspond roughly to the orientations of cultural anthropology, psychology and sociology respectively.

Yet even within any one of these disciplines, with particular reference to psychology, there is by no means unanimity. To a large extent this is a reflection of the particular theory of child development that happens to be prevalent at the time. For example, as long as learning theory was the predominant point of view, the child was seen as an essentially passive organism, shaped by whatever forces he happened to encounter in his environment. Socialization was thus seen as a kind of clay-moulding process: the child, that is, arrives in the world as a formless lump of clay and society, as represented by mothers, fathers, teachers and other authority figures, proceeds to mould him into whatever shape it desires. The end product would thus be wholly explicable in terms of the external forces which the child encountered, and if by chance this product turned out to be undesirable it could be regarded as entirely the responsibility of the socializing agents. It follows that all attempts to understand how socialization comes about must involve an analysis of the behaviour of the adults with whom the child comes into contact: the child's own part was confined simply to observing, learning, retaining, imitating and reproducing whatever occurred in front of him.

The advent of Piagetian theory put an end to this one-sided view—though only to substitute another equally one-sided account. From birth on, Piaget maintained, the child's behaviour shows form and organization. Far from being a *tabula rasa* the neonate is already equipped with certain behavioural structures by means of which he acts on the environment and which enable him to influence others as well as be influenced by them. Far from being a passive being, the infant interacts spontaneously with his surroundings; far from responding to every stimulus to which the environment happens to expose him he carefully selects those aspects of his surroundings that fit in with his predilections. A considerable body of empirical research on infant behaviour has now spelled out the details of psychological competence in the early months and years of life and demonstrated the many avenues open to the infant to make contact with others. The child-rearing literature echoed this change of orientation: from a concern with the socializing adult's action it switched to a concern with the socialized child's action, and a primarily child-centred approach thus came into being—one which focused solely on the child and took the environment for granted, neglecting its variations and treating it simply as a constant. We thus see a swing from one extreme to the other, from a preoccupation with environmental forces to a preoccupation with the individual child without any reference to that environment. In each case a unidirectional view is taken which neglects one half of the picture.

It is only more recently that a *dyadic* view has emerged. Socialization, thus conceived, is based on interaction and its function is to smooth the conduct of such interaction. It always involves two (or more) participants, each already equipped with his own set of predispositions, aims, intentions and predilections, and any interaction between them must therefore inevitably involve a negotiating process, as a result of which progressive modification in the behaviour of both participants takes place. Zigler and Child (1973) bring us nearest to this point of view with their characterization of socialization as 'the whole process by which an individual develops, *through transactions with other people*, his specific patterns of socially relevant behaviour and experience' (italics ours). To understand the socialization process means therefore that these transactions must be examined in detail, for by attending to the behaviour of *both* parties we can learn how the child becomes gradually transformed into an increasingly acculturated being.

This also means, however, that our concern is no longer solely with long-term effects—with just the final product that eventually emerges in maturity. Much of previous research involved efforts to link early experi-

ence in child-rearing situations to personality characteristics in maturity—
efforts that (as reviews by Orlansky, 1949, and Caldwell, 1964, have shown)
have resulted in ambiguous and often negative results. It is now apparent
that the attempt to forge such links over time is too fraught with methodological and conceptual difficulties to make simple antecedent-consequent
statements possible (Clarke and Clarke, 1976). Instead, consideration needs
to be given to all the intermediate steps, i.e. to the here-and-now effects
that indicate how the child and his adult caretakers progressively modify
each other.

That children's behaviour is changed as a result of interacting with
socializing agents, and that this change occurs in particular directions which
reflect the values of the society in which they live, is, of course, not in question. How the change is brought about, however, is still open to debate. In
the past socialization has generally been treated as though a model of 'potty
training' were applicable to it all: as though, that is, it is solely concerned
with preventing the child from doing what is natural and forcing him to
comply with some quite arbitrary requests by powerful adults for new and
unnatural behaviour. Such a view sees the child as being in fundamental
opposition to society, and conceives of socializing techniques as those forces
(often punitive) that push the child into compliance. Many such techniques
have been suggested in the past (Hoffman, 1970), power assertion and
withdrawal of love being perhaps the most common. Thus much of the
socialization literature is concerned with sanctions and with the way in which
socially desirable behaviour is reinforced and undesirable behaviour punished.

There are a number of criticisms of this view that one can make: the
slippery nature of the concept of reinforcement and the consequent difficulty of ever proving or disproving it; the fact that the techniques suggested are rarely derived from observing what parents actually do; the highly
constrained model of the rewarding or punishing parent which laboratory
studies of social reinforcement generally assume, and so on. But more
important, it neglects the basic mutuality between mother and child that
recent studies have so strongly emphasized and that forms the framework
within which any attempt to understand the socialization process must be
placed.

Mother-Child Mutuality

Much of the literature concerned with the child's earliest stages of social
development has centred on the concept of attachment (see Ainsworth,
1974; Bowlby, 1969; Schaffer, 1971). A considerable body of research has
now accumulated around this topic; most of this, however, treats attachment as an essentially individual-based characteristic, i.e. as though it were
the property of individual children which they must acquire in the course
of development and which from then on forms part of their personality.
The questions asked by investigators have accordingly concerned such topics as the age when attachments first become evident, the behaviour patterns whereby they are expressed, the variations in intensity of both an
intra- and an interindividual nature, the persons to whom they are directed,

and so on. The focus of study, in other words, is on the child *per se*, with relatively little attention being paid to his social partners and the interaction with them.

It is only recently that a new direction has been taken in the way in which early social development is approached, with emphasis given to the interactive quality of social behaviour (Schaffer, 1977a). The mother-child relationship is seen, in other words, as a total dyadic system in which both partners play a part in achieving mutual synchrony. Accordingly, the questions now asked by investigators are different: they concern the nature of these early dyadic systems, their characteristics at different developmental stages, and the respective contributions which mother and child make to the interaction.

Some Early Social Interactions

Let us first acknowledge the fact that from birth onwards an infant participates in interpersonal behaviour sequences of many types, of varying degrees of sophistication and intricacy, and involving different channels of communication (visual, vocal, tactual, and so on), but all already bearing some of the hallmarks that characterize interpersonal dialogues. Some examples, though drawn from very different situations, show the communality that exists among these early dialogues.

The sucking response is the first means whereby an infant comes into close contact with another being. A great body of work (reviewed by Kessen et al., 1970) testifies to the intricacy of this response; in particular, we have learned a great deal in recent years about the innately based temporal organization underlying sucking. This normally takes the form of a burst-pause pattern, i.e. sucks tend to occur in a series of bursts, with pauses interspersed. We are thus confronted with a high-frequency micro-rhythm—an apparently simple motor activity that is in fact organized in complex time sequences regulated by an endogenous mechanism in the brain (Wolff, 1967). It is perhaps ironic that a highly social response such as sucking has, until recently, usually been abstracted from the interpersonal context in which it generally occurs and studied in isolation. Yet, as the work of Kaye (1977) indicates, by adopting a wider focus of study and including the mother's as well as the baby's behaviour during feeding, sucking emerges as just one part of an interpersonal dialogue that takes place in this situation. In particular, Kaye has shown that mothers tend to interact with their babies in precise synchrony with the burst-pause pattern of sucking. During bursts they are generally quiet and inactive; during pauses, on the other hand, they jiggle, stroke and talk to the baby, thereby setting in motion an alternating pattern in which first one and then the other is principal actor while the other remains passive. This is primarily brought about, however, because the mother allows herself to be paced by the infant's spontaneous behaviour: she fits in with his natural sucking pattern, responds to his ceasing to suck as though it were a signal to her, and in this way sets up a dialogue between them.

This example provides us with a prototype for a great deal of early interaction. In particular, it emphasizes that the interpersonal synchrony generally observed between mother and infant is based on the integration of the two participants' responses *over time,* and that it is accomplished on the basis of two main factors: first, the baby's spontaneously occurring behaviour, temporally organized according to endogenous mechanisms, and second, the mother's sensitivity to such periodicity and her willingness to fit in with this pattern. The precision and smoothness which generally characterize the interaction is thus the resultant of these two factors.

A second example concerns vocal interchange. One common way of ensuring the smoothness of many forms of interaction is by means of an alternating pattern of dialogue. This is especially evident in adults' verbal conversations, where an intricate set of rules for turn taking and the smooth exchange of speaker- and listener-roles can be discerned (Duncan, 1973). A study by Schaffer et al. (1977) has shown, however, that formal characteristics of verbal interchange such as turn taking antedate the appearance of language: the vocal exchanges of preverbal infants with their mothers in a free play situation were just as much characterized by an alternating pattern as those of older, verbal children. Moreover, among the former the exchanges of speaker- and listener-roles were just as easily handled, with the same kind of split-second timing, as was found in the older group.

Among adults the turn-taking pattern is, of course, usually brought about by the *joint* action of the two participants: they both know the rules and both attend to the signals on which these rules are based. It seems highly unlikely that this applies to infants too; instead, a much more likely explanation is that the responsibility is almost wholly assumed by the mother. The infant's vocalizations, that is, occur in bouts and, by carefully attending, the mother is then able to fill in the pauses between the bouts. Thus— as with sucking—we find that the interaction starts with the infant's spontaneous behaviour and that the mother, by virtue of her sensitivity to the temporal patterning of her baby's responses, then incorporates these into a mutual exchange in which she acts *as if* his behaviour had truly communicational significance.

One further example comes from a study by Collis and Schaffer (1975) on the way in which mothers and infants establish mutual attention to features of the environment. Observations in a novel environment containing a number of attention-compelling foci (large, brightly coloured toys placed at a distance from the pair) highlighted two findings. First, it was noted that there was a strong tendency for both partners to be attending to the same object at the same time (a phenomenon termed 'visual co-orientation'), and, second, when one examines how such mutual attention is brought about it emerges that almost invariably it was the baby that led and the mother that followed. The baby, that is, showed spontaneous interest in the various toys, the mother closely monitored his behaviour almost continuously and then, as if allowing herself to be led by him, she looked in that direction too. Visual co-orientation means that the couple share a topic of interest and it thus may become the first step in a whole series of further interactions involving this topic (talking about it, manipulating it, and so forth). More important to our present concern is that once again we have an illustration of a type of interaction that is initiated by the infant but converted by the mother into a dyadic experience.

Social interactions, even those involving young infants, generally give the impression of 'smoothness'. Somehow the various participants manage to enmesh their individual responses into a synchronous dyadic flow with all the appearance of dialogue. Yet these early interactions are really 'pseudo-dialogues', for the two partners do not play an equal role. In each of the examples we have examined the infant sets the pace and the mother allows herself to be phased by his behaviour. Reciprocity, in the sense of both partners taking equal responsibility for maintaining the interaction by assuming interlocking and exchangeable roles, is not yet evident.

The Infant's Contribution

It is apparent that the 'smoothness' of these early interactions is due to contributions from both mother and infant. As to the infant, it has been pointed out elsewhere (Schaffer, 1978) that his behaviour has all the hall-marks of being socially pre-adapted, i.e. that by virtue of its endogenous characteristics it is from the beginning specifically suited to social interaction. Two aspects of social pre-adaptation may be distinguished, namely *structural* and *functional* aspects. The former refer to those bodily structures which serve to bring the infant into contact with other people, such as the oral apparatus that is precisely adapted to cope with the nipple and food that the mother will provide, his visual structures that are highly sensitive to those aspects of stimulation that tend to emanate from other people's faces, and his auditory equipment that is selectively attuned to the human voice. Functional aspects refer to the way in which these structures are used, and may be seen in particular in the fact that from the first weeks of life the different behaviour patterns of the child (suckling, smiling, crying, and so on) are organized according to specific temporal sequences. Thus the biological rhythms that underlie such responses as sucking have a regularity which make it possible for the mother to anticipate the infant's behaviour, and it may well be that the split-second timing that characterizes so much of interactive behavior is the result of such anticipation. And furthermore, the on-off nature of so much of sensorimotor activity (seen, for example, in the bout structure of vocalization) provides the pauses that enable the other person to take turns with the infant and in this way to set up the pseudo-dialogues so characteristic of the infant's early social life.

A basic compatibility between the infant and his caretakers is thus ensured. In due course, through repeated participation in interactive sequences, the infant's primitive temporal patterns become transformed into vastly more complex and flexible structures. Pseudo-dialogues become dialogues, in that *both* partners take a share in sustaining them and playing mutually integrative and exchangeable roles (speaker and listener, actor and spectator, giver and taker, and so forth). For this to come about, however, the child's social partners must be willing to afford the necessary opportunities for interaction through involvement in dialogue-like exchanges.

The Mother's Contribution

It is apparent that a considerable onus lies with the mother to ensure that the infant's social experience is appropriately structured. How does she play this part and, for that matter, how may one best study what she does?

In the past the examination of the mother's relationship with her child has been based to a considerable extent on the use of interviews and questionnaires, in which the individuals involved reported on their own behaviour. The advantage of such global techniques lies, of course, in their economy: within the space of a few minutes a mother can make generalized statements about her behaviour within the last twenty-four hours, the last week or the last few years. She has, moreover, access to parts of the family's daily life that outsiders would not normally penetrate, and in addition she can endow events with an emotional significance that might well be missed by an impartial observer.

Yet the disadvantages of such an approach have gradually come to outweigh the advantages. In part this arises from increasing doubts about the reliability of data so obtained: for instance, in an unfortunately only too rare attempt at replication Yarrow et al. (1968) completely failed to confirm the classical study of Sears et al. (1957), in which reports from the mothers of 379 five-year-old children had been obtained regarding the rearing practices they had adopted at various phases of the child's life. Using the same techniques and measures of Sears et al. in order to examine the child-rearing antecedents of dependence, aggression and conscience formation, Yarrow and her colleagues were unable to find the patterns of relationships previously obtained, and were thus forced to conclude that the assumed link between maternal influence and child behaviour has as yet no roots in solid data and that its verification thus remains a subject for future research.

Equally compelling, however, was the gradual disillusionment with the kinds of concepts that were used for elucidating parental behaviour—concepts like warmth, rejection, authoritarianism, and so forth. Adopted originally because of their wide-ranging nature, it gradually became clear that they were far too global and arbitrary for explanatory purposes. As summary variables they average out parental characteristics over time and situation and as a result not only neglect some of the most meaningful nuances of the relationship but also fail to act as predictors of child behaviour. Concepts need to arise out of the behavioural data to which they refer rather than be imposed on them.

Accordingly, a much more observationally based approach to the study of the mother-child relationship has now been adopted—impelled to a considerable extent by the growth of human ethology (Blurton Jones, 1972). It has also become apparent that when this approach is employed at a highly detailed, micro-analytic level of description, a great many new phenomena may be uncovered which throw light on the way in which mother and child establish mutuality (Schaffer, 1977a). In particular, it is now becoming possible to specify much more precisely just what dyadic techniques a mother employs in interacting with children at various ages (see Schaffer, 1977b, for further discussion).

That mothers carefully and continuously adjust the type of stimulation offered to an infant throughout the course of an interactive episode and that they most sensitively, though generally quite unconsciously, adjust their behaviour towards him in the light of their perception of his capacities, has been documented by a number of writers. For example, analyses of speech addressed by mothers to their children show that linguistic complexity varies quite systematically with the child's age: the younger the child, the simpler the verbal input which the mother provides (Snow, 1972; Phillips, 1973). Similarly, as Stern et al. (1977) have described, the behaviour of a mother talking to a three-months-old infant is characterized by the highly repetitive nature of her vocal and gestural acts, the grossly exaggerated form of her facial expressions, and the slowing down of her vocalizations. Not only the content but also the form of her behaviour is adjusted to the infant—as though she were aware of his limited capacity for information processing and hence wanted to ensure that she would not lose his interest. Stimulation is thus offered in such a way that it matches the infant's ability to assimilate it.

These are illustrations of the sensitivity that mothers—indeed most adults—quite naturally display in their interactions with young children. That same sensitivity was also highlighted in our previous discussion of visual co-orientation, vocal interchange and feeding, for in all of these cases we see the extent to which mothers are aware of the often very rapid sequential patterning of the infant's behaviour and are able to enmesh their own responses with his into one continuing flow. The dialogue thus produced may be a one-sided one in its dependence on the mother's willingness to sustain it, but it is already one of exquisite precision of timing and patterning.

Sensitivity is surely the single most salient general quality which one can discern in maternal behaviour. Whether it can be treated as a unitary entity that remains relatively constant across time and situation is an open issue that need not occupy us here any further; suffice it that this is the quality that makes possible the very prompt response to and anticipation of the infant's behaviour that we find repeatedly in dyadic situations. The conditions that give rise to it in the mother's history, the reasons for its absence in some pathological cases, and the extent to which it can be improved through training and experience are all further issues to which we have as yet no answer. What is clear is that sensitivity involves a close monitoring of the child's actions, the ability to respond appropriately and to monitor in turn the effects on him of the mother's own behaviour, and the willingness subsequently to change that behaviour in the light of these effects. It represents a basic condition for the occurrence and development of mother-infant dialogues.

The infant's active role in determining the course and content of social interactions clearly deserves emphasis. Let us, however, also note that most of the recent work in this area has been based on situations specifically set up to bring out this fact, i.e., they have maximized the possibility for the infant to take the initiative, confining the mother to following his lead and adapting to his particular requirements. However, in acknowledging the reality of this phenomenon there is a danger that we may swing from one extreme to another: from seeing mother as a dictator (albeit benevolent) to seeing her as a nonentity (albeit an alert one). In other words we would no longer be acknowledging the obvious fact that mothers do have to take the initiative from time to time, that they do have purposes and goals and needs of their own which they wish to convey to their children and with which the children have to fit in. The more assertive aspects of maternal behaviour must thus also be accounted for if we are to do justice to the total range of mother-child interaction: accordingly we shall turn to an examination of maternal control techniques in the next section.

Maternal Controls

Given the new approach to the study of mother-child interaction, with its emphasis on the dyadic nature of the relationship and the use of micro-analytic techniques to examine its structure in detail, it is time to return to an old problem with a fresh look and ask the question that lies at the heart of the socialization issue, namely *what do mothers in fact do when they wish to direct their children's behaviour into particular channels?*

This problem arises in its most acute form in the second year of life. It has been suggested that 'obedience' cannot be expected until the end of the first year (Stayton et al., 1971); in any case, the onset of independent mobility around this time means that there is now a pressing need for controlling tactics that are rapidly administered and effective. Fortunately at this time too the child begins to reveal a rudimentary comprehension of spoken language, and the need to control behaviour from a distance is thus partly met. Whereas in the first year the mother's control techniques are likely to assume a primarily non-verbal form (i.e. through physical manipulation of the child and his environment), the development of language comprehension and the greater understanding of gestures on the part of the child offer a vastly increased scope for methods of influencing the course of his behaviour. The nature of these methods and their functioning need describing.

We have recently been studying maternal control techniques in two groups of mother-infant dyads, involving children aged fifteen and twenty-four months respectively. Each mother-child pair is observed under free play conditions for a period of eight minutes. There is a large number of toys in the room in which the observations are made, and to ensure that she takes an active role in the interactions the mother is instructed to encourage the child to play with as many toys as possible and not to have him spend all the time with one or two toys. The entire procedure is video-recorded from behind a one-way screen and it is the fine-grain analysis of the records of these social encounters that provides the basis for our discussion on control techniques.

The Nature of Control Techniques

It is important to emphasize that control techniques, as the term is used here, should not be understood in a purely negative fashion, denoting force, inhibition, punishment, and so on. Rather, *control techniques are all those methods employed by the adult with the aim of changing the course of the child's behaviour.* Such methods may take many diverse forms, by no means all of a negative nature. In each case, however, the adult has some particular end-result in mind that he wants the child to achieve, and it is his task therefore to communicate his purpose in such a way that the child will come to share this purpose. How such a relatively assertive role is played— didactically, bolt-out-of-the-blue fashion, or by preserving the same mutuality

that the study of other aspects of mother-infant interaction has highlighted, is an empirical problem to which we need to give attention.

Sociologists (e.g. Bernstein, 1971) see control techniques as stemming
from some specific policy designed to evoke a particular moral, cognitive
and affective awareness in the child as part of his acculturation. Our concern here, however, is far less with the socialization policy that underlies a
parent's behaviour and the values it expresses, and far more with the
behaviour patterns themselves that are used to bring about control, i.e. that
are intended to result in the child's compliance with the adult's wishes. We
are also not concerned with the long-term effects on the child, i.e. with the
internalization of the social values conveyed to him. The primary need at
present is to examine control techniques in terms of their here-and-now
impact.

The Range and Variety of Control Techniques

Any attempt at detailed description of how mothers set out to influence their children's ongoing behaviour must do justice to the extraordinarily wide range of techniques employed by them. However, analysis of
the play sessions observed by us suggested a way of organizing these techniques within one global taxonomic scheme, which is illustrated diagram-
matically in Figures 1 and 2. A discussion of the distinctions drawn
within this scheme may serve to convey some flavour of the variety of control techniques applied to children in the second year of life.

Verbal controls.   A fundamental distinction is that between controls administered through the medium of language and those manifest in other, non-
verbal, aspects of the mother's behaviour. As to the former, approximately
half of all maternal utterances in both the age groups observed by us were
judged to be verbal control utterances. It would be a mistake, however, to
analyse these simply in terms of the categories commonly applied to direc-

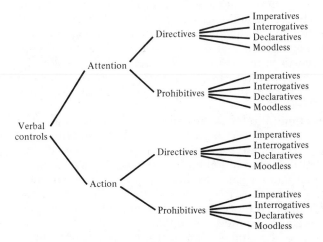

Figure 1 Classification of verbal control techniques

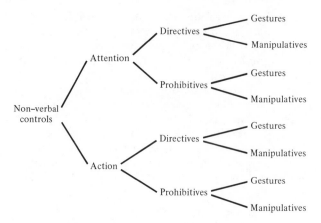

Figure 2   Classification of non-verbal techniques

tive speech found in adult social encounters (e.g., Ervin-Tripp, 1976), for such a procedure would not respect the special features of speech addressed to young children. In particular, one salient difference to which an examination of the latter points is that between utterances pertaining to the *control of attention* and those pertaining to the *control of action.*

Action controls aim to modify the course of the child's behaviour by specifying some activity that he is expected to perform. Thus they involve verbs such as 'push', 'fetch,' 'kick,' etc., designed to initiate some response that the child is not at the time engaged in. However, action controls may also be intended to modify an activity that is already underway; the action verb may then be implicit, e.g. 'Do that again over here!' By these means the child's behaviour is constrained or channelled in some respect; the degree of constraint, however, may vary considerably according to the nature of the utterance and the extent to which it permits a variety of 'appropriate' responses. Thus, at one extreme, a mother is highly explicit in what is expected from the child: 'Push the car to me!,' specifying action, object and location; at the other extreme a statement such as 'Play with the car!', while also a command, is far less specific as to what the child is to do and leaves a wide range of choices open to him. There may well be an important dimension of maternal differences in this respect that deserves to be explored; a mother's controls can be viewed in terms of the range of options they provide for compliance, and the question of consistent individual differences can thus be raised.

Attention controls attempt to focus the child's visual or auditory attention ('Look at that lovely ball!'; 'Listen to the noise it makes!') and thus serve to introduce an object (or a locality) into the sphere of play. The child is thereby expected to identify or locate something, generally as a prelude for the performance of some action related to that object. That action is, however, left unspecified: a remark such as 'Look, there's teddy!', made to a child pushing an empty pram, is more like a 'gentle hint' and thus displays a kind of subtlety that is actually quite commonplace.

Influencing the course of a child's behaviour involves not only initiating activities but also terminating or preventing activities. This distinction is made with the terms *directives* and *prohibitives*. While directives control behaviour by guiding in into specified channels, prohibitives control it by blocking channels, the child being told *not* to act or *not* to attend.

However, the aim of preventing or terminating an activity is not exclusively served by prohibitives. Consider a mother coping with a child who has put a toy in his mouth: she may, it is true, issue a straightforward prohibitive, 'Don't eat teddy!'; on the other hand, she may attempt to achieve the same aim with 'Take teddy out of your mouth!' or even 'Put teddy in the pram!' These more subtle ways of preventing some action deemed undesirable by the mother are especially characteristic of attention controls for which prohibitives, although possible, occur only infrequently. The task of shifting a child's attention away from something is usually achieved by distraction, i.e. by providing an alternative and, ideally, more interesting focus—thus, to the child who has seen an electric socket: 'Look [instead] at this lovely spinning top!' Speech containing many prohibitives is usually regarded as authoritarian, and it may well be important to distinguish maternal strategies that are highly reliant on the use of prohibitives. It is clear, however, that a mother may be just as restrictive but achieve her end in more positive ways, i.e. by the skilful and timely use of directives.

The examples of verbal controls with which we have illustrated the discussion so far, and the widespread view that speech addressed to young children tends to be highly simplified (e.g., Snow, 1972), might suggest that control utterances are always delivered in the simple grammatical form appropriate to commands, i.e. the *imperative*. This, however, is by no means so; action and atention can also be manipulated by *interrogatives, declaratives* and by *moodless* utterances (i.e. those lacking a verb, c.f. Sinclair and Coulthard, 1975).

The imperative category does, of course, provide the most unambiguous examples of verbal control: 'Throw me the ball!,' 'Look at those bricks!' Interrogatives tend to be much more varied, and to an adult different interrogative constructions can provide questions with subtle variations in meaning (Ervin-Tripp, 1976). Consider, for example, 'Shall we sit teddy over there?', 'Can you sit teddy over there?', 'Will teddy sit over there?', 'Why not sit teddy over there?' It seems unlikely that very young children can discriminate the shades of meaning that distinguish these utterances, and available evidence (Shatz, 1978) suggests that children in the second year react to such questions much as they would to imperatives. One way of viewing these interrogative utterances is as embedded imperatives, in that the interrogative construction precedes the explicit agent, action and object as a formal addition. The embedded imperative form is, however, less characteristic of attention interrogatives. These frequently are variations of naming or finding games in which the explicit attention verbs such as 'look' or 'see' do not appear, e.g. 'What's this here?' or 'Where's teddy?'

Declaratives provide the mother with another form of 'indirect' command. Taken literally, they usually convey information and thus may seem the least forceful of the various grammatical forms. An action is sometimes specified, again in the manner of an embedded imperative: 'You have to push it right down,' but it may be even less explicit, as in 'I think the top comes off'. Attention declaratives are generally used to identify the location of an object: 'There's the wheelbarrow,' 'It's over there'. With such statements the mother may be providing the child with information, just as with interrogatives she appears to be asking for information; in each case, however, the intended outcome may be to bring about a change in the child's behaviour regarding the object referred to.

Moodless controls incorporate those clipped utterances that are inserted into a child's ongoing activity in order to modify its progress: 'Careful', 'Over there,' 'Round the other way'. The child must relate them to what he is currently doing and perhaps also to a preceding more complete verbal control: 'Push it down . . . gently now'.

Non-verbal controls.   Some of the same classificatory distinctions that we have used for verbal controls can also be made with regard to non-verbal controls (see Figure 2). This does not apply, of course, to the formal linguistic categories (imperatives, interrogatives, declaratives and moodless) we have previously discussed; instead, a distinction between *gestures* and *manipulatives* can be usefully made. These two categories differ with respect to whether something, object or child, is directly acted upon or not: gestures, being symbolic in nature, do not generally involve such contact; manipulatives, on the other hand, do entail an action bringing the individual into direct contact with the object.

Gestures are frequently used to supplement verbal controls. As Murphy and Messer (1977) have shown, mothers' use of pointing in order to focus the infants' attention on some feature of the environment tends to be synchronized (in a most precise manner) with verbal references to that feature. Pointing persists as one of the most common discourse gestures, particularly in situations such as that described here where interaction takes place primarily via a number of objects scattered around at a distance. Among other classes of gestures that can be identified are receiving gestures, either of an object (by holding out the hands) or of the child (by beckoning); pantomimes of an action the child is expected to perform upon a toy; and approval or disapproval gestures (e.g. head nodding or finger shaking). All can be said to serve control purposes.

Manipulatives make some form of physical contact with either the child or an object. They may be divided into three classes. *Location* manipulatives result in a changed position for some object relative to the child: the mother may, for example, discretely put a toy within reach of the child or, rather more assertively, pick up a child and carry him away from a door he was attempting to open. This strategy is very typical of interactions with younger infants whose own mobility is limited and whose lack of language comprehension makes verbal controls relatively ineffective. *Demonstrating* manipulatives have an obviously instructive character. The function, structure or properties of some object is illustrated, usually by acting upon the object in question, e.g. the mother guides her child's hands as he attempts a difficult task like spinning a top. *Attracting* manipulatives are used to direct the child's attention towards some object by touching it or moving it about its location. The consequence is to generate a more interesting visual or auditory stimulus; a common example is the shaking of a toy in front of the child.

The other classificatory distinctions made for non-verbal controls are the same as those for verbal controls. Thus the former too may serve either to direct attention to objects or to specify some action. Pointing, for example, is used to attract attention to an object; other gestures, such as pantomimes, indicate actions for the child to perform. Similarly, location manipulatives can direct attention to a toy, while demonstrating manipulatives specify the action that can be performed on that toy. The distinction between directives and prohibitives is also applicable; thus attention to some object may be effectively initiated or terminated by altering its location with respect to the child.

Maternal Strategies and Child Behavior

A detailed examination of mothers' behaviour makes it very apparent that the techniques used to influence children's activities assume a great many different forms. The mode of the technique (verbal or non-verbal), its positive or negative character (directive or prohibitive), the aspect of the child's behavior to which it is addressed (attention or action), the construction of the utterance (imperative, interrogative, declarative or moodless) and the nature of the non-verbal technique (gesture or manipulative), all indicate something of the rich stock from which the mother is, potentially at least, able to draw whatever is relevant for any given set of circumstances in order to convey her purpose to the child and affect his behaviour accordingly. And, in particular, it becomes clear that the directness with which she attempts to achieve her purpose is also highly varied: the parade-ground-like command that perhaps most people initially associate with the notion of control is in fact observed far less frequently than a great range of highly subtle and indirect tactics that are much less forceful but that, nevertheless, may serve just as effectively as controls.

Such variety raises two main questions. First, how are individual controls organized together into coherent strategies, involving the simultaneous integration of verbal and non-verbal elements and the successive integration of sequences of controls? Second, what determines the occurrence of different controls—in particular, how are they related to ongoing child behaviour? These are both highly complex problems, and we can but briefly touch upon them here.

As to interrelationships among control techniques, it is apparent that individual controls are associated in a far from haphazard manner. Thus gestures rarely occur without some simultaneous, appropriate verbal utterance: a mother pointing to an object will almost invariably accompany her gesture with some reference to the object or at the very least with a request to look at it—even when the child addressed is a pre-verbal infant. The additional information conveyed by non-verbal elements may be particularly useful in cases of ambiguity in speech, such as that resulting from the use of pronouns and of deictic terms. Thus the younger the child the greater the incidence of simultaneous verbal and non-verbal cues that one can expect. And similarly, the sequential arrangement of controls is frequently of an orderly nature; for example, attention controls tend to precede action controls, in that a mother must first ensure that her child's attention is on the appropriate object before she requests him to act upon it. Also, strings of verbal directives all referring to the same object and act (repeated because the child did not comply at once) are rarely identical; invariably the mother will modify her original remark, sometimes by elaborating upon it but often by simplifying it through a process of abbreviation or ellipsis.

In the particular situation observed by us the mother's role was one of initiating and maintaining play around half a dozen or so toys. Under such circumstances a great many of a mother's control utterances are organized in sequences (or 'episodes'), in which all the constituent controls refer to the same object (e.g. 'Go and fetch the ball . . . go on, pick it up . . . bring it over here . . . now throw it to me . . .'). While within each episode the mother's focus remains upon one particular toy, the question arises as to how episodes are first initiated: does the mother decide arbitrarily, bolt-out-of-the-blue fashion when the child is to play with a new toy, or does she take note of what he is currently doing and time her directive accordingly?

We can answer this question by taking the beginning of each episode, i.e. the first utterance that mentions a toy not referred to in the previous episode, and consider what the child is doing at the time. When this analysis is performed it emerges that a considerable proportion of the mothers' verbal controls concerning a new toy follow *an initiative taken by the child*. Thus, for the younger and older children respectively, 59.7 per cent and 74 per cent of these maternal directives occur after the child himself has already made contact with the toy or at least focused upon it. The age difference is particularly notable, for it appears to reflect the generally much more active and exploratory character of the older children's play: with increasing age the child is much more likely to initiate toy shifts himself, the mother merely coming in with requests for new actions.

What happens in the remaining cases, however, when the mother takes the initiative for a toy shift? In most of these instances (87.2 per cent and 78.8 per cent respectively for the two age groups) the shift is attempted with an attention directive; action controls tend to be reserved until attention is captured and focused. In other words, to a child busily engaged with building bricks, the mother will not suddenly shout: 'Kick the ball!'. Rather, having decided it is time he turned to something else, she will first use various attention-attracting devices (verbal and non-verbal) in order gently to introduce the ball, wean him away from the bricks, and only when she has succeeded in doing so will she issue an action directive such as to kick the ball. Such a strategy has, however, to be employed far more frequently with younger children: in our fifteen-months-old group we found mothers using twice as many attention directives as in the twenty-four-months group, despite the fact that action directives occurred with approximately the same frequency. The greater tendency of the younger children to get 'stuck' on a particular toy meant that their mothers had to work harder in tempting them to other toys; in most of such instances, however, they first made sure that the child was oriented to the new toy before indicating some action to be performed upon it.

These observations highlight once again the skill with which mothers phase their own actions and requirements into what the child is doing at the time. Their aim may be to control the child by directing his behaviour into particular channels; more often than not, however, this is accomplished in a most sensitive, not a dictatorial manner.

Conclusions

Mothering is a most varied, multi-faceted activity and its analysis correspondingly complex. It is, therefore, not surprising that different investigators have resorted to different approaches in order to understand its nature and its relationship to child behaviour. These approaches have been described in detail elsewhere (Schaffer, 1977b); they may be roughly grouped into the following four categories:

Mothering as physical care activity, where attention is given primarily to such practices as feeding, weaning and toileting, in that (following Freudian theory) variations in these practices are thought to account for particular personality constellations in later life.

Mothering as a set of attitudes, the crucial variables here being rather broader aspects of the relationship, i.e. dimensions (such as warmth-coldness and permissiveness-restrictiveness) which are assumed to underlie a wide range of parental behaviour.

Mothering as stimulation, an approach which pays particular attention to the way in which the mother mediates and suitably selects the environmental stimulation the child requires for fostering development.

Mothering as interlocution. It is this approach with which we have been particularly concerned here, for it is based on the notion that mothering is part of an interactional pattern in which both partners must adapt to one another. Just as in a conversation the two interlocutors continually synchronize their responses according to a shared set of rules for regulating the relationship, so mother-child interaction also involves a highly sophisticated integration of the two sets of responses into one consistent flow. As we have seen, much of the responsibility for establishing such interpersonal synchrony during infancy lies with the mother: it is her skill in knowing not only *how* but also *when* to respond that is crucial in maintaining a dialogue.

According to this view, mutuality is the keynote in the relationship between mother and even the very youngest infant. What one does is affected by what the other is doing; neither is acting upon an inert organism. Thus the mother's task, in acting as a socializing agent, is not to create something out of nothing—it is rather to slot her responses into the ongoing stream of the child's behaviour, with due respect to its temporal and content characteristics, in order thus to bring about a 'smooth' interaction and a predictable outcome. The fact that from the beginning an infant is active, not passive, that he is capable of spontaneous, organized behaviour, means that in social interactions he is often an initiator, not merely a responder, and that the mother is thus frequently cast into the role of follower, not leader.

This conclusion is reached by various studies of mother-infant interaction, some of which were described in the earlier part of this chapter. However, while many of these were specifically set up to highlight the infant's determining role, it is noteworthy that even in a situation where the mother is asked to adopt a more assertive, task-oriented part the evidence for mutuality is still to be found. In part this is provided by the way in which the mother times her controls, in that even this type of behaviour is sensitively linked to the child's activity at the time; and in part by the way in which maternal behaviour changes according to the child's age, showing how mother can adjust the nature of her demands to the capabilities of the child. Both points underline the fact that mothers do not act as though they see the child as a mere lump of clay to be shaped at will, but rather that they appear at all times acutely aware of what is appropriate to a given child at a given moment and that they are prepared then to adjust their requirements and actions accordingly.

Socialization thus emerges as a process based on mutuality. It is not an arbitrary imposition by a powerful being on another, utterly passive being. If a mother wishes to bring about some change in her child she needs to start within the context of his own behaviour. Socialization is based on a two-way relationship, and any theoretical model that neglects this basic feature will fail to account for its very essence.

REFERENCES

AINSWORTH, M. D. S. (1974) The development of infant-mother attachment. In B. M. Caldwell and H. N. Ricciuti (eds) *Review of Child Development Research, Vol. 3*. Chicago: University of Chicago Press.

BERNSTEIN, B. (1971) Language and socialization. In N. Minnis (ed.) *Linguistics at Large*. London: Gollancz.

BLURTON JONES, N. (ed.) (1972) *Ethological Studies of Child Behaviour*. London: Cambridge University Press.

BOWLBY, J. (1969) *Attachment and Loss, Vol. 1*. London: Hogarth.

BRONFENBRENNER, U. (1971) *Two Worlds of Childhood: U.S. and U.S.S.R.* London: Allen and Unwin.

CALDWELL, B. M. (1964) The effects of infant care. In M. L. Hoffman and L. W. Hoffman (eds) *Review of Child Development Research, Vol. 1*. New York: Russell Sage Foundation.

CLARKE, A. M. AND CLARKE, A. D. B. (1976) *Early Experience: Myth and Evidence*. London: Open Books.

COLLIS, G. M. AND SCHAFFER, H. R. (1975) Synchronization of visual attention in mother-infant pairs. *Journal of Child Psychology and Psychiatry 16*: 315–20.

DUNCAN, S. (1973) Toward a grammar for dyadic conversation. *Semiotica 9*: 29–46.

ERVIN-TRIPP, S. (1976) Is Sybil there? the structure of some American English directives. *Language and Society 5*: 25–66.

FERGUSSON, C. A. (1964) Baby talk in six languages. *American Anthropologist 66*: 103–14.

HARTUP, W. W. (1970) Peer interaction and social organization. In P. H. Mussen (ed.) *Manual of Child Psychology, Vol. 2*. New York: Wiley.

HOFFMAN, M. L. (1970) Moral development. In P. H. Mussen (ed.) *Manual of Child Psychology*, Vol. 2. New York: Wiley.

KAYE, K. (1977) Toward the origin of dialogue. In H. R. Schaffer (ed.) *Studies in Mother-Infant Interaction*. London: Academic Press.

KESSEN, W., HAITH, M., AND SALAPATEK, P. H. (1970) Human infancy: a bibliography and guide. In P. H. Mussen (ed.) *Manual of Child Psychology, Vol. 1*. New York: Wiley.

LAMB, M. E. (1976) *The Role of the Father in Child Development*. New York: Wiley.

LE VINE, R. (1969) Culture, personality, and socialization: an evolutionary view. In D. A. Goslin (ed.) *Handbook of Socialization Theory and Research*. Chicago: Rand-McNally.

MEAD, M. (1935) *Sex and Temperament in Three Primitive Societies*. New York: Morrow.

MURPHY, C. M. AND MESSER, D. J. (1977) Mothers, infants and pointing: a study of a gesture. In H. R. Schaffer (ed.) *Studies in Mother-Infant Interaction*. London: Academic Press.

ORLANSKY, H. (1949) Infant care and personality. *Psychological Bulletin 46*: 1–48.

PHILLIPS, J. R. (1973) Syntax and vocabulary of mothers' speech to young children: age and sex comparisons. *Child Development 44*: 182–5.

SCHAFFER, H. R. (1971) *The Growth of Sociability*. Harmondsworth: Penguin Books.

SCHAFFER, H. R. (1977a) Early interactive development. In H. R. Schaffer (ed.) *Studies in Mother-Infant Interaction*. London: Academic Press.

SCHAFFER, H. R. (1977b) *Mothering*. London: Open Books; Cambridge, Mass: Harvard University Press.

SCHAFFER, H. R. (1978) Acquiring the concept of the dialogue. In M. Bornstein and W. Kessen (eds) *Psychological Development from Infancy*. Hillsdale, NJ: Erlbaum.

SCHAFFER, H. R., COLLIS, G. M., AND PARSONS, G. (1977) Vocal interchange and visual regard in verbal and pre-verbal children. In H. R. Schaffer (ed.) *Studies in Mother-Infant Interaction*. London: Academic Press.

SEARS, R. R., MACCOBY, E. E. AND LEVIN, H. (1957) *Patterns of Child Rearing*. Evanston, Ill.: Row, Peterson.

SHATZ, M. (1978) Children's comprehension of their mothers' question-directives. *Journal of Child Language 5:* 39–46.

SINCLAIR, J. MCH. AND COULTHARD, R. M. (1975) *Towards an Analysis of Discourse*. London: Oxford University Press.

SNOW, C. E. (1972) Mothers' speech to children learning language. *Child Development 43:* 549–65.

STAYTON, D. J., HOGAN, R. AND AINSWORTH, M. D. S. (1971) Infant obedience and maternal behavior: the origins of socialization reconsidered. *Child Development 42:* 1057–69.

STERN, D. N., BEEBE, B., JAFFE, J. AND BENNETT, S. J. (1977) The infant's stimulus world during social interaction. In H. R. Schaffer (ed.) *Studies in Mother-Infant Interaction*. London: Academic Press.

WOLFF, P. H. (1967) The role of biological rhythms in early psychological development. *Bulletin of Meninger Clinic 31:* 197–218.

YARROW, M. R., CAMPBELL, J. D. AND BURTON, R. V. (1968) *Child Rearing: An Inquiry into Research and Methods*. San Francisco: Jossey-Bass.

ZIGLER, E. F. AND CHILD, I. L. (eds) (1973) *Socialization and Personality Development*. Reading, Mass.: Addison-Wesley.

PART IX

Women's Lives:
Tradition and Change

The Western world in the last two decades has seen dramatic changes in the roles and scope of women's lives. The most prominent of these is the unprecedented entry of women, including those with young children, into the work force. Perhaps the most pressing reason for this phenomenon is economic, but other related factors also are behind it. Increased educational achievement and career opportunities, postponement of marriage and childbearing, smaller families, and greater social acceptance of working mothers have combined to create the shift to the world outside the home, effecting major changes in the lives many women lead.

When part of a social system changes, the rest of it must adapt to that change. The process is attended by strain, tension, and often disruption as old customs and attitudes are challenged by proponents of the new order. Today's woman feels this, too. The middle-aged housewife, having followed all the rules, hears that her life of domesticity is less esteemed in the new scheme of things. And even if she did work outside the home, she knows that her job might be of low status and poorly rewarded compared to the jobs of her male counterparts, or compared to what she herself could have done had she not dedicated all those years to the care and well-being of others.

The younger woman looks at her mother and says, "It won't happen to me." So she continues her education, or works part-time while the children are young, or continues with a full-time commitment, babies or no babies. But for many the old expectations are still there, and studies of dual-career couples show that women come home from work and, without missing a beat, pick up where they left off that morning: caring for children and doing housework.

Women of college age and younger have other kinds of problems. While still uncommitted to social, personal, or career goals, they have choices their mothers never had. They feel the burden of having to make decisions. What do I want to do with my life? Should I get married? Should I have children? How can I combine a satisfying personal life with the work I want to do? Where can I find someone who will willingly share the work at home so that both of us can explore other arenas as fully as we wish?

Women today are experiencing life across a wider spectrum than ever before. But tradition, layered through centuries, yields slowly to change, especially in areas invested with powerful emotions and deep personal meanings. The papers in this section deal with just such areas in women's lives.

The ambivalence, the difficulties, the soul-searching that women experience as they think of their futures, attempt to plan their lives, and attempt to implement their plans are the subject of Pamela Daniels's paper, "Dream vs. Drift in Women's Careers: The Question of Generativity." *Generativity*, a term coined by Erik Erikson, includes whatever a person creates, produces, and leaves behind. Traditionally a woman's generativity has unfolded through motherhood and her work as nurturer and provider of love, whereas man's has been reflected in his occupational identity, his works and ideas. Today, as more and more women sense that their vitality depends on more than motherhood, and as a result are seeking challenge in other work as well, the concept of generativity for women has begun to transcend the stereotypes and to become more androgynous. This means lives of increasing complexity for women, as they want to expand their generativity to include not only motherhood but the production of "work and ideas" as well.

How can women do this successfully? The question gives rise to the issue of the importance of "the Dream" in men's lives, an anticipatory vision of his adult years and how he will use them. The Dream, while not always made real, can be a guiding principle for the focus of his energy and the direction of his efforts. Women, by contrast, often expect to derive their happiness and satisfaction vicariously through the Dream of others; only belatedly do some of the most talented drift into careers of their own. In spite of the cultural pressure toward marriage and motherhood, some women have their Dream, too. Daniels presents the stories of four women who from childhood wanted careers in medicine and tells how for each of them the Dream was either dismissed, deferred, pursued, or claimed. But a good Dream, she reminds us, can center a life and can give us the momentum we need to choose our works and our loves as we shape our lives.

For women, the importance of other women in our lives has been observed, explained, and interpreted in various ways. Our first love relationship and our primary identification were with our mother, predisposing us, one would believe, to a readiness for intimacy with other women. But early on we learned of the relatively inferior status of our gender and came to share with men the sense of ourselves and those like us as less important and less valuable. We experienced the intense "best friend" relationships of girlhood and passionate crushes on adored women teachers or aunts. But as we matured the quality of female friendships became more tenuous as we waited for the "real" relationship to come along. And when it did, our female friends took second place, or we drifted away from them as we became absorbed with the man in our lives.

The women's movement, with its creed of the sisterhood of all women, has had an effect on women's relations with each other. Women have become more conscious of the value of other women as friends. Researchers have become interested in the differences in the ways that men and women relate to others of the same gender as well as to each other. "Friendships of Women and of Men," by Robert Bell, is a study of Conventional and Nonconventional women and men and their feelings about friendship and aloneness. Nonconventionals have a desire to influence change, to seek pleasure, to exert control over their lives, and to take chances in their lives. Conventionals are opposite Nonconventionals on each of these dimensions. The study showed that, while gender differences in friendship clearly exist, the effects of the personality variable of Conventionality yield more refined information, when combined with gender, than does the study of gender alone. Values and attitudes related to one's outlook on life and one's beliefs about men and women can, it seems, cut across gender where some aspects of friendship and being alone are concerned. Nonconventional women and men, Bell found, are more like each other on these qualities than are Conventional and Nonconventional women *or* men.

The family is generally regarded as the basic unit of society. Within its bounds we are born, are nurtured, develop personalities, mature, and move on to form families of our own. Traditional families, whether extended or nuclear, have prescribed different roles for women and men and have distributed power unequally. Male dominance in the family was secured by the man's role as provider and by the traditional rules of patriarchy, "the law of the father." But changes in the roles and status of women have begun to have profound effects on this institution. In "Equality and the Family," I examine those effects as they are fostered by egalitarian ideology. In addition to an analysis of role segregation in the family, the review focuses on some variables that affect equality, such as the division of labor along sex lines; trends such as later marriage, smaller families, and employment of women, all of which potentially give women more power; and implications of equality for the family, ranging from conservative adaptations to new models free of distinctions based on sex and gender.

Most of the research on role conflict among women has focused on the experiences of heterosexual women, conflict, for example, between the work role and the wife / mother role. In "Working Lesbians: Role Conflicts and Coping Strategies," Sandra Shachar and Lucia Gilbert investigate inter- and intrarole conflicts and coping strategies of working / lesbian women. As expected, the most commonly reported interrole conflict was between the worker and lover roles, a conflict that seemed independent of their lesbianism. The favored strategy was direct communication in order to negotiate a settlement. By contrast, their lesbianism was highly related to their intrarole conflicts, most frequently in the roles of worker and daughter. In coping with these conflicts, the women were more likely to assume that the demands of others for the role (parent, boss) were unchangeable and that there was no satisfying way to deal with them. For example, the conflict in her role as daughter might emanate from her desire for her parents' acceptance and her belief that they would never accept her lesbianism. While the strategy of choosing not to disclose her lesbianism might keep the relationship smooth, it might decrease her happiness and morale. The authors suggest that different strategies may be chosen by individuals to cope with specific role conflicts.

Living in a society characterized by rapid social change, we are no longer guided by traditional values and expectancies handed down from one generation to the next. Nor have we yet built a society that is truly egalitarian and tolerant of pluralistic life styles, where women and men are free from the old constraints that defined behavior along lines laid down by anatomy.

The change, though, is an authentic one. Today a woman may marry and spend the rest of her life engaged in domestic activities. Or she may combine domestic roles with a job or a lifelong career. Or she may choose to remain single and spend as much time in the work force as a typical man does. Variants of these patterns, modified by such contingencies as divorce and widowhood, account for the ways that most women spend their lives. Increased understanding of the options and what they entail as ways to live may make the transition to the brave new world a little smoother.

29

Dream vs. Drift in Women's Careers
The Question of Generativity

Pamela Daniels

Women's lives have been profoundly affected by the social and historical changes of the last thirty-five years, changes that are gradually permeating the thinking and planning of individual women, and even more gradually being incorporated into our theories of women's development.[1]

The most dramatic change is the lengthening of woman's life cycle *coupled with* the shortening of the time within it devoted to childbearing and childrearing. However intense its pleasures and obligations while our children are young, we can no longer expect motherhood to occupy a lifetime.[2]

Second, economic and social facts of life, such as soaring living costs and forbidding divorce statistics, are compelling women, whether they are on the threshhold of adulthood or "displaced" as homemakers in mid-life, to contribute to their own and their family's livelihood—to become providers as well as nurturers.

Third, the feminist movement has generated a revolution in women's individual and collective consciousness by striking down structural barriers to accomplishment in the public worlds of education and employment, and by creating intimate and political networks of recognition, advocacy and support. While change in the fundamental contours of woman's life cycle conveys the *inevitable*, and shifts in economic and social realities document the *probable*, the rise of feminism opens up our awareness of the *possible*. As we move into the 1980s, women are asking more of themselves, of each other, and of life. The traditional "Woman's Life Plan," as Sara Ruddick

(1977) has called it—"to marry well, to bear and raise children who thrive, to accept age and one's children's children"—is plainly an insufficient prescription for our lives. Whether we are midlife family women stretching for postparental careers, or midthirties career women waging an inner debate about whether to have a child, or newly launched young women groping for a life plan that will include both family and career, we are experiencing not so much a crisis of identity (Barnett and Baruch, 1978) as a profound and hopeful restlessness in our sense of generativity.

Generativity is not a familiar word, nor is it an easy idea to grasp. Yet to understand its developmental significance is to give us new ways of conceptualizing, shaping and re-shaping our experience. Generativity is a term coined by Erik Erikson (1959, 1968) to designate the seventh developmental stage in the human life cycle which he named "Generativity vs. Stagnation." In its primary variation, generativity is "the concern for establishing and guiding the next generation" (1968, p. 138). It is reflected in our capacity for care, most literally expressed in parenthood.

Given Erikson's protean way with ideas, however, generativity refers to more than a particular life stage, and encompasses more than parenthood. It also has to do with "the instinctual power behind various forms of selfless caring," and it potentially includes "whatever a man generates and leaves behind, creates and produces" (1964, p. 131). As it is spelled out in Erikson's writings (1964, 1967), the emphasis in women's and men's generativity differs—reflecting the division of labor and lives of prefeminist times. For Erikson, as for the culture in which he was writing, woman's generativity unfolds primarily through her intimate relationships with others, and becomes focused in motherhood and in the invisible maintenance work of love. In contrast, man's generative experience reflects and draws upon his occupational identity, is expressed in his *"love for his works and ideas as well as for his children,"* and resonates in the "necessary self-verification which adult man's ego receives, and must receive, from his labor's challenge" (1964, pp. 131, 132; italics in original). It is this artificial separation of women's and men's experience, based on traditional sex-role assignments—woman as nurturer of men and children in the intimate private world, man as generator of works and ideas in the public world of policy and enterprise, woman confined to domestic careers, man to worldly one—that is undergoing challenge and revision in our times. It no longer makes sense to view love as woman's essential and exclusive work, and work as man's essential and exclusive love. For both sexes, both love and work are the means of taking care.

While women must not repudiate or forfeit the distinctive place in our lives of intimacy, connection and sensitivity to the needs of others (Miller, 1976; Gilligan, 1979), at the same time we are realizing, as we must, that for women as for men a sense of vitality, of remaining alive in work and love, depends on more than parenthood. Generativity is potentially an androgynous concept. For women as for men it includes production as well as procreation, aspiration for achievement as well as capacity for nurturance, confirmation of autonomy and competence as well as expression of compassion and care, pursuit of our own dreams as well as creating the conditions in which others can grow and flourish. Women, like men, began to shrivel inside when deprived of that self-verification that comes from meeting the challenge of chosen work, when we are excluded from stretching and testing ourselves through "love for our works and ideas as well as for our children."

In the past, women of course have held jobs and worked for pay. Participation in the labor force is not new for women; what *is* new is that more and more women are investing themselves in their work away from home, viewing career development and accomplishment as intrinsic to psychological and moral well-being. Our agenda, as women, as feminists, as psychologists, then, is how to create a concept of female generativity and purpose that transcends the stereotypes. To change and grow as adults—to be able to transform or transcend the recurrent moments of stagnation, confinement and aborted promise that are the dark side of generativity—depends upon a sense of purpose, the feeling of being in control of our lives, in a position to make choices that will work out over a lifetime in such a way that identity is extended, elaborated and renewed in patterns of love and work and care that are both fruitful and feasible. That is the ideal. How do we attain it?

Daniel Levinson and his colleagues at Yale (1978) have identified and spelled out the developmental importance of "the Dream" in men's construction of their adult lives. "More formed than a pure fantasy, yet less articulated than a fully thought-out plan," the Dream, Levinson writes, has the quality of an anticipatory "vision of a life," of what a man will do with his adult years, how he will use them. It is "an imagined possibility that generates excitement and vitality" (p. 91). Whatever the nature or the content of the Dream, men in their young adult years have the developmental task of giving it form and definition, of finding ways to live it out—to plunge into the intricate (and lifelong) work of articulating the possibilities with the realities. "If the Dream remains unconnected with [a man's] life," Levinson writes, "it may simply die, and *with it his sense of aliveness and purpose*" (pp. 91, 92; italics are mine). Timing is critical to forming and testing the Dream, for it is part of the necessary developmental work of making the transition to adulthood.

What is the place of the Dream in women's lives? In the experience of the men Levinson interviewed, forming a Dream frequently hinges upon occupational decisions. The life Dream is often indistinguishable from the occupational Dream. For women, the Dream is at least as important as it is for men, and much more complicated, for it must *integrate* imagery of self-in-family with self-in-the-world, self-in-relation-to-others with self-in-work-of-one's-own. To project our identity into ambitious and inclusive patterns of generativity, we must engage the Dream early in two senses: first, in its occupational version, a Career Dream itself; and second, in the wider sense of an imaginative groundplan that will guide and nourish the career piece, that piece of the dream that has been dismissed or eclipsed in the approved Woman's Life Plan.

In lives saturated with the expectancy of deriving much of life's satisfaction through the lives and Dream of others, women have sometimes drifted belatedly into careers or dreams of their own. In those rare, "dream-bitten" lives (in Toni Morrison's [1977] phrase), women have often had to pay a high price to pursue their own Dream—the actual or anticipated pain of isolation and loneliness, the loss of the pleasures of intimacy and motherhood, the loss of conventional status awarded to those who lived out the approved Dream.

Small wonder, then, that many gifted, creative, and successful women, innovators in their lives and work, feel that they initially drifted into their accomplishments, their successes, their careers: "I do not have the sense of having been at the center of my life, directing its course," writes philosopher and teacher Amelie Rorty (1977, p. 41). In an interview at thirty-nine, Joni Mitchell, song poet, when asked whether and how she had prepared for her success, replied:

> I never thought that far ahead. I never expected to have this degree of success. *Music was a hobby that mushroomed.* I was *grateful* to make one record . . . I wrote poetry and I painted all my life. I always wanted to play music and dabbled with it, but I never thought of putting them all together. It never occurred to me. (1979; italics added)

Alice Rossi, originator of some of the classic documents of contemporary feminist research, reflects on the steps by which she became a sociologist:

> It never occurred to me the whole time I was churning out pages for the Research Center that I had a dissertation there. It was "just work" to be turned out for that project, for that agency. If I had defined it in terms of a private standard of performance, of what I would *want* as my dissertation, I would not have done a good job—certainly not a *quick* job . . . But it became my dissertation. That's part of what I mean by the "drift phenomenon" in women's careers. You drift into things. You don't set a goal and work toward it. You're tapped on the shoulder with, "Oh, what a good girl *you* are. Look what fine work you can do. Why don't you get a Ph.D. instead of an M.A.? Try your hand at research." And so on and on. (1976)

For the past three years, Kathy Weingarten and I have been doing research on the timing of parenthood (Daniels and Weingarten, in preparation, 1981). We have interviewed parents of different ages and different family timing patterns to find out what difference it makes, initially and over the course of the life cycle, *when* people have their children. In these interviews, the imagery of drift and dream emerged again and again as women accounted for their generativity.

Four women in our study had a Dream of going into medicine, a Dream that defied the odds, the stereotypes and the patriarchal establishment. All four women wanted both children and work of their own. Two of them became mothers in their early twenties, two in their early thirties. Their stories reveal the interplay between the timing of motherhood and the evolution of the occupational Dream in women's lives. Moreover, they do so in an emblematic way, for in no other profession are the dilemmas of combining family life and organizational career, of integrating domestic and public accomplishment and involvement more clear or more complex than in medicine. In the first place, women have found it difficult, to say the least, to dream themselves into such a male-dominanted, male-identified profession (Howell, 1973). Although one out of four first-year medical students is a woman, women make up only ten percent of the nation's practicing physicians. The costs for women of both training and establishment in a successful practice are high: the long years of apprenticeship edging into prime childbearing time, the depleting pace, the disheartening competitiveness of peers, the inflexible career timetable, and the scarcity of both professional mentors and models of an inclusive and flexible generativity, that is, others who would (in Arlie Hochschild's phrase) "throw you a psychic lifeline" (1975, p. 56). In such circumstances it takes a powerful Dream to sustain the Dreamer.

Dismissing the Dream

Chris Cole[3] is the forty-year-old mother of three sons, the first of whom was born when she was twenty-one. The daughter of a small-town physician, she grew up in a family that lived and breathed medicine. When she and her friends "played hospital," she insisted on being the doctor. After all, she was the one with the stethoscope! In high school she blossomed into a very beautiful woman and exchanged the stethoscope for the tulle formals and pleated kilts she modeled in local fashion shows.

> "From then on," she said, "I was always torn between the worlds of fashion and medicine. I would drift back and forth without being able to make up my mind one way or the other.
>
> "I've always worked. Summers I would work on a fashion board or as a model in some fancy store. I'd have a wonderful time for the first month or so, making good money, and then I couldn't stand it anymore. I'd be so bored I'd quit, and go to work as a nurse's aide at fifteen cents an hour. And what I was doing in the hospital was fascinating. I was never bored. Still, in college I definitely didn't take pre-med courses. *I did not prepare myself to become a doctor in any way.* And yet there was always the problem with fashion; it didn't include any humanitarian goal, any bigger purpose."

Chris married in college and became pregnant her senior year—an unconscious ensurance that she would not have to take her embryonic medical Dream seriously, that she could postpone dealing with the ambivalence, with the war in her emerging identity between the glamorous and the humanitarian. The possibilities of the "dream" remained just a tug of conscience in her consciousness.

Later, at thirty-four, her last child in school, Chris found herself with the time and the overwhelming desire to revive and develop those unexpressed generative goals and "to do something more."

> "I wanted to spend more time doing something important for myself, on my own," she said. "But I just could not see my way to it. I found myself thinking about medicine again. I thought about wanting to go to medical school. I considered it for a while . . . was serious about wanting to, but *I could never, at that point in my life, see it as a reality.* And now I'm appreciating my freedom instead. I don't know whether it's an accommodation I've made, or whether this is the 'real me' and the other was a fantasy. I don't know."

Over the course of the next few years, with increasing conviction and deliberateness, Chris drifted into a part-time job "on the edge of medicine." She works in an administrative capacity in a family services clinic, a job which began with attendance "out of idle curiosity" at some counseling lectures, which led to volunteer work at the clinic, which became a casual paid job, which finally became a regular thirty-hour-a-week commitment.

In men's lives, the decade of the twenties are the critical years of giving the Dream form, of translating it into reality. When women devote full time in their twenties and early thirties to the consuming work of mothering, an inchoate Dream may remain unformed, unactivated, "untranslated"—a pure fantasy. Without being out in the world serving what Levinson calls an "occupational novitiate" (1978), without participating in the daily substance and rituals of career preparation, without being exposed to teachers, mentors, critics and a network of friends-at-work, women can neither try out their career dreams nor give them content. The dream isn't transformed into the skill, experience, groundwork and credentials that are the baseline of most professional careers. For all intents and purposes the Dream is dismissed. It goes underground, perhaps to surface later, as it did with Chris, in work on the fringe of the profession.

Deferring the Dream

We are all daughters of our times. Women of Chris's generation had to contend with resistance to career dreams, in the culture and inside themselves, in the form of the approved and certified Dream, the traditional Woman's Life Plan. "Unless you were a burning genius," one woman told us, "motherhood was *the* career. There was no deliberating, no dreaming about it."

Ann Abelard came of age in a later era, a time of feminist-influenced cultural "permission" to hold to her Dream—to postpone it perhaps, but not to sacrifice it. At thirty-two, a full-time mother at home, she has deferred the idea of professional medicine. Ann grew up wanting to be a doctor. She also wanted children, and she has three, the youngest an infant. Unlike Chris, Ann took pre-med courses in college, and finished a Master's degree in chemistry. She married close to medicine; her husband does cancer research. They had their (planned) first child when she twenty-two, two years after their marriage—"early" parenthood by current standards among women of her education and ambition, but "late" by the criteria of her large, close-knit Roman Catholic family "where babies are supposed to come nine months after marriage." Although she completed her Master's paper while nursing her first child, motherhood at twenty-two and the close spacing of the next two children meant that Ann put off medical school plans. She has by no means abandoned them. Vehemently she says,

> "The idea is still there now, you know. I never thought that having a family could keep me from going on and doing what I wanted to do afterwards, anyway. The crunch will come when I actually try to do it."

Ann holds to the Dream. The issue is not closed for her. The evidence is not in.

> "I've been in the syndrome of being a mother-with-young-children ever since our eldest child was born. I've accepted what I've done during these years.

Who knows what the future will bring? Come back in ten years," she said with a provocative grin.[4]

Ann's Dream is alive and well, and she intends to try to realize it.

Some of the mothers in our study who had their children young, women without defined career goals or a manifest vision of the future course or content of their lives, found the motherhood years to be a useful "career moratorium" in the Eriksonian sense, "a period of delay of adult commitment granted to somebody who is not ready to meet an obligation or forced on somebody who should give [herself] time" (1968, p. 157). Domestic time-in proved, for some, to be a useful time-out from work-in-the-world—time in which to think through and work out latent career dreams, to construct a life and work after motherhood (Weingarten and Daniels, 1978).

> "I was grateful for the chance motherhood gave me to think about things," said one woman who had put career thoughts "on hold" when her first child was born, "because when I actually did make a decision it was a decision that I had had time to ponder. I never felt that I was ready after college to move into something earth-shattering. I wanted time to think. Having a child around the house is hardly time to think," she laughed ruefully, "but it *was*, actually. As a mother I had a job, and a reason for being. I also had space and time to think."

Pursuing the Dream

If early motherhood means we run the risk of foreclosing opportunities of transforming the Dream into a workable reality, of precluding an early launch into a life work, the postponement of children—while affording no guarantee—leaves the decade of the twenties open for the activation of an occupational Dream into the rudiments of a career, a strategy that seems critical for women struggling to envision and fashion a life work in traditionally male professions such as medicine, in which the timing of a career progression is as arbitrary as clockwork (Hochschild, 1975).

Thirty years ago, even twenty years ago, only a maverick pursued a career Dream in her twenties, for to do so was to risk personal and cultural penalties for repudiating the Woman's Life Plan. Such women were rare; the exceptions proved the rule. Faith Fromm, a fifty-year-old psychiatrist who consciously put family thoughts "on hold" during her twenties, giving birth to the first of her two children at thirty-one, is one such woman. A self-described maverick, she had an early, unconditional commitment to a life work beyond motherhood. The daughter of a physician and of a "mother who did not work," Faith "always wanted to be a physician and always wanted to have kids." For her to have both, the late-motherhood timetable was crucial, for it enabled her not only to complete the prescribed agenda of medical training, but subsequently to integrate her two careers, to make them "all of a piece," without any of the strands of her generativity unraveling.

> "I wanted to be finished with at least something before I became pregnant," she said. "I didn't want to take time out until I was through with my residency.

Then I wanted to have my family quickly, because I wanted to get back to work. I planned it quite carefully in my head . . . I would have had a hell of a time if I had had children earlier. It would have been almost impossible to come where I've come professionally."

Faith's aspiration and accomplishment in both work spheres vividly document the importance of engaging our Dreams early not only to give us the experiences and the skills, the mentors and credentials to "move up," but to provide us as well with the inner momentum to negotiate subsequent conflicts with, and/or time out for, mothering.

"I chose to take time out when my children were small. I wanted very much to have a family, and I had a wonderful time, not being on a tight schedule and being able to give myself to my kids . . . If you are a maternal person, when you have *little* babies you concentrate a lot of emotional energy on them, and your external involvements fade for a while. But when the youngest child is six or seven, somewhere in there, it comes back, the outside interests. The passion for the work you'd set aside. The *passion* for it, not just the doing of it. From then on, for me, it was a steady progression of involvement and ambition."

A Variation: Nurturing the Dream

Faith Fromm knew what she wanted professionally and she was certain about how to get there. The career path was laid down and well marked. However, in some careers, for some Dreams—artistic ones, for example—a different kind of "pursuit" is called for: a way of approaching work that is more in tune with the inner life than with institutional requirements, more responsive and receptive, profoundly patient and seemingly random. In this variation of pursuing the Dream it may be equally important to hold the twenties free from the cares of motherhood in order to allow for the gestation of the Dream by creating the time and the space for it to take its own shape.

Florence Faison, a successful painter in her fifties, postponed parenthood until her early thirties not in order to serve a prerequisite apprenticeship in a defined career, but to let her imagination play, her ideas and images take shape, her work "come together." She referred to this time, to her *use* of this time, as "the knowing, necessary drift."

"If I had had children younger," she said, "my work would never have formed itself. In my life, the twenties were the years when I was putting everything together, *without even knowing what I was doing,* and evolving a style and getting my work going. Having children in those years would have been an enormous upheaval and disruption of the creative process."

The evidence of women's experience suggests that until we have laid out career paths that work *for us,* that accommodate the imperatives of our private lives, we can and sometimes must bring early Dreams to fruition through a process of lucid drifting.

Claiming the Dream

If Faith Fromm pursued her Dream of medicine and Florence Faison nurtured hers of art, the only word to describe Deborah Diamond's way of becoming a doctor is "claim"—"to demand as one's due," "to assert," "to state to be true." A forty-year-old neurologist with two school-age children born after she was thirty, Deborah claimed her dream step by step. Overcoming conscious conflict and unconscious ambivalence, she gathered confidence and certainty in her ambition and its legitimacy. For, as Arlie Hochschild has written (1975, p. 55), "Ambition is no static or given thing, like having blue eyes. It is more like sexuality, variable, subject to influence, and attached to past loves, deprivations, rivalries, and many events long erased from memory."

As a girl, Deborah had "many grandiose dreams—the impossible dream of becoming President of the United States, the inevitable dream of having a family." She became interested in science and biology in high school, and thought she would be a medical technologist.

> "In college, I got a little more adventuresome," she continued, "and thought I would go on and get a Ph.D. in virology. Chipping away at the hedges, senior year, I said, 'Hell, I'm going to be a doctor. That's what I really want to be.'"

At that, she almost sabotaged the fledgling Dream. A "wrong" love affair delayed her application to medical school. Once disentangled from that romance she proceeded briskly through the prescribed training sequence, married, completed her residency, and embarked upon parenthood in her early thirties. The pattern in her twenties is not unlike that of Faith Fromm.

Deborah, however, had always planned to take a full time out during the early years of her children's lives. "What we did was so 'traditional,'" she said, "only we did it later." She finished her residency three days before her first child was born, and entered soon therafter into a contract to write a textbook on neurology, which she felt was "a good interim solution."

> "Eighteen months of work at a pace of about twenty hours a week—writing a book seemed like a terrific solution," Deborah recalled. "I felt that as an intern and as a resident I had worked as hard as any human being had ever worked, and I thought that when I had a baby the little creature would sleep sweetly and I would sit down and write a book during naptimes. As soon as he went to sleep I would go to the typewriter, and as soon as he woke up, I would stop. But it wasn't that easy, for he woke up a lot, and *I* was the one on call. If we had had any idea how easy it was to have a child, and how difficult to raise one, I would have thought twice about agreeing to do that book."

Deborah accommodated her Dream in the early parenting years "when decisions about motherhood were paramount over any other thing" by improvising. Her improvisation was brilliant, yet difficult to sustain. It was a way of turning resolutely toward motherhood while at the same time nourishing a piece of her career, of "keeping her oar in." She construed the time as a career lull, a step off the established track that jeopardized her professionally; yet with book and baby she was actually working more than full time—as hard as she ever had. The availability of the Dream as a baseline was crucial during these years. It was something to come back to, again and again, whenever she was besieged by doubts—her own and those of others. For all her eventual success as evidenced by her royalties, while she was writing she worked in virtual isolation—out of phase with the traditional timetable for medical careers and out of contact with peers and colleagues, mentors and supervisors. (Later, setting up a practice after ten years was painfully difficult.) While she was writing she often found herself wondering whether the book "counted"—in the view of the medical establishment, in the eyes of her husband, in her own estimation.

> "Dan expected me to be my same old self, somehow. Writing this book and caring for this baby. Although the late 1960's weren't very traditional days, we still had very traditional thoughts and ways. And I thought to myself, 'After all, what am I? I'm just a housewife. I'm writing this book which nobody may buy.' I couldn't say to Dan, 'Look, *you* change the diapers, *you* take care of the baby for one afternoon, I'm writing a book. I, too, have work.' I was always waiting for him to say (he never did) 'No, that's not work. That's play.' So, I carried all these worries around. I carried the load of parenting close to 100 percent in those days, *and* the house, *and* the book—and I felt that that was what I *ought* to be doing. *And more.*"

At the same time, women around her, feminist peers, maintaining a safe inner distance from the realities of her (and their?) overloaded circuits, were critical of Deborah's improvisation, of her decision temporarily to compromise career for motherhood. Ignoring the cultural values and institutional arrangements that require such compromises of women but not of men, they interpreted her decision to take time out to care for her children as an untimely retirement and impolitic betrayal: "You can't retire now! You *owe* it to women, to the movement, to stay in there. You're letting us down and becoming just what men say we become." To which Deborah answered: "Don't you think I *owe something* to this baby I've given birth to?"

The experience of all these women—whether they dismissed the Dream, deferred it, drifted into it, pursued it, nurtured it, or claimed it—provides cumulative evidence of the value of a Dream (in both its occupational and more inclusive meanings) in prefiguring, substantiating and sustaining a sense of generativity in women's lives. Levinson stresses the importance of the Dream as an underlying source of motivation that can carry men through the transitions and problematic moments of their life cycle. At this moment in our social history, women may need the Dream as developmental fuel even more than men do. We need it to overcome the *inner conflicts* that are the residue of female childhood in a patriarchal world; and we need it to improvise our way, as Deborah Diamond did, through the *circumstantial conflicts* of lives increasingly defined by not one, but two, spheres of generativity.

The legacy of drift in women's careers reflects the developmental ambiguities and ambivalent cues of female socialization in childhood—ambiguities and mixed messages that leave emotional scar tissue in the form of deeply ingrained prejudices against ourselves and our capacities. It also reflects the internalization of patriarchal taboos against purposes and dreams of our own, against admitting, even to ourselves, that we might "love our work as much as husband and children, *need* it as much, perhaps more" (Gilbert, 1977, pp. 318, 319). Until we change profoundly the way we raise our daughters (and sons) and consistently encourage a sense of initiative and adventure in children of both sexes, we are all jeopardizing our ability to envision a wide canvas for our lives. In the meantime, a bootstraps operation in Dream recognition is called for. Wherever women are in their individual life cycles, lacking sufficient role models and mentors in generativity, we owe it to ourselves and to the women around us—our friends, our sisters, our students, our mothers, our daughters—to acknowledge and support a Dream where we see it, to nourish the merest promising fragment, and incorporate it into the gist of our lives.

Activating a Dream is a way of traversing the minefields of the inner world. A powerful Dream also serves as fuel through the external circumstantial conflicts and transitions characteristic of female adulthood. Given the variability of women's lives, the logistical and chronological intricacies of our double generativity, we need to draw upon the energy of a life Dream even more than men do. As the stories of Chris and Ann, Faith, Florence, and Deborah, abundantly demonstrate, women's generativity experience is fraught with complexity and compromise. Our careers unfold more slowly. Interruptions are the rule—daily, and over time. Increasing numbers of women have no intention of forefeiting career for motherhood, or vice versa. Overloaded circuits are common. A good Dream is a groundplan for improvisation, for negotiating the explicit role conflicts that emerge all along the way. Long-lasting, a good Dream can see us through an unpredictable life sequence of "times-in" and "times-out." A good Dream can center a life. If we engage a life Dream—and within it, a career Dream—early on, we can build some of the momentum we need to choose our works and our loves again and again, in ever new and ever different combinations.

The lives of all of us are marked by the tension between dream and drift, between pursuing the plums and letting the ripe fruit fall. The triumph of generativity over a sense of stagnation is, of course, a combination of dream and drift, a life so empowered by a vivid guiding vision of the possibilities that there are time and space throughout the life cycle for creative and re-creative drift.

REFERENCE NOTES

1. This paper draws, in part, on my research with Kathy Weingarten funded by the Northeastern Pooled Common Fund. It has been informed and inspirited by many conversations with Kathy Weingarten, Vicky Steinitz and Beiden Daniels.
2. It used to be that a woman's entire adult life might be consumed in maternal activity. Today, by contrast, a family of two children spaced two or three years apart means that daily absorption in the care of preschool children lasts for nine years at most—only one-sixth of a woman's projected adult life (Rossi, 1972).
3. The women's names are pseudonyms. Identifying features of their lives, including details extrinsic to the Dream, have been altered to safeguard individual identities.
4. The 1970s have seen a slow trickle of "early re-entry" women into medicine, women with children applying to medical school, being admitted, completing their training, and beginning to practice (Howell, 1973).

REFERENCES

BARNETT, ROSALIND, AND BARUCH, GRACE. Women in the middle years: A critique of research and theory. *Psychology of Women Quarterly,* 1978, *3*(2), 187–197.

DANIELS, PAMELA. Birth of the amateur. In S. Ruddick and P Daniels (eds.), *Working it out,* New York: Pantheon, 1977.

DANIELS, PAMELA AND WEINGARTEN, KATHY. *Sooner or later: The timing of parenthood in adult lives.* New York: Norton, 1981.

ERIKSON, ERIK H. Human strength and the cycle of generations. In *Insight and Responsibility,* New York: Norton, 1964.

———. Identity and the life cycle: Selected papers. *Psychological Issues,* 1959, *1* (1).

———. *Identity: Youth and crisis.* New York: Norton, 1968.

———. Inner and outer space: Reflections on womanhood. In Robert Jay Lifton (ed.), *The woman in America.* Boston: Beacon Press, 1967.

GILBERT, CELIA. The sacred fire. In S. Ruddick and P. Daniels (eds.), *Working it out.* New York: Pantheon, 1977.

GILLIGAN, CAROL. Woman's place in man's life cycle. *Harvard Educational Review,* 1979, *49*(4).

HOCHSCHILD, ARLIE R. Inside the clockwork of male careers. In Florence Howe (ed.), *Women and the power to change.* New York: McGraw Hill, 1975.

HOWELL, MARY. *Why should a girl go into medicine?* Old Westbury, N.Y. The Feminist Press, 1973.

LEVINSON, DANIEL J. *The seasons of a man's life.* New York: Knopf, 1978.

MILLER, JEAN BAKER. *Toward a new psychology of women.* Boston: Beacon Press, 1976.

MITCHELL, JONI. Interview with Cameron Crowe, *Rolling Stone,* July 26, 1979, pp. 46–53.

MORRISON, TONI. *Song of Solomon.* New York: Knopf, 1977.

RORTY, AMELIE O. Dependency, individuality, and work. In S. Ruddick and P. Daniels (eds.), *Working it out.* New York: Pantheon, 1977.

ROSSI, ALICE. Family development in a changing world. *American Journal of Psychiatry,* 1972, *128*.

———. Personal communication, July 1976.

RUDDICK, SARA. A work of one's own. In S. Ruddick and P. Daniels (eds.), *Working it out.* New York: Pantheon, 1977.

RUDDICK, SARA, AND DANIELS, PAMELA. (eds.), *Working it out: 23 women writers, artists, scientists, and scholars talk about their lives and work.* New York: Pantheon, 1977.

WEINGARTEN, KATHY, AND DANIELS, PAMELA. *Family-career transitions in women's lives.* Paper presented at the American Psychological Association, Toronto, August, 1978.

30
Friendships of Women and of Men

Robert R. Bell

This study examines the responses of four groups of persons as to their feelings about friendship and aloneness. The four groups are defined on the basis of gender and their Conventionality vs. Nonconventionality of values and attitudes toward life. It was found that the friendships of women are more personal and emotionally based than those of men. It is suggested that Nonconventional women and men may have more in common than do Conventional and Nonconventional women or men.

Friendship is a voluntary, close and enduring social relationship. How enduring is difficult to answer, but it can go on for years. Eisenstadt (1974) writes about the concept of solidarity as a special quality that binds friends together. He suggests that relationships of friendship appear to be based on attributes of solidarity that go beyond the primordial, the sacred and the civil types.

Other writers place a high importance on the primary nature of friendship. In this context primary refers to a predisposition to enter into a wide range of activities. This suggests that friendship is broad and involves significantly large parts of a person's life. It is also primary because of the positive effect which is manifested in the mutual expression of concern, the development and repeating of private tradition, and the feeling of right on each one's part to be able to make demands on the other (Booth & Hess, 1974).

There must always be a quality of exchange between friends. While who gives what and how much relative to the other may often vary in different friendships or even in a given friendship over time, it can not be too one way. If the exchange becomes too loaded in one direction this implies an inequity in the relationship. On a general sociological level friendship can be defined to include choice being made on a voluntary level and without any kind of coercion and as having extensive effect by each on and with the other. This implies many things and activities important to the persons as well as a sense of binding together, a "we" feeling of having something special and private.

"Friendships of Women and of Men" by Robert R. Bell in *Psychology of Women Quarterly*, 1981, 5, 3, 402–417. Copyright © 1981 by Human Sciences Press, Inc. Reprinted by permission.

Basic to the social psychology of friendship is the relationship which is positively evaluated. Any strong indication of self-interest is seen as a discredit to the relationship. A friend appreciates the objective qualities, private property, or social characteristics of a friend only because they represent the person rather than some external value given to the person. Furthermore, any exchange between friends must be seen on private and individual levels. "It is inappropriate to express friendship by making a gift that is not of value to the other's real self irrespective of the general value placed on the gift" (Suttles, 1970, p. 100).

Simmel (1950) talked about differentiated friendships which effect the degrees of friendship relations. These are friendships based on different social and psychological factors. There are differentiated friendships that connect us with one individual in terms of affection, with another in terms of intellectual aspects, with a third in terms of religious impulses and with a fourth in terms of common experiences.

Intimacy and closeness between friends is also reflected in the values extended to friends and beliefs about friendships. In part to say that we have a friend is to say we are not alone and we matter to at least that one other significant individual. Furthermore we can share some things that are important to both of us. Along with this are the positive psychological feelings, the pleasures to be derived from friendship. Possibly most important the pleasure of having a friend gives the good feeling of being reaffirmed and reassured by a significant other.

Friendship carries with it other kinds of pleasures. There can be the pleasure of laughter, of excitement and of emotional release. The dimension of laughter is very important because it means we can trust the other and relax with them to the point of sharing the good and tickling sensations of life. For friends laughing is sharing and being exuberant and not being superior or patronizing. Greeley (1971) writes that being friends is a "very serious business and that is why they have no choice but to be comedians" (p. 29).

Gender and Friendship

In recent years the emergence of the women's movement has had effects on women's friendships with each other. Seiden and Bart (1975) believe that among women in the movement there has developed some special feelings about friendship. They point out that while people make friends in all types of social movements the women's movement has had as a part of its ideology the belief in sisterhood. They report that in a pilot study of twenty women active in the women's movement the overwhelming majority reported that they had always had warm and significant relationships with women.

> It was not that they first found these friendships in movement activities, but rather that the movement supported them in *conceptualizing the value of friendship*. Previously, female friendships had often had a 'pastime' quality, being regarded as outside the arena of major action, something you do until the "relationship" comes. Friendships with women had a quality of "play," while

friendships with men had a quality of being an "investment" in terms of marriage prospects, dating experience which might enhance marriage prospects, and the like (p. 193).

Often men interact with others in terms of roles. Because men are often outward oriented they tend to construct roles about behavior. They frequently see persons not as total human beings but as persons filling particular roles. They may see another man as a lawyer, a competitor in tennis, a co-worker or a drinking partner. In this sense, many men do not see women as full human beings. They rather turn to their sets of role expectations and assign them to the woman in the light of the role in which they see her. They may choose whatever role seems most appropriate to them under given circumstances and offer their responses accordingly. Oxley (1974), in his study of mateship in Australia, found that male friendships were seldom intimate and were limited to particular contexts: "The well integrated man plays bowls with one group, goes fishing with another, drinks regularly with another, and so on. He is not likely to have a small circle of special friends with whom he does everything; the small circle of all-purpose friends is more likely to be found among women" (p. 100).

American men have long been able to deal with the inanimate objects of the world more easily than with other human beings. Men grow up to build things and shape things, and the interpersonal worlds have never been highly valued by men. Traditionally, if there have been emotional needs to deal with they have been left to women. Often men find it difficult to face up to the fears and anxieties they are not supposed to have if they are really masculine. Even recognizing how they feel, they may be unable to do anything about it. They may have been so effectively socialized that they can't confide in their wives or friends. They often find it difficult to confide in others sharing the reality in question—the competitive and striving nature of masculinity will make it especially difficult to share family fears with family members or work worries with work-mates. The risk of having such fears confirmed as well-founded seems too great. The fact that men are stuck within themselves has come through clearly in our interviews. Women will overwhelmingly reveal many of their fears, anxieties and insecurities to their best friends, while men overwhelmingly will not. The close friend relationship between women is generally defined as one which is self revealing and accepting, whereas the close friend relationship between men is subjectively defined in terms of doing things together.

Friendships of Women and of Men

This section will report and examine some findings from a study dealing in part with friendships of women and of men. The stress will be placed on some positive aspects of friendships in the lives of individuals.

In March 1976, I started interviewing people about friendship and aloneness, as well as their evaluations and feelings about their lives—where their lives had been and where they wanted to go. An assessment was made on their state of well being and desire for change. This assessment was on the basis of the following factors discussed during the interview: desire to influence change, to seek pleasure or greater happiness, to exert more control over their lives; overall satisfaction with life combined with willingness to take gambles in their lives. I have defined this group as *Nonconventional*. They indicated a clear difference in interpersonal norms and values from the second group, the *Conventional*, who were at the opposite pole with regard to these dimensions.

The persons interviewed were Australians and Americans. There were no significant differences between the two groups. Among the 87 women, 37 were Australian and 50 American. Among the 54 men, 16 were Australian and 38 American. The average age of the women was 34.5 years and for the men 33.4 years. About half of both the men and women were married, about one-quarter never married and one-quarter were separated or divorced (but not remarried). In education and occupation the respondents were highly successful. About 15 percent of both sexes were students (mostly graduate students). Over one-half were in the professions and the rest in the arts or the business worlds. Everyone in the study who was not a student was involved in a full-time occupation. The respondents were overwhelmingly upper middle class—at least according to educational and occupational variables.

During the interviews I tried to determine the meaning and importance attached to aloneness. Among the Nonconventional women 92% either said they had enough time alone or would like to have more. For the Conventional women the corresponding figure was 48%. Among the Nonconventional men it was 90% and 47% for the Conventional. In the interview the respondents were asked how they would feel about living alone for the next three months. Among the Nonconventional women 83% were living alone and liking it or said they would like to. This was true of only 31% of the Conventional women. Among the men the corresponding percentages were 68% and 25%. The evidence suggests that aloneness was a common characteristic as well as one valued by the Nonconventional women and men.

One measurement of the importance of friendship to the persons studied was the number of very good friends they reported having. Part of the interview was to ask questions about why persons were defined as friends. This allowed for a common basis of comparison between the interviewees. It is assumed that more very close friends suggests greater significance attached to friendship. For the same-sex friends the average number for the Nonconventional women was 5.6 while for the Conventional women it was 3.1. The corresponding averages for the men were 4.0 and 2.6. As to very close friends of the opposite sex for the Nonconventional women the average was 3.6 and for the Conventional women, 2.0. For the men the corresponding figures were 3.3 and 1.7.

Drawing from the total interview experience four group portraits were created around the respondents' feelings and behavior about friendship as well as some aspects of their personal privacy. That is, given the association of aloneness and friendship to the lives of the Nonconventional, in what ways and with what kinds of feelings are they manifested? The four group portraits presented are structured on the basis of gender and whether or not they were defined as Nonconventional or Conventional.

Nonconventional Women (55 respondents)

There is a body of evidence showing that close relationship or confidant relationship between women has taken on increasing importance. A study by Booth (1972) found that female friendship ties were richer in spontaneity and confidances than those for males. It has been suggested that for women the intimacy of friendship means a closeness: sharing ideas; sharing the secret corners of the self; expressing feelings; becoming vulnerable (Seiden & Bart, 1975).

In looking at their same-sex friends this group has more friends than any of the other three groups. When they are compared with the Conventional women they reveal far more about themselves to their friends. Two-thirds (65%) said they would reveal anything about themselves to at least some of their very best friends. One woman said: "I have four close women friends. I can be absolutely honest and self-revealing because they know everything about me. I can talk about all kinds of personal things. I think that friendships are more important than marriage. No friends would be worse than no marriage." Another woman reported: "We have total acceptance of each other—we don't have to prove anything. I share and they accept and don't make value judgments about me. We can tell each other anything and that is why we are best friends."

Almost three-fourths (74%) of the Nonconventional women said that what made good friends were such things as common experiences, interests and values. Also those with whom they can relax, receive support, or care and share. They further described their feelings toward their best friends as love, affection, warmth, comfortableness or support. By contrast, the Conventional women were more apt to stress trust, reliability, and mutual help. One Nonconventional woman said "they know who I am and are willing to accept me as I think I am. They are warm and doing something they like to do. They are very generous in sharing thoughts, feelings and are open about them. They have a real desire to understand."

The Nonconventional women more frequently (52%) report that other women more often see them as best friends than they see those women to be. To be more often viewed as best friends is less true of the Conventional women (31%). It appears that the aliveness and vibrancy of Nonconventional women are attractive to other women and they are drawn toward them. About three-quarters of both groups felt there were some unique experiences of femaleness that contributed to a special nature of friendship with other women. They often referred to the common growing up process that they had been through. One woman said "womenness does matter because of the same socialization. All of us have experienced being crapped on. But I don't think it is any sort of basic femaleness. I think the women's movement has made it deeper and more open. It has made me feel free to want and to be friends with women."

Nonconventional women have fewer close male friends than they do close female friends. And fewer of them are apt to reveal everything to at least some of their close female friends (65%). But there are far more of them willing to reveal everything to male friends than is true for Conventional women (4%). The Nonconventional women are clearly the most comfortable and satisfied in their relationships with men. When asked what makes men very good friends, they are likely to describe such values as honesty, give-and-take and supportiveness. These values were often presented during the interview as not involving any sexual discrimination and involving a complete sense of equality with their male friends. While there often was a sexual dimension to their interactions, that was secondary to the nonsexual nature of the relationship. However, most women said they would define their same sex friends as generally closer to them than their opposite sex friends. But more Nonconventional women (44%) either felt there was no difference or felt closer to their male friends than did the Conventional women (14%).

It is a common assumption that a woman and a man may develop a sexual relationship without any degree of friendship. But friendship without sexual involvement is often seen as more problematic. Privacy and exclusiveness are qualities commonly found in friendship. But these are often seen as important qualities of a love (or sexual) relationship between a woman and a man. Therefore, such a relationship is often assumed to exist in almost all situations involving adults of the opposite sex (Bell, Note 1).

Some of the women interviewed believed there was an inevitability of sex interfering with friendship. One woman said: "some of my male friendships have had to end because of attempts to move it into the bedroom. I have never had one male friend who has accepted the friendship without wanting to move into sexual involvement." But most of the Nonconventional women have positive values and experiences with sexuality and friendship. Fifty-eight percent of them said they wanted a sexual dimension in a least some friendships and believed the experience often to be good. This positive view was reported by only 14% of the Conventional women. As to sexual experience, over two-thirds of the Nonconventional women report strong attraction or the maintaining of a friendship with a former lover while this was reported by about one-quarter of the Conventional women. Quoting several women illustrates how they viewed sexuality and friendship. One woman said: "I realize the subtlety of sexual attraction is there. It is a valuable addition to friendship. If a good friendship could develop into a good sexual relationship I think that would be great." Another woman said: "I rely on my male friends for my sense of sexuality because that self-image is given to me by men. I would be very upset if a man did not find me attractive. So my relationships with my close male friends all have a sexual dimension."

As earlier suggested, the Nonconventional place a strong importance on aloneness as well as spending more time alone. One woman said: "Aloneness is very important to me—it has allowed me to survive. I could get away by myself, shut the door and not answer it. Aloneness has meant I found myself. I needed it and it has given me what I have and it has allowed me to become pleased with what I am." Another woman said: "My biggest cry is that I have no time to myself. I tell my husband to get out and take the kids and give me some time. I spend 45 minutes in the shower early every morning just to have some time to myself. I would just love to live alone—that would be great." Slightly more than half of the Nonconventional women felt that having time alone was very important, but this was true of only about one-third of the Conventional women.

Almost all of the women in the study said they felt loneliness at various times in their lives. And there were no differences in the two groups as to the kinds of situations where it had occurred. Over two-thirds of all the women said loneliness was feeling unwanted, of not fitting or of suffering through broken relationships.

One woman described how she was lonely when she started back to the university. "I think it is hard to eat alone. I would sit next to people and listen to their conversations and pretend I was part of the group. After about three months someone called me by name for the first time and what a thrill." Another woman said: "My major period of depression and desperate loneliness was when my marriage was ending. I had friends around but I couldn't get from them and I felt desperately lonely. This was bound up with my unhappiness in marriage. I kept wondering and worrying about how I would cope on my own. It was the fear of being alone more than the experiences of actual loneliness."

Conventional Women (32 respondents)

As mentioned, fewer of the Conventional women reveal fully about themselves to their best friends. One explained "I wouldn't talk about my private sex life or about my marriage because of a sense of loyalty to my husband. I do talk about a few of my personal problems, anxieties, etc. But on the whole I try not to tell too much. I have different friends for different levels." These women also place greater limits on what they will reveal. For example, almost half of them say there are some insecurities they would not reveal or they will reveal some happiness, but not sorrow (this was true of only 13% of the Nonconventional women). As earlier suggested they place greater value on helping one another and not being judgmental in what makes a good friend. For them there is a greater tendency to stress the negotiable and external aspects of friendship rather than the internal and emotional. One woman said: "Most of my friendships developed when I needed them the most. We will help each other, there is a reciprocal give and take." About two-thirds of these women feel that about the same number of women view them as good friends as they do them. Relatively few see themselves in special demand as friends.

These women have fewer close friends among men and for those who do they reveal much less to the men. They are especially more apt to hold back on revealing sexual or marital matters than are Nonconventional women. Well over one-third of them could offer no positive statements as to close male friends nor of having any personally good feelings about men as friends. Over one-fifth (21%) of these women said they had no close male friends. Some saw friendship with men as inappropriate or threatening in various ways. One woman said, "I have no close male friends because my husband would not allow it. In our relationships with couples if I talk to the man alone he raises hell. He is jealous—both sexually and because I have interests with the other man he is not a part of." About four out of five of the Conventional women said they felt less close to any male friends than to female friends. One woman said, "With women I can share and relate because they can have children and fake orgasms. Men don't know how to companion. They don't have the ability to just *do*. They have to have a purpose."

The Conventional women are more apt to feel there are sexual dangers in friendships with men (42% vs. 11%). As one said, "to have a sexual relationship with a male friend is threatening. I have had friendships end because sex entered. Once sex enters, the relationship is not kept in the proper perspective and all sorts of emotions, jealousies, etc. may begin." Almost two-thirds (61%) of these women believe there are usually strong pressures to move the friendship toward overt sexuality.

The Conventional women are also less interested in being alone. One woman said, "I find that when I go into my room to study I don't like to be alone and come out and work where the others are, even with the noise of the children and the television. I sometimes say I would like to have more time alone but I really don't mean it." Close to two-thirds of the women do not feel there is any importance to being alone. One woman said, "aloneness is not important to me to have time to myself. I actively seek people out. I hate being alone. I could never live alone for three days, let alone for three months."

A brief description will summarize some of the qualities of the Nonconventional women as they are contrasted to the Conventional ones. They have more friends of both sexes and reveal more about themselves to those friends. Friends are important to them but they do not dominate their lives. The extent and depth of their friendships greatly influence their lives and their friendships are within the emotional relationships of love, warmth and comforting. They do not usually see their friends in terms of what these friends can do for them. They more often see themselves as providing more friendship for others than in receiving friendship. The women tend to be the kind of persons that others are drawn to for close relationships. And in their friendships the Nonconventional women often place a high value on what they can give to those who come to them in friendship. These women most often have high values and high positive experiences in their interactions with men. Most of them have had with some male friends strong sexual attractions or experiences and have found those to be good and desirable. These women also place a high value on their aloneness and see it as contributing a great deal to their sense of self-awareness and personal development.

Nonconventional Men (22 respondents)

The Nonconventional men have fewer friends than do Nonconventional women but have significantly more than the Conventional men. Two-thirds (67%) of these men say they reveal everything to at least some of their best male friends. But this is true of only 12% of the Conventional men. It may be that Nonconventional men reveal more because they have a more positive view about themselves and what they have to reveal. By contrast, the Conventional man may have all kinds of negative feelings and thoughts that limit what he can comfortably tell about himself. Almost three-fourths of these men believe that what makes good friends is being supportive, understanding, sympathetic or sharing.

Well over half of the Nonconventional men believe that more same sex individuals viewed them as best friends than they do them. Somewhat less than half (45%) of these men believe that the common experience of maleness contributes something special to male friendship. These men do not offer support for the belief in any strong and special kind of male relationship. One man said, "I don't find any special qualities in male friendship. In fact, in the sense of mateship or bonding I find I am turned off by those ideas."

About as many Nonconventional men say they would reveal everything (59%) to at least some close female friends as they do to close male friends. But this was true of only 6% of the Conventional men. In their friendships with women over half (58%) believed that honesty, supportiveness and willingness to listen were important traits. And over half (53%) of the Nonconventional men expressed feelings of love, affection and warmth for their close women friends. These men see both sexes about equally as best friends and express no differences in the experience and feelings they found in both kinds of relationships. One man said, "My women friends are bright, have strong personalities, a sense of humor and are sensitive people. They are all people I trust. I would and have revealed anything to them, not the same things to all but only because it never has been relevant. If anything I may reveal too much about myself."

When these men were asked to compare the closeness of female friendships to those of male friends, over three-fourths felt there were no differences or that they felt closer to at least some of their female friends. One said, "I have always felt I could be much closer to a woman as a friend than to any man. It is a real gut feeling I have." Another man said, "Right now, and in the future, my female friends are far more important to me than my male friends, although that was not true in the past. I am beginning to think that 'macho' threatens male friendship and that is not true with women. It gets down to there being trust with women that is not there with men."

About half (52%) of the Nonconventional men say there are strong feelings of sexuality at least some of the time in some of their relationships with female friends. One man said "sexuality enters all my relationships with women in that there is some sexual attraction on my part. In some cases it has led to sexual relations and that has been very good. It is possible to maintain a friendship after the sexuality ends but there is probably a level of feeling that will be lost."

As shown earlier, the Nonconventional men have a stronger attachment to aloneness than do the Conventional. About one-third of them felt that aloneness was very important but this was true of only 8% of the Conventional men. One man said, "Aloneness is very important to me. It would give me more relaxation because in social situations I do not feel relaxed. Most of my thinking and fantasy would be much easier if I had more time alone. I would certainly like to have more aloneness. The idea of living alone for three months excites me." About two-thirds of the men felt that aloneness was important for greater self-awareness and expression. One man said "I must be alone at times—it allows me the feeling of forming myself rather than being attacked and formed by constant external influences. It is time to experience selfness."

Almost all the men described various experiences with loneliness in their lives. Almost two-thirds (61%) said they had felt loneliness when feeling unwanted or not fitting in with others. One man said "I have felt lonely a lot. Mainly when I fall out with my wife and there was no one to whom I could relate. When I feel lonely I feel unwanted, unappreciated, unsuccessful, unnecessary—I feel a failure. I cut myself off and then suffer in my isolation." Another said "I have had acute periods of loneliness. The greatest was as my marriage was coming apart. That was mainly because I was looking for something in the relationship that wasn't there. She had moved away from me very rapidly and I was left behind clinging to what wasn't there and may never have been."

Conventional Men (32 respondents)

Most of these men said there were some things about themselves they would not reveal. Over two-thirds say there are some insecurities about their selves they would not tell about. In contrast to the Nonconventional men they are most apt to stress helping characteristics in their best friend relationships. The restrictions on what they will reveal is illustrated by what one man said: "I would not reveal to them sexual feelings or experiences in my marriage. Maybe some emotional and financial things but not much. After that I would reveal most everything. Because we grew up together there is some competitiveness and a certain false pride in wanting to impress each other. So on some things I wouldn't tell the truth even if pressed."

Only about one-third (37%) of these men see more men viewing them as best friends than they view. They are very strong in their view of the importance of same sexness for friendship with three-fourths believing that the common experience of maleness contributes something special. One man said "maleness contributes heavily to friendship. The uniqueness of being male, women just wouldn't be the same, I find it very difficult to get close to women." Another man said, "there is a special quality to being friends with men and it wouldn't be the same with women. With my male friends there is something special—I don't know what but it isn't there with women."

Only a few have close friendships with women and almost all of them (94%) place restrictions on what they would reveal. What they typically would not reveal would be sexual matters, personal feelings and any sorrows or insecurities they might be feeling. One man said, "I avoid serious discussion with women because basically I see them as intellectually inferior." Another said, "I don't think I have ever had close female friends. I can't relate freely. Can't drink with them or camp out in the bush. Intimacy can't approach that with men." Among a number of the Conventional men there came through in the interviews fairly strong anti-female feelings. These men are characterized by traditional and basically sexist views of female and male behavior.

Over half of the men believe there is a strong potential risk of sexual involvement with women friends and feel that if that happens it will destroy the friendship. Therefore, sexual involvement is usually seen as antithetical to opposite sex friendship. One man commented, "Women who are sexually attractive to me are usually different from those that I reveal much to—I tend to make that kind of distinction. If a woman really turned me on I would not reveal very much to her."

Nine out of ten of the Conventional men do not believe that aloneness is important. One man said, "aloneness is important—but not very much. I sometimes want to be alone to work with the kids away. But I don't enjoy coming home to an empty house. I will always use contacts if alone for awhile. I am really afraid of being alone. I really do need people most of the time." Another man said, "Three months alone? I would not like it. I am miserable in the house on my own. I would go to any length to avoid being alone. For this reason I may have stopped my wife from expanding, because she knows I don't like being alone." The Conventional men are the largest group of any of the respondents to say they have never felt lonely. This was reported by 21% of them, as against 5% of the Nonconventional men. One man said "I don't think I have ever felt lonely. If I start to feel that way I seek out people to relieve or stop it from happening."

When the Conventional men mention loneliness it usually refers to conflict or broken relationships. Their loneliness centers on what they see as interpersonal conflicts rather than internal personal frustrations or anxieties. One man said, "I sometimes can lie in bed with my wife and feel lonely and alienated. I feel there is nothing more there for me. When I feel alienated with people I feel lonely." Another man said, "I remember standing in the window for hours feeling lonely and wondering when she would come home and who would bring her." Still another said "I have felt lonely with my wife. Sometimes she makes me angry and for days I will have this frustration and this is a very lonely situation. Then I wonder why I ever got married and I feel trapped and alone."

A brief description will summarize some of the qualities of the Nonconventional men. They have more friends of both sexes than do the Conventional men and they reveal more about themselves to those friends. They are more apt to stress the emotional and feeling aspects of friendships with both men and women. More of them see other men viewing them as close friends than they so view. One of their most striking characteristics is that many of them place very high value on their friendships with women. They tend to be generally free of sexism and place very high values on women as people and what they can and do give in friendship. These men have generally positive experiences and values toward their women friends. It may be that they are not able to deal with this in male friendships. That is, some may not have been socialized to a free expression of these feelings. Men looking for interaction involving these kinds of feelings may have to find them by turning to women.

Both groups of Nonconventional women and men have had frequent experiences and hold positive values about sexuality being related to good cross-sex friendships. Sexuality appears to be much less stressful for them than for the Conventional respondents of both sexes.

Both groups of Nonconventional women and men place a high value on aloneness and the two have had experiences with loneliness. And both groups most often define loneliness as related to not fitting, of feeling

448   Robert R. Bell

unwanted or of not being a part of a group. Loneliness is typically associated with a failure to relate to or belong with others on a level of intimacy they would like to have. Both groups of Nonconventional persons place high values on aloneness and on friendship. But our interviews suggest that the setting for these experiences are mainly within the emotional and private realm of the self and less in the pragmatic and ends-serving areas as is much more common among the Conventional persons.

This paper reports a part of a pilot study into friendship and the private world of the self. The findings presented in this paper generate two hypotheses that will be put to further tests in the ongoing research. The two hypotheses are:

(1) Generally the friendship of women is more personal and emotionally based than that of men. Men's friendships are more often characterized by how they relate to others and how they do things with their friends.

(2) The general social psychological state of Conventional vs. Nonconventional cuts across gender lines in describing friendship. To be Nonconventional may explain the importance of interpersonal and aloneness qualities more than does gender. Nonconventional women and men may have more in common than do Conventional and Nonconventional women *or* men.

REFERENCE NOTE

1. Bell, R.R. *Friendship and aloneness in a "select" group of women.* Paper presented at Sociological Association of Australia and New Zealand, Melbourne, Australia, August 1976.

REFERENCES

BOOTH, A. Sex and social participation. *American Sociological Review,* April 1972, p. 183–192.
BOOTH, A. & HESS,E. Cross-sex friendships. *Journal of Marriage and the Family,* February 1974, p. 38–47.
EISENSTADT, S.N. Friendship and the structure of trust and solidarity in society. In E Leyton, (Ed.), *The compact: Selected dimensions of friendship.* Canada: University of Newfoundland Press, 1974.
GREELEY, A. *The friendship game.* New York: Doubleday, 1971.
OXLEY, H.C. *Mateship in local organization,* Australia: University of Queensland Press, 1974.
SEIDEN, A.M. & BART, P.B. Women to women: Is sisterhood powerful? In N. Glazer-Malbin, (Ed.) *Old family/New family.* New York: Van Nostrand, 1975.
SIMMEL, G. *The sociology of George Simmel* Wolfe, K. Trans. Glencoe, Illinois: Free Press, 1950.
SUTTLES, G.D. Friendship as a social institution. In C.J. McColl, (Ed.), *Social Relationships.* Chicago: Aldine, 1970.

31
Equality and the Family
Juanita H. Williams

The effects on the family of recent social changes fostered by egalitarian ideology have begun to attract the attention of theoreticians and researchers. This review focuses on (a) traditional role segregation in the family, (b) major variables relevant to equality in the family, (c) birth struggles of egalitarianism in the family, and (d) implications of equality for the family and for the quality of family life.

Between Alice Rossi's (1964) "immodest proposal" for equality between the sexes (which now seems modest indeed) and Joan Landes' (1977–78) analysis of housework from a Marxist feminist perspective, we have witnessed the appearance of a robust literature on the effects of egalitarian ideology on the family. Its style and method range from the theoretical, analytical, and empirical to the rhetorical, angry, and personal. The family, now battered by storms of social change, is an institution intimately familiar to all of us, being the nexus of our developing lives. Now we are mandated, as professionals, to analyze and to understand its role in our lives and in society. We need to consider its values and its limitations, to question old assumptions inherent in its form and substance, and to evaluate its resilience and flexibility as new ideals of egalitarianism conflict with its old modes of division of labor and unequal distribution of power and dominance.

After defining the terms whose relationship concerns us, I want to focus on these topical areas: (a) analysis of traditional role segregation in the family, (b) major variables in effecting equality, (c) birth struggles of egalitarianism in the family, and (d) implications of equality for the family and for the quality of family life.

Since unanimity of opinion on definition of the family is not present in the writings of scholars on the subject, I must clarify the concept for this discussion. Reiss (1974) has proposed a "universal" definition of the family which he believes is valid across all cultures: "The family institution is a small kinship-structured group with the key function of nurturant socialization of the young" (p. 332). Implicit in this definition is the presence of two generations (at least), and since our topic concerns sexual equality, I stipulate that the kinship structure include a man and a woman who provide the nurturant context for one or more children.

Even though family role specialization seems to be universal (Hartmann, 1976), my comments will be focused for the most part on the family in our own society.

Among the many meanings of equality, the one most relevant here is from a stimulating analysis by Dixon (1976): "Equality occurs with the abolition of the social division of labor based on gender" (p.20). Dixon proposes that the potential for equality of women with men depends on their positions in five spheres; sexual relations, reproduction, homemaking and socialization, education and economic production, and political decision making. In each sphere, equality requires that both sexes be equally represented, equally active in the exercise of the role's rights and responsibilities, and equally rewarded psychologically as well as materially.

Traditional Role Segregation in the Family

In Western society the institution of the family has always featured segregation of familial roles by sex and the unequal exercise of power. Theories of ubiquitous patriarchy hold that the family as we know it arose from the reciprocal exchange of women. Levi-Strauss (1969), for instance, has contended that the elaboration of kinship systems made possible the formation of alliances based on ceremonial exchanges of women and other valuables. The giving away of sisters and daughters became a form of survival insurance, greatly strengthening the original family. The significance of this for our discussion is that an important sex difference was made: it was men who were exchanging women. The opposite, as far as we know, has never occurred in any human society (Mitchell, 1974). "The reciprocal bond basic to marriage is not set up between men and women, but between men and men by means of women, who are only the principal occasion for it" (Levi-Strauss, 1949, cited in Mitchell, 1974, p. 373).

This power differential and its corollary, the identification of woman as property, combined with woman's sexual and reproductive attributes to effect a division of labor by sex. To the man was assigned his role of economic provider with its attendant need for training/education, assertion in the outside world, and the opportunity to participate in the affairs of the society. To the woman was assigned the sphere of the home, its duties including the bearing and rearing of children and the maintenance of order and domestic serenity.

Although this sexual division of labor is now hierarchical, with men on top, there is some evidence that it was not always thus. Draper (1975), for example, described the !Kung, a hunter-gatherer people in South West Africa, among whom the women have considerable autonomy. Draper attributed this to the women's contribution of 60-80 percent of the food, gathered by them over a range equal to that of the male hunters; the flexibility of sex roles (with the exceptions that women did not hunt, and men did not clean the noses of children!); and the absence of physical aggression.

The importance of this work for our subject is that it shows how the evolution of sexual status from relative equality to inequality and the subordination of women might have occurred. While Draper was doing her fieldwork among the !Kung, some of them were beginning to abandon their nomadic lifestyle and to settle into villages where the women planted gardens and the men herded animals. The women were thus kept close to home while the men ranged and had contact with other social groups. Sex roles became more rigid, and girls and boys began to be socialized into them. Males acquired more power because of their work and their contacts and knowledge of the wider world, and the status of women declined as their attention to family and home concerns increased. Thus, the public sphere became identified with men and the private sphere with women; and the former was invested with more importance, more power, and more rewards.

Thus, male hegemony could have emerged along with the sexual stratification of labor and the devaluing of women and their products. As capitalism emerged with the creation of a wage-labor force, its promoters took advantage of the power structure to exploit women and children who were more vulnerable because of their lesser status and their economic disadvantage. Hartmann (1976) in her analysis of occupational segregation states that the low status of women in today's society and the division of labor by sex is the result of just such an interaction between patriarchy and capitalism.

It was not until women began their exodus from the home that behavioral scientists became interested in "woman's work," and then the main concern was centered on the effects of her absence on her children and her marriage. Wortis (1974), for example, analyzed the widespread acceptance of the concept of the maternal role by behavioral scientists and its implications for women. Serious analyses of the work that women do at home and its *meaning* for women, men, and the family, had to wait for the raised consciousness of the 70's. These have been reviewed in detail by Glazer-Malbin (1976).

Women have been invisible until recently in all the scholarly disciplines, mainly because the kinds of work that women do are not considered to be important and are not recognized as work. Oakley (1974) in *Sociology of Housework* traced the reasoning behind this: (a) women belong in the family, while men belong "at work;" (b) therefore men work, while women do not work; (c) therefore housework is not a form of work. To this Glazer-Malbin (1976) adds: (d) monetary and social rights belong to those who work; (e) women do not work but are parasitic; (f) therefore women are not entitled to the same economic and social rights as are men. "Thus the invisibility of their work provides a rationale for women's second-class status in both public and private domains" (p. 906).

In an essay on economic equality for women and men, Lekachman (1975) provided poignant support for the miserably poor esteem accorded housework in a quote from a British newspaper. It seems that a magistrate sentenced an offender to clean an old-age-pensioner's flat as punishment for a minor crime. Other judges saw the merit of this and followed suit. Observing this growing practice, a female reporter commented: "It may come as a surprise to the magistrate that thousands of women in this country are interned for varying periods of time, week in and week out, performing the new ultimate deterrent known as 'housework.' Many are finding it increasingly difficult to remember what offense they committed in the first place" (p. 94).

The salience of traditional role segregation in the family and its necessary allocation of women to secondary status continues relatively unaffected by social changes whose direction is toward equality. In a study of almost six hundred women, Lopata (1971) investigated the roles of women in contemporary society. These women, urban and suburban, employed and nonemployed, were emphatic in giving the home roles of women the greatest importance. Asked to rank thirteen possible roles of women, they gave top places to mother, wife, and housewife. At the bottom were career woman, worker, and member of the community. To the counterpart question for men, they agreed that their main role is economic provider, followed by father and husband.

The "two-person career" (Papanek, 1973) is a widely prevalent marital phenomenon which exemplifies traditional middle-class family roles in their purest form. In such a career, both husband and wife are heavily involved and committed, though only he is employed by the institution. His achievement is direct, while hers is vicarious, by virtue of her identification with him and with his job, and her performance of the duties and expectations required of a wife by the employer. The prototype of the two-person career is that of the corporate executive and his wife, though the military, academic, and high level professional man likewise depends on having a "suitable" wife to furnish the support system he needs for the advancement of his career. Parenthetically, Papanek notes that the preparation of women to participate in a two-person career marriage is an important if latent, function of many colleges: "Training suitable wives for important men is a function which is only now beginning to be challenged"(p. 865).

What happens to traditional roles of married couples when the wife goes to work? Reason would suggest that, with both members of the couple employed outside the home, both would share in the home tasks of child care and domestic maintenance. But in this most intimate of life's arenas, reason does not prevail. Considerable research clearly shows that home and children continue to be viewed by both as her responsibility (Bryson et al., 1976; Herman & Gyllstrom, 1977; Lloyd, 1975; Poloma & Garland, 1971).

Poloma and Garland (1971) quote a woman pediatrician married to a pathologist. Asked if her husband helped around the house, she replied:

> He helps a lot. I don't ask him to clean up the living room or to wash the diapers—I have a maid to clean. It's the little things that are most important. If I am tired, he will take the baby . . . and he is not at all demanding. If I am busy, he doesn't mind having a TV dinner for supper (p. 750).

Imagine that the speaker is male, and substitute female pronouns for male. The resulting incongruity will demonstrate who is responsible for the baby and the dinner.

Patriarchy and the subordination of women are living and potent institutions. Studying the status of married, employed, middle-class women living on a predominantly black island in the West Indies, Moses (1977) found that notions of what constitutes women's work and men's work are grouped along sex lines. Both women and men consider housework unsuitable for men, and men do not do it. Closer to home, Bryson et al. (1976) reported on psychologists married to other psychologists and found that, with regard to domestic activities, equality was nonexistent. Wives had the major responsibility for cooking, marketing, laundry, and caring for children of all ages. Outside help, not husbands, did the housecleaning. They concluded that sharing a profession did not mean sharing the housework.

Major Variables Affecting Equality

We have said that equality requires the abolition of the division of labor along sex lines. The brevity and simplicity of this statement notwithstanding, it has radical implications for the institutions of our society. Far more than surface changes, such as "allowing" women equal access to jobs and their rewards, such equality would require basic changes in the values and beliefs which have historically prevailed in American society and which underlie and support our institutions. Two key institutions which are the very fabric of our social life are the family and the marketplace. We have seen how unequal is the participation of women and men in these arenas. A look at what equality would require conveys a sense of the depth of proposed changes and of their essentially counternormative nature, revealing the resistance which is inherent in our way of life.

Dixon's (1976) paper on measuring equality presents a model which clearly shows what equality would look like and what has to happen to effect it. Figure 1 represents the traditional division of labor. For women,

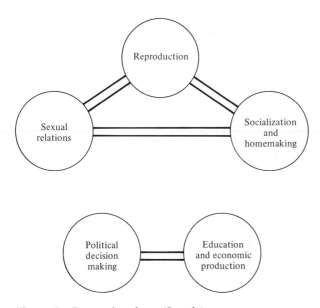

Figure 1   Domestic sphere (female)

sexuality, reproduction, and socialization of the young and homemaking
are strongly linked together, fixing them in the domestic life and precluding their entry into the public spheres, which comprise the male domain.
Figure 2 shows a new model wherein women and men are equally represented in the spheres and share equally in their responsibilities and rewards.
For equality to occur, the strong linkages which preserve the exclusivity of
the two domains must be broken. Sexuality becomes independent of reproduction with effective birth control. Sharing of domestic tasks, including
arrangements for child care, means that the woman's responsibility for
socialization and homemaking does not inexorably follow upon her reproductive behavior. More flexible working arrangements, such as part time
work, job sharing, and paid parental leaves would facilitate the entry of
more women into the public spheres and make it possible for men to be
equally represented among those who stay at home. The abolition of the
sexual division of labor, then, requires that societal systems undergo major
changes in their structures as well as in the value systems supporting them.
Until recently, as Zellman (1976) points out, it was widely held that the
individual woman had to find personal solutions for surmounting institutional barriers, almost always at great cost to her. Increasingly, it appears
that the systematic denial of access by women to the public domain is a
societal problem which can only be solved by basic changes in the social
institutions themselves.

Dixon's identification of the variables effecting equality is supported
in a different kind of analysis by Etheridge (1978). She compared four
"experimental" family systems to the nuclear family with regard to their
positions on variables which seemed relevant to egalitarian family living.
The Oneida Community, Israeli Kibbutzim, certain Mountain communes,

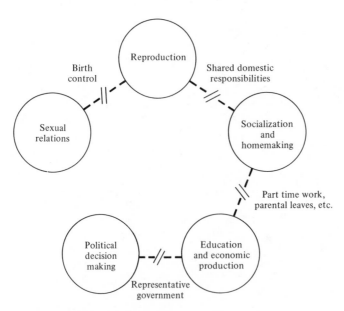

Figure 2   Public sphere (male)

and Dual-Career Families offered considerable variability on the variables of size of adult unit, economic dependency, task allocation, ideology, the parent-child link, and sexual access; and each varies as well from the nuclear family model. Etheridge concluded that four major interdependent variables are critical to equality in the family: egalitarian ideology, economic independence for women and men, equal task allocation in public and private domains, and collective childrearing.

While egalitarian ideology might seem to be sine qua non, its importance is more than semantic lip service. Attempts at radical change require a strong ideological commitment on the part of individuals and the society. While economic independence of women from men (and vice versa) helps to even out the distribution of power, it is too difficult to achieve short of totally equal task allocation in both the private and public domains. Helping women to become economically independent by giving them equal access to jobs does not convey equality in the family if women must come home and pick up with their other responsibilities of children and housework.

Etheridge's studies of the dual-career families convinced her of the interdependence of task allocation and child rearing. If both parents participate equally in the public and private domains, some child care must be provided by external agents. Dual-career families typically feel overloaded, and it may well be that equality of role sharing is less efficient than the division of labor. In fact, the belief that it is, given that efficiency is a powerful value in our society, has long supported the traditional family model: "To a considerable extent, the idea of shared work is incompatible with the most efficient division of labor. Much of the progress of our modern economy rests upon the increasing specialization of labor" (Blood and Wolfe, 1960, p. 48.). If we are proposing social changes which challenge such values, then the importance of ideological commitment is clarified.

Birth Struggles of Egalitarianism in the Family

What observations suggest to us that equality in the family is an emerging value and that attempts to implement it are reflected in evolutionary if not revolutionary changes? We have seen what are the important variables related to equality. It appears that among them progress toward the goal is uneven, though changes are observable in all in recent years.

Sexual relations in marriage continue to reflect a double standard (Williams, 1979), though women are reporting higher frequencies of sexual intercourse and orgasm. More women are expressing their sexual desires openly, abandoning the posture of passive recipient for more active participation. Sex research, such as that of Masters and Johnson (1966), Sherfey (1973), and Hite (1976) has brought to women a new awareness and appreciation of their own sexuality and its potential. With such information now available to large numbers of the population, women's expectations for the sexual part of their lives are changing in the direction of liberation from old inhibitions. Some married women are feeling freer to initiate as well as to refuse sex. In a study of employed professional women, Whitley and Poulsen (1975) found that assertive women were more likely to report sexual satisfaction as well as more diverse sexual activity.

Since women will continue to have the babies for the foreseeable future, one wonders if it makes sense to talk about equality in the reproductive area. We can, however, as Dixon (1976) suggests accept a goal of control of reproduction, with chosen biological motherhood as the norm. Although the ideal method does not yet exist, techniques for birth control are widely available. Contraception, including use of the Pill and IUD, and abortion, legally available since 1973, continues to be women's responsibility, with effective male contraception being far in the future (Bremner and de Kretser, 1975). Surgical sterilization for both women and men has increased greatly. It is estimated that about 10,000,000 sterilizations have been performed in the United States (*Sexuality Today*, Dec. 25, 1978).

Women are marrying later, postponing childbearing, having fewer children, and, in some cases choosing to remain childless. The median age at first marriage has risen almost a full year in the past 25 years. During the late 50's, 70% of white women had their first child in the first two years of marriage; 10 years later, only 60% did so. In 1974, the birth rate in this country reached a record low of 14.8 per 1,000 population. In 1974, only 8% of women aged 18–24 expected to have four or more children, compared with 38% in 1955. In that same year, the number of wives under 30 who planned to remain childless had increased by 23% in 3 years (Van Dusen & Sheldon, 1976).

Equality seems least evident in the area of child care and homemaking. Community care for preschool children continues to be low priority in influencing public policy. Public day care is available only for the lowest income levels, and private facilities often strain the budgets of young families. Mothers continue to assume the major responsibility of the early socialization and care of children. Even among dual-career families, with their greater resources and higher incomes, children tend to be their mother's responsibility (St. John-Parsons, 1978; Weingarten, 1978; Bryson et al., 1976). As for household tasks, sex-typing of roles continues to be the norm (Bryson et al., 1976; Glazer-Malbin, 1976; Lopata, 1971; Oakley, 1974). On the positive side, however, some studies show that when married women work outside the home, they tend to do less housework while their husbands do more (Williams, 1977). This phenomenon seems to be a conservative adaptation to role shifts rather than a restructuring of task allocations in the interest of equality.

If the private roles of men seem not to have changed much, the public participation of women in some areas has reached notable proportions. Nearly half of bachelor's and master's degrees are now earned by women, though they still receive less than 1 in 5 doctor's degrees. Enrollment of women in law and medical schools has increased fourfold since 1960, now constituting about 10% of total enrollment. Also, the number of women between the ages of 25 and 34 who are in college has increased by more than 100% since 1970, indicating that women are less likely to abandon their educational plans during the peak years of childbearing (Van Dusen & Sheldon, 1976).

Women have entered the labor force in droves during the past decade, and the greatest increase has been among young married women with children. In addition, newly married women are more likely to continue to work, and older women in their 40's and 50's are entering the labor market in record numbers (Van Dusen & Sheldon, 1976). Even so, women are greatly underrepresented among managers, professionals, and other high-level workers and are greatly overrepresented among clerical, service, and other low-level and poorly paid employees (Dixon, 1976). Not only does the sex typing of occupations continue unabated, but women workers receive on the average only about 60% of the earnings of men. Though women today have greater visibility in the public domain than ever before, equality is a long way off. Power in that world remains strongly invested in males.

Perhaps the strongest influence toward the emergence of egalitarian values and toward equality in practice in family life is the women's movement. Promoting the essential value of the equality of women with men in all sectors, its ideals and actions have elevated the consciousness of people everywhere and have brought about changes in expectations, in public policy, and in behavior, both public and private. It has caused the rethinking of old theories and ideas about human nature and has generated new knowledge which informs us and potentially changes our lives.

Implications of Equality for the Family

Given that the family is responsive to any social or economic change of any importance (Wrigley, 1978), it follows that the expansion of egalitarian ideology to include sectors of the society heretofore not covered by it will bring about change in the old institution. If the division of labor by sex becomes obsolete, then women wil contribute to the economic fortunes of the family and men will share equally in the domestic responsibilities. Persons of both sexes will be equally represented in the public and private sectors of the society. What will this mean for the family and its members?

Visions of the future range from conservative adaptations, within the family, to the social changes we have been talking about, to revolutionary models existing within a totally restructured society free of distinctions based on sex, age, race, and class. While the former are closer to the witness of our lifetime, the latter may be the experience of those who inherit the future.

An optimistic analysis of the near future of the family is Lipman-Blumen's (1976) examination of demographic trends and what they predict for new directions in sex roles. As women free themselves from their old dependencies on men, they will recover control of their sexuality, and sexual relationships will be divested of their barter connotations and will reflect mutual desire and control. The erosion of the value of sexual exclusivity will lead to more realistic perceptions of extramarital relationships as arrangements that fill the needs of some persons. The trend toward fewer children will continue, and voluntary childlessness will be an alternative for many. The positive effects of this lifestyle for marriage have already been demonstrated (Renne, 1976). Women's work roles will assume comparable importance with men's and, as their economic contribution to the family increases, women's power in decision-making roles will be strengthened. Changes in the work world, such as flex-time, job-sharing, and a shorter work week, will result in enhancement of the role of fathering, as well as more time for avocational interests and other activities, such as study and travel, which enrich life and broaden perspectives.

> As traditional roles begin to crumble, authentic, if not totally carefree, individuals will emerge. We shall have to confront and begin to understand our real selves and the real selves of others. Life will be more unpredictable, but also more challenging. . . . This will be a time for new creativity, strength, patience, adaptability, and knowledge. (Lipman-Blumen, 1976, p. 79)

Many who have thought about the implications of equality, however, believe that it is an illusory goal within the prevailing socioeconomic order with its values of competition, aggressive "winning," and the hierarchical distribution of power (Dixon, 1976; Hartmann, 1976; Hunt & Hunt, 1977; Lekachman, 1975). "If sexual equality is finally to become a central social value, it cannot realistically be expected to coexist with social institutions which are the outgrowths of the excesses of a patriarchal society" (Hunt & Hunt, 1977, p. 414). Even the dual-career family, they believe, cannot provide a generalized solution to the problem of inequality. Such a solution would require:

1. Radical redistribution and restructuring of work and compensation so that all persons, including children, could share in a nonexpanding economy:
2. Reduction of the amount of domestic service expected by persons, so that no class of persons would have to work just to provide a more privileged lifestyle for others;
3. The establishment of informal, intergenerational social units for the rearing of children as participating members of human communities.

The radical vision of the family was articulated as part of a feminist revolution by Shulamith Firestone (1974). In her view, the family, based on biological reproduction, is incompatible with equality and needs to be replaced by households of people of varing ages, wherein children would be cared for by many adults and older children, and relationships would be based on love alone, not biological kinship. Housework would be rotated equitably, and eventually eliminated, along with all other drudgery, by cybernetic technology. People would be freed from toil, and "work" divorced from wages in an economy wherein money would be distributed equally to all, regardless of age, work, prestige, or sex. Thus patriarchy and capitalism, with their social, political, and economic inequities, would be abolished, and all the old human dilemmas inherent in their basic unit, the family, would be resolved.

The one observation with which no one argues is that, while traditional family patterns and dynamics are still very much a part of the scene, the emergence of the value of equality for all people is effecting dramatic shifts in the old alignments of role and place. Arrangements which were only recently seen as marginal and exotic are now becoming accepted and normative. We must be cognizant of both the changes and the stresses they produce. To thus direct our work is to affect the future of the family in the direction of adaptations and alternatives which are both viable and humane.

REFERENCES

BLOOD, R.O., JR., & WOLFE, D. *Husbands and Wives.* Glencoe, Ill.: Free Press, 1960.

BREMNER, W.J., & DE KRETSER, D.M. "Contraceptives for Males." *Signs: Journal of Women in Culture and Society,* 1 (1975), 387–396.

BRYSON, R.B., BRYSON, J.B., LICHT, M.H., & LICHT, B.G. "The Professional Pair: Husband and Wife Psychologists." *American Psychologist,* 31 (1976), 10–16.

DIXON, R. "Measuring Equality Between the Sexes." *Journal of Social Issues,* 32 (1976) 19–32.

DRAPER, P. "!Kung Women: Contrasts in Sexual Egalitarianism in Foraging and Sedentary Contexts." *Toward an Anthropology of Women.* Ed. R. Reiter. New York: Monthly Review Press, 1975.

ETHERIDGE, C.F. "Equality in the Family: Comparative Analysis and Theoretical Model." *International Journal of Women's Studies,* 1,1 (1978), 50–63.

FIRESTONE, S. "The Ultimate Revolution." *Marriage and the Family.* Ed. C.C. Perrucci and D.B. Targ. New York: David McKay, 1974.

GLAZER-MALBIN, N. "Housework." *Signs: Journal of Women in Culture and Society,* 1 (1976), 905–922.

HARTMANN, H. "Capitalism, Patriarchy, and Job Segregation by Sex." *Signs: Journal of Women in Culture and Society,* 1 (1976), 137–169.

HERMAN, J.B., & GYLLSTROM, K.K. "Working Men and Women: Inter-and Intra-Role Conflict." *Psychology of Women Quarterly,* 1 (1977), 319–333.

HITE, S. *The Hite Report.* New York: Macmillan, 1976.

HUNT, J.G., & HUNT, L.L. "Dilemmas and Contradictions of Status: The Case of the Dual-Career Family." *Social Problems,* 24 (1977), 407–416.

LANDES, J. "Women, Labor and Family Life." *Science and Society,* 41 (1977–78), 386–409.

LEKACHMAN, R. "On Economic Equality." *Signs: Journal of Women in Culture and Society,* 1 (1975), 93–102.

LEVI-STRAUSS, C. *The Elementary Structures of Kinship.* London: Eyre & Spottiswoode, 1969.

LIPMAN-BLUMEN, J. "The Implications for Family Structure of Changing Sex Roles." *Social Casework,* 57 (1976), 67–79.

LOPATA, H. *Occupation: Housewife.* New York: Oxford University Press, 1971.

MASTERS, W., & JOHNSON, V. *Human Sexual Response.* Boston: Little, Brown, 1966.

MITCHELL, J. *Psychoanalysis and Feminism.* New York: Pantheon, 1974.

MOSES, Y.T. "Female Status, the Family, and Male Dominance in a West Indian Community." *Signs: Journal of Women in Culture and Society,* 3 (1977), 142–153.

OAKLEY, A. *The Sociology of Housework.* New York: Pantheon, 1974.

PAPANEK, H. "Men, Women, and Work: Reflections on the Two Person Career." *American Journal of Sociology,* 78 (1973), 852–872.

POLOMA, M.M., & GARLAND, T.N. "The Myth of the Egalitarian Family: Familial Roles and the Professionally Employed Wife." *The Professional Woman.* Ed. A. Theodore. Cambridge, Mass.: Schenkman, 1971.

REISS, I.L. "The Universality of the Family." *Marriage and the Family.* Ed. C.C. Perrucci and D.B. Targ. New York: David McKay, 1974.

RENNE, K.S. "Childlessness, Health, and Marital Satisfaction." *Social Biology,* 23 (1976), 183–197.

ROSSI, A. "Equality Between the Sexes: An Immodest Proposal." *Daedelus,* 93 (1964), 607–652. *Sex, Discrimination and the Division of Labor.* Ed. C.B. Lloyd. New York: Columbia University Press, 1975.

SHERFEY, M.J. *The Nature and Evolution of Female Sexuality.* New York: Random House, 1973.

ST. JOHN-PARSONS, D. "Continuous Dual-Career Families: A Case Study." *Psychology of Women Quarterly,* 3 (1978), 30–42.

VAN DUSEN, R.A., & SHELDON, E. "The Changing Status of American Women: A Life Cycle Perspective." *American Psychologist,* 31 (1976), 106–116.

WEINGARTEN, K. "The Employment Pattern of Professional Couples and their Distribution of Involvement in the Family." *Psychology of Women Quarterly,* 3 (1978), 43–52.

WHITLEY, M.P., & POULSEN, S.B. "Assertiveness and Sexual Satisfaction in Employed Professional Women." *Journal of Marriage and The Family,* 37 (1975), 573–581.

WILLIAMS, J.H. *Psychology of Women: Behavior in a Biosocial Context.* New York: Norton, 1977.

WILLIAMS, J.H. "Sexuality in Marriage." *Handbook of Human Sexuality*. Ed. B. Wolman. New York: Prentice-Hall, 1979.

WORTIS, R.P. "The Acceptance of the Concept of the Maternal Role by Behavioral Scientists: Its Effects on Women." *Intimacy, Family, and Society*. Ed. A. Skolnick and J.H. Skolnick. Boston: Little, Brown, 1974.

WRIGLEY, E.A. "Reflections on the History of the Family." *The Family*. Ed. A.S. Rossi, J. Kagan, & T.K. Hareven, New York: Norton, 1978.

ZELLMAN, G.L. "The Role of Structural Factors in Limiting Women's Institutional Participation." *Journal of Social Issues*, 32 (1976), 33–46.

32

Working Lesbians
Role Conflicts and Coping Strategies

Sandra A. Shachar and Lucia A. Gilbert

This study investigated areas of interrole and intrarole conflict reported by 79 lesbian working women and factors influencing the types of coping strategies these women used. The three coping strategies identified by Hall (1972) were used to code responses to a questionnaire sent to women on the mailing list of a local lesbian newsletter. The most frequently reported interrole conflicts were between the work and lover roles, and the most frequently reported intrarole conflicts involved the work and daughter roles. Subjects viewed being lesbian as contributing little to their interrole conflicts and, as hypothesized, used predominantly role restructuring strategies (Types I and II) to deal with the conflicts. Also, as hypothesized, higher self-esteem was reported by individuals using restructuring strategies than by those using reactant strategies (Type III). In contrast, subjects viewed being lesbian as highly related to their intrarole conflicts, and, contrary to predictions, used reactive strategies almost as frequently as role restructuring strategies. Moreover, self-esteem did not differ among subjects using the three strategy types. The unexpected findings for intrarole conflict are discussed in terms of the potential benefits of reactant-avoidant strategies in work situations.

Being heterosexual typically is not considered relevant to career competency and qualifications. Being homosexual, on the other hand, can become an issue, whether covert or overt, once it is known. Thus, although working lesbians engage in the same roles as heterosexual women, because of the negative social status ascribed to homosexuality, they may face unique conflict situations in the work environment (Abbott & Love, 1972; Martin & Lyon, 1972).

Research on the conflicts women experience in fulfilling their work role has focused on the experiences of heterosexual women (Gilbert & Holahan, Note 1; Holahan & Gilbert, 1979; Nevill & Damico, 1975). A major purpose of the present study was to identify salient areas of role conflict reported by a sample of working women who are lesbian. In contrast to previous studies in which conflicts between roles (e.g., Goode, 1960; Hall, 1972) were explored, this study investigated both interrole and intrarole conflicts (i.e., conflict within a particular role). Of particular interest was whether subjects perceived that their lesbianism influenced their experience of interrole and intrarole conflicts. A second purpose was to compare the strategies used in coping with the identified areas of role conflict. Finally, we investigated the influence of self-esteem on the experience of role conflict and the strategies employed to deal with the role conflict.

The model of conflict resolution employed was initially developed by Hall (1972). He identified three basic coping mechanisms in dealing with interrole conflict: Structural Role Redefinition, Personal Role Redefinition, and Reactive Behavior. These strategies are each designed to alter one of the three role components defined by Levinson (1959): structurally given demands, personal conceptions of roles, and role performance or behavior. In Structural Role Redefinition (Type I coping), the individual deals directly with those communicating demands or expectations for the role (role senders) to negotiate a mutually satisfying set of role expectations. Personal Role Redefinition (Type II coping) involves changing one's own perceptions of roles and role demands rather than changing the external environment or role context. The individual using Reactive Behavior (Type III coping) assumes that role demands are unchangeable and admits, denies, or tries to meet all role demands.

Hall (1972), in a study of college-educated women, found that women choosing either a Type I or Type II strategy generally reported greater satisfaction with their role performance than those choosing a Type III strategy. Gilbert and Holahan (Note 1) applied Hall's typology in analyzing the strategies for dealing with conflict between professional and parental roles reported by female university professors in dual-career marriages. Their results are generally consistent with the prediction that Type I and II strategies would result in less stress and greater satisfaction with coping than would Type III.

Although Hall (1972) proposes that Type I is the most adaptive of the three strategies because it involves direct negotiation with role senders, subsequent studies do not support this view (e.g., Harrison & Minor, 1978). It seems likely that both Type II and Type I strategies would result in greater coping satisfaction and lower stress than would a strategy which assumed that all role demands had to be admitted, met, or denied (Type III). Lesbians, for example, whose personal identity may be in conflict with role demands, may find a strategy which redefines their internal perceptions of a role (Type II) to be as functional a strategy as one which restructures the external role demands (Type I).

Certain personality variables may be related to the experience of role conflict and to the strategies employed in coping with role conflict. Rogers' self theory provides a framework for clarification of the influence of lesbianism on the experience of role conflict. According to self theory, the accurate perception and subsequent integration of social expectations with personal values are essential to adaptive development (Rogers, 1961). The social expectations for sex-appropriate sexual preference may conflict with lesbians' personal values. That is, if society's and important role senders' beliefs about sexual preference do not correspond with what individuals want for themselves or with how they think others want them to be, then, according to Rogerian theory, psychological conflict results.

Individuals who have achieved a congruence between their personal values and social expectations feel a greater sense of self-acceptance and self-competence than those who have not (Rogers, 1961) and thus may experience less conflict in their interactions with various role senders. In addition, because of their stronger sense of self, they may be more apt to use strategies which involve active negotiation with role senders (Type I) and/or strategies that focus on personal redefinition. To test this possibility, self-esteem was used as a personality variable in the present study.

In the study, a sample of lesbians completed a questionnaire describing important areas of interrole and intrarole conflict, indicated the degree to which their lesbianism contributed to their conflicts, and described their characteristic coping strategies. A measure of self-esteem was also completed. The following hypotheses were advanced for both interrole and intrarole conflict: (a) subjects using strategy Types I and II would report less stress due to role conflict and greater satisfaction with coping than would subjects using Type III, and (b) subjects using strategy Types I and II would report higher self-esteem than would subjects using Type III. No hypotheses were made about how the perceived degree of lesbianism contribution might be related to the kind of role conflict or type of coping strategy.

Method

Subjects and Procedure

A research questionnaire with explanatory cover letters was mailed to all 220 women on the mailing list of a local lesbian newsletter by the newsletter staff. The friendship network of one investigator also was utilized to distribute an additional 43 questionnaires. Both newsletter and friendship network participants were assured of the anonymity and confidentiality of their responses, which were to be returned by mail in the stamped, addressed envelope provided.

A total of 79 questionnaires (30%) were returned. Of these, nine questionnaires were not used because the subjects classified themselves as heterosexual or bisexual on the Kinsey Scale of Sexual Orientation (Kinsey, Pomeroy, Martin & Gebhard, 1953). The remaining 70 subjects (53 from the newsletter, and 17 from the friendship network) classified themselves on the seven-point Kinsey Scale as Exclusively or Predominantly Lesbian. Three-fourths of the participants were currently in lesbian primary relationships, and of these 82% lived with their lover. Over half (56.5%) had been in heterosexual marriages or primary relationships, but only 10% of the sample had children. Subjects ranged in age from 21 to 58, with a median age of 28.3; they were primarily Anglo (92.6%) and well educated, with 94% having at least a college degree; and 91.4% were presently working (defined as paid employment or full-time student enrollment). Further informatior. on subjects' characteristics is available from the authors.

Measures

Three kinds of data were collected: (a) ratings on aspects of the role conflict experienced, hereafter referred to as "role-conflict related variables" (stress, coping satisfaction, and degree of lesbian contribution), (b) self-esteem scores, and (c) strategies for dealing with role conflict.

Role-conflict related variables.   Participants were provided with definitions of role, role senders, and interrole and intrarole conflict. Interrole conflict was described as the felt difficulty in meeting the perceived demands for two or more roles; intrarole conflict as the felt difficulty in meeting perceived demands or expectations from others regarding behavior within a particular role.

Subjects were then asked, "What do you consider to be the most important pair of roles for which you have in the past or currently experience conflict?" After identifying these roles, subjects described the conflict and rated the three role-conflict related items on a six-point scale ranging from one (not at all) to six (very). Most subjects (90.7%) said the conflict described was current.

The role-conflict items were: "How stressful is (or was) this conflict for you?"; "How satisfied are you with the way you dealt with this conflict?"; "How much do you feel being lesbian contributes to this conflict?" A parallel set of questions was used for intrarole conflict.

Of the 70 respondents, 86% described an area of intrarole conflict, 78% an area of interrole conflict, and 70% both areas. All subjects reported conflict in one area or the other.

Self-esteem.   A 16-item, short form of the Texas Social Behavior Inventory (TSBI) was used to measure self-esteem (Helmreich & Stapp, 1974). This instrument is designed to determine individuals' self-confidence and competence in interpersonal situations and is generally considered to be a measure of social self-esteem. Coefficient alphas typically range from .87 to .92. Each item is scored from zero to four and total scores range from zero to 64. Lower scores are associated with lower self-esteem.

Coping strategies.   Subjects were asked to respond to the open-ended question, "How would you describe how you have dealt with this conflict?" Responses were coded independently by three raters trained in Hall's (1972) classification system for coping strategies. Subjects who used multiple coping styles were coded according to the predominant type of coping strategy used. The rate of agreement between the first two raters was 74% for interrole conflict, and 71% for intrarole conflict. The third rater independently coded responses on which the first two raters did not agree. The third rater invariably agreed with one of the other two raters.

Examples of responses coded in each strategy type are as follows:

1. For conflict within the daughter role, subject "told my father I am a lesbian two-and-one-half years ago. He knows by now that I am not just going through a 'phase'."

This strategy was called *Type I*—Self-disclosure to change role sender's expectations.

2. For conflict between lover and work roles, subject "tried to look at my image at work as acting a role while not losing myself to it."

This strategy was coded *Type II*—Changed attitudes toward roles.

    3. For conflict between lover and work roles, subject "tries not to bring up the conflict at all."

This strategy was coded *Type III*—Avoids conflict.

Results

Analyses

Directional hypotheses were tested by one-tailed t-tests. Because 70% of the respondents reported both kinds of conflict, comparisons between responses for interrole conflict and intrarole conflict were made by t-tests for correlated means. Intercorrelations of subjects' responses among the three role-conflict related items and self-esteem scores were typically low (absolute median $r = .16$). Thus, each was treated as a separate dependent variable. Finally, comparisons of responses from subjects obtained from the newsletter and the friendship network indicated no differences between these two groups on the various dependent measures. Thus, the groups were combined.

Descriptions of Role Conflicts

Interrole conflict. The most frequent interrole conflict reported was between the lover and work roles (40.8%). Other areas of interrole conflict mentioned less frequently were between work and political activist (12.9%), lover and daughter (7.4%), and lover and political activist (5.5%) roles. Of the remaining role conflicts identified by subjects (e.g., lover vs. mother), none was reported by more than one respondent.

Conflicts between lover and work roles generally concerned allocation of time and energy to the two roles and conflict between the needs or interests of the role senders (lovers and employers). Examples are:

> The relationship between myself and my employer is that I would rearrange my schedule if I'm needed to work any overtime and my lover cannot cope with the conflict of my work and time I spend with her.

> My lover wants the security of staying in one area and spending much time with me; I am very busy with my career . . . and I must move frequently to gain experience / opportunities.

In general subjects viewed their interrole conflicts as quite stressful ($M = 4.52$) and their lesbianism as contributing only moderately to the conflict ($M = 3.26$). Satisfaction with coping was moderate ($M = 3.11$).

Intrarole conflict. For intrarole conflict, the work role was mentioned most often ($n = 20$, 32.8%), followed in order by the daughter ($n = 18$, 29.5%) and lover ($n = 10$, 16.4%) roles. Subjects identifying these three areas of intrarole conflict did not differ in self-esteem or in their ratings of the role conflict experience. Of the remaining roles identified by subjects (e.g., mother, friend), none was selected by more than three respondents.

Conflicts within the role of work typically involved feeling socially unacceptable in a heterosexual, male-dominated work environment. For example,

> Expectations of co-workers and boss (all male) that I be heterosexual (dress, act, and have evidence of so being) when I really wish I could just be who I am at work. I cannot, usually, because I am afraid of what'd result.

> I would like to be completely myself at work. I enjoy my job, however, I can never discuss my home or personal life.

Intrarole conflict in the daughter role typically involved expectations of parents which subjects could not or did not wish to meet. Examples include:

> My father would prefer that I were heterosexual and that I marry and produce grandchildren.

> I want to be a loving daughter but cannot always meet my mother's demands, i.e., that I visit her often, etc.

In general, subjects viewed their intrarole conflict as quite stressful (M = 4.61) and their lesbianism as contributing substantially to the conflict (M = 4.61). Satisfaction with coping was moderate (M = 3.56).

Comparisons of Two Kinds of Role Conflicts

Subjects reported that their lesbianism contributed more to intrarole conflict (4.61) than to interrole conflict (3.26), $F(1,113) = 3.67, p < .001$. The two kinds of conflict, however, were rated as equally high in stress (interrole, 4.52; intrarole, 4.61). Ratings of the degree of satisfaction in coping with each kind of conflict also were similar (interrole, 3.11; intrarole 3.56).

Coping strategies employed for conflicts in each area are summarized in Table 1. A Type III strategy was used more frequently for intrarole conflicts than for interrole conflicts and a Type I strategy more frequently for interrole conflicts than for intrarole conflicts, $X^2(2) = 6.43, p < .05$.

Comparisons of Types of Coping Strategies Employed

It should be noted that only 25% of the subjects employed the same strategy for both their interrole and intrarole conflict.

Table 1 Frequency of coping types for interrole and intrarole conflict

Coping strategy	Interrole (n = 54) %	Interrole (n = 54) frequency	Intrarole (n = 61) %	Intrarole (n = 61) frequency
Type I	54	(29)	44	(27)
Type II	28	(18)	16	(10)
Type III	18	(10)	40	(24)

Table 2 Summary of mean item ratings and scale scores for subjects using the three types of coping strategies

| | Coping styles | | | | | |
| | Type I | | Type II | | Type III | |
Variables	M	(S.D.)	M	(S.D.)	M	(S.D.)
Interrole Conflict	(n = 29)		(n = 15)		(n = 10)	
Stress of conflict[a]	4.52	(1.18)	4.33	(1.45)	4.80	(1.48)
Coping Satisfaction[a]	3.66	(1.34)	4.07	(1.39)	4.30	(1.77)
Degree of lesbian contribution[a]	2.89	(2.04)	3.93	(2.05)	3.30	(2.06)
Self-esteem	46.24	(11.49)	47.73	(8.35)	40.60	(9.80)
Intrarole Conflict	(n = 28)		(n = 9)		(n = 23)	
Stress of conflict[a]	4.68	(1.25)	4.67	(1.00)	4.43	(1.20)
Coping satisfaction[a]	4.07	(1.33)	4.11	(1.17)	2.48	(1.27)
Degree of lesbian contribution[a]	4.57	(1.73)	4.44	(1.94)	4.87	(1.94)
Self-esteem	46.93	(10.18)	41.89	(12.06)	43.87	(8.73)

Note: Higher scores are associated with a greater endorsement of the variable.
[a] Ratings were made on a 6-point scale.

Interrole conflicts. As predicted, subjects using Type III strategies reported lower self-esteem than those using Type II strategies, but not Type I, $t(23) = 1.95$, $p < .05$, and $t(37) = 1.39$, $p > .05$, respectively. Contrary to our hypothesis, no differences were found among the strategy types on stress due to role conflict or on satisfaction with coping. The degree to which lesbianism contributed to role conflict also did not differ among strategy types. The mean values are summarized in Table 2.

Intrarole conflicts. As predicted, subjects using Type III strategies reported significantly less satisfaction with coping than those using Type I and Type II strategies $t(37) = 4.33$, $p < .001$, and $t(23) = 3.33$, $p < .001$, respectively. Contrary to expectations, however, no differences in self-esteem and in stress due to role conflict were reported. As with interrole conflict, no differences were found on the degree to which lesbianism contributed to the role conflict.

Discussion

Interrole Conflict

The most frequently reported interrole conflict was between the work and lover roles. Subjects' written descriptions of their work-lover conflict and their response that lesbianism contributed little to the conflict suggest that this kind of interrole conflict occurs independently of one's sexual orientation. Rather, these findings, like those reported for heterosexual women in the workforce (Holahan & Gilbert, 1979), underscore the difficulties of meeting the multiple demands of work and primary relationships.

Different coping strategies typically were used for dealing with interrole and intrarole conflict. For interrole conflict, the Type I strategies clearly predominated (54%), with 28% of respondents using Type II and only 18% using Type III. Thus, most respondents used the coping strategies typically viewed as the more effective (i.e., Types I and II). As anticipated, higher self-esteem was reported by individuals using these strategies than those using Type III. Thus, individuals who have higher self-esteem and confidence appear more likely to use restructuring strategies for interrole conflict than do persons with lower self-esteem and confidence. (Using Type I and II strategies may also enhance self-esteem.) Contrary to expectations, however, using strategy Types I and II as opposed to Type III did not result in significantly lower stress due to interrole conflict or to higher satisfaction with coping.

This similarity among the stress and satisfaction variables associated with the different strategies is perplexing. The diversity of interrole conflicts identified by subjects may have produced too much variability in subjects' responses to detect differences among those using the three strategies. Harrison and Minor (1978), for example, found that the type of coping strategy used by black working mothers was influenced by the kind of interrole conflict being assessed. Degree of conflict and ratings of effectiveness may also be influenced by kind of interrole conflict. Unfortunately, our sample was too small to allow comparisons of self-esteem, stress, and effectiveness across the three coping styles within a specific area of interrole conflict (e.g., lover-work).

Intrarole Conflict

In contrast to interrole conflicts, subjects viewed being lesbian as highly related to their intrarole conflicts. Conflicts within the most frequently mentioned roles of work and daughter concerned expectations or demands from role senders which subjects could not or did not want to meet because of their sexual preference. These situations, then, involve the struggles with integration of social expectations and personal values described in Rogers' self theory. Subjects identifying work as their most important intrarole conflict area, for example, may be working in an environment in which being known as lesbian would jeopardize one's job security and career development. Similarly, relationships with parents are important in our society and the inability or unwillingness to meet parents' expectations can cause problems. Furthermore, if subjects have internalized parents' (and society's) definitions of the daughter role (e.g., the importance of marriage or of a child), their role situation may be even more stressful.

Regarding coping, for intrarole conflict, the Type III strategies were used almost as frequently as Type I. This more frequent use of Type III for intrarole than for interrole conflicts may be related to the finding that subjects described their lesbianism as contributing more to intrarole conflicts than to interrole conflicts.

Of the respondents choosing a Type III strategy for intrarole conflict, 95% said they either could not "see any way to deal with it" or avoided the conflict. Thus, a lesbian may find herself in a no-win situation with regard to parents' or employers' expectations. If she chooses a Type I strategy, she may disclose her lesbianism and risk loss of affection or employment. If she chooses a Type II strategy by attempting to change her perception of the role rather than the actual situation, she may increase the personal strain of maintaining a heterosexual image. Thus, "I can't see any way to deal with it" may be the result of careful deliberation about the risks and benefits of confrontation, as well as of an awareness of societal factors. Similarly, avoidance could be a very effective strategy for certain conflicts. Lazarus (Note 2) distinguishes between denial of conflict and actual avoidance. Whereas the former represents efforts to negate a problem, the latter represents efforts not to think about or act upon a problem once one is aware of the social or personal reality surrounding the problem. Such effective avoidance could occur in cases where a lesbian deals with an antihomosexual employer by not mentioning her personal life at work.

The much lower satisfaction with coping reported by individuals using Type III strategies rather than Type I and II for intrarole conflict is consistent with this explanation. That is, Type III strategies may be the most effective politically although not very satisfying personally. Also, in contrast to interrole conflicts, subjects using the various coping strategies did not differ in self-esteem, again suggesting that environmental reality dictates choice of coping style for intrarole conflict more than for interrole conflict.

As with interrole conflict, comparisons of strategies within specific areas of intrarole conflict are needed. Although our sample size was too small to detect statistically significant differences, our data suggest that Type III strategies were used most frequently within the work role whereas Type I strategies were used most frequently in conflicts with the daughter or lover roles.

These suggestive findings together with the difference in strategies employed for intrarole and interrole conflicts indicate that people, by and large, may *not* use the *same* strategy for different role conflicts. Moreover, the strategy type used for a particular interrole conflict may change with time and circumstances. For example, a lesbian may wisely use a Type III strategy in an antigay work situation as long as the environmental constraints do not cause undue stress and job dissatisfaction. Should the latter occur, however, a restructuring type strategy would be in order.

Generalizations from our findings are limited by the small sample size, the use of self-report, the nature of the sample, and the data collection procedure. Lesbians who subscribe to a lesbian newsletter in the southwest are not representative of all lesbians. Also, the low return rate may reflect a self-selection bias. One could also argue that those subjects who did respond may have tried to present themselves, or lesbians as a group, in a favorable light. The high stress reported by respondents, however, indicates otherwise. Finally, respondents were not asked to rate the effectiveness of their coping strategies. As was noted in the discussion of intrarole conflicts, effectiveness and satisfaction with coping may represent separate dimensions.

This study provides some clarification on the kinds of role conflicts experienced by working lesbians and the factors influencing the types of coping strategies used. Additional research is needed to identify variables relevant to strategies for coping with specific role conflicts. Further evaluation of coping effectiveness is also important. Lazarus (Note 2) points out that coping effectiveness has several dimensions (i.e., social functioning, morale, and somatic health). Thus, while one strategy may enhance social functioning (choosing not to disclose one's lesbianism), it may simultaneously decrease morale.

REFERENCE NOTES

1. Gilbert, L. A., & Holahan, C. K. Conflict with the parent role: The perceived cost of effective coping. Paper presented at the annual meeting of the American Psychological Association, New York, September 1979.
2. Lazarus, R. The stress and coping paradigm. Paper presented at the conference, The Critical Evaluation of Behavioral Paradigms for Psychiatric Science, Gleneden Beach, Oregon, November 1978.

REFERENCES

ABBOTT, S., & LOVE, B. *Sappho was a right-on woman.* New York: Stein & Day, 1972.

GOODE, W. A theory of role strain. *American Sociological Review,* 1960, *25,* 483–496.

HALL, D. A model of coping with role conflict: The role behavior of college educated women. *Administrative Science Quarterly,* 1972, *17,* 471–486.

HARRISON, A., & MINOR, J. Interrole conflict, coping strategies, and satisfaction among black working wives. *Journal of Marriage and the Family,* 1978, *40,* 799–805.

HELMREICH, R., & STAPP, J. Short form of the Texas Social Behavior Inventory (TSBI). *Psychonomic Bulletin,* 1974, *4,* 473–475.

HOLAHAN, C. K., & GILBERT, L. A. Conflict between major life roles: The women and men in dual career couples. *Human Relations,* 1979, *32,* 451–467.

KINSEY, A. C., POMEROY, W. B., MARTIN, C. E., & GEBHARD, P. H. *Sexual behavior in the human female.* Philadelphia: Saunders, 1953.

LEVINSON, D. Role, personality, and social structure in organizational settings. *Journal of Abnormal and Social Psychology,* 1959, *58,* 170–180.

MARTIN, D., & LYON, P. *Lesbian/woman.* New York: Bantam, 1972.

NEVILLE, D., & DAMICO, S. Role conflict in women as a function of marital status. *Human Relations,* 1975, *28,* 487–498.

ROGERS, C. *On becoming a person.* Boston: Houghton-Mifflin, 1961.

PART X

Psyche and Society: Women in Conflict

To be born female in our society confers on girls an early advantage. Female infants have fewer congenital defects, are less likely to be stillborn, and, if premature, are more likely to survive. They have a lower mortality rate and are more robust in response to childhood diseases. Throughout childhood they have a lower incidence of all kinds of problems, both physical and behavioral, than boys have. They are much less likely to come to the attention of school psychologists, mental health clinics, and juvenile courts, and to exhibit behavior that is likely to bring them into conflict with authority. Several factors have been suggested to account for their smoother course. The genetic material on the second X chromosome protects girls from some sex-linked disorders that can add stress to the life of the affected individual; girls' advanced developmental maturity may facilitate early socialization, giving them an edge in developing interpersonal skills; the "feminine" tone of the early environment, in which girls are cared for and later taught by women, may make simpler for them than for boys the developmental tasks of childhood, such as identification with persons of one's gender; and their lower level of aggressive and resistive behaviors may facilitate their adaptation to adult expectations.

Following puberty, however, the picture changes. Through adolescence and adulthood, conflicts and problems of adjustment become common for women, as they are for men, though the patterns of these, as we shall see, are somewhat different. The reported crime rate for women, though still much lower than for men, has dramatically increased in the past few years, and women are overrepresented among the clients of mental health professionals. Many explanations have been advanced for these phenomena. Regarding crime, it is asserted by some that the changed social climate wherein women are freer and more likely to be employed outside the home, such that for some their lives are more like men's, has weakened old restraints and increased opportunities for them to commit crimes. It is also possible that police and the courts are less likely to apply a double standard to the criminal behavior of women and men than they once were. Regarding the biased representation of women among those who seek help for psychological problems, a network of hypotheses has been presented: women's adult roles as housewife and low-paid employee are frustrating and unsatisfying; women are more likely to express their problems and to seek help; women can more easily enter the role of client or patient, since the therapist is most likely to be male, and women are accustomed to being in a dependency role with male authority figures. An old and resilient explanation ties women's psychological problems to their bodies. The menstrual cycle in particular has been held to affect women so that by nature they are nervous, anxious, and erratic in behavior.

The papers in this section are concerned with problem behavior in women, theories to account for such behaviors, and society's attempts to deal with them. In "Difficulties Experienced by Women in Prison," Suzanne Sobel presents data on the inequalities between occupational and educational programs offered in women's prisons and those in men's prisons. The average men's prison offers about five times as many vocational programs as does the average prison for women, and those for women are usually gender-typed, such as cosmetology, food services, and nurse's aide. Too, health and mental health services are often inadequate, with personnel who are less available and less well-trained than those found in men's prisons. Prisons for women are more isolated and inaccessible than are those for men, making it difficult for families and children to visit. Since most women in prison are mothers, the separation puts an unnecessary strain on them and their families. While no one claims that men's prisons are model institutions, the sexist practices described by Sobel put unique psychological strains on women. Her recommendations for change encourage elimination of the inequities and greater sensitivity to the family-oriented needs of women.

Though a very small percentage of the prison population is female, a somewhat different picture emerges when we look at the population of persons being treated for mental and emotional disorders. The total rates of functional mental disorders are not higher for women than for men, and women are not overrepresented in mental hospital populations. More women than men, however, are outpatient clients of clinical psychologists and other mental health professionals. Analysis of the major subclassifications of mental disorders reveals that the rates of manic-depressive disorder and of the psychoneuroses are higher for women, while the rates of personality disorders are higher for men. It has been suggested that the common denominator for the former is depression, while the common denominator for the later is irresponsible and antisocial behavior. This explanation fits well with the observation that the typical client of the mental health professional is a woman, while the typical prison inmate is a man. Of course, there is much overlap between male and female populations on these variables, as there is for all behavioral characteristics. But to the extent that systematically different trends appear, it is important to understand what there is in the female experience and in the male experience that biases them toward different kinds of maladaptive behavior.

Study after study reports that more women than men suffer from depressive disorders. Gerald Klerman and Myrna Weissman in "Depressions among Women: Their Nature and Causes" discuss theories of the causes of depression and explanations for the preponderance of women suffering from depression. Since studies show that 20–30 percent of women have a depressive episode at some time in their adult lives, the topic is obviously of great importance to mental health professionals and to women and their families.

Theories of the causes of depression are many and varied. A popular early theory related the onset of depression to stress following loss and separation. Freudians and neo-Freudians believe that depression is repressed hostility turned against the self. Family studies indicate a genetic basis for vulnerability to depression, while drug-related research relates depression to a deficit in certain brain neurotransmitter chemicals. Still others relate depression to negative views of the self, the outside world, and the future. Some of the theories come out of a biological approach, others from an environmental perspective wherein stress may precipitate depression in a vulnerable person. Why are more women depressed? Is this finding real, or is it an artifact? Studies show that women do not report more stressful events in their lives than men do, but that they do report more symptoms related to depression. They go to doctors more often, get more prescriptions, and take more mood-altering drugs. The authors believe that the sex difference in incidence of depression is real, and they offer a theory that integrates the effects of stress with physiological and psychological balances in the individual. The evidence, they believe, supports a pluralistic theory of the causes and treatment of depressions.

Marlene Boskind-Lodahl's paper, "Cinderella's Stepsisters: A Feminist Perspective on Anorexia Nervosa and Bulimia," is a fine example of a feminist analysis of a pair of peculiarly female eating disorders that have received considerable attention by earlier generations of traditional theoreticians. Anorexia nervosa is prolonged self-starvation, which sometimes alternates with bulimia, gorging on food following by purging by induced vomiting. Typical psychoanalytic explanations of these two disorders, (both mostly manifested by young women), draw on hatred of the mother, rejection of the feminine role, and conflicts between fears of oral impregnation and desire for pregnancy. Boskind-Lodahl's theory, however, is that such women, far from rejecting the stereotyped model of femininity, are completely captured by it. Having identified with it since childhood, they have learned a passive and accommodating approach to life, which has two opposing tensions: a desperate requirement of self-validation from a man, and, at the same time, a fear of men because of their power to reject. Success is defined as the ability to attract and to hold a man, and these patients are preoccupied with a fear of failure, of not being good enough to please a man. Thus the problem is basically one of self-worth and self-esteem.

Boskind-Lodahl notes that traditional approaches to therapy with women would recommend a male therapist for such women on the grounds that he could replace her inadequate father with a good father and would not be identified with her bad mother. The author argues, however, that such women need female therapists, positive role models to contrast with their experiences of their mothers, to help them grow toward a healthier, more independent sense of self.

The institution of psychotherapy, too, has been affected by the impact of feminism. Since the typical therapist is male and the typical client is female, much of what we have said above applies to this relationship as well. Annette Brodsky, in her paper "A Decade of Feminist Influence on Psychotherapy," reviews the evidence for sex bias in therapy practice and concludes that because of methodological problems it is hard to say with confidence what the relationship is between therapy and sex bias. Such bias clearly exists however, in individual cases, and the feeling among feminists therapists and many women clients is that many if not most women clients will be better served by women therapists. Dramatic progress has been observed in some areas, such as rape counseling, family violence, and abortion counseling, as well as in understanding of some mental disorders that afflict mostly women, such as agoraphobia and hysterical personality. Brodsky ends on an encouraging note. Progress has been made, as anyone can observe by looking at pre-1970s psychotherapy journals and noting their attitudes toward women. Perhaps by the end of the 1980s today's more subtle sexism will seem just as blatant.

Thus we see that in some ways men and women are different in certain behaviors that deviate from important social norms that define and regulate antisocial behavior and define and treat mental disorders. Fewer women are incarcerated in prisons, but fewer efforts are made to prepare them for resuming life in the world, and they suffer from punitive separation from their children and families. Women are more likely than men to develop depressive disorders, which involve self-recrimination and the definition of the self as powerless, while men have a higher incidence of antisocial and "acting-out" kinds of behavior, as well as of substance abuse. It is not far fetched to conclude that some part of these differences is embedded in social values, sex roles and tradition, which differentially affect women and men.

More research is needed on disorders that are peculiarly female, such as anorexia nervosa and bulimia. Here again, one sees a connection between the Gestalt of the disorder and the socialization process whereby some young women believe that they must alter their bodies to fit a rigid mold that they both desire and fear.

Finally, our consciousness is raised in regard to our traditional treatment and to beliefs about us by the medical and mental health professions. While the first response was anger, we see in these analyses that progress has been made, and that gives us hope for the future.

33
Difficulties Experienced by Women in Prison

Suzanne B. Sobel

This article assembles data that identify some problems experienced by women incarcerated in prisons in the United States. Inequalities in occupational and educational programs offered in women's prisons in comparison with those offered in prisons for men are discussed. The impact of inadequate health and mental health services on the lives of these women is explored, and separation problems encountered by the woman prisoner and her family are examined. Some recommendations for change are suggested.

Women offenders comprise a small portion of arrested and convicted persons incarcerated in state, county, and local jails and prisons. In 1970, of the 296,000 inmates reported as being incarcerated in state and federal prisons, only 5600 (approximately 3%) were women (Simon, 1975). McArthur's data (1974) showed that on any one day, there were approximately 15,000 women incarcerated in jails and prisons, about 4% of all persons incarcerated in criminal justice settings.

Recent arrest statistics indicate that there has been an increase in the number of arrests, especially within the property crime category (Adler, 1975; Crites, 1976; Simon, 1976). As a result, the ratio of females to males arrested is increasing. Some writers have attributed these increases to the changing role of women in our society. Simon (1975, 1976) and Adler (1975) have speculated that as women become more involved in jobs and careers, they will be more likely to engage in crimes for which their occupations provide the opportunity. Regardless of the reason for the increase in the numbers of women involved with the criminal justice system, the fact remains that women prisoners have been subjected to differential treatment and to sex-tracked policies and programs which result in health and mental health problems. The purpose of this article is to explore some of the difficulties that women prisoners experience.

Institutional Milieu

Contrasted with men's prisons, women's institutions are usually more physically attractive. They tend to be located in pastoral country settings, and the tall brick fences, concrete walls, gun towers, and barbed wire typical of men's prisons are not present (Simon, 1975). The female inmate's quarters often have more privacy than the quarters of male inmates. The woman is usually permitted to wear street clothes and to decorate her room as she desires. This pastoral facade is deceiving, however, because in most ways women's prisons are more punitive. In fact, the country setting itself is punitive.

Giallombardo's (1966) description of the daily life of an inmate at the Federal Penitentiary for Women at Alderson, West Virginia, paints a picture of the difficulties that face women prisoners. The State Advisory Committee Reports to the United States Commission on Civil Rights and the National Study of Women's Correctional Programs (Glick & Neto, 1977) shed light on the types of privileges, rights, and routines to which women prisoners must adhere. Mitford (1974) also documents the initial phases of placement in an institution in the District of Columbia. These accounts show that a woman in prison is expected to obey and to conform to a set of rules, some of which are unrealistic and not adaptive to community living. The prison becomes the inmate's "parent" and has total control over the woman's life (Burkhardt, 1976). She is not afforded the opportunity to develop skills in coping with the outside world nor to explore new ways of relating. This lack of opportunity to develop coping and social skills interferes with the personality development of the offender. One can question whether this type of institutional milieu, which has existed for years in criminal justice settings, is in any way treatment oriented or rehabilitative.

Accounts of policies and programs in women's prisons, when contrasted with those of men's prisons, lead one to conclude that women's prisons tend to be more punitive and punishment oriented and to lack the opportunities for vocational, educational, social, and personal development that are present in many prisons for male offenders. Information reported by Burkhardt (1976), Simon (1975), and Bird (1979), and data presented in the Reports to the U.S. Commission on Civil Rights (e.g., Georgia Advisory Committee, 1976; Louisiana Advisory Committee, 1976) support these differences.

"Typical" Women's Prison Populations

There are a number of characteristics that tend to be common to prisons for women. Most noticeable is that the physical locations of women's prisons are usually more isolated and inaccessible than the locations of men's prisons (Adler, 1975; Simon, 1975). None of the women's prisons have provisions for women to have their children live with them, although some have nurseries where their infants can stay for varying lengths of time (McGowan & Blumenthal, 1976). In areas where public transportation is not available, women may not see their families for the duration of their sentences. In fact, some prisons prohibit visits for children under 16 years of age, which only increases the women's isolation from their families.

The populations in women's prisons are more heterogeneous than in men's prisons (Simon, 1975) and contain all types of offenders of all ages. While states often have more than one prison for male offenders, which permits grouping them by age and / or seriousness of offense, this does not occur with female offenders owing to their smaller numbers. Glick and Neto[1] (1977) noted that in the states they studied two-thirds of the women inmates were under 30 years of age, and there was an overrepresentation of Blacks and Native Americans in the prison population.

Do Women's Prisons Offer Equal Programs?

Women's prisons often do not have available services designed to facilitate re-entry into the community (Glick & Neto, 1977; Simon, 1975). Comparing vocational programs, educational programs, and job assignments offered at women's prisons to those in men's prisons highlights the dearth of opportunities for women (Alabama Advisory Committee, 1974; Arditi, Goldberg, Hartle, Peters, & Phelps, 1973; Georgia Advisory Committee, 1976; Glick & Neto, 1977; Louisiana Advisory Committee, 1976; Nebraska Advisory Committee, 1974; New York Advisory Committee, 1974).

A study of 47 prisons for men and 15 prisons for women (Arditi et al., 1973) revealed that the average men's prison offered 10 vocational-industrial programs while women's prisons offered an average of only 2.7 programs. The programs offered in women's prisons were usually sex-typed and thus did not offer the female inmate new career choices. While male prisoners had a choice of about 50 vocational programs, the women's choices were basically limited to cosmetology, clerical training, food services, or nurse's aide. Of industries available at the institutions, that is, work opportunities that can provide income for prisoners, there were an average of 3.2 industries for men in prison and 1.2 industries in prisons for women.

The following examples illustrate some inequities within the female prison system. Inmates at the Georgia Rehabilitation Center for Women are required to work in the kitchen or laundry at Central State Hospital before gaining the opportunity for training or education in other areas. A few of the women prisoners work as aides on the hospital's ward for the criminally insane, and four of the women prisoners are given the opportunity to live at a work release center in Altanta while serving as maids in the Governor's mansion (Georgia Advisory Committee, 1976). Inmates in the North Carolina Correctional Center for Women have programs which provide the opportunity to sew, launder, cook, and work in the dining room (North Carolina Advisory Committee, 1976).

However, Oregon's Women's Correctional Center has developed a system which allows its inmates to participate in training programs available at Oregon State Prison, the nearby facility for male prisoners. These women inmates have the opportunity to take business education courses, to learn computer programming, keypunching, or drafting, and to enroll in a college program in conjunction with the state college system (Oregon Advisory Committee, 1976). Also, the Perdy Correctional Center for Women in

the state of Washington has developed some innovative educational programs (Adler, 1975; Glick & Neto, 1977). More of these programs are needed
nation-wide.

Availability of Health and Mental Health Services

Availability of medical care is often inadequate in women's prisons. Most
of the prisons Glick and Neto (1977) surveyed did not have total health
care programs, although all had some type of medical care available, provided primarily in response to an inmate's illness or injury. They reported
that only four of the institutions had full-time physicians, while many of
the others had only part-time medical help on staff.

The reports of eight State Advisory Committees to the U.S. Commission on Civil Rights confirmed the bleak picture of inadequate medical
treatment for women prisoners. For instance, the Georgia report (Georgia
Advisory Committee, 1976) noted that only one physician was available for
only an hour a day at the women's prison. While the prisons for men had
part-time medical doctors once or twice a week, the North Carolina Correctional Center for Women had four nurses but utilized medical specialists on an on-call basis only (North Carolina Advisory Committee, 1976).
The Bedford Hills Facility for Women in New York had a nurse who held
a daily sick call. However, the New York Advisory Committee (1974) concluded that medical services were inadequate throughout the state's prison
system. Although prisons for men employed full-time physicians, the Kansas Correctional Institution for Women employed only a nurse who held a
daily sick call (Kansas Advisory Committee, 1974). The Nebraska facility
had a full-time nurse (Nebraska Advisory Committee, 1974) and the Alabama Women's facility had a full-time medical assistant (Alabama Advisory
Committee, 1974). Prenatal care was generally provided by local hospitals.
The data suggest that personnel providing health services in women's prisons are less available and not as well trained as those providing services in
men's prisons.

Glick and Neto's (1977) study revealed that the most frequent medical
complaints were gynecological problems, second were nerves (anxiety and
depression), third were headaches, and fourth were respiratory infections.
Two reasons may account for the emphasis on gynecological problems. First
is the lack of trained gynecologists as consultants or staff members. Thus
diagnosis and treatment of diseases of the female reproductive system may
not be sophisticated since those delivering the services are not specialists.
Problems may go undetected or misdiagnosed as a result. Second is the
relationship of medical problems to psychological disability and stress.
Research indicates that psychosomatic disorders are frequently associated
with deprivations. In this case, it is quite possible that the psychosocial deprivation experienced by women inmates may be the underlying cause of
the gynecological problems. The emphasis on nervous disorders serves as
documentation of the stress experienced by women inmates, and the reported
high incidence of headaches of unknown origin also may have psychosomatic roots. One can speculate that many women inmates develop physical
symptoms as an indication of their emotional distress and as a response to

their lack of opportunity to express their psychological conflicts in a constructive manner.

In Glick and Neto's sample, the most frequently dispensed medications were pain-killers. Prescriptions for tranquilizers and psychotropic medications ranked second. With the lack of medical staff available to deliver health services and the dearth of psychiatrists in women's prisons, inappropriate use of behavior-altering medications becomes a problem. However, the inappropriate use of minor tranquilizers by women is a general problem that is not specific in prison populations (Special Populations Subpanel, 1978).

Associated with the poor availability of medical services is the almost uniform lack of availability of psychiatric and/or psychological services in women's prisons. While many of the prisons for male offenders provide a thorough psychiatric and psychological evaluation as part of the initial diagnostic placement process, this rarely occurs in any women's prison. Generally, women's prisons do not have psychotherapeutic services available to their inmates on a regular basis, and thus do not provide the opportunity for the prisoner to enhance her personality development.

Counselors: Therapists or Guards

In her study of the Alderson facility in West Virginia, Giallombardo (1966) traced the transition from a custodial model to a treatment model for prison settings. As part of this transition, the role of the guard has undergone a change: originally just an enforcer of rules, guards now play the dual roles of counselor and rule enforcer. Thus, counseling services most available to prisoners are generally those provided by the institutional counselors (guards), who are on duty around the clock. Usually these counselors have had little or no training in counseling skills. At some facilities, university students in training provide counseling to inmates as part of their field experience.

Many institutions indicate that they offer group counseling to their residents. However, group counseling must be clearly differentiated from group sessions which have a primary purpose of insuring smooth management and functioning in the unit. Frequently, data on management-oriented and treatment-oriented groups become confused, thus leading to possible erroneous conclusions about the availability of personal counseling services to a female inmate.

Relationships to Families

Incarceration in a prison which is distant from the woman's home places a great strain on the offender's relationship to her family. Women in our society are considered the major caretaker of children. Thus the separation from her children places a great strain on the family. The lack of transportation to the facility except by private means serves, in some cases, to exacerbate an already difficult family relationship. This geographic separation, with its consequent emotional separation, affects not only the woman inmate's relationships with her family and community while she is imprisoned, but also presents an obstacle to a smooth transition during her return to her family and re-entry into her community.

McGowan and Blumenthal (1976) surveyed administrators and residents in correctional facilities reported to hold more than 25 female inmates. Returns were received from 74 institutions which confined about 9,379 women. They found 67.1% were mothers who averaged 2.4 dependent children. Sixty-two percent of the children were younger than 10 years. Most of the children resided with their mother prior to her arrest; about one quarter did not. During their mother's incarceration, most of the children lived with relatives. McGowan and Blumenthal reported that many women felt their contacts with their children were not frequent enough, citing geographic distance and restrictive visiting and telephone policies as major obstacles.

In Glick and Neto's (1977) 15-state sample, 25.6% of the female inmates had not borne children, and 25.6% did not have their children living with them prior to incarceration. The average number of children among women who were mothers was 2.48, a finding almost identical to that of McGowan and Blumenthal.

State laws and administrative procedures for placement of children in foster care during a parent's imprisonment vary. Data on this particular problem, which is heavily laden with issues relevant to the mental health of women, are quite sparse.

At the Perdy Institution for Women in the state of Washington, every effort is made to place the children in a foster home close to the prison if the mother requests it. The overall philosophy of the Perdy Institution reflects the importance of the family (Burkles & LaFazie, 1973). This program involves a contractual agreement between the foster mother and the inmate mother about the care of the children. The foster mother agrees to provide care for the children for the duration of the inmate mother's sentence. Additionally, the foster mother agrees to bring the children to the inmate mother at the prison for a specified number of visits per month, and allows the inmate mother to go to the foster home and care for the children at designated times. Arrangements such as these help to facilitate the adjustment of the woman and her children to this most difficult situation. At the other extreme is Oregon, where state statutes permit the state, if it deems it advisable or necessary, to automatically assume custody of the inmate's children when the parent is to be incarcerated for more than three years. Although this law exists, it is rarely used. In fact, Oregon Women's Correctional Center has developed a program in which the public welfare worker becomes part of the team working with the prisoner (McGowan & Blumenthal, 1976).

Being labeled a "bad mother" is one of the painful stigmas that female offenders have to bear (Burkhardt, 1976). The separation causes anxieties and fears for all family members, but little attention has been paid to their needs (McGowan & Blumenthal, 1976). Inadvertently, the criminal justice system may possibly destroy a family relationship by not providing planning for the inmate's children which minimizes their stress, by not coordinating with the welfare department, and by making decisions which do not take into account the woman's family obligations. Burkhardt described some of the negative consequences of these practices on the woman and her family relationship. Most who have studied the criminal justice system as it applies to women agree that counseling services are definitely needed.

The lack of counseling / psychotherapy services to assist the mutual adjustment of the mother and her children to her imprisonment, and to facilitate her adjustment and return to the community present another problem for the inmate mother. In fact, McGowan and Blumenthal reported that the administrators in their sample placed emphasis on the need for child welfare workers to serve as liaison and for provision of counseling services for children and mothers. Implementation of these services would require the involvement of social service staffs in the community working in close cooperation with the staffs at the prison. Given the geographic isolation of many of the women's prisons, this ideal may in reality be impossible to attain. There does remain a nationwide need for additional mental health services for inmates in women's prisons as well as a need for development of stronger combined efforts on the part of the community social services and the prison's social services staffs (Sobel, 1980).

Training Programs for Mental Health Professionals in Criminal Justice Work

There are few training programs for mental health professionals which involve work in criminal justice settings. Brodsky (1973) surveyed psychology graduate programs and found that only 11 programs offered a total of 14 courses in the areas of law and practice of psychology. Additionally, he noted only 5 programs which specifically offered graduate level training for work in criminal justice settings. None of these courses were specifically designed to explore the special problems of the woman prisoner. However, the University of Alabama has developed a correctional-clinical psychology program (Fowler & Brodsky, 1978) since Brodsky's (1973) survey.

The American Psychological Association does not have an approved internship in a criminal justice setting (American Psychological Association, 1977, 1978; Fowler & Brodsky, 1978). It is suspected that most psychiatric residency programs do not involve work within a prison except for some possible supervision in how to examine and testify on issues of competency to stand trial and / or criminal responsibility. In-service training programs within criminal justice settings tend to be deficient in amount of time devoted to them. Little emphasis has been placed on the special mental health problems of women in prison in academic and in-service training courses.

There is a need for training mental health professionals to work effectively with female offenders. With this, however, there is a need for refocusing and rethinking popular theories of personality development and their relationship to the functioning of the female inmate. For the woman in prison, training focused away from the traditional maternal, submissive, domestic role of women is necessary.

Some Ideas for Change

The preceding data illustrate that women incarcerated in prison are the innocent victims of a sexist correctional system which delivers fewer services and offers fewer opportunities than those available to male prisoners. Many reports have been prepared which demonstrate the negative consequences of sexism on the health and mental health of women. The report of the President's Commission on Mental Health (1978) and the report of the Special Populations Subpanel on Mental Health of Women (1978) document the problems resulting from sexist practices which affect all ethnic, racial, and social groups. Proponents of the Equal Rights Amendment (ERA) point to its passage as at least establishing that there must be equal access to educational and vocational opportunities for individuals (Bird, 1979). Thus some of the currently existing procedures and policies in the programs at women's prisons might not continue to exist if the ERA were passed.

Mental health professionals have not been active in providing policy makers wirh data to substantiate the negative impact of sex-stereotyped programs on women prisoners and their families. While books have been written on theories and research relating to sexist practices (Garskof, 1971; Miller, 1976), little has been publicized about the plights of women in prison and the unique psychological strains that imprisonment places on them. A few recommendations which, if implemented, would decrease the inequalities and negative effects of sexism in prison settings are:

1. Adequate health and mental health services must be provided in women's prisons. These services should be delivered by professionals trained in nonsexist theories and techniques.

2. Prisons for women must develop educational and vocational opportunities for their inmates which are broad and allow the prisoner to explore her work potential. With adequate job skills, women offenders can look forward to returning to their communities and earning salaries commensurate with those received by men. The state prisons for women must insure that their inmates have equal opportunities with male inmates for involvement in work release programs. It is important to develop these programs in order to insure that women prisoners are no longer treated differently from male prisoners.

3. Training programs for mental health professionals should include courses and supervised practicum experiences on the problems that characterize the female offender in prison. In-service training models should have the goal of increasing staff sensitivity to the special problems of women prisoners.

4. Greater sensitivity to the stresses experienced by women in prison as a result of the separation from family should lead to the development of inexpensive public transportation systems to the prisons and of programs whose goals are to assist the adjustment of prisoners and their families to imprisonment. Development of transitional services for all offenders returning to their communities should be a priority.

REFERENCE NOTE

1. The states surveyed by Glick and Neto (1977) were California, Colorado, Florida, Georgia, Illinois, Indiana, Massachusetts, Michigan, Minnesota, Nebraska, New York, North Carolina, Texas, and Washington.

REFERENCES

ADLER, F. A. *Sisters in crime.* New York: McGraw-Hill, 1975.

Alabama Advisory Committee to the U.S. Commission on Civil Rights. *Alabama prisons.* Washington, D.C.: U.S. Commission on Civil Rights, 1974

American Psychological Association. APA-approved predoctoral internships for doctoral training in clinical and counseling psychology: 1977. *American Psychologist,* 1977, *32,* 1089–1091.

American Psychological Association. Supplement to listing of APA-approved doctoral and internship training programs. *American Psychologist,* 1978, *34,* 418.

ARDITI, R.R., GOLDBERG,F., JR., HARTLE, M. M., PETERS J.H., & PHELPS, W.R. The sexual segregation of American prisons: Notes, *Yale Law Journal,* 1973, *82,* 1229–1273.

BIRD, C. *What women want.* New York: Simon and Schuster, 1979.

BRODSKY, S. L. *Psychologists in the criminal justice system.* Urbana: University of Illinois Press, 1973.

BURKHARDT, K. *Women in prison.* New York: Popular Library, 1976.

BURKLES, D., & LAFAZIE, M. A. Child care for mothers in prison. In B. Ross & C. Chireman (Eds.), *Social work practice and social justice.* New York: National Association of Social Workers, 1973.

CRITES, L. Women offenders: Myth vs. reality. In L. Crites (Ed.), *The female offender.* Lexington, Mass.: D. C. Heath and Co., 1976.

FOWLER, R.D., & BRODSKY, S. L. Development of a correctional-clinical psychology program. *Professional Psychology,* 1978, 9, 440–447.

GARSKOF, M.H. (Ed.) *Roles women play: Readings towards women's liberation.* Belmont, Ca.: Brooks / Cole, 1971.

Georgia Advisory Committee to the U.S. Commission on Civil Rights. *Georgia prisons.* Washington, D.C.: U.S. Commission on Civil Rights, 1976.

GIALLOMBARDO, R. *Society of women.* New York: Wiley, 1966.

GLICK, R. M., & NETO, V. V. *National study of women's correctional programs.* (National Institute of Law Enforcement and Criminal Justice, LEAA), Washington, D.C.: U.S. Government Printing Office, 1977.

Kansas Advisory Committee to the U.S. Commission on Civil Rights. *Inmate rights and the Kansas state prison system.* Washington, D.C.: U.S. Commission on Civil Rights, 1974.

Louisiana Advisory Committe to the U.S. Commission on Civil Rights. *A study of adult corrections in Louisiana.* Washington, D.C.: U.S. Commission on Civil Rights, 1976.

MCARTHUR, V. A. *Fom convict to citzen: Programs for the woman offender.* Washington, D. C.: District of Columbia Commission on the Status of Women, 1974.

MCGOWAN, B.G., & BLUMENTHAL. K. L. Children of women prisoners: A forgotten minority. In L. Crites (Ed.), *The female offender.* Lexington, Mass.: D.C. Heath and Co., 1976.

MILLER, J. B. *Toward a new psychology of momen.* Boston: Beacon, 1976.

MITFORD, J. *Kind and usual punishment.* New York: Vintage Books, 1974.

Nebraska Advisory Committee to the U.S. Commission on Civil Rights. *Inmate rights and institutional response: The Nebraska state prison system.* Washington, D.C.: U.S. Commission on Civil Rights, 1974.

New York Advisory Committee to the U.S. Commission on Civil Rights. *Warehousing human beings.* Washington, D.C.: U.S. Commission on Civil Rights, 1974.

North Carolina Advisory Committee to the U.S. Commission on Civil Rights. *Prisons in North Carolina.* Washington, D.C.: U.S. Commission on Civil Rights, 1976.

Oregon Advisory Committee to the U.S. Commission on Civil Rights. *Civil and human rights in Oregon state prisons.* Washington, D.C.: U.S. Commission on Civil Rights, 1976.

President's Commission on Mental Health. *Report to the President* (Vol. 1). Washington, D.C.: U.S. Government Printing Office, 1978.

SIMON, R. J. *The contemporary woman and crime* (Crime and Delinquency Issues: A Monograph Series, DHEW Publication No. (ADM) 76-161). Washington, D.C.: U.S. Government Printing Office, 1975.

SIMON, R. J. American women and crime. *Annals of the American Academy of Political and Social Science,* 1976, *423,* 31–46.

SOBEL, S. B. Women in prison: Sexism behind bars. *Professional Psychology,* 1980, *11,* 331–338.

Special Populations Subpanel on the Mental Health of Women, President's Commission on Mental Health. *Task panel reports submitted to the President's Commission on Mental Health (Vol. 3 Appendix). Washington, D.C.: United States Government Printing Office, 1978.*

34

Depressions among Women
Their Nature and Causes

Gerald L. Klerman and
Myrna M. Weissman

Previous [studies] have examined in some detail utilization data from mental health facilities and have reviewed epidemiological data on mental health problems. Given these utilization data, it is clear that women are *not* over-represented in mental hospital patient populations. It is clear, however, that women exceed men in their rate of treatment for depression. Moreover, there is considerable evidence from community surveys that untreated depression is disproportionately more prevalent among women (Weissman & Klerman, 1977). Furthermore, there is evidence that the rate of untreated depression, especially among young women, may be rising (Weissman, 1975).

A repeated conclusion in epidemiologic studies of depression is that women predominate. Observations of a sex difference in the frequency of any disorder attract attention and stimulate explanations. Depression has recently gained the attention of biologists, sociologists, feminists, and the educated public. Is it a true finding that women are more prone to depression? Or are the observations the result of confounding factors in case reporting or in the organization of the health care system? If the finding is "real," what processes, biological or psychosocial, best explain the differences?

The topic is timely for a number of reasons. All aspects of women's roles and experience are currently under scrutiny. Demographic changes in this century have increased longevity for women more than for men. However, while these changes have resulted in a larger population of women aged 60–80, the greater number of older women in itself cannot account for the predominance of depressed women found in epidemiologic studies. The preponderance of women is not only in the absolute numbers of depressed patients, but, more significantly, in rates per population group adjusted for age. At every age group, rates of depression are higher for women. Moreover, there is evidence for a lowering in the modal age of onset of depression. Whereas pre-World War II textbooks characterized the age of onset of depression as the fourth decade of life, recent reports emphasize onset of depression in young adults, again females predominating.

A number of explanations for this showing have been offered. One set of explanations questions whether the finds are real and speculates that they are an artifact accounted for by women's perceptions of stress and by their coping responses, their willingness to express psychological symptoms, and the high rate at which they seek medical help. Alternatively, the finding is considered a true phenomenon and attributed to female biological susceptibility or to psychosocial causes.

How can these important sex differences be understood? To understand these trends, it is necessary to re-examine the nature of depression and its causes, and then analyze the causal explanations offered for the higher rates of depression among women. In this chapter, we will first review the most important current views on clinical depressions, their antecedents, and their consequences.

The Nature of Depressions

Descriptions of depressions are as old as written documents; recognizable accounts of depressive states occur in ancient Egyptian, Greek, and Biblical texts. Excellent portraits of depressed persons occur in Shakespeare's plays and in the novels of the eighteenth and nineteenth centuries.

Since the early part of this century, mental health clinicians and investigators have grouped the depressions and other related emotional states into the category of "affective disorders." Although a broad spectrum of symptoms, behaviors, and states are included within this category, the dominant feature common to these otherwise diverse disorders is that the patients' disturbance is expressed in their mood and emotional distress. As the most common conditions included among the affective disorders, the depressions are clinical states in which persistent abnormal emotional symptoms are associated with feelings of worthlessness, guilt, helplessness, and hopelessness; anxiety, crying, suicidal tendencies; loss of interest in work and other activities; impaired capacity to perform everyday social functions; and hypochondriasis, or bodily alterations including anorexia, weight change, and constipation; psychomotor retardation; and agitation.

Mania and other elations are the less frequently seen, but the more dramatic, conditions within the category of affective disorders. Most manic patients (over 80%) also have depressive episodes at some points in their lives, but the converse is not true: Only a small fraction of depressed patients (about 10%) also have manic episodes. However, the close association of these two affective conditions led Kraepelin and other nineteenth-century clinicians to define the manic-depressive illness category. While manic-depressive is one important form of depression, it represents only a small fraction of depressions and affective disorders.

Some authorities also include anxiety and tension in the affective disorders, but current research evidence supports the classification of anxiety states separately from depression. However, over one-half of depressed persons also experience anxiety, tension, and related symptoms.

Depressions are similar in many aspects to other broadly defined clinical syndromes in general medicine, like anemia, congestive heart failure, or jaundice. Like these other medical conditions, patients present common clinical features that may be due to diverse causes. The clinical depressive syndrome has the common feature of intensity of emotion and multiple etiological forces (genetic, environmental, or biochemical); it allows for multiple treatments such as psychotherapy, drugs, and so on.

Epidemiological studies in the United Kingdom, Scandinavia, and the United States have documented the fact that large proportions of individuals among the general population, and perhaps as many as 20–30% of all females experience depressive episodes at some point in their adult lives, often of moderate severity. However, only one-quarter of those with depressive symptoms and behaviors seek professional attention from physicians, let alone from psychiatrists. There is a large group of distressed individuals who, because of stigma, shame, or inability or unwillingness to gain access to medical care do not receive treatment.

The heterogeneity of the clinical manifestations within the depressive disorders should be emphasized. Though clinicians identify these depressed states on symptomatic and behavioral criteria, they would ideally like to make diagnoses based on etiologic criteria. This ideal is far from being realized in psychiatry in general, and in the affective disorders in particular. Multiple etiological factors are involved: genetic, biochemical, personality, stress and life events, and social background. Some affective syndromes, like the bipolar form of manic-depressive illness; (i.e. persons who have both highs and lows) almost certainly have major genetic determinants. Other depressions are the consequence of drugs such as amphetamines or rauwolfia. However, in the majority of depressions, the proximate etiology is uncertain and clinicians' and patients' explanations invoke varying combinations of stress, personality, changes in the central nervous system (CNS) catecholamines, and other factors. However, our current knowledge of these etiological factors is limited, and at best, relies on evidence far removed from the immediate clinical situation.

Some Problems of Terminology

The meaning of the term "depression" does not remain constant in different fields—neurophysiology, pharmacology, psychology, and psychiatry all employ the term, but with varying definitions. The resulting confusion makes some attempt at clarification of its psychiatric meaning and use appropriate. For the neurophysiologist, depression refers to any decrease in electrophysiological activity, as, for example "cortical depression." To the pharmacologist, depression refers to drug actions which decrease the activity of the target organ; thus the "CNS depressants" include the barbiturates and the anesthetics, which are not related clinically or pharmacologically to antidepressant drugs. The experimental psychologist uses the term "depression" for any decrement in optimal performance, such as a slowing of psychomotor activity or a reduction of intellectual functioning. For the clinical psychiatrist or psychologist, however, depression covers a wide range of changes in affective state, ranging in severity from the normal mood fluctuations of everyday life to severe melancholic psychotic episodes.

Unfortunately, the use of the same term in a number of scientific fields has perpetuated the view, and also the hope, that there are common mechanisms unifying the neurophysiological, pharmacological, and clinical phenomena. In the past, clinical psychopathological states have been ordered on a continuum according to alteration in patients' psychomotor activity; thus manic excitements were presumably due to excessive CNS excitation and were contrasted with depressive symptoms presumably due to inhibition of generalized or specific CNS functioning. This polarity concept has also been applied to Pavlovian conditioning and to psychoanalytic theory. Moreover, the selection of therapy was rationalized by this polarity model. Using the traditional classification of drugs into stimulant and depressant categories, treatment drugs were chosen if their actions were opposite to the presumed CNS activity. This "stimulant-depressant continuum" has been the classical model for drug treatment, and was popular during the period when the amphetamines and barbiturates were the major CNS agents. And recent proposals relating catecholamines to affective disorders parallel to the older characterization of a stimulant-depressant continuum. However, the complexity of actions of newer psychotropic drugs, particularly the phenothiazines and tricyclic depressants, makes the stimulant-depressant continuum model overly simplistic and obsolete. Lithium's actions in preventing recurrence of both manic and depressed episodes suggest that there are neurochemical processes common to both elation and depression or to one's predisposition to these states. In the absence of firmly established neurophysiological, biochemical, or even psychodynamic mechanisms in the etiology or pathophysiology of depressive disorders, assessment, diagnosis, and therapeutic decisions continue to be based almost entirely on clinical criteria.

Distinguishing Normal Mood from Depressive Illness

As a mood, depression is part of normal human living. The capacity to experience depression is part of humanity's evolutionary heritage and has contributed greatly to the survival and growth of the species. Feelings of sadness, disappointment, and frustration are within the vicissitudes of the human condition. The distinction between normal mood and abnormal depression is not always clear, and psychiatrists do not always agree on the full range of emotional phenomena to be diagnosed as pathological.

The fact that the depressions involve an accentuation in intensity and / or duration of otherwise normal emotions has mixed consequences for clinical judgment. On the one hand, this fact promotes the empathic understanding of clinicians and family members to patients' difficulties. Almost all human beings experience unhappy, sad, depressed, and discouraged periods, and thus it is often easy to identify the individuals' emotional state and empathize with his or her distress. However, this very familiarity some-times renders clinical assessment and differential diagnosis difficult, in that there may be a lack of appreciation that the individual has crossed the boundary area between the normal and abnormal. Particularly among fam-ily and friends of the patients, there is a tendency to minimize the severity of the patient's difficulties because the manifestations may seem like a nor-mal emotional state. Similarly, clinicians also tend to minimize the severity of affective reactions even when precipitating stressful events are apparent.

In severe forms, most depressed states are easily judged as pathologi-cal by criteria of intensity, pervasiveness, persistence, and interference with usual social and bodily functioning. The difficult problems arise in distin-guishing normal states from the many mild depressive illnesses.

In addition to the dominant disturbances of mood, depressive illness usually involves some combination of the following features:

1. Impairments of bodily functioning, as manifested by disturbances in sleep, appetite, sexual interest, autonomic nervous system, and gastroin-testinal activity.

2. Reduced desire and ability to perform usual expected social roles in the family, at work, in marriage, in school, etc.

3. Suicidal thoughts or acts.

4. Disturbances in perception, cognition, and reality testing, as mani-fested by delusions, hallucinations, confusion, etc.

While suicidal thought and acts and impairment of reality testing are rela-tively infrequent, their presence usually indicates that the patient's behav-ior is no longer to be considered in the range of normal mood swings, but requires psychiatric attention. Features indicative of depression are listed in Table 1.

The Depressive Syndromes

Very rarely do depressed patients experience only one of the many symptoms described; most often patients report multiple symptoms. The patient with a depressive illness usually manifests depressed mood plus a significant number (four to five) of other associated symptoms. Because some symptoms occur together with greater-than-chance expectation, terms such as "symptom configuration", "cluster", "constellation", or "syndrome" are used to refer to the coexistence and covariance of associated depressive symptoms and behaviors. Recently, factor analysis and other multivariate correlational statistics have been applied to symptom ratings and person-ality tests to identify such symptom groupings.

Moreover, it is important to recognize that there is no *one* depressive syndrome. There is no universal agreement as to the bases upon which the various depressive syndromes should be identified and separated. Most theorists and investigators accept the principle that heterogeneity exists within the affective disorders. The official nomenclature designates multiple affective states such as manic-depressive illness, involutional states, psycho-neurotic depression, and so on. The retarded-agitated typology and the psychotic-neurotic separations are two conventional subtypes of depression which have been partially useful in clinical work. Other subtypes involve

Table 1 Symptoms and behaviors of states of depressions

 1. Depressed mood characterized by reports of feeling sad, low, blue, despondent, hopeless, gloomy, etc.
 2. Changes in posture, facial expressions, speech, dress, grooming
 3. Change in appetite, usually leading to weight loss
 4. Sleep difficulty, usually insomnia
 5. Loss of energy; fatigue, lethargy, anergy
 6. Anxiety
 7. Bodily complaints
 8. Agitation (increased motor activity experienced as restlessness)
 9. Retardation of speech, thought, and movements
10. Decrease in capacity to experience pleasure
11. Decrease in sexual interest and activity
12. Loss of interest in work and usual activities
13. Diminished ability to think or concentrate, with complaints or "slowed thinking" or "mixed-up thoughts"
14. Feeling of worthlessness, self-reproach, guilt, shame
15. Fall in self-esteem
16. Feelings of helplessness
17. Pessimism and helplessness
18. Thoughts of death and/or suicide attempts

the primary-secondary separation and the endogenous-neurotic distinction.

Theories of the Causes of Depressions

Having described the characteristics of depressions as clinical states and some of the features that may distinguish the forms of it which should be treated from the normal mood, we will now review the major theories explaining this common condition currently under investigation. It should be noted that these theories usually refer to the problem of depression in general and not to the special problem of explaining the preponderance of this emotional condition among women. We shall address this latter issue in the next section of this chapter, after reviewing the general theories of depression.

Theories about depression have had a long and controversial history. Depressive syndromes have been ascribed to biological factors, social causes, stress reaction, and recently, to social labeling. The concept of depression as a mental illness, developed by Kraepelin during the late nineteenth century, has had, and continues to have, the greatest influence in the medical and psychiatric professions. His work on manic-depressive illness (Kraepelin, 1921) emphasized biological causation, mostly genetic and metabolic in nature, and allowed little room for social, environmental, or psychological explanations.

Adolph Meyer's (1957) theory of psychobiology offered an alternative to the nineteenth century conception of mental illness as exclusively biologically caused. Kraepelin's (1921) biological disease concept of depression and Meyer's reactive concept of depression continued to be theoretically opposed to each other for over 70 years. In 1933, Aubry Lewis (1967) offered evidence strongly contradictory to Gillespie's view of endogenous depression, and supporting Meyer's concept of depression as a psychobiological reactive form. In Western Europe and North America, most theorizing and teaching adopted Meyer's ideas of psychobiology and a unitary view of depression. This unitary view of depression emphasized the common features among various types of depressive episodes, and stressed the continuity between every day "moods," mild depression, and psychotic episodes of melancholia. According to this theory the vicissitudes of the life experience were a possible cause of depression. The Meyerian perspective tended to minimize classification systems, and to downplay the importance of constitutional and genetic factors.

Currently, theorists and clinicians tend to hold that neither Kraepelin's concept of depression as a disease, nor the Meyerian view of depression as a reaction form, is completely satisfactory. But definitional confusion and disagreement about terminology has seriously hampered the progress of research on depression. Recently, there has been an upsurge of interest in biological theories, emphasizing hereditary, hormonal, and genetic influences in the incidence of depression. Since World War II, treatment has concentrated on psychotherapeutic methods. The host of highly effective antidepressant drugs developed over recent years have focused discussion and research on the interaction between biological and psychosocial explanations of depression.

Loss and Stress

The most widely held theory about depression relates its onset and quality to the stress accompanying loss and separation. This theory is based upon the close similarities between the normal emotional reactions to loss and separation and the clinical state of depression. The prototype of the reaction to loss and separation is, of course, that of grief and mourning which follows the death of a loved one. The emotional, behavioral, and biological similarities of the grief and mourning state to clinical depression have been observed for centuries, and since the beginning of modern psychiatry, have formed the basis for psychological understanding of the state. There is good anthropological and comparative animal behavioral data indicating that the capacity to become depressed is based upon the evolutionary heritage of the human species, in reactions to loss, and that the response of humans is similar to that of animals. The responses of children to loss and separation have been widely studied, particularly by psychoanalysts such as Spitz (1946), A. Freud (1965), and Bowlby (1969). It is their observations that have formed the basis for the loss theory. Similarly, observations of reactions of adults to catastrophe and disaster, such as those made by Lindemann (1944) in the Coconut Grove fire disaster, indicate that the grief and mourning state may, if not adequately resolved, lead to clinical depression as well as to other clinical states.

In recent years, the concept of loss has been extended to include not only separation and death, but also symbolic losses and other forms of threats to self-esteem and impairment of interpersonal relations. This extension has generated a considerable amount of clinical and theoretical controversy.

The concept of loss has also been broadened to include the general concept of stress, particularly after the studies of Selye (1956) on the hormonal and physiological responses of organisms to various forms of stress. Research efforts to quantify stress using the techniques of Holmes and Rahe have led to fruitful research which indicates that among depressed patients, experiences of loss and separation occur more frequently than they do in a matched normal sample. However, direct loss and separation cannot account for all forms of depression; thus it is necessary to include in the concept of loss symbolic loss and other forms of stress.

Psychodynamic Theories

The literature concerning the psychodynamic variables involved in depression is extensive. It also becomes increasingly complex as qualifications are added to the earliest Freudian theories to account for evidence from personality and sociological research. However, most psychodynamically oriented workers agree that the depressive condition is related to personality needs, especially orality, internalized aggression, strong superego, and extreme narcissism. Furthermore, they hypothesize that the early years of life are especially important in forming the individual's predisposition to adult depression. Theorists often disagree as to the role of superego factors in depression and the intrapsychic mechanisms and identifications found in depression. Freud (1957), Abraham (1927), and the classic psychoanalysts depicted depression as a basically hostile response to a lost love object. The hostility, in the process of being repressed, is turned against the self, and clinically results in self-destructive impulses. The neo-Freudians have directed attention to interpersonal functioning as part of the broadening of psychodynamic thinking and clinical experience. Widely held views about the predisposing personalities of depressives emphasize that depression-prone people are inordinately dependent on others in order to maintain their own self-esteem. Their frustration tolerance is low and they employ a variety of techniques such as manipulation, submission, coercion, pity, and demands to maintain those desperately needed but still ambivalent relationships with external or internalized objects (Bonime, 1976).

These ideas have had extensive influence on theory and clinical practice. They are most influential in psychotherapeutic practive. But extensive research efforts have only partially verified their scientific bases (Chodoff, 1972, 1974), and until further evidence is generated, the psychodynamic theories must be regarded as stimulating but still tentative and not fully established.

Genetic Transmission Theories

Extensive evidence supports the existence of a genetic factor causing or predisposing certain individuals toward depression. Family studies have examined the rates of illness within families, and the evidence indicates that affective disorders are more likely to occur in first degree relatives of diagnosed patients than in the general population (Klerman & Barrett, 1973). Twin studies which compare illness rates for monozygotic twins indicate that they show a higher concordance rate for affective disorders. Cross-rearing studies following high-risk children raised in adoptive homes (Kety, Rosenthal, Wender, Schulsinger, & Jacobson, 1975) attempt to separate out the proportional influence of genetics and environment. These types of family studies indicate a genetic basis for at least an inherent vulnerability to depression, particularly the manic-depressive forms.

A more sophisticated method for studying the genetics of depression is linkage studies, in which known genetic markers are used to follow traits throughout the family network. X-linkage markers are particularly important for testing sex differences in rates of depression disorder. If the gene for depression is located in the X chromosome and the trait is dominant, females, who have two X chromosomes, will be more often affected than males, who have only one X chromosome. However, if the trait is recessive, males will be more often affected than females. However, different types of depression, such as in bipolars and unipolars, complicate the testing of the X-linkage hypothesis. Some family studies demonstrate X-linkage transmission for unipolars, but not for bipolars, while others suggest the opposite; still others provide no evidence at all for any sex linkage.

Kidd, Reich, and Kessler (1974) proposed a polygenic model of inheritance in addition to the conventional single genic pattern. Perhaps there exists a genetically determined differential threshold to stress in the environment, with women having a lower threshold and therefore greater susceptibility to a depressive response to specific environmental stresses.

Pharmacological and Neurochemical Theories

Drug-related research in the last 10 years has produced an intriguing neurochemical theory of depression. This line of research has generated the amine hypothesis of affective disorders, which relates depression to a functional deficit of one or more brain neurotransmitter amines at specific central synapses. Conversely, mania, in this view, is associated with a functional excess of one or more of these amines. There are critical synapses in brain areas which are related to vegetative and affect regulatory behavior. Norepinephrine, dopamine, and serotonin are the neurotransmitter amines regulating the flow of impulses in these brain areas. At the synaptic junction, the neurotransmitter serves as a chemical transducer which converts electrical energy into chemical energy, which is then reconverted into electrical energy. Complex processes are responsible for synthesis, storage, release, re-uptake, and metabolism of the amine neurotransmitters. When electrical impulses arrive at the nerve endings, the storage granules containing norepinephrine release some of the transmitter substance, which then reacts with the receptor and causes an electrochemical event at the receptor site.

Two concurrent pharmacological observations initiated the amine hypothesis. The first occurred in the treatment of hypertension with reserpine, when it was observed that a large proportion of patients so treated for hypertension became depressed (Goodwin & Bunney, 1971). Another research team (Shore & Brodie, 1957) finds that reserpine depleted serotonin and norepinephrine in the brain. Monoamine oxidase (MAO) inhibitor drugs are capable of elevating brain amine levels, and in animals, treatment with MAO inhibitors could inhibit or reverse symptoms of depression caused by reserpine.

Another piece of evidence appeared with the tricyclic antidepressants. Although they do not directly alter the amine levels in the brain, they do block the presynaptic re-uptake of the amines so that there is a functional increase in amines at the synaptic juncture. Lithium, an effective drug in the treatment of mania, enhances the re-uptake of amines at the synapse, therefore lowering the amount of amines at the synaptic cleft. These drug actions indirectly support the general hypothesis that depression is a deficit of brain neurotransmitter amines and that mania is an excess of these amines at specific synapses.

This amine theory, in the ensuing years, required modification according to the different classifications of depression (i.e., unipolar and bipolar) and mania, and the pharmacological responses to the many types of drugs by those taking them. Unexpected reactions of patients responding or not responding to certain drug therapies in opposition to what was anticipated suggest that the chemical interactions and shifts during depression are extremely complex, and that more careful research is necessary.

Cognitive Theories

Many clinicians and researchers have hypothesized that the psychological deficit in depression involves a cognitive problem. Beck (1974) in particular has studied the cognitive themes of depressed patients. These patients misinterpret or exaggerate the real or imagined loss, and attach extravagant meanings to their difficulties. The depressed person views everything in his life, his attributes, his relationships, and his achievements with a sense of inadequacy and failure, past, present, and future. In his sufferings, the depressed person attributes the cause of the difficulty to himself. A chain reaction is triggered in which the patient personalizes the defect, magnifies any deficiencies, devastates his own self-esteem, and then harshly reproaches and criticizes himself. Pessimism alternates with apathy as the patient regards his own state of affairs. In dreams and in verbal productions, depressed patients center on three interdependent themes: a negative view of the self, of the outside world, and of the future. Beck suggests that this set of idiosyncratic patterns, which he labels the "cognitive triad," pervades the conscious experiences of the depressed person.

One strength of this cognitive model lies in its potential for a new psychotherapy. An extremely low self-concept can be treated by presenting a hierarchy of cognitive tasks and to demonstrate, through these tasks, the invalidity of the patient's self-reproaches. This allows the therapist not only to generally approve of the depresssed person, but to offer an objective evaluation of the patient's ability to perform a cognitive task.

Attempts have been made to specify what types of reinforcement for a cognitive task are more likely to raise self-esteem. Dweck (1975) hypothesizes that a person who has learned helplessness believes failure to be a result of his absence of ability or a result of external factors beyond his control. A person who believes failure to be a result of his own lack of motivation will be likely to escalate his effort in an attempt to obtain a goal. The cognitive theory, a relatively recent one, attempts to link experimental psychological research with clinical observation and systematic therapeutic intervention.

Behavioral Approaches

Behavior theory views depression in stimulus and response terms. Depression is characterized by a reduction in the frequency of many kinds of activity and an increase in the frequency of others, usually avoidance and escape. The depressed person's complaints, requests, bizarre behaviors, and repetitions are, functionally speaking, avoidance and escape behaviors, since they are reinforced by the removal of the aversive stimulus. Moreover, there is a deficit of positively reinforced activities in a depressed person's repertoire. The psychological treatment often consists of restoring the normal balance between negatively and positively reinforced activities.

Ferster (1974) identifies some specific behavior mechanisms that account for the frequency of the depressed person's actions and thus explain, in part, the infrequency of certain activities by the depressed person. He hypothesizes that fixed reinforcement schedules which require a large and regular amount of activity for each reinforcement are more apt to produce depression than variable reinforcement schedules. For instance, he suggests that the housewife and the professional who are both performing within a standard routine are more susceptible to depression than the struggling young executive or substitute teacher in a school system. According to Ferster, the uncertainty and variability in the reinforcement for the young executive and substitute teacher are less likely to produce strain than the stiff schedule associated with a stable work situation in which a constant daily amount of activity is needed to achieve a required goal.

Changes in the person's environment, or within himself, produce a disorientation and a shifting of dependable reinforcers. When changes are too drastic, the person may not be able to locate reinforcers for his particular repertoire of behaviors, and so may choose not to act. This lack of acceptable positive reinforcers, it is theorized, produces depression.

A low frequency of positively reinforced behaviors perpetuates the distorted perception of the patient's own inability to influence the environment. Low frequency of verbal activity indicates a patient's unwillingness to interact with the environment and to locate specific negative and positive contingencies in the environment. In Ferster's words (1974), "The patient has (1) a limited view of the world, (2) a 'lousy' view of the world, and (3) an unchanging view of the world [p. 39]."

Lewinsohn (1974) used this social reinforcement model as the basis for his behavioral approaches. He observes that a low rate of response-contingent, positive reinforcement elicits certain aspects of the depressive syndrome, such as inactivity, fatigue, etc. The low rate of response-contingent, positive reinforcement is predicted by three factors: potentially reinforcing events in the environment, the availability of reinforcement in the environment, and the instrumental behavior of the individual. Depression is predicted when there is little probability that the individual's behavior will be followed by positive reinforcement and when there is great probability that the individual will be reinforced when he does not emit the behavior.

Depressed persons are observed to be deficient in social skills; that is, they lack the ability to behave in such a way as to receive positive reinforcement from others. Measures of social skill, such as amount of behavior, modes of interaction, interpersonal range, positive reactions, and action latency indicate the patient's lack of interest in either giving or receiving positive reinforcement in their social interactions.

Learned Helplessness Theories

Recent experiments on animal behavior have created a condition in animals that parallels depression in humans. Seligman (1975) observes that dogs, after receiving a few trials of inescapable shock, accepted shock passively, without attempting to escape. The dog "learned" that it could not control the shock, and that no response succeeded in producing relief; the dog thus "learned" that it was totally "helpless." Continued laboratory trials suggested that an animal which had "learned helplessness" had extreme difficulty in "learning" that there were times when a response would produce relief from shock.

The behaviors of learned helplessness in animals are similar to features of clinical depression. One outstanding similarity is passivity. Animals and humans who have experienced an inability to control reinforcing contingencies in their environment thereafter demonstrate fewer voluntary responses, acting less on their own initiative. Helpless animals and depressed people also maintain a negative, cognitive set. That is, they have difficulty learning that their own responses can produce useful outcomes. The pessimism of the depressed patient is focused on his own inability to act in a skillful and influential enough manner to produce a change or reaction to anything or anyone in his surroundings. A third similarity between learned helplessness and depression relates to the timing of depression. If helplessness is induced in animals by a single session of uncontrollable shock, that sense of helplessness will dissipate in time. But if the animal undergoes multiple trials of inescapable shock, the helplessness persists for longer periods. In humans, a single catastrophic incident, such as the death of a child, produces grief and a sense of depression. This form of extreme depression is usually relieved with the passage of time. But if a person is subjected to continued experiences of inability to control what is happening in his life, there is a likelihood that he will maintain the symptoms of a depression for a longer time. The fourth similarity, that of lessened aggression, is the subject of much controversy in the field of depression. Helpless animals initiate fewer aggressive and competitive responses, and their status within the group diminishes. In the same way, clinically depressed patients seldom act in an aggressive or hostile manner, although the content of their dreams and conversation may be intensely aggressive. Helpless animals and depressed humans act alike in that they both will manifest loss of appetite, loss of weight, and lack of interest in sexual behavior. There are also strong similarities in the physiological and chemical changes that accompany the behaviors, although the chemical basis of depression has not been completely explicated. Helpless rats show norepinephrine depletion, while antidepressant drugs have the common ability to increase norepinephrine available at certain brain synapses.

In addition to these similarities, Seligman (1975) argues that helplessness is caused by learning that responding is independent of reinforcement; or in depression terms, that action is futile. Contrary to many other theories of depression, Seligman's holds that it is not the loss of reinforcement, but the loss of *control* over reinforcement that causes depression.

Relating Behavioral and Biological Theories

Seligman's theory of learned helplessness in animal studies and depression in humans has been challenged by physiological evidence. Laboratory experiments (Weiss, Glazer, & Pohorecky, 1974) indicate that the animal's inability to effectively act in the learned helplessness situation is due to a decrease of the norepinephrine in the animal's brain. The neurochemical shift is caused by environmental stress; when the stress, such as inescapable shock, is relieved, the neurochemical levels slowly return to normal, and the helpless animal then regains the ability to respond instrumentally.

Evidence that there is this biochemical mechanism rather than a learning mechanism derives from a series of animal studies. Helpless dogs, when tested 24 hours after inescapable shock, fail to jump the hurdle, but dogs tested 48 hours after inescapable shock can and do respond by jumping. This suggests that the early lack of response was due not to a learning phenomenon, but rather to a temporary biochemical depletion. Supplementary experiments with rats make this hypothesis more tenable. A group of rats exposed to a 3½ minute swim in cold water which reduced brain norepinephrine levels could not respond to avoid shock immediately afterwards. However, animals swimming in warm water showed no difficulty in escaping shock. But since norepinephrine primarily affects motor activity, rats in warm or cold water were shown to be able to avoid shock by responding to a task which required little motor activity, such as poking their noses through a hole to shut off the shock. In addition, drugs which are known to compensate for decreased norepinephrine levels protect animals against response deficits in a learned helplessness paradigm.

This biochemical-behavior research is intriguing because it relates stress to brain norepinephrine levels. It offers a possible mechanism for relating the chemical theories of depression to behavioral theories of depression, and accommodates both the catecholamine hypothesis of norepinephrine depletion in the brain and the environmental theories that implicate stress as a causative factor in clinical depression. However, there are still too many gaps in the research to allow for any conclusive synthesis of the findings.

It is apparent that there is no final agreement as to the causes of depression. Although there is moderate agreement among clinicians as to the differences between clinical states and the normal emotional mood of depression, this concordance does not extend to the causes of the depressive syndromes, nor to the best manner as to the classification of the various clinical states. Increasingly, it is being recognized that a single cause is unlikely to emerge, and that more complex, multicausal explanations are necessary to understand this complex human experience.

Explanations for Preponderance of Women Suffering from Depression

There is very good evidence that rates of depression amongst the sexes differ, both in the United States and elsewhere. Various explanations have been offered for this sex difference. There is a possibility that the trends are spurious, caused by faults and inconsistencies in the varying methods of reporting symptoms. The sex differences may be real and attributable to the biological susceptibility of women due to genetic factors or to the female endocrine system; or to psychosocial factors such as social discrimination; or to the learned helplessness of women.

Evidence that Women Predominate among Depressives

The available evidence of the predominance of females among depressives comes from four sources: observations of patients coming into treatment; community surveys of persons not under treatment; studies of suicide and suicide attempters; and studies of grief and bereavement. These data are reviewed in earlier chapters of this book and in Weissman and Klerman (1977).

Some of the sex variations in depression rates can be explained by differences in methodology, particularly in case definition. However, the methodological difficulties notwithstanding, it is striking that the findings show, with amazing consistency, a preponderance of females among depressives.

Of the various sources of evidence, the most compelling are from community surveys. Since rates of treated cases do not represent true prevalence, epidemiologic analysis requires data from community surveys. Such surveys usually involve a random sample drawn from a total community, and therefore provide information on many persons who have the disorder but have not received treatment.

Data are available from a number of community surveys in the United States and elsewhere. In clinical studies of diagnosed cases, the sex ratios show some minor variations; but in the community surveys, there are no variations, with the exception of bereaved widows, who will be discussed separately. Women predominate in all countries and all time periods.

The Problem of Artifact Due to Reporting of Stress and Symptoms

There have been frequent discussions as to whether this predominance of women among those diagnosed as depressed may be an artifact of the methodology. Reports from data sources as diverse as clinical observations, community surveys, and suicide studies indicate that women are overrepresented in the diagnostic category of depression. Are women really more depressed, or do they show up in the statistics more often for other reasons? Perhaps this preponderance of women is the result of their more frequently being under stress; perhaps it is their willingness to admit to stress. Or maybe women's response biases make them appear to be more depressed. It is possible that the same stress has different effects on men and women. Variations in the help-seeking patterns of men and women may mean that more female depressives show up in doctor's offices and therefore represent a larger proportion of the statistics.

Are Women under More Stress?

Before the sex differences in rates of depression can be regarded as an artifact, the possibility must be considered that women are under more stressful life events and therefore run a greater risk of succumbing to depression. Many clinicians, observing that stressful events occur before the onset of clinical depression, concluded that these events precipitate the depression. Holmes and Rahe (1967) provided great impetus to these studies by developing a simple quantitative scale for assessing the life events used in epidemiologic and clinical studies. Their results support the hypothesized relationship between stressful life events and the onset and severity of numerous medical illnesses and psychiatric disorders, particularly depression. Consistent sex differences in stress reports have appeared.

Uhlenhuth, Lipman, Balter, and Stern (1974) conducted elegant studies to examine the relationship between actual and perceived stress, using newer life events scales and reports of symptoms by patients in both psychiatric settings and normal populations in community studies. Uhlenhuth *et al.* find a direct relationship between stress and symptom intensity, but do not find that women reported more stressful life events. At the same levels of stress, women reported symptom intensities about 25% higher than men. This study was repeated with similar results in a probability sample of all households in Oakland, California.

Dohrenwend (1973) and others discuss the thesis that life event stresses act in an additive manner with health problems of all kinds. The basic hypothesis is that stressful life events include all major life changes, whether positive or negative. Most life event scales measure stresses as dramatic as divorce or loss of spouse, loss of job, relocation, and also minor stresses, like giving up smoking or changing a typical routine. Major life event stresses are equally distributed between men and women. However, it is possible that the minor stresses associated particularly with the role of married women may have been previously underweighted in the scoring of life event scales, and should be given much more importance in assessing a woman's susceptibility to depression. New life event scales (Atkinson, 1975) are being developed and tested to more accurately depict the subtle and relative stresses on men and on women.

Current stress scales emphasize discrete life events and acute changes in life conditions. They are relatively insensitive to certain chronic conditions such as poverty, large family size, or health problems, which might have a greater impact on women than men. However, pending empirical research, the available evidence is that women do not experience or report more stressful events.

Do Women Weigh Events as More Stressful?

While women may not report experiencing greater numbers of stressful life events, they may evaluate these events as more stressful than do men. To study the weight given to stress, Paykel, Prusoff, and Uhlenhuth (1971) asked patients and their relatives to judge the degree to which various life events were upsetting. They found no sex differences. Men did not appear to evaluate the standard lists of life events as having a very different impact upon their lives than did women.

Women Report More Symptoms, Especially of Affective Distress

One hypothesis proposed to account for the excess of depressive symptoms among women is that women respond to stress with affective distress because they feel freer to acknowledge symptoms. Clancy and Gove (1973), examining the possible role of social disapproval in the reporting of symptoms and find no significant sex difference. Women did not report more desire for social approval than men did; neither did they judge having psychiatric symptoms as less undesirable than did men. Clancy and Gove conclude that sex differences in symptom reporting appear to reflect actual differences and are not an artifact of response bias: women actually experienced more symptoms.

Women Go to Doctors More Often

Women cope with problems by visiting doctors, and, by every measure of utilization of the general health care system, women predominate. They have higher rates than men of use of outpatient facilities, of visiting physicians, of getting prescriptions, and taking psychotropic drugs.

Consistent with this are the findings for seeking help. Women will come for aid for minor complaints. Women seek treatment for depression more often, while men have a higher suicide rate. In our society, the public assumption of the role of being sick is interpreted by men as a sign of weakness. Moreover, the health care system is organized in ways that make it difficult for most men to get treatment, since office hours usually conflict with hours of employment. But help-seeking patterns alone cannot account for the predominance of depressed women in community surveys, since the majority of persons classified as depressed in community surveys have not been treated in psychiatric clinics, and thus have not been included in any official treatment rates.

Alcoholism and Deviance

The male-female statistics are more balanced if one considers alcoholism as a disorder and compares rates of alcoholism among men and women with those for depression. Apparently families and social conventions can tolerate depressed women and alcoholic men, but not depressed men and alcoholic women (Winokur, Rimmer, & Reich, 1971). Perhaps depressed men drink in order to lessen their feelings of despair physiologically (Mayfield, 1968) or emotionally, through their drinking groups. Alcoholic patients often have serious depressive symptoms (Tyndel, 1974); clinically depressed patients often have histories of alcoholism (Reich, Davies, & Himmelhoch, 1974). Although studies have solidly linked alcoholism and depression, the causal sequence is still unclear.

500 Gerald L. Klerman and Myrna M. Weissman

However, the two types of behavioral deviance, that is, depression and alcoholism, lead to very different directions of help seeking. While women predominate in the health care system, men predominate as inmates in correctional institutions. Better reporting by traditional psychiatric facilities and correctional institutions could more accurately depict the role of depression in the institutionalization of men and women.

More males than females have alcohol problems; thus some unknown proportion of depressed men appear in the alcoholism rates but are not identified as depressed. There are debates, however, as to whether or not these men are really depressed. Accurate diagnostic assessments are required to determine the morbid risk of depression and the time of its onset in relation to the beginning of the alcoholism problem. Similar factors must be considered regarding the possibility that depressed men are to be found in the correctional system. Pending future research, this remains an interesting, but unproven, hypothesis.

When all these possibilities are assessed, our conclusion is that the female preponderance is not an artifact.

The Female Preponderance Is Real and Is Possibly Due to Biological Factors

We conclude that the sex differences are real findings and now must examine the possible explanations. Some of the hypotheses involve biological susceptibility; among these, the investigations have been made as to the role of genetic transmission and of female endocrine physiological processes.

The possibility that there is a genetic factor in the etiology of depression has regularly attracted attention. There are four main sources of evidence for the genetic hypothesis: family aggregation studies, which compare illness rates within and between generations of a particular family based on the fact that members of the same family share the same genes to varying degrees; studies of illness rates in monozygotic and dyzygotic twins; cross-rearing studies; and linkage studies, in which known genetic markers are used to follow other traits through several generations or in siblings. The majority of genetic research in depression is concerned with evidence from family aggregation or twin studies.

The available evidence summarized by several investigators shows an increased morbid risk of affective disorder in the first-degree relatives of diagnosed patients as compared with the general population, and a higher concordance rate for affective disorders in monozygotic than dyzygotic twins. Taking into consideration all the studies, there is reasonable evidence of the existence of a genetic factor operating in depression.

Much of the recent evidence suggests X-linkage for inheritance of the manic-depressive form of depression. This mode of genetic transmission could explain unequal female-male rates. However, the available evidence is limited in quantity and inconsistent in direction, and pending further research, the genetic explanation must be acknowledged as possible, but not established.

Interest in the possible relationships between female sex hormones and affective states derives from observations that clinical depression tends to occur in association with events in the reproductive cycle, including the menstrual cycle, the use of contraceptive drugs, the postpartum period, and menopause. The female endocrine system has been widely proposed as the cause of mood swings and affective disorders in women. Yet many women accept premenstrual tension, postpartum depression, and menopausal changes as expected realities in their lives.

Ivey and Bardwick (1968) report that anxiety (measured by analyses of verbal samples) peaks during the premenstrual phase. Thirty to 50% of the 839 women responding to the Moos Menstrual Distress Questionnaire (Moos, 1968, 1969) reported that cramps, backache, headache, irritability, mood swings, and / or depression were associated with menstruation. Coppen and Kessel (1963) find through their questionnaire that premenstrual symptoms are significantly correlated with neuroticism. Zimmerman and Parlee (1973), who analyze cyclic phase and its relation to mood swings, find no significant differences between phases.

However, recent critical reviews, such as Sommer (1973) and Parlee (1972), describe the methodological problems inherent in many of these hormonal studies that may distort results. Other inaccuracies may arise from individual variations in the cycle phase among women examined and by response biases among the women surveyed. Many women often describe themselves as being tense, irritable, anxious, and depressed about 4 to 5 days before the onset of menses (see Moos, 1968, 1969, Paige, 1971). Parlee (1973) administered the Moos Menstrual Distress Questionnaire to both male and female subjects with instructions that they should "describe symptoms that women sometimes experience" during the menstrual and premenstrual phases of the cycle. Both women and men selected similar types of symptoms in response to Parlee's questioning. Although a number of physiological and psychological theories have been offered to explain the premenstrual syndrome, none of them convincingly presents a coherent biological process as the cause of estrogen drop and mood changes. There is still not sufficient evidence to conclusively link depression with the menstrual cycle.

However, the postpartum period is one phase of the life cycle where research provides solid data implicating hormones in mood changes. The significant hormonal shifts after giving birth are accompanied by mood disturbances. In the postpartum period, women do have a higher rate of serious psychiatric disorders, especially depression. Several studies which surveyed admission rates in psychiatric facilities (Paffenbarger & McCabe, 1966, Pugh, Jerath, Schmidt, & Reed, 1963) verified the increase in psychoses and mental disorders during the first to third month after delivery. A concurrent finding is that pregnant women are *less* likely to be incapacitated by mental disorders (Gordon & Gordon, 1959). Researchers cannot yet define how specific endocrines and endocrine changes influence postpartum psychiatric illness and protect against prenatal mental illness. It is clear that the social and emotional factors surrounding the birth of a child may contribute to this pattern as much as the concurrent hormone levels do.

The menopausal period of a woman's life is often depicted as a particularly depressing time. This has historically and officially been labelled involutional melancholia. Symptoms such as agitation, hot flushes, obsessions, and hypochondriasis increase. Depression has commonly been believed to accompany this change in life. But in an extensive study of over 800 women aged 38–60 (Hallstrom, 1973), no significant differences in the one-year incident rates of mental illness or depressive states were found in the different age categories. And Winokur (1973b) finds that there is no greater risk of depression during menopause than during other times of the life span. Thus a category of menopausal depression causally related to regular hormonal activity is not currently tenable.

The pattern of the relationship of the female endocrine system to clinical states is inconsistent. There is good evidence that premenstrual tension and use of oral contraceptives increase depressive mood, but these effects are probably of small magnitude. There is excellent data to show an increase in depression in the postpartum period. Contrary to widely held views, there is good evidence that the menopause does not increase rates of depression.

But there is little to substantiate a finding relating these mood changes and clinical states to altered endocrine balance or specific hormones. No study could be located which correlated clinical state with female endocrines, utilizing modern endocrinological methods or sensitive quantitative hormonal assays. Here is an area for fruitful collaboration of further research between endocrinology and psychiatry. As of now, it can be said that while some portion of the sex differences in depression, probably during the childrearing years, may be explained endocrinologically, this factor is not sufficient to account for the large ratio of sex differences in rates of depression.

Psychosocial Explanations

Psychologists, sociologists, feminists, and others concerned with women's problems have increasingly looked to psychosocial factors to explain why more women than men become depressed. The conventional wisdom holds that the longstanding disadvantaged social status of women has psychological consequences that result in depression. This persistence of social status discrimination is proposed to explain the long-term trends of female predominance in depression. In addition to this hypothesis, explanations based on views of female personality and on historical changes associated with social stress are offered.

Psychological Disadvantages of Women's Social Status

Various hypotheses have been proposed specifying the ways in which women's disadvantaged status might contribute to their pronounced rates of clinical depression. Our review of these hypotheses indicates two main pathways. One emphasizes the low social status, and the legal and economic discrimination against women; the other focuses on women's internalization of role expectations, which results in a state of learned helplessness.

The first pathway, which we call the *social status hypothesis*, is widely accepted in the recent discussions of social discrimination against women. Many women find their life situations depressing, since real social discriminations make it difficult for them to achieve mastery by direct action and self-assertion, which only further contributes to their psychological distress. It is suggested that these inequities lead to legal and economic helplessness, dependency on others, chronically low self-esteem, low aspirations, and ultimately, clinical depression.

The second pathway, which we call the *learned helplessness hypothesis*, proposes that socially conditioned, stereotypical images produce in women a cognitive set against assertion, which is reinforced by societal expectations. In this hypothesis, the classic "femininity" values are redefined as a variant of the "learned helplessness," characteristic of depression. Young girls learn to be helpless during their socialization and thus develop a limited response repertoire when under stress. These self-images and expectations are internalized in childhood so that the young girl comes to believe in the stereotype of femininity, especially its emphasis on youthfulness, beauty, and passivity.

Women and Learned Helplessness

The findings of the learned helplessness experiments of Seligman (1974, 1975) have been extrapolated to apply to the social status of women. Although the learned helplessness theory does not provide any immediate explanations for the sex difference in depression, certain aspects of the theory are particularly apt in describing the situation of women. Women are particularly susceptible to loss because they generally depend more than men upon social statuses, which are easily lost. Today's greater geographic and economic mobility mean that women are more likely to leave family and friends as they move and establish themselves in new jobs and in new neighborhoods. Within the family, the man's dependence on a job takes priority over the woman's dependence on her socioemotional network. Therefore women realistically may have less of a sense of control over their lives, and greater feelings of helplessness and loss.

As for treatment, if we look at animal experiments, the most effective way to overcome learned helplessness in dogs is to force them to respond. In other words, dogs must be *made* to jump in order to avoid shock. For the depressed patients, there are many therapies geared to teach the patient that she or he can solve a problem or perform a task. Electroconvulsive shock has also been shown to be effective in reducing depression and helplessness in humans and dogs. The prevention of succumbing to learned helplessness depends on the person's previous experience in mastering reinforcements in his or her own behavior. In depression, people who have been victimized, with few opportunities to influence positively and change their uncomfortable situation, are particularly susceptible to depression.

The role of women throughout history and even currently in our society is marked by a sense of powerlessness, an inability to produce a substantial influence on the course of events. The stereotypical feminine role tends to be defined as passive. The stereotypical areas of expertise for females, such as housework and cooking, tend to become not so much a matter of mastery as of routine.

Women's roles and occupations are seldom evaluated honestly. Therefore, it is thought, women, because of their roles, are predisposed to feelings of learned helplessness over a considerable period of time. If, because of their less powerful social roles, women have experiences which reinforce their feelings, of helplessness, they are likely to acquire depressive symptoms. This correspondence between Seligman's concepts of learned helplessness and the powerlessness of women's roles in society has been explicated more clearly and carefully by various feminist theorists.

Marital Role and Depression

In one of the few attempts to test the hypothesis that the high rates of depression are related to the disadvantages of women's social status, particular attention has been given to the difference in rates of mental illness of married and unmarried women. If the social status theory is correct, marriage should be a greater disadvantage to the woman than to the man, since married women are then more likely to fulfill the traditional stereotyped role and should, therefore, have higher rates of depression. Gove (1972), in particular, has researched rates of mental illness among married women as compared to the rate among unmarried women and married men.

Studies about the role performance of depressed women provide information about social conflicts of depressed patients. In a matched study, Weissman, Klerman, Paykel, Prusoff and Hanson (1974) observed that depressed women are extremely impaired in their roles as spouse, mother, and participant in close family relationships. Relationships with friends and extended family relations cause less difficulty for the depressed women. It appears that depressed women who are employed outside the home exhibit fewer differences in social functioning than comparable nondepressed women. Depressed women, then, are less maladjusted in instrumental roles than in expressive roles.

Based on these findings, Mostow and Newberry (1975) studied women workers and housewives coming for treatment of depression. In the initial sample, there appeared to be no significant difference in the severity and type of depression experienced by 21 matched worker and housewife subjects. After 1 month of treatment, the mental states of the two groups of sample subjects were still similar to each other. However, after 3 months, there were indications that the worker women were beginning to adjust socially while the housewives reported impaired performance, disinterest, feelings of inadequacy, and economic difficulties. It is important to consider that the working women were participating in sterotypically nongratifying jobs, such as those falling in the 4 and 5 categories of the Hollingshead Scale, and yet they still felt more competent than the housewives at their work. This is an indication that the work role, at any level, can support and benefit the depressed woman.

The association of poor interpersonal relations within the marriage and clinical depression is further supported by studies of depressed women during psychiatric treatment. The New Haven group (Paykel *et al.*, 1969) finds that marital discord was the most common event reported by depressed patients as having occurred in the previous six months. Weissman and Paykel (1974) found that acutely depressed women as compared to matched normal groups reported considerably more problems in marital intimacy, especially in their ability to communicate with their spouses. Moreover, these marital problems often were enduring and did not completely subside with symptomatic remission of the acute depression.

The strains of the marriage role were cited by Gove (1972) as a causal factor in higher rates of mental illness among women. Since the selective process of marrying filters out the mentally ill, the married of both sexes have lower rates of mental illness than the unmarried. However, Gove (1972) indicates that an important sex difference occurs in the rates of mental illness among married persons. Being married "protects" men against mental illness; for women, however, marriage produces difficulties which promote mental illness. The married woman's role is usually more stressful since it involves only one major source of gratification, the home life. The role of housewife is unstructured and invisible, with self-imposed rather than objective standards of performance. Also, many of the women's instrumental roles, such as the jobs they often fill, are frustrating, involve little skills and few challenges, and are not very prestigious. If a married woman does work outside the home, she is generally in a less satisfactory position in terms of pay, upward mobility, and scheduling. The expectations for a woman are unclear and diffuse. Rather than attaining clearcut individual goals, women spend much time adjusting to external contingencies.

On the other hand, the roles of single men and women are fairly similar, particularly for jobholders lacking close interpersonal ties. But after marriage and / or divorce, rates of depression among women are higher than among men, suggesting that women must cope with more role conflicts outside their control than men.

The data showing that unmarried women have lower rates of mental illness than unmarried men, but that married women have higher rates than married men, are cited as evidence that the excess of symptoms in married women is not entirely due to biological factors intrinsic to being female, is partly caused by the conflicts generated by the traditional female role.

Psychoanalytic Explanations

Among mental health clinicians, a widely held explanation for the high rates of depression among women attributes it to women's specific intrapsychic conflicts. Interestingly, two relatively independent psychoanalytic theories related to this issue developed in the early decades of this century, but theories were not linked together until recently with the emergence of the feminist critique. One is the psychoanalytic theory of female psychological development; the other, psychodynamic theory of the psychogenesis of depression.

As to the former, Freud and other psychoanalysts proposed that the personality of adult women, normal and neurotic, is characterized by narcissism, machochism, low self-esteem, dependency, and inhibited hostility, as a consequence of the young girl's special resolution of her Oedipal complex. This theory had been extensively criticized by Clara Thompson and Karen Horney, and more recently by Kate Millett. The classic psychodynamic theory of depression emphasized that individuals prone to depression had difficulties in close relationships, showed excess dependency, had suffered early childhood deprivation, felt excessive guilt, and manifested a tendency to turn hostility against themselves. According to this theory, the immediate precipitant for the overt clinical depression was hypothesized to be a loss, either actual or symbolic.

These two theories grew parallel with each other for almost 50 years. But few psychoanalysts attempted to link the epidemiologic fact that women predominate among depressives with their presumed characteristic psychic conflicts regarding narcissism, low self-esteem, dependency, and childhood experiences of penis envy. Although these two theories have been widely accepted among clinicians in one form of another, empirical evidence to support them has been meager.

The Possible Contribution of the Mental Health System

The prominence of these psychodynamic views among clinicians has stimulated criticism of the mental health system by feminists. They claim that women's difficulty in freeing themselves from the feminine stereotype has been consistently reinforced in public by "experts" on child development and psychology. Keller, Kirsh and other critics assert that psychotherapeutic treatment too often reiterates the negative self-image of women and perpetuates problems of women suffering symptoms arising from their life situations.

The most often-quoted work on the existence of sex role stereotypes among mental health professionals was undertaken by Broverman, Broverman, Clarkson, Rosenkrantz, and Vogel (1970), who asked mental health clinicians what behaviors they considered healthy in men, women, and adults whose sex was unspecified. The study found a powerful negative assessment of women. The standard for a healthy adult was the same as that for a healthy man but *not* as for a healthy woman. Healthy women were seen as differing from healthy men in that the healthy women were supposed to be submissive, dependent, subjective, emotional, and easily hurt. Thus, a double standard of mental health was found which parallels the sex-role stereotypes in our society. Moreover, both sexes incorporated the best or worst aspects of the stereotypical role in their image of themselves; women tended to have a more negative self-image than men.

Feminist critics have been intense in their assertions that psychiatry is a male-oriented profession which has perpetuated male-dominated theories (Chesler, 1972). Attempts have been made to encourage women to seek female therapists and to join groups for consciousness-raising. Before these feminist criticisms can be accepted, the results of studies on the attitudes and views of female mental health practitioners need to be appraised. From these studies, it can be seen that, in response to various case histories, male psychotherapists judged protocols of female patients less stringently than did female counselors. Thus, male mental health professionals were not necessarily bound by their ideology to discriminate against women.

How well psychiatric theory can explain depression in women has been strongly debated in recent years. Some believe that psychoanalytic theory does not provide a coherent personality system for women, nor the model of a strong, nonstereotypical woman. A number of critics (Franks & Burtle, 1974) assert that the mental health practice continues to support stereotyped roles for women by concentrating on women in relationship to their love objects—men—as fathers or spouses. They say that psychotherapy places a woman in a passive stance as a patient, encouraging expressiveness and a transference of trust to the psychoanalyst.

This is a crucial attack since the majority of therapists and psychiatrists who work with women are men. Case studies and experimental studies have pointed up sex discrimination and sexual preoccupation in therapy (Masling & Harris, 1969). Observations of testing sessions have indicated that male mental health professionals extended treatment sessions for females and used more sexual romantic projective tests and discussions with women (Barocas & Vance, 1974).

This suspicion of the male mental health professional has encouraged the use of female therapists and psychiatrists. Feminist therapists have organized and proclaimed themselves as more able to understand and deal with the mental health needs of women. However, some recent studies (Abramowitz & Abramowitz, 1973) indicate that female mental health practitioners are, in fact, quicker to infer greater maladjustments in females than in males. There is as yet little evidence to suggest that males support sex stereotypes in their depressed female patients more so than do female professionals. It appears that mental health personnel of both sexes maintain stereotypical and sex-biased notions or role adjustments.

Labeling Theory and Professional Stereotypes

Building on these findings, labeling theorists would explain the sex differences in depression not as an artifact in methodology or help-seeking patterns, but rather as a consequence of professional behavior. These theorists cite society's reaction to and labeling of symptoms as the source of any differences in diagnoses patterns. Szasz (1970), for instance, holds that a diagnosis of mental illness tends to produce conformity to society's standards (Szasz, 1970). Scheff's (1966) influential sociological approach proposes that virtually everyone at some time commits an act that corresponds to the public stereotype of mental illness. If and when the public acknowledges these acts, the person, depending on his status in society, may be labeled as mentally ill. These views place the onus of diagnosis on external standards and evaluations in mental health.

A major factor in the labeling of mental illness is the sex of the individual patient. The Broverman *et al.* (1970) study of clinicians' evaluations of mental health documented the existence of sex-role stereotypes among mental health professionals. The existence of such stereotypes has led to speculation that the diagnosis of depression is a labeling category applied selectively to women. The sex differences in rates of depression, according to this view, are "caused" by the labeling process, rather than to the actual differences in the numbers of men and women suffering from depression.

Although it is clear that professional and social attitudes towards sex roles influence the diagnosis and treatment of depression, the labeling view seems too simplistic to explain the complicated interactions between sex role and depression. For example, it cannot explain why in epidemiological studies, women consistently describe themselves as much more depressed than men. In epidemiological studies, societal labeling and stereotyping are not influencing factors. However, both the stereotypic female role and women's attitudes toward themselves within that role may contribute to the higher likelihood of women to maintain the symptoms of and be diagnosed with depression. Yet this does not seem to be the explanation for the high rates of women among untreated depression cases.

Historical Change, Rising Expectations, and Increasing Rates of Depression among Women

Any attempt to understand the female preponderance in depression must explain both the long-term and the short-term trends. Conventional explanations have assumed that the female predominance in depression has been a long-term trend. Data from the nineteenth century does indicate a female predominance of depression. That these trends are long-standing can be interpreted as supporting either the biological or the social status theory.

On the other hand, recent evidence suggests short-term trends. There has been an increase in the rates of depression, especially among young women, manifested by their rising rate of suicide attempts and by the high attendance of women at psychiatric outpatient clinics. This has prompted speculation about the possible contributory role of recent social changes, especially the presumed increased psychological stresses of modern life.

Rising expectations, changing demographic trends, increased life events, separations, and loss of attachment bonds are all factors creating risks of depression which have been suggested as mechanisms by which social change can create psychic stress. It is proposed that these stress factors have a greater impact on women because of their more vulnerable social position.

Increases in depression have been reported during other periods of rapid social change. The possible historical parallels to the current era in the late Elizabethan and early seventeenth century England, when depression was described to have reached epidemic proportions, have been described. One explanation during this period attributed the rise in mental illness to the "wear and tear of a civilization," and speculated on the reasons for the sex differences in rates of prevalence of mental disorder.

Rising expectations, access to new opportunities and efforts to redress the social inequalities of women have been suggested as possible explanations for the recent increase in depression among women. Depressions may occur not when things are at their worst but when there is possibility of improvement, and a discrepancy between one's rising aspirations and the likelihood of fulfilling these wishes. The women's movement, governmental legislation, and efforts to improve educational and employment opportunities for women have created higher expectations. But social and economic achievement often have not kept pace with the promises, especially in a decreasing job market, where long-standing discriminatory practices perpetuate unequal job opportunities.

These new role expectations may also create personal conflicts, particularly for women who value their traditional family tasks but who also desire employment and recognition outside the family. While the women's movement has mainly involved middle- and upper-class and educated women, it has had an impact on women from other social classes where opportunities for work outside the home, management of money, and dominance in the marriage may be crucial. Even for the educated and economically comfortable women, ambivalence and conflict continue about careers not conventionally seen as feminine. The documented increase in suicides and suicide attempts among women suggests that social changes may be exacting psychological costs for many young women. In this regard, Gove and Tudor (1973) note that communities which are extremely closeknit, stable, traditionally family-oriented, and culturally isolated, have lower rates of mental illness in general, with the women having even lower rates than the men.

Although support can be adduced for the hypothesis that participation in the women's movement is associated with psychological distress, it is unlikely that this is a major factor for the high rate of depression among women. The rate differences long predate the women's movement. While short-term changes may be disruptive, over a long period, a new equilibrium may be reached and the high female rates may begin to decrease. Such a reduction in women's rate of depression would be indirect confirmation of the hypothesis that the excess of depression among women is due to the psychological disadvantages of the female role. As social behaviors of the sexes become more equivalent, females may begin to employ modes of coping with stress similar to those used by men. There are some indications that the female rates of alcoholism, suicide, and crime—which are usually male behaviors—have begun to rise. Alternatively, the sex ratios for depression could become equal because of an increase in depression among men due to the stress produced by the new status of women, and the uncertainty of the male role. In this regard, it would be interesting to determine the rates of depression among educated and emancipated women. Similarly, are the rates of depression equalized between the sexes in cultural subgroups where sex role allocations are less rigid or nonconventional?

Summary of the Psychosocial Explanation

The most convincing evidence that social role plays an important role in the vulnerability of women to depression is the data that suggest that marriage has a protective effect for males but a detrimental effect for women. This supports the view that elements of the traditional female role may contribute to depression. Further understanding of social stress and its interactions with components of female vulnerability in the traditional role is a promising area of research. This research would need to take into account intervening variables such as women's employment and the quality of their marriages. Any comprehensive theory, including those based in biological explanations, must account for both the long-term rates and recent changes in rates.

Conclusion

The male-female differences in rates of depression are real. The evidence in support of these differential rates is best established in Western industrialized societies. Further studies in non-Western countries, particularly in Africa and in Asia, are necessary before any conclusions can be drawn as to the universality of these rate differences.

There is little doubt, however, that the sex differences found in depression are a promising lead which require a considerably broader based inquiry in epidemiology. It is highly unlikely that any one of the explanations already discussed will account for the phenomena, nor that every type of depressions will be associated with the same risk factors. As was shown, the explanations cross such a wide variety of disciplines that it is rare to find one group of investigators entertaining all of them. There has been an unfortunate tendency for fragmentation, so that the investigators in genetics, social psychology, or endocrinology are not specifically aware of attempts by colleagues in other fields to deal with similar phenomena. The purpose of this review has been to assess different positions and, hopefully, to guide future research.

We propose an integrative theory based on the concept of adaptation. Clinical depression is a maladaptive outcome of partially successful attempts of adaptation (Klerman, 1974). To support this thesis, Klerman has reviewed the adaptive functions of emotions and affects, especially sadness and depression, throughout the evolutionary process: social communication, physiological arousal, subjective awareness, and psychodynamic defense. Evidence for the communication function of affects came from the separation-loss paradigm in animal studies (Harlow, Harlow & Suomi, 1971). A baby monkey separated from the biological mother, cloth mother, or peer, communicates the need for maternal or peer support with actions that replicate the affect of depression. Just as separated animals maintain a fear-flight-arousal system, the depressed human is preparing for meeting and dealing with dangers. A "conservation-withdrawal" response, as seen by Schmale and Engel (1967), involves reduced activity, lowered metabolism, and increased parasympathetic activity.

Internalized and subjective affects also play important functions in psychic reflection. They permit goal-setting and self-evaluation, which are again representative of evolutionary attainments. Psychodynamic thinking has stressed the important role of affect in stimulating defense mechanisms which protect against danger to the ego's self-esteem. It is clear from these examples that the affective state of depression has been adaptive, from an evolutionary perspective, particularly for primates and human infants.

The adult depressive, however, still utilizes patterns such as dependency, passivity and helplessness, which were once adaptive in the child's developmental schemes, but are useless in the adult. The depressive episode is often initiated as a response to helplessness and fallen self-esteem, but this attempted adaptation fails. Depression does not facilitate social communication and interpersonal relationships. It does not prepare the organism to meet with the environmental contingencies. It causes a misperception in awareness of self, and employs defensive mechanisms that have negative consequences.

A combined model of learned helplessness and life event stresses with concurrent physiological changes may accommodate a new theory about the development of depression which accounts for the sex differences found in depressive symptoms. According to the sociopsychological explanation for depression, we could expect to find the highest rates of depression among that group of people who experience the greatest number of stressful events life demands, and at the same time the fewest actual possibilities for mastery of them.

We suggest that a balance of external stress and individual vulnerability predisposes women to this maladaptive response. While stress does contribute to the timing and precipitation of acute depressive episodes, stressful events are not universal or specific to depression. We advocate an adaptive model to integrate external stress and internal physiological and psychological balances. We foresee a future theory that will accommodate and link loss and separation changes, social order, genetic vulnerability and changes in the CNS biogenic amines. Animal studies testing the various effects of antidepressant drugs with concurrent behavioral indices will help to specify particular chemical-behavioral relationships. It is clear that different types of drug therapies, such as tricyclical antidepressants, monoamine inhibitors, estrogens, and so on, prove to have varying degrees of effectiveness on certain classifications of depression. All the evidence supports a pluralistic theory of the causes and treatments of depressions.

NOTE

1. The material in this section of the chapter derives in large part from abstracting Weissman, M. M., and Klerman, G. L. Sex differences and the epidemiology of depression, *Archives of General Psychiatry*, 1977, *34*:98–111.

REFERENCES

ABRAHAM, K. *Selected papers of Karl Abraham, M.D.* London: Hogarth Press, 1927.
ABRAMOWITZ, S. I., & ABRAMOWITZ, C. V. Should prospective women clients seek out women practitioners? Intimations of a "ding-bat" effect in clinical evaluation. *Proceedings, 81st Annual Convention, American Psychological Association*, 1973, *8*(1), 503–504.
ATKINSON, C. Personal communication, 1975.
BAROCAS, R., & VANCE, F. Physical appearance and personal adjustment counseling. *Journal of Counseling Psychiatrists*, 1974, *21*, 96–100.
BECK, A. T. The development of depression: A cognitive model. In Friedman, R. J., & Katz, M. M. (Eds.), *The psychology of depression: Contemporary theory and research*. Washington, D.C.: V. H. Winston and Sons, 1974.
BONIME, W. The psychodynamics of neurotic depression. *Journal of the American Academy of Psychoanalysis*, 1976, *4*, 301.
BOWLBY, J. *Attachment*. New York: Basic Books, 1969.
BROVERMAN, I. K., BROVERMAN, D. M., CLARKSON, F. E., ROSENKRANTZ, P. S., & VOGEL, S. R. Sex-role stereotypes and clinical judgments of mental health. *Journal of Consulting and Clinical Psychology*, 1970, *34*(1), 1–7.
CHESLER, P. *Women and madness*. New York: Doubleday, 1972.
CHODOFF, P. The depressive personality. Archives of General Psychiatry, 1972, *27*, 666.
CHODOFF, P. The depressive personality: A critical review. In Friedman, R. J., & Katz, M. M. (Eds.), *The psychology of depression: Contemporary theory and research*. Washington, D.C.: V. H. Winston and Sons, 1974.
CLANCY, K., & GOVE, W. Sex differences in mental illness: An analysis of response bias in self reports. *American Journal of Sociology*, 1974, *80*(1), 205–216.
COPPEN, W. R., & KESSEL, N. Menstruation and personality. *British Journal of Psychiatry*, 1963, *109*, 711–721.
DOHRENWEND, B. S. Life events as stressors: A methodological inquiry. *Journal of Health and Social Behavior*, 1973, *14*, 167–175.
DWECK, C. S. The role of expectations and attributions in the alleviation of learned helplessness. *Journal of Personality and Social Psychology*, 1975, *31*(4): 674–685.
FERSTER, C. B. Behavioral approaches to depression. In Friedman, R. J., & Katz, M. M. (Eds.),

The psychology of depression: Contemporary theory and research. Washington, D.C.: V. H. Winston and Sons, 1974.

FLEISS, J. L. *Statistical methods for rates and proportions.* New York: Wiley, 1973.

FRANKS, V., & BURTLE, V. (Eds.). *Women in therapy: New psychotherapies.* New York: Brunner / Mazel, 1974.

FREUD, A. *Normality and Pathology in Childhood.* New York: International Universities Press, 1965.

FREUD, S. Mourning and melancholia. In *Standard Edition of the Complete Psychological Works of Sigmund Freud,* Vol. 14. London: Hogarth Press, 1957.

GOODWIN, F. K., & BUNNEY, W. E., JR. Depression following reserpine: A reevaluation. *Seminars in Psychiatry,* 1971, *3,* 435.

GORDON, R., & GORDON, K. Social factors in the prediction and treatment of emotional disorders of pregnancy. *American Journal of Obstetrical Gynecology,* 1959, *77,* 1074–1083.

GOVE, W. R. The relationship between sex roles, marital status, and mental illness. *Social Forces,* 1972, *51*(1), 34–44.

GOVE, W., & TUDOR, J. Adult sex roles and mental illness. *American Journal of Sociology,* 1973, *78,* 812–835.

HALLSTROM, T. *Mental disorder and sexuality in the climacteric.* Goteberg, Sweden: Orstadius Boktrystreu A. B., 1973.

HARLOW, H. F., HARLOW, M. K., & SUOMI, S. J. From thought to therapy: Lessons from a primate laboratory. *American Scientist,* 1971, *59,* 538–549.

HOLMES, T. H., & RAHE, R. H. The social readjustment rating scale. *Journal of Psychosomatic Resarch,* 1967, *11,* 213–218.

IVEY, M., & BARDWICK, J. M. Patterns of affective fluctuation in the menstrual cycle. *Psychosomatic Medicine,* 1968, *30,* 336–345.

KETY, S. S., ROSENTHAL, D., WENDER, P. H., SCHULSINGER, F., & JACOBSEN, B. Mental illness in the biological and adoptive families of adopted individuals who have become schizophrenic: A preliminary report based on psychiatric interviews. In Fieve, R. R., Rosenthal, D. & Brill, H. (Eds.), *Genetic Research in psychiatry.* Baltimore: Johns Hopkins University Press, 1975.

KIDD, K. K., REICH, T., & KESSLER, S. Sex effect and single gene: The relevance of sex effect in discriminating between genetic hypotheses. In Weissman, and Klerman, unpublished manuscript, 1975.

KLERMAN, G. L. Depression and adaptation. In Friedman, R. J. & Katz, M. M. (Eds.), *The psychology of depression: Contemporary theory and research.*

KLERMAN, G. L., & BARRETT, J. E. The affective disorders: Clinical and epidemiological aspects. In Gershon, S., & Shopsin, B (Eds.), *Lithium: Its role in psychiatric research and treatment.* New York: Plenum, 1973.

KRAEPELIN, E. *Manic-Depressive Insanity and Paranoia.* Edinburgh: E. and S. Livingstone, 1921.

LEWINSOHN, P. M. "A Behavioral Approach to Depression." In Friedman, R. J., & Katz, M. M. (Eds.), *The psychology of depression: Contemporary theory and research.* Washington, D.C.: V. H. Winston and Sons, 1974.

LEWIS, A. *Inquiries in Psychiatry.* New York: Science House, Inc., 1967.

LINDEMANN, E. The symptomatology and management of acute grief. *American Journal of Psychiatry,* 1944, *101,* 141.

MASLING, J., & HARRIS, S. Sexual aspects of TAT administration. *Journal of Consulting Clinical Psychology,* 1969, *33,* 166–169.

MAYFIELD, D. G. Psychopharmacology of alcohol: I. affective change with intoxication, drinking, behavior and affective state. *Journal of Nervous Mental Disorders,* 1968, *146*(4), 314–321.

MEYER, A. *Psychobiology: A Science of Man.* Springfield, Ill.: Charles C Thomas, 1957.

MOOS, R. H. The development of a menstrual distress questionnaire. *Psychosomatic Medicine,* 1968, *30,* 853–867.

MOOS, R. H. Typology of menstrual cycle symptoms. *American Journal of Obstetrics and Gynecology,* 1969, *103,* 390–402.

MOSTOW, E., & NEWBERRY, P. Work role and depression in women: A comparison of workers and housewives in treatment. *American Journal of Orthopsychiatry,* 1975, *45*(4), 538–548.

PAFFENBARGER, R., & MCCABE, L. The effect of obstetric and prenatal events on risk of mental illness in women of child-bearing age. *American Journal of Public Health,* 1966, *56,* 400–407.

PAIGE, K. E. Effects of oral contraceptives on affective fluctuations associated with the menstrual cycle. *Psychosomatic Medicine,* 1971, *33,* 515–537.

PARLEE, M. B. Comments on "roles of activation and inhibition in sex differences in cognitive abilities" by Broverman, Klaiber, Kobayashi, and Vogel. *Psychological Review*, 1972, *79*, 180–184.

PARLEE, M. B. The premenstrual syndrome. *Psychological Bulletin* 1973, *80*(6), 454–465.

PAYKEL, E. S., MEYERS, J. K., DIENELT, M. N., KLERMAN, G. L., LINDENTHAL, J. J., & PEPPER, M. P. Life events and depression: A controlled study. *Archives of General Psychiatry*, 1969, *21*, 753–760.

PAYKEL, E. S., PRUSOFF, B., & UHLENHUTH, E. H. Scaling of life events. *Archives of General Psychiatry*, 1971, *25*, 340–347.

PUGH, T. F., JERATH, B. K., SCHMIDT, W. M., & REED, R. B. Rates of mental disease related to childbearing. *The New England Journal of Medicine*, 1963, *268*(22), 1224–1228.

REICH, L. H., DAVIES, R. K., & HIMMELHOCH, J. M. EXCESSIVE ALCOHOL USE IN MANIC-DEPRESSIVE ILLNESS. AMERICAN JOURNAL OF PSYCHIATRY, 1974, *131*(1), 83–86.

SCHEFF, T. *Being mentally ill: A sociological theory*. Chicago: Aldine, 1966.

SCHMALE, A. H., & ENGEL, G. L. The giving up-given up complex illustrated on film. *Journal of the American Psychoanalytic Association*, 1967, *15*, 344.

SELIGMAN, M. E. P. Depression and learned helplessness. In Freedman, R. J. & Katz, M. M. (Eds.) *The psychology of depression: Contemporary theory and research*. Washington, D.C.: V. H. Winston and Sons, 1974.

SELIGMAN, M. E. P. *Helplessness: On depression, development, and death*. San Francisco: W. H. Freeman, 1975.

SELYE, H. *The Stress of Life*. New York: McGraw Hill, 1956.

SHORE, P. A., & BRODIE, B. B. Influence of various drugs on serotonin and norepinephrine in the brain. In Garattini, S. & Ghetti, V. (Eds.), *Psychotropic drugs*. Amsterdam; Elsevier. 1957).

SOMMER, B. The effect of menstruation on cognitive and perceptual-motor behavior: A reivew. *Psychosomatic Medicine*, 1973, *35*(6), 515–534.

SPITZ, R. A. *Anaclitic Depression: The Psychoanalytic Study of the Child*, vol. 2. New York: International Universities Press, 1946.

SZASZ, T. S. Repudiation of the medical model. In Sahakian W. S. (Ed.), *Psychopathology Today*. Itasca, Ill.: F. E. Peacock, 1970.

TYNDEL, M. Psychiatric study of one thousand alcoholic patients. *Canadian Psychiatric Association Journal*, 1974, *18*(1), 21–24.

UHLENHUTH, E. H., LIPMAN, R. S., BALTER, M. B. & STERN, M. Symptom intensity and life stress in the city. *Archives of General Psychiatry*, 1974, *31*, 759–764.

WEISS, J. M., GLAZER, H. I., & POHORECKY, L. A. Neurotransmitters and helplessness: A chemical bridge to depression? *Psycholgoy Today*, 1974, 58–60.

WEISSMAN, M. M. Depressed women: Traditional and nontraditional therapies. In *Effective psychotherapy*. Symposium presented at the meeing of the Texas Research Institute of Mental Science, Houston, November 1975.

WEISSMAN, M. M., & KLERMAN, G. L. Sex differences and the epidemiology of depression. *Archives of General Psychiatry*, 1977, *34*, 98–111.

WEISSMAN, M. M., KLERMAN, G. L., PAYKEL, E. S., PRUSOFF, B., & HANSON, B. Treatment effects on the social adjustment of depressed patients. *Archives of General Psychiatry*, 1974, 30(June), 771–778.

WEISSMAN, M. M. & PAYKEL, E. S. *The depressed woman: A study of social relationships*. Chicago: University of Chicago Press, 1974.

WINOKUR, G. Depression in the menopause. *American Journal of Psychiatry*, 1973, *130*(1), 92–93.

WINOKUR, G., RIMMER, J., & REICH, T. Alcoholism IV: Is there more than one type of alcoholism? *British Journal of Psychiatry*, 1971, *118*, 525–531.

ZIMMERMAN, E., & PARLEE, M. B. Behavioral changes associates with the menstrual cycle: An experimental investigation. *Journal of Applied Social psychology*, 1973, *3*(4), 335–344.

35

Cinderella's Stepsisters
A Feminist Perspective on Anorexia Nervosa and Bulimia

Marlene Boskind-Lodahl

Reading the literature on female socialization reminds one of the familiar image of Cinderella's stepsisters industriously lopping off their toes and heels so as to fit into the glass slipper (key to the somewhat enigmatic heart of the prince)—when of course it was never intended for them anyway. [1]

During my early months of internship in 1974 in the mental health section of a university clinic, I encountered Anne, a lively, attractive, and slim young woman of eighteen. For three years she had been on a cycle of gorging and starving which had continued without relief. She felt desperate and out of control.

Anne was the first in a series of 138 binger-starvers that I was to treat. It became clear that the exaggerated gorging and purging reported by these patients was part of a self-perpetuating syndrome that was primarily a problem of women.[2] The women I interviewed were consumed by constant but self-defeating attempts to change their bodies so that they might each fit into the glass slipper. Anne was well informed about her symptoms. She even recommended books for me to read. I searched the traditional literature for insights into her problem. Bruch, who has written extensively on eating disorders, has most clearly diagnosed the starvation or anorexic aspect of this syndrome. According to her, characteristics of primary anorexia nervosa are: (1) severe weight loss; (2) a disturbance of body image and body concept which Bruch calls "delusional"; (3) a disturbance of cognitive interpretation of body stimuli, combined with the failure to recognize signs of nutritional need; (4) hyperactivity and denial of fatigue; (5) a paralyzing sense of ineffectiveness; (6) a family life in which (*a*) self-expression was neither encouraged nor reinforced. (*b*) the mother was frustrated in career aspirations, subservient to her husband, and generally conscientious and overprotective, (c) the father was preoccupied with outer appearances, admired fitness and beauty, and expected proper behavior and measurable achievements from his children.[3] Little else, however, was helpful. Most writers treated the starvation and the binge-ing (bulimia) as separate and distinct diseases, although several researchers had noted in passing the compulsion of the self-starver to binge.

This paper is intended to provide the nucleus of a new approach. Relating anorexia to bulimia, it may also help to stimulate successful therapies for the young women whom I shall describe as "bulimarexics."

Psychoanalytic Interpretation of Anorexia and Bulimia

The view of anorexia as a rejection of femininity which often manifests itself as a fear of oral impregnation is widely held (see fig. 1). Szyrynski observes:

> They appear to be afraid of growing and maturation and they find it difficult to accept . . . their sexual identity. In the case of girls, fear of pregnancy often dominates the picture; pregnancy being symbolized by food, getting fat means becoming pregnant. Such fantasies are also quite often formulated as oral impregnation. The girl, after kissing a boy for the first time, gets panicky lest pregnancy should follow. She pays particular attention to her gaining weight and not infrequently a casual remark of a visitor, a relative, or a friend, that she is looking well and probably has gained some weight will unleash the disastrous ritual of self-starvation.[4]

Behind such fears is said to be an unconscious hatred of the mother, who is ineffective and discontent but castrating. Wulff, writing in the early 1930s, describes such psychodynamics.

> This neurosis is characterized by the person's fight against her sexuality which, through previous repression, has become greedy and insatiable. . . . This sexuality is pregenitally oriented and sexual satisfaction is perceived as a "dirty meal." Periods of depression in which patients stuff themselves and feel themselves "fat," . . . "dirty," or "pregnant," . . . alternate with "good" periods in which they behave ascetically, feel slim and conduct themselves normally. . . . Psychoanalysis discloses that the unconscious content of the syndrome is a preoedipal mother conflict, which may be covered by an oral-sadistic Oedipus conflict. The patients have an intense unconscious hatred against their mothers and against femininity.[5]

Lindner, describing the case of Laura in *The Fifty-Minute Hour,* is a more modern proponent of traditional theory.[6] His patient, Laura, complained of the same gorging-fasting symptoms as my patient, Anne, but his interpretation of these symptoms diverges sharply from mine. He fits Laura neatly into a stereotyped feminine role, maintaining that her symptoms show a neurotic, unhealthy resistance to that role. His cure involves putting an end to that hatred of femininity by helping the woman learn to accept and to act out the traditional female role, often described as accommodating, receptive, or passive. What Lindner's Laura "really wanted" was to become pregnant. He observes Laura's desperate desire for a man, but

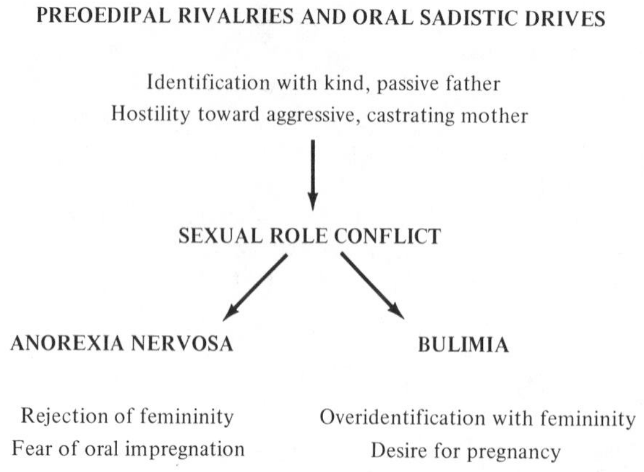

PREOEDIPAL RIVALRIES AND ORAL SADISTIC DRIVES

Identification with kind, passive father
Hostility toward aggressive, castrating mother

SEXUAL ROLE CONFLICT

ANOREXIA NERVOSA   BULIMIA

Rejection of femininity   Overidentification with femininity
Fear of oral impregnation   Desire for pregnancy

Figure 1 Psychoanalytic model of anorexia nervosa and bulimia

presupposes that it is healthy for a woman to feel desperate without a man and likewise to feel completely fulfilled once she is in a relationship.

Bruch writes more critically on the oral impregnation interpretation. She states that "modern psychoanalytic thinking has turned away from this merely symbolic, often analogistic etiological approach and focuses now on the nature of the parent-child relationship from the beginning." However, she confirms that "even today fear of oral impregnation is the one psychodynamic issue most consistently looked for."[7] The fact that most anorexic women suffer from amenorrhea, interruption of the menstrual cycle, is seen as further evidence that these women are rejecting their "femininity."[8] Medical evidence has shown, however, that amenorrhea is consistently observed in women with abnormally low body weight who do not have symptoms of primary anorexia. This suggests that it is low body weight that is the key factor in initiating hormonal changes associated with amenorrhea.[9]

Women Who Become Bulimarexic

My experience with bulimarexics contradicts standard psychoanalytic theory (see fig. 2). Far from rejecting the stereotype of femininity—that of the accommodating, passive, dependent woman—these young women have never questioned their assumptions that wifehood, motherhood, and intimacy with men are the fundamental components of femininity. I came to understand that their obsessive pursuit of thinness constitutes not only an acceptance of this ideal but an exaggerated striving to achieve it.[10] Their attempts to control their physical appearance demonstrate a disproportionate concern with pleasing others, particularly men—a reliance on others to validate their sense of worth.[11] They have devoted their lives to fulfilling the feminine *role* rather than the individual person. None has developed a basic sense of personal power or of self worth.

Bruch says that these women have a basic *delusion* "of not having an identity of their own, of not even owning their body and its sensations, with the specific inability of recognizing hunger as a sign of nutritional needs." She attributes this to, among other things, "the mother's superimposing on the child her own concept of the child's needs." [12] Thus the child, believing that she is hungry because her mother says so, has little sense of what hunger is about internally. In my experience with these women, the feeling of not having any identity is not a delusion or a misperception but a reality which need not be caused solely by the stereotyped protective mother but by other cultural, social, and psychological pressures as well.

Anne, for example, was a good, generally submissive child. She had lived her life the way "she was supposed to"—precisely her problem. She had been socialized by her parents to believe that society would reward her good looks: "Some day the boys are going to go crazy over you." "What a face! With your good looks you'll never have to worry about getting a job." Clinging and dependent, she could not see herself as a separate person. Our early sessions had an unreal quality. I searched for a glimpse of unique

CHILDHOOD

Powerless and controlling mother + "hero" father

Suffocating demands for conformity

Child who defines herself by perceived reactions of others

ADOLESCENCE

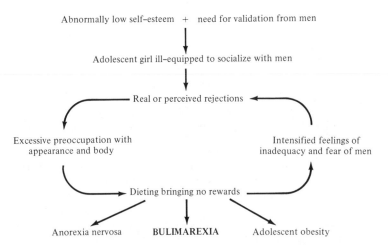

Abnormally low self–esteem + need for validation from men

Adolescent girl ill–equipped to socialize with men

Real or perceived rejections

Excessive preoccupation with appearance and body

Intensified feelings of inadequacy and fear of men

Dieting bringing no rewards

Anorexia nervosa   **BULIMAREXIA**   Adolescent obesity

Figure 2   Development of bulimarexic behavior

character, but Anne had no identifiable sense of self from which to project a real person. Her dependency on others prevented any development of self. Most of the women in my study had been rewarded for their physical attractiveness and submissive "goodness," while characteristics such as independence, self-reliance, and assertiveness were generally punished by parents, grandparents, teachers, and peers. Peggy said, "I was always a tomboy. In fact at the age of ten to twelve I was stronger and faster than any of the boys. After I won a race against a boy, I was given the cold shoulder by the rest of the boys in my class. The girls teased me and my parents put pressure on me to 'start acting like a girl should.' I did, and stopped having as much fun."

Wulff refers to an intense, unconscious mother hate in these women. In my experience they were, on the contrary, painfully conscious of despising their mothers, most of whom they described as weak and unhappy, women who had abandoned careers in order to raise children. "My mother wanted to be a lawyer but gave it all up when she married my father." Though the mothers are painted as generally ineffectual, they do exercise power in one limited realm: over their children. There, as if they are compensating for their misery elsewhere, they are often suffocating, dominating, and manipulative. Rather than rejecting the passive aggressive behavior of their mothers and with it the more destructive results of such behavior, the women to whom I listened described their struggle for a social acceptance that would allow them to enact their mother's role. Most of them also strongly identified with their fathers, despite the fact that many fathers spent little time with their families. Instead, they concentrated on interests outside the home. Some of the women reported that the fathers were more persistent in their demands for prettiness and feminine behavior than the mothers. Fathers were objects of hero worship, even though they were preoccupied, distant, or emotionally rejecting.

A distorted concept of body size, a characteristic of the anorexics described by Bruch and of the bulimarexics I have studied, is related to the parental and societal expectations that emphasize physical appearance. At the first session with Anne, I was struck by the utter distortion of her body size. She complained frequently of how fat she was; I saw her as exceedingly thin.

> M. B.–L.   Why don't you stand up and point out to me where you experience yourself as fat.
>
> ANNE   Here . . . here . . . everywhere. [She jabbed and pulled.]

I noted at this session that Anne's "distorted body image" was linked to a complete lack of confidence in her own ability to control her behavior. She reported that she felt inadequate as a woman and that she had never been able to sustain a loving relationship with a man.

As well as striving to perfect and control their physical appearance, the bulimarexics displayed a need for achievement. All the women were high achievers academically and above average in intellect. However, in most cases the drive to achieve had as its goal pleasing parents and marrying "well." Continued success in academe was essential to feelings of self worth, but the pressure to achieve, with its rewards, was expected to be forgotten and tucked away in exchange for the fulfillments that marriage and childbearing could bring. These women saw achievement mainly in terms of what rewards it could provoke from others. For example, a doctor is more likely to meet and desire for a mate a woman who is educated; a woman is most likely to meet this man in a university. Achievement was not seen in terms of intrinsic rewards to the self.

Obviously, women who grew up struggling to perfect the female role expect that perfection to be rewarded by fulfillment. Their expectations are founded on what they perceive to be the expectations and standards of the rest of the world for them. It is expectation that has left the women I interviewed sadly vulnerable to rejection. In adolescence they begin to look eagerly for their reward, for the men who will see them as they have struggled to be seen. But rather than being offered rows of handsome princes waiting to court, many women suffer male rejection about this time. For others the rejection was *perceived* rather than actual (i.e., these adolescent girls felt rejected if they were not pursued by males and socially active). The experience of male rejection often precipitates dieting. The girl somehow believes that the appearance of her body must be related to the reason for her rejection. Bruch describes a young woman who could trace the beginning of her anorexic behavior to an incident she experienced as a rejection.

> Celia (No. 12) had begun her noneating regimen during her second year in college, when her boyfriend commented that she weighed nearly as much as he. He was of slight build weighing only 130 lbs. and was sensitive about this, feeling that his manliness was at stake. He expressed the desire that she lose a few pounds and she went on a diet in an effort to please him. However she resented that he had "fixed" their relationship at a certain weight. When she first talked about this she said, "I completely lost my appetite"; later she added that she had been continuously preoccupied with food but denied it to herself. . . . As she began to lose weight she experienced a great sense of strength and independence.[13]

Some women reported that they were, in fact, chubby at this time, but others described themselves as slim but not slim enough, according to their ideal image of what they believed a beautiful body should look like. Along with these slimming efforts, other attempts were sometimes made to beautify the body; three women reported having their noses straightened. However, these dieting attempts also do not produce anticipated rewards (i.e., male attentiveness).

When the expectations of these women of being desired and pursued by men did not materialize, they believed themselves to be undesirable, unattractive, and unworthy. These beliefs reinforced their already existing pervasive sense of inadequacy. Fear of rejection then became a crucial motivating force in their behavior. A rejection, real or perceived, shatters the self-image of the person who has constructed that image around the expectations of others. The person adopts a behavior that will protect her against future rejection. Lee supports this view: "There was an overwhelming preoccupation with weight and a tendency to view others according to their weight as a way of defending against feelings of inadequacy and fear of rejection by others. The struggle consists of a 'relentless pursuit of thinness.' "[14]

A fear of rejection as a source of Anne's symptoms appeared rather dramatically one day. After three months, she had not been able to recall her first food binge or the circumstances that had led to it. This day she was describing a binge she had had the night before. Using Gestalt techniques, I suggested she try a role-playing fantasy, something with which she was familiar.

> M. B.–L.   OK—in that chair is your *body*. The chair you are sitting in is *the food*. Now *be the "food"* and tell your body what you are doing and why.
> ANNE   I'm your food and I'm going into you now . . . stuffing you . . . making you disgusting . . . fat. I'm your shame and I'm making you untouchable. No one will ever touch you now. That's what you want . . . that no one will touch you. [She looked up in surprise.]
> M. B.–L.   Are you surprised about something you just said?
> ANNE   About not being touched . . . [silence]
> M. B.–L.   Is that something you feel you could get into talking about now?
> ANNE   Yes, I guess it might be important. . . . When I was fifteen [three years ago] I was on a cruise down the Snake River. I impulsively decided I didn't want to be a virgin anymore and since I liked the boat man, I decided to let him make love to me. The only thing is I got drunk, passed out, and that's when he did it to me. I didn't remember anything the next day except feeling miserable and disgusted with myself. And the worst part was this guy didn't want anything to do with me after that. After this happened I lost some weight because I felt maybe I was too fat and that this is what had turned him off. Shortly after I lost weight I had my first binge, and it's gone on ever since.

The first rejection often becomes a pattern. Many women revert to dependent behavior, which assures the repetition of the rejection. Anne would meet a man, "fall in love," and eventually drive him away by growing increasingly possessive and clinging. She then tried to compensate for what she perceived as a failure, attempting to alter herself through fasting in order to accommodate to some mysterious standard of perfection men held. Other women become supercritical of most men they encounter, thereby eliminating the possibility of warm and loving relationships.

Another of my patients, Linda, petite, soft-spoken, and lovely, says of her first binge:

> Well, my mother thinks it all started after I was rejected by a boy in my junior year of high school . . . [silence] . . . he was my first boyfriend, and I was really crazy about him. One day he just dropped me without any explanation. . . . I never did find out what I had done. It was so confusing. . . . I was really depressed. Shortly after I had my nose fixed and began to diet. I wasn't fat, but it was the Twiggy era, and I can't remember exactly, but I started to binge somewhere around that time, but I don't really know if there's any connection.

The Psychodynamics of the Binge and Purge

The cycle the bulimarexic endures can be physically damaging (see fig. 3). The women report fasting, habitual forced vomiting, and amphetamine

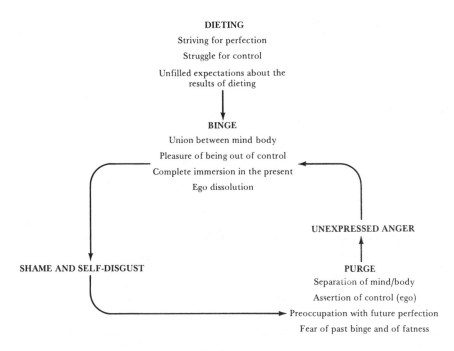

Figure 3   The psychodynamics of bulimarexia

and laxative abuse as means to counteract a binge. However, for these young women who have been "good" girls, and who are afraid of parental disapproval and the rejection that might result from sexual activity, food is one of the few elements in their tightly regulated lives that they can choose to indulge excessively. For the person who is struggling to meet unrealistic goals by imposing severe and ascetic control over herself, the binge is a release.

> ANNE   When I am into a binge it doesn't matter if I have just eaten . . . I just go crazy . . . completely out of control. Whatever is around I eat . . . candy . . . four or five bars . . . a whole quart of ice cream. If I am in the cafeteria, I fill my plate with everything. I then go back for seconds, thirds, and even more. I eat until I feel sick. After I binge I feel disgusted with myself and start my fast. I don't eat anything except liquids for a few days. I usually stick to this for as long as a week.

Moreover, the binge brings about a union between the mind and body. One gives one's self to the food, to the moment completely. There is a complete loss of control (ego). It is an absolute here-and-now experience, a kind of ecstasy.

However, the giving over of one's self to this kind of experience leads to shame and guilt. Socialization and cultural pressures intrude to initiate the purification rites, purging or fasting. The purging represents a concentration on past and future. In reliving the past, the self is a helpless child, rewarded for beauty and feminine passivity, punished for being assertive and rebellious. In anticipating the future, the self preoccupies itself with the repercussions of having a fat body in American culture, which will bring about male rejection. For the bulimarexic, ego manifests itself in social symbols (i.e., beautiful body = male approval = self-validation). Because the binge will bring about an ugly body, it carries with it the threat of ego dissolution and social humiliation. In purging, the mind separates itself from the body by focusing on the shame of being out of control.

A feature of fasting that feeds the persistence of the syndrome is the false sense of power that the faster derives from her starvation. The woman feels "good," "in control," and "disciplined" when her life has narrowed to self-denial. Bruch refers to anorexia as a "struggle for control for a sense of identity, competence, and effectiveness." She writes that many of these youngsters "had struggled for years to make themselves over and to be perfect in the eyes of others." [15] What her otherwise reasonable interpretation of the syndrome overlooks is the fact that the fasting behavior in this syndrome also strives for power and control over the bulimic behavior. Thus, the bulimarexic is involved in a struggle against a part of the self rather than a struggle toward a self. In the early stages of the syndrome, the adolescent girl may be asserting ownership rights over her body. She also may be using this behavior as a passive-aggressive reaction to her mother whom she perceives as controlling and suffocating. The refusal of food—along with compulsive masturbation, nailbiting, etc.—are all behaviors that the parents cannot completely control. The child chooses privacy and isolation for her acting out. However, when bulimia first occurs the nature of the syndrome undergoes a transformation. The underlying beliefs about one's self ("I am unlovable, unattractive, and inadequate") are pervasive and make the woman extraordinarily sensitive to the reactions of other people toward her. The most minor or insignificant slight is exaggerated and distorted, creating massive self-loathing, and is used as an *excuse* for binge-ing. The anger the woman feels toward her imagined rejector is not acknowledged, and this unexpressed anger is turned inward, adding to the fury of the binge.

The fast-binge cycle of the bulimarexic is confining. It consumes enough energy to prevent the woman from looking beyond it or outgrowing it. It serves to keep her socially isolated. Binge-ing wards off people with a "wall of [perceived] fat." It is a way of "filling up" without needing others. A fairly typical example from Anne's case supports this hypothesis. Anne was invited to go out to dinner by a boy she really liked; she wanted to go but was on the fasting part of her cycle. She feared the temptation and thus worked herself into a high state of anxiety, fearing a binge and vacillating between going and staying home. On the date, she ate moderately and had an enjoyable time. When the man dropped her off, she proceeded to binge grotesquely.

The fact that the behavior is a secret one, carried out in private, further isolates the bulimarexic. For her food becomes a *fetish,* as Becker uses the term in "Fetishism as Low Self-Esteem."

> "General inactivity," "low self-esteem," and "sense of inadequacy" indicate that the fetishist is a person who has sentenced himself (herself) to live in a certain kind of object world. It will be shallow in terms of the complexity and richness

of its objects; it will represent a narrow commitment instead of a broad and flexible one; yet it will be a segment of the world which has to bear a full load of life meaning. In other words, the fetishist will be a behaviorally poor person, who has the resourceful task of creating a rich world. As we said, the record of that resourceful contriving is the fetish behavior itself.[16]

A Feminist Perspective

None of the women in this study had ever experienced a satisfying love relationship in spite of their attractiveness and high intelligence. All longed for one. Most were virgins. Others froze up when sexual overtures were made or developed severe anxiety or depression during or after sex. The sexual conflicts that are evident in these women do not reflect a rejection of femininity or a bizarre fear of oral impregnation.[17] Rather, these women have already learned a passive and accommodating approach to life from their parents and their culture. This accommodation is combined with two opposing tensions: the desperate desire for self-validation from a man, and an inordinate *fear of men* and their power to reject. Since most of the women have already experienced a real or perceived rejection by a male or males, this perpetuates the already larger than life belief in the power and importance of men. The sexual fears of these women are often associated with intercourse, which is viewed as an act of surrender exposing their vulnerability to rejection. Rather than finding an obsession with bizarre fantasies (oral impregnation), I found a preoccupation with the fear of rejection in sex, of not being good enough to please a man.

If the woman is able to find a male companion who loves her, in spite of the obstacles her behavior presents to the relationship, a remission of symptoms might occur. This relationship, while relieving the surface of the bulimarexic's problem, can be more ultimately destructive. If the woman has not strengthened her sense of self and self-worth, the future of the relationship can be at best uncertain; failure of the relationship can be devastating.

Why is it that the bulimarexic gives men the power to reject her? Why does she give up her own power and make men larger than life? A reasonable answer, one more direct than that found in a theory of the innate psychology of women, lies in our heritage of sexual inequality. As Miller says, "our male dominated society creates a system of values in which men and women tend to believe that the only meaningful relationships are with men. Men attempt to win esteem by achievement and their attention lies in the sphere outside the family. And since the women define themselves in terms of their success in holding the love of men, a system of mutual frustration develops and the children become the repository."[18] Between the ages of thirteen to seventeen, these adolescent girls find that society in general and men in particular do not reward them as they have been socialized by both their parents and their culture to *expect*. Obviously this image of men affects a woman not only as a daughter but as a mother. It is my conviction that the mothers of these women became what they are for the same reasons that their daughters became bulimarexics. Most women are socialized to dependency to some degree. Laws has summarized ways in which this affects women:

> Social dependence, as a habit of responding, has a number of consequences. . . . First, the reliance on rewards coming from others makes the individual very flexible and adaptable, ready to alter her behavior (or herself) in response to words and threats. Second, she is limited to others as a source of rewards, including self-esteem, for two reasons: (1) the necessity of being accommodating and responsive works against the development of a sense of self which might oppose the demands of others, and (2) any evidence of the development of the self as a source of approval or of alternative directions is punished by others. The "responsiveness" and the sole reliance on social support make the woman extraordinarily vulnerable to rejection (meaning failure).[19]

Many traditional approaches to therapy with women see men as solutions to problems of low self-esteem. Szyrynski exaggerates these assumptions when he suggests that "since a great majority of such patients are adolescent girls, a male therapist may be probably more effective than a woman. He can replace for the girl her inadequate father figure; on the other hand, he will not be identified by the patient with her hostile mother."[20] I believe, on the contrary, that female therapists can provide positive female role models for these women which are a marked contrast to the negative experiences they recount in relationships with their mothers. In addition, it is unrealistic to expect that the presence of a man, or any other person, can compensate for a nonexistent sense of self. It is equally unrealistic to expect a man to want to serve this function. I can only offer a pessimistic prognosis for the woman who looks at the accession of an approving man as the solution to her psychological conflicts.[21] Since anorexia nervosa and bulimarexia are appearing with greater frequency,[22] I can only hope that the increasing number of women suffering from these syndromes can avail themselves of a humane therapy to help alleviate the low self-esteem that is at the root of their problems.

NOTES

1. Judith Long Laws, "Woman as Object," *The Second XX* (New York: Elsevier Publishing Co., in press).
2. Four men who reported the binge-ing-starving behavior were also treated. I saw three of these men in individual therapy. Since the writing of this paper I have been engaged in therapeutic interventions and research designed to test some of these theoretical arguments. Taking advantage of a new philosophical and innovative movement within our mental health clinic, I attempted an outreach program designed to break through the isolation and shame experienced by women who are food bingers. In September 1974, an ad was placed in our university newspaper describing the symptom and offering a group experience with a feminist orientation that would utilize Gestalt and behaviorist techniques. Sixty women responded; fifteen were admitted to the group. Some of the before, after, and follow-up measurements administered were: questionnaires specifically dealing with the binge-fast behavior and early childhood training; a body cathexis test (P. Secord and S. Jourard, "The Appraisal of Body-Cathexis: Body-Cathexis and the Self," *Journal of Consulting Psychology* 17 [1953]: 343–47); and the Sixteen Personality Factor questionnaire (R. B. Cattell, *The 16 P-F* [Champaign, Ill.: Institute for Personality and Ability Testing, 1972]). Based on the success of this initial group, two subsequent groups have been run and data collected. Our outreach program, designed as a preventive intervention, re-

vealed a much larger population manifesting this behavior than had been suspected. After seeing 138 women and four men in two years at our clinic and systematically studying eight of these with a variety of tests and other measurements, we are now working on developing an operational definition of the bulimarexic syndrome, analyzing our data for publication, and outlining a new therapeutic approach to this problem.

3. Hilda Bruch, *Eating Disorders* (New York: Basic Books, 1973), pp. 82, 251–54.

4. V. Szyrynski, "Anorexia Nervosa and Psychotherapy," *American Journal of Psychotherapy*, 27, no. 2 (October 1973): 492–505.

5. M. Wulff, "Ueber einen interessanten oralen Symptomenkomplex und seine Beziehung zur sucht," in *The Psychoanalytic Theory of Neuroses*, ed. Otto Fenichel (New York: W. W. Norton & Co., 1945), p. 241.

6. Robert Lindner, "The Case of Laura," *The Fifty-Minute Hour* (New York: Holt, Rinehart & Winston, 1955).

7. Bruch, p. 217.

8. J. V. Waller, R. M. Kaufman, and F. Deutsch, "Anorexia Nervosa: A Psychosomatic Entity," *Psychosomatic Medicine* 2 (September 1940): 3–16.

9. R. M. Boyer et al., "Anorexia Nervosa: Immaturity of the 24-Hour Luteinizing Hormone Secretory Pattern," *New England Journal of Medicine* 291 (October 24, 1974).

10. I am indebted to Dr. Ronald Leifer for his insights into the implications of bulimarexic behavior and to Janet Snoyer and Holly Bailey for their assistance.

11. The four male bingers I interviewed exhibited the following striking commonalities with the women in the study: (1) all complained of feelings of inadequacy and helplessness and exhibited abnormally low self-esteem; (2) all were extremely dependent and passive individuals who worked very hard at pleasing their parents through academic achievement; (3) all expressed feeling inadequate because they had never been able to sustain relationships with women, and, indeed, all had suffered female rejection in adolescence, which left them fearful of women and further encouraged their isolation; (4) all described their parents as excessively repressive. Unlike the women in the study, the men strongly identified with their mothers and expressed hostility toward their fathers whom they experienced as demanding and authoritarian. All had been pushed into athletics at an early age by their fathers. Although none were overweight as children and some were, in fact, slight of build, they became preoccupied with weight because of their desire to maintain slim and athletic bodies.

12. Hilda Bruch, "Children Who Starve Themselves," *The New York Times Magazine* (November 10, 1974), p. 70.

13. Bruch, *Eating Disorders*, p. 268.

14. A. O. Lee, "Disturbance of Body Image in Obesity and Anorexia Nervosa," *Smith College Studies in Social Work* 44 (1973): 33–34.

15. Bruch, *Eating Disorders*, p. 251.

16. Ernest Becker, *Angel in Armor* (New York: Free Press, 1969), pp. 18–19.

17. Normal adolescent girls often express a fear of oral impregnation. These fears occur between the ages of ten and thirteen and usually are connected with inaccurate sexual information and imagined parental disapproval. Since such fears are so often experienced by normal women, I can see no basis for assuming that these fears foster anorexic behavior.

18. Jean B. Miller, "Sexual In-Equality: Men's Dilemma; a Note on the Oedipus Complex, Paranoia, and Other Psychological Concepts," *American Journal of Psychoanalysis* 32, no. 2 (April 1972): 140–55.

19. Laws (n. 1).

20. Szyrynski (n. 4), p. 502. In the cases of the three men I saw in individual therapy, the same Gestalt-behaviorist approach used with women was utilized. It emphasized awareness, responsibility, assertiveness training, and male consciousness raising. In all cases, at a particular stage in the therapy it was decided that a male therapist would be useful to deal with issues of sexuality, and these patients were then referred to a male counselor with a similar therapeutic orientation. All eventually gave up the bulimarexic behavior and reported many positive changes in their attitudes toward themselves, women, and their parents.

21. The extent to which such attitudes prevail in our culture is indicated by the account of a "cured" anorexic. "I fell in love. By no means do I want to suggest that love is the answer to everything. For me, loving someone shifted my attention away from the compulsive, convoluted world of self I had created inside me, toward another person. Finally, I felt some self-esteem because I had been found worthy by someone else" (Kathryn Lynch, "Danger! You Can Overdo Dieting," *Seventeen* 24 [March 1974]: 107).

22. With a few exceptions, most of the literature on these behaviors has not acknowledged this upward trend. One exception is the British study by May Duddle, "An Increase of Anorexia Nervosa in a University Population," *British Journal of Psychiatry* 123 (December 1973): 711–12. Most of the food bingers I have encountered know of other women who binge. I suspect that most cases are seen in a high school guidance office or college mental health service. Many more women probably suffer secretly from this compulsion and do not seek help because of inordinate shame about their behaviors.

36

A Decade of Feminist Influence on Psychotherapy

Annette M. Brodsky

The last decade has seen some major impacts of feminism on the institution of psychotherapy regarding theories, treatment techniques, and assessment instruments. The changes in attitudes toward women as therapists and as clients have reflected the general advances of the women's movement in that women clients are more likely to seek women therapists and to receive treatments specifically developed for crises affecting women such as rape, pregnancy and domestic violence. The difficulties in designing empirical studies to demonstrate bias in psychotherapy have resulted in a confusing state of the art because only the higher-order interactions have consistently been significant. Attempts of some women to resist changes brought about by the women's movement and the apathy and levity of others have also presented problems in the path of progress. However, movement toward the long-range goal is encouraging when one compares the writing on women and psychotherapy in recent professional journals with examples from the 1960s.

In 1963, as the first female clinical psychology intern in the U.S. Army, I was assigned a 40-year-old woman client who refused to accept me as her therapist because I was younger than she, and a woman. She was convinced that she was assigned to the lowly female intern because her husband was only a sergeant. Her parting words as we aborted our tenuous relationship were something like, "I'm a difficult case, honey. It's not your fault. I hope someday you'll be another Joyce Brothers."

On the other hand, recently a woman client peeked into my office after leaving our initial session and commented, "You know, I'm glad you're a woman. I don't think I could be as honest with a man. I would be worrying too much about whether or not he approved of me."

These two comments reflect more than differences in personality, age, marital status, or some unknown variable. They reflect almost two decades of change in attitudes toward women in positions of authority. They also reflect a change in knowledge of women's roles in society. Individual women may not have made the personal changes that the women's movement has fostered, but they are aware of the potential for such changes and have a sense of where they fit in. Instead of seeing themselves as "difficult cases" that only a strong man can handle, they are more receptive to being independent of men and working with other women.

Women and Psychotherapy

There has probably been more said and written about the subject of women and psychotherapy in the last decade than in the 50 preceding years. During this period, the women's movement has had a strong influence on many areas of our lives, including new life styles, work situations, and relationships between the sexes. We have been examining and reexamining our stereotypes and their scientific or lack of scientific bases.

Observers of psychotherapy have made very little progress toward a better understanding of what is helpful in insuring that clients achieve mental health and self-actualization. Critics of the institution of psychotherapy, especially women (Fields, 1975; Tennov, 1975), have been vocal about this. The field of psychotherapy appears to have developed laterally more than it has linearly. There are now hundreds of systems of psychotherapy, each with its own vocabulary, process, and specific goals. Little common ground exists among the psychotherapies other than the assumption that the client, who is experiencing some sort of distress, enters into a verbal relationship with an expert, who through use of specified techniques based on a particular theory of personality, facilitates growth toward remediation and well-being.

What we do know from empirical research about the ingredients of good therapy is limited and often elusive. We know that, in general, clients report they feel better after therapy than they did before, no matter what type of therapy they have received (Aronoff & Lesse, 1976). Women report more satisfaction with therapy than men (Orlinsky & Howard, 1976), but we do not know if their reports of satisfaction correlate with behavioral criteria of improvement. We know that therapy cannot be completely value free, and we suppose that clients are often seen as improved because they become more like their therapists (Welkowitz, Cohen, & Ortmeyer, 1967). We have evidence that it is the therapist more than the therapeutic technique that may make the difference in whether or not a client improves (Dent, 1978), and we know, therefore, that the therapist's personal traits, values, attitudes, and impressions of the client have a major impact on the client and the course of therapy (Abramowitz & Dokecki, 1977).

The influence of therapist variables has only recently been recognized. The empirical basis for evaluating the benefits of psychotherapy remains shaky, even though researchers have for many years been painstakingly trying to isolate the components that make for good psychotherapy outcome. The variables involved in therapy are enormously complex, and researchers have examined effects of therapist, process, and client dimensions, alone and in combination with one another (Strupp & Luborsky, 1962). However, the ethics of dealing with human beings in need, controlling pertinent variables, isolating therapy segments from their total context, and so forth have understandably restricted the extent of knowledge that empirical research has been able to provide (Bergin & Strupp, 1972).

Sex Bias in Psychotherapy

From this limited research base, feminists have attempted to examine sex bias in psychotherapy. As a variable superimposed on those applicable to psychotherapy in general, sex bias presents almost formidable problems to the researcher. After all, bias, by definition, implies a lack of awareness of one's actual behavior. Deception therefore becomes necessary in most experimental research designs to avoid any artificial sensitization of subjects to sex role bias that does not reflect the typical behavior of therapists in the field.

In spite of these difficulties, a need arose to validate empirically the gut feelings of feminists that biases were rampant in therapy. The clinical experiences of feminist therapists and clients convinced them that sex bias and sex role stereotyping were very real and not at all rare (APA, 1975). Thus, an era emerged of investigation of therapist, client, and process variables related to sex roles. We started the decade by examining relevant demographic statistics. Several researchers (Chester, 1971; Gove & Tudor, 1973) alerted us to the fact that therapists are mostly male, whereas their clients are mostly female, and that the longest treatment relationships are most likely to be between attractive young male therapists and attractive young female clients. Next we learned that diagnostic labels vary by sex; women are deemed depressed, hysterical, anxiety neurotics, and phobic, whereas men are deemed alcoholic, organic, and antisocial (Gove & Tudor, 1973; Howard & Howard, 1974).

Reeling with this information, we invaded the mechanics of the therapist-patient relationship. Very few main effects indicative of bias were found, however. Sex of the therapist, for example, has not proven to be an important variable in the majority of published studies that investigated sex role bias toward clients. The impact of the most often cited study that did find a sex of therapist effect (Haan & Livson, 1973) was softened when Werner and Block (1975) reanalyzed the data using a more appropriate error term and found no differences. However, the original Haan and Livson study is still being cited today, perhaps because the need to validate personal experience that sex bias in psychotherapy exists is so strong that researchers feel almost compelled to demonstrate it empirically. Even feminist researchers, however, fail to find the effect they seek (Billingsley, 1977; Gomes & Abramowitz, 1976; Kaschak, 1978). The inability to validate one's personal experiences is frustrating.

In an article in the *American Psychologist*, Stricker (1977) sharply criticized the research on sex bias on a number of methodological grounds. Although he insists that empirical studies be the final determinant of whether bias occurs, his own need to proceed without such empirical evidence surfaces later when he chastizes the Task Force on Sex Bias and Sex Role Stereotyping (APA, 1975) for bothering to survey the obvious by asking women psychologists for examples of sexist practices. We certainly would prefer not to have to research what we consider obvious, but many of our colleagues will not believe our experiences unless we are able to present data to validate them. All research is colored by the biases of the investigator and as long as a certain segment of the profession believes that sex bias does not exist, we will have to demonstrate what we, with feminist biased eyes and ears, know to be true. I am not particularly worried about a Rosenthal (1966) effect in feminist research, as I am fully confident that our detractors are actively counterbalancing it with their own equal and opposite experimenter biases. Feminist research originally emerged to challenge a male bias that has existed for many years.

To return to our failure to find sex of therapist as a significant variable, however, our insights, clinical experiences, and surveys of women therapists (APA, 1975; Sherman, Koufacos, & Kenworthy, 1978) are being supported empirically, not through main effects, but through higher-order interactions. We are where the more generic psychotherapy research was about 20 years ago. We are finding that only by taking into account the interaction of many relevant variables affecting psychotherapy will we find the effects of sex bias. Thus, for example, Orlinsky and Howard (1976) found the relationship of therapist sex to the therapy experiences of women depended on factors such as age, marital status, and independence of the woman client. Although the dependent variable in this study was not a behavioral indicator from a therapy session but a report by the client after termination, this finding nevertheless is representative of where we are in answering such questions as "should women clients see male therapists?"

At the beginning of the decade, Phyllis Chesler (1972) concluded that the answer to this question was no. Today, if we believe clients' retrospective reports, there are more likely to be two answers: (a) "no" for young single women uncertain as to their direction in life, or in their relationships with men, or both; and (b) "yes" if the client is older, or married. We do not, however, know what other factors, yet to be studied, may also have a bearing on the answer.

In general, we do not have enough empirical support from well-designed and executed studies to state relationships between psychotherapy and sex bias or sex role stereotyping with confidence. Because our methodology is restricted, we may never be able to "prove" that certain attributes relevant to sex bias are prominent among therapists. We can point to such attributes in individual cases, however, and we can prepare clinicians for their vulnerability to sexist behavior. Sherman, Koufacos, and Kenworthy (1978) point out from their survey regarding the practices and knowledge about women clients of Wisconsin therapists that there may be less bias than misinformation about women's problems.

There is a bright side to the status of our knowledge about women in therapy, however. For while some feminists have invested their energies in demonstrating empirically that women have suffered, others have approached the issues from more applied perspectives. There is much that we can use now as a result of the theoretical and applied efforts of feminist practitioners in psychotherapy during the last decade.

Feminist Influences in Assessments

With the rise of the new feminist movement, some women rejected the psychological professions entirely and took advantage of consciousness-raising groups, finding that they could help each other where traditional psychological sources of help had failed. This was in the context of the development of other self-help techniques that enabled women to learn about their bodies, pregnancy, and childbirth. Women also shared their expertise and compassion with each other in crisis situations, such as rape or abortion counseling. Rape centers were established by radical feminists who were not professionals. Feminists in the helping professions were often involved, and it was in this atmosphere of working with women who rejected professional health care that women in psychology and psychiatry began to look at how their own professions were contributing to this widespread dissatisfaction.

With the birth of the Association for Women in Psychology in 1968, presentations on the psychology of women began to surface at APA conventions and in the feminist literature. Naomi Weisstein (1970) attacked the misguided wisdom on which clinical stereotypes were based, and Phyllis Chesler's *Women and Madness* (1972) became an impetus for clinical researchers to examine assessment and treatment issues. Julia Sherman (1971) and others reviewed studies that refuted psychoanalytic concepts used to reify penis envy, moral inferiority of women, and "inner space."

In the area of sexual functioning, Masters and Johnson (1966) reported that women had multiple orgasms. The physiological response to sexual arousal was comparable between men and women, with the clitoris being the major if not the sole source of orgasms in women. These discoveries led to a tremendous amount of debate and discussion of the nature of female sexuality. The psychoanalytic insistence that orgasms experienced during sexual intercourse were superior to those felt through clitoral stimulation was simply physiologically incorrect. Thus the analogous insistence that passivity is a biologically determined trait for sexually mature women was likewise refuted.

Meanwhile, other feminists were challenging the assessment measures used to equate nonconformity with pathology in the female. Thus counseling psychologists became concerned that the Strong Vocational Inventory, with its pink and blue forms for female and male, was prejudiced by having three times as many scorable occupations for males as for females. It was noted that many counselors were giving the male forms to females when they expressed an interest in a more "masculine" occupation. The Campbell-Strong Revision (Campbell, 1974) eliminated the male-female dichotomy and provided norms that included women. Intelligence tests also were scrutinized for items slanted toward males. The new revision of the WISC (Wechsler, 1974) includes an arithmetic problem involving the counting of hair ribbons.

The Dictionary of Occupational Titles became suspect when feminist researchers discovered that occupations were rated with higher status if they were traditionally male rather than traditionally female. Thus a dog trainer was considered to have more skill dealing with persons, data, and concepts than was a kindergarten teacher (Briggs, 1971). In the new revision, titles of occupations have become nonsexist. Thus the former mailman is now a postal worker, and the stewardess is a flight attendant, but the ratings have not yet been changed to reflect more accurately the status of the skills involved (Witt & Nahenny, 1975).

When we move into the area of projective testing and evaluation of personality, we approach even more sensitive issues. A study that reanalyzed hundreds of assessment reports of adolescents discovered that descriptors of female clients did not differentiate women from each other, but merely served to stereotype women as a class regardless of their personality characteristics. Thus when a report described a woman as emotional, it did nothing to aid in evaluation other than to indicate that the person described was probably female (Haller, 1975). Some Rorschach interpreters were distressed when it was discovered in the early seventies that the symmetrical figures on Card III were producing new norms. Clients were increasingly reporting one figure as female and the other as male. One male psychiatrist even suggested that this reflected sexual identity confusion caused by unisex dressing in our culture. Regardless of the interpretation given, however, there was at least the demonstration that perceptions of women were indeed changing.

Feminist Treatment Alternatives

It is in the area of providing direct psychotherapeutic services that the most dramatic progress has occurred. In the area of rape, for example, the last several years have seen the protest against the identification of rape victims as seducers and the recognition of the rape trauma syndrome to understand the dynamics of the victim and to work with her on reintegrating her life after the assault. Burgess and Holstrum (1973) reported on the sequence of shock, disorganization of everyday life, and eventual reintegration of the rape victim. The shock is less that of being sexually violated than the threat of death or the experience of loss of control over one's body. Since then, we have seen the development of support systems, family counseling, and follow-up services for rape victims, as well as direct emergency aid for the victims. The updating of archaic corroboration rules of evidence, and the differentiation of degrees of rape (so that victims and juries do not feel that a conviction means the death sentence in all cases) were partly a response to the rape crisis center movement.

Another spin-off was concern about family violence, where feminist psychologists had much input on theoretical and practical application. Factors such as poverty, low self-esteem, stigma, and so forth, countered the victim-precipitation explanation for the low incidence of reporting. Victims had little free choice to leave their situations due to economic and psychological bondage to their assailants. Needs of battered wives thus emerged as an area of psychological attention, and we are seeing some feminist analyses of the situation that do not blame the victim (Walker, 1978).

With regard to abortion, the last decade has seen the legalization of the procedure, changing the counseling process into a more personal decision rather than one based on ability to find and risk the dangers involved. This topic is still fraught with great emotion and controversy on moral grounds. Now, however, at least there is access to a variety of alternatives for the women who have the economic means and good fortune to live in a community that does not try to circumvent the law by enacting local statutes requiring the reading of propaganda including pictures of aborted fetuses.

We are also seeing some changes in the concepts of disorders that are frequently diagnosed for females. For example, many women were laughingly passed off as hysterical personalities because they were flamboyant in dress and manner, constantly demanding attention, seductively and often desperately seeking approval of men, and demeaning of other women. Such a woman was usually termed manipulative and considered to have a style of life that was difficult to change in therapy, because her manipulations usually included her male therapist. Now hysterical personality disorders are being understood as exaggerations of the traditional feminine sex role, an overconditioned reaction in vulnerable women to their dependency on males for their self-esteem. This "disorder" turns out to be something they acquired in the normal process of being rewarded for cute dressing and acting coyly toward their fathers and of being fawned on by adults for performing and catering to their superficial needs (Wolowitz, 1972). As adults, these women have continued to manifest these traits past their usefulness and have leaned on approval of others, particularly males, as their sole source of self-esteem. Traditional therapies deal with insight into the inability of the manipulations to work and the substituting of less dramatic means to gain approval. The feminist perspective emphasizes the development of an independent self-identity and self-determination, so that the need for approval diminishes.

The area of depression in women has also seen strong feminist influence as a result of Pauline Bart's (1972) work on "the empty nest syndrome." Women had been socialized to become "supermoms" who depended entirely on this role for a sense of usefulness. Previously we had not paid much attention to the meaninglessness of the role of women who completed their childrearing tasks by the age of 40 and who were not prepared for any other role to occupy their next 40 years. Depression has also been associated with a mourning for the lives women have not permitted themselves to pursue and their sense of helplessness in determining the course of their current lives (Beck & Greenberg, 1974). The contribution of role conflicts to postpartum and involutional depressions has also been examined (Melges, 1972).

Feminists have become involved in a closer look at phobias in women. We are just beginning to discover the extent of inhibiting fears that keep women housebound and dependent. Most agoraphobics are women, and the great majority are married (Fodor, 1974). Socialization of dependence in women fosters development of phobic reactions. In fact, assertive training has surfaced as a technique applied so predominantly to women that books and workshops on assertive training for women are requested by men.

Backlash, Regression, and Apathy

Not all women, however, are reaping the benefits of the procedures that can help them to counteract the years of socialization that convinced them they had no right to put their own needs on a level with that of the rest of the family. Many women do not yet believe they should have this right. In a letter to the editor of the *Tuscaloosa News,* a woman wrote explaining her objection to the ERA and ended with the statement, "I have no desire to be equal to anyone, especially a man."

For all the progress that has been made in working with women in therapy in the last decade, there are also discouraging aspects to the story. Rapid advances always leave some casualties behind. As Bardwick and Douvan (1972) noted, one way to deal with an expected change with which you are not yet ready to cope is to deny the need for adoption of new behaviors by a reactionary exaggeration of the necessity and desirability of the outmoded roles. Thus in the seventies we have not only contended with the exciting new possibilities and options for women, but we must also deal with a flight to exaggerated, stereotyped feminine roles as prescribed by Marabel Morgan's *The Total Woman* (1975) or Andelin's *Fascinating Womanhood* (1974).

These superfeminine women sincerely believe that the new roles are destructive for them and others, and they hear the women's movement telling them that they have wasted their lives. A therapist cannot tell a 50-year-old housewife that she has lived her life in vain, that it was not necessary to make all those sacrifices, or that her children should not be expected to repay her for them. Her self-esteem is at stake. Holding on to the last glorious remnants of the past era is one way to survive a confusing transition period. In her *Playboy* (Kelly, 1978) interview, Anita Bryant, a friend of Marabel Morgan, told how frightened she was when she realized that she was under great stress and needed psychological help. She finally went to a religious retreat after having rejected the possibility of being helped by a traditional psychiatrist.

So fear of the power and influence of the therapist over the client is not restricted to feminists wanting to be free of stereotypes, but extends also to antifeminists who fear the prospect of change and its responsibilities. In fact, keeping therapists objective and ethical has been a prime goal of feminists in the psychotherapeutic professions.

The Task Force on Sex Bias commissioned by the American Psychological Association (APA, 1975) collected data from women psychologists in 1974 and derived a set of guidelines for therapy with women (APA, 1978). Division 17 of the APA (1978) has just endorsed a set of principles for counseling women. So identification of the problem areas has been accomplished; but getting therapists to abide by these guidelines will be an enormous task. No one identifies him or herself as sexist. It is very difficult to examine one's own prejudices. It takes openness, sensitivity, and dedication to recognize one's flaws, to learn from them, and thus to modify one's behavior. In a survey Jean Holroyd and I conducted on erotic practices of licensed psychologists (Holroyd & Brodsky, 1977), 5.6% (1 in 20) of the males and .6% (1 in 200) of the females admitted to having sexual intercourse with their opposite-sex clients. The general consensus of those who engaged in such practices was that the incident was destructive to either client, therapist, or both, but most of those who engaged in the activity were repeaters.

This study at least provided some data on the prevalence of a blatantly unethical act after a decade of feminist concern and attention to the practice. The victory, however, was only one battle in the war. The reactions to the study included, "Oh, is that all, I thought the rate would be much higher." *Playboy* magazine treated it with a comment under *Sex News* (1978) in a piece entitled "Kiss my Couch." They noted that, "It is as hard to find a good therapist these days as it is to find a good masseuse."

Like violence on TV, there is the danger that the public and profession will become immune to the reports of sex in the therapy hour. When the news no longer is hot, who will continue to monitor the behavior? Interest in rape victims has already passed its prime. Rape centers are struggling for financial support which is now being diverted to newly exposed abuses of children and battered wives and, most recently, the elderly. We will need steady monitoring to assure reasonable long-term attention to issues that present mental health delivery problems past their hour in the spotlight.

An Encouraging Word

In concluding, I think we can feel encouraged by the distance we have traveled in the last decade. Certainly there are still incidents of gross sexism and ignorance of women's unique problems, and large segments of the therapist population are unwilling to admit they may have any biases, much less be educated on how to remediate them. It only seems that we are losing ground every time we see a throwback to the rampant sexism of the fifties and sixties. To appreciate our progress one has to revisit some old issues of our psychotherapy journals. In a 1967 issue on the sexual revolution (*Voices,* 1967), under the title of "Women and Other Revolutionaries" (O'Donovan, 1967), an author shares with the reader his insights about the women's movement.

> Having obtained many rights, they are dissatisfied with not having more. . . . Indeed there are definite advantages to their present status. There is also some biological evidence supporting their present status. They have not been trained for equal status and responsibility. They seem naturally adapted to their less free, less responsible, more serving role. They are in danger of losing what makes them unique and lovable if they gain equal status.

On the preceding page of this issue is a cartoon of a female client lying nude on the office couch, while the therapist at the open door says to a colleague, "I tell you Fred, it's a shame to cure her." I think our professional journals have improved, even though we may still find much covert sexism. I do not have the fantasy that sexism can be eliminated entirely, but I do feel that by the next decade today's seemingly more subtle sexist publications and offhand comments will seem just as blatant to everyone as the 1967 issue of *Voices* seems today.

REFERENCES

ABRAMOWITZ, C. V., & DOKECKI, P. R. The politics of clinical judgment: Early empirical returns. *Psychological Bulletin,* 1977, *84,* 460–476.
American Psychological Association. Report of the Task Force on Sex Bias and Sex-Role Stereotyping in Psychotherapeutic Practice. *American Psychologist,* 1975, *30,* 1169–1175.
American Psychological Association. Task Force on Sex Bias and Sex Role Stereotyping in

Psychotherapeutic Practice. Guidelines for therapy with women. *American Psychologist,* 1978, *33,* 1122–1123.

American Psychological Association Division 17 Ad Hoc Committee on Women. Principles concerning the counseling and therapy of women. Paper presented at Annual Meeting of the American Psychological Association, Toronto, Canada, 1978.

ANDELIN, H. B. *Fascinating womanhood.* New York: Bantam Books, 1974.

ARONOFF, M. S., & LESSE, S. Principles of psychotherapy. In B. B. Wolman (Ed.), *The therapist handbook: Treatment methods of mental disorders.* New York: Van Nostrand Reinhold, 1976.

BARDWICK, J. M., & DOUVAN, E. Ambivalence: The socialization of women. In J. M. Bardwick (Ed.), *Readings on the psychology of women.* New York: Harper & Row, 1972.

BART, P. Depression in middle aged women. In J. M. Bardwick (Ed.), *Readings on the psychology of women.* New York: Harper & Row, 1972.

BECK, A. T., & GREENBERG, R. L. Cognitive therapy with depressed women. In V. Franks & V. Burtle (Eds.), *Women in therapy.* New York: Brunner/Mazel, 1974.

BERGIN, A. E., & STRUPP, H. H. New directions in psychotherapy research: A summary statement. *Changing frontiers in the science of psychotherapy.* Chicago, Ill.: Aldine/Atherton, 1972.

BILLINGSLEY, D. Sex bias in psychotherapy: An examination of the effects of client sex, client pathology, and therapist sex on treatment planning. *Journal of Consulting and Clinical Psychology,* 1977, *45,* 250–256.

BRIGGS, N. Prejudice: Being down on something you are not up on. The Forum: (Report No. 2) Wisconsin Psychiatric Institute, University of Wisconsin, Madison, Wisc., 1971.

BURGESS, A., & HOLMSTROM, L. Rape trauma syndrome. *American Journal of Psychiatry,* 1973, *131,* 981–986.

CAMPBELL, D. P. *Manual for the Strong-Campbell Interest Inventory.* Palo Alto, Calif.: Stanford University Press, 1974.

CHESLER, P. Patient and patriarch: Women in the psychotherapeutic relationship. In V. Gornick & B. K. Moran (Eds.), *Women in sexist society.* New York: Basic Books, 1971.

CHESLER, P. *Women and madness.* New York: Doubleday, 1972.

DENT, J. K. *Exploring the psycho-social therapies through the personalities of effective therapists.* Rockville, Md: U.S. Department of Health, Education and Welfare, 1978.

FIELDS, R. M. *Psychotherapy: The sexist machine.* Pittsburgh: Know, 1975.

FODOR, I. G. The phobic syndrome in women: Implications for treatment. In V. Franks & V. Burtle (Eds.), *Women in therapy.* New York: Brunner/Mazel, 1974.

GOMES, B., & ABRAMOWITZ, S. I. Sex-related patient and therapist effects on clinical judgment. *Sex Roles: A Journal of Research,* 1976, *2,* 1–13.

GOVE, W. R., & TUDOR, J. F. Adult sex roles and mental illness. *American Journal of Sociology,* 1973, *78,* 50–73.

HAAN, N., & LIVSON, N. Sex differences in the eyes of expert personality assessors: Blind spots? *Journal of Personality Assessment,* 1973, *37,* 486–492.

HALLER, D. L. Attribution of sex-stereotypic descriptors to adolescent females in psychotherapy. Unpublished Master's thesis, The University of Alabama, 1975.

HOLROYD, J. C., & BRODSKY, A. M. Psychologists' attitudes and practices regarding erotic and non-erotic physical contact with patients. *American Psychologist,* 1977, *32,* 843–849.

HOWARD, E. M., & HOWARD, J. L. Women in institutions: Treatment in prisons and mental hospitals. In V. Franks & V. Burtle (Eds.), *Women in therapy.* New York: Brunner/Mazel, 1974.

KASCHAK, E. Therapist and client: Two views of the process and outcome of psychotherapy. *Professional Psychology,* 1978, *9,* 271–277.

KELLY, K. Playboy interview: Anita Bryant. *Playboy Magazine,* 1978, *25,* 240–241.

MASTERS, W. H., & JOHNSON, V. E. *Human sexual response.* Boston: Little, Brown, 1966.

MELGES, F. Postpartum psychiatric syndromes. In J. M. Bardwick (Ed.), *Readings on the psychology of women.* New York: Harper & Row, 1972.

MORGAN, M. *The total woman.* New York: Simon & Schuster, 1975.

O'DONOVAN, D. Women and other revolutionaries. *Voices,* 1967, *3,* 38–39.

ORLINSKY, D. E., & HOWARD K. I. The effects of sex of therapist on the therapeutic experiences of women. *Psychotherapy: Theory, Research and Practice,* 1976, *13,* 82–88.

ROSENTHAL, R. *Experimenter effects in behavior research.* New York: Appleton-Century-Crofts, 1966.

Sex news. *Playboy Magazine,* 1978, *25,* 264.

SHERMAN, J. A. *On the psychology of women.* Springfield, Ill.: C. C. Thomas, 1971.

SHERMAN, J. A., KOUFACOS, C., & KENWORTHY, J. A. Therapists: Their attitudes and information about women. *Psychology of Women Quarterly*, 1978, *2*, 299–313.

STRICKER, G. Implications of research for psychotherapeutic treatment of women. *American Psychologist*, 1977, *32*, 14–22.

STRUPP, H. H., & LUBORSKY, L. *Research in psychotherapy (Vol. 2)*. Washington, D.C.: American Psychological Association, 1962.

TENNOV, D. *Psychotherapy: The hazardous cure*. New York: Abelard-Schuman, 1975.

Voices: The Art and Science of Psychotherapy, 1967, *3* (Special issue, *The Sexual Revolution*).

WALKER, L. E. Treatment alternatives for battered women. In J. R. Chapman & M. Gates (Eds.), *The victimization of women*. Beverly Hills, Calif.: Sage, 1978.

WECHSLER, D. *Manual for Wechsler Intelligence Scale for Children (Rev.)* New York: Psychological Corporation, 1974.

WEISSTEIN, N. Kuche, Kirche as scientific law: Psychology constructs the female. In R. Morgan (Ed.), *Sisterhood is powerful*. New York: Vintage Books, 1970.

WELKOWITZ, J., COHEN, J., & ORTMEYER, D. Value system similarity: Investigation of patient-therapist dyads. *Journal of Consulting Psychology*, 1967, *31*, 48–55.

WERNER, P., & BLOCK, J. Sex differences in the eyes of expert personality assessors: Unwarranted conclusions. *Journal of Personality Assessment*, 1975, *39*, 110–113.

WITT, M., & NAHENNY, P. K. *Womens work-up from 878. Report on D.O.T. research project*. Madison, Wisc.: University of Wisconsin Extension Resources, 1975.

WOLOWITZ, H. M. Hysterical character and feminine identity. In J. M. Bardwick (Ed.), *Readings on the psychology of women*. New York: Harper & Row, 1972.

PART XI
Middle Age and Aging

The population of the United States is growing older as people live longer and fewer babies are born. This shift in numbers, together with the higher educational levels of those moving toward middle age and beyond, promises an increase in power for older people and changes in attitudes toward them as well. Such cultural changes have important implications for women for at least two reasons: since women live longer than men do and have a lower mortality rate at all ages, the ratio of women to men increases significantly as a function of age; and women have traditionally suffered more than men from prejudice against people who are no longer young.

In a society that rewards youthful beauty and lifestyle, the perception of oneself as aging can be sobering. Physically, aging brings changes associated with a slowing of physical and mental processes, with diminished flexibility and muscle tone, with the appearance of lines and wrinkles. Psychologically, the experience is often associated with a motif of loss—loss of youth, loss of vigor, loss of children, and sometimes loss of job or spouse. In our society, cultural attitudes toward aging and older people have generally been negative, constructing an unattractive model for the middle and later years. By contrast, many who are middle-aged and older report feelings of buoyancy and freedom, greater financial security, and appreciation of mature values and attitudes. Many are glad to be relieved of the stormy pressures of their youthful years.

While people vary greatly in their adaptations to aging, our society has typically structured different meanings of aging for women and men. Women have been valued primarily for their sexual and reproductive functions, both expressed chiefly in the context of youth. Men are more likely to be rewarded for achievement and economic productivity, features of their maturity. A glance at any newsstand will confirm that the favored model of womanhood is the "girl," who above all is young and sexually attractive. Men, on the other hand, have greater permission to be seen as socially and sexually desirable into middle age and older.

While differential valuing of aging for men and women is a reflection of cultural attitudes and perceptions, there are also realities that discriminate between the experiences of their mature lives. Women who are socialized to build their lives and identities around the primary roles of wife and mother find these roles attenuated or lost as children leave home and husbands die or go elsewhere. This role loss occurs earlier for women than it does for men, who typically occupy their major role of worker until they are well into their seventh decade or older. For such women, the diminution or loss of those roles that gave their lives meaning and purpose may lead to feelings of depression: loss of enthusiasm for life, apathy, boredom. On the brighter side, many women, especially those with interests beyond the walls of home, find this time of life, with its freedom from pregnancy and childrearing and the unending concern with the well-being of others, filled with challenge for the development of themselves and the identifying of new objectives.

In our society, characteristically valuing women first as sex objects and then as mothers, aging single women, presumably performing neither of these functions, have in the past been the subjects of negative stereotypes, such as the old maid, the embittered spinster. Scientists, too, have not been drawn to study them. The past few years, however, have seen changes in this sector of the social value system, as well as in the many others we have looked at. The numbers of women who are choosing to remain single or not to remarry after divorce are growing. With their increased numbers and visibility, their status becomes less deviant, and the stereotype becomes obsolete. Even so, empirical knowledge of such women is scattered and scarce. Particularly valuable, then, is the first study in this section, "A Study of Satisfactions and Stresses of Single Women in Midlife," by Sophie Loewenstein and her colleagues.

Using both spontaneous responses and semistructured interviews, the investigators probed such areas as relationships, sexuality, work, and health in the lives of sixty midlife single women, attempting to see how these were related to life satisfaction. The results suggest a robust denial of the stereotype of the unhappy spinster. Most of the women reported being well satisfied with their lives. Associated with life satisfaction were such variables as health, living arrangements, friends, and work. They named many advantages of being single: freedom, ability to pursue career goals, personal growth, and privacy. Some were less happy. Disadvantages named by them included lack of mate and children, financial problems, attitudes of society, and loneliness. While recognizing the need for further research on this understudied group, the authors conclude that some women in our society manage to lead a fulfilling life without the benefits of sex, marriage, or motherhood.

Since women live longer than men, and since most women tend to marry men who are a few years older than they are, married women in our society have a high probability of becoming widows as they grow older. Since loss of one's husband usually means loss of an important relationship, what resources does the widow turn to for help in meeting both her interpersonal emotional and instrumental needs? In "Intimacy in Widowhood," Carol Barrett explores those intimate relationships that may be available to widowed women. Though some friends may move away from the now unmarried woman, others, particularly those who are themselves unmarried, remain fast. Physical intimacy, even touching, is an unmet need for many. Daughters increase all types of interactions with their mothers, while sons increase only those involving the giving of tangible aid. Neighbors and fellow members of church or social organizations may provide some supportive interaction. Poignantly, not a few widows continue to relate to the deceased husband through illusions of his presence, talking to him, writing to him, even sleeping on his side of the bed. Some women meet their emotional needs through their relationship with God, while others make themselves the object of their nurturance and care. Barrett notes that the experiences of widows in meeting their intimacy needs reveals some untested assumptions in our theories and research. These include the assumptions that intimacy is possible only between living humans, with close age-mates, within a dyad, between two of the opposite sex. The research with widows shows that these assumptions have questionable validity, with important implications for research.

And what of the future? In "Women and Aging: A Futurist Perspective," Sharon McIrvin Abu-Laban projects what it will be like to be an older woman in the years between 2000 and 2025. Her analysis is based on the assumption that important contemporary trends in women's lives will continue. These include later marriage and childbearing, fewer children, increased incidence of divorce and living together without marriage, increased labor force participation, more sexual and reproductive freedom. If these trends continue, older women of the future may have greater access to the mechanisms of power, as well as increased access to emotional and support ties, than do their counterparts of today. The author, however, provides a cautionary caveat to this optimistic vision. An antifeminist neoconservatism is exemplified by an expansion of fundamentalist religious systems. Embedded in these are ideologies supporting the subordination of women and the elevation of patriarchy. Should this movement prove viable into the future, then our granddaughters, who will be the older women of the early twenty-first century, may find their position quite similar, with respect to power, prestige, and interpersonal issues, to that of older women in today's society.

Running through the literature on the meanings of middle age and aging for women are two themes. One we may identify metaphorically as "the closing of the gates," in Helene Deutsch's phrase; the other, in happier terms, as the opening of the gates. The first, carrying the conception that the most important part of life is over, is expressed in terms of loss—loss of youth with its beauty and grace, loss of fertility, loss of the mother role as children leave, and perhaps loss of the wife role when husband dies—and has been the more prevalent theme in both the research literature and the popular consciousness. But more recent data emerging in a new social climate call for a reevaluation of that conception. Middle age can be the beginning of a time of life when one is freer than ever before from the old exigencies of role and place, when time and opportunity become available for exploration of oneself and of one's relation to an expanded world, less bound than in earlier years by the necessity of putting others first and oneself second. Qualities that many women acquire in maturity, independence, self-confidence, and a sense of identity, enhance a woman's attractiveness to herself and to others, resulting in happier consequences for the second part of the passage through life.

37

A Study of Satisfactions and Stresses of Single Women in Midlife

Sophie Freud Loewenstein, Natalie Ebin Bloch, Jennifer Campion, Jane Sproule Epstein, Peggy Gale, and Maggie Salvatore

Sixty single women 35 to 65 years old, previously married or never married, were interviewed about the satisfactions and stresses of the single status. Respondents were categorized as having high, medium, or low life satisfaction. Life satisfaction was found to be significantly correlated to such factors as good health, not being lonely, living with a female housemate, having many casual friends, and being invested in work. Half the women mentioned having sexual needs, which were or were not fulfilled. The other half stated that they did not have sexual needs. These two groups did not differ in life satisfaction. Regrets about not having had children occurred in one-quarter of the childless women, without necessarily implying low life satisfaction. Only 15% of the entire sample had low life satisfaction, a percentage similar to that found in the general population.[1]

"Whenever one is unhappy, everyone assumes it's because you're alone. It just isn't so."
                                                                    —*Single woman in her late thirties*

Single midlife women have become an important segment in the changing American Landscape (Lipman-Blumen, 1976). Such women form a disparate group. They may be single by choice, having rejected marriage, opted for divorce, and / or avoided remarriage; or, like poor Sheila Levine (Parent, 1972), they may not have been able to find a mate or may have been abandoned by their husbands through death or divorce. However, in midlife such women face somewhat similar issues of economic, social, and emotional survival in a society that has traditionally been organized around family groups and in which women have learned to define themselves through their relationships with husband and children (Miller, 1976).

Although life satisfaction research in the last two decades has dramatically disrupted the stereotype of gay bachelors and disappointed, bitter spinsters (Campbell, 1975; Gove, 1972), our understanding of these women remains fragmented and uncertain. We continue to have conflicting literary images of the liberated successful single professional woman—delineated by Lynn Caine (1978), for example, or the beautiful strong teacher in *Spinster* (Ashton-Warner, 1959)—and the poignant picture of total isolation depicted in *The Lonely Passion of Judith Hearne* (Moore, 1955).

Systematic research studies of such women are quite limited. We find a few studies of previously married women, such as Lopata's study of widowhood (1973), Goode's study of divorced women (1956) and recent books by O'Brien (1973), Bequaert (1976), Adams (1976), and Stein (1976), which highlight the advantages of the single lifestyle but are based primarily on theoretical speculations, randomly chosen interviews, or much younger samples. Women who make life choices should do so with full knowledge of the stresses and advantages of alternatives to the traditional married state. Systematic research of the lives of single women is needed; our study is a modest step in this direction.

We have attempted to study the stresses and rewards in the lives of a sample of single women and the way these are related to life satisfaction. We address ourselves to unresolved questions in the psychology of women such as whether there are universally felt needs for sexual outlets, for child rearing, and for one major intimate relationship, and whether the fulfillment of such needs is necessarily related to a personally satisfactory life.

Study Design

For the purpose of this study, single women were defined as those who were never-married, widowed, divorced, or separated and *who defined themselves as single.*

The focus of interest was on women for whom the single lifestyle was more likely an ongoing rather than a transitional stage. Hence, we interviewed rarely studied midlife women, 35 to 65 years old.

Women who had lost a partner within the last year were excluded, as they might have been in a transitional crisis. Also excluded were women with dependent children under 18 living at home, since single parenting presents a different set of issues.

The research was undertaken by a faculty member (the senior author) and five graduate students (the coauthors). We gained access to various organizational units in the Boston community, consisting of two college communities (comprising 33 and 8 women, respectively); the clerical staff of a school system (6 women); the staff of a community service agency (5 women); a religious association (4 women); the clerical staff in a unit of a manufacturing company (2 women); the social service staff of a hospital (2 women). Once the cooperation of an organizational unit was obtained, all 73 women who could be identified as meeting the above critera were contacted. All but 13 women consented to be interviewed. We thus had a final sample of 60 women drawn from seven organizations. Although the sample is not random, it avoided the limitations of self-selection.

We began each interview with an open-ended question, which allowed for spontaneous responses regarding the satisfactions and stresses in the women's lives. It was followed by semi-structured interviews which lasted from one to two hours. The interviews focused on facts and feelings in the areas of relationships, sexuality, work, religion, health, help-seeking, and living arrangements, all of which were thought possibly to be associated with life satisfaction. We also explored subjects' regrets, hopes, fears, and wishes. The interviewers subsequently filled in a prepared schedule of questions for each respondent. Data were coded and frequency counts and chi squares were obtained with the aid of a computer program. In view of our central research question, the major dependent variable chosen was Life Satisfaction, which was correlated against all other independent variables in the study.

Description of the Sample

The sample consisted of 60 women: 38 never-married, 14 divorced or separated, and 8 widows. Fifty-eight women were White; 2 were Black. Twenty were in the decade 35 to 45, 14 were aged 46 to 55, and 26 women (almost half the sample) were between 56 and 65 years old.

We found a high level of educational and professional status among respondents, which was probably due to the inclusion of two college communities. However, the literature indicated that highly educated women are most apt to remain single or avoid remarriage (Lipman-Blumen, 1976, p. 71). Ten women held doctoral degrees, 19 master's degrees, and 14 bachelor's degrees; 13 had technical training and / or some college, and only 4 had a high school education or less. Almost two-thirds of the sample held professional or administative positions; the rest were in clerical or related jobs.

Religious affiliation of these women reflects approximately that of the general population of Boston, where this study took place: 54% Protestant, 34% Catholic, and 12% Jewish.

At the time of the study, 49 women (65%) rented their living quarters; the others owned their own home. More than half the respondents lived alone, and the rest were living in equal numbers with parents, other relatives (sisters, aunts, an adult son or daughter), or a female roommate.

Criteria for Assessment of Life Satisfaction

Specific responses to certain of the questions in the "feeling area," as well as general clinical impressions, were used to determine each women's level of life satisfaction. We rated each subject "high," "medium," or "low" on each of the following five criteria:

> 1. Verbal and nonverbal expression(s) of enjoyment or contentment with life
> 2. Expressions of hope or optimism
> 3. Lack of chronic anxiety or worry
> 4. Sense of control over life
> 5. No major regrets about life (High was "no major regrets," medium was "some regrets but none pervasive," low was "one or more intense regrets.")

Care was taken not to use independent variables to define life satisfaction. To determine the overall level of satisfaction for each woman, 4 or more highs were to indicate High Life Satisfaction (henceforth referred to in the text as HLS), 4 or more lows were to indicate Low Life Satisfaction (LLS), and other combinations were defined as Medium Life Satisfaction (MLS). Short profiles of one women in each category will illustrate our rating scheme.

A, a 57-year-old energetic youthful-looking widow is an example of a HLS woman. A's voice was animated, her demeanor cheerful. She mentioned with pleasure her recent promotion, confident that she could master the difficult tasks ahead. Her husband's death 10 years ago had been a severe blow, but she had recovered and was now able to enjoy the freedom that the single life-style offered her. She was glad that she had resisted pressures to remarry. She expressed some concern about the premature marriage of her daughter, but this concern did not overshadow her optimism. Life, with all its good and bad aspects, was rich and exciting and A was ready to meet its challenges.

B, a never-married 38-year-old nurse, was rated as having MLS. She told about a childhood of social isolation dominated by an emotionally troubled mother. She suffered from a severe depression in her late twenties, and the psychiatric help she received was like a rebirth for her, a first step into self-awareness and trust. She successfully overcame her severe obesity, started to enjoy life for the first time, and learned to reach out to people. B felt herself on the threshold of a new life and expressed optimism about the future. She was anxious, however, about the many recent transitions in her life—a new job, a new apartment—and wondered whether she could sustain all her gains. She regretted her wasted youth and hoped that she could make up for lost years, find a husband, and have children.

C, a never-married 44-year-old administrator, is an example of LLS. In a low and sad voice, she reported having been depressed since the death of her father three years ago. She was particularly disappointed not to have had children and wished she had the courage to adopt a child. She also lacked courage, she said, to change her secure job, although she experienced it as meaningless and monotonous. Life seemed empty and joyless to her.

Final decisions on the ratings of Life Satisfaction for each woman were made by the entire research group after discussion and comparison of each individual case.

Satisfaction and Stresses of the Single Status

Life Satisfaction was generally high among these largely well-educated single working women. While 85% (51 women) of these 60 women had High (29 women) or Medium (22 women) Life Satisfaction, only 15% (9 women) had Low Life Satisfaction.

Variables Associated with Life Satisfaction

The variables associated with Life Satisfaction in this study are listed in Table 1. Health provided the most striking association with Life Satisfaction. Health was divided into three categories—Good, Fair, and Poor—

Table 1   Levels of significance *(p)* between selected variables and
levels of life satisfaction using the chi-square test $(N = 60, df = 4)$

Variable[a]	Level of significance (p)[a]
Strong correlations	
Health	.001
Loneliness	.007
Living situation (alone or with others)	.034
Having many casual friends	.042
Subjective importance of work	.043
Perceived salary fairness	.053
Weaker correlations	
Perceived current financial security	*ns*
Status of job	*ns*
Home ownership	*ns*
Helpfulness of parents	*ns*
Educational level	*ns*
Satisfaction with hell-seeking experience	*ns*

[a] A significance of $p < .05$ or lower is considered to indicate a strong correlation.

depending on the number and severity of current health problems, the amount of time missed from work, and the extent to which chronic conditions affected a woman's daily functioning. An instance of Fair Health is a respondent who defines herself as "a very emotional and nervous person" whose health has been affected by stress at work. She feels unable to relax while working under the pressure of deadlines and this has resulted in a "nervous" stomach and diverticulitis. She uses tranquilizers daily and takes additional medication for hypertension. An example of Poor Health was found in a woman who suffered a disabling illness which severely impaired her freedom of activity. Of the entire group, 46 women enjoyed Good Health and only 3 women suffered from Poor Health. These 3 women also had LLS ratings. While Good Health did not guarantee HLS, it seems to have played a major positive role. Health was a major concern for some women who felt that they did not have "built-in assistance" in case of sickness. Eight women were preoccupied with their state of health, and one-third of the sample mentioned "good health" as one of their major three wishes.

Another important variable was Living Arrangements. The presence of a peer companion in the household was closely as sociated with HLS $(p < .03)$. Seven of the 8 women living with a housemate had HLS, and the remaining woman had MLS. Most of the women listed their housemates as one of their most intimate friends, with whom they shared joys, sorrows, and frustrations. For example, "The loss of my roommate would be a catastrophe for me." It is interesting that only 9 out of 60 women chose such a satisfactory living arrangement. Other living arrangements were randomly associated with satisfaction.

Some associations that one might expect did not occur. Anticipating that age would be a factor in Life Satisfaction, we divided the sample into 3 age groups—35–45 years; 46–55 years; and 56–65 years—and compared the life satisfactions between the age groups. We found that Age did not affect life satisfaction in this sample. $(p < .73)$

Life satisfaction was also unrelated to Religious Involvement, although 44% of women felt that religion was either a spiritual or social resource for themselves. Education was found to be only weakly related to Life Satisfaction ($p<.19$), with LLS occurring more rarely in the more highly educated group.

Surprisingly, Marital Status was statistically unrelated to Life Satisfaction ($p<.55$), although there was a slight trend of the divorced group being less satisfied with life than the other two groups. About one-third of divorced women had LLS, while this was true for only approximately 10% of the other two groups.

Campbell (1975) found that single women over 30 tend to be relatively content with their lives. "Perhaps this is because the longer a woman remains single, the more she likes it, or at least adjusts to it; and because she is more likely to hold a satisfying, better-paying job, and to have a well-defined career" (p. 38). This finding is true for the women in our sample as well. However, we did not see the same marked dissatisfaction among divorced women that Campbell (1975, p. 43) noted. Among the 14 divorced women, 5 had HLS, 5 had MLS, and 4 had LLS. Among the 5 divorced women with HLS, 3 were highly educated (2 Ph.D.s and 1 M.A.), which protected them from the poverty usually associated with a divorce status. A fourth woman adopted a lesbian lifestyle after her divorce, while the fifth woman, a clerical worker, simply preferred the single lifestyle. "I can come and go as I please; I don't have to answer to anyone."

Campbell (1975) found life satisfaction among widows quite high, and this was true for our study as well. Four widows had HLS, 3 had MLS, and only 1 widow had LLS. The fact that marital status did not make for major differences in LS agrees with Bequaert's contention (1976) that there are more similarities than differences between women who have been divorced, widowed, and or never-married.

Loneliness, Friendship, and Work Situations had strong associations with Life Satisfaction, and will be discussed later.

Advantages of the Single State

In response to our first open-ended question about the single status, women mentioned a range of advantages that could be grouped into one or several of four categories.

The first category included freedom, independence, pride, and self-respect, mentioned by 43 women. Some comments were "Whatever I've achieved I've done all by myself, and I feel proud of that." "I live in the best of all worlds. I enjoy my nieces and nephews without the burden of motherhood. I can spend money as I please, eat what I want and when I want it. I love my independence and freedom to come and go as I choose."

The second category was the pursuit of career goals, mentioned by 15 women. "I wouldn't have been free to develop myself in so many different directions. I might have compromised, since I like to please others. I wouldn't have been so productive."

The third area was personal growth and friendship, which was mentioned by 11 respondents: "I'm a social creature, perhaps more social because I live alone."

Fourth, 6 women cited privacy as an advantage of single life: "I tend to be a private person. I don't talk about myself or my feelings."

Among the 60 women, 52 saw some positive features in their single status, while only 8 saw no advantages.

Disadvantages of the Single State

Many disadvantages difficult to categorize were also mentioned. They included no mate or children, financial problems, lack of companionship or sexual partner, sole care of family members, making decisions alone, maintenance problems, attitudes of society, and loneliness ("I could drop dead tomorrow and no one would care"). Two women mentioned the difficulty for single women in making certain major financial institutional investments, such as buying a home. Three women expressed fear of the future in terms of health, finances, and loneliness: "There is no one to take care of me if I lose my job." Several women expressed with some bitterness that they are in a stigmatized position in society and even in their own family group: "People think being single is a misfortune." Some women mentioned the pressure toward marriage, especially earlier in life, and the subtle or overt questions they were asked about being single. One woman felt bitter about her family's expectation that she would take the burden of caring for her aging sick parents. Another described her pain over her parents' disappointment at not having grandchildren. Unease about being at parties in the company of couples, or being unwelcome at such parties, was mentioned repeatedly. "It's a completely different social life," said one separated woman, "I've been dropped for the most part by my married friends."

Some never-married women deplored the fact that single women cannot move freely in society: "You can't walk into a bar and have a drink." "I'd like to go to a disco or take a walk at night. Men still symbolize protection."

Forty-seven women mentioned disadvantages, while 13 women had found none. "Life is blissful" said one of them.

Why Women Do Not Marry

Nine of the 38 never-married women indicated that they were single by choice: "I've never been interested in getting married. I don't feel myself to be a social person and am too impatient for motherhood . . . I have no regrets."

Five women ascribed their single status to the break-up of one or several unhappy love affairs, which seemed sad at the time, but were fortunate from their current perspective: "At 18 I thought I wanted to get married and almost died of a broken heart. Now I realize it would've been a dreadful mistake. I would have chosen the wrong man, since I was immature, and it would have hampered my career development."

Twenty-one women, more than half of the never-married group, indicated that they had drifted into the single state through circumstances that they still considered unfortunate. "I just didn't find the right person, with similar high standards and values, and was not willing to settle for second-

best." "I was obese and isolated as an adolescent and never dated or participated in social activities."

The other 3 women stayed single because they thought marriage and
career were incompatible.

The Wish to Marry or Remarry

Both formerly married and never-married women mentioned the difficulty of finding a suitable mate: "I would remarry if a really nice guy came
along." "If you find a good man, bring him over." "Men my age seek younger
women."

Several women, especially in the younger age group, either counted
on, or hoped to marry or remarry. Others felt that marriage would not
necessarily improve their lives: "I'd marry if it would be a richer, fuller life,
but I'm not sure it would be." "I'm now more ready for marriage, but have
less need for it."

We examined both "major regrets" and "wishes" to see if disappointment about not being married or the hope of still finding a suitable mate
were widespread and of high priority among these single women. Seventeen never-married and 11 ever-married women (half of each group)
expressed a wish for a mate or companion of either sex, with or without
marriage. The yearning for steady companionship was widespread in spite
of the HLS of the majority of the women. We are reminded of Bernard's
interpretation (1972, pp. 49–51) that single women do not consider themselves as happy as married women, since marriage is the preferred social
status, even though they give otherwise good evidence of leading full and
contented lives.

Emotional Relationships of Single Women

We attempted to identify the most significant emotional attachment in these
women's lives by asking whose loss would cause them greatest upheaval and
distress. Many women mentioned more than one person: 19 identified female
friends, 16 said "family members," 14 named sisters, 14 named children,
13 said "mother"; others mentioned brothers, male friends, housemates,
an ex-husband and a fiancé. One mentioned her dog. Three women named
no specific figure. Unexpectedly, these 3 women had HLS. D illustrates the
style of the latter women.

> D was in her mid-forties, a never-married professional woman who described
> her life as "blissful." She was an ebullient person who had an active life involv-
> ing many physical activities and social contacts. She couldn't imagine how any-
> one could possibly be lonely. Her doorbell and phone were always ringing; her
> house was open; she adored people, but did not need the intimate confidences
> or daily support that others do. She could not mention any one person to
> whom she was intimately attached. She had many opportunities for marriage,
> but did not like to pursue them since she did not like to gamble. Her father
> had taught her to be competent and self-sufficient.

Although many people would not appreciate this woman's life style, it was satisfactory to her.

Thus, the absence of Intimate Friendships did not preclude HLS, nor did the presence of major relationships assure HLS. Two LLS women, who suffered from ill health, chronic worry, and family difficulties described having many intimate friends. By contrast, HLS did relate to the presence of many casual friends in these 60 women's lives. Of women with HLS, 73% had many casual friends, while 75% of those with LLS had few casual friends ($p<.04$).

Family Relationships did not seem to contribute greatly to Life Satisfaction. Neither the emotional importance, helpfulness, nor geographic distance of parents, siblings, or children were related to Life Satisfaction. It did appear that responsibility for sick elderly parents affected Life Satisfaction, quite dramatically in some instances. One woman was tied to the home by a senile, incontinent mother, her sister caring for the parent during the day while she worked. Her mother did not tolerate visitors, and the woman had no opportunities to engage in recreation outside the home. Her anxiety, concern, and anger about her mother pervaded the interview. Another woman felt financially strapped by housekeeper fees and was socially restricted by her mother's physical demands. Such responsibilities exacted a heavy toll from these women's lives.

Is Motherhood Necessary?

Since a recent movement has sought to make "nonmotherhood" an acceptable choice for women (Rollin, 1972), it was of special interest to see how women felt about their childlessness in middle life.

Thirteen out of 40 childless women regretted the absence of children in their lives. This relatively small number may be reassuring to those who plan childlessness. It must be added, however, that the lack of children was a major and intense regret for a few women who had not chosen the single lifestyle, throwing a shadow of disappointment over their lives.

Twenty-four of the never-married women had sought and found a way of having relationships with children, such as nieces, nephews, godchildren, and the children of friends. For some women these relationships were of great importance, while for others they were only peripheral. A number of our respondents were teachers who felt that their students met their needs for nurturing and contributing to the next generation.

Some social scientists have suggested that "generativity" (Erikson, 1959, p. 97) or "opportunity for nurturance" (Weiss, 1976, p. 23) are indispensable aspects of a mentally healthy, rewarding life. In this study 5 women experienced HLS without having made room for such relationships in their lives, and opportunity for nurturance was not statistically associated with HLS.

A Profile of Lonely Women

Loneliness was a problem for some women, and it was highly correlated with LLS, ($p<.0007$). Of the 14 lonely women, only 1 had HLS, while 5 had LLS.

The lives of these 14 women reveal a striking common denominator of loss and emotional deprivation. Eight were separated, divorced, or widowed—within the past five years after many years of marriage. They spoke of the enormous adjustment required to resume the single status: "One has to rebuild one's social life." "Loneliness? Yes and no. I've learned to live with it. I'm often glad to close the door on the world. I don't notice it on the average. But on holidays . . . Christmas morning is just like any other day. Here come the weekends and what do you do? Loneliness then."

Two women had experienced traumatic loss in childhood, and one never-married woman had recently lost a sibling and a close relative. Four of the 6 never-married lonely women were either burdened by caring for a disabled older relative or were over-involved with a demanding, possessive mother. A fifth never-married woman had recently broken a love relationship and currently had neither a major attachment figure nor any intimate friends.

Social life for 11 of the women was limited. Ten women lived alone, wishing for either marriage (7) or a female roommate (3). Chronic loneliness seems to be the most serious psychic danger that threatens single women.

"Sex and the Single Girl"

It is commonly believed that lack of sexual satisfaction leads to anxiety or frustration. The data did not confirm these expectations. All but 3 women were willing to candidly discuss their sexuality with us. We believe these findings to be valid for this sample of women.

Twenty-six women talked about experiencing sexual needs, deprivations, or longings, while 31 women said that they did not have such feelings. The 26 women who acknowledged sexual needs met them in various ways. Thirteen were heterosexually active, with 9 having intimate long-term relationships and 4 mentioning "casual lovers." One woman lived in a committed lesbian relationship; 5 met their needs through masturbation; 7 talked about sublimating their sexual needs through sports, poetry, music, nursing care, interesting conversations, and hugging friends or family.

Masturbation was generally not much practiced in this sample. Only 5 women in the total sample mentioned practicing masturbation, while others marked on inhibition in this area: "I am sorry I have never been able to enjoy masturbation."

Some of the 26 women with sexual needs expressed frustration and disappointment in regard to their sexual lives: "Sexual tension has been a strong area of stress at different times." Six women mentioned lack of a sexual partner as an important disadvantage of the single state.

The data for Presence of Sexual Needs for women of different marital status revealed a striking correlation between widowhood and lack of current sexual desires. ($p<.058$) Gebhard (1971) reports that the widows in the Kinsey sample "could figuratively take sex or leave it" (p. 99); he adds that "this attitude had no necessary relationship to orgasmic capacity: such a woman can have marital coitus with orgasm for years, be widowed and then live years of abstinence with little or no sexual frustration" (p. 99). These observations apply to the widows in this sample. Six out of 7 widows (1 unknown) stated a lack of current sexual need, and 5 of them mentioned high sexual satisfaction during marriage. One widow engaged initially in "meaningless affairs," but discontinued this when she could not recapture outside the intimacy of marriage her prior sexual satisfaction. Three widows felt that sex without an intimate relationship was unacceptable to them and that such relationships were difficult to find for women of their age.

Seven of 13 divorced women (1 unknown) stated that they had no sexual needs. Four of these reported unsatisfactory sexual relations during marriage with some permanent bitterness toward men and a concomitant disinterest in sex. Of 37 never-married women (1 was unknown) 18 said they had no sexual needs; 22 had never engaged in coitus: "I don't experience much sense of loss, maybe because I don't know what I'm missing." "The importance of sex is much overstated." Several women mentioned that sexual activity outside marriage was incompatible with their standards: "My moral values require repression of sexual needs—sex is almost irrelevant."

Neither the presence nor absence of sexual needs, nor the mode of current sexual fulfillment, were in any way related to Life Satisfaction. Among the 29 women with HLS, 14 felt the presence of sexual needs and 14 did not (1 was unknown). Among the 9 women with LLS, 4 mentioned the presence and 4 mentioned the absence of sexual needs (1 was unknown). The 13 women who had lovers were evenly distributed among the 3 types of Life Satisfaction.

These midlife women raised in an era of sexual taboos, do not reflect the merry widows, gay divorcées, or swinging singles of the popular media. Sexual indifference, rather than sexual frustration or sexual repression, would describe many of these women's attitudes.

Investment in Work

The perceived high importance of work for these single women was dramatically related to Life Satisfaction ($p<.42$). Only 1 out of the 29 HLS women rated their work as unimportant. And for some women with LLS, work was the one bright spot in their lives: "It's important for single women to have a job to keep from disintegrating." In comparing women with professional and nonprofessional jobs, there was some association between high-status work and Life Satisfaction, but it was weaker than might have been expected ($p<.10$).

Fifty-two women described their work as "very important." It was not only seen as a necessary economic activity but also gave meaning to their lives. Some comments were "Professionally my life is very satisfying. I'm proud of my accomplishments;" "I feel respected at work;" "I get so much satisfaction out of my work, it meets so many of my needs, that I never have time on my hands."

Work connected women socially with the wider world, as it does men. "Being with people keeps me from being lonely." "I don't feel 'single.' I'm an important member of an institution, involved in a set of loving relationships with my students, working with colleagues and my professional community."

Work was also indispensable for economic survival. Perception of sal-

ary fairness, which varied even within the same salary group, was significantly related to Life Satisfaction ($p<.05$). Half of the 40 women who
considered their salary fair had HLS, compared to one-third of the 20 women
who considered their salary unfair.

Poverty is often considered the major problem of single women
(Bequaert, 1976), but this was not true for this predominantly highly educated professional group. Forty-four felt currently financially secure and
this was weakly related to HLS, ($p<.09$), while 38 felt confident about their
future financial security. The importance of satisfying work and fair salaries for single women is highlighted by these data.

Help Seeking

There was no relationship between Life Satisfaction and seeking therapeutic help. Twenty-nine women had sought help, of which 16 had sought
help once, 10 had sought help twice, and 3 had done so three times. Thirty-
one respondents had no experience with help-seeking.

Eight of the women saw female therapists and 21 saw males. Twelve
of the providers were psychiatrists, 5 were social workers, 4 were psychologists, 5 were pastoral counselors, and 3 served in other capacities. For
their first help-seeking experience, 57% of the women were satisfied; 75%
were satisfied with further experiences. Reasons for seeking help included
losses, decision-making, depression, and problems with relationships or work.
For example, E, a 45-year-old social worker, sought help in her early twenties about a decision to get married to a man from a different religious
background. This specific need for help evolved into two years of therapy
with a male psychiatrist. At 35, after a job promotion, E felt overwhelmed
by work pressure and saw a woman psychologist for a brief, two-month
therapeutic intervention. Several women sought help after being rejected
or betrayed in love relationships.

There were several instances in which therapy had dramatically affected
someone's life. One 39-year-old woman had experienced a traumatic childhood characterized by not "good-enough mothering." Following her divorce
in her early twenties, she became quite disturbed and spent the next 10
years in therapy with three different psychiatrists involving several hospi-
talizations. Her life was turned around when she met a therapist whom she
perceived as deeply understanding her, leading to a dramatic recovery. She
was currently finding rewarding new life goals.

Among women who did not seek help, comments included the following: "I never felt the need;" "If I need help I might seek it in the future;"
"I prepare for the worst, so if it comes I can bear it." "Help-seeking seems
a luxury."

Summary and Conclusion

The majority of women in this sample can be considered highly satisfied or
reasonably content, with only 15% experiencing considerable dissatisfaction with their lives. The data are unfortunately limited by lack of a control

group of comparable married women; however, we can turn to Campbell's description (1975) of the life satisfaction of a random sample of 2,164 Americans: "Fewer than 10 percent described their lives in sour terms . . . and far more than half think their lives are worthwhile." (p. 38) The women in our sample seem to be about as content as other Americans: and when single midlife women seek help, mental health professionals should not assume that their unmarried status is necessarily the cause of their distress. As one respondent said, "Each situation has its advantages; it depends which set you want to live with." A statistical composite of a HLS single woman of this sample would be a highly educated woman in a professional, well-compensated job in which she is deeply invested. She lives with her roommate in her own house, does not feel lonely, and is in good health. She enjoys some intimate and many casual friendships. LLS women were found to suffer from ill health and loneliness, which were either the cause or the consequence of LLS.

Although the great majority of women relied on one or two major intimate relationships and many of the childless women "borrowed" children to meet their nurturing needs, neither the fulfillment of "attachment" needs in Weiss' sense (1976) nor the "opportunity for nurturance" (Weiss, 1976) were found to be an indispensable part of a satisfactory life. Especially striking were the large number of contented women who did not experience sexual needs.

It must be emphasized that this sample was heavily skewed in the direction of educated, high-status working women, the majority of whom found their work highly rewarding. In addition, the women in this study were exempt from the stresses of single parenthood.

We recognize the exploratory nature of this small-scale, modest study. It is hoped that further studies on midlife single women can be conducted on a more ambitious scale, with the goal of assessing the different life satisfactions of women of different age groups and educational levels, as well as allowing for distinctions between never-married, widowed, and divorced women who live with or without dependent children.

Our data suggest that some women in this society lead a satisfactory, fulfilling life without the benefits of sex, marriage, or motherhood.

NOTE

1. The authors wish to express sincere appreciation to George Loewenstein for his aid with the computer analysis of the data.

REFERENCES

ADAMS, M. *Single blessedness: Observations on the single status in married society.* New York: Basic Books, 1976.
ASHTON-WARNER, S. *Spinster.* New York: Simon & Schuster, 1959.
BERNARD, J. *The future of marriage.* New York: World, 1972.
BEQUAERT, L. *Single women, alone and together.* Boston: Beacon, 1976.
CAINE, L. *Lifelines.* Garden City, N. Y.: Doubleday, 1978.
CAMPBELL, A. The American way of mating. *Psychology Today,* 1975, *9*, 37–43.

ERIKSON, E. Growth and crises of the healthy personality. *Psychological Issues*, 1959, *1*, 50–100.

GEBHARD P. Post-marital coitus among widows and divorcees. In P. Bohannon (Ed.), *Divorce and after*. New York: Anchor, 1971.

GOODE W. *Women in divorce*. New York: Free Press, 1956.

GOVE, W. The relationship between sex roles, marital status and mental illness. *Social Forces*, 1972, *51*, 34–44.

LIPMAN-BLUMEN, J. The implications for family structure of changing sex roles. *Social Casework*, 1976, *57*, 67–79.

LOPATA, H. *Widowhood in an American city*. Cambridge, Mass: Schenkman, 1973.

MILLER, J. B. *Toward a new psychology of women*. Boston: Beacon, 1976.

MOORE, B. *The lonely passion of Judith Hearne*. Boston: Little, Brown, 1955.

O'BRIEN, P. *The woman alone*. New York: Quadrangle, 1973.

PARENT, G. *Sheila Levine is dead and living in New York*. New York: Bantam, 1972.

ROLLIN, B. Motherhood: Who needs it? In L. K. Howe (Ed.), *The future of the family*. New York: Simon & Schuster, 1972.

STEIN, P. *Single*. Englewood Cliffs, N.J.: Prentice-Hall, 1976.

WEISS, R. S. The provision of social relationships. In Z. Rubin (Ed.), *Doing unto others*. Englewood Cliffs, N. J.: Prentice-Hall, 1976.

38
Intimacy in Widowhood
Carol J. Barrett

This article explores all intimate relationships potentially available to the widowed woman. Friends, relatives, professionals and nonprofessional associates are considered, in addition to the deceased spouse, God, and the widow herself. The author concludes that traditional resources are inadequate to meet the widow's intimacy needs. The issue of reciprocity is addressed. The widow's experience stands opposed to human values which needlessly limit definitions of intimacy to dyadic, human relationships among opposite sex age peers. Research is needed to evaluate the correspondence between relationship styles in marriage and those in widowhood, to assess the interdependency of the widow's relationships, and to examine individual differences in the intimacy patterns of widows.

The study of intimate relationships in widowhood is important for three reasons. The first concerns the human lives at stake. The widow's needs are intense, yet few traditional resources are available. The second reason is that alternative forms of intimacy evolve in wodowhood which have received remarkably little attention in the professional literature. The unique intimate relations developed by widowed women are intriguing in and of themselves. But they also challenge our definitions of intimacy, our conceptual framework, and the range of human behavior we are compelled to acknowledge. Thus, the topic is also important because of the theoretical implications for research on intimacy in other contexts.

The widow's relationship needs stem from six sources: the need for human dialogue to help her work through the loss of her husband, the need for alternative sources of gratification of the intimacy needs previously met by her husband, the need to integrate secondary losses (e.g., income, position, home, lifestyle, friends) resulting from her husband's death, the need to deal with the consequent changes in her relationship with other persons, the continuation of relationship needs experienced prior to the husband's death and unaffected by it, and the emergence of new interpersonal needs developing out of her altered lifestyle and goals.

Since intimacy requires at a minimum the establishment of a relationship, those relationships in which the *potential* for intimacy exists are reviewed. The probability of experiencing intimacy in some of the relationships discussed is not high. But an overview of the widow's limited relationship resources is essential to understanding both the intensified demands for intimacy in existing relationships, and the widow's utilization of nontraditional resources in meeting her intimacy needs.

Relationships with Friends

In most cases, widowhood results in the dissolution of close friendships the widow and her husband previously enjoyed with couples (Barrett, 1977; Strugnell, 1974). The reasons for this loss of potential intimates are many: the frequent location of the original bond within the husband's work associates (Lopata, 1970), the dominant socializing pattern of couples, the discomfort married persons feel in confronting the reality of widowhood, the wives' experience of the widow as a sexual threat, coupled with the very real sexual advances by the husbands (Schlesinger, 1971; Lopata, 1973c). The friendships the widow may have had with unmarried women or men are more likely to survive the death of her husband. The widow's friendship network in a small town may be more enduring than those in larger communities (Pihlblad & Adams, 1972; Arling, 1976a).

The development of new friendships is difficult for the widow, owing in part to financial hardship (Barrett, 1977; Harvey & Bahr, 1974) and the rustiness of skills for initiating, as opposed to maintaining, close relationships (Lopata, 1973c). Despite disdain for the "society of widows," stemming from the general devaluation of relationships among women, new and lasting relationships among widows have been demonstrated in widows' groups (Barrett, 1978). The availability of other widows as friends may be partly responsible for the better psychological adjustment of older widows (Barrett & Becker).[1]

New relationships with men suffer a variety of constraints. Widows outnumber widowers by about four to one (Barrett, 1977). Although the majority of widows do not wish to remarry, this option is very unrealistic (Cleveland & Gianturco, 1976), despite increasing examples of intimacy between older women and younger men, and an increasing flexibility in the ages of spouses in second marriages (Presser, 1975).

Only very limited data on the sexuality of widowed women are available. Clayton and Bornstein (1976) interviewed 65 widows with an average age of 60 approximately 13 months after the death of their husbands. Only four had dated; none did so within the first four months of bereavement. Only one had experienced sexual intercourse. The lack of a standard sexual code was problematic for some. But the lack of a partner is clearly the number one cause of sexual inactivity in older women (Burnside, 1975).

In the widows' groups which I have led, I initially approached the theme of sexuality with some reluctance, operating with the mistaken assumption that most widows would be too embarrassed to discuss it openly. My revised conviction is that most widows are aware of unmet sexual needs, although early in bereavement sexual interests are generally nil. Their needs have sometimes led them into sexual involvements they find abusive, repulsive, or "wrong." Some have discovered or re-discovered masturbation. Many recognize that statistically their most likely partners are other women. The frequency with which lesbian relationships evolve among widows who have not experienced such relationships previously is not known.

The need for physical intimacy must be understood in the context of what is often a severe deprivation of human *touch*. It is not just sexual intercourse that is missed, it is the hugs and squeezes, the strokes and pats that are denied. More than one widow has told me she goes to church for the handshake she will receive by the door, on the way out.

The importance of friends in maintaining the widow's morale and general psychological adjustment cannot be overemphasized (Arling, 1976b; Maddison, 1968; Maddison & Raphael, 1975). But the limitations in relationships with friends are obvious when we consider that loneliness is the most consistent problem widows endure (Lopata, 1969; Barrett, 1977).

Relationships with Relatives

The emotional demands on the widow are increased by the necessity to assume total responsibility for parenting of any young children. The widow's relationships with young children give her some satisfaction, but also cause her considerable anxiety (Schlesinger, 1971; Silverman & Englander, 1975). Younger children rarely talk with her about the mutual losses they are experiencing and their own changing perceptions of each other.

Those widows whose children are adults face a different set of relationship issues. Marris (1958) found that most widows did not experience an increase in contact with grown children since the death of the husband / father. Adams (1968) analyzed the interaction patterns of sons and daughters separately, and found differences. The particular functions of visits with children were specified. Whereas daughters increased almost all types of interaction with their widowed mothers, sons only increased interactions aimed specifically at tangible aid to the mother. Lopata also found that the daughters of older widows appeared more often in their emotional support networks than sons.[2]

Childless widows constituted about one fourth of Lopata's (1973c) over-50 sample. While some may never have had children, the children of elderly widows may have died. Thus we cannot assume that there will be children available to attend to the widow's needs.

The widow's own parents may or may not be living. Given the increased life expectancy of women in this country, it is far more likely that today's widow will be able to talk to her (widowed) mother than was possible in previous decades or centuries. If the mother is living, contact between the young widow and her siblings is likely to be much more frequent (Marris, 1958), and sisters are likely to be particularly helpful (Glick, Weiss & Parkes, 1974). However, among older widows, whether the mother is living or not has little bearing on the frequency of contact among the widow and her brothers and sisters (Marris, 1958). Lopata (1973b) reported that two thirds of her sample of older widows had little or no contact with siblings.

The available research on the widow's relationships with her husband's family is even more discouraging than that on her own kin. Both Marris (1958) and Adams (1968) confirmed a definite decline in the frequency of interaction between the widow and her in-laws after the husband's death. Trends within the family interaction were consistent; rarely did a widow see more of one in-law and less of another (Marris, 1958). The widow is often distressed by her in-laws' insinuations that her loss is less profound than their own (Maddison, 1968). Young widows have complained to me that the husband's parents object to their inclinations to seek the company of other men, may torment them with guilt-inducing accusations, or attempt to instill what they consider to be false images of the deceased in the widows' children. However, a number of young widows studied by Glick, Parkes and Weiss (1974) reported sincere appreciation for their new relationships with a *brother* of the deceased.

There is some exciting research emerging on the potential closeness of grandparent-grandchild relationships (Kahana & Kahana, 1971; Robertson, 1976). But little is known about the ways in which these relationships are affected by the death of one of the grandparents.

Relationships with Others

The primary persons apart from friends and family with whom the widow may frequently interact are her associates at work or in the classroom, the neighbors near whom she lives, and her peers in voluntary organizations. Limited research suggests that work associates are inadequate in meeting the new intimacy needs of the widow (Abrahams, 1972). She may belong to organizations with a political, recreational, altruistic or religious function. The literature on the change in religious participation at widowhood is conflicting (Barrett & Larson).[3] While membership in social organizations characteristically declines, the widow's educational level is an important intervening variable (Lopata, 1973a; Arling, 1976a, Berardo, 1967).

Another group of potential intimates are the service providers in the widow's life. Relationships with physicians, social workers, police and lawyers may in fact be injurious to the widow's self-esteem (Weiss, 1973). Aside from the need for attention to physical distress, we may postulate that the widow seeks *emotional* support from her physician in the form of dialogue about her life circumstances and feelings, in order to alleviate despair and loneliness. In short, she may seek intimacy. The doctor's office is one place she will be touched, and she is likely to be accustomed to the coexistence of physical and emotional intimacy. Physicians, however, receive little training in treating loneliness. The role of nurses as assistant mourners (Kramer, Dunlap & Kramer, 1966) also needs expansion.

The response of the clergy in assisting the widow after the funeral service may be summed up in one word: disappointing (e.g., Strugnell, 1974). In addition to inadequate preparation for grief counseling among the clergy (as among other counselors), the widow's new single status may contribute to the male clergy's reluctance to continue a close relationship with her. Church sponsorship of specific services for the widowed is a hopeful development (Silverman, Mackenzie, Pettipas & Wilson, 1974).

Despite wide-spread distrust of funeral directors, the available research documents that many widows feel gratitude to the individual in this role (Glick, et al., 1974). The funeral director may be the one person who does not withdraw at signs of grief. As a professional group, they have also provided tangible support to widowed persons services (Silverman et al., 1974).

The potential role of the mental health professional as an intimate friend of the widow is often curtailed by traditional diagnosis, excessive reliance on tranquilizers and anti-depressants, and an inadequate opportunity for grief work in the therapeutic relationship.

We come now to the service providers without formal professional credentials: clerks, tellers, mail carriers, store owners, auto mechanics, etc. The bereft widow is particularly vulnerable to exploitation by individuals who possess goods or services she requires. However, nonprofessional service providers can relate with genuine compassion to the widow. In one city restaurant, I have observed an elderly widow exchange extended conversation with the owner, deposit her week's correspondence near the cash register for him to mail, and write a check to cover the amount, not only of the meal, but the stamps. This is her one-stop social service station, and she is there every Sunday afternoon. In bad weather, he will see that she gets safely to the bus.

Unique Relationships

Given the widow's limited opportunities for responsive relations with a variety of living persons, is it possible that she meets some of her emotional needs through a continuing relationship with her deceased spouse? The evidence comes from a variety of sources, which when considered together, are overwhelming in their implication.

Foremost among the documentation is the phenomenon of the illusion of the spouse's presence—physically, visually, auditorily, psychologically, or spiritually. Marris (1958) was the first to document the high frequency of such occurrences among British widows. Some simply felt his presence; others talked to his photograph and imagined him giving advice; still others attended seances. In a later study of London widows, Parkes (1970b) reported that some began to act or think like the spouse, developed symptoms resembling those he experienced in the last illness, or felt that he was now inside one of the children or the widow herself. In a description of the search for the lost love, Parkes (1970a) indicated that 15 out of 22 widows were comforted by the husband's presence, and remarked, "It almost seems that for these people the search has been successful."

While the early interpretations of the bereaved person's illusions of the deceased in the psychiatric literature described them as symptomatic of *pathological* grief, recent research disputes this perspective. Rees (1971; 1975) interviewed 227 widows and 66 widowers in Wales. Almost half (46.7%) had experienced illusions of the deceased spouse. The presence of the spouse was felt by 39.2% of the sample; 14% experienced visual "hallucinations", 13.3% auditory "hallucinations" and 2.7% tactile "hallucinations." More than 11% had talked to the dead spouse. These experiences often lasted many years, although the incidence was higher among those widowed less than ten years. It was also higher among those who reported happy marriages, those who had been married longer, and those who were older when widowed. The incidence was not related to the subject's sex, current age, current social isolation or history of depression; nor was the suddenness of death a factor. Although 68.8% of the subjects felt helped by these experiences, only 27.7% had ever disclosed them to anyone previously.

Research with widows in Japan (Yamamoto, Okonagi, Iwasaki, & Yoshimura, 1969) suggests that the prevalence of illusions of the spouse is even higher when the prevailing religious doctrine sanctions rather than discourages them.[4]

The most systematic study in this country of the widow's experience of the presence of her husband, reported this occurrence among nearly 60 percent of the sample (Kalish & Reynolds, 1974). In my own conversations with widows, such illusions are often initially shared with some reluctance; the widow may be apprehensive that they are indicative of mental illness. When she is reassured that such illusions are very common in bereavement, she experiences relief, and is apt to remark on the positive meaning of these experiences.

Behaviors which may connote a continuing relationship with the deceased range widely, from the more dramatic example of verbal conversations with the spouse, to writing letters to him (Beck, 1965; Robson, 1974), to such mild behavioral alterations as sleeping on "his" side of the bed, wearing "his" clothing, or preferring "his" favorite chair. My professional experience indicates that memories of the deceased may serve a similar psychological function. Events in which the spouse was involved—other than those associated with his death—are often recalled with considerable pleasure. Memories enable continuity with the deceased, and insure his impact on her life even after death. Even those widows who frequently recall very negative experiences with the husband appear to derive momentum from them in planning for the future.

Given the lack of *human* intimates available to the widow, an alternative source of intimacy might be her relationship with God. Despite the presumption of renewed faith among widows by the public and professionals alike, Glick et al. (1974) found no consistent reorientation to God in their sample of young widows. Scattered comments in other reports also fail to present a convincing picture of greater trust, strength or serenity based in God after the husband's death. Understanding the widow's relationship with God requires a consideration of her personal, theological conception of God. Some view God as a human-like being. For the widow of this persuasion, God may become an enemy. Would-be comforters who offer the solace that her husband is now with God or who imply that God knows best—at a time when her existence is wrenched with pain—probably unwittingly contribute to her wrath at God (Schiff, 1977).

Anger at God can be seen as a projection of the widow's (unexpressed) rage at her husband for abandoning her. This projection might be inhibited among widows for whom God is a woman, rather than a being with a male persona. A female God might be more conducive to a supportive relationship with the widow. (In consciousness-raising groups where this issue has come up, widows are uniformly delighted with my statement that perhaps God is a widow.)

Others conceive of God as love. For such a widow, a major personal source of God has vanished, along with the probable erosion of love from friends and relatives. In a third view, God is a symbol for a valued principle or force, e.g., being, spirit, nature, universe, beauty, justice or truth. For the widow who views God as an abstraction, intimacy based on the alleviation of emotional needs is not likely to evolve. Of course, if the widow does not subscribe to any conception of God, it is moot to discuss her relationship with deity.

There is another being who may meet some of the widow's relational needs: the widow herself. I know of no formal research which conveys the experience of widows actively engaged in interaction with the self as a distinct being, and hence will rely on my observations during intensive dialogues with them. Those who are able to meet socio-emotional needs by relating to themselves are not typical. But their style of coping intrigues and sometimes inspires others. These widows make *themselves* the objects of their compassion, nurturance and care. Each believes she is her own best friend, and actively seeks to respond to felt needs. The relationship has a quality of discovery—of getting to know "someone" better, of sharing innermost thoughts and feelings, and of finding a responsive reactor. We may be tempted to infer psychopathology in these conversations with the self.[5] To the contrary, the widows I am describing are not depressed; they are not out of touch with reality. They are alive with energy, able to learn from new experience, and to respond to others. Their self-esteem is high, and their joy in living is evident.

There are several alternative sources of intimacy for the widow, about which I have only very limited experiential data. Some widows may develop intense relationships with pets. The absence of physical touching in widowhood, the quietness of an otherwise empty house, and the fear of intruders may propel the widow to cherish the comfort of a pet she would have regarded with rather mild affection while married.

Fantasy objects are another potential source of (imagined) intimacy in solitude. We do not know whether widows are more likely to engage in fantasized relationships (with living persons) than women in other marital status groups. My experience leads me to suspect that this is not a frequent source of gratification among widows, although Lopata (1975) has pointed out that some widows may assume intensified vicarious relationships with television characters.

Finally, there is the emotional, intellectual, and perhaps spiritual relationship possible with works of art. I do not know of any data indicating whether bereaved persons seek and enjoy such experiences more often than others. The observation that wealthy widows are firmly numbered among the nation's art patrons suggests that this question might be worth pursuing; art may offer the beholder a sense of permanence and enduring value which those who have suffered loss may find reassuring.

Implications

The review of the widow's relationships with individuals on whom she might traditionally depend for intimacy is a fairly stark accounting of possibilities. In light of the importance of reciprocity in intimate relationships (e.g., Arling, 1976b), it would be well to consider what the widow has to offer her potential intimate. I will identify here the special "gifts" which the widow possesses as a result of her bereavement, which enhance the likelihood that her intimate encounters will be genuinely reciprocal.

The experience of sharing grief with the bereaved can be rewarding to the non-bereaved in several ways. Barrett & Becker[1] have documented that married women with widow friends are more prepared for widowhood than those without. Intimate dialogue with someone who is experiencing loss may also help to integrate *previous* losses. Aside from these influences on past and future grief, intimacy with someone who is widowed can be valuable for the experience it offers in the *now*. Death brings intense pain, which increases sensitivity. The widow becomes more responsive to subtle nuances in her relationships with others; she feels relationship shifts more quickly and intensely. This heightened awareness can enhance the level of intimacy possible with someone who is willing to be involved.

In addition to this sensitizing of grief, affective experiences with the widow potentially include deep serenity or joy. That the prospect of death or its actual occurrence sometimes brings a powerful surge of positive emotional feelings has not to my knowledge been systematically documented. But occasional reports of such experiences have been published. Cassem's (1975) discussion of bereavement as indispensible for growth is persuasive. Transcendence of loss is evident in this excerpt from a young widow's letter to friends soon after the death of her husband:

> To all of you, I would say (as I'm sure Mark would wish me to)—live out your love for one another now. Don't assume the future; don't assume all kinds of healing time for the bruised places in your relationships with others. Don't be afraid to touch and share deeply and openly all the tragic and joyful dimensions of life. (Cassem, 1975, p. 16.)

Encounters with someone who has such a perspective can be very enriching. How frequently widows come to feel such an intense respect for life experience is not known. Barrett[6] found that seven percent of the widows in her sample made recommendations to married women consistent with this love-of-life philosophy.[7]

Despite what the widow has to offer potential intimates, traditional forms of intimacy are not often forthcoming, and alternatives emerge. The data on the relationship between the widow and her deceased spouse have some provocative implication for theories of death and dying. Some may argue that the sympathetic treatment of illusions of the deceased in this report only serves to augment the *denial* of death. However, these experiences can only be considered ramifications of death denial when we view death as nothingness. To the extent that we view death as having substance or form, relationship issues naturally evolve.

Some may view the persistence of the relationship with the (dead) husband as insidious testimony to the denial of woman's freedom. While I have some sympathy with this point of view, freedom implies the right to choose, including the right to choose monogamous intimacy with a man for life (death). We must also ask whether the freeing of bonds to the husband is accomplished by insisting on the absence of a relationship. How many feminist psychotherapists would encourage the working-through of a living relationship by advising the client to forget all about it?

The experience of widows brings to light some assumptions about intimacy which have prevailed in our theory, research, and social customs. The first is that we assume intimacy is possible only between human beings—not between human beings and deity, the dead, the self, animals, fantasy or art objects. Our future research needs to examine seriously the similarities between intimacy as traditionally conceived and behavior of the kinds reported here. If the same psychological functions are served, it is pedantry to insist on a definition of intimacy which excludes nonhuman participants.

The widow's experience also challenges the prevailing assumption that intimacy is possible only among close age-mates. Can a forty-year-old woman have an intimate, nonexploitive relationship with her four-year-old child? What about the 18-year-old and his or her 80-year-old widowed grandparent? Empirical exploration of such relationships from the vantage point of reciprocal needs should be enlightening.

The experience of widows in groups raises a question also raised by women's C-R groups. To what extent can one be intimate with a group? A traditional (androcentric) assumption is that intimacy is by nature *dyadic* (Davis, 1973). That our literature also reflects the assumption that genuine intimacy is only possible between individuals of the opposite sex almost goes without saying.

There are other questions we need to raise about sexuality. Should the opportunity to engage in a sexual relationship be considered a right, or is it a privilege available only to some? Should widows be encouraged to relate sexually to men if they so desire? Even if by demographic necessity that means married men? Are cultures which sanction polygyny in this respect less oppressive to women? How best can the option of sexual intimacy with a woman be presented to widows?

Among the pressing research issues are the consequences of various marital relationships in limiting or expanding the intimacy potential of the widow, the roots of individual differences in the intimacy patterns of widows, and the repercussions of changes in one relationship in widowhood for other relationships. We need to know the relationship consequences of interventions such as peer support programs, psychotherapy, and the deliberate legitimation of relationships with the deceased. An intriguing quesion is whether the explicit provision of opportunities for intimacy in widowhood will reduce the need for intimacy in pre-existing relationships, or conversely, will ease the stress in these relationships, and paradoxically enable more intense intimacy. Barrett (1978) found that 14% of her widowed clients spontaneously reported improvement in relationships with relatives (primarily children) after participation in a widows' discussion group. Information on these themes can help us desire more responsive institutional, clinical and personal interventions to accommodate the human needs of America's widows.

REFERENCE NOTES

1. Barrett, C. J. & Becker, R. M. *Prediction of adjustment to widowhood from social and demographic data.* Paper presented at the Western Social Science Association Annual Meeting, Denver, April 27, 1978.
2. Lopata, H. Z. *Support systems involving widows.* Paper presented at the American Psychological Association Annual Convention, Chicago, September 1975.
3. Barrett, C. J. & Larson, D. *Psychological functions of religion in widowhood: Attribution versus evidence.* Manuscript submitted for publication.

4. Beyond our own culture, there are further examples of the behavior of bereaved persons which may represent a relationship with the deceased. Sixty-five out of sixty-six societies studied by Rosenblatt (1975) evidenced a belief in ghosts.
5. History is filled with examples of women managing competently on their own and being rewarded with labels of deviance (Chesler, 1972).
6. Barrett, C. J. *Strategies for preventing the stresses of widowhood.* Paper presented at the Southwestern Psychological Association Annual Meeting, New Orleans, Louisiana, April 21, 1978.
7. From the standpoint of facilitating bereavement, such advice may be well-founded. The wife who loves deeply and well will have fewer regrets when opportunities are later lost, and is less likely to be encumbered with guilt as a widow.

REFERENCES

ABRAHAMS, R. B. Mutual help for the widowed. *Social Work*, 1972, *17*(5), 54–61.

ADAMS, B. N. The middle-class adult and his widowed or still-married mother. *Social Problems*, 1968, *16*, 50–59.

ARLING, G. Resistance to isolation among elderly widows. *International Journal of Aging and Human Development*, 1976a, 7(1), 67–86.

ARLING, G. The elderly widow and her family, neighbors and friends. *Journal of Marriage and the Family*, 1976b, *38*(4), 757–767.

BARRETT, C. J. Women in widowhood: Review essay. *Signs: Journal of Women in Culture and Society*, 1977, *2*(1), 856–868.

BARRETT, C. J. Effectiveness of widows' groups in facilitating change. *Journal of Consulting and Clinical Psychology*, 1978, *46*(1), 20–31.

BECK, F. *The Diary of a Widow.* Boston: Beacon Press, 1965.

BERARDO, F. M. *Social adaptation to widowhood among a rural-urban aged population.* Bulletin #689, Washington, D.C.: Department of Agriculture, December 1967.

BURNSIDE, I. M. *Sexuality and aging.* Los Angeles: Ethel Percy Andrus Gerontology Center, University of Southern California, 1975.

CASSEM, N. Bereavement as indispensible to growth. In B. Schoenberg et al. (Eds.), *Bereavement: Its psychosocial aspects.* N.Y.: Columbia University Press, 1975, 9–17.

CHESLER, P. *Women and madness.* Garden City, N.Y.: Doubleday, 1972.

CLAYTON, P. J. & BORNSTEIN, P. E. Widows and widowers. *Medical Aspects of Human Sexuality*, 1976, *10*(9), 27–53.

CLEVELAND, W. P. & GIANTURCO, D. T. Remarriage probability after widowhood: A retrospective method. *Journal of Gerontology*, 1976, *31*(1), 99–103.

DAVIS, M. S. *Intimate Relations.* N.Y.: Free Press, 1973.

GLICK I. O., WEISS, R. S., & PARKES, C. M. *The first year of bereavement.* N.Y.: Wiley, 1974.

HARVEY, C. D., & BAHR, H. M. Widowhood, morale, and affiliation. *Journal of Marriage and the Family*, 1974, *36*(1), 97–106.

KAHANA, E., & KAHANA, B. Theoretical and research perspectives on grandparenthood. *Aging and Human Development*, 1971, *2*, 261–267.

KALISH, R. A., & REYNOLDS, D. K. Widows view death: A brief research note. *Omega*, 1974, *5*(2), 187–192.

KRAMER, C. H., DUNLOP, H. E., & KRAMER, J. R. Resolving grief. *Geriatric Nursing*, 1966, *2*, 14–17.

LOPATA, H. Z. Loneliness: Forms and components. *Social Problems*, *1969*, *17*, 248–261.

LOPATA, H. Z. The social involvement of American widows. *American Behavioral Scientist*, 1970, *14*(1), 41–57.

LOPATA, H. Z. The effect of schooling on social contacts of urban widows. *American Journal of Sociology*, 1973a, *79*(3), 604–619.

LOPATA, H. Z. Social relations of black and white widowed women in a Northern metropolis. *American Journal of Sociology*, 1973b, *78*(4), 1003–1010.

LOPATA, H. Z. *Widowhood in an American city.* Cambridge, MA: Schenkman, 1973c.

LOPATA, H. Z. On widowhood: Grief work and identity reconstruction. *Journal of Geriatric Psychiatry*, 1975, *8*, 41–55.

MADDISON, D. The relevance of conjugal bereavement for preventive psychiatry. *British Journal of Medical Psychology*, 1968, *41*(3), 223–233.

MADDISON, D., & RAPHAEL, B. Conjugal bereavement and the social network. In B. Schoenberg et al. (Eds.) *Bereavement: Its psychosocial aspects*. N.Y.: Columbia University Press, 1975, 26–40.

MARRIS, P. *Widows and their families*. London: Routledge & Kegan Paul, 1958.

PARKES, C. M. "Seeking" and "finding" a lost object: Evidence from recent studies of the reaction to bereavement. *Social Science and Medicine*, 1970a, *4*, 187–201.

PARKES, C. M. The first year of bereavement. *Psychiatry*, 1970b, *33*, 444–467.

PIHLBLAD, C. T., & ADAMS, D. L. Widowhood, social participation and life satisfaction. *Aging and Human Development*, 1972, *3*(4), 323–330.

PRESSER, H. B. Age differences between spouses: Trends, patterns and social implications. *American Behavioral Scientist*, 1975, *19*(2), 190–205.

REES, W. D. The hallucinations of widowhood. *British Medical Journal*, 1971, *4*, 37–41.

REES, W. D. The bereaved and their hallucinations. In B. Schoenberg et al. (Eds.) *Bereavement: Its psychosocial aspects*. N.Y.: Columbia University Press, 1975, 66–71.

ROBERTSON, J. F. Significance of grandparents: Perceptions of young adult grandchildren. *Gerontologist*, 1976, *16*, 137–140.

ROBSON, K. S. Letters to a dead husband. *Journal of Geriatric Psychiatry*, 1974, *7*(2), 208–232.

ROSENBLATT, P. C. Uses of ethnography in understanding grief and mourning. In B. Schoenberg et al. (Eds.). *Bereavement: Its psychosocial aspects*. N.Y.: Columbia University Press, 1975.

SCHIFF, H. S. *The bereaved parent*. N.Y.: Crown, 1977.

SCHLESINGER, S. The widowed as a one-parent family unit. *Social Science*, 1971, *46*, 26–32.

SILVERMAN, P., MACKENZIE, D., PETTIPAS, M., & WILSON, E. (Eds.). *Helping each other in widowhood*. N.Y.: Meilen, 1974.

SILVERMAN, P., & ENGLANDER, S. The widow's view of her dependent children. *Omega*, 1975, *6*(1), 3–20.

STRUGNELL, C. Who the widow-to-widow program served. In Silverman, P., Mackenzie, D., Pettipas, M., & Wilson, E. (Eds.). *Helping each other in widowhood*. N.Y.: Meilen, 1974, 31–50.

WEISS, R. S. Helping relationships: Relationships of clients with physicians, social workers, priests, and others. *Social Problems*, 1973, *20*(3), 319–328.

YAMAMOTO, J., OKONOGI, K., IWASAKI, T., & YOSHIMURA, S. Mourning in Japan. *American Journal of Psychiatry*, 1969, *125*(12), 1660–1665.

39

Women and Aging
A Futurist Perspective

Sharon McIrvin Abu-Laban

Many of the inequities characteristic of the female position tend to crystallize in older age. Under the assumed continuation of trends involving family life, reproductive freedom, sexuality and labor force participation, aging women of the future may find improvement with respect to personal status and socio-emotional rewards. However, incipient counter trends, made strong by religious conservatism, must be noted. Should such counter trends gain in strength, the lot of aging women of the future may be but a version of the status quo ante.

For contemporary women, aging and old age give small cause to rejoice; not only are there physically imposed liabilities, but there are major, socially imposed limitations on life opportunities. Aging is differentially disadvantageous; its impact varies by sex. Compared to their male counterparts, the current generations of older women in America are economically, politically and interpersonally disadvantaged. Older women are more likely than older men to be poor (Chen, 1977); to be widowed (Atchley, 1977); to be living alone (Cutler & Harootyan, 1975, p. 65); to be dismissed as desirable sex partners (Bell, 1970); to have their physical attractiveness belittled (Sontag, 1972); to have diminished access to mechanisms of prestige and power (Nielsen, 1978); and to be institutionalized (Hendricks & Hendricks, 1977, p. 66). Yet, older women are likely to outlive men of their age by an average of seven years. In older age, women are numerically dominant, outnumbering men by a ratio of 144:100 in the 65-and-over age group and by a ratio of 171:100 in the 75+ age group (Brotman, 1977).

Projections concerning the future of women must, of necessity, include an examination of the future of older women, for in many ways the inequities which characterize the female condition appear to crystallize in old age. To be an old woman often means to bear the brunt of both ageism and sexism; it is no utopia. The current generations of aging women labor under severe disadvantages. These women are the products of traditional sex role socialization and generation specific opportunities. What of old women of the future? Most of the women who will comprise the aged and

"Women and Aging: A Futurist Perspective" by Sharon McIrvin Abu-Laban in *Psychology of Women Quarterly*, 1981, 6, 1, 85–98. Copyright © 1981 by Human Sciences Press, Inc. Reprinted by permission.

aging of the first quarter of the 21st century have already been born. Is their aging likely to be different? Does the future hold promise of an amelioration of current inequities?

As defined here, the "future" will refer to the 25-year period between 2000 and 2025 and, recognizing the relativity of old age, it will encompass the "middle-aged" (45–64); the "young-old" (65–74) and the "old-old" (75+). The women who will be 45, 65 and 75 years of age in the year 2000 were born in 1955, 1935 and 1925, respectively. Those women who will form the 75+ age group of 2025 are currently in their thirties; those who will be 65 are entering their twenties; and those who will comprise the young middle-aged of 2025 are infants or yet unborn. Each age cohort will have been exposed to differing socio-cultural opportunities and limitations at differing phases of the developmental cycle. Thus, even those experiences which most would have commonly shared (e.g., the social-historical climate of the year 1979) would presumably have differential impact. It should be noted, then, that the possible consequence of the trends to be discussed will necessarily vary by the extent and timing of each cohort's exposure.

Predicting the social future is fraught with the possibility of error. While some demographic and technological forecasts may be made with a comfortable margin of certitude, it is far more difficult to accurately predict changes in the attitudes and values which constitute the crucial social environment. Viable projections must consider competing trends, and in a complex society such as the United States, competing trends are usually evident. Given this, the first part of this discussion examines and contrasts the future of aging women under the major assumption that there will be a continuation of certain important contemporary trends. The latter part of the paper examines specific, already discernible, counter trends, which, should they gain prominence, may have quite differing implications for older women of the future.

Some Current Trends and Their Implications

Several contemporary trends give promise of a rather dramatic shift in the life chances of aging women. These include: a delay in the incidence of first marriage, a delay in childbearing and an increase in childlessness (Glick, 1975; Van Dusen & Sheldon, 1976); increased incidence of divorce, remarriage and numbers of unmarried couples living together (Population Reference Bureau, 1978); increased female labor force participation (Chafe, 1976; earlier sexual experience and greater tolerance of variant forms of sexual expression (Hunt, 1974; Sorensen, 1973; Zelnik & Kantner, 1972) and increased reproductive freedom including access to birth control techniques, voluntary sterilization and abortion. Should these trends continue, older women of the future may have increased access to mechanisms of prestige and status and increased access to interpersonal affect and support ties.

Access to Prestige and Status

Contemporary women may experience the most apparent "prestige" and "power" (of sorts) at the stage in life where they are defined as most attractive. Physical attractiveness is a power base, even if not a legitimated one (Nielsen, 1978). However, status based on current definitions of female beauty declines with visible aging. Society does not reward the physical appearance of an aging woman, much less than of an old woman. Hence, a woman's status may begin its decline in the middle years, at a time when status for males is often at its peak.

> The young girl of 18 or 25 may well believe that her position in society is equal to, or even higher than that of men. As she approaches middle age, however, she begins to notice a change in the way people treat her. Reflected in growing indifference of others toward her looks, toward her sexuality (read 'toward her as a sex object'), she can see and measure the decline of her worth, her status in the world. (Bell, 1970, p. 75).

Several writers have noted a double standard of aging with respect to appearance (Bell, 1970; Moss, 1970; Nowak, 1977; Preston, 1975; Sontag, 1972). The physical changes, primarily facial, which accompany aging are more likely to be seen as tolerable or even attractive in males, while they are something to be hidden or removed in females. Further, older males are more likely to have access to bases of prestige other than appearance, e.g., occupation, power or money.

With advancing age, a woman's social worth may be measured basically in terms either of her importance to the members of her immediate family or her derived status as a social appendage of her spouse. In the world outside the home she is frequently ill-equipped to command respect or admiration in her own right.

While stress on physical fitness and society's increasing acceptance of cosmetic surgery may help the financially advantaged of the future defer the visual evidence of age, these physical changes cannot be eradicated by any means presently known to science; there is an inevitability to their progression.

One more common alternative avenue of prestige in the future may result from the fact that more young women (the old of the future) are gainfully employed and increasing proportions are deeply attached to work and hence less likely to withdraw from the labor force (Kreps & Leaper, 1976). Increased and prolonged labor force participation lends to the possibility of acquiring occupational prestige. If not this, there is the possibility of deriving on-the-job esteem, i.e., such women have the opportunity to be socially recognized and valued for their specific job performance (a quality which is "hidden" in the job of a full-time homemaker).

In the future, derived status from a husband's occupation is less likely to be the determining factor in a married woman's prestige. With delay in marriage and delay or even avoidance of childbearing, a woman has more time to identify with her occupational role and is more likely to be identified by others with that occupation. Further, with more time having been given to building their credentials as workers, even women who withdraw from the labor force for child rearing stand an improved chance of making a job re-entry at a level more secure than would have been the case in the past.

Although American society has been moving toward more flexible work styles and greater appreciation of leisure activities, those women who, because of family responsibilities, experience lengthy interruptions in their work careers, are likely to be the ones who will take advantage of the relaxation of mandatory retirement laws. For "late bloomers," deferral of retirement gives more opportunity to move through the customary phases of a career (Atchley & Corbett, 1977). In line with this, the future labor force participation of women 45–64 and 65+ is likely to increase, in contrast to decreases in the labor force participation of males in these age categories (Sheppard, 1975). Thus, increasing proportions of women will be retaining occupational roles and titles, together with their associated prestige, well into older age.

In retirement, these women will have access to monetary benefits which are not linked to the private pension plans or Social Security benefits of a spouse and hence are not subject to dramatic reduction should that spouse die. This suggests that in the future more women will be less economically dependent in older age.

The skills of contemporary older women are often rather sex-specific, confined to the parameters of the traditional wife-mother role, and as such include learned incompetencies, e.g., occupational, mechanical or financial ineptitudes (Bernard, 1972). These learned incompetencies lend to feelings of personal vulnerability, particularly in the absence of a male partner, and increase the stress of coping with widowhood. Further, such incompetencies detract from societal assessments of stature. However, increased participation in the public sphere of gainful employment as well as greater experience with autonomous living arrangements independent of a spouse or parents, should contribute to a broadening of the range of women's life skills. Thus, women's status in advanced age will be enhanced by a strengthened repertoire of societally valued personal competencies.

Should aging women of the future have increased access to alternative bases of prestige which go beyond age-linked physical attractiveness or the derived status of a wife, they will then have access to some of the very same mechanisms which currently contribute to the prestige of aging males.

Access to Interpersonal Affect and Support

Contemporary older women were socialized to view marriage as the normal, optimal, and enduring framework for an adult life. Yet these same women are much more likely to be the singled survivors of marriages which have been broken by death (experience with divorce is relatively low for current older people). Given the tendency to marry males older than they and the sex differentials in life expectancy, the majority of contemporary older women spend their later years in an unmarried state. In 1970, among people 65–69 years of age, 49% of women were married in contrast to 77% of men; among those 80–84, only 15% of women were married, in contrast to 53% of men (U. S. Bureau of the Census, 1973). Demographic forecasts usually assume a continuance of the sex differentials in life expectancy, at least into the near future (Cutler & Harootyan, 1975; Science Council of Canada, 1976).

There is a form of preparatory experience, ongoing today, which may help women of the future to cope with some of the painful inevitabilities of old age, particularly the death of a mate. Such women will be more likely to have had experience with transitory living / loving relationships, including living with partners outside a legal marriage, divorce, and a greater number of sexual partners. All of these represent experience with adapting to the beginning and ending of relationships; as such, they can provide a training ground for coping with loss and learning to rely on a more self-sufficient and self-directed life style.

Those who are widowed are a high risk population with respect to both morbidity and mortality rates (Holmes & Rahe, 1967). Marriage tends to provide important supports in older age (Abu-Laban, 1978). Yet remarriage possibilities are differentially available. Divorced women are less likely to remarry than divorced men, and the same is true for widowed women in contrast to widowed men. Furthermore, women's chances for remarriage lessen as they age (Treas & Van Hilst, 1976). While women are expected to marry men approximately the same age or older, men, as they age, have a theoretically expanding age-range of potential mates. Further, the traditional direction of age differences between brides and grooms is usually even greater with second marriages (Presser, 1975). This not only signals a shortage of "eligible" men for older women but also means that women in second marriages face an increased probability of experiencing widowhood and, as well, a longer period of single survivorship.

However, older women of the future may find greater equalization of partner survivorship, an increased range of choice, and a new (for them) buttress against some of the disadvantages of old age: marriage to a younger man. There are several factors which, in interaction, suggest that current sanctions against older women marrying younger men are likely to diminish. 1) The drop in births since 1960 means that as men at the tail end of the "baby boom" years move through this century and marry and remarry, they will find an insufficient number of potential mates in the younger, "birth-dearth," appropriate age groups (Van Dusen & Sheldon, 1976). Such demographic realities may initiate a transition which acts to ease the traditional expectations regarding the correct direction of age differentials between mates. 2) With the increase in age at first marriage and the increased incidence of remarriage at later ages, the differences of a few years are likely to seem less important. For example, a 54-year-old woman marrying a 42-year-old man, or a 32-year-old woman marrying a 27-year-old man may seem less socially reprehensible than a 24-year-old woman marrying a 19-year-old man. 3) As more older women are gainfully employed, they are in contact with men of various ages, in non-domestic settings which are likely to emphasize similarities rather than differences and increase the possibility of knowing the person behind the age label. 4) As recognition is given to the childless relationship as a viable, even desirable, option, this will reduce the importance of the menopause and female fertility. 5) As older women are able to develop and maintain independent avenues of personal prestige, their appeal as potential mates goes beyond that of age-linked physical attractiveness.

With respect to sexual expressiveness in the later years, although Masters and Johnson's (1966, p. 247) research optimistically asserts that "there is no time limit drawn by advancing years to female sexuality," in fact there are currently real limitations on the sexuality of aging women. Stringent socialization, the likelihood of being widowed, the unlikelihood of remarriage in later age, and social pressure all act to diminish sexual expression. Several writers, speculating on the future, have discussed the benefits of polygyny after sixty, with the unchallenged notion that, given the deficit of men in later years, several aging women might share one older man (e.g., Cavan, 1973; Kassel, 1966). While the supportive advantages of communal living can and have been argued, the idea that in the future one older man could meet the sexual needs of several older women is shortsighted, at best.

The comparatively sophisticated older women of the early 21st century are not as likely as contemporary older women to be satisfied with sublimation or abstinence. Women's sexual socialization is beginning earlier, is more experimental, less restricted, more open, and involves more partners (Hunt, 1974; Sorensen, 1973; Zelnik & Kantner, 1972). Older women of the future will be less inhibited in speech, expectations, and actions. They are far more likely to put a high premium on sexuality than the current generation which was exposed to strong doses of Victorian repressiveness. The functioning sexuality of future older women may be expressed not only in the longer maintenance of the active sexual side of marriages, but also, reflecting increased societal tolerance toward homosexuality and less pressure on singles to restrict themselves to sex only in marriage, an increase in other forms of initimacy, both heterosexual and homosexual. Given the sex ratio in later years, this suggests an advantage for women who are homosexual or bisexual. Additionally, however, for the reasons outlined earlier it is probable that older women of the future will have greater access to younger male partners. Thus, not only is the frequency of older women's sexual behavior likely to increase but the range of potential sex partners may well broaden to include same-sex as well as a wider age-range of males.

An often important socio-emotional tie in older age is that between a woman and her adult child or children. There tends to be reciprocal help between the generations (Adams, 1968; Shanas, 1967). As with a spouse, the presence of an adult child is a support in the face of the normal dependencies of advanced age and a deterrent to institutionalization (Atchley, 1977, p. 116). Soldo and Meyers (Note 1) argue that in contrast to women who have borne three or more children, childless women and those with few children have a 15% greater chance of being institutionalized before the age of 75. Women who reach the age of 65–75 in the year 2000 will actually have *more* adult children as potential supports than did the women of earlier generations (Neugarten, 1975). These women, born during the depression years of the 1930's, had an unusually high birth rate (Glick, 1975). However, the birth declines which began in the 1960's will be reflected in fewer adult children available to women who will be 55–65 at the close of the first quarter of the new century.

It is women who have tended to maintain the socio-emotional links between family members—visiting, corresponding, arranging family celebrations, and caring for the sick (Adams, 1968; Garigue, 1956; Sweetzer, 1968). These supports have been of help to women as they age and cope with the life changes associated with advancing years. Yet increasing female labor force participation suggests an alteration, if not an attenuation, of younger women's past supportive role to dependent aged parents or parents-in-law. Hence, the sheer physical existence of adult children (specifically daughters) in 2000–2025, may be less of an indicator of potential emotional support for an aged woman than it is in the present.

An extension of family-like support can be found through friendships. These can become particularly important in advanced age with the possible dispersal of adult children, death of spouse and general shrinkage of the family circle. Older women have long found rewards from close companionship with other women. Lowenthal and Haven (1968) found older married women to be twice as likely as older married men to indicate someone other than their spouse as their confidant. Clark and Anderson (1967) found that older women, in contrast to older men, are less passive about their friendships and appear to regard them as more important. Older widows may form very strong support networks (Blau, 1961; Hochschild, 1973). Such supports and near-kin relationships may be even stronger in the future. As contemporary young women increasingly participate in a range of activities, independent of male escort, the intimation that the absence of a man signifies social failure and / or personal vulnerability should become uncommon, if not obsolete. Single older women of the future (both the widowed and the divorced) are less likely than current older women (Lopata, 1970, p. 62) to find it stigmatic or a drop in status to be in the company of other women only.

To conclude, under the assumed continuation of specified trends with respect to family life, sexuality, reproductive freedom, and labor force participation, the future of aging and aged women looks, in many ways, increasingly advantageous. There is the possibility of improvement in their status as well as in their access to socio-emotional rewards (save, possibly, rewards from adult children). The question arises, can the continuation of these trends be comfortably assumed?

Countervailing Trends: A Caveat

Prognostications about the future must consider counter trends. Futurists too often assume unilinearity and irreversibility with respect to societal transformations, thereby disregarding the possible devolutionary changes which in fact abound in history (Tilly, 1970). For example, although a society may develop increasingly sophisticated and complex technology, this does not assure that it will move in the direction of increasing liberalization of values, with a resulting liberation from traditional sex roles. To assume such for a complex, pluralist society underestimates the possibility of value confrontations or even reversals. It may also overlook the powerful potential of rapid mass communication to convey and sanction alternate values.

Societal values and social movements are crucially relevant to predictions concerning older women of the future. An example, critical to the subject at hand, is that of an apparently shifting religious climate in the United States. The mid-1960s witnessed a movement away from religious traditionalism toward a new, more secular era. Theologians debated the "death of God" (Cox, 1967). Moralists discussed "situational ethics" and then superstar John Lennon asserted that the Beatles were more popular than Jesus Christ (Heenan, 1973). There appeared to be a growing emphasis on rational, "cerebral" religion. Yet, in the few years since then, there appears to have been a significant move away from religious rationalism, toward more emphasis on religious feeling and emotionalism. Greeley (1974) and Kokosalakis (1974), among others, report the emergence of neofundamentalism and a retreat from the analytical to religions "'of the heart." Bellah (1976, p. 351) sees the likelihood of a return to traditional authoritarianism in American society, arising from a base in "right-wing Protestant fundamentalism." Gallup (1976), in a national survey, reported some 34% of Americans indicating that they had had the experience of being "born again." McCready and Greeley (1976), in another national sample, report 4 out of 10 Americans indicating that they had had some forms of mystical religious experience. While mainline, liberal, Protestant denominations have experienced membership declines, conservative churches have been growing at rates exceeding the growth of the general population; this includes groups such as the Jehovah's Witnesses, Church of the Nazarene, Pentecostal Holiness, the Church of Jesus Christ of Latter-day Saints (Mormons), and the largest, still growing, denomination in the United States, the Southern Baptist Convention (Kelley, 1972; Wilson, 1978).

An important consideration is the extent to which contra-feminist movements are embedded in these expanding, conservative religions. While shifts away from religious rationalism need not be linked with paternalistic orientations toward women, the nexus between these groups and biblical literalism (Abu-Laban, 1975) would appear to presage this role. In this perspective biblical writings are seen as the literal words of God and not (as in the more cosmopolitan, liberal, churches) fallible truths written by spiritual inspired humans. Religions which adhere to beliefs in biblical inerrancy tend to single out conservative passages regarding the female role, emphasizing the subordination of woman and elevating patriarchal family patterns (Daly, 1973; Hageman, 1974; Ruether, 1974).

It should not go unnoticed that two recent popular books, *Fascinating Womanhood* (Andelin, 1975) and *Total Woman* (Morgan, 1975), which are often used in formal courses which aim specifically at female self-improvement and promise marital happiness to the pupil who is able to acquire "true femininity," have emerged from conservative religious traditions (the Mormon and Southern Baptist, respectively). Further, the significance of religious values is reflected in the fact that conservative religious backing and justifications have been behind movements to defeat the Equal Rights Amendment, to restrict the civil rights of homosexuals, and (particularly with respect to Roman Catholicism) to oppose legalization of the right to abortion. Opposition to abortion is often interconnected with many other issues, including divorce, birth control, the subservience of wives, and the exclusion of women from religious hierarchies (Daly, 1977, p. 93). Such counter movements, working to impose traditional values with respect to women's place and conduct, are likely to condemn and attempt to reverse the contemporary trends discussed earlier.

The potential power of an anti-feminist backlash, in combination with expanding conservative and fundamentalist religions, suggests neither increasing liberation from sex role ideologies, nor a projected maintenance of the *status quo*, but rather suggests the possibility of a future return to a version of the *status quo ante*. There are historical examples which should temper the optimism of those who assume the eventual triumph of feminist issues. For example, in 1880 abortion was not illegal in any jurisdiction in the United States. It was practiced freely and openly, even advertised, through much of the last century. However by 1900, after a concerted campaign which involved physicians and Roman Catholic and Protestant clergy and linked abortion with undesirable feminist trends, abortion was controlled and made almost wholly illegal in virtually all jurisdictions (Mohr, 1978).

To the extent that contemporary, conservative religious movements embody restrictions which constrain women's access to prestige mechanisms other than those based on age-linked attractiveness or derived from a husband, to the extent that they restrict women to wife / mother roles as the *only* meaningful and appropriate roles, then future women of advancing age will be exceptionally vulnerable to declines in status, and, as well, vulnerable to several forms of socio-emotional deprivation.

Increasing proportions of the population are entering middle and older age. The median age of the population is shifting upward. This suggests numerical power which, coupled with the greater education of the coming old, gives promise of the potential strength of future movements aimed at eliminating ageism. These age-protest movements are ones with which both sexes can well identify, for men also age and grow old. While this fact may appear to bode well for aging women of the future, such is not necessarily the case. Ageism and sexism, while often joint concerns of socially conscious women, offend and arouse different segments of the population. Men may identify with the liabilities of old age, but it is far more difficult for them to identify with femaleness and its deprivations and limitations. Further, while organized religions and religious cults have little stake in the perpetuation of a lowered status for older people (in fact, given older people's frequent support of religious traditions this may be to an organization's disadvantage), the subordination of women is often consistent with and embroidered into religious teachings.

Futurists would do well to heed the findings of Simmons' (1945) cross-cultural examination of age and prestige in 71 societies. While advances in the status of old women may favor improved status for old men, it does not follow that societies which give prestige to their old men will give similar prestige to their old women:

> Wherever aged women have been respected, old men have rarely been without honor; but prestige for aged men has offered no assurance of the same status for women. If either sex has lost respect in old age, it has been more likely to be the women than the men. (Simmons, 1945, p. 81)

In conclusion, current, seemingly dominant, societal trends hold promise for improvements in the situation of older women of the future. Yet a comprehensive projection would suggest that the strength and ultimate viability of the feminist movement, as well as of age-protest movements, must be judged not only in terms of current trends but also in terms of incipient counter trends. Despite the longer duration of gender liberation movements, it is possible that advances in the elimination of ageism may outdistance advances in the elimination of sexism. Although the lot of older women would be improved as a concomitant to improvements in the lot of the old in general, prophecies of "deliverance" for older women, *as women,* are not assured. The burgeoning counterforces of religious conservatism, particularly when fueled by less cerebral "faiths of the heart," have implications which may well bode elements of "heartlessness" for future generations of aging women. Should contemporary conservative forces gain headway with respect to traditionalist prescriptions and proscriptions regarding females, the future of aging women may hold striking similarities to the interpersonal, prestige, power, and financial inequities experienced by the older women of today.

REFERENCE NOTE

1. Soldo, B. J. & Meyers, G. C. The effects of total fertility on living arrangements among elderly women: 1970. Paper presented at the Annual Meeting of the Gerontological Society.

REFERENCES

ABU-LABAN, S. M. The family life of older Canadians. *Canadian Home Economics Journal*, 1978, *28*, 16–25.

ABU-LABAN, S. M. Stereotypes of middle east peoples: An analysis of church school curricula. In B. Abu-Laban & F. Zeadey (Eds.), *Arabs in America: Myths and realities.* Wilmette, Illinois: Medina University Press, 1975, 149–169.

ADAMS, B. N. *Kinship in an urban setting.* Chicago: Markham, 1968.

ANDELIN, H. B. *Fascinating womanhood.* New York: Bantam, 1975.

ATCHLEY, R. C. *The social forces in later life.* (2nd ed.). Belmont, California: Wadsworth, 1977.

ATCHLEY, R. C. & CORBETT, S. L. Older women and jobs. In L. Troll, J. Israel & K. Israel, *Looking ahead.* Englewood Cliffs, N. J.: Prentice-Hall, 1977.

BELLAH, R. N. New religious consciousness and the crisis in modernity. In C. V. Glock & R. N. Bellah (Eds.), *The new religious consciousness.* Berkeley: University of California Press, 1976.

BELL, I. P. The double standard. *Transaction* 1970, *8*, 75–80.

BERNARD, J. *The future of marriage.* New York: Bantham, 1972.

BLAU, Z. S. Structured constraints on friendships in old age. *American Sociological Review*, 1961, *26*, 429–439.

BROTMAN, H. Population projections: Part 1. Tomorrow's older population (to 2000). *The Gerontologist*, 1977, *17*, 203–210.

CAVEN, R. S. Speculations on innovations to conventional marriages in old age. *The Gerontologist*, 1973, *13*, pp. 409–411. Reprinted in R. C. Atchley & M. M. Seltzer (Eds.), *The sociology of aging.* Belmont, California: Wadsworth 1976.

CHAFE, W. H. Looking backward in order to look forward. In J. M. Kreps (Ed.), *Women and the American economy.* Englewood Cliffs. N. J.: Prentice-Hall, 1976.

CHEN, Y. P. The economic status of the aged. In R. A. Kalish (Ed.), *The later years.* Monterey, California: Brooks / Cole, 1977.

CLARK, M. & ANDERSON, B. *Culture and aging.* Springfield, Illinois: Charles C. Thomas, 1967.

COX, H. The death of God and the future of theology. In W. R. Miller (Ed.), *The new Christianity.* New York: Delacorte, 1967.

CUTLER, N. & HAROOTYAN, R. A. Demography of the aged. In D. S. Woodruff & J. E. Birren (Eds.), *Aging: Scientific perspectives and social issues.* New York: Van Nostrand, 1975.

DALY, M. *Beyond God the father: Toward a philosophy of women's liberation.* Boston: Beacon, 1973.

DALY, M. Feminism and the prospects for change. In R. Fernandez (Ed.), *The future as a social problem.* Santa Monica: Goodyear, 1977.

GALLUP, G. Poll finds 34% share "born again" feeling. *New York Times*, September 26, 1976, p. 18.

GARIGUE, P. French-Canadian kinship and urban life. *American Anthropologist*, 1956, *58*, 1090–1101.

GLICK, P. C. A demographer looks at American families. *Journal of Marriage and the Family*, 1975, *37*, 15–26.

GREELEY, A. Religion in a secular society. *Social Research*, 1974, *41*, 226–240.

HAGEMAN, A. L. (Ed.), *Sexist religion and women in the church: No more silence*. New York: Association, 1974.

HEENAN, E. F. The Jesus generation. In E. F. Heenan (Ed.), *Mystery, Magic and miracle: Religion in a post-aquarian age*. Englewood Cliffs, N.J.: Prentice-Hall, 1973.

HENDRICKS, J. & HENDRICKS, G. D. *Aging in mass society*. Cambridge, Massachusetts: Winthrop, 1977.

HOCHSCHILD, A. R. *The unexpected community*. Englewood Cliffs, N. J.: Prentice-Hall, 1973.

HOLMES, T. H. & RAHE, R. J. The social readjustment rating scale. *Journal of Psychosomatic Research*, 1967, *11*, 213–248.

HUNT, M. *Sexual behavior in the 1970's*. Playboy Press, 1974.

KASSEL, V. Polygamy after 60. *Geriatrics*, 1966, *21*, 214–218.

KELLEY, D. M. *Why conservative churches are growing*. New York: Harper & Row, 1972.

KOKOSALAKIS, N. The contemporary metamorphosis of religion. *The Human Context*, 1974, *6*, 243–249.

KREPS, J. M. & LEAPER, R. J. Home work, market work and the allocation of time. In J. Kreps (Ed.), *Women and the American economy*. Englewood Cliffs, N. J.: Prentice-Hall, 1976.

LOPATA, H. Z. The social involvement of American widows. In E. Shanas (Ed.), *Aging in contemporary society*. Beverly Hills: Sage, 1970.

LOWENTHAL, M. F. & HAVEN, C. Interaction and adaptation: Intimacy as a critical variable. *American Sociological Review*, 1968, *33*, 20–30.

MASTERS, W. H. & JOHNSON, V. *Human sexual response*. Boston: Little, Brown, 1966.

MCCREADY, W. C. & GREELEY, A. M. *The ultimate values of the American people*. Beverly Hills: Sage, 1976.

MOHR, J. C. *Abortion in America: The origins and evolution of national policy*. New York: Oxford University Press, 1978.

MORGAN, M. *The total woman*. Markham, Ontario: Simon & Schuster of Canada, 1975.

MOSS, Z. It hurts to be alive and obsolete, or, the aging woman. In R. Morgan (Ed.), *Sisterhood is powerful*. New York: Vintage, 1970.

NEUGARTEN, B. L. The future and the young old. *The Gerontologist* 1975, *15*, 4–9.

NIELSEN, J. M. *Sex in society: Perspectives on stratification*. Belmont, California: Wadsworth, 1978.

NOWAK, C. Does youthfulness equal attractiveness? In L. Troll, J. Israel, & K. Israel (Eds.), *Looking ahead*. Englewood Cliffs, N. J.: Prentice-Hall, 1977, 59–64.

Population Reference Bureau. *Interchange*, 1978, 7, 1–4.

PRESSER, H. B. Age differences between spouses. *American Behavioral Scientist*, 1975, *19*, 190–205.

PRESTON, C. An old bag: The stereotype of the older woman. In Institute of Gerontology, *No longer young: The older woman in America*. Ann Arbor: University of Michigan & Wayne State University, 1975.

RUETHER, R. R. (Ed.) *Religion and sexism: Images of women in the Jewish and Christian traditions*. New York: Simon and Schuster, 1974.

Science Council of Canada. *Perceptions 2*. Ottawa: Minister of Supply and Services, 1976.

SHANAS, E. Family help patterns and social class in three societies. *Journal of Marriage and the Family*, 1967, *29*, 257–266.

SHEPPARD, H. L. The status of women, 1993–1998: Financial aspects. In Institute of Gerontology, (Ed.) *No longer young: The older woman in America*. Ann Arbor: University of Michigan & Wayne State University, 1975.

SIMMONS, L. *The role of the aged in primitive society*. New Haven: Yale University Press, 1945.

SONTAG, S. The double standard of aging. *Saturday Review*. Octobver, 1972, *55*, no. 39, 29–38.

SORENSEN, R. *Adolescent sexuality in contemporary America*. New York: World Publishing, 1973.

SWEETZER, D. A. The effect of industrialization on intergenerational solidarity. In R. F. Winch and L. W. Goodman (Eds.), *Selected studies in marriage and the family*. New York: Holt, Rinehart and Winston, 1968.

TILLY, C. Clio and Minerva. In J. C. McKinney and E. A. Tiryakian (Eds.), *Theoretical sociology: Perspectives and developments*. New York: Appleton-Century-Crofts, 1970.

TREAS, J. Family support systems for the aged. *The Gerontologist*, 1977, *17*, 486–491.

TREAS, J. & VAN HILST, A. Marriage and remarriage rates among older Americans. *The Gerontologist*, 1976, *16*, 132–136.

United States Bureau of the Census. *Census of Population: 1970. Volume, 1, Characteristics of the Population, Part I, United States Summary, Section 1.* Washington, D. C.: U.S. Government Printing Office, 1973.

VAN DUSEN, R. A. & SHELDON, E. The changing status of American women: A life cycle perspective. *American Psychologist,* 1976, *31,* 106–116.

WILSON, J. *Religion in American society; The effective presence.* Englewood Cliffs, N. J.: Prentice-Hall, 1978.

ZELNIK, M. & KANTNER, J. F. Sexuality, contraception and pregnancy among young unwed females in the United States. In the U.S. Commission on Population Growth and the American Future, *Demographic and Social Aspects of Population Growth,* Volume 1, Washington, D. C.: U. S. Government Printing Office, 1972.